D0979372

DAMIEN SIMONIS

BARCELONA
CITY GUIDE

Off-the-wall Casa Batlló (p105) is one of Gaudí's eye-catching masterpieces

JEAN-PIER

Sun-kissed and lapped by the Mediterranean, Barcelona is a dynamo where people work hard and play hard. A magnet for architecture buffs, foodies and night owls, it is a pleasure for all the senses.

Life pulsates at high pressure through the streets of this seaside city. An economic powerhouse 'Barna' displays a zest for life, artistic genius and sense of style few cities can rival. It also seem to be in a permanent state of self-renewal, its skyline constantly altering as neglected distric come in for their beauty treatment.

Barcelona's medieval boom period left it with one of Europe's most impressive Gothic leg-cies. Centuries later the Modernistas, led by Antoni Gaudí, cast an unparalleled whimsical A Nouveau splash across the city. Today a phalanx of international design stars is adding to th impressive heritage with landmark 21st-century buildings.

In this cauldron of culinary activity, monument-gazing can create a substantial appeti Traditional restaurants and alfresco seafood eateries rub shoulders with designer dens run b the city's avant-garde chefs.

Barcelona's hedonistic streak infects everyone, from the voluble gents playing dominos at I Barceloneta's beaches to the gay bodybuilders sun-worshipping nearby. Club sounds waft ov the sand from waterfront chill-out lounges. At night students pack century-old taverns whi fashionistas sip *caipirinhas* in designer cocktail bars before hitting the clubs.

BARCELONA LIFE

With 1.62 million inhabitants (and 3.4 million more in the greater Barcelona area), Barcelona is Spain's second city. Compact and densely inhabited, it manages to exude a metropolitan *and* small-town air. It has some enviable trump cards: a beautiful medieval core, the wacky delights of Modernista architecture and a sunny disposition.

The bulk of *barcelonins* wouldn't live anywhere else. Many outsiders seem to agree – the city's resident foreign population tripled between 2000 and 2008 but has since dropped a little, largely due to the world economic slowdown that has hit Spain especially hard. With 286,000 officially resident foreigners in the city, about 17.5% of the city's population is of foreign origin, almost half Latin American and a quarter from elsewhere in the European Union.

Tourism brings in millions more, although there has been a drop since 2007, with 6.7 million visitors arriving in 2008. Nonetheless, the sector employs some 80,000 people and generates up to €8 billion a year.

The city's leaders promote Barcelona as a business, conference and research centre. In March 2010, the Alba sincroton, or particles accelerator, was unveiled, which is one of the most important scientific research centres ever established in Spain. Half the city's visitors are there on business and Barcelona is second only to Milan in available trade-fair space in Europe.

Sensitivity over regional identity is never far from Spanish political debates. A new devolution statute (the Estatut) hammered out in 2006 was held up in the Constitutional Court four years later, after the rightwing Partido Popular lodged an appeal against its constitutionality. Perhaps angered by this, hundreds of towns and villages across the region staged (in three waves) symbolic referenda on Catalan independence from December 2009 to April 2010. Little more than 20% of eligible voters turned out, although 95% of them voted in favour of independence. Barcelona did not participate.

Another source of controversy is the high-speed railway tunnel to run 6km across the city centre in 2010–11 linking Estació Sants with Sagrera train station. The tunnel will run below streets flanking two Antoni Gaudí masterpieces: La Sagrada Família (p102) and La Pedrera (p104).

As Mayor Jordi Hereu announced in 2010 that Barcelona would try to host the Winter Olympic Games in 2022, the father of that city's 1992 Olympic effort and longtime head of the International Olympic Committee, Juan Antonio Samaranch, died aged 89 in April 2010.

IZZET KERIBAR

Prepare your taste buds for a culinary explosion in a tapas bar (p168)

BARCELONA HIGHLIGHTS

KRZYSZTOF DYDYNSKI

BARRI GÒTIC & LA RAMBLA

The medieval heart of old Barcelona is an endless tangle of crooked lanes where Roman remnants are obscured by timeless old taverns and curious shops. Gourmet restaurants jostle for attention with grunge bars and half-hidden clubs. Past it all runs La Rambla, Barcelona's signature boulevard.

NEIL SETCHFIELD

CHRIS MELLOR

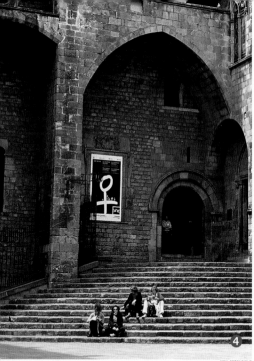

❶ La Catedral
Barcelona's medieval masterpiece, centuries in the making (p59)

❷ Plaça de Sant Jaume
Site of the Roman forum and home of the town hall and regional government (p65)

❸ La Rambla
Spain's liveliest and best-known strolling boulevard (p57)

❹ Plaça del Rei
A picturesque medieval square and subterranean slice of Roman Barcino in the Museu d'Història de Barcelona (p63)

❺ Plaça Reial
A square with lighting by Gaudí and a host of bars, clubs and eateries (p57)

❻ Temple Romà d'August
Graceful, soaring columns of what remains of Barcelona's greatest Roman temple (p68)

NEIL SETCHFIELD

KRZYSZTOF DYDYNSKI

NEIL SETCHFIELD

EL RAVAL

Long the dodgiest part of old Barcelona, the chaotic district on La Rambla's west flank remains a conundrum. Contemporary art museums, hip hotels and an engaging mix of historic taverns are given added colour by a multinational migrant community. The lower, waterfront end retains a louche feel with hookers, drug-dealers and pickpockets.

NEIL SETCHFIELD

BILL WASSMA

❶ Palau Güell
A Gaudí flight of fantasy built for his patrons, the Güell family (p76)

❷ Museu d'Art Contemporani de Barcelona (Macba)
Macba is the place to go to catch up on contemporary art trends (p76)

❸ Església de Sant Pau del Camp
An ancient church with a Visigothic entrance and graceful Romanesque cloister (p77)

❹ Antic Hospital de la Santa Creu
This former medieval hospital houses fine Gothic library reading rooms (p73)

❺ Rambla del Raval
A colourful boulevard lined by restaurants, bars and a design hotel (p47)

NEIL SETCHFIE

LA RIBERA

Marked by the majesty of the Església de Santa Maria del Mar and flanked by the Parc de la Ciutadella, La Ribera offers anything from Picasso and high-brow concerts in the Palau de la Música Catalana to alternative fashion and bustling nightlife around Passeig del Born.

KRZYSZTOF DYDYNSKI

KRZYSZTOF DYDYNSKI

❶ Església de Santa Maria del Mar
Barcelona's finest church is a noble work of grand Gothic construction (p80)

❷ Museu Picasso
Get to know early Picasso, from his childhood oils to the Blue Period (p80)

❸ Mercat de Santa Caterina
The undulating roof lends a cheeky splash of colour to this modern market (p85)

❹ Palau de la Música Catalana
Admire the Modernista decor at the Palace of Catalan Music (p84)

❺ Carrer de Montcada
Promenade on this medieval street, flanked by Gothic and Baroque buildings (p80)

❻ Passeig del Born
Where jousts were once held, crowds now linger in eateries, bars and gourmet food shops (p79)

❼ Parc de la Ciutadella
Relax in Barcelona's most central park, home to parliament, the zoo and some unique buildings (p85)

© BOB MASTERS / ALAMY

PORT VELL & LA BARCELONETA

With its pricey marina, Maremàgnum shopping-mall-on-water, IMAX cinema and aquarium, the Old Port attracts strollers from all points. La Barceloneta, a former working-class neighbourhood that retains true grit despite timid gentrification, has beaches and backstreet eateries that are beloved of locals and visitors alike.

❶ La Barceloneta beach
Hang out on Barcelona's handiest city beach before or after doing some sights (p89)

❷ Museu d'Història de Catalunya
Check out the history of Catalonia in this intriguing museum (p91)

❸ Streets of La Barceloneta
Explore La Barceloneta's narrow streets and countless seafood eateries (p89)

KARL BLACKWELL

JEAN-PIERRE LESCOURET

PORT OLÍMPIC, EL POBLENOU & EL FÒRUM

Born of the Olympic Games, Port Olímpic and the beaches to its north are the seaside face of a continuing transformation. El Poblenou, once industrial, is attracting high-tech companies and loft-seeking gentry. Where the beaches peter out is Barcelona's new skyscraper district of El Fòrum.

NEIL SETCHFIELD

KRZYSZTOF DYDYNSKI

❶ Beaches
Get some sea and sun before sipping cocktails in the beach bars (p94)

❷ El Fòrum
Cycle and skate around this leisure and conference area, or come for a concert (p95)

❸ Torre Agbar
Jean Nouvel's towering landmark resembles a crystal finger pointing heavenwards (p95)

❹ Cementiri de l'Est
The East Cemetery is loaded with curious funerary statuary (p94)

L'EIXAMPLE

The late-19th-century grid pattern city extension beyond Barcelona's old town is laced with the whimsical wonders of the Modernistas, from La Sagrada Família to countless gems by fantasy-driven architects. Busy with shops, small businesses, hotels and offices, it remains a largely middle-class area.

RACHEL LEWIS

KRZYSZTOF DYDYNSKI

❶ La Sagrada Família
Gaudí's unfinished symphony, an extraordinary work of soaring religious devotion (p102)

❷ Casa Batlló
Looking like a mythical beast, Casa Batlló is one of Gaudí's strangest creations (p105)

❸ La Pedrera
This one-time residence is a masterpiece of Gaudí's swirling imagination (p104)

❹ Casa Amatller
This mock medieval fantasy is a hallmark of Modernista Puig i Cadafalch (p105)

❺ Fundació Antoni Tàpies
A Modernista home for the works of Barcelona's greatest living modern artist (p107)

❻ Hospital de la Santa Creu i de Sant Pau
A hospital full of ceramic delights and Modernista quirks (p109)

❼ Casa de les Punxes
Witch's-hat towers on this Modernista mansion stand out in central Barcelona (p111)

KIMBERLEY COOLE

GRÀCIA & PARK GÜELL

Gràcia was a working-class bastion whose narrow streets still bear names like Fraternity and Liberty. Its streets and a series of pleasant squares are lined with all manner of curious shops, taverns, eateries and bars. Beyond stretches Gaudí's green contribution to the city, Park Güell.

❶ Park Güell
Gaudí's intriguing park offers Modernista swirls and panoramic city vistas (p115)

❷ Hotel Casa Fuster
A luxury hotel that is a sight in itself, Casa Fuster invites admiration and offers a street level lounge (p240)

❸ Carrer de Verdi
With cinemas, bars and shops, Carrer de Verdi is one of Gràcia's liveliest streets (p115)

RACHEL LEWIS

RACHEL LEWIS

NEIL SETCHFIELD

LA ZONA ALTA

Taking in the high ground from Tibidabo to Pedralbes, the districts of the High Zone are where the serious money lives. Scattered across the area is an eclectic range of sights, from a medieval monastery to an amusement park, and chic dining, drinking and shopping.

KRZYSZTOF DYDYNSKI

GUY MOBERLY

❶ Camp Nou
Football fans make solemn pilgrimage to FC Barcelona's home stadium (p121)

❷ Museu-Monestir de Pedralbes
Seek peace in the beautiful cloisters of this one-time monastery (p121)

❸ Parc d'Atraccions
Head to the mountain for amusement park thrills and panoramic views (p133)

❹ Palau Reial de Pedralbes
Ceramics, decorative arts and textile displays come together in this villa (p124)

❺ Jardins del Laberint d'Horta
Get lost in the maze of these elegant gardens (p134)

❻ Torre de Collserola
Take the lift up Sir Norman Foster's communications tower for breathtaking views (p134)

ALFREDO MAIQUEZ

MONTJUÏC, SANTS & EL POBLE SEC

The castle-topped hill of Montjuïc, with its gardens and myriad museums, is a perfect day out. Admire Miró's oeuvre, take in the views and study the flora. Clinging to the hillside, the streets of El Poble Sec are loaded with eateries and bars.

❶ Castell de Montjuïc
'Invade' the castle and enjoy the views over city, port and sea (p142)

❷ Fundació Joan Miró
This purpose-designed building houses a grand display of Joan Miró's works (p143)

❸ Museu Nacional d'Art de Catalunya
The gamut of Catalan art, from Romanesque frescoes to Gaudí furniture (p138)

❹ CaixaForum
This Modernista exhibition centre is worth a visit in its own right (p139)

❺ Estadi Olímpic
Explore the stadium that hosted the 1992 Olympics (p144)

❻ Font Màgica
Marvel at the watery sound and light show of the Magic Fountain (p144)

❼ Pavelló Mies van der Rohe
A faithful reproduction of the 1929 German Pavilion, raised here for Barcelona's World Exhibition (p145)

❽ Poble Espanyol
See all of Spain in a day at Spain Town (p145)

NEIL SETCHFIELD

NEIL SETCHFIELD

GUY MOBERLY

12

CONTENTS

THE AUTHOR

Damien Simonis

In 1990, during a continental foray from a rain-sodden London, Damien found himself in pre-Olympics Barcelona. He had never before set foot in Spain. What was it about this town? The crowded produce markets, the dimly lit *colmados* (treasure caverns of all sorts of weird and wonderful foods), the gaily noisy terraces where chatter mixed so easily with wine, the Gaudí colours, the mysterious narrow lanes of the Barri Gòtic, the seaside? Perhaps it was all this and some unifying, indefinable quality that got under his skin. Eight years later, Damien turned up in a Rambla-side *pensión* on assignment for Lonely Planet. And that old magic started doing its work again. A chat with a fellow in a bar and he had a room in a top-floor flat in Gran Via. Barcelona was for years a second home for Damien and is now our restless correspondent's main base.

DAMIEN'S TOP BARCELONA DAY
A great way to kick-start the day is with everyone else, leaning up against a bar over a *cafè amb llet* (coffee with milk), an orange juice and a pastry (preferably something nice and creamy like a *canya*). A quick read of the paper to find out where we stand on the latest round of squabbling over Catalan autonomy, ETA, the bishops' spat with the Socialists and FC Barcelona's results and it's time to hit the streets.

There are few monuments in the world like La Sagrada Família, not only for its uniqueness but because it is one of the few where you never quite know what this work-in-progress will look like each time you happen by! A visit to the Museu Picasso or the CaixaForum, to catch the latest temporary art exhibition, takes care of the day's spiritual nourishment and lunch beckons.

I head into the narrow lanes of La Barceloneta for a slap-up meal of fish or finger-licking *mariscos* (seafood). The choice of area has a double purpose, for what's a day in Barcelona without a couple of hours' lazing on the beach? Time permitting, I like to wander back through El Born, poking my nose into cheese and sweet shops, lingering for a glass of wine at La Vinya del Senyor and working my way north to the Mercat de Santa Caterina. A little gourmet shopping here and off home for a late siesta before heading out again into the night.

First, an elegant meal in one of the many gems scattered across the grid maze of L'Eixample. From there, it's a short taxi ride into the heart of the Barri Gòtic for some jazz at the Harlem. If the spirit is willing, another taxi whisks us up into the Zona Alta for a little clubbing at Sutton the Club. As dawn breaks, it is but a short, somewhat dazed, stroll home.

Compact and easy to get around by public transport, Barcelona is geared to tourism and you will find plenty of information on all major tourist attractions. At the same time, it is full of mystery and invites you to spend long days of meandering and discovering. The monuments and museums, mainly concentrated in a relatively small area, could keep you busy for a week or more, but inevitably some of your time will be dedicated to simply hanging out in cafes, bars, eateries and at the beach. Consider setting aside a day or two for excursions (p244), most easily done by train. Consider booking hotels, sought-after restaurants and shows before leaving home (see p20). Take care, particularly on arrival, as petty crime directed at tourists laden with cameras and bags is, unfortunately, common.

WHEN TO GO

Barcelona is a year-round destination; as ideal for a long weekend city break as for a six-month sabbatical. It is a good idea to time a trip with one eye on events and the other on the weather (see p276). Many associate Barcelona with the summer sun, but August can be a poor choice – the city broils and swarms with tourists as the locals disappear to more salubrious climes. It is certainly better to come around mid-June or September. If beach time is not a priority, you can easily find sunny (if chilly) weather and fewer visitors in January and February. You stand a good chance of striking rain from April to May and October through November.

FESTIVALS

Whether it's being chased by fire-spitting demons or joining parades of giants, meandering through the decorated streets of Barcelona's *barris* (neighbourhoods) with beer in hand, or crowding into a mega-concert at the Fòrum, the city proffers a plethora of festivals. Many are steeped in colourful tradition, while others are modern affairs focused on concerts, theatre or sport. Some envelop the entire city; other lively local *festes* are limited to a particular *barri*. Events take place throughout much of the year, although there is more activity in

the warmer months. For a list of official public holidays in Barcelona, see p280.

January

ANY NOU/AÑO NUEVO (NEW YEAR'S DAY)

Like Cap d'Any/Noche Vieja (New Year's Eve) anywhere, this occasion can create but not always fulfil expectations. Many locals arrange parties in their homes as restaurants, bars and clubs fill to bursting and charge like wounded bulls. Rowdy folks also gather around Plaça de Catalunya.

REIS/REYES

Epifanía (Epiphany) on 6 January is also known as the Dia dels Reis Mags/Día de los Reyes Magos (Three Kings' Day), or simply Reis/Reyes, perhaps the most important day on a Barcelona kid's calendar. According to tradition, this is when they receive gifts (although Christmas has made heavy inroads). The holiday itself is quiet, but on 5 January children delight in the Cavalcada dels Reis Mags (Parade of the Three Kings), a colourful parade of floats and music, during which countless sweets are launched from the floats into the crowds.

FESTES DELS TRES TOMBS

A key part of the festival of Sant Antoni Abat, the patron saint of domestic and carriage animals, is this Feast of the Three Circuits, a parade of horse-drawn carts in L'Eixample near the Mercat de Sant Antoni every 17 January.

February

BARCELONA VISUALSOUND
www.bcnvisualsound.org, in Catalan
This 10-day festival brings together audio-visual creators in a celebration of emerging stars in the making of anything from video to multimedia art.

BARNASANTS
www.barnasants.com, in Catalan
Each year the city's main live-music venues host a bevy of Catalan, Spanish and Latin

American singer-songwriters for concerts spread over a period from the end of January until about mid-March.

CARNESTOLTES/CARNAVAL
Celebrated in February or March, this festival involves several days of fancy-dress parades and merrymaking, ending on the Tuesday 47 days before Easter Sunday. The *Gran Rua* (Grand Parade) takes place on the Saturday evening from 5.30pm. Down in Sitges (p255) a much wilder version takes place. The gay community stages gaudy parades and party-goers keep the bars and clubs heaving for several days running.

DE CAJÓN FESTIVAL FLAMENCO
www.theproject.es/en
A major flamenco fest running over different dates each year (a series of 16 major concerts from mid-February to mid-April in 2010) and held in venues across town.

FESTES DE SANTA EULÀLIA
www.bcn.cat/santaeulalia
Coinciding roughly with Carnaval, this is the feast of Barcelona's first patron saint, Eulàlia (or 'la Laia' for short). The Ajuntament (town hall) organises a week of cultural events, from concerts through to performances by *castellers* (human-castle builders; see p228).

FESTIVAL DE JAZZ
www.jazzterrassa.org, in Catalan
A major season of jazz concerts from late January to the end of February in the nearby city of Terrassa.

March & April
DIVENDRES SANT/VIERNES SANTO (GOOD FRIDAY)
Transport yourself to southern Spain with the Easter processions from the Església de Sant Agustí in El Raval on Good Friday. They start at 5pm and end in front of La Catedral three hours later.

RAL.LI BARCELONA-SITGES
www.rallyesitges.com
Dozens of classic cars converge on Barcelona towards the end of March for this annual rally. You can see the cars on show on the Saturday morning in Plaça de Sant Jaume, or position yourself on the route here or in Sitges.

DIA DE SANT JORDI
Catalonia celebrates the feast of its patron saint, St George, on 23 April. At the same time, the Dia del Llibre (Day of the Book) is observed – men give women a rose, women give men a book, publishers launch new titles and La Rambla and Plaça de Sant Jaume fill with book and flower stalls. In some years the day is marked, as in 2010, by a mega-concert in the Club Sant Jordi on Montjuïc (Map p140).

FERIA DE ABRIL DE CATALUNYA
Andalucía comes to town with this traditional southern festival staged by and for the city's big Andalucian population. It lasts for about a week from late April and is held in the Parc del Fòrum.

FESTIVAL DE MÚSICA ANTIGA DE BARCELONA
www.auditori.com
A month-long festival from mid-April to mid-May of ancient music, which reaches back centuries and across cultures to create a varied series of concerts at l'Auditori.

May
L'OU COM BALLA
A curious tradition, the 'Dancing Egg' is an empty shell that bobs on top of the flower-festooned fountain in the cloister of La Catedral. This spectacle is Barcelona's way of celebrating Corpus Christi (the Thursday following the eighth Sunday after Easter Sunday), which can also fall in June. You can see *sardanes* (traditional Catalan folk dance) being danced on Plaça de Sant Jaume from 7pm on this day.

FESTA DE SANT PONÇ
To commemorate the patron saint of beekeepers and herbalists, locals fill Carrer de l'Hospital in El Raval on 11 May with the chatter and bustle of a street market.

FESTA DEL PASSATGE LLUÍS PELLICER
The intriguing little lane in L'Eixample (Map p100), lined with several interesting restaurants, really comes to life for three days in May with its folksy festival, featuring concerts and locals feasting at tables set up along the lane.

PRIMAVERA SOUND
www.primaverasound.com

For three days in late May (or early June) the Auditori Fòrum and other locations around town welcome a host of international DJs and musicians.

FESTIVAL DE FLAMENCO DE CIUTAT VELLA
www.tallerdemusics.com

One of the best occasions to see great flamenco in Barcelona, this concentrated festival is held over four days at the Centre de Cultura Contemporània de Barcelona (CCCB). In the district of Nou Barris, a smaller three-day festival is usually held around the middle of the month in a local civic centre. Keep your eyes open for flyers.

June
SÓNAR
www.sonar.es

Sónar is Barcelona's celebration of electronic music and is said to be Europe's biggest such event. Locations and dates change each year.

FESTIVAL DEL GREC
www.barcelonafestival.com, in Catalan

This eclectic programme of theatre, dance and music runs for most of the summer. Performances are held all over the city, including at the Teatre Grec (Map p140; Passeig de Santa Madrona; Ⓜ Espanya) amphitheatre on Montjuïc, from which the festival takes its name.

DIA DE SANT JOAN/DÍA DE SAN JUAN BAUTISTA
The night before the Feast of St John the Baptist (24 June), the people of Barcelona hit the streets or hold parties at home to celebrate the Berbena de Sant Joan (St John's Night), which involves drinking, dancing, bonfires and fireworks.

PRIDE BARCELONA
www.pridebarcelona.org, in Catalan

The Barcelona Gay Pride festival is a week of celebrations held towards the end of June with a crammed programme of culture and concerts, along with the traditional Gay Pride march on the last Sunday of the month.

DÍA DE LA MÚSICA
www.diadelamusica.com, in Spanish

On 21 June a bevy of bands converge on Barcelona and other cities for an evening of indie music performances, usually held in Maremàgnum.

August
FESTA MAJOR DE GRÀCIA
www.festamajordegracia.org, in Catalan

This local festival, which takes place over about nine days around 15 August, is one of the biggest in Barcelona. More than a dozen streets in Gràcia are decorated by their inhabitants as part of a competition for the most imaginative street. People pour in to listen to bands in the streets and squares, fuel on snacks and drink at countless street stands.

FESTA MAJOR DE SANTS
www.festamajordesants.net, in Catalan

The district of Sants launches its own week-long version of decorated mayhem, held around 24 August, hard on the heels of Gràcia.

FESTES DE SANT ROC
For four days in mid-August, Plaça Nova in the Barri Gòtic becomes the scene of parades, *correfoc* (fire race), a market, traditional music and magic shows for kids.

September
DIADA NACIONAL DE CATALUNYA
Catalonia's national day commemorates, curiously, Barcelona's surrender on 11 September 1714 to the Bourbon monarchy of Spain, at the conclusion of the War of the Spanish Succession (see p25).

FESTES DE LA MERCÈ
www.bcn.cat/merce

This four-day fest sparks a final burst of pre-winter madness. Nostra Senyora de la Mercè (Our Lady of Mercy), Barcelona's co-patron saint, is celebrated in the city's *festa major*. There's a swimming race across the harbour, a fun run, outstanding free concerts (such as Barcelona Acció Musica, or BAM; www.bcn.cat/bam) and a bewildering programme of cultural events. Adding to the local colour are all the ingredients of a major Catalan *festa: castellers, sardanes,* parades of *gegants* and *capgrossos* (giants and big heads), and a huge *correfoc*.

MOSTRA DE VINS I CAVES DE CATALUNYA
An excellent chance to taste a wide range of Catalan wine and *cava,* this expo is usually held at Maremàgnum over four days towards the end of September.

FESTA MAJOR DE LA BARCELONETA
Barcelona's party-goers usually have only a short wait until the next opportunity for merrymaking. Although on a small scale, La Barceloneta's gig, to celebrate the local patron saint, Sant Miquel, on 29 September, lasts about a week and involves plenty of dancing and drinking (especially on the beach).

October
FESTIVAL DE TARDOR
www.ribermusica.org, in Catalan
Five days of live music, workshops and more in bars and other locations around La Ribera.

November
FESTIVAL INTERNACIONAL DE JAZZ DE BARCELONA
www.theproject.es
For most of the month, the big venues (from the Auditori down) across town host a plethora of international jazz acts. At the same time, a more home-spun jazz fest takes place for about a month in bars across Ciutat Vella.

December
FESTIVAL MIL.LENNI
www.festivalmillenni.com
Stretching into April of the following year, this concert series offers an eclectic range of performances, mainly in the Palau de la Música Catalana, from flamenco to Joan Baez.

NADAL/NAVIDAD (CHRISTMAS)
Catalans tend to have their main Christmas dinner on Christmas Eve, although many have a big lunch the following day. An odd event to mark the occasion is the annual (freezing) 200m swimming dash from Maremàgnum in Port Vell to the Moll de les Drassanes.

PRIMAVERA CLUB
www.primaverasound.com
The winter equivalent of Primavera Sound in May.

COSTS & MONEY
Long gone are the days when Barcelona could be considered a cheap destination. A 2009 study placed Barcelona in 38th spot in a ranking of more than 100 cities by expense. A midrange hotel double room can cost anything from €70 to €250, and a midrange dinner averages €21 to €70. On the other hand, simple, filling set lunchtime meals cost around €10. Many museums have free admission days (see the Neighbourhoods chapter, p91). Staying in a modest hotel, sticking to set lunches and dining out well (but without splurging), you can bargain on spending €100 to €150 a day.

POO-POOING CHRISTMAS
A Catalan Christmas wouldn't be the same without the *pessebres* (nativity scenes). A giant one is set up in Plaça de Sant Jaume and you can see a display of them in an annex of the Església de Betlem (p57). These cribs are common throughout the Catholic world, particularly in the Mediterranean.

What makes them different here is the scatological presence – along with the baby Jesus, Mary, Joseph and the three kings – of the *caganer* (crapper), a chap who has dropped his pants and is doing number twos (a symbol of fertility for the coming year).

On a similar note, the *caga tió* (poop log) is a wooden beast that 'lives' in the kitchen or dining room in the run-up to Christmas and has to be 'fed' (traditionally things like dry bread and water) so that on Christmas Day it will *cagar* (shit) gifts. Once, the gifts were sweets. In some families they tend to be more substantial nowadays.

The whole thing developed from a country tradition of placing a huge *tió* (tree trunk) in the fireplace – its gifts in the misty past were simply the benefits of heat and light. Somewhere along the line the story became more, shall we say, sophisticated. You can buy your own *caganers* and let kids have a go hitting a *caga tió* with a stick to get a present at the Fira de Santa Llúcia, a market in front of La Catedral, in the weeks leading up to Christmas.

ADVANCE PLANNING

You might want to book a few things in advance. Many of the more popular hotels fill up fast, especially during trade fairs. To know which dates to avoid, check the trade-fair calendar at www.firabcn.com.

If you are keen to eat in certain restaurants, book a table (by phone or, in some cases, online) to avoid disappointment on arrival. Similarly, those planning a night at the opera or similar outings should consider booking through the venues' websites or ticketing agencies like: Tel-Entrada (www.telentrada.com); ServiCaixa (www.servicaixa.com); Ticket Master (www.ticketmaster.es) and El Corte Inglés (www.elcorteingles.es/entradas, in Spanish). Football fans anxious to catch a match with FC Barcelona should also book ahead (see p227).

Those on a strict budget, who stay in hostel dorms and survive on *entrepans* (filled rolls) or make up their own meals, should be able to get by on about €50 a day.

INTERNET RESOURCES

The following sites will get you started on a virtual research tour of Barcelona:

Barcelona (www.bcn.cat/en) The town hall's official website, with plenty of links.

Barcelona Turisme (www.barcelonaturisme.com) The city's official tourism website.

Barcelonareporter.com (www.barcelonareporter.com) An English language news site on Catalonia.

Barcelona Yellow (www.barcelonayellow.com) A general site with plenty of links and information on everything from Gaudí to gourmet dining.

Le Cool (http://lecool.com) A free weekly guide to what's happening in Barcelona (and other cities).

Lonely Planet (www.lonelyplanet.com/spain/barcelona)

Ruta del Modernisme (www.rutadelmodernisme.com) The site that covers Barcelona's Modernista heritage, sites, events and more.

SUSTAINABLE BARCELONA

Water shortages are a problem throughout Spain. The situation in Barcelona, at one point so critical in 2008 that boatloads had to be imported from Almería (southern Spain) and Marseille (France), has been alleviated by the opening of a major desalination plant in nearby El Prat de Llobregat in 2009. It can process 200 million litres of water a day, providing up to 20% of Barcelona's water needs. It is costly in terms of energy, however, and is brought to maximum production only if dam water supplies are lacking.

You can do your part to keep water consumption down, for example, by not sending off towels for washing each day in your hotel and making sure you don't litter in the streets (a problem that has led to the hosing down of the city every night).

Air pollution is a problem (see p46) and driving around Barcelona is impractical anyway, so use public transport (more than a quarter of buses run on natural gas and diesel-powered buses are continually being phased out). Bike hire is an option but the introduction of a system of bicycles as public transport, the exponential explosion of bike tour companies and the inadequate network of bike lanes can, at times, make getting around by bike frustrating for cyclists, pedestrians and drivers alike!

Instead of flying to Barcelona, consider lengthening your trip and travelling there by train. Direct overnight sleepers run from Paris, Geneva and Milan. From London you could start with the Eurostar and spend a day in Paris en route.

Catalonia and 40 other European regions (including Tuscany and Provence) are members of a sustainable tourism network aimed at rendering tourism compatible with the environment, local quality of life and maintenance of local traditions.

HISTORY

SIGNS FROM THE DISTANT PAST

The area around present-day Barcelona was certainly inhabited prior to the arrival of the Romans in Catalonia in 218 BC. By whom, and whether or not there was an urban nucleus, is open to debate.

Pre-Roman coins found in the area suggest the Iberian Laietani tribe may have settled here. As far back as 35,000 BC, the tribe's Stone Age predecessors had roamed the Pyrenees and begun to descend into the lowlands to the south. In 1991 the remains of 25 corpses were found in Carrer de Sant Pau in El Raval – they had been buried around 4000 BC. It has been speculated that, in those days, much of El Raval was a bay and that the hillock (Mont Tàber) next to Plaça de Sant Jaume may have been home to a Neolithic settlement.

Other evidence hints at a settlement established around 230 BC by the Carthaginian conqueror (and father of Hannibal), Hamilcar Barca. It is tempting to see in his name the roots of the city's own name. Some archaeologists believe that any pre-Roman town must have been built on the hill of Montjuïc.

ROMANS, VISIGOTHS & ISLAM

The heart of the Roman settlement of Barcino (much later Barcelona) lay within what would later become the medieval city – now known as the Barri Gòtic. The temple was raised on Mont Tàber. Remains of city walls, temple pillars and graves all attest to what would eventually become a busy and lively town. Barcino was not a major centre, however. Tarraco (Tarragona) to the southwest and the one-time Greek trading centre of Emporion (Empúries) to the north were more important. The Latin poet Ausonius, however, paints a picture of contented prosperity – Barcino (founded in the reign of Caesar Augustus) lived well off the agricultural produce in its hinterland and from fishing. Oysters, in particular, appeared regularly on the Roman menu in ancient times. Wine, olive oil and *garum* (a rather tart fish paste and favourite staple of the Romans) were all produced and consumed in abundance.

As the Roman Empire wobbled, Hispania (as the Iberian Peninsula was known to the Romans) felt the effects. It is no coincidence that the bulk of Barcelona's Roman walls, vestiges of which remain today, went up in the 4th century AD. Marauding Franks had visited a little death and destruction on the city in a prelude to what was to come – several waves of invaders flooded across the country like great Atlantic rollers. By 415 the comparatively Romanised Visigoths had arrived and, under their leader Athaulf (a narrow lane in the Barri Gòtic is named after him), made a temporary capital in Barcino before moving on to Toletum (Toledo) in the 6th century. In the wake of their departure, the town and surrounding territory was left largely lawless. As various epidemics struck, local revolts against weak Visigothic rule were frequent.

TIMELINE

c 4000 BC	218 BC	15 BC
Jasper implements discovered around Carrer del Paradís indicate that a Neolithic settlement may have thrived around the present-day Plaça de Sant Jaume at this time.	In a move to block supplies to the Carthaginian general Hannibal, waging war against Rome in Italy itself, Roman troops under Scipio land at Empúries, found Tarraco (Tarragona) and take control of the Catalan coast.	Caesar Augustus grants the town of Barcino, possibly established under his auspices, the rather long-winded title of Colonia Julia Augusta Faventia Paterna Barcino.

top picks

BOOKS ON THE HISTORY OF BARCELONA

- Barcelona (Robert Hughes; 1992) A witty and passionate study of the art and architecture of the city through history. It is neither flouncing artistic criticism nor dry history, rather a distillation of the life of the city and people and an assessment of its expression. He followed up with the briefer, more personal Barcelona the Great Enchantress in 2004.
- Barcelona – A Thousand Years of the City's Past (Felipe Fernández-Armesto; 1991) A fascinating history of the city from medieval days to the 20th century, organised not in chronological order but rather by themes such as Barcelona and the Sea, and Barcelona and Europe.
- Anarchism and the City: Revolution and Counter-Revolution in Barcelona, 1898–1937 (Chris Ealham; 2010) Ealham explores the dyamics of an industrial city that was home to Europe's biggest anarchist hotbeds, examining the fluid fabric of the city in the run-up to the Spanish Civil War.
- Homage to Catalonia (George Orwell; 1938) Orwell's classic account of the first half of the 1936–39 Spanish Civil War as he lived it in Barcelona and on the front line in Catalonia, moving from the euphoria of the early days in Barcelona to disillusionment with the disastrous infighting on the Republican side.
- Historia de Barcelona (María Pomés & Alicia Sánchez; 2001) Spanish readers will appreciate this straightforward, chronological account of the city, which presents plenty of curious social history alongside the usual political events.

In 711 the Muslim general Tariq landed an expeditionary force at present-day Gibraltar (Arabic for Tariq's Mountain). He had no trouble sweeping across the peninsula all the way into France, where he and his army were only brought to a halt in 732 by the Franks at Poitiers.

Barcelona fell under Muslim sway but they seem not to have been overly impressed with their prize. The town is mentioned in Arabic chronicles but it seems the Muslims resigned themselves early on to setting up a defensive line along the Riu Ebro to the south. Louis the Pious, the future Frankish ruler, retook Barcelona from them in 801.

The comtes (counts) installed here as Louis' lieutenants hailed from local tribes roaming on the periphery of the Frankish empire. Barcelona was a frontier town in what was known as the Frankish or Spanish March – a rough-and-ready buffer zone south of the Pyrenees.

A HAIRY BEGINNING

The plains and mountains to the northwest and north of Barcelona were populated by the people who by then could be identified as 'Catalans' (although surviving documentary references to the term only date from the 12th century). Catalan, the language of these people, was closely related to the langue d'oc, the post-Latin lingua franca of southern France (of which Provençal is about the only barely surviving reminder).

The March was under nominal Frankish control but the real power lay with local potentates (themselves often of Frankish origin, however) who ranged across the territory. One of these rulers went by the curious name of Guifré el Pelós, or Wilfred the Hairy. This was not a reference to uneven shaving habits: according to legend, old Guifré had hair in parts most people do not (exactly which parts was never specified!). He and his brothers gained control of most of the Catalan counties by 878 and Guifré entered the folk mythology of Catalonia. If Catalonia can be called a nation, then its 'father' was the hirsute Guifré.

AD 415	718	801
Visigoths under Athaulf, with captured Roman empress Galla Placidia as his wife, make Barcino their capital. With several interruptions, it remains so until the Visigoths move to Toledo (central Spain) in the 6th century.	Only seven years after the Muslim invasion of Spain launched from Morocco at Gibraltar, Barcelona falls to Tariq's mostly Arab and Berber troops on their blitzkrieg march north into France.	After a year-long siege, the son of Charlemagne and future Frankish king Louis the Pious, wrests Barcelona from Muslims and establishes the Spanish March under local counts.

Guifré and his immediate successors continued, at least in name, to be vassals of the Franks. In reality, his position as 'Comte de Barcelona' (Count of Barcelona; even today many refer to Barcelona as the *ciutat comtal*, or city of counts) was assured in his own right.

THE COMTES DE BARCELONA

By the late 10th century, the Casal de Barcelona (House of Barcelona) was the senior of several counties (whose leaders were all related by family ties) that would soon be a single, independent principality covering most of modern Catalonia except the south, plus Roussillon (today in France).

This was the only Iberian Christian 'state' not to fall under the sway of Sancho III of Navarra in the early 11th century. The failure of the Franks to come to Barcelona's aid when it was plundered by the Muslims under Al-Mansur in 985 led the counts to reject Frankish suzerainty. So a new entity – Catalonia – acquired tacit recognition across Europe.

Count Ramon Berenguer I was able to buy the counties of Carcassonne and Béziers, north of Roussillon, and Barcelona would maintain ambitions in France for two more centuries – at one point it held territory as far east as Provence. Under Ramon Berenguer III (1082-1131), sea trade developed and Catalonia launched its own fleet.

A system of feudal government and law evolved that had little to do with the more centralised and absolutist models that would emerge in subsequent centuries in Castilla, reconquered from the Muslims. A hotchpotch of Roman-Visigothic laws combined with emerging feudal practice found its way into the written bill of rights called the 'Usatges de Barcelona' from around 1060.

Justice in those days was a little rough by modern standards: '…let them (the rulers) render justice as it seems fit to them: by cutting off hands and feet, putting out eyes, keeping men in prison for a long time and, ultimately, in hanging their bodies if necessary.' Was there an element of misogyny in the Usatges? 'In regard to women, let the rulers render justice by cutting off their noses, lips, ears and breasts, and by burning them at the stake if necessary…'

MARRIAGE OF CONVENIENCE?

In 1137 Ramon Berenguer IV clinched what must have seemed an unbeatable deal. He was betrothed to Petronilla, the one-year-old heiress to the throne of Catalonia's western neighbour Aragón, thus creating a joint state that set the scene for Catalonia's golden age.

This state, known as the Corona de Aragón (Crown of Aragon), was ruled by *comtes-reis* (count-kings, ie counts of Barcelona and kings of Aragón). The title enshrined the continued separateness of the two states, and both retained many of their own laws. The arrangement was to have unexpected consequences as it tied Catalonia to the destiny of the rest of the peninsula in a way that ultimately would not appeal to many Catalans. In the meantime, however, the combined state had the critical mass needed for expansion. Curiously, while the bulk of the following centuries' conquests and trade would be carried out by the Catalans from Barcelona, the name Catalonia would be largely subsumed into that of Aragón. After all, the counts of Barcelona were from hereon the kings of Aragón. Strictly speaking, there never was a Catalan kingdom.

MEDITERRANEAN EMPIRE

Not content to leave all the glory of the Reconquista to the Castilians, Jaume I (r 1213–76) set about his own spectacular missions. At only 21 years of age, he set off in 1229 with fleets from

985	1137	1225–29
Al-Mansur (the Victorious) rampages across Catalan territory and devastates Barcelona in a lightning campaign. The city is largely razed and much of its population marched off as slaves to Córdoba.	Count Ramon Berenguer IV is betrothed to one-year-old Petronilla, daughter of the king of Aragón, creating a new combined state that would be known as the Corona de Aragón.	At 18 years old, Jaume I takes command of the realm and four years later he conquers Muslim-held Mallorca, the first of several dazzling conquests that lead him to be called El Conqueridor (the Conqueror).

Tarragona, Barcelona, Marseilles and other ports. His objective was Mallorca, which he won. Six years later he had Ibiza and Formentera. Things were going so well that, prodded by the Aragonese, for good measure he took control of Valencia (on the mainland) too. This was no easy task and was only completed in 1248 after 16 years of grinding conquest. Still, it would be hard to begrudge the tireless king his sobriquet of El Conqueridor (the Conqueror). All this activity helped fuel a boom in Barcelona and Jaume raised new walls that increased the size of the enclosed city tenfold.

The empire-building shifted into top gear in the 1280s. Jaume I's son Pere II (1240–85) took Sicily in 1282. The easternmost part of the Balearics, Menorca, fell to Alfons II in 1287 after prolonged blood-letting. Most of its people were killed or enslaved and the island remained largely deserted throughout its occupation. Malta, Gozo and Athens were also briefly taken. A half-hearted attempt was made on Corsica but the most determined and ultimately fruitless assault began on Sardinia in 1323. The island became the Corona de Aragón's Vietnam.

In spite of the carnage and the expense of war, this was Barcelona's golden age. It was the base for what was now a thriving mercantile empire and the western Mediterranean was virtually a Catalan lake.

THE RISE OF PARLIAMENT

The rulers of the Casal de Barcelona and then the *comtes-reis* of the Corona de Aragón had a habit of regularly making themselves absent from Barcelona. Initially, local city administration was in the hands of a viscount, but in the course of the 12th and 13th centuries local power began to shift.

In 1249 Jaume I authorised the election of a committee of key citizens to advise his officials. The idea developed and, by 1274, the Consell dels Cent Jurats (Council of the Hundred Sworn-In) formed an electoral college from which an executive body of five *consellers* (councillors) was nominated to run city affairs.

In 1283 the Corts Catalanes met for the first time. This new legislative council for Catalonia (equivalent bodies sat in Aragón and Valencia) was made up of representatives of the nobility, clergy and high-class merchants to form a counterweight to regal power. The Corts Catalanes met at first annually, then every three years, but had a permanent secretariat known as the Diputació del General or Generalitat. Its home was, and remains, the Palau de la Generalitat.

The Corts and Council increased their leverage as trade grew and their respective roles in raising taxes and distributing wealth became more important. As the *comtes-reis* required money to organise wars and other enterprises, they increasingly relied on business barons who were best represented through these two oligarchic bodies.

Meanwhile, Barcelona's trading wealth paid for the great Gothic buildings that bejewel the city to this day. La Catedral (59), the Capella Reial de Santa Àgata (p64) and the churches of Santa Maria del Pi (p66) and Santa Maria del Mar (p80) were all built within the city's boundaries during the late 13th or early 14th centuries. King Pere III (1336–87) later created the breathtaking Reials Drassanes (Royal Shipyards; p73) and also extended the city walls yet again, this time to include the El Raval area to the west.

DECLINE & CASTILIAN DOMINATION

Preserving the empire began to exhaust Catalonia. Sea wars with Genoa, resistance in Sardinia, the rise of the Ottoman Empire and the loss of the gold trade all drained the city's coffers. Com-

1283	1323	1348
The Corts Catalanes, a legislative council for Catalonia, meets for the first time and begins to curtail unlimited powers of sovereigns in favour of the nobles and the powerful trading class in the cities.	Catalan forces land in Sardinia and launch a campaign of conquest that would only end in 1409. Their most fierce enemy was Eleonora de Arborea, a Sardinian Joan of Arc. Sporadic revolts continue until 1478.	An outbreak of plague devastates Barcelona. Two-thirds of the city's population may have died. Further waves of the Black Death, a plague of locusts in 1358 and an earthquake in 1373 deal further blows.

merce collapsed. The Black Death and famines killed about half of Catalonia's population in the 14th century. Barcelona's Jewish population suffered a pogrom in 1391.

After the last of Guifré el Pelós' dynasty, Martí I, died heirless in 1410, a stacked council elected Fernando (known as Ferran to the Catalans) de Antequera, a Castilian prince of the Trastámara house, to the Aragonese throne. This Compromiso de Caspe (Caspe Agreement) of 1412 was engineered by the Aragonese nobility, which saw it as a chance to reduce Catalan influence.

Another Fernando succeeded to the Aragonese throne in 1479 and his marriage to Isabel, queen of Castilla, united Spain's two most powerful monarchies. Just as Catalonia had been hitched to Aragón, now the combine was hitched to Castilla.

Catalonia effectively became part of the Castilian state, although it jealously guarded its own institutions and system of law. Rather than attack this problem head on, Fernando and Isabel sidestepped it, introducing the hated Spanish Inquisition to Barcelona in 1487 (a local, milder version of the Inquisition had operated on Catalan territory since 1242, with headquarters in the Palau Episcopal – see p63). The local citizenry implored them not to do so as what was left of business life in the city lay largely in the hands of *conversos* (Jews at least nominally converted to Christianity) who were a particular target of Inquisitorial attention. The pleas were ignored and the *conversos* packed their bags and shipped out their money. Barcelona was reduced to penury. Fernando and Isabel's successors, the Habsburg Holy Roman Emperor Carlos V (Carlos I of Spain), and his son, Felipe II, tightened Madrid's grip on Catalonia, although the region long managed to retain a degree of autonomy.

Impoverished and disaffected by ever-growing financial demands from the crown, Catalonia revolted in the 17th century in the Guerra dels Segadors (Reapers' War; 1640–52) and declared itself to be an independent 'republic' under French protection. The countryside and towns were devastated, and Barcelona was finally besieged into submission.

WAR OF THE SPANISH SUCCESSION

By the beginning of the 18th century Spain was on the skids. The last of the Habsburgs, Carlos II, died in 1700 with no successor. France imposed a Bourbon, the absolutist Felipe V, but the Catalans preferred the Austrian candidate, Archduke Carlos, and threw in their lot with England, Holland, some German states, Portugal and the House of Savoy to back Austria. In 1702, the War of the Spanish Succession broke out. Catalans thought they were onto a winner. They were wrong and in 1713 the Treaty of Utrecht left Felipe V in charge in Madrid. Abandoned by its allies, Barcelona decided to resist. The siege began in March 1713 and ended on 11 September 1714.

There were no half measures. Felipe V abolished the Generalitat, built a huge fort (the Ciutadella) to watch over Barcelona, and banned writing and teaching in Catalan. What was left of Catalonia's possessions were farmed out to the great powers.

A NEW BOOM

After the initial shock, Barcelona found the Bourbon rulers to be comparatively light-handed in their treatment of the city. Indeed, its prosperity and productivity was in Spain's national interest. Throughout the 18th century, the *barcelonins* concentrated on what they do best – industry and commerce.

1670	1714	1770
Barcelona's first bullfights are held for the Viceroy, the Duke of Osuña, in the Pla del Palau. Fourteen bulls succumb to the toreros in an activity that would become popular in the 19th century.	Barcelona loses all autonomy after surrendering to the Bourbon king, Felipe V, on 11 September at the end of the War of the Spanish Succession.	A hurricane strikes Barcelona, causing considerable damage. Among other things, the winds destroy more than 200 of the city's 1500 gaslight street lamps.

The big break came in 1778, when the ban on trade with the Spanish American colonies was lifted. Since the Conquistadors opened up South America to Spanish trade, Barcelona had been sidelined in a deliberate policy to favour Seville and its satellite ports, which was deemed as being loyal to Madrid. That ban had been formalised after the defeat of 1714. Some enterprising traders had already sent vessels across the Atlantic to deal directly in the Americas – although this was still technically forbidden. Their early ventures were a commercial success and the lifting of the ban stimulated business. In Barcelona itself, growth was modest but sustained. Small-scale manufacturing provided employment and profit. Wages were rising and the city fathers even had a stab at town planning, creating the grid-based workers' district of La Barceloneta.

Before the industrial revolution, based initially on the cotton trade with America, could really get underway, Barcelona and the rest of Spain had to go through a little more pain. A French revolutionary army was launched Spain's way (1793–95) with limited success, but when Napoleon turned his attentions to the country in 1808 it was another story. Barcelona and Catalonia suffered along with the rest of the country until the French were expelled in 1814 (Barcelona was the last city in the hands of the French, who left in September).

By the 1830s, Barcelona was beginning to ride on a feel-good factor that would last for most of the century. Wine, cork and iron industries developed. From the mid-1830s onwards, steamships were launched off the slipways. In 1848 Spain's first railway line was opened between Barcelona and Mataró.

Creeping industrialisation and prosperity for the business class did not work out so well down the line. Working-class families lived in increasingly putrid and cramped conditions. Poor nutrition, bad sanitation and disease were the norm in workers' districts, and riots, predictably, resulted. As a rule they were put down with little ceremony – the 1842 rising was bombarded into submission from the Montjuïc castle. Some relief came in 1854 with the knocking down of the medieval walls but the pressure remained acute.

In 1869 a plan to expand the city was begun. Ildefons Cerdà designed L'Eixample (the Enlargement) as a grid, broken up with gardens and parks and grafted onto the old town, beginning at Plaça de Catalunya. The plan was revolutionary. Until then it had been illegal to build in the plains between Barcelona and Gràcia, the area being a military zone. As industrialisation got underway this building ban also forced the concentration of factories in Barcelona itself (especially in La Barceloneta) and surrounding towns like Gràcia, Sant Martí, Sants and Sant Andreu (all of which were subsequently swallowed up by the burgeoning city).

L'Eixample became (and to some extent remains) the most sought-after chunk of real estate in Barcelona – but the parks were mostly sacrificed to an insatiable demand for housing and undisguised land speculation. The flourishing bourgeoisie paid for lavish, ostentatious buildings, many of them in the unique, Modernista style.

There seemed to be no stopping this town. In 1888 it hosted a Universal Exhibition. Little more than a year before, work on the exhibition buildings and grounds had not even begun, but they were all completed only 10 days late. Although the exhibition attracted more than two million visitors, it did not generate the international attention some had hoped for.

Still, changing the cityscape had become habitual in modern Barcelona. La Rambla de Catalunya and Avinguda del Paral.lel were both slammed through in 1888. The Mirador de Colom and Arc de Triomf, rather odd monuments in some respects (Columbus had little to do with Barcelona and tangible triumphs were in short supply), also were built that year.

1808	1873	1895
In the Battle of Bruc outside Barcelona, Catalan militiamen defeat occupying Napoleonic units in June. Nonetheless, Barcelona, Figueres and the coast remain under French control until Napoleon is ejected from Spain in 1814.	Antoni Gaudí, 21 years old and in Barcelona since 1869, enrols in architecture school, from which he graduates five years later, having already designed the street lamps in Plaça Reial.	Málaga-born Pablo Picasso, 13, arrives in Barcelona with his family. His art teacher father gets a job in the Escola de Belles Artes de la Llotja, where Pablo is enrolled as a pupil.

BARCELONA REBORN

Barcelona was comparatively peaceful for most of the second half of the 19th century but far from politically inert. The relative calm and growing wealth that came with commercial success helped revive interest in all things Catalan.

The Renaixença (Renaissance) reflected the feeling in Barcelona of renewed self-confidence. The mood was both backwards- and forwards-looking. Politicians and academics increasingly studied and demanded the return of former Catalan institutions and legal systems. The Catalan language was readopted by the middle and upper classes and new Catalan literature emerged as well.

In 1892 the Unió Catalanista (Catalanist Union) demanded the re-establishment of the Corts in a document known as the *Bases de Manresa*. In 1906 the suppression of Catalan newssheets was greeted by the formation of Solidaritat Catalana (Catalan Solidarity, a nationalist movement). Led by Enric Prat de la Riba, it attracted a broad band of Catalans, not all of them nationalists.

Perhaps the most dynamic expression of the Catalan Renaissance occurred in the world of art. Barcelona was the home of Modernisme, Catalan Art Nouveau. While the rest of Spain stagnated, Barcelona was a hotbed of artistic activity, an avant-garde base with close links to Paris. The young Picasso spread his artistic wings here and drank in the artists' hangout, Els Quatre Gats (p70), a Modernista tavern that today is a somewhat mediocre eatery.

An unpleasant wakeup call came with Spain's short, futile war with the US in 1898, in which it lost not only its entire navy, but its last colonies (Cuba, Puerto Rico and the Philippines). The blow to Barcelona's trade was enormous.

MAYHEM

Barcelona's proletariat was growing fast. The total population grew from 115,000 in 1800 to over 500,000 by 1900 and over one million by 1930 – boosted, in the early 19th century, by poor immigrants from rural Catalonia and, later, from other regions of Spain. All this made Barcelona ripe for unrest.

The city became a swirling vortex of anarchists, Republicans, bourgeois regionalists, gangsters, police terrorists and hired *pistoleros* (gunmen). One anarchist bomb at the Liceu opera house on La Rambla in the 1890s killed 20 people. Anarchists were also blamed for the Setmana Tràgica (Tragic Week) in July 1909 when, following a military call-up for Spanish campaigns in Morocco, rampaging mobs wrecked 70 religious buildings and workers were shot on the street in reprisal.

In the post-WWI slump, unionism took hold. This movement was led by the anarchist Confederación Nacional del Trabajo (CNT), or National Workers' Confederation, which embraced 80% of the city's workers. During a wave of strikes in 1919 and 1920, employers hired assassins to eliminate union leaders. The 1920s dictator General Miguel Primo de Rivera opposed bourgeois-Catalan nationalism and working-class radicalism, banning the CNT and even closing Barcelona football club, a potent symbol of Catalanism. But he did support the staging of a second world fair in Barcelona, the Montjuïc World Exhibition of 1929.

Rivera's repression only succeeded in uniting, after his fall in 1930, Catalonia's radical elements. Within days of the formation of Spain's Second Republic in 1931, leftist Catalan nationalists of the ERC (Esquerra Republicana de Catalunya), led by Francesc Macià and Lluís

1898	1914	July 1936
Spain loses its entire navy and last remaining colonies (the Philippines, Cuba and Puerto Rico) in two hopeless campaigns against the USA, dealing a heavy blow to Barcelona businesses.	The Mancomunitat de Catalunya, a first timid attempt at self-rule (restricted largely to administrative matters) and headed by Catalan nationalist Enric Prat de la Riba, is created in April.	General Franco launches the Spanish Civil War in Morocco. In Barcelona, General Goded leads army units to take the city for Franco but is defeated by a combination of left-wing militia, workers and loyalist police.

Companys, proclaimed Catalonia a republic within an imaginary 'Iberian Federation'. Madrid pressured them into accepting unitary Spanish statehood, but after the leftist Popular Front victory in the February 1936 national elections, Catalonia briefly won genuine autonomy. Companys, its president, carried out land reforms and planned an alternative Barcelona Olympics to the official 1936 games in Nazi Berlin.

But things were racing out of control. The left and the right across Spain were shaping up for a showdown.

THE CIVIL WAR

On 17 July 1936, an army uprising in Morocco kick-started the Spanish Civil War. Barcelona's army garrison attempted to take the city for General Franco but was defeated by anarchists and police loyal to the government.

Franco's Nationalist forces quickly took hold of most of southern and western Spain; Galicia and Navarra in the north were also his. Most of the east and industrialised north stood with Madrid. Initial rapid advances on Madrid were stifled and the two sides settled in for almost three years of misery.

For nearly a year, Barcelona was run by anarchists and the Partido Obrero de Unificación Marxista (POUM; the Marxist Unification Workers' Party) Trotskyist militia, with Companys president only in name. Factory owners and rightists fled the city. Unions took over factories and public services, hotels and mansions became hospitals and schools, everyone wore workers' clothes (in something of a foretaste of what would later happen in Mao's China), bars and cafés were collectivised, trams and taxis were painted red and black (the colours of the anarchists) and one-way streets were ignored as they were seen to be part of the old system.

The anarchists were a disparate lot ranging from gentle idealists to hardliners who drew up death lists, held kangaroo courts, shot priests, monks and nuns (over 1200 of whom were killed in Barcelona province during the civil war), and also burnt and wrecked churches – which is why so many of Barcelona's churches are today oddly plain inside. They in turn were shunted aside by the communists (directed by Stalin from Moscow) after a bloody internecine battle in Barcelona that left 1500 dead in May 1937.

Barcelona became the Republicans' national capital in autumn 1937. The Republican defeat in the Battle of the Ebro in southern Catalonia in summer 1938 left Barcelona undefended. Republican resistance crumbled, in part due to exhaustion, in part due to disunity. In 1938 Catalan nationalists started negotiating separately with the Nationalists. Indeed, the last resistance put up in Barcelona was by some 2000 soldiers of the Fifth Regiment that had fought so long in Madrid! The city fell on 25 January 1939.

That first year of occupation was a strange hiatus before the full machinery of oppression began to weigh in. Within two weeks of the city's fall, a dozen cinemas were in operation and the following month Hollywood comedies were being shown between rounds of Nationalist propaganda. The people were even encouraged to dance the *sardana*, Catalonia's national dance, in public (the Nationalists thought such folkloric generosity might endear them to the people of Barcelona).

On the other hand, the city presented an exhausted picture. The Metro was running but there were no buses (they had all been used on the front). Virtually all the animals in the city zoo had died of starvation or wounds. There were frequent blackouts, and would be for years.

March 1938	1939	1940
In just three days of day and night air raids on Barcelona carried out by Fascist Italian bombers based in Franco-controlled Mallorca, 979 people are killed and 1500 wounded.	On 26 January, the first of Franco's troops, along with Italian tanks, roll into Barcelona from Tibidabo and parade down Avinguda Diagonal. Thousands flee the city towards the French border.	Hitler's henchman and chief of the SS, Heinrich Himmler visits Barcelona, stays at the Ritz, enjoys a folkloric show at Poble Espanyol and has his wallet stolen.

By 1940, with WWII raging across Europe, Franco had his regime more firmly in place and things turned darker for many. Catalan Francoists led the way in rounding up victims and up to 35,000 people were shot in purges. At the same time, small bands of resistance fighters continued to harry the Nationalists in the Pyrenees through much of the 1940s. Lluís Companys was arrested in France by the Gestapo in August 1940, handed over to Franco, and shot on 15 October on Montjuïc. He is reputed to have died with the words 'Visca Catalunya!' ('Long live Catalonia!') on his lips. The executions continued into the 1950s. *Barcelonins* reacted in different ways. Most accepted the situation and tried to get on with living, while some leapt at opportunities, occupying flats abandoned by 'Reds' who had been forced to flee. Speculators and industrialists in bed with Franco began to make money hand over fist while most people barely managed to keep body and soul together.

FROM FRANCO TO PUJOL

Franco had already abolished the Generalitat in 1938. Companys was succeeded as the head of the Catalan government-in-exile in Mexico by Josep Irla and, in 1954, by the charismatic Josep Tarradellas, who remained its head until after Franco's demise.

Franco, meanwhile, embarked on a programme of Castilianisation. He banned public use of Catalan and had all town, village and street names rendered in Spanish (Castilian). Book publishing in Catalan was allowed from the mid-1940s, but education, radio, TV and the daily press remained in Spanish.

In Barcelona, the Francoist Josep Maria de Porcioles became mayor in 1957, a post he held until 1973. That same year, he obtained for the city a 'municipal charter' that expanded the mayor's authority and the city's capacity to raise and spend taxes, manage urban development and, ultimately, widen the city's metropolitan limits to absorb neighbouring territory. He was responsible for such monstrosities as the concrete municipal buildings on Plaça de Sant Miquel in the Barri Gòtic. His rule marked a grey time for Barcelona. Barely regulated urban expansion was the norm and decades of grime accumulated on the face of the city, hiding the delightful flights of architectural fantasy that today draw so many visitors.

By the 1950s, opposition to Franco had turned to peaceful mass protests and strikes. In 1960, an audience at the city's Palau de la Música Catalana concert hall (p84) sang a banned Catalan anthem in front of Franco. The ringleaders included a young Catholic banker, Jordi Pujol, who would later rise to pre-eminence in the post-Franco era. For his singing effort he wound up in jail for a short time.

Under Franco a flood of 1.5 million immigrants from poorer parts of Spain, chiefly Andalucía, Extremadura and the northwest, poured into Catalonia (750,000 of them to Barcelona) in the 1950s and '60s looking for work. Many lived in appalling conditions. While some made the effort to learn Catalan and integrate as fully as possible into local society, the majority came to form Spanish-speaking pockets in the poorer working-class districts of the city and in a ring of satellite towns. Even today, the atmosphere in many of these towns is more Andalucian than Catalan. Catalan nationalists will tell you it was all part of a Francoist plot to undermine the Catalan identity.

Two years after Franco's death in 1975, Josep Tarradellas was invited to Madrid to hammer out the Catalan part of a regional autonomy policy. Eighteen days later, King Juan Carlos I decreed the re-establishment of the Generalitat and recognised Josep Tarradellas as its president.

1957	1980	1992
The Francoist Josep Maria de Porcioles becomes mayor of Barcelona and remains in charge until 1973. He presides over a willy-nilly building spurt in the city and builds the first *rondas* (ring roads).	Right-wing Catalan nationalist Jordi Pujol is elected president of the resurrected Catalan regional government at the head of the CiU coalition; he remains in power without interruption until 2003.	Barcelona is catapulted to the world stage as it hosts the summer Olympic Games. In preparation for the games, the city undergoes a radical renovation programme whose momentum continues to the present.

Twenty years after his stint in Franco's jails, Pujol was elected Tarradellas' successor at the head of the rightwing Catalan nationalist Convergència i Unió (CiU) coalition in April 1980. A wily antagonist of the central authorities in Madrid, he waged a quarter-century war of attrition, eking out greater fiscal and policy autonomy and vigorously promoting a re-Catalanisation programme, with uneven success.

Politics aside, the big event in post-Franco Barcelona was the successful 1992 Olympics, planned under the guidance of the popular Socialist mayor, Pasqual Maragall. The Games spurred a burst of public works and brought new life to areas such as Montjuïc, where the major events were held. The once-shabby waterfront was transformed with promenades, beaches, marinas, restaurants, leisure attractions and new housing.

A LEFTWARD LURCH & TUNNEL VISION

Pujol remained in power until 2003, when he stepped aside to make way for his designated successor, party colleague Artur Mas. Things didn't go according to plan, as Pasqual Maragall pipped Mas at the post and formed an unsteady three-party coalition government in November 2003.

Maragall's principal achievement was reaching agreement between his Partit Socialista de Catalunya (PSC), his coalition partners Iniciativa Verds-Esquerra Unida (Green Initiative-United Left) and independence-minded Esquerra Republicana de Catalunya (ERC, Republican Left of Catalonia), and the opposition CiU on a new autonomy statute (*Estatut*). Since the demise of Franco, Spain has devolved considerable powers to the regions, which are officially known as *comunidades autónomas* (autonomous communities).

The proposed statute was submitted to the national Spanish parliament for consideration in 2005 and was the subject of tough bargaining. In early 2006, Prime Minister José Luis Rodríguez Zapatero's governing Partido Socialista Obrero Español (PSOE, Spanish Socialist Workers' Party, of which the PSC is a branch) and CiU struck a deal, behind Maragall's back, to approve a modified version of the *Estatut*.

Maragall reluctantly went along with the deal but his ERC allies protested and forced the dissolution of the Catalan parliament and snap elections in autumn 2006. Maragall, accused of weakness in the face of the ERC by the PSOE, was obliged to make way for Madrid's preferred candidate, José Montilla. In a virtual rerun, Montilla won by such a narrow margin that he was forced to re-establish the weak three-party coalition of his predecessor.

DIVE, DIVE, DIVE

It could have been the Spanish Navy's V2, a late-19th-century secret weapon. Narcís Monturiol i Estarriol (1819–85), part-time publisher and all-round utopian, was fascinated by the sea. In 1859, he launched a wooden, fish-shaped submarine, the *Ictíneo*, in Barcelona. Air shortages made only brief dives possible but Monturiol became an overnight celebrity. He received, however, not a jot of funding.

Undeterred, he sank himself further into debt by designing *Ictíneo II*. This was a first. It was 17m long, its screws were steam driven and Monturiol had devised a system for renewing the oxygen inside the vessel. It was trialled in 1864 but again attracted no finance. Four years later, the vessel was broken up for scrap.

If the Spaniards had had a few of these when they faced the US Navy off Cuba and in the Philippines in 1898, perhaps things might have turned out differently!

January 1994	2003	2006
The Gran Teatre del Liceu, Barcelona's opera house, burns to the ground as a spark from a welder's blowtorch sets the stage area alight. It is rebuilt and reopens in 1999.	Popular former mayor of Barcelona, Pasqual Maragall becomes the first Socialist president of Catalonia (with a wobbly three-party coalition) in tight elections after Pujol steps aside in favour of CiU's Artur Mas.	The Catalan government negotiates a new autonomy statute with Madrid in a compromise that leaves many unsatisfied and ultimately leads to the fall of Maragall. His replacement, after snap elections, is fellow Socialist José Montilla.

BARCELONA, OPEN CITY

It made little difference to Benito Mussolini, General Franco's overbearing Fascist comrade-in-arms, that Barcelona possessed few military targets worthy of note beyond its port and railway, or that it had been declared an open city precisely to avoid its destruction.

In a trial run for the horrors that would rain down on Europe in WWII, Italian bombers based in Mallorca (joined towards the end of the war by Germany's terrifying Junkers JU87 Stuka dive-bombers) carried out air raids on the largely defenceless city (only three Italian planes were brought down over Barcelona in the entire war) regularly from 16 March 1937 to 24 January 1939, a day before Nationalist troops marched in. Mussolini ordered the raids with or without Franco's blessing, which the latter often withheld, realising that indiscriminate bombing of civilians would hardly boost his popularity. Indeed, Franco prohibited attacks on urban centres in March 1938, after three days of relentless raids that cost almost 1000 lives, but the Italians paid no heed. By the end of the war, almost 3000 Barcelonins had been killed, with 7000 wounded and 1800 buildings destroyed.

In a radio broadcast on 18 June 1940, as the Battle of Britain began, Winston Churchill declared: 'I do not underrate the severity of the ordeal which lies before us but I believe our countrymen will show themselves capable of standing up to it like the brave men of Barcelona.' He might have added women and children, who together formed the bulk of the bombers' victims.

Catalans approved the new Estatut in a referendum in 2006 but within months the rightwing Partido Popular launched an appeal in the Constitutional Court to repeal the Estatut, which it claims grants too much autonomy. Four years later, the court was still wrangling over it.

For years, Barcelona and the regional Catalan government have railed against Madrid's lack of investment in infrastructure in Catalonia, from transport to electricity supply. In 2009, the central government agreed to a record €4.8 billion in infrastructure finance for Catalonia in that year alone – a long overdue record figure, according to the Catalan government. This came at a time when statistics were showing Madrid's economy coming ever closer to toppling Catalonia from its number one spot. The Catalans were hanging on with a GDP of €6.3 billion.

Jordi Hereu, the PSC candidate who had replaced Joan Clos as mayor in 2006, came out on top in the city's 2007 polls and formed a shaky minority government with Iniciativa Verds-Esquerra Unida. Many observers predict a first-ever defeat for the PSC in the next elections, due in 2011.

In 2009, the city was rocked by a scandal in one of its most emblematic institutions, the Palau de la Música Catalana (p84). The president of the foundation that runs the Palau, a certain Felix Millet, was forced to resign over charges of embezzling Palau funds. By September 2009, he had admitted to creaming off €3.3 million but as investigations continued, it appeared the true figure might be considerably more.

ARTS

Once home to Picasso and Miró, Barcelona has had an on-and-off run as a centre of artistic creation. Today, art galleries and museums abound, world-class exhibitions are standard fare and there is a hum in the air. While cinema is largely the preserve of Madrid, Barcelona is Spain's publishing capital and many of the country's top writers are Catalans. If only to reach a broader market, many of them choose to write in Spanish. On the other hand, a bevy of musicians, from stalwarts with an international following to eager young rock bands, cheerfully

March 2008	September 2009	January 2010
Socialist Prime Minister, José Luis Rodríguez Zapatero wins second four-year term in office at Spanish national elections, with 169 seats (seven short of an absolute majority) to the right-wing opposition Partido Popular's 153 seats.	The President of the Palau de la Música, Felix Millet, shocks the establishment as he confesses to misappropriating more than €3 million in this iconic cultural institution's funds. Forced to resign, he's later accused of misappropriating more than €10 million.	The mayor of Barcelona, Jordi Hereu, announces that the city will be a candidate for the 2022 Olympic Winter Games.

top picks

NOTABLE BUILDINGS

- Casa Amatller (p105) Puig i Cadafalch's Modernista-Gothic romp has a Dutch air about it.
- Casa Batlló (p105) Gaudí renovated this block of flats to make it look like a sinewy deep-sea beast.
- Edifici Fòrum (p95) A strange blue triangle hovers by the beach like an enormous UFO.
- Església de Santa Maria del Mar (p80) Broad and noble, and constructed in record time, this is Barcelona's proudest Gothic church.
- Hospital de la Santa Creu i de Sant Pau (p109) With its dainty pavilions, ceramic décor and gardens, this hospital works artistic as well as medical wonders.
- La Pedrera (p104) Its detractors called it 'the quarry' for its wavy stone structure.
- La Sagrada Família (p102) Gaudí's unfinished masterpiece is still in construction.
- Palau de la Música Catalana (p84) This Modernista caprice is home to Catalan music.
- Pavelló Mies van der Rohe (p145) A touch of interwar German new wave building brought back to life.
- Torre Agbar (p95) Jean Nouvel's multicoloured cucumber illuminates Barcelona's night sky.

belt out their songs in Catalan, a tradition that started in part as a way of flouting Francoist cultural repression. For many a young local, Catalan rock rocks!

ARCHITECTURE

How odd that the many weird and wonderful buildings that attract planeloads of tourists to Barcelona every day barely raised an eyebrow until the 1990s. As seaside tourism took off in Spain from the 1960s, Barcelona was ignored. The bulk of its Modernista (Catalan Art Nouveau) masterpieces lay buried under decades of grime, neglected by locals and unknown to outsiders. Business-minded Barcelona was sitting on a goldmine, but nobody realised it.

Gaudí was vaguely known for his unfinished architectural symphony, La Sagrada Família. But no-one gave a fig for La Pedrera, his gracefully curvaceous piece of whimsy on Passeig de Gràcia.

How things have changed. Gaudí stood at the pinnacle of Modernisme, which since the 1992 Olympic Games has been rediscovered for the burst of joyous creativity its architects brought to construction in Barcelona from the late 1800s to the 1920s. For more on this turn to p125.

Barcelona's last such building boom had come at the height of the Middle Ages, when its great Gothic churches, mansions and shipyards were raised, together creating what survives to this day as one of the most extensive Gothic old city centres in Europe.

Although the medieval wrecking balls put paid to most of it, there was architecture before Gothic. On the site of the original Roman town rose a busy centre full of Romanesque monuments. Some evidence of both periods can still be admired.

Roman Remnants

What Caesar Augustus and friends called Barcino was a standard Roman rectangular (more or less) town. The forum lay about where Plaça de Sant Jaume is and the whole place covered little more than 10 hectares.

There remain some impressive leftovers of the 4th-century walls that once comprised 70 towers. In the basement of the Museu d'Història de la Ciutat (p63) you can inspect parts of a tower and the wall, as well as a whole chunk of the Roman town unearthed during excavations. On the edge of what was the forum stand stout columns of the temple raised for emperor worship, the Temple Romà d'August (p68). A little further north along what was once one of the roads leading out of the Roman town, sarcophagi of modest Roman tombs (p68) are visible.

Romanesque

Little remains of Barcelona's Romanesque past – largely swept aside to make way for what were considered greater Gothic spectacles. A tour through northern Catalonia should more than satisfy your curiosity as to what form the Catalan version of this first great wave of Christian-European architecture took.

Lombard artisans from northern Italy first introduced the Romanesque style of building to Catalonia. It is characterised by a pleasing simplicity, although its roots lie in grander buildings of the imperial Roman age. Churches tended to be austere, angular constructions, with tall, square-based bell towers. There were a few notable concessions to the curve – almost always semicircular or semicylindrical. These included the barrel vaulting inside the churches and the apse (or apses).

The main portal and windows are invariably topped with simple arches. If builders were feeling daring, they might adorn the main entrance with several arches within one another. From the late 11th century, stonemasons began to fill the arches with statuary.

In Barcelona you can see only a few Romanesque remnants. In La Catedral the 13th-century Capella de Santa Llúcia (p63) survives, along with part of the cloister doors. The 12th-century former Benedictine Església de Sant Pau del Camp (p77) is also a good example, especially the cloisters.

The counterpoint to Romanesque architecture was the art used to decorate churches and monasteries built in the style. Contrary to popular belief, these buildings were not bare stone, but gaily painted inside and out. Barcelona is the place to see this art, as the best Romanesque frescoes from around Catalonia are preserved in the Museu Nacional d'Art de Catalunya (p138).

Gothic Grandeur

This soaring style took off in France in the 13th century and spread across Europe. Its emergence coincided with Jaume I's march into Valencia and the annexation of Mallorca and Ibiza, accompanied by the rise and rise of a trading class and a burgeoning mercantile empire. The enormous cost of building the grand new monuments could thus be covered by the steady increase in the city's wealth.

The style of architecture reflected the development of building techniques. The introduction of buttresses, flying buttresses and ribbed vaulting in ceilings allowed engineers to raise edifices that were loftier and seemingly lighter than ever before. The pointed arch became standard and great rose windows were the source of light inside these enormous spaces. Think about the hovels that labourers on such projects lived in and the primitive nature of building materials available, and you get an idea of the awe such churches, once completed, must have inspired. They were not built in a day. It took more than 160 years, a fairly typical time frame, to finish La Catedral (p59), although its façade was not erected until the 19th century. Its rival, the Església de Santa Maria del Mar (p80), was one for the record books, taking only 59 years to build.

Catalan Gothic did not follow the same course as the style typical of northern Europe. Decoration here tends to be more sparing and the most obvious defining characteristic is the triumph of breadth over height. While northern European cathedrals reach for the sky, Catalan Gothic has a tendency to push to the sides, stretching its vaulting design to the limit.

The Saló del Tinell (p64), with a parade of 15m arches (among the largest ever built without reinforcement) holding up the roof, is a perfect example of Catalan Gothic. Another is the present home of the Museu Marítim, the Drassanes (p73), Barcelona's medieval shipyards. In their churches, too, the Catalans opted for a more robust shape and lateral

top picks

BARCELONA ARCHITECTURE BOOKS

- Barcelona Architecture & Design (Jürgen Forster) A handy guide to all sorts of buildings, parks, designer hotels and restaurants for the contemporary design lover.
- Catalunya: Guía de la Arquitectura Moderna 1880–2007 (Col.legi d'Arquitectes de Catalunya) An exhaustive presentation (available in English) of modern Catalan architecture (missing a few of the latest items) in and beyond Barcelona.
- El Gòtic Català (Francesca Español) Full of photos, this is as close to a specialised look at Catalan Gothic building as you'll find (in Catalan).
- Gaudí: The Man & His Work (Joan Masso Bergos) A beautifully illustrated study of the man and his architecture, based on the writings of one of his confidants.
- La Ruta del Modernisme (Published by Barcelona Town Hall) An extensive guide to 115 Modernista buildings across the city. It comes with discounted entry to many sights.
- Gaudí (Gijs van Hensbergen) A nicely crafted biography of one of architecture's most extraordinary yet elusive characters.

space – step into the Església de Santa Maria del Mar or the Església de Santa Maria del Pi (p66) and you'll soon get the idea.

Another notable departure from what you might have come to expect of Gothic north of the Pyrenees is the lack of spires and pinnacles. Bell towers tend to terminate in a flat or nearly flat roof. Occasional exceptions prove the rule – the main facade of Barcelona's Catedral, with its three gnarled and knobbly spires, does vaguely resemble the outline that confronts you in cathedrals in Chartres or Cologne. But then it was a 19th-century addition, admittedly to a medieval design.

Perhaps the single greatest building spurt came under Pere III. This is odd in a sense because, as Dickens might have observed, it was not only the best of times, but also the worst. By the mid-14th century, when Pere III was in command, Barcelona had been pushed to the ropes by a series of disasters: famine, repeated plagues and pogroms.

Maybe he didn't notice. He built, or began to build, much of La Catedral, the Drassanes, the Llotja stock exchange, the Saló del Tinell, the Casa de la Ciutat (which now houses the town hall) and numerous lesser buildings, not to mention part of the city walls. The churches of Santa Maria del Pi and Santa Maria del Mar were completed by the end of the 14th century.

Gothic had a longer use-by date in Barcelona than in many other European centres. By the early 15th century, the Generalitat still didn't have a home worthy of its name, and architect Marc Safont set to work on the present building on Plaça de Sant Jaume (p65). Even renovations carried out a century later were largely in the Gothic tradition, although some Renaissance elements eventually snuck in – the façade on Plaça de Sant Jaume is a rather disappointing result.

Carrer de Montcada (p80), in La Ribera, was the result of a late-medieval act of town planning. Eventually, mansions belonging to the moneyed classes of 15th- and 16th-century Barcelona were erected along it. Many now house museums and art galleries. Although these former mansions appear forbidding on the outside, their interiors often reveal another world, of pleasing courtyards and decorated external staircases. They mostly went through a gentle baroque make-over in later years.

Most of Barcelona's Gothic heritage lies within the boundaries of Ciutat Vella but a few examples can be found beyond, notably the Museu-Monestir de Pedralbes (p121) in Sarrià.

Renaissance To Neoclassicism

The strong *barcelonin* affection for Gothic, coupled with a decline in the city's fortunes that slowed urban development, seems to have largely closed Barcelona to the Renaissance and baroque periods that blossomed elsewhere in Europe (and elsewhere in Spain). The handful of examples of baroque in Barcelona are generally decorative rather than structural.

Among the more important but restrained baroque constructions are the Església de la Mercè (p69), home to the medieval sculpture of Mare del Déu de la Mercè (Our Lady of Mercy; Barcelona's co-patron with Santa Eulàlia); the Església de Sant Felip Neri (p71); and the Jesuits' Església de Betlem (p57), largely destroyed in the civil war and since rebuilt. Also worth a look is the courtyard of the Palau de Dalmases (p80), in Carrer de Montcada, which has been reworked from the original Gothic structure.

The Palau de la Virreina (p57), just across Carrer del Carme from the Església de Betlem, is, depending on which expert you read, a rococo or neoclassical building raised in the 1770s. If anything, it is hybrid. More definitely neoclassical and built around the same time is Palau Moja (p57), across La Rambla.

OH, HOW AWFULLY GOTHIC!

The lofty Gothic buildings of medieval Europe inspire awe in their modern visitors. But as early as the 16th century, when Renaissance artists and architects turned to the clean lines of Classical Antiquity for inspiration, all things medieval looked crude, rough and, well, frankly barbarian, just like the ancient Germanic tribes of Goths that had stormed across Europe centuries before. To label something Gothic became the ultimate insult. This attitude spread across Europe. In Barcelona, many private homes built in Gothic style would get a baroque make-over later, but thankfully most of the major monuments were left alone. Not until the 19th century did this extraordinary heritage again awaken admiration, to such an extent that in some north European countries in particular it led to a wave of Gothic revival building.

top picks

BEST MUSEUM FOR...

- Ancient History Buffs: Museu d'Història Barcelona (p63)
- Lovers of the Sea and Gothic Architecture: Museu Marítim (p73)
- Devotees of Romanesque Art: Museu Nacional d'Art de Catalunya (p138)
- Aficionados of Pre-Colombian Art: Museu Barbier-Mueller d'Art Pre-Colombí (p81)
- Kids and Chocoholics: Museu de la Xocolata (p86)

The Napoleonic wars and successive outbursts of political trouble did little to encourage interesting architectural developments in the course of the 19th century. Then, around 1880, an exhilarating movement emerged that would forever change the city's look. For more on the Modernistas and contemporary architecture, turn to p125.

PAINTING & SCULPTURE

The Middle Ages

Many anonymous artists left their work behind in medieval Catalonia, mostly in the form of frescoes, altarpieces and the like in Romanesque and Gothic churches – the Museu Nacional d'Art de Catalunya (MNAC; p138) houses a magnificent collection of these.

But a few leading lights managed to get some credit. Gothic painter Ferrer Bassá (c 1290–1348) was one of the region's first recognised masters. Influenced by the Italian school of Siena, his few surviving works include murals with a slight touch of caricature in the Monestir de Pedralbes (p121).

Bernat Martorell (1400–52), a master of chiaroscuro who was active in the mid-15th century, was one of the region's leading exponents of International Gothic. As the Flemish school gained influence, painters like Jaume Huguet (1415–92) adopted its sombre realism, lightening the style with Hispanic splashes of gold, as in his *Sant Jordi* in the MNAC. Another of his paintings hangs in the Museu Frederic Marès (p64).

In the latter museum you may be overwhelmed by the collection of medieval wooden sculpture. Mostly anonymous sculptors were busy throughout Catalonia from at least the 12th century, carving religious images for the growing number of churches. Although saints and other characters sometimes figured, by far the most common subjects were Christ crucified and the Virgin Mary with the Christ child sitting on her lap.

Another source of exquisite sculpture lies in VIP sarcophagi. Examples range from the alabaster memorial to Santa Eulàlia in La Catedral (p70) to the pantheon of count-kings in the Reial Monestir de Santa Maria de Poblet (see boxed text, p261) outside Barcelona.

Fortuny's Century

Little of greatness was achieved in Catalan painting and sculpture from the end of the Middle Ages to the 19th century. Barcelona neither produced nor attracted any El Grecos, Velázquezs, Zurbaráns, Murillos or Goyas.

By the mid-19th century, Realisme was the modish medium on canvas, reaching a zenith with the work of Marià Fortuny (1838–74). The best known (and largest) of his paintings is the 'official' version of the *Batalla de Tetuán* (Battle of Tetuán; 1863), depicting a rousing Spanish victory over a ragtag Moroccan enemy in North Africa. Fortuny, whom many consider the best Catalan artist of the 19th century, left his native turf for Italy in 1857, where he died in Rome. He had lived for a time in Venice, where his lodgings now constitute a gallery of his works.

Modernisme & Noucentisme

Towards the end of the 19th century, a fresher generation of artists emerged – the Modernistas. Influenced by their French counterparts (Paris was seen as Europe's artistic capital), the Modernistas allowed themselves greater freedom in interpretation than the Realists. They sought not so much to portray observed 'reality' as to interpret it subjectively and infuse it with flights of their own fantasy.

Ramón Casas (1866–1932) and Santiago Rusiñol (1861–1931) were the leading lights of Modernista painting. The former was a wealthy dilettante of some talent, the latter a more

BACKGROUND ARTS

earnest soul who ran a close second. Both were the toast of the bohemian set in turn-of-the-20th-century Barcelona. The single best collection of works by these two artists is on show in the Museu Nacional d'Art de Catalunya (MNAC; p138).

In a similar class was Josep Llimona (1864–1934), the most prolific and prominent sculptor of the late 19th century and on into the 1930s. His works can be seen scattered about town today, ranging from the statue of Ramon Berenguer el Gran on the square of the same name just off Via Laietana to friezes on the Mirador de Colom (p67). A handful of his statues are also on display in the Museu del Modernisme Català (p110). He is often classed as a Modernista but his style was in constant development across a long career.

From about 1910, as Modernisme fizzled, the more conservative cultural movement Noucentisme (loosely '20th centuryism') sought, in general, to advance Catalonia by looking backwards. The Noucentistas demanded a return to a 'healthier' classicism, clarity and 'Mediterranean light' after the 'excesses' of the Modernistas. From about 1917, a second wave of Noucentistas challenged these notions, which had begun to feel like an artistic straitjacket.

Among the Noucentistas, Joaquim Sunyer (1874–1956) and Isidre Nonell (1876–1911) were clearly influenced by the likes of Cézanne; some of their works can be seen in the MNAC. They were soon to be overshadowed by true genius.

Twentieth-Century Masters

PABLO PICASSO

Born in Málaga in Andalucía, Pablo Ruiz Picasso (1881–1973) was already sketching by the age of nine. After a stint in La Coruña (in Galicia), he landed in Barcelona in 1895. His father had obtained a post teaching art at the Escola de Belles Artes de la Llotja (then housed in the stock exchange building) and had his son enrolled there too. It was in Barcelona and Catalonia that Picasso matured, spending his time ceaselessly drawing and painting.

After a stint at the Escuela de Bellas Artes de San Fernando in Madrid in 1897, Picasso spent six months with his friend Manuel Pallarès in bucolic Horta de Sant Joan, in western Catalonia – he would later claim that it was there he learned everything he knew. In Barcelona, Picasso lived and worked in the Barri Gòtic and El Raval (where he was introduced to the seamier side of life in the Barri Xinès).

By the time Picasso moved to France in 1904, he had explored his first highly personal style. In this so-called Blue Period, his canvases have a melancholy feel heightened by the trademark dominance of dark blues. Some of his portraits and cityscapes from this period were created in and inspired by what he saw in Barcelona. Plenty of pieces from this period hang in the Museu Picasso (p80).

This was followed by the Pink (or Rose) Period, in which Picasso's subjects became merrier and the colouring leaned towards light pinks and greys.

Picasso was a turbulent character and gifted not only as a painter but as a sculptor, graphic designer and ceramicist. Down the years, his work encompassed many style changes. With *Les Demoiselles d'Avignon* (Ladies of Avignon; 1907), Picasso broke with all forms of traditional representation, introducing a deformed perspective that would later spill over into cubism. The subject was supposedly taken from the Carrer d'Avinyó in the Barri Gòtic, in those days populated with a series of brothels.

By the mid-1920s, he was dabbling with surrealism. His best-known work is *Guernica* (in Madrid's Centro de Arte Reina Sofia), a complex painting portraying the horror of war, inspired by the German aerial bombing of the Basque town Gernika in 1937.

Picasso worked prolifically during and after WWII and he was still cranking out paintings, sculptures, ceramics and etchings until the day he died in 1973.

JOAN MIRÓ

By the time the 13-year-old Picasso arrived in Barcelona, his near contemporary, Joan Miró (1893–1983), was cutting his teeth on rusk biscuits in the Barri Gòtic, where he was born. He spent a third of his life in Barcelona but later divided his time between France, the Tarragona countryside and the island of Mallorca, where he ended his days.

Like Picasso, Miró attended the Escola de Belles Artes de la Llotja. He was initially uncertain about his artistic vocation – in fact he studied commerce. In Paris from 1920, he mixed with Picasso, Hemingway, Joyce and friends, and made his own mark, after several years of struggle, with an exhibition in 1925. The masterpiece from this, his so-called realist period, was *La Masia* (Farmhouse).

It was during WWII, while living in seclusion in Normandy, that Miró's definitive leitmotifs emerged. Among the most important images that appear frequently throughout his work are women, birds (the link between earth and the heavens), stars (the unattainable heavenly world, the source of imagination), and a sort of net entrapping all these levels of the cosmos. The Miró works that most people are acquainted with emerged from this time – arrangements of lines and symbolic figures in primary colours, with shapes reduced to their essence.

In the 1960s and '70s, Miró devoted more of his time to creating sculpture and designing textiles, largely employing the same kinds of symbolic figures as those in his paintings. He lived in Mallorca, home of his wife Pilar

top picks

GALLERIES

- CaixaForum (p139) A beautifully restored Modernista factory that hosts top art exhibitions.
- Museu Picasso (p80) A unique insight into the early years of Picasso's career.
- Fundació Joan Miró (p143) A grand canvas of this local boy's life's work.
- Museu d'Art Contemporani de Barcelona (p76) Barcelona's main contemporary art palace, with constantly changing exhibitions.
- Fundació Antoni Tàpies (p107) A Modernista home for a selection of the great Catalan contemporary painter's work and exhibitions of other artists.

Juncosa, from 1956 until his death in 1983. The Fundació Joan Miró (p143), housed in Montjuïc, has the single largest collection of Miró's work in the world today.

SALVADOR DALÍ

Although he spent precious little time in Barcelona, and nothing much of his can be seen in the city, it would be churlish to leave Salvador Dalí i Domènech (1904–89) out of the picture. He was born and died in Figueres, where he left his single greatest artistic legacy, the Teatre-Museu Dalí (p249).

Prolific painter, showman, shameless self-promoter or just plain weirdo, Dalí was nothing if not a character – probably a little too much for the conservative small-town folk of Figueres.

Every now and then a key moment arrives that can change the course of one's life. Dalí's came in 1929, when the French poet Paul Éluard visited Cadaqués with his Russian wife, Gala. The rest, as they say, is histrionics. Dalí shot off to Paris to be with Gala and plunged into the world of surrealism.

In the 1930s, Salvador and Gala returned to live at Port Lligat on the north Catalan coast, where they played host to a long list of fashionable and art-world guests until the war years – the parties were by all accounts memorable.

They started again in Port Lligat in the 1950s. The stories of sexual romps and Gala's appetite for young local boys are legendary. The 1960s saw Dalí painting pictures on a grand scale, including his 1962 reinterpretation of Marià Fortuny's *Batalla de Tetuán*. On his death in 1989, he was buried (according to his own wish) in the Teatre-Museu he had created on the site of the old theatre in central Figueres, which now houses the single greatest collection of Dalí's work.

The Present

Artistic life did not come grinding to a halt with the demise of Miró and Dalí. Barcelona has for decades been a minor cauldron of activity, dominated by the figure of Antoni Tàpies (1923–), an elder statesman of Catalan contemporary art. Early in his career (from the mid-1940s onwards) he seemed keen on self-portraits, but also experimented with collage using all sorts of materials from wood to rice. Check out his Fundació Antoni Tàpies (p107).

Joan Brossa (1921–98) was a cultural beacon in Barcelona, a poet, artist and man of theatre. His 'visual poems', lithographs and other artworks in which letters generally figure, along with

BACKGROUND ARTS

all sorts of objects, make his world accessible to those who can't read his Catalan poetry. Get a taste at the Fundació Joan Brossa (p112).

Barcelona-born Jaume Plensa (1955–) is possibly Spain's best and most prolific contemporary sculptor. His work ranges from sketches and sculpture through to video and other installations that have been shown around the world. At the time of writing he had a major outdoor exhibition of works in public places throughout Vancouver (until 2011), paintings on display in a Madrid gallery, other sculptures and statuary in New York, and some major exhibitions in public places planned as far and wide as Abu Dhabi and Japan for 2010. He has left grand pieces of public sculpture in more than 35 locations around the world.

Joan Hernández Pijuan (1931–2005) was one of the most important 20th-century abstract painters to come out of Barcelona. Having studied, like Picasso and Miró, at the Llotja, he produced work concentrating on natural shapes and figures, often using neutral colours on different surfaces.

Xavier Corberó (1935–), influenced by his friend Salvador Dalí, has created a mixed oeuvre of difficult-to-classify sculptures that betray something of the dream-nightmare quality so often apparent in Dalí's work. He splits his time between a loft in New York City and his main workshop in Esplugues de Llobregat, on the periphery of Barcelona.

Susana Solano (1946–) is a painter and sculptor, one of the most important at work in Spain today and certainly one of Barcelona's best. She often uses steel in her works, such as *Huella Desnuda Que Mira* (Naked Trace Looking), and frequently designs for large open spaces. But her palette is broad, extending to video installations, collages, photography, jewellery and smaller-scale sculpture.

Jordi Colomer (1962–) makes heavy use of audiovisual material in his artworks, creating highly imaginative spaces and three-dimensional images. Somewhat hallucinatory videos such as *Simo* and *Pianito* shot him to fame in the late 1990s, and video continues to play an important part in his work. He's a man of many parts, however, as his puppet-like series of sculptures, *Heroes*, which went on show in Mexico in 2009, shows.

Some of the paintings of Joanpere Massana (1968–), born in the province of Lleida but educated in Barcelona, are a little reminiscent of Tàpies, with his use of different materials

STREET TREATS

Barcelona hosts an array of street sculpture, from Miró's 1983 Dona i Ocell (Map p140), in the park dedicated to the artist, to Peix (Fish; Map p96), Frank Gehry's shimmering, bronze-coloured headless fish facing Port Olímpic. Halfway along La Rambla, at Plaça de la Boqueria, you can walk all over Miró's *Mosaïc de Miró*. Picasso left an open-air mark with his design on the façade of the Col.legi de Arquitectes (Map p60) opposite La Catedral in the Barri Gòtic.

Others you may want to keep an eye out for are Barcelona's Head (Map p90) by Roy Lichtenstein at the Port Vell end of Via Laietana and Fernando Botero's characteristically tumescent El Gat (Map p74) on Rambla del Raval.

Just plain weird is what looks like a precarious pile of square rusty containers on Platja de Sant Sebastià. Made in 1992 by Rebecca Horn, it is called Homenatge a la Barceloneta (Tribute to La Barceloneta; Map p90). Odd tribute. A little further south is the 2003 Homenatge als Nedadors (Tribute to the Swimmers; Map p90), a complex metallic rendition of swimmers and divers in the water by Alfredo Lanz. Odder still, while on the subject of tributes, is Antoni Tàpies' 1983 Homenatge a Picasso (aka *L'Estel Ferit*, the Wounded Star; Map p82) on Passeig de Picasso, a glass cube set in a pond and filled with, well, junk.

Antoni Llena's David i Goliat (Map p96), a massive sculpture of tubular and sheet iron, in the Parc de les Cascades near Port Olímpic's two skyscrapers, looks like an untidy kite inspired by Halloween. Beyond this, Avinguda d'Icària is lined by architect Enric Miralles' so-called *Pergoles* – bizarre, twisted metal contraptions.

And who is taking the mickey at the bottom end of Rambla de Catalunya? The statue of a thinking bull is simply called Meditation (Map p106), but one wonders what Rodin would make of it.

One of the best known pieces of public art whimsy is Xavier Mariscal's Gamba (Prawn, although it is actually a crayfish; Map p90) on Passeig de Colom. Stuck here in 1987 on the roof of the Gambrinus bar, when this strip was lined by popular designer bars (which unfortunately disappeared in the late 1990s), it has remained as a kind of seafood symbol of the city (and was restored in 2004).

For a comprehensive look at street art (and much more), go to the city of Barcelona's main website (www.bcn.cat) and click on Art Públic (under La Ciutat/The City). Here you will find a host of files on public sculpture, along with a host of other categories of art and architecture.

and broad brushstrokes to create striking images. He also does installation art. David Casals (1976–) has behind him an impressive series of exhibitions for his paintings, which include thoughtful landscapes done in acrylic on paper or wood, such as his 2009 work, *La Nostra Pluja* (Our Rain).

Other young Catalan artists to keep an eye on include Laura Cuch, Mar Garcia, Daniel Gasol, Míriam Grau, Mercè Hernández, Antonio Hervás, Tamara Kuselman, Daniel Lumbreras and Ariadna Mangrané.

To see the work of local and foreign contemporary artists head to the Museu d'Art Contemporani de Barcelona (Macba; p76), where you will get a good introductory look at what is happening in contemporary art through various exhibitions. Some of the works on show are usually from the museum's own reserves. CaixaForum (p139) and the Centre d'Art Santa Mònica (p57) are excellent public galleries. The latter concentrates on contemporary artists, including a bevy of emerging Catalan talent.

The private commercial gallery scene has traditionally been concentrated on and around Carrer del Consell de Cent, between Passeig de Gràcia and Carrer d'Aribau. A handful of classic galleries operate in the Barri Gòtic, of which the long-standing Sala Parés (p152) is the most interesting if you want to tap into shows by a broad range of Catalan artists working today. Also worth keeping an eye on is the Art Barcelona association of more than 25 art galleries (www.artbarcelona.es). You can see what's on show in these galleries on the website. A bigger umbrella group of more than 100 art galleries throughout Catalonia is the Gremi de Galeries d'Art de Catalunya. Check out its useful website (www.galeriescatalunya.com).

LITERATURE

Barcelona is the beating heart of Spanish publishing. All the literary big-hitters, such as Tusquets Editores, Seix-Barral, Anagrama, Planeta and Quaderns Crema, are based here. Catalonia teems with world-class writers.

From Law Codes to the Segle d'Or

The earliest surviving documents written in Catalan date from the 12th century and include the *Homilies d'Organyà*, a religious work.

The first great Catalan writer was Ramon Llull (1235–1315), who eschewed the use of Latin and Provençal. His two best-known works are *El Llibre de les Bèsties* (Book of Beasts) and *El Llibre d'Amic i Amat* (Book of the Friend and the Loved One), the former an allegorical attack on feudal corruption and the latter a series of short pieces aimed at daily meditation.

The count-king Jaume I was a bit of a scribbler himself, writing a rare autobiographical work called *Llibre dels Feyts* (Book of Deeds) in the late 13th century.

Everyone has a 'golden century', and for Catalan writers it was the 15th. Ausiàs March (1400–59), from Valencia, forged a poetic tradition that inspires Catalan poets to this day.

Several European peoples claim responsibility for producing the first novel. The Catalans claim it was Joanot Martorell (c 1405–65), with *Tirant lo Blanc* (Tirant the White Knight). Cervantes himself thought it the best book in the world. Martorell was a busy fighting knight and his writing tells of bloody battles, war, politics and sex. Some things don't change!

Renaixença

Catalan literature declined after the 15th century and only began to make a comeback with the economic boom of the 19th century, which brought a renewal of interest in intellectual circles in all things Catalan. The revival of Catalan literature is commonly dated to 1833, when homesick Carles Aribau (1798–1862) penned the rather saccharine poem *A la Pàtria* (To the Homeland) in Madrid. Catalonia's bard was, however, a country pastor called Jacint Verdaguer (1845–1902), whose *L'Atlàntida* is an epic that defies easy description. Verdaguer's death in a farmhouse outside Barcelona (Parc de Collserola; see p133) was greeted as a national tragedy.

Modernisme's main literary voice was the poet Joan Maragall (1860–1911). Also noteworthy is the work of Víctor Català (1873–1966), actually Caterina Albert. Her principal work, *Solitud* (Solitude), charts the awakening of a young woman whose husband has taken her to live in the Pyrenees.

Into the 20th Century

What Verdaguer was to poetry, Josep Pla (1897–1981) was to prose. He wrote in Catalan and Spanish and his work ranged from travel writing (after Franco's victory in 1939 he spent many years abroad) to histories and fiction.

Mercè Rodoreda (1909–83), who spent many years in exile after the Spanish Civil War, published one of her best-known works, *Plaça del Diamant* (The Time of the Doves) in 1962. It recounts life in Barcelona before, during and after the war, through the eyes of a struggling working-class woman.

In the 1930s, George Orwell (1903–50) was one of many idealistic leftists who flooded into Barcelona to join the fight against Franco's Nationalist forces. His account of those difficult days, *Homage to Catalonia,* is a classic.

Juan Goytisolo (1931–), who lives in Marrakech, started off in the neo-Realist camp but his later works, such as the trilogy made up of *Señas de Identidad* (Marks of Identity), *Reivindicacion del Conde Don Julián* (Count Julian) and *Juan sin Tierra* (John the Landless), are decidedly more experimental and by far his most powerful writings. Much of his work revolves around sexuality, as he equates sexual freedom (he is bisexual) with political freedom.

Goytisolo's contemporary, Jaime Gil de Biedma (1929–90), was one of Spain's key 20th-century poets. Although his output was not extensive, it had an enormous impact on modern Spanish poetry. *Las Personas del Verbo,* which first came out in 1975, was updated in 1982 and, combined, contains work from the 1960s until 1982. His is an elegiac style with a recurring hint of eroticism.

Montserrat Roig (1946–91) crammed a lot of journalistic and fiction writing (largely in Catalan) into her short life. Her novels include *Ramon Adéu* (Goodbye Ramon) and *El Temps de les Cireres* (The Time of the Cherries).

Manuel Vázquez Montalbán (1939–2003), one of the city's most prolific writers, was best known for his Pepe Carvalho detective novel series and a range of other thrillers. Montalbán shared with his character Pepe a predilection for the semi-obscurity of El Raval, where he ate frequently at Casa Leopoldo (p174). Among his works available in English are thrillers such as *Murder in the Central Committee* and *Galíndez.* The latter is about the capture, torture and death of a Basque activist in the Dominican Republic in the 1950s. The kinds of character that pop up in Carvalho's world would have had a lot in common with the tortured French writer, Jean Genet, whose 1949 novel, *Journal du Voleur* (Diary of a Thief) is set in the then much dodgier streets of El Raval.

One Barcelona writer who deserves more attention than he gets is Joan Sales i Vallès (1912–1983). He left behind a powerful novel, *Incerta Glòria* (Uncertain Glory), which narrates the lives of various Catalans caught up in the fighting in the Spanish Civil War. It is a story also of personal love and defeat, of incomprehension and changes in fate. It is followed up by *El Vent de la Nit* (Night Wind), which traces the lives of many of those characters in the years after the war.

Jorge Semprún (1923–), who wound up in a Nazi concentration camp for his activities with the French Resistance in WWII, writes mostly in French. His first novel, *Le Grand Voyage* (The Long Voyage), is one of his best. It is his account of the agonising journey of a young Spaniard who had fought with the French Resistance on his way to the Buchenwald concentration camp – it is his own story.

Mario Lacruz (1929–2000) was better known as a publisher than as a novelist but after his death a curious manuscript, written in English in the 1960s, was discovered. *Gaudí, Una Novela,* posthumously published in Spanish and Catalan, is an intriguing novel about the architect.

top picks

BOOKS

- La Sombra del Viento (The Shadow of the Wind; 2004), Carlos Ruiz Zafón
- La Ciudad de los Prodigios (The City of Marvels; 1986), Eduardo Mendoza
- Homage to Catalonia (1938), George Orwell
- Dublinesca (2010), Enrique Vila-Matas
- Plaça del Diamant (The Time of the Doves; 1962), Mercè Rodoreda

The Present

One of Montalbán's contemporaries, Juan Marsé (1933–) is another iconic figure on the Barcelona literature scene. Among his outstanding novels is 1993 *El Embrujo de Shanghai* (The Shanghai Spell). Set in Gràcia, it was brought to the screen in a memorable film by Fernando Trueba in 2002. The story revolves around characters struggling along in the wake of the civil war and a 14-year-old's timid discovery of love. Rather more rough and tumble is *Canciones de Amor en el Lolita's Club* (Love Songs in Lolita's Club), an excursion into the seedy world of prostitution and pimps.

Eduardo Mendoza (1943–) is one of Barcelona's finest contemporary writers. His *La Ciudad de los Prodigios* (The City of Marvels) is an absorbing and at times bizarre novel set in the city in the period between the Universal Exhibition of 1888 and the World Exhibition of 1929. Much more recent was a quite off-the-wall novel, *El Asombroso Viaje de Pomponio Flato* (The Amazing Journey of Pomponio Flatus), about the journey of a Roman around the empire, in which he winds up in Nazareth solving a murder mystery.

Enrique Vila-Matas (1948–) has won fans way beyond his native Barcelona and his novels have been translated into a dozen languages. In *Paris No Se Acaba Nunca* (Paris Never Ends), Vila-Matas returns to the 1970s, when he rented a garret in Paris from Marguerite Duras and penned his first novel. His latest novel, however, has been broadly greeted as his best. *Dublinesca* recounts a retired editor's trip to Dublin to celebrate the death of the printed word, mixes the story in with references to James Joyce's *Ulysses* and so creates a contemporary literary romp.

Those with an interest in the flavour of medieval Barcelona could do worse than read the debut effort by Barcelona lawyer Ildefonso Falcones (1945–), *La Catedral del Mar* (Cathedral of the Sea), a historical novel that tells the story of the construction of the Església de Santa Maria del Mar (p80) in La Ribera, a Gothic beauty raised in recordbreaking and, for many of its workers, backbreaking time. It is not timeless literature but offers interesting insights into medieval life in Barcelona. Falcones shot back into the bestseller lists in 2009 with *La Mano de Fátima* (The Hand of Fatima), another historical novel that is something of a love story of a baptised Moor in 16th-century Andalucía.

Barcelona-born, US-based Carlos Ruiz Zafón (1964–) earlier had huge success with his *La Sombra del Viento* (The Shadow of the Wind), an engaging, multilayered mystery story that plays out over several periods in Barcelona's 20th-century history. Having sold millions of copies, it has made Zafón one of Spain's most successful international novelists. The prequel, *El Juego del Ángel* (The Angel's Game), is set in the Barcelona of the 1920s and '30s.

Playing to a more local audience, Quim Monzó (1952–) is perhaps the highest profile author writing in Catalan today, and one of the world's great short-story writers. He churns out a stream of short stories, columns and essays. His wide-ranging work is marked by a mordant wit and an abiding interest in pornography. He revised his best stories and published them in one volume, *Vuitanta-sis Contes* (Eighty-six Short Stories), in 1999. Available in English is *La Magnitud de la Tragèdia* (The Enormity of the Tragedy).

A rarity on the local literary scene is Matthew Tree, a born and bred Brit who has lived in Catalonia since the mid-1980s and writes predominantly in Catalan. His *Aniversari* (2005) is a penetrating look at his adopted home, at once an insider's and outsider's view.

MUSIC
Contemporary
Curiously, it was probably the Franco repression that most helped foster a vigorous local music scene in Catalan. In those dark years, the Nova Cançó (New Song) movement was born in the

LONGING FOR CUBA

The oldest musical tradition to have survived to some degree in Catalonia is that of the *havaneres* (from Havana) – nostalgic songs and melancholy sea shanties brought back from Cuba by Catalans who lived, sailed and traded there in the 19th century. Even after Spain lost Cuba in 1898, the *havanera* tradition (a mix of European and Cuban rhythms) continued. A magical opportunity to enjoy these songs is the *Cantada d'Havaneres*, an evening concert held in Calella, on the Costa Brava, on or around 1 July. Otherwise, you may stumble across performances elsewhere along the coast or even in Barcelona, but there is no set programme.

1950s to resist linguistic oppression with music in Catalan (getting air time on the radio was long close to impossible), throwing up stars that in some cases won huge popularity throughout Spain, such as the Valencia-born Raimon (1940–).

More specifically loved in Catalonia as a Bob Dylan–style 1960s protest singer-songwriter was Lluís Llach (1948–), much of whose music was more or less anti-regime. Joan Manuel Serrat (1943–) is another legendary figure. His appeal stretches from Barcelona to Buenos Aires. Born in the Poble Sec district, this poet-singer is equally at ease in Catalan and Spanish. He has repeatedly shown that record sales are not everything to him. In 1968 he refused to represent Spain at the Eurovision song contest if he were not allowed to sing in Catalan. Accused of being anti-Spanish, he was long banned from performing in Spain.

A specifically local strand of rock has emerged since the 1980s. Rock Català (Catalan rock) is not essentially different from rock anywhere else, except that it is sung in Catalan by local bands that appeal to local tastes. Among the most popular and long-lived groups are Sau, Els Pets (one of the region's top acts), Lax'n Busto and the Valenciano band, Obrint Pas.

For years, the annual summer Senglar Rock music festival was *the* date for Catalan rock music, usually spiced up with some international acts. It was not held in 2009 and a shadow remains over its future.

The Pinker Tones are a Barcelona duo that has quickly scaled the heights of international popularity with an eclectic electronic mix of music, ranging from dizzy dance numbers to film soundtracks. Their second album, *The Million Colour Revolution,* is their best, although *Wild Animals* (2008) received good reviews too. Another Barcelona band with international ambitions and flavours is Macaco. Their latest album, *Puerto Presente,* is an eloquent expression of this, with a musical mix inspired by anything from rocksteady to Barcelona rumba. Various guests participate in the album, including actor Javier Bardem. When people talk about '*Raval sound*' (after the name of the still somewhat seedy old town district), this is the kind of thing they mean.

Far greater success across Spain has gone to Estopa, a male rock duo from Cornellà, a satellite suburb of Barcelona. The guitar-wielding brothers sing a clean Spanish rock, occasionally with a vaguely flamenco flavour. Their compilation album, *Estopa X Anniversarium*, brings it all together. Pastora is a Barcelona trio that peddles a successful brand of soft Spanish pop, mixing electric sounds with a strong acoustic element that produces a pleasing, clean music.

Sabadell-born Albert Pla (1966–) is one of the most controversial singer-songwriters on the national scene today. Swinging between his brand of forthright rock lyrics, stage and cinema, he is a multifaceted maestro. His latest CD, *La Diferencia,* is one of the more interesting, with 11 songs about tragic love, cruelty and the USA burning because of a spark that falls from the head of the last descendant of the Aztecs!

For a pleasing combination of rock and folk, Mesclat, who are particularly popular on their home turf, are a group to watch out for. Band members come from all over Catalonia. They have three CDs, *Mesclat, Manilla* and Cròniques Colonials

To get a further look into the Barcelona music scene, have a listen to Scanner.BCN (www.bcn.cat/scannerbcn). Jazz lovers curious about what's cooking in Barcelona can tune into Barcelonajazzradio (www.barcelonajazzradio.com).

THE POWER OF PAU

Pau Casals (1876–1973) was one of the greatest cellists of the 20th century. Born in El Vendrell, in southern Catalonia, he was playing in the orchestra of the Teatre del Liceu by the age of 20 and, in 1899, he debuted in London and Paris. He chose exile in southern France after Franco's victory in the civil war. In 1946 he declared he would not play in public any more as long as the Western democracies continued to tolerate Franco's regime. One of the most moving moments of his career came when he accepted a request to play before the UN General Assembly in New York in 1958. The concert was transmitted by radio around the world and that same year he was a candidate for the Nobel Peace Prize.

In his later years he worked increasingly as a conductor. He was also a prolific composer of operatic songs, although the bulk of his works remain unpublished. He died in Puerto Rico in 1973, and his remains were brought back to El Vendrell in 1979. You can visit the beachside Museu Pau Casals (☎ 977 68 42 76; www.paucasals.org; Avinguda Palfuriana 67, Sant Salvador, near El Vendrell) in the house he had built as a summer retreat in 1910. Take the regular *rodalies* train from Barcelona (Passeig de Gràcia) to Sant Vicenç de Calders (€4.65, one hour 10 minutes). And don't forget your swimming costume!

THE RETURN OF LA RUMBA

Back in the 1950s, a new sound mixing flamenco with Latin (salsa and other South American dance flavours) emerged in *gitano* (Roma people) circles in the bars of Gràcia and the Barri Gòtic. The main man was Antonio González, known as El Pescailla (married to the flamenco star Lola Flores). The guy who took this eminently Barcelona style to a wider (eventually international) audience was Mataró-born *gitano* Peret. By the end of the 1970s, however, rumba Catalana was running out of steam. Peret had turned to religion and El Pescailla lived in Flores' shadow in Madrid. A plaque to the latter's memory graces Carrer Fraternitat 1, in Gràcia. But Buenos Aires-born Javier Patricio 'Gato' Pérez discovered rumba in 1977 and gave it his own personal spin, bringing out several popular records, such as *Atalaya*, until the early 1980s. After Pérez, it seemed that rumba was dead. Not so fast! New rumba bands, often highly eclectic, have emerged in recent years. Papawa, Barrio Negro and El Tío Carlos are names to look out for. Others mix rumba with anything from reggae to ragga.

Classical, Opera & Baroque

Spain's contribution to the world of classical music has been modest, but Catalonia has produced a few exceptional composers. Best known is Camprodon-born Isaac Albéniz (1860–1909), a gifted pianist who later turned his hand to composition. Among his best-remembered works is the *Iberia* cycle.

Lleida's Enric Granados i Campiña (1867–1916) was another fine pianist. He established Barcelona's conservatorium in 1901 and composed a great many pieces for piano, including *Danzas Españolas*, *Cantos de la Juventud* and *Goyescas*.

Other Catalan composers and musicians of some note include Eduard Toldrà (1895–1962) and Frederic Mompou (1893–1987).

Montserrat Caballé is Barcelona's most successful voice. Born in Gràcia in 1933, the soprano made her debut in 1956 in Basel (Switzerland). Her hometown launch came four years later in the Gran Teatre del Liceu (p67). In 1965, she performed to wild acclaim at New York's Carnegie Hall and went on to become one of the world's finest 20th-century sopranos. Her daughter, Montserrat Martí, is also a singer and they occasionally appear together. Another fine Catalan soprano was Victoria de los Ángeles (1923–2005), while Catalonia's other world-class opera star is the renowned tenor Josep (José) Carreras (1946–).

Jordi Savall (1941–) has assumed the task of rediscovering a European heritage in music that predates the era of the classical greats. He and his wife, soprano Montserrat Figueras, have, along with musicians from other countries, been largely responsible for resuscitating the beauties of medieval, Renaissance and baroque music. In 1987, Savall founded La Capella Reial de Catalunya and two years later he formed the baroque orchestra Le Concert des Nations. You can sometimes catch their recitals in locations such as the Església de Santa Maria del Mar (p80).

CINEMA

In 1932 Francesc Macià, president of the Generalitat, opened Spain's first studios for making 'talkies' and a year later Metro Goldwyn Mayer had a dubbing studio in Barcelona. But since Franco's victory in 1939, pretty much all cinematic production has taken place in Madrid.

José Juan Bigas Luna (1946–) is one of Catalonia's best known directors, responsible for the hilarious *Jamón, Jamón* (1992). His latest flick, *Yo Soy la Juani* (I am Juani; 2006), takes us into the life of a modern young woman in the tough world of Barcelona's outer suburbs.

Ventura Pons (1945–) is a veteran of Catalan theatre and film-making who cranks out movies with almost frightening speed (one a year since 1989, skipping three years). *Barcelona (Un Mapa)*, which came out in 2007, looks at six urban characters gathered together but essentially lonely in an L'Eixample apartment.

Gràcia-born Isabel Coixet (1960–) has had some ups and downs with some original films. She reached a high point (and four Goyas, the Spanish equivalent of the Oscars) for *Vida Secreta de las Palabras* (The Secret Life of Words; 2005), in which a taciturn nurse arrives on a moribund North Sea oil platform to take care of a burns patient. She turns out to be a torture victim of the wars in the former Yugoslavia. Her last film, *Map of the Sounds of Tokyo* (2009) was an uneven but intriguing exploration of the Japanese through some odd characters that include the Spanish wine purveyor played by Catalan star Sergi López.

Vicente Aranda (1926–) is an eclectic and surprising director capable of anything from the not altogether successful 2006 blockbuster based on the medieval classic tome of derring-do, *Tirant Lo Blanc*, to his adaptation of Juan Marsé's rather more subtle *Canciones de Amor en el Lolita's Club*, which he wrote and directed, in 2007.

Barcelona's tourism folk have set up a website (www.barcelonamovie.com) with suggested walking tours taking in spots where various films have been shot in Barcelona. Print 'em out and follow in the footsteps of Almodóvar or Jean-Baptiste Grenouille, the unpleasant protagonist in *Perfume: The Story of a Murderer*.

THEATRE

Barcelona rivals Madrid as a centre of theatrical production in Spain. The bulk of dramatic theatre on Barcelona's stages is done in Catalan, whether local fringe stuff or interpretations of Ibsen and Shakespeare.

Several outstanding local theatre companies have a far wider appeal. One of the world's wackiest theatre companies is La Fura dels Baus (www.lafura.com). These guys turn theatre spaces (or warehouses, or boats…) into a kind of participatory apocalypse and can, as with their *Boris Gudonov* act in 2008, in which they turned their audiences into hostages in a terrorist situation, reach (or pass) the limits of what many might consider good taste. For more on them, see p219. Tricicle (www.tricicle.com) is a three-man mime team easily enjoyed by anyone. Els Comediants (www.comediants.com) and La Cubana (www.lacubana.es) are highly successful comedy groups that owe a lot to the impromptu world of street theatre. Els Joglars (www.elsjoglars.com) are not afraid to create pieces full of social critique, while Dagoll Dagom (www.dagolldagom.com) is Catalonia's very own bells-and-whistles musical theatre company. Lavish and somewhat all-over-the-place performances are their speciality, with lots of kitschy high drama. They switch between homegrown material and original interpretations of Broadway classics.

See p218 for theatrical locations.

DANCE
Contemporary

Barcelona is the capital of contemporary dance in Spain. Ramon Oller is the city's leading choreographer, working with one of the country's most established companies, Metros, which he created in 1986. Its dance is rooted in a comparatively formal technique.

top picks

FILMS SHOT IN BARCELONA

- **Perfume: The Story of a Murderer** (Tom Tykwer; 2006) Starring Ben Wishaw as the psychopathic Jean-Baptiste Grenouille, this film is based on the extraordinary novel by Patrick Süsskind and is partly shot on locations across town and around Catalonia (including Girona, the Castell de Sant Ferran in Figueres and Tarragona).
- **Vicky Cristina Barcelona** (Woody Allen; 2008) – Barcelona was all agog in 2007 as Woody Allen, Scarlett Johansson, Penelope Cruz (who won an Oscar for her part in this film) and Javier Bardem wandered around shooting Allen's vision of Barcelona. Bardem's character, a painter, gets Cruz and Johansson all hot and sweaty in this light romantic romp.
- **Todo Sobre Mi Madre** (All About My Mother; Pedro Almodóvar; 1999) One of the Spanish director's most polished films, partly set in Barcelona. A quirky commentary that ties together the lives of the most improbable collection of women (including a couple of transsexuals).
- **L'Auberge Espagnole** (The Spanish Apartment; Cédric Klapisch; 2002) A young Parisian from the suburbs, Xavier, goes to Barcelona to learn Spanish for business. It ain't easy when university classes are given half the time in Catalan, but Xavier has no yen to return to Paris.
- **Manuale d'Amore** (Giovanni Veronesi; 2006) Four love stories are linked through a radio program on the subject in this Italian social comedy. Two stories take their protagonists to Barcelona, a gay couple and a couple seeking to have a child through artificially assisted means. Italians seem to be obsessed with Barcelona, a city they see as liberal.

CASANOVA IN JAIL AGAIN

That incorrigible Venetian lover and one-time inmate of the Piombi jail in Venice's Palazzo Ducale, Giacomo Casanova (1725–98), arrived in Barcelona in 1769, having been expelled from Paris, and spent some time trundling around Spain in search of a little peace and work. Seemingly unable to keep out of trouble, Casanova got tangled up with a lively ballerina, who happened to be the lover of the governor of Catalonia. It is perhaps unsurprising that Casanova wound up behind bars in the Ciutadella castle. After 40 days' incarceration, he was set free and moved on to Perpignan, back on French territory, where he presumably breathed a sigh of relief.

Other dance companies worth keeping an eye out for are Cesc Gelabert (www.gelabertazzopardi.com), run by the choreographer of the same name; Mudances (www.margarit-mudances.com), run by Àngels Margarit; Lanònima Imperial (www.lanonima.com), run by Juan Carlos García; and Mal Pelo (www.malpelo.org), run by Maria Muñoz and Pep Ramis. All tend to work from a base of 'release technique', which favours 'natural' movement, working from the skeleton, over a reliance on muscular power. Sol Picó (www.solpico.com) is a younger company that does provocative dance sets on a big scale. Butoh style aficionados should check out the work of Andrés Corchero and Rosa Muñoz.

Flamenco

For those who think that the passion of flamenco is the preserve of the south, think again. The *gitanos* (Roma people) get around, and some of the big names of the genre come from Catalonia. They were already in Catalonia long before the massive migrations from the south of the 1960s, but with these waves came an exponential growth in flamenco bars as Andalucians sought to recreate a little bit of home.

First and foremost, one of the greatest *bailaoras* (flamenco dancers) of all time, Carmen Amaya (1913–63) was born in what is now Port Olímpic. She danced to her father's guitar in the streets and bars around La Rambla in pre-civil war years. Much to the bemusement of purists from the south, not a few flamenco stars today have at least trained in flamenco schools in Barcelona – dancers Antonio Canales (1962–) and Joaquín Cortés (1969–) are among them. Other Catalan stars of flamenco include *cantaores* (singers) Juan Cortés Duquende (1965–) and Miguel Poveda (1973–), a boy from Badalona. He took an original step in 2006 by releasing a flamenco album, *Desglaç,* in Catalan. Another interesting flamenco voice in Catalonia is Ginesa Ortega Cortés (1967–), actually born in France. She masters traditional genres ably but loves to experiment. In her 2002 album, *Por los Espejos del Agua* (Through the Water's Mirrors), she does a reggae version of flamenco and she has sung flamenco versions of songs by Joan Manuel Serrat and Billie Holliday.

An exciting combo formed in Barcelona in 1996 and which defies classification is the seven-man, one-woman group Ojos de Brujo (Wizard's Eyes), who meld flamenco and rumba (see boxed text, p43) with rap, ragga and electronic music. Their third CD, *Techari,* is the smoothest and most exciting, although their latest effort *Aocaná,* isn't far behind.

See p217 for information on where to see flamenco performances.

Sardana

The Catalan dance *par excellence* is the *sardana,* whose roots lie in the far northern Empordà region of Catalonia. Compared with flamenco, it is sober indeed but not unlike a lot of other Mediterranean folk dances.

The dancers hold hands in a circle and wait for the 10 or so musicians to begin. The performance starts with the piping of the *flabiol,* a little wooden flute. When the other musicians join in, the dancers start – a series of steps to the right, one back and then the same to the left. As the music 'heats up' the steps become more complex, the leaps are higher and the dancers lift their arms. Then they return to the initial steps and continue. If newcomers wish to join in, space is made for them as the dance continues and the whole thing proceeds in a more or less seamless fashion.

For information on where and when to see locals indulging in their traditional two-step, see p218.

ENVIRONMENT & PLANNING

A report published in 2007 claimed that, with an average 50 micrograms of toxic particles per cubic metre of air, Barcelona had a worse air pollution problem than such megalopolises as New York, Mexico City and Tokyo. The single biggest source (85%) of unhealthy air is private vehicles, although industry plays its part and, paradoxically, sea breezes don't help either.

In reaction, parking and traffic restrictions in central Barcelona have been tightened. In 2008 a speed limit of 80km/h throughout Barcelona and 16 surrounding municipalities (including on highways) was introduced with the aim of cutting emissions by 30% in the metropolitan area.

It worked. By 2010, the level had dropped to 38 micrograms in central Barcelona. However, nitrogen dioxide (NO2) emissions (which affect breathing), were going up (it is speculated because of the growing use of diesel-powered cars). City authorities noted that NO2 rates were up in other European cities too.

The city's buses are being progressively replaced by new models powered by compressed natural gas – 296 are in service and the figure is expected to reach 500, about half the fleet, by 2015. The city transport authority is experimenting with hydrogen fuel cell and hydrogen combustion powered buses, as well as with bio-diesel fuelled buses. In the short term this contributes to reducing air pollution. However, combined with the growing density and efficiency of public transport networks, which encourage people to ride not drive, it is hoped to make a real impact in the long term.

Noise pollution is a problem, especially in parts of the old city (notably around El Born and in El Raval). Rowdy traffic, late-night rubbish collection, day-long construction and road works, and the screaming and shouting of revellers, all contribute to insomnia. Main roads are gradually getting a layer of noise-reduction asphalt to reduce traffic noise. But for many, double or even triple glazing is the only answer (not particularly comfortable in summer).

Although much depends on the goodwill of citizens, rubbish disposal is not too bad. Large, brightly coloured containers have been scattered about the city for the separated collection of paper, glass, cans and compost, and they are emptied daily. Emptying is one thing, but the disposal of waste produced in Barcelona is a major problem. Some of it is transported as far off as Murcia, in southern Spain!

Every night the city streets are hosed down, but every day they wind up dirty again. Some areas (such as much of Ciutat Vella) are worse than others (such as L'Eixample). This does not exactly contribute to reducing water consumption. Water is a big issue throughout Spain. Reports in 2008 estimated that, throughout Catalonia, about a quarter of water was lost through leakage on its way from distribution centres to end-users. Drought pressure on Barcelona was greatly eased by the opening in 2009 of a desalination plant in El Prat de Llobregat. It covers about 20% of Barcelona's needs. According to one local study, Barcelona is far from being the most wasteful city with water – consuming 116L per person a day, compared with 162L in Paris, 504L in New York and 666L in Beijing!

Barcelona gets a lot of sun and the huge photovoltaic panel at El Fòrum is symbolic of the city's stated intentions to increase solar energy output. Town bylaws require the installation of solar panels on new buildings of more than 12 apartments, although ecologists doubt this rule is being enforced.

THE LAND

Barcelona spreads along the Catalan coast in what is known as the Pla de Barcelona (Barcelona Plain), midway between the French border and the regional frontier with Valencia. The plain averages about 4m above sea level. Mont Tàber, the little elevation upon which the Romans built their town, is 16.9m above sea level. To the southwest, Montjuïc is 173m high.

Urban sprawl tends to be channelled southwest and northeast along the coast, as the landwards side is effectively blocked off by the Serralada Litoral mountain chain, which between the Riu Besòs and Riu Llobregat is known as the Serra de Collserola. Tibidabo is the highest point of this chain at 512m, with commanding views across the whole city.

Badalona to the northeast and L'Hospitalet to the southwest mark the municipal boundaries of the city – although, as you drive through them, you'd never know where they begin and end.

To the north, the Riu Besòs (so successfully cleaned up in recent years that otters have been spotted in it for the first time since the 1970s!) in part marks the northern limits of the city. The Riu Llobregat, which rises in the Pyrenees, empties into the Mediterranean just south of L'Hospitalet. On the southern side of the river is El Prat de Llobregat and Barcelona's airport.

GREEN BARCELONA

Serious concentrations of green are few and far between in Barcelona, but there are some exceptions. Closest to the town centre is the pleasant Parc de la Ciutadella.

The main green lung is Montjuïc, which rises behind the port. Extensive landscaped gardens surround the Olympic stadium, swimming pools, art galleries, museums, cemeteries and the fort, making it a wonderful spot for walks.

The city is bordered to the west by the Serra de Collserola, which serves as another smog filter and is laced with walks and bicycle paths. Declared a Natural Park in September 2006, it has for years been under pressure from urban development (much of it illegal) around and in it. In 2008 the town hall announced plans to limit further construction and, in some cases, to tear down existing, illegal residences. That said, the same town hall enthusiastically backed the construction of a giant roller coaster in the Parc d'Atraccions, to the consternation of some neighbours.

About 35% of the trees that line Barcelona's streets and parks are plane trees. Others include acacias and nettle trees.

URBAN PLANNING & DEVELOPMENT

The eminent British architect and town planner, Lord Richard Rogers, declared in 2000 that Barcelona was 'perhaps the most successful city in the world in terms of urban regeneration'.

That process, which got under way in earnest with the 1992 Olympic Games, thunders ahead. No sooner is one area given a new look, than another becomes the subject of modernisation.

Development continues at the mini-Manhattan that is the Diagonal Mar project on the northeast stretch of coast. A great chunk of El Poblenou (117 blocks to be precise), once an industrial and warehouse zone, is slowly being converted into a hi-tech business district, dubbed 22@bcn, or 22@for short. Although take-up of office space by such cutting-edge firms has been slow to date, the 22@ development was hailed by the CNBC European Business magazine in 2008 as one of the best urban renewal projects in Europe.

To the north, the Sagrera area will be transformed by the new high-speed railway station and transport interchange, while the completion of the giant new trade fair area, a single giant justice and courts complex, and nearby office complexes along Gran Via de les Corts Catalanes in L'Hospital de Llobregat and in the Zona Franca has already changed the look of this area between the city centre and the airport beyond recognition. For more on landmark buildings in these areas, see p129.

Further funds have been released for the renovation of the city centre. Slowly, parts of the Barri Gòtic, La Ribera and El Raval that were depressed and abandoned have been or are being brought back to life. In El Raval a new boulevard, La Rambla del Raval, was opened in 2001 and is finally attracting attention. Flanked by eateries and bars, the largely pedestrian boulevard is now also graced with a state-of-the-art design hotel. Some streets around it remain dodgy but the area has changed out of sight since the Rambla was opened.

Many other depressed parts of the city (such as the densely populated hillock area of El Carmel) have been singled out for major improvements in the coming years too. No-one can say that Barcelona is resting on its laurels.

GOVERNMENT & POLITICS

The Generalitat de Catalunya (the regional Catalan government) was resurrected by royal decree in 1977. Its power as an autonomous government is enshrined in the statutes of the Spanish constitution of 1978, and by the Estatut d'Autonomia (devolution statute). The Govern (executive) is housed in the Palau de la Generalitat on Plaça de Sant Jaume, while parliament sits in the Parlament de Catalunya in the Parc de la Ciutadella. The Generalitat has wide powers over matters such as education, health, trade, industry, tourism and agriculture.

The Ajuntament (town hall) stands opposite the Palau de la Generalitat in Plaça de St Jaume and has traditionally been a Socialist haven. Never has the Socialists' hold on city government been so tenuous. Since the 2007 municipal elections, Jordi Hereu has led a minority government with the Greens, totalling 18 seats (three shy of an absolute majority). Opposition comes from the moderately right-wing Catalan nationalist CiU coalition under Xavier Trias (12 seats), their independence-minded left-wing counterparts ERC (Jordi Portabella), with four seats, and the PP with seven slots. For more on the recent machinations at city and regional level, see p30.

Elections to the Ajuntament (next due in 2011) and Generalitat (due in late 2010) take place every four years. They are free and by direct universal suffrage. The members of each house then vote for the mayor and president of the Generalitat.

Barcelona is divided into 10 *districtes municipals* (municipal districts), each with its own *ajuntament*.

MEDIA

Much of the Spanish media makes little effort to hide its political affiliations. The respected national daily, *El País*, born out of the early days of democracy in the 1970s, is closely aligned to the PSOE (Spanish Socialist Workers' Party). Many Catalans find its political coverage overwhelmingly biased towards that party. *ABC,* on the other hand, is a long-standing organ of the conservative right and readily identified with the Partido Popular. More stridently hawkish is *El Mundo*.

Catalans, by their choice of paper, make political statements. Reading the local Spanish-language and slightly conservative *La Vanguardia* is a clear vote for local product, while *Avui*, a subsidised loss-maker, is vociferously Catalan nationalist.

It is little different in the electronic media. While they sometimes have interesting programming, the most important local stations, such as the Catalan government's TV-3 and Canal 33, push an almost constant Catalanist line. Documentaries on the civil war, the horrors of the Franco period and so forth abound, while investigative journalism on some of the dodgier sides of Catalan government since 1980 are noticeable by their absence.

FASHION

For years, Barcelona and Madrid ran competing *haute couture* shows but the end came in 2006 when the Generalitat pulled the plug on funding. Alternative shows were staged in 2007, but by 2008 it was all over.

The shows may come and go, but Barcelona teems with its own designers. Names range from the ebullient Custo Barcelona to the international *prêt-a-porter* phenomenon of Mango. Based outside the city in the Vallès area, it has more than 900 stores throughout the world (in locations as far-flung as Vietnam and London's Oxford St), and has come a long way since opening its first store on Passeig de Gràcia in 1984. Mango is one of Spain's largest textile exporters, specialising mainly in women's fashion.

Other local design names worth keeping an eye out for include Joaquim Verdú (who has been making men's and women's clothes since 1977); Antonio Miró (who designed the Spanish team's uniforms for the 1992 Olympic Games and also does a line in furniture); David Valls; Josep Font; Armand Basi; Purificación García; Konrad Muhr; Josep Abril; Sita Murt and TCN. Another popular young brand with Barcelona roots is Desigual. Along with

MUCHO GUSTO, MR CUSTO

Custo (actually Custodio Dalmau) and his brother David, from Lleida and now based in Barcelona, have become hot fashion property since breaking into the tough US women's fashion market in the early 2000s. Indeed, the light and breezy brand has become something of a cult obsession with women around the world. Their ever-cosmopolitan, inventive and often provocative mix of colours, especially in their hallmark tops, are miles away from the more conservative, classic fashion tastes that still dominate some sectors of Barcelona high society.

the Dalmau brothers of Custo Barcelona, another runaway renegade is Uruguay-born but Barcelona-bred Jordi Labanda. Better known in his earlier days as a cartoonist and illustrator (the cheerful Sandwich&Friends fast food outlets are gaily decorated with his distinctive, bright, clear-cut urban murals), he was propelled to international fame and fortune as a fashion designer after moving to New York in 1995 and, after publishing illustrations in the *New York Times*, switching his pen to hip women's design. You can buy his colour items online at www. jordilabandashop.com.

With so much talent popping up around them, it is hardly surprising that *barcelonins* like to dress with such style – they have no shortage of outlets in which to hunt down offerings from their favourite designers. The city's premier shopping boulevards, Passeig de Gràcia, Rambla de Catalunya and Avinguda Diagonal, are lined with the best of both international and Spanish rag-trade fashion labels. If L'Eixample is the brand-happy shopping mecca for fashion victims, there's plenty more in the old town. Both the Barri Gòtic and La Ribera are peppered with boutiques purveying all sorts of youthful fashion, unfettered by convention or macroeconomic considerations. Conversely, if it's grunge and secondhand clothing you're after, we highly recommend heading for Carrer de la Riera Baixa in El Raval.

LANGUAGE

Barcelona is a bilingual city. The mother tongue of born-and-bred locals is Catalan, which belongs to the group of Western European languages that grew out of Latin (Romance languages), including Italian, French, Spanish and Portuguese. By the 12th century, it was a clearly established language with its own nascent literature. The language was most closely related to

WAR OF WORDS

Since Barcelona was crushed in the War of the Spanish Succession in 1714, the use of Catalan has been repeatedly banned or at least frowned upon. Franco was the last of Spain's rulers to clamp down on its public use.

People in the country and small towns largely ignored the bans, but intellectual circles in Barcelona and other cities only 'rediscovered' Catalan with the Renaixença at the end of the 19th century (see p27). Franco loosened the reins from the 1960s on, but all education in Catalan schools remained exclusively in Spanish until after the dictator's demise in 1975.

Since the first autonomous regional parliament was assembled in 1980, the Generalitat (Catalan government) has waged an unstinting campaign of *normalització lingüística* (linguistic normalisation). The Generalitat reckons 95% of the population in Catalonia understand Catalan and nearly 70% speak it. In Valencia, about half the population speak it, as do 65% in the Balearic Islands. The big problem is that not nearly as many write it. Even in Catalonia, only about 40% of the population write Catalan satisfactorily.

In Catalonia today it is impossible to get a public-service job without fluency in Catalan. And just as Franco had all signs in Catalan replaced, Spanish road signs and advertising are now harder to find. On the other hand, dubbing of films into Catalan is nearly non-existent and studies show that adolescents mostly watch Spanish-language TV. In 2008 the regional government decided to pour €2.4 million into the promotion of dubbing films in Catalan and €36 million into subsidies to encourage the production of Catalan-language movies. Two years later, the government toughened its stance and passed a law that obliges movie distributors to dub half the copies of films shown in Catalan cinemas into Catalan. The big US film producers reacted angrily and some gloom and doomers in Barcelona predicted many films (especially from the USA) would simply not be shown in Catalonia. At the time of writing, such a drastic reaction was not yet readily apparent.

The Catalan schooling model, in which all subjects are generally taught in Catalan (although Spanish is frequently the main vehicle of communication between kids in the playground), has drawn praise from the European Commission, which sees it as a successful model for the preservation of Catalan. It has also attracted venom from the right-wing Partido Popular, which claims Spanish is being driven underground. Depending on who you ask, both languages are on the edge of extinction! In fact, both are probably perfectly safe.

The media play a key role in the diffusion and preservation of Catalan and complex content rules mean that certain radio and TV stations must include a minimum fixed percentage of programming in Catalan (including even music played). On certain chat programmes you'll occasionally strike hosts speaking Catalan, with their interlocutors answering in Spanish.

The Catalan government hailed the decision in 2005 allowing the use (albeit not obligatory) of Catalan in EU institutions as 'historic'.

langue d'oc, the southern French derivative of Latin that was long the principal tongue in Gallic lands. The most conspicuous survivor of *langue d'oc* is the now little-used Provençal. Catalan followed its speakers' conquests and was introduced to the Balearic Islands and Valencia. It is also spoken in parts of eastern Aragón, and was for a while carried as far afield as Sardinia (where it still survives, just, in Alghero).

Alongside Catalan, Spanish is also an official (and for many non-Catalans the only) language. It is probably fair to say that Spanish is the first language of more people in the greater Barcelona area than Catalan. For more information, see the Language chapter on p287.

NEIGHBOURHOODS

top picks

NEIGHBOURHOODS

For *barcelonins,* the *barri* (*barrio* in Spanish), meaning 'local district', is everything. Those born and raised in them are proud to say '*Sóc del barri!*' ('I am from this neighbourhood!'). A *barri* has little to do with official municipal boundaries (Barcelona is officially divided into 10 districts); in fact, it can often be a vague term that might mean just the surrounding few streets.

We start in the Barri Gòtic and La Rambla, the medieval heart of the municipal district known as Ciutat Vella (Old City), which also covers edgy El Raval and lively La Ribera.

El Raval stretches southwest of La Rambla, Spain's best-known boulevard, and was long a sordid slum, home to prostitutes, drug dealers and a louche nightlife. A whiff of those bygone days remains, but for years hip bars, restaurants and hotels have been springing up all over, along with art galleries, university faculties and, in the years to come, the brand new Filmoteca de Catalunya, the region's film library under construction in a zone that even now remains the territory of streetwalkers and drug vendors.

The southern half of La Ribera was medieval Barcelona's financial district, where bars have long since replaced the bourse. La Ribera was cut off from the 'Gothic Quarter' by the creation of the rumbling traffic corridor of Via Laietana in 1908.

The old town is fronted by Port Vell and La Barceloneta. The 'Old Port' is a combination of pleasure-boat marina and leisure zone with restaurants, cinemas and bars. A brief, sunny stroll takes you into the narrow lanes of the one-time working-class zone of La Barceloneta, a cauldron of seafood eateries with clear signs of gentrification. Beyond its narrow streets, the Mediterranean laps the city's crowded central beaches.

Where La Barceloneta ends, a new chapter in Barcelona's urban history begins. Port Olímpic, El Poblenou and El Fòrum reflect contemporary Barcelona's drive to renew itself. The port was built for the 1992 Olympics, as were the apartments stretching behind it in the southwest edge of the city's former factory district, El Poblenou. The hi-tech tenants are moving into a growing array of shiny new buildings as the mammoth task of remaking this extensive one-time industrial district continues (see p47). Long shunned as a place to live, its warehouse lofts and big apartments have increasingly attracted homebuyers' attention since the late 1990s. Crowds flock to the nearby beaches that stretch northeast of Port Olímpic. The strands peter out in El Fòrum, a residential, business and pleasure district where skyscrapers sprouted out of nothing in the first years of the 21st century.

The last time Barcelona went on such an urban-planning drive was towards the end of the 19th century, with the creation of L'Eixample. Its Modernista treasures, from La Pedrera to La Sagrada Família, attract hordes of visitors to its gridded streets, which also hide countless gems for foodies, drinkers and shoppers.

L'Eixample filled the gap between Barcelona, Gràcia and Park Güell. Originally a separate town, with its sinuous, narrow lanes and web of lively squares, Gràcia retains an atmosphere utterly its own, with Park Güell a Gaudí fantasy to its north.

From here, the city rises up towards the hills of Parc de Collserola. The slopes of Barcelona in the district of Sarrià-Sant Gervasi are known as La Zona Alta (meaning 'The High Zone', synonymous with snobbery) and take in sought-after Pedralbes and Tibidabo, with its amusement park. For simplicity's sake, we include the more down-to-earth Les Corts, south of Avinguda Diagonal, in this section. It is a residential district and home to the Camp Nou football stadium.

Finally, we visit Montjuïc, Barcelona's Olympic hill and green lung; El Poble Sec, a once-poor area now home to a growing Latin American population; and Sants, a busy working-class neighbourhood that offers little for visitors but is full of life.

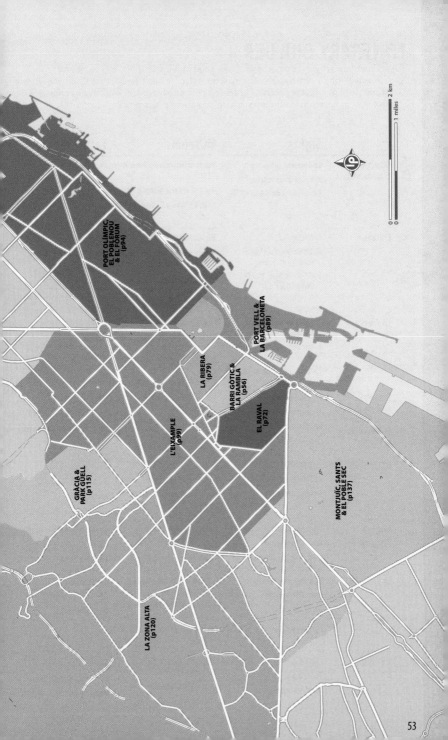

PORT OLÍMPIC,
EL POBLENOU
& EL FÒRUM
(p94)

PORT VELL &
LA BARCELONETA
(p89)

LA RIBERA
(p79)

BARRI GÒTIC &
LA RAMBLA
(p56)

EL RAVAL
(p72)

L'EIXAMPLE
(p99)

GRÀCIA &
PARK GÜELL
(p115)

MONTJUÏC, SANTS
& EL POBLE SEC
(p137)

LA ZONA ALTA
(p120)

0   1 miles
0   2 km

ITINERARY BUILDER

Barcelona is remarkably compact and boasts good public transport, making it easy to see a lot. You can use the Metro to reach key attractions (La Sagrada Família, Park Güell, the Barri Gòtic and perhaps even the beaches) in one long but satisfying day. Walkers can criss-cross most of central Barcelona without even thinking about a Metro ticket.

AREA	Sights	Museums	Eating
Barri Gòtic & La Rambla	La Catedral (p59) Mirador de Colom (p67) Gran Teatre del Liceu (p67)	Museu d'Història de Barcelona (p63) Museu Frederic Marès (p64) Centre d'Interpretació del Call (p67)	Pla (p173) Agut (p173) Bar Celta (p174)
El Raval	Palau Güell (p76) Antic Hospital de la Santa Creu (p73) Església de Sant Pau Del Camp (p77)	Museu Marítim (p73) Museu d'Art Contemporani de Barcelona (Macba) (p76) Centre de Cultura Contemporània de Barcelona (CCCB) (p77)	Casa Leopoldo (p174) Bar Central (p175) Biocenter (p176)
La Ribera	Església de Santa Maria del Mar (p80) Palau de la Música Catalana (p84) Parc de la Ciutadella (p85)	Museu Picasso (p80) Museu Barbier-Mueller d'Art Pre-Colombí (p81) Museu de la Xocolata (p86)	Cal Pep (p176) Bubó (p177)
Port Vell, La Barceloneta, Port Olímpic, El Poblenou & El Fòrum	L'Aquàrium (p89) Transbordador Aeri (p92) Beaches (p94)	Museu d'Història de Catalunya (p91)	Can Majó (p179) Vaso de Oro (p179) Xiringuito d'Escribà (p180)
L'Eixample	La Sagrada Família (p102) La Pedrera (p104) Casa Batlló (p105)	Museu de la Música (p109) Fundació d'Antoni Tàpies (p107) Fundación Francisco Godia (p109)	Casa Darío (p181) Restaurant Me (p182) Inopia (p184)
Gràcia & Park Güell	Park Güell (p115) Casa Viçenc (p117) Mercat de la Llibertat (p117)	Fundació Foto Colectania (p117)	Restaurant Roig Robí (p186) Bilbao (p187) Cal Boter (p187)
La Zona Alta	Parc de Collserola (p133) Parc d'Atraccions (p133) Camp Nou (p121)	CosmoCaixa (Museu de la Ciència) (p120) Museu-Monestir de Pedralbes (p121) Palau Reial de Pedralbes (p124)	Coure (p189) Can Travi Nou (p190) Bar Tomàs (p190)
Montjuïc, Sants & Poble Sec	Castell de Montjuïc (p142) Poble Espanyol (p145) Jardí Botànic (p146)	Museu Nacional d'Art de Catalunya (p138) Fundació de Joan Miró (p143) CaixaForum (p139)	Xemei (p191) La Tomaquera (p192) Quimet i Quimet (p192)

HOW TO USE THIS TABLE

The table below allows you to plan a day's worth of activities in any area of the city. Simply select which area you wish to explore, and then mix and match from the corresponding listings to build your day. The first item in each cell represents a well-known highlight of the area, while the other items are more off-the-beaten-track gems.

Shopping	Drinking & Nightlife	Arts, Sports & Activities
Caelum (p154)	Soul Club (p199)	Gran Teatre del Liceu (p217)
Herboristeria del Rei (p155)	Manchester (p198)	Sala Tarantos (p217)
Papabubble (p153)	Harlem Jazz Club (p199)	Poliesportiu Frontó Colom (p225)
El Indio (p156)	Bar Marsella (p200)	Mailuna (p224)
Teranyina (p156)	Boadas (p200)	Teatre Romea (p219)
	Moog (p201)	Teatre Llantiol (p219)
Casa Gispert (p158)	La Fianna (p202)	Palau de la Música Catalana (p217)
Custo Barcelona (p157)	La Vinya del Senyor (p202)	Aire de Barcelona (p224)
Vila Viniteca (p157)	Magic (p203)	
Maremàgnum (p158)	CDLC (p203)	Poliesportiu Marítim (p225)
	Beach bars (p204)	Club Natació Atlètic-Barcelona (p225)
	Razzmatazz (p204)	Yelmo Cine Icària (p221)
Cubiña (p160)	Dry Martini (p205)	L'Auditori (p217)
Camper (p162)	Michael Collins Pub (p206)	Teatre Nacional de Catalunya (p219)
Xampany (p160)	Antilla BCN (p207)	Teatre Tívoli (p219)
Érase una Vez (p163)	La Baignoire (p209)	Sala Beckett (p218)
Red Market (p163)	Raïm (p209)	Teatreneu (p220)
	Sabor a Cuba (p209)	Flotarium (p224)
La Botiga del Barça (p164)	Berlin (p210)	Football at Camp Nou (p227)
Lavinia (p163)	Otto Zutz (p211)	Rituels d'Orient (p224)
	Mirablau (p211)	Renoir-Les Corts cinema (p220)
	Barcelona Rouge (p212)	Tablao de Carmen (p218)
	Maumau Underground (p212)	Teatre Mercat de les Flors (p218)
	Sala Apolo (p213)	Teatre Lliure (p219)

BARRI GÒTIC & LA RAMBLA

Drinking & Nightlife p198; Eating p172; Shopping p152; Sleeping p231

La Rambla is Spain's most talked-about boulevard. It certainly packs a lot of colour into a short walk, with bird stalls, flower stands, historic buildings, a pungent produce market, overpriced beers and tourist tat, and a ceaselessly changing parade of people from all walks of life. Once a river and sewage ditch on the edge of medieval Barcelona, it still marks the southwest flank of the Barri Gòtic, the nucleus of old Barcelona.

The medieval city was constructed on the Roman core, which in succeeding centuries slowly spread north, south and west. The Barri Gòtic is a warren of narrow, winding streets and unexpected, uneven squares, and is home to a dense concentration of budget hotels, bars, cafes and restaurants. Few of its great buildings date from after the early 15th century – the decline Barcelona went into at that time curtailed grand projects for several centuries. An early port of call for new visitors to Barcelona is Plaça de Catalunya, which roughly marks the northern boundary of the Barri Gòtic. Apart from transport connections, it is also home to the main branch of the city's tourist office (see p284).

The square hums for much of the day. South American pan-flute bands often set up at its La Rambla end, and other buskers can be seen hard at work in front of the punters sipping coffee at Cafè Zurich. Shoppers stream in and out of El Corte Inglés and the El Triangle shopping centre, while hordes charge down from here into La Rambla.

La Rambla proceeds 1.25km southeast gently downhill towards the waterfront. Yes, it's clichéd, but it is a lively introduction to the city.

top picks

BARRI GÒTIC & LA RAMBLA

- La Rambla (see opposite)
- La Catedral (p59)
- Museu d'Història de Barcelona (p63)
- Museu Frederic Marès (p64)
- Plaça de Sant Jaume (p65)

Human statues compete for the attention of passers-by with news-stands seemingly burdened with half the city's porno-magazine supply. Flower stands and bird stalls follow one another. Among the sober 18th-century mansions are scattered overpriced eateries and bars, Dunkin' Donuts and Burger King, and the enticing Mercat de la Boqueria. The highbrow Liceu opera house offers theatre inside...and outside. Around here at night the local transvestite population comes out to play, vying for attention with female prostitutes further down La Rambla. In September 2009, police cleared the area of this activity but by early 2010 there were signs that streetwalkers were beginning to return. As the night wears on, revellers cascade up, down and across the boulevard, in search of the next bar or a rare taxi.

Imagine the northeast side of La Rambla lined by a brooding medieval wall. Inside lies the labyrinth of the Barri Gòtic. To penetrate quickly to its core, follow Carrer de Ferran, an early-19th-century scar through the city, to Plaça de Sant Jaume, lined by the seats of city and regional governments. A step away stand the remaining columns from the city's Roman temple and further north is its successor, the grand Gothic La Catedral. This is the core of the 2000-year-old city. To the west of the Palau de la Generalitat unfold the tiny lanes of what was once the Call, the Jewish quarter. Between the cathedral and Plaça de Catalunya are busy shopping streets, a street dedicated to hot chocolate, another lined with antique shops and remnants of a Roman cemetery.

Heading southeast towards the sea, there is a noticeable change. Although much has been improved since the early 1990s, the streets around Plaça Reial still exude a slight whiff of lawlessness. Pickpockets are on the move (be careful on and around Carrer dels Escudellers too) and a crew of substance abusers congregates around the triangular Plaça de George Orwell (locally known as Plaça del Trippy). Taverns, tearooms and food options from ham to sushi abound. Bars of all sorts, from pseudo-Irish pubs to ill-lit holes in the wall, populate this area, and the acrid smell of urine in the streets late at night is testimony to the roaring trade they do.

With three Metro lines, FGC trains all *rodalies* trains all arriving at Plaça de Catalunya, not to mention airport buses and trains, and night buses and taxis, there is no problem arriving at the northern end of the Barri Gòtic. Other strategic Metro stops include Liceu and Drassanes on Línia 3 and Jaume I on Línia 4.

LA RAMBLA Map p60

Ⓜ Catalunya, Liceu or Drassanes

Flanked by narrow traffic lanes and plane trees, the middle of La Rambla is a broad pedestrian boulevard, crowded every day until the wee hours with a cross-section of *barcelonins* and out-of-towners. Dotted with cafes, restaurants, kiosks and news-stands, and enlivened by buskers, pavement artists, mimes and living statues, La Rambla rarely allows a dull moment.

It takes its name from a seasonal stream (*raml* in Arabic) that once ran here. From the early Middle Ages, on it was better known as the Cagalell (Stream of Shit) and lay outside the city walls until the 14th century. Monastic buildings were then built and, subsequently, mansions of the well-to-do from the 16th to the early 19th centuries. Unofficially, La Rambla is divided into five sections, which explains why many know it as Las Ramblas.

The initial stretch from Plaça de Catalunya is La Rambla de Canaletes, named after a turn-of-the-20th-century drinking fountain, the water of which supposedly emerges from what were once known as the springs of Canaletes. It used to be said that *barcelonins* 'drank the waters of Les Canaletes'. Nowadays, people claim that anyone who drinks from the fountain will return to Barcelona, which is not such a bad prospect. This is the traditional meeting point for happy FC Barcelona fans when they win cups and competitions.

The second stretch, La Rambla dels Estudis (Carrer de la Canuda to Carrer de la Portaferrissa) is also called La Rambla dels Ocells (birds) because of its twittering bird market.

Just north of Carrer del Carme, the Església de Betlem was constructed in baroque style for the Jesuits in the late 17th and early 18th centuries to replace an earlier church destroyed by fire in 1671. Fire was a bit of a theme for this site: the church was once considered the most splendid of Barcelona's few baroque offerings, but leftist arsonists torched it in 1936.

La Rambla de Sant Josep, named after a former monastery dedicated to St Joseph, runs from Carrer de la Portaferrissa to Plaça de la Boqueria and is lined with verdant flower stalls, which give it the alternative name La Rambla de les Flors.

The Palau de la Virreina (La Rambla de Sant Josep 99) is a grand 18th-century rococo mansion (with some neoclassical elements) housing an arts/entertainment information and ticket office run by the Ajuntament (town hall). Built by the then corrupt captain-general of Chile (a Spanish colony that included the Peruvian silver mines of Potosí), Manuel d'Amat i de Junyent, it is a rare example of such postbaroque building in Barcelona. In a series of exhibition rooms, including the bulk of the 1st floor, it houses the Centre de la Imatge (☎ 93 316 10 00; www.bcn.cat/virreinacentredelaimatge), scene of rotating photo exhibitions; admission prices and opening hours vary.

Across La Rambla at No 118 is an equally rare example of a more pure neoclassical pile, Palau Moja, which houses government offices, the Generalitat's bookshop and exhibition space. Its clean, classical lines are best appreciated from across La Rambla.

Next, you are confronted by the bustling sound, smell and tastefest of the Mercat de la Boqueria. It is possibly La Rambla's most interesting building, not so much for its Modernista-influenced design (it was actually built over a long period, from 1840 to 1914, on the site of the former St Joseph monastery) as for the action of the food market (see p186).

At Plaça de la Boqueria, where four side streets meet just north of Liceu Metro station, you can walk all over a Miró – the colourful Mosaïc de Miró in the pavement, with one tile signed by the artist.

La Rambla dels Caputxins (aka La Rambla del Centre), named after another now non-existent monastery, runs from Plaça de la Boqueria to Carrer dels Escudellers. The latter street is named after the potters' guild, founded in the 13th century, whose members lived and worked here (their raw materials came principally from Sicily). On the western side of La Rambla is the Gran Teatre del Liceu (p67).

Further south on the eastern side of La Rambla dels Caputxins is the entrance to the palm-shaded Plaça Reial. Below this point, La Rambla gets seedier, with the occasional strip club and peep show. The final stretch, La Rambla de Santa Mònica, widens out to approach the Mirador de Colom (p67) overlooking Port Vell. La Rambla here is named after the Convent de Santa Mònica, which once stood on the western flank of the street and has since been converted into an art gallery and cultural centre, the Centre d'Art Santa Mònica (☎ 93 567 11 10; www.artssanta-monica.cat; La Rambla de Santa Mònica 7; admission free; ☺ 11am-9pm Tue-Sun & holidays; Ⓜ Drassanes).

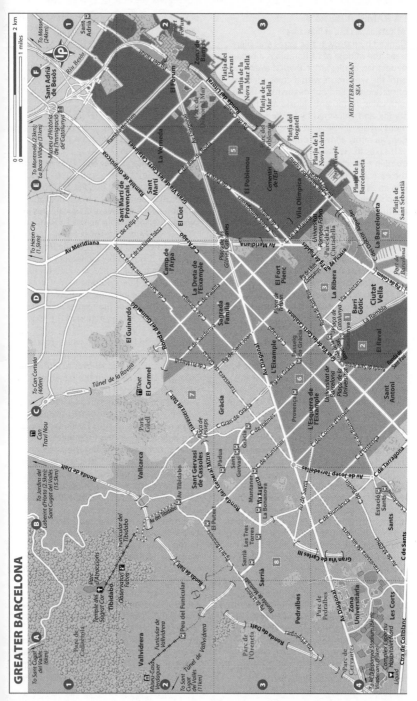

GREATER BARCELONA

58

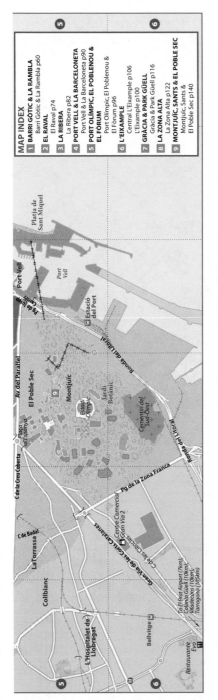

LA CATEDRAL & AROUND Map p60

☎ 93 342 82 60; www.website.es/catedralbcn,
in Catalan & Spanish; Plaça de la Seu; admission
free, special visit €5; ☽ 8am-12.45pm & 5.15-8pm
Mon-Sat, special visit 1-5pm Mon-Sat, 2-5pm Sun &
holidays; Ⓜ Jaume I

Approached from the broad Avinguda de
la Catedral, Barcelona's central place of
worship presents a magnificent image. The
richly decorated main (northwest) facade,
laced with gargoyles and the stone intrica-
cies you would expect of northern European Gothic, sets it quite apart from other
churches in Barcelona. The facade was
actually added in 1870 (and is receiving
a serious round of restoration), although
it is based on a 1408 design. The rest of
the building was built between 1298 and
1460. The other facades are sparse in
decoration, and the octagonal, flat-roofed
towers are a clear reminder that, even
here, Catalan Gothic architectural principles prevailed.

The interior is a broad, soaring space divided into a central nave and two aisles by
lines of elegant, slim pillars. The cathedral
was one of the few churches in Barcelona
spared by the anarchists in the civil war,
so its ornamentation, never overly lavish,
is intact. The faithful frequently notice the
absence of holy water in the church's fonts.
This is not because of a scarcity of holy
water, but a preventive measure taken in
the face of fear over the 2009–10 swine flu
(H1N1) epidemic.

In the first chapel on the right from the
northwest entrance, the main Crucifixion
figure above the altar is Sant Crist de Lepant. It is
said Don Juan's flagship bore it into battle at
Lepanto and that the figure acquired its odd
stance by dodging an incoming cannon-
ball. Further along this same wall, past the
southwest transept, are the wooden coffins
of Count Ramon Berenguer I and his wife Al-
modis, founders of the 11th-century Romanesque predecessor to the present cathedral.
Left from the main entrance is the baptismal
font where, according to one story, six North
American Indians brought to Europe by
Columbus after his first voyage of accidental
discovery were bathed in holy water.

In the middle of the central nave is the
late-14th-century, exquisitely sculpted
timber coro (choir stalls; admission €2.20). The coats
of arms on the stalls belong to members of
the Barcelona chapter of the Order of the
Golden Fleece. Emperor Carlos V presided

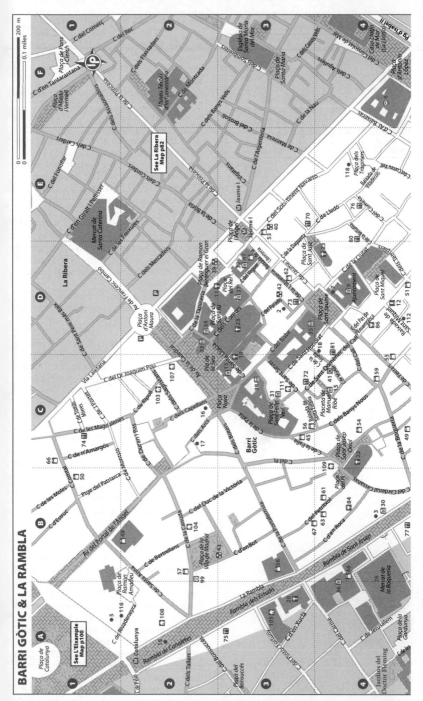

BARRI GÒTIC & LA RAMBLA

See L'Eixample Map p100

See La Ribera Map p82

Plaça de Catalunya

La Ribera

Barri Gòtic

La Rambla

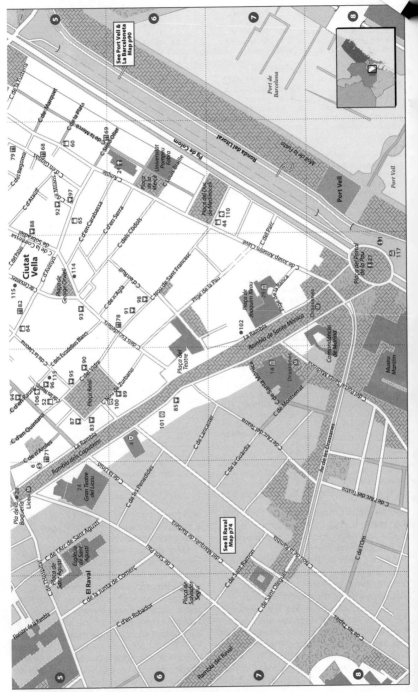

See Port Vell &
La Barceloneta Map p90

See El Raval
Map p74

Ciutat
Vella

El Raval

Port Vell

Port de
Barcelona

Ronda del Litoral

Moll de la Fusta

Pg de Colom

Museu
Marítim

Plaça del Portal
de la Pau

Rambla de Santa Mònica

Plaça de
Joaquim Xirau

La Rambla

Plaça del
Teatre

Rambla dels Caputxins

Gran Teatre
del Liceu

Plaça de la
Boqueria

Rambla del Raval

over the order's meeting here in 1519. Take the time to look at the workmanship up close – the Virgin Mary and Child depicted on the pulpit are especially fine.

A broad staircase before the main altar leads you down to the crypt, which contains the tomb of Santa Eulàlia, one of Barcelona's two patron saints and more affectionately known as Laia. The reliefs on the alabaster sarcophagus, executed by Pisan artisans, recount some of her tortures and, along the top strip, the removal of her body to its present resting place.

For a bird's-eye view (mind the poop) of medieval Barcelona, visit the cathedral's roof

and tower by taking the lift (€2.20) from the Capella de les Animes del Purgatori near the northeast transept.

From the southwest transept, exit by the partly Romanesque door (one of the few remnants of the present church's predecessor) to the leafy claustre (cloister), with its fountains and flock of 13 geese. The geese supposedly represent the age of Santa Eulàlia at the time of her martyrdom and have, generation after generation, been squawking here since medieval days. They make fine watchdogs! One of the cloister chapels commemorates 930 priests, monks and nuns martyred during the civil war.

Along the northern flank of the cloister you can enter the Sala Capitular (Chapter House; admission €2; ☻ 10am-12.15pm & 5.15-7pm Mon-Sat, 10am-12.45pm & 5.15-7pm Sun). Although it's bathed in rich red carpet and graced with fine timber seating, the few artworks gathered here are of minor interest. Among them figure a *pietà* by Bartolomeo Bermejo. A couple of doors down in the northwest corner of the cloister is the Capella de Santa Llúcia, one of the few reminders of Romanesque Barcelona (although the interior is largely Gothic). Walk out the door on to Carrer de Santa Llúcia and turn around to look at the exterior – you can see that, although incorporated into La Catedral, it is a separate building.

Upon exiting the Capella de Santa Llúcia, wander across the lane into the 16th-century Casa de l'Ardiaca (Archdeacon's House; ☻ 9am-9pm Mon-Fri, 9am-2pm Sat), which houses the city's archives. You may stroll around the supremely serene courtyard, cooled by trees and a fountain; it was renovated by Lluis Domènech i Montaner in 1902, when the building was owned by the lawyers' college. Montaner also designed the postal slot, which is adorned with swallows and a tortoise, said to represent the swiftness of truth and the plodding pace of justice. You can get a good glimpse at some stout Roman wall in here. Upstairs, you can look down into the courtyard and across to La Catedral.

You may visit La Catedral in one of two ways. In the morning or afternoon, entrance is free and you can opt to visit any combination of the choir stalls, chapter house and roof. To visit all three areas, it costs less (and is less crowded) to enter for the so-called 'special visit' between 1pm and 5pm.

Across Carrer del Bisbe is the 17th-century Palau Episcopal (Palau del Bisbat; Bishop's Palace). Virtually nothing remains of the original 13th-century structure. The Roman city's northwest gate stood here and you can see the lower segments of the Roman towers that stood on either side of the gate at the base of the Palau Episcopal and Casa de l'Ardiaca. In fact, the lower part of the entire northwest wall of the Casa de l'Ardiaca is of Roman origin – you can also make out part of the first arch of a Roman aqueduct.

Across Plaça Nova from La Catedral your eye may be caught by childlike scribblings on the facade of the Col.legi de Arquitectes (Architectural College). It is, in fact, a giant contribution by Picasso from 1962. Representing Mediterranean festivals, it was much ridiculed by the local press when it was unveiled.

MUSEU D'HISTÒRIA DE BARCELONA
Map p60

☎ 93 256 21 00; www.museuhistoria.bcn.cat; Carrer del Veguer; adult/child under 7yr/senior & student €7/free/5, from 4pm 1st Sat of month and from 3pm Sun free; ☻ 10am-2pm & 4-7pm Tue-Sat Oct-Mar, 10am-8pm Tue-Sat Apr-Sep, 10am-8pm Sun, 10am-3pm holidays; Ⓜ Jaume I
Leap back into Roman Barcino with a subterranean stroll and then stride around parts of the former Palau Reial Major (Grand Royal Palace) on Plaça del Rei (King's Sq, the former palace's courtyard), among the key locations of medieval princely power in Barcelona, in what is one of Barcelona's most fascinating museums. The square is frequently the scene of organised or impromptu concerts and is one of the most atmospheric corners of the medieval city.

Enter through Casa Padellàs, just south of Plaça del Rei. Casa Padellàs was built for a 16th-century noble family in Carrer dels Mercaders and moved here, stone by stone, in the 1930s. It has a courtyard typical of Barcelona's late-Gothic and baroque mansions, with a graceful external staircase up to the 1st floor. Today it leads to a restored Roman tower and a section of Roman wall (whose exterior faces Plaça Ramon de Berenguer el Gran), as well as a section of the house set aside for temporary exhibitions

MUSEUMS WITHIN A MUSEUM

One combined ticket, which has no expiry date, can be used to visit all the components of the Museu d'Història de Barcelona. The main centre is the Plaça del Rei complex, where you can discover parts of Roman and medieval Barcelona. The ticket also includes the Museu-Monestir de Pedralbes (p121), the Centre d'Interpretació in Park Güell (p115), the civil war air raid shelter, Refugi 307 (p147), and the Via Sepulcral Romana (p68). Other sites included in the ticket (although these are all free anyway) are the Temple Romà d'August (p68), Centre d'Interpretació del Call (p67), Museu-Casa Verdaguer in Collserola (p133) and the Espai Santa Caterina in the Mercat de Santa Caterina (p85).

(these can be visited independently to the rest of the museum for €2).

Below ground is a remarkable walk through about 4 sq km of excavated Roman and Visigothic Barcelona. After the display on the typical Roman *domus* (villa), you reach a public laundry (outside in the street were containers for people to urinate into, as the urine was used as disinfectant). You pass more laundries and dyeing shops, a 6th-century public cold-water bath and more dye shops. As you hit the Cardo Minor (a main street), you turn right then left and reach various shops dedicated to the making of *garum*. This paste, a fave food across the Roman Empire, was made of mashed-up fish intestines, eggs and blood. Occasionally prawns, cockles and herbs were added to create other flavours. Further on are fish-preserve stores. Fish were sliced up (and all innards removed for making *garum*) and laid in alternate layers with salt to preserve, sitting in troughs for about three weeks before being ready for sale and export.

Next come remnants of a 6th- to 7th-century church and episcopal buildings, followed by winemaking stores, with ducts for allowing the must to flow off and ceramic, round-bottomed *dolia* for storing and ageing wine. Ramparts then wind around and upward, past remains of the gated patio of a Roman house, the medieval Palau Episcopal (Bishops' Palace) and into two broad vaulted halls with displays on medieval Barcelona.

You eventually emerge at a hall and ticket office set up on the north side of Plaça del Rei. To your right is the Saló del Tinell, the banqueting hall of the royal palace and a fine example of Catalan Gothic (built 1359–70). Its broad arches and bare walls give a sense of solemnity that would have made an appropriate setting for Fernando and Isabel to hear Columbus' first reports of the New World. The hall is sometimes used for temporary exhibitions, which may cost extra and mean that your peaceful contemplation of its architectural majesty is somewhat obstructed.

As you leave the *saló* you come to the 14th-century Capella Reial de Santa Àgata, the palace chapel. Outside, a spindly bell tower rises from the northeast side of Plaça del Rei. Inside, all is bare except for the 15th-century altarpiece and the magnificent *techumbre* (decorated timber ceiling). The altarpiece is considered to be one of Jaume Huguet's finest surviving works.

Head down the fan-shaped stairs into Plaça del Rei and look up to observe the Mirador del Rei Martí (lookout tower of King Martin), built in 1555, long after the king's death. It is part of the Arxiu de la Corona d'Aragón (see below) and so the magnificent views over the old city are now enjoyed only by a privileged few.

From Plaça del Rei, it's worth taking a detour northeast to see the two best surviving stretches of Barcelona's Roman walls, which once boasted 78 towers (as much a matter of prestige as of defence). One is on the southwest side of Plaça Ramon de Berenguer Gran, with the Capella Reial de Santa Àgata atop. The square itself is dominated by a statue of count-king Ramon de Berenguer Gran done by Josep Llimona in 1880. The other is a little further south, by the northern end of Carrer del Sots-tinent Navarro. The Romans built and reinforced these walls in the 3rd and 4th centuries AD, after the first attacks by Germanic tribes from the north.

PALAU DEL LLOCTINENT Map p60
Carrer dels Comtes; admission free; ☯ 10am-7pm; Ⓜ Jaume I

The southwest side of Plaça del Rei is taken up by this palace, built in the 1550s as the residence of the Spanish *lloctinent* (viceroy) of Catalonia and later converted into a convent. From 1853, it housed the Arxiu de la Corona d'Aragón, a unique archive with documents detailing the history of the Crown of Aragón and Catalonia, starting in the 12th century and reaching to the 20th. Gracefully restored in 2006, its courtyard is worth wandering through. Have a look upwards from the main staircase to admire the extraordinary timber *artesonado*, a sculpted ceiling made to seem like the upturned hull of a boat. It was done in the 16th century by Antoni Carbonell. Exhibitions, usually related in some way to the archives, are sometimes staged. When you walk outside the main entrance, look at the *putti* on the right side of the main facade below the window – one seems to be shoving a bellows up the other's backside.

MUSEU FREDERIC MARÈS Map p60
☎ 93 256 35 00; www.museumares.bcn.es; Plaça de Sant Iu 5-6; Ⓜ Jaume I

Closed for renovation until 2011, this eclectic collection is housed in what was once part of the medieval Palau Reial Major, on

Carrer dels Comtes. A rather worn coat of arms on the wall indicates that it was also, for a while, the seat of the Spanish Inquisition in Barcelona. Frederic Marès i Deulovol (1893–1991) was a rich sculptor, traveller and obsessive collector. He specialised in medieval Spanish sculpture, huge quantities of which are displayed in the basement and on the ground and 1st floors – including some lovely polychrome wooden sculptures of the Crucifixion and the Virgin. Among the most eye-catching pieces is a reconstructed Romanesque doorway with four arches, taken from a 13th-century country church in the Aragonese province of Huesca.

The top two floors hold a mind-boggling array of knick-knacks, from toy soldiers and cribs to scissors and 19th-century playing cards, and from early still cameras to pipes and fine ceramics. A room that once served as Marès' study and library is now crammed with sculpture. The shady courtyard houses a pleasant summer cafe (Cafè de l'Estiu) and a series of interactive screens that allow visitors to get an idea of the collection while the museum remains closed.

MUSEU DIOCESÀ Map p60

Casa de la Pia Almoina; ☎ 93 315 22 13; www. arqbcn.org, in Catalan; Avinguda de la Catedral 4; adult/child under 7yr/senior & student €6/free/3; ☯ 10am-2pm & 5-8pm Tue-Sat, 11am-2pm Sun; Ⓜ Jaume I

Barcelona's Roman walls ran across present-day Plaça de la Seu into what subsequently became the Casa de la Pia Almoina. The city's main centre of charity was located here in the 11th century, although the much-crumbled remains of the present building date to the 15th century. Today it houses the Museu Diocesà (Diocesan Museum), where a sparse collection of medieval religious art is on display, usually supplemented by a temporary exhibition or two.

PLAÇA DE SANT JAUME Map p60

Ⓜ Jaume I

In the 2000 or so years since the Romans settled here, the area around this square (often remodelled), which started life as the forum, has been the focus of Barcelona's civic life. Facing each other across it are the Palau de la Generalitat (seat of Catalonia's regional government) on the north side and the Ajuntament (town hall) to the south. Both have fine Gothic interiors, which, unhappily, the public can enter only at limited times.

Founded in the early 15th century on land that had largely belonged to the city's by then defunct Jewish community to house Catalonia's government, the Palau de la Generalitat (☯ free guided visit 10am-1pm 2nd & 4th weekend of month, open doors 23 Apr, 11 Sep & 24 Sep) was extended over the centuries as its importance (and bureaucracy) grew. For weekend visits, you need to book online at www.gencat.cat. Click on *Guia Breu de la Generalitat*, then on *Visites guiades al Palau de la Generalitat* under *Activitats* to reach the booking form.

Marc Safont designed the original Gothic main entrance on Carrer del Bisbe. The modern main entrance on Plaça de Sant Jaume is a late-Renaissance job with neoclassical leanings. If you wander by in the evening, squint up through the windows into the Saló de Sant Jordi (Hall of St George) and you will get some idea of the sumptuousness of the interior.

If you *do* get inside, you're in for a treat. Normally you will have to enter from Carrer de Sant Sever. The first rooms you pass through are characterised by low vaulted ceilings. From here you head upstairs to the raised courtyard known as the Pati dels Tarongers, a modest Gothic orangery (opened about once a month for concert performances of the palace's chimes; see p216). The 16th-century Sala Daurada i de Sessions, one of the rooms leading off the patio, is a splendid meeting hall lit up by huge chandeliers. Still more imposing is the Renaissance Saló de Sant Jordi, whose murals were added last century – many an occasion of pomp and circumstance takes place here. Finally, you descend the staircase of the Gothic Pati Central to leave by what was, in the beginning, the building's main entrance.

Facing the Palau de la Generalitat, and otherwise known as the Casa de la Ciutat, the Ajuntament (☎ 010; admission free; ☯ 10am-1pm Sun) has been the seat of city power for centuries. The Consell de Cent, from medieval times the city's ruling council, first sat here in the 14th century, but the building has lamentably undergone many changes since the days of Barcelona's Gothic-era splendour.

Only the original, now disused, entrance on Carrer de la Ciutat retains its Gothic ornament. The main 19th-century neoclassical facade on the square is a charmless riposte to the Palau de la Generalitat. Inside, the Saló de Cent is the hall in which the town council once held its plenary sessions. The broad vaulting is pure Catalan Gothic and the *artesonado* ceiling demonstrates fine work. In fact, much of what you see is comparatively recent. The building was badly damaged in a bombardment in 1842 and has been repaired and tampered with repeatedly. The wooden neo-Gothic seating was added at the beginning of the 20th century, as was the grand alabaster *retablo* (retable, or altarpiece) at the back. To the right you enter the small Saló de la Reina Regente, built in 1860, where the Ajuntament now sits. To the left of the Saló de Cent is the Saló de les Croniques – the murals here recount Catalan exploits in Greece and the Near East in Catalonia's empire-building days.

Behind the Ajuntament rise the awful town hall offices built in the 1970s over Plaça de Sant Miquel. Opposite is a rare 15th-century gem, Casa Centelles, on the corner of Baixada de Sant Miquel. You can wander into the fine Gothic-Renaissance courtyard if the gates are open.

PLAÇA DE SANT JOSEP ORIOL & AROUND Map p60
Ⓜ Liceu

This small plaza is the prettiest in the Barri Gòtic. Its bars and cafes attract buskers and artists and make it a lively place to hang out. It is surrounded by quaint streets, many dotted with appealing cafes, restaurants and shops.

Looming over the square is the flank of the Església de Santa Maria del Pi (⏲ 9.30am-1pm & 5-8.30pm Mon-Fri, 9.30am-1pm & 4-8.30pm Sat, 9.30am-2pm & 5-8.30pm Sun & holidays), a Gothic church built in the 14th to 16th centuries. The bulk of it was completed in 1320–91. With its 10m diameter, the beautiful rose window above its entrance on Plaça del Pi is claimed by some to be the world's biggest. The interior of the church was gutted when leftists ransacked it in the opening months of the civil war in 1936 and most of the stained glass is modern. Perhaps one happy result of the fire was the destruction of the 19th-century, neo-Gothic seating, which therefore had to be replaced by the 18th-century baroque original.

The third chapel on the left is dedicated to Sant Josep Oriol, who was parish priest here from 1687 to 1702. The chapel has a map showing the places in the church where he worked numerous miracles (he was canonised in 1909). According to legend, a 10th-century fisherman discovered an image of the Virgin Mary in a *pi* (pine tree) that he was intent on cutting down to build a boat. Struck by the vision, he instead built a little chapel, later to be succeeded by this Gothic church. A pine still grows in the square.

PLAÇA REIAL & AROUND Map p60
Ⓜ Liceu

Just south of Carrer de Ferran, near its La Rambla end, Plaça Reial is a traffic-free plaza whose 19th-century neoclassical facades are punctuated by numerous eateries, bars and nightspots. It was created on the site of a convent, one of several destroyed along La Rambla (the strip was teeming with religious institutions) in the wake of the Spainwide disentailment laws that stripped the Church of much of its property. The lamp posts by the central fountain are Antoni Gaudí's first known works in the city.

Residents have a rough time of it, with noise a virtual constant as punters crowd in and out of restaurants, bars and *discotecas* (clubs) at all hours. Downright dangerous until the 1980s, the square retains a restless atmosphere, where unsuspecting tourists, respectable citizens, ragged buskers, nonchalant cops, down-and-outs and sharpwitted pickpockets come face to face. Don't be put off, but watch your pockets.

The southern half of the Barri Gòtic is imbued with the memory of Picasso, who

---

MANIC MONDAYS

Many attractions shut their doors on Monday, but there are plenty of exceptions. Among the more enticing ones are Casa-Museu Gaudí (in Park Güell, p115); Gran Teatre del Liceu (see opposite); Jardí Botànic (p146); La Catedral (p59); La Pedrera (p104); La Sagrada Família (p102); Mirador de Colom (see opposite); Museu d'Art Contemporani de Barcelona (p76); Museu de l'Eròtica (p69); Museu de la Xocolata (p86); Museu del Futbol Club Barcelona (near Camp Nou, p121); Museu del Modernisme Català (p110); Museu Marítim (p73); Palau de la Música Catalana (p84) and the Pavelló Mies van der Rohe (p145).

lived as a teenager with his family in Carrer de la Mercè, had his first studio in Carrer de la Plata (now a rather cheesy restaurant) and was a regular visitor to a brothel at Carrer d'Avinyó 27. That experience may have inspired his 1907 painting *Les Demoiselles d'Avignon*.

GRAN TEATRE DEL LICEU Map p60

☎ 93 485 99 14; www.liceubarcelona.com; La Rambla dels Caputxins 51-59; admission with/without guide €8.70/4; ☾ guided tour 10am, unguided visits 11.30am, noon, 12.30pm & 1pm; Ⓜ Liceu

If you can't catch a night at the opera, you can still have a look around one of Europe's greatest opera houses, known to locals as the Liceu. Smaller than Milan's La Scala but bigger than Venice's La Fenice, it can seat up to 2300 people in its grand horseshoe auditorium.

Built in 1847, the Liceu launched such Catalan stars as Josep (aka José) Carreras and Montserrat Caballé. Fire virtually destroyed it in 1994, but city authorities were quick to get it back into operation. Carefully reconstructing the 19th-century auditorium and installing the latest in theatre technology, technicians brought the Liceu back to life in October 1999. You can take a 20-minute quick turn around the main public areas of the theatre or join a one-hour guided tour.

On the guided tour you are taken to the grand foyer, with its thick pillars and sumptuous chandeliers, and then up the marble staircase to the Saló dels Miralls (Hall of Mirrors). These both survived the 1994 fire and the latter was traditionally where theatregoers mingled during intermission. With mirrors, ceiling frescoes, fluted columns and high-and-mighty phrases in praise of the arts, it all exudes a typically neobaroque richness worthy of its 19th-century patrons. You are then led up to the 4th-floor stalls to admire the theatre itself.

The tour also takes in a collection of Modernista art, El Cercle del Liceu, which contains works by Ramon Casas. It is possible to book special tours, one that is similar to the guided tour described above but including a half-hour music recital on the Saló dels Miralls. The other tour penetrates the inner workings of the stage and backstage work areas.

MIRADOR DE COLOM Map p60

☎ 93 302 52 24; Plaça del Portal de la Pau; lift adult/child under 4yr/senior & child 4-12yr €2.50/ free/1.50; ☾ 9am-8.30pm Jun-Sep, 10am-6.30pm Oct-May; Ⓜ Drassanes

High above the swirl of traffic on the roundabout below, a pigeon-poop-coiffed Columbus keeps permanent watch, pointing vaguely out to the Mediterranean (to his home town of Genoa?). Built for the Universal Exhibition in 1888, the monument allows you to zip up 60m in the lift for bird's-eye views back up La Rambla and across the ports of Barcelona. It was in Barcelona that Columbus allegedly gave the delighted Catholic monarchs a report of his first discoveries in the Americas after his voyage in 1492. In the 19th century, it was popularly believed here that Columbus was one of Barcelona's most illustrious sons. Some historians still make that claim.

ESGLÉSIA DE SANTS JUST I PASTOR

Map p60

☎ 93 301 74 33; www.basilicasantjust.cat, in Catalan; Plaça de Sant Just 5; admission free; ☾ 11am-2pm & 5-9pm Wed-Fri, 5-9pm Sat, 10am-1.30pm Sun, 11am-2pm & 5-8pm Tue; Ⓜ Liceu or Jaume I

This somewhat neglected, single-nave church, with chapels on either side of the buttressing, was built in 1342 in Catalan Gothic style on what is reputedly the site of the oldest parish church in Barcelona. Inside, you can admire some fine stained-glass windows. In front of it, in a pretty little square that was used as a set (a smelly Parisian marketplace) in 2006 for *Perfume: The Story of a Murderer*, is what is claimed to be the city's oldest Gothic fountain.

On the morning of 11 September 1924, Antoni Gaudí was arrested as he attempted to enter the church from this square to attend Mass. In those days of the dictatorship of General Primo de Rivera, it took little to ruffle official feathers, and Gaudí's refusal to speak Spanish (Castilian) to the overbearing Guardia Civil officers who had stopped him earned him the better part of a day in the cells until a friend came to bail him out.

CENTRE D'INTERPRETACIÓ DEL CALL

Map p60

☎ 93 256 21 00; www.museuhistoria.bcn.cat; Placeta de Manuel Ribé; admission free; ☾ 10am-2pm Wed-Fri, 11am-6pm Sat, 11am-3pm Sun & holidays; Ⓜ Jaume I or Liceu

Once a 14th-century house of the Jewish weaver Jucef Bonhiac, this small visitors' centre is dedicated to the history of Barcelona's Jewish quarter, the Call. Glass sections in the ground floor allow you to inspect Mr Bonhiac's former wells and storage space. The house, also known as the Casa de l'Alquimista (Alchemist's House), hosts a modest display of Jewish artefacts, including ceramics excavated in the area of the Call, along with explanations and maps of the one-time Jewish quarter.

The area between Carrer dels Banys Nous and Plaça de Sant Jaume was the heart of the city's medieval Jewish quarter, or Call Major, until the Jews were expelled in the late 15th century. The Call Menor extended across the modern Carrer de Ferran as far as Baixada de Sant Miquel and Carrer d'en Rauric. The present Església de Sant Jaume on Carrer de Ferran was built on the site of a synagogue.

Even before their expulsion in 1492, Jews were not exactly privileged citizens. As in many medieval centres, they were obliged to wear a special identifying mark on their garments and had trouble getting permission to expand their ghetto as the Call's population increased (as many as 4000 people were crammed into the tiny streets of the Call Major).

SINAGOGA MAJOR Map p60

☎ 93 317 07 90; www.calldebarcelona.org; Carrer de Marlet 5; admission €2 donation; ☉ 10.30am-6pm Mon-Fri, 10.30am-3pm Sat & Sun; Ⓜ Liceu
When an Argentine investor bought a run-down electrician's store with an eye to converting it into central Barcelona's umpteenth bar, he could hardly have known he had stumbled onto the remains of what could be the city's main medieval synagogue (some historians cast doubt on the claim). Remnants of medieval and Roman-era walls remain in the small vaulted space that you enter from the street. Also remaining are tanners' wells installed in the 15th century. The second chamber has been spruced up for use as a synagogue. A remnant of late-Roman-era wall here, given its orientation facing Jerusalem, has led some to speculate that there was a synagogue here even in Roman times. There were four synagogues in the medieval city, but after the pogroms of 1391, this one (assuming it was the Sinagoga Major) was Christianised by the placing of an effigy of St Dominic on the building. A guide will explain what is thought to be the significance of the site in various languages.

TEMPLE ROMÀ D'AUGUST Map p60

Carrer del Paradis; admission free; ☉ 10am-2pm & 4-7pm Tue-Sat, 10am-8pm Sun, 10am-3pm holidays Oct-Mar, 10am-8pm Tue-Sat, 10am-8pm Sun, 10am-3pm holidays Apr-Sep; Ⓜ Jaume I
Opposite the southeast end of La Catedral, narrow Carrer del Paradis leads towards Plaça de Sant Jaume. Inside No 10, itself an intriguing building with Gothic and baroque touches, are four columns and the architrave of Barcelona's main Roman temple, dedicated to Caesar Augustus and built to worship his imperial highness in the 1st century AD. You are now standing on the highest point of Roman Barcino, Mont Tàber (a grand total of 16.9m, unlikely to induce altitude sickness). You may well find the door open outside the listed hours. Just pop in.

VIA SEPULCRAL ROMANA Map p60

☎ 93 256 21 00; www.museuhistoria.bcn.cat; Plaça de la Vila de Madrid; admission €2; ☉ 10am-8pm Tue-Sun, 10am-3pm holidays Apr-Sep, 10am-2pm & 4-7pm Tue-Sat, 10am-8pm Sun, 10am-3pm holidays Oct-Mar; Ⓜ Catalunya
Along Carrer de la Canuda, a block east of the top end of La Rambla, is a sunken garden where a series of Roman tombs lies exposed. The burial ground stretches along either side of the road that led northwest out of Barcelona's Roman predecessor, Barcino. Roman law forbade burial within city limits and so everyone, the great and humble, were generally buried along roads leading out of cities. A smallish display in Spanish and Catalan by the tombs explores the Roman road and highway system, burial and funerary rites and customs. A few bits of pottery (including a burial amphora with the skeleton of a three-year-old Roman child) accompany the display.

DOMUS ROMANA Map p60

☎ 93 256 21 00; www.museuhistoria.bcn.cat; Carrer de la Fruita 3; ☉ 10am-3pm Sat, Sun & holidays; Ⓜ Liceu
The remains of a Roman domus (town house) have been unearthed and opened to the public. The house (and vestiges of three small shops) lay close to the Roman forum and the owners were clearly well off. Apart from getting something of an idea of daily Roman life through these remains, the location also contains six medieval grain

silos installed at the time the Jewish quarter, the Call, was located in this area. The whole is housed in the mid-19th century Casa Morell. So, in an unusual mix, one gets a glimpse of three distinct periods in history in the same spot.

MUSEU DE L'ERÒTICA Map p60

Erotica Museum; ☎ 93 318 98 65; www.erotica-museum.com; La Rambla de Sant Josep 96; adult/senior & student €9/8; ☺ 10am-9pm Jun-Sep, 10am-8pm Oct-May; Ⓜ Liceu

Observe what naughtiness people have been getting up to since ancient times in this museum, with lots of Kama Sutra and 1920s flickering porn movies. The museum caters to all tastes. For those red-faced about entering such a scurrilous place, there really is a lot of sound historical material, such as Indian bas-reliefs showing various aspects of tantric love, 18th-century wood carvings depicting Kama Sutra positions (can normal people really engage in all these gymnastics?), Japanese porcelain porn and the like. An array of modern, vaguely erotic artwork also lends intellectual weight to the exercise. Altogether more fun are the 18th-century torture room, the rather complicated, dildo-equipped 'pleasure seat' and early-20th-century skin flicks.

MUSEU DE CERA Map p60

☎ 93 317 26 49; www.museocerabcn.com; Passatge de la Banca 7; adult/child under 5yr/senior, student & child 5-11yr €12/free/7; ☺ 10am-10pm daily Jun-Sep, 10am-1.30pm & 4-7.30pm Mon-Fri, 11am-2pm & 4.30-8.30pm Sat, Sun & holidays Oct-May; Ⓜ Drassanes

Inside this late-19th-century building, you can stand, sit and lounge about with 300 wax figures. The visit is just as interesting for the tour around this former bank, with its grand internal stairway and salons, none of which seemed to have changed much in many decades. Frankenstein is here, along with a rather awkward-looking Prince Charles with Camilla. In the same hall and grouped together willy-nilly are Hitler, Bill Clinton, Mussolini, Che Guevara, Fidel Castro, General Franco and head of the former Catalan government-in-exile Josep Taradellas. Elsewhere are groups of great Catalan leaders, artists, musicians and the like, as well as a section on explorers, ranging from Captain James Cook to Morocco's Ibn Bat-

tuta. Towards the end, *Star Wars* characters prance in sci-fi style.

ESGLÉSIA DE LA MERCÈ Map p60

Plaça de la Mercè; Ⓜ Drassanes

Raised in the 1760s on the site of its Gothic predecessor, the baroque Església de la Mercè is home to Barcelona's most celebrated patron saint. It was badly damaged during the civil war. What remains is, however, quite a curiosity. The baroque facade facing the square contrasts with the Renaissance flank along Carrer Ample. The latter was actually moved here from another nearby church that was subsequently destroyed in the 1870s.

DALÍ ESCULTOR Map p60

Carrer dels Arcs 5; admission €8; ☺ 10am-10pm; Ⓜ Liceu

One of the best things about this collection is its superb location in the Reial Cercle Artístic (Royal Art Circle) building just near La Catedral. This somewhat hyped display offers 60-odd little-known sculptures by a man who was largely renowned for his paintings. Documents, sketches and photos by and of the artist complete the picture. If you can't visit his museum-mausoleum (p249) in Figueres, this is no substitute, but does provide some clues to the life and work of the mustachioed maestro.

MUSEU DEL CALÇAT Map p60

Footwear Museum; ☎ 93 301 45 33; Plaça de Sant Felip Neri 5; admission €2.50; ☺ 11am-2pm Tue-Sun; Ⓜ Jaume I

This obscure museum is home to everything from Egyptian sandals to dainty ladies' shoes of the 18th century. The museum and cobblers' guild, which has its roots in the city's medieval past, were moved here shortly after the civil war.

HIDDEN TREASURES IN THE BARRI GÒTIC
Walking Tour
1 Roman Tombs

On Plaça de la Vila de Madrid is a sunken garden with various Roman tombs (see opposite) lined up and a small explanatory museum attached. It was customary to line highways leading out of cities with tombs and it is believed this

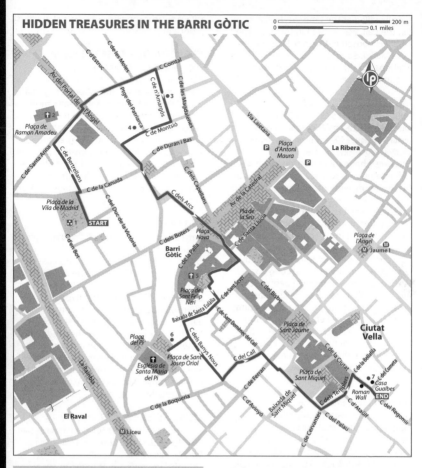

HIDDEN TREASURES IN THE BARRI GÒTIC

WALK FACTS

Start **Roman Tombs**
Finish **Centre Cívic Pati Llimona**
Distance **1.5km**
Duration **30 minutes**
Transport Ⓜ **Catalunya or Liceu**

road connected Roman Barcino with the Via
Augusta, which linked Rome and Cádiz.

2 Església de Santa Anna

In a tranquil square just off busy Carrer de
Santa Anna lies this rarely visited church. It
dates from the 12th century, but little remains
of the original Romanesque structure. The
Gothic cloister is a shady haven – if you can
get in. It's open sporadically.

3 Palace Walls of Guifré el Pelós

Stroll along Carrer de N'Amargos and muse
on the plaque at No 8. It claims the palace
garden walls of the first Comte (Count) of
Barcelona, Guifré el Pelós (Wilfred the Hairy;
see p22), stood here. Carrer de N'Amargos
was the first street in Barcelona to get gas
lighting.

4 Els Quatre Gats

Near the supposed site of Wilfred's palace
is a Modernista icon at Carrer de Montsió
3. 'The Four Cats', a colourful if mediocre
restaurant, started life as Casa Martí (1896),
built by Puig i Cadafalch. From 1897 to 1903,
it was *the* hang-out for Modernista artists and
other bohemians, from Picasso to composer
Enric Granados.

5 Església de Sant Felip Neri

The baroque facade of the Església de Sant Felip Neri (completed in 1752) has been shattered by the impact of machine-gun fire. One story says that pro-Franco troops carried out summary executions here shortly after they marched into the city in 1939. An eerie silence hangs over the square.

6 Palau de Fiveller

Gracing Plaça de Sant Josep Oriol (at No 4), just opposite the silent stone flank of the Església de Santa Maria del Pi (p66), stands Palau de Fiveller, a one-time private mansion dating from 1571. The facade dates from the 18th century.

7 Centre Cívic Pati Llimona

Remains of Roman Barcino's southernmost city gate, as well as parts of the 3rd- and 4th-century city wall, line Carrer de Regomir. To get a closer look at the ruins, enter the Centre Cívic Pati Llimona (☎ 93 268 47 00; admission free; ⊙ 9am-9pm Mon-Fri, 10am-2pm & 4-8pm Sat). Just beyond the gate at No 13 stands a 15th-century mansion, Casa Gualbes.

EL RAVAL

Drinking & Nightlife p200; Eating p174; Shopping p155; Sleeping p232

Long one of the most rough-and-tumble parts of Barcelona, El Raval is becoming so hip in a grungy, inner-city way that *barcelonins* have even invented a verb for rambling around El Raval: *ravalejar*.

El Raval (an Arabic word referring to the suburbs beyond the medieval walls that long lined La Rambla) has had a chequered history. Its bottom half is better known as the Barri Xinès, a seedy red-light zone that, even today, after decades of efforts to clean it up, retains a touch of its dodgy feel.

For centuries the area has been home to prostitutes, louche lads and, at times, a bohemian collection of interlopers. In the 1920s and '30s especially, it was a popular playground for *barcelonins* of many classes, busy at night with the rambunctious activity in taverns, cafes, concerts, cabarets and brothels. Carrer Nou de la Rambla, where Picasso lived for a while, was particularly lively. By the 1960s, many of the brothels and bars had shut down, but there was still plenty of activity, especially when the American Sixth

top picks

EL RAVAL

- Museu Marítim (see opposite)
- Antic Hospital de la Santa Creu (see opposite)
- Palau Güell (p76)
- Església de Sant Pau del Camp (p77)
- Museu d'Art Contemporani de Barcelona (p76)

Fleet, with its three aircraft carriers, came to town. Those visits were frequent, providing a ready clientele for bars and prostitutes, until they came to an end in 1988. This was also the haunt of Pepe Carvalho, the dissolute star of Barcelona writer Manuel Vázquez Montalbán's much-loved detective stories (see p40).

Waves of immigration have changed the make-up of El Raval, which boasts a busy Pakistani population, with sizeable contingents from North Africa and the Philippines. Migrants have gone from 3% of El Raval's popualtion to around 50% since the mid-1990s.

Just as great an impact has come from the explosion of bars and restaurants. While it may never attain the popularity of El Born (see La Ribera, p79), El Raval attracts swarms of adventurous locals and curious visitors who search out a growing and eclectic range of places to while away the days and evenings. Just about all tastes are catered for, from those wanting a cheap beer in a timelessly grungy old bar to fastidious gourmets in need of elegance and fine flavours.

Bounded by La Rambla in the east and Ronda de Sant Antoni, Ronda de Sant Pau and Avinguda del Paral.lel to the west and south, El Raval started life as a higgledy-piggledy suburb of medieval Barcelona. Here and there, we stumble across reminders of the area's long history, from Romanesque cloisters to the medieval shipyards of Les Drassanes.

Carrer de l'Hospital, named after the city's 15th-century hospital and once the road to Madrid, roughly divides the area in two. The northern half has an almost respectable air about it. It is certainly full of diversity. From the Le Méridien hotel on expensive Carrer del Pintor Fortuny, you are a couple of blocks away from the colourful Mercat de la Boqueria produce market, a feast of contemporary art at the Museu d'Art Contemporani de Barcelona, art galleries, the Universitat de Barcelona's history, geography and philosophy faculties (with some 6000 students), the journalism school of Universitat Ramon Llull and the Massana conservatorium. At night, students fill the bars on Carrer de Valldonzella and Carrer de Joaquín Costa.

Carrer de l'Hospital marks a crossroads. Home to an unassuming mosque (virtually opposite the national library and one of three in the district), the street is lined with bars that are more reminiscent of Tangier than Spain. The street fills with faithful male Muslims around midday on Fridays for the week's main prayers. The western end of the street has been largely taken over by Pakistanis and North Africans, who have opened cafes, halal butcher shops and barber shops. In La Rambla del Raval, which replaced a whole slum block in 2000, Pakistanis sometimes play cricket, while a youthful set of hedonists checks out kebab shops and an assortment of bars and well-heeled patrons wander in and out of the striking cylindrical designer hotel Barceló Raval (p233) and its fashionable restaurant.

Between Carrer de l'Hospital and the waterfront, El Raval retains some of its dodgy flavour of yore. The city's new central cinema archive (Filmoteca de Catalunya) is being built near the Barceló Raval hotel in the area bounded by the Rambla del Raval and Carrer de Sant Pau (where excavations have uncovered traces of the city's 17th-century women's prison). For the moment, Carrer de Sant Pau remains a haunt of junkies and dealers, while Carrer de Sant Ramon is particularly busy with streetwalkers – some traditions die hard. Several fine old bars have stood the test of time in these streets.

El Raval is encircled by three Metro lines. Línies 1, 2 and 3 stop at strategic points around the district, so nothing is far from a Metro stop. The Línia 3 stop at Liceu is a convenient exit point.

MUSEU MARÍTIM Map p74

☎ 93 342 99 20; www.mmb.cat; Avinguda de les Drassanes; adult/child under 7yr/senior & student €2.50/free/1.25, 3-8pm Sun free; ☷ 10am-8pm; Ⓜ Drassanes; ⌘

Venice had its Arsenal and Barcelona the Reials Drassanes (Royal Shipyards), from which Don Juan of Austria's flagship galley was launched to lead a joint Spanish-Venetian fleet into the momentous Battle of Lepanto against the Turks in 1571.

These mighty Gothic shipyards are not as extensive as their Venetian counterparts but they're an extraordinary piece of civilian architecture nonetheless. Today the broad arches shelter the Museu Marítim, the city's seafaring-history museum and one of the most fascinating museums in town.

The shipyards were, in their heyday, among the greatest in Europe. Begun in the 13th century and completed by 1378, the long, arched bays (the highest arches reach 13m) once sloped off as slipways directly into the water, which lapped the seaward side of the Drassanes until at least the end of the 18th century.

The centre of the shipyards is dominated by a full-sized replica (made in the 1970s) of Don Juan of Austria's flagship. A clever audiovisual display aboard the vessel brings to life the ghastly existence of the slaves, prisoners and volunteers (!) who at full steam could haul this vessel along at 9 knots. They remained chained to their seats, four to an oar, at all times. Here they worked, drank (fresh water was stored below decks, where the infirmary was also located), ate, slept and went to the loo. You could *smell* a galley like this from miles away.

Fishing vessels, old navigation charts, models and dioramas of the Barcelona waterfront make up the rest of this engaging museum. Temporary exhibitions, often on wholly unrelated subjects, are also held. The museum was being largely overhauled at the time of writing. While this work continues, only Don Juan's flagship and a limited selection of the museum's objects can be seen.

The pleasant museum cafe offers courtyard seating and wi-fi.

Outside and partly obscured by rampant vegetation on the Avinguda del Paral.lel side of the building are remnants of the city walls erected in the 13th century and later extended under count-king Pere el Ceremoniós (1336–87).

ANTIC HOSPITAL DE LA SANTA CREU Map p74

☎ 93 270 23 00; www.bnc.cat; Carrer de l'Hospital 56; Ⓜ Liceu

Behind the Mercat de la Boqueria stands what was, in the 15th century, the city's main hospital. The restored Antic Hospital de la Santa Creu (Former Holy Cross Hospital) today houses the Biblioteca de Catalunya (Library of Catalonia; admission free; ☷ 9am-8pm Mon-Fri, 9am-2pm Sat), as well as the Institut d'Estudis Catalans (Institute for Catalan Studies).

The library is the single most complete collection of documents (estimated at around three million) tracing the region's long history. The hospital, which was begun in 1401 and functioned until the 1930s, was considered one of the best in Europe in its medieval heyday.

Entering from Carrer de l'Hospital, you find yourself in a delightfully bedraggled, vaguely tropical garden that is home to bums, earnest students on a break and a cheerful bar-cafe. Off the garden lies the entrance to the prestigious Massana conservatorium and, up a sweep of stairs, the library. You can freely visit the most impressive part, the grand reading rooms beneath broad Gothic stone arches, where you can also see temporary displays of anything

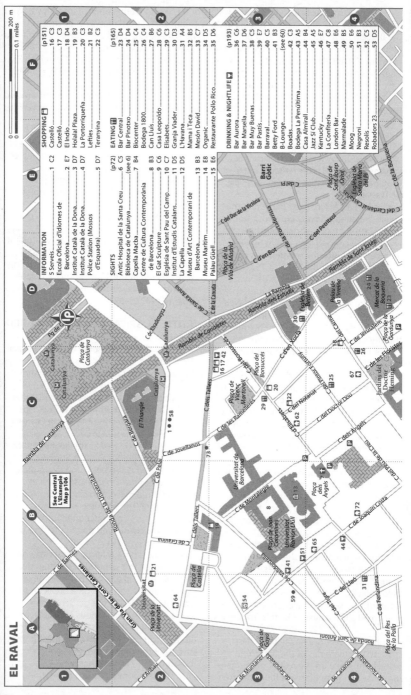

EL RAVAL

0 .... 200 m
0 .... 0.1 miles

See Central L'Eixample Map p106

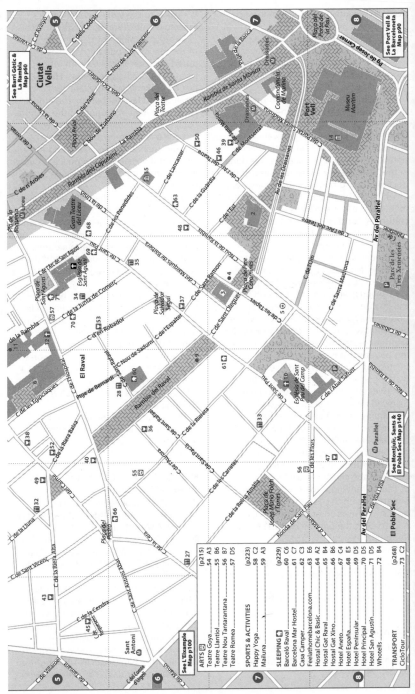

See L'Eixample
Map p100

See Barri Gòtic &
La Rambla
Map p60

Ciutat
Vella

See Port Vell &
La Barceloneta
Map p90

See Montjuïc, Sants &
El Poble Sec Map p140

El Raval

Sant
Antoni

Sant Antoni

El Poble Sec

Av del Paral·lel

Port
Vell

Museu
Marítim

Plaça del
Teatre

Gran Teatre
del Liceu

Plaça de
Sant Agustí

Plaça de
Salvador
Seguí

Plaça de la
Boqueria

La Rambla

Rambla de Santa Mònica

Rambla dels Caputxins

Rambla del Raval

Plaça de
Josep Miró Folch
i Torres

Plaça del
Pedró

Parc de les
Tres Xemeneies

Església de Sant
Pau del Camp

Església de
Sant Agustí

75

from old records to medieval monastic hymnals.

Otherwise, it is possible to join a tour on 23 April (Sant Jordi) and one day late in September (the date changes), when the entire building throws itself open for guided visits.

The guided visit takes you through the library's public areas and others usually closed to the public, such as the Museu del Llibre Frederic Marès, a former private ward in the hospital, whose bright tile decoration of the stations of the cross was done in the 17th century. Marès donated 1500 documents and books to the library, some of which are on display. He also sculpted medallions of great figures of Catalan culture. Antoni Gaudí wound up in the Via Crucis ward in 1926 after being run over by a tram; he died here.

Approaching the complex down a narrow lane from Carrer del Carme or from Jardins del Doctor Fleming (the little park with swings), you arrive at the entrance to the institute, which sometimes opens its doors for expositions. If it's open, wander into what was the 17th-century Casa de Convalescència de Sant Pau, which housed recovering patients from the hospital. At first, it hosted just seven men and five women. By the end of the 17th century, there were 200 beds and 400 mattresses and patients received meat and desserts (which is more than many might have hoped for outside). The hospice operated until the early 20th century. The building, which centres on a cloister, is richly decorated with ceramics (especially the entrance vestibule). In the centre of the cloister you'll find a statue of St Paul, after whom the house is named. Situated up on the 1st floor at the far end is what was an orange garden, now named after the Catalan novelist Mercè Rodoreda.

The former hospital's Gothic chapel, La Capella (☎ 93 442 71 71; www.bcn.cat/lacapella; admission free; ⏰ noon-2pm & 4-8pm Tue-Sat, 11am-2pm Sun & holidays) is worth poking your nose into for the frequent temporary exhibitions.

PALAU GÜELL Map p74

☎ 93 317 39 74; www.palauguell.cat; Carrer Nou de la Rambla 3-5; admission free; ⏰ 10am-2.30pm Tue-Sat; Ⓜ Drassanes

Welcome to the early days of Gaudí's fevered architectural imagination. This extraordinary Modernista mansion, one of the few major buildings of that era raised in Ciutat Vella, gives an insight into its maker's prodigious genius. He built it just off La Rambla in the late 1880s for his wealthy and faithful patron, the industrialist Eusebi Güell. Although a little sombre compared with some of his later whims, it is still a characteristic riot of styles (Gothic, Islamic, art nouveau) and materials. After the civil war, the police occupied it and tortured political prisoners in the basement.

Up two floors are the main hall and its annexes (closed for renovation at the time of writing). The hall is a parabolic pyramid – each wall an arch stretching up three floors and coming together to form a dome. The roof is a mad Gaudíesque tumult of tiled colour and fanciful design in the building's chimney pots.

Picasso – who, incidentally, hated Gaudí's work – began his Blue Period in 1902 in a studio across the street at Carrer Nou de la Rambla 10. Begging to differ with Señor Picasso, Unesco declared the Palau, together with Gaudí's other main works (La Sagrada Família, p102; Casa Batlló, p105; La Pedrera, p104; Park Güell, p115; Casa Vicens, p117; and Colònia Güell crypt, p149) a World Heritage Site.

The ground floor and basement reopened to the public in early 2008 after renovation. When the rest will open is unclear.

MUSEU D'ART CONTEMPORANI DE BARCELONA Map p74

Macba; ☎ 93 412 08 10; www.macba.cat; Plaça dels Àngels 1; adult/concession €7.50/6; ⏰ 11am-8pm Mon & Wed, 11am-midnight Thu & Fri, 10am-8pm Sat, 10am-3pm Sun & holidays late Sep, 11am-7.30pm Mon & Wed-Fri, 10am-8pm Sat, 10am-3pm Sun & holidays late Sep-late Jun; Ⓜ Universitat

The ground and 1st floors of this great white bastion of contemporary art are generally given over to exhibitions from the gallery's own collections (some 3000 pieces centred on three periods: post-WWII; around 1968; and the years since the fall of the Berlin wall in 1989, right up until the present day). You may see works by Antoni Tàpies, Joan Brossa, Paul Klee, Miquel Barceló and a whole raft of international talent, depending on the theme(s) of the ever-changing exposition. The gallery also presents temporary visiting exhibitions and has an extensive art bookshop. Outside, the spectacle is as intriguing as inside. While skateboarders dominate the space south of the museum (considered one of Europe's great skateboard locations), you may well find Pakistani kids enjoying a game of cricket in Plaça de Joan Coromines.

Across the main skateboard-infested square, the renovated 400-year-old Convent dels Àngels houses the Capella Macba (Plaça dels Àngels; Ⓜ Universitat), where the Macba regularly rotates selections from its permanent collection. The Gothic framework of the one-time convent-church remains intact.

CENTRE DE CULTURA CONTEMPORÀNIA DE BARCELONA
Map p74

CCCB; ☎ 93 306 41 00; www.cccb.org; Carrer de Montalegre 5; 2 exhibitions adult/child under 16yr/senior & student €6/free/4.50, 1 exhibition €4.50/free/3.40, free 1st Wed of month, 8-10pm Thu, 3-8pm Sun; Ⓨ 11am-8pm Tue, Wed & Fri-Sun, 11am-10pm Thu; Ⓜ Universitat

A complex of auditoriums, exhibition spaces and conference halls opened here in 1994 in what had been an 18th-century hospice, the Casa de la Caritat. The courtyard, with a vast glass wall on one side, is spectacular. With 4500 sq metres of exhibition space in four separate areas, the centre hosts a constantly changing program of exhibitions, film cycles and other events.

ESGLÉSIA DE SANT PAU DEL CAMP
Map p74

☎ 93 441 00 01; Carrer de Sant Pau 101; admission free; Ⓨ cloister 10am-1pm & 4-7pm Mon-Sat; Ⓜ Paral.lel

Back in the 9th century, when monks founded the monastery of Sant Pau del Camp (St Paul in the Fields), it was a good walk from the city gates amid fields and gardens. Today, the church and cloister, erected in the 12th century and partly surrounded by the trees of a small garden, are located on a fairly down-at-heel street and surrounded by dense inner-city housing. The doorway to the church bears rare Visigothic sculptural decoration, predating the Muslim invasion of Spain. Inside, the beautiful Romanesque cloister is the main reason for dropping by.

MODERNISTA WINING & DINING IN EL RAVAL
Walking Tour
1 Casa Almirall
Long run by the Almirall family that opened it in the mid-19th century, this corner tavern (p201) on Carrer de Joaquín Costa preserves much of its Modernista decor, especially in the picture windows opening on to the street and the counter and display cabinet.

2 Bar Muy Buenas
You'll recognise similarly sinuous curves as you enter Bar Muy Buenas (p200), on Carrer del Carme. Opened as a milk bar in the late 19th century, it retains much of its original decoration. It's a welcoming, cosy spot for a tipple and snacks.

3 La Confitería
On Carrer de Sant Pau, past the Romanesque church, drop by La Confitería (p201), once a barber shop and then a long-time confectioner's. It was lovingly restored for its reconversion into a bar in 1998. Most of the elements, including facade, bar counter and cabinets, are the real deal.

4 Hotel España
This recently renovated hotel (p233) is known above all for its dining rooms, part of the 1903 design by Domènech i Montaner. The Sala Arnau (Arnau Room) features a magnificent alabaster fireplace designed by Eusebi Arnau. Moderately priced traditional Catalan fare is served.

5 Palau Güell
While wandering around El Raval, you should not miss its Modernista star, one of Gaudí's earlier big commissions, Palau Güell (p76), a remarkable building. If passing by at night while doing a round of the bars, make a note to return here by day!

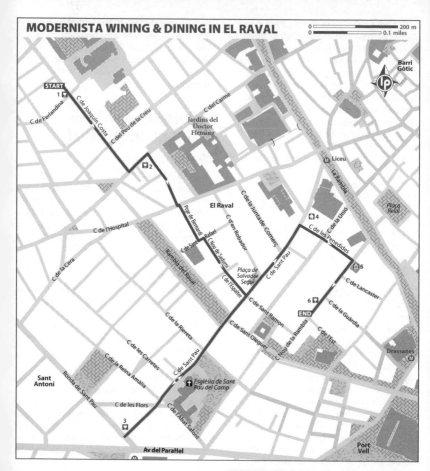

MODERNISTA WINING & DINING IN EL RAVAL

START
1

C de Ferlandina
C de Joaquín Costa
C del Peu de la Creu
C del Carme

Jardins del Doctor Fleming

2

El Raval

C de l'Hospital
C de la Cera
Rambla del Raval
Ptge de Bernardí
C de Sant Rafael
C de Sedinn
C en Robador
C de la Junta de Comerç
Nou de la Rambla

Liceu

La Rambla

Plaça Reial

Barri Gòtic

4
C de la Unió
C de les Penedides
C de Sant Pau
Plaça de Salvador Seguí
C de l'Espalter
C de Sant Ramon
5
C de Lancaster
6
END
C de la Guàrdia
C de Sant Oleguer
C Nou de la Rambla
C de l'Est

C de la Riereta
C de les Carretes
C de Sant Pau

Drassanes
M

Sant Antoni
Ronda de Sant Pau
C de la Reina Amàlia
C de Sant Pau
Església de Sant Pau del Camp

C de les Flors
C de l'Abat Safont

3

Av del ParaHel

Port Vell

6 London Bar

A classic of Barcelona nightlife for over a century, the London Bar (p201) displays Modernista decor and is run by the family of the waiter who founded it in 1910. In its heyday, it stayed open 24 hours and attracted the likes of Picasso and Miró for countless swift beers.

WALK FACTS

Start Casa Almirall
Finish London Bar
Distance 2km
Duration 45 minutes
Transport Ⓜ Liceu

LA RIBERA

Drinking & Nightlife p202; Eating p176; Shopping p156; Sleeping p234

In Roman times, a scattering of *villae* (country houses) and small farms covered the fields here beyond Barcino's walls. In the 6th century, the area was dominated by a Christian necropolis. The first monastery was raised in the 11th century.

By the beginning of the 13th century, two busy communities had developed: Vilanova de Sant Pere, clustered around the convent of Sant Pere de les Puelles; and Vilanova de la Mar, huddled around the Romanesque predecessor to the present Església de Santa Maria del Mar. Between the two, a busy tradesmen's district thrived around Carrer dels Corders (Ropemakers' St). Many streets retain the names of the trades once practised along them.

Vilanova de la Mar, from where merchants carried out their vital trade across the Mediterranean, became the richest part of the city. It was later known as La Ribera, a name that most now use to refer to the whole area (although the city council gives it the rather long-winded appellation of Sant Pere, Santa Caterina i la Ribera).

Carrer de Montcada was laid to link the tradesmen's workshops with the then-waterfront merchants and soon became *the* address. Its rich legacy of Gothic and baroque mansions attests to its primacy until well into the 18th century, when the creation of the Ciutadella swept away a whole chunk of La Ribera and trade focus shifted to Port Vell.

top picks

LA RIBERA

- Església de Santa Maria del Mar (p80)
- Museu Picasso (p80)
- Palau de la Música Catalana (p84)
- Museu Barbier-Mueller d'Art Pre-Colombí (p81)
- Parc de la Ciutadella (p85)

Passeig del Born was Barcelona's main square from the 13th to the 18th centuries. Jousting tournaments, executions and other public entertainments took place here in the Middle Ages (a remnant of Gothic facade remains at No 16) and it was the hub of the city's vital maritime trade. *Barcelonins* used to say *'roda el món i torna al Born'* (go around the world and return to the Born), and the merchants and ship owners who lived and dealt around here no doubt saw it as the navel of their world. Not far away, one of Europe's first stock exchanges came to life at Casa Llotja de Mar (p87).

Via Laietana, a rumbling, traffic-choked thoroughfare that connects the waterfront with the east side of L'Eixample, marks the southwest side of La Ribera, while the Parc de la Ciutadella (p85) closes off its northeastern flank. The creation of Via Laietana in 1908 saw the destruction of 2000 houses and the displacement of 10,000 people. A great swathe of Barcelona's medieval history thus disappeared in what many considered little more than a speculative manoeuvre.

To the south, parallel ribbons of main road and highway cut it off from the sea and La Barceloneta, and the grid streets of L'Eixample round it off to the north.

Carrer de la Princesa, ramrod straight between Via Laietana and the park, was laid in the 1820s and cuts La Ribera in half. The gentrified southern half is generally known as El Born, after busy, bar-lined Passeig del Born. Capped at one end by the magnificent Gothic Església de Santa Maria del Mar, it runs into the former Mercat del Born.

Several important streets feed south into El Born. From the Jaume I Metro stop, restaurant-lined Carrer de l'Argenteria (whose name dates to the 16th century, when it was lined with silversmiths) leads to the Església de Santa Maria del Mar. Carrer de Montcada, with its majestic houses (now mostly occupied by the Museu Picasso, other museums and art galleries), reaches El Born from Carrer de la Princesa.

Although there were only a few dowdy bars and eateries in the early 1990s, El Born is now jammed with colourful restaurants, packed bars and endless fashion outlets, with the likes of Custo Barcelona (p157) leading the way. It is a heterodox, cosmopolitan jumble in a magnificent Middle Ages setting.

Northwest of Carrer de la Princesa, the area's physiognomy changes. A mess of untidy streets wiggles northwards around the striking modern reincarnation of the Mercat de Santa Caterina and on towards the Modernista Palau de la Música Catalana. North African and South American immigrant communities call this part of La Ribera home.

The expanse of the Parc de la Ciutadella is a rare gift in a city so densely packed and lacking in serious greenery, but it started life as an ominous 18th-century citadel, of which little more than the name remains.

Metro Línia 4 coasts down the southwest flank of La Ribera, stopping at Urquinaona, Jaume I and Barceloneta. Línia 1 also stops nearby, at Urquinaona and Arc de Triomf (the nearest stop for the Parc de la Ciutadella).

ESGLÉSIA DE SANTA MARIA DEL MAR Map p82

☎ 93 319 05 16; Plaça de Santa Maria; admission free; ☉ 9am-1.30pm & 4.30-8pm; Ⓜ Jaume I

At the southwest end of Passeig del Born stands the apse of Barcelona's finest Catalan Gothic church, Santa Maria del Mar (Our Lady of the Sea). Built in the 14th century, Santa Maria was lacking in superfluous decoration even before anarchists gutted it in 1909 and 1936.

Built with record-breaking alacrity for the time (it took just 59 years), the church is remarkable for its architectural harmony. The main body is made up of a central nave and two flanking aisles separated by slender octagonal pillars, creating an enormous sense of lateral space. This was built as a people's church. The city's porters (bastaixos) spent a day each week carrying on their backs the stone required to build the church from royal quarries in Montjuïc. Their memory lives on in reliefs of them in the main doors and stone carvings elsewhere in the church.

Keep an eye out for music recitals, often baroque and classical, here. The uneven acoustics are more than made up for by the setting.

Opposite the church's southern flank, an eternal flame burns brightly over an apparently anonymous sunken square. This was once El Fossar de les Moreres (The Mulberry Cemetery), named after the mulberry trees that grew here, and was originally the site of a Roman cemetery. It's also where Catalan resistance fighters were buried after the siege of Barcelona ended in defeat in September 1714.

CARRER DE MONTCADA Map p82

Ⓜ Jaume I

An early example of town planning, this medieval high street was driven down towards the sea from the road that in the 12th century led northeast from the city walls. It would, in time, become the snootiest address in town for the city's merchant class. The bulk of the great mansions that remain today date to the 14th and 15th centuries, although they were often tampered with later. This area was the commercial heartland of medieval Barcelona.

Five of the mansions on the east side of the street have been linked to house the Museu Picasso (see below). Across the road, others house the Museu Barbier-Mueller d'Art Pre-Colombí (see opposite) and the Disseny Hub (see opposite). Several other mansions on this street are commercial art galleries where you're welcome to browse. The biggest is the local branch of the prestigious Parisian Galeria Maeght (No 25; see p157) in the 16th-century Palau dels Cervelló. If you can, peek into the baroque courtyard of the originally medieval Palau de Dalmases (☎ 93 310 06 73; ☉ 8pm-2am Tue-Sat, 6-10pm Sun) at No 20; you can sip wine in the evening while listening to baroque music or operatic snippets.

At the corner of Carrer dels Corders and the northern end of the street, just beyond the 19th-century Carrer de la Princesa, stands a much-meddled-with Romanesque chapel, the Capella d'en Marcús, once a wayfarers' stop on the road northeast out of medieval Barcelona.

MUSEU PICASSO Map p82

☎ 93 256 30 00; www.museupicasso.bcn.es; Carrer de Montcada 15-23; adult/senior & child under 16yr/student €9/free/6, temporary exhibitions adult/student/seniors & children under 16 yr €5.80/2.90/free 3-8pm Sun & all day 1st Sun of month; ☉ 10am-8pm Tue-Sun & holidays; Ⓜ Jaume I

The setting alone, in five contiguous medieval stone mansions, makes the Museu Picasso worth the detour (and the probable queues). The pretty courtyards, galleries and staircases preserved in the first three of these buildings are as delightful as the collection inside is unique. One word of warning: the collection concentrates on the artist's formative years, sometimes disappointing for those hoping for a feast of his better-known later works (best found in Paris).

The permanent collection is housed in Palau Aguilar, Palau del Baró de Castellet and Palau Meca, all dating to the 14th century. The 18th-century Casa Mauri, built over medieval remains (even some Roman leftovers have been identified), and the adjacent 14th-century Palau Finestres accommodate temporary exhibitions.

The collection, which includes more than 3500 artworks, is strongest on Picasso's earliest years, up until 1904, but there is enough material from subsequent periods to give you a deep impression of the man's versatility and genius. Above all, you feel that Picasso is always one step ahead of himself, let alone anyone else, in his search for new forms of expression.

A visit starts with sketches and oils from Picasso's earliest years in Málaga and La Coruña – around 1893–95. Some of his self-portraits and the portraits of his father, which date from 1896, are evidence enough of his precocious talent. *Retrato de la Tía Pepa* (Portrait of Aunt Pepa), done in Málaga in 1897, is a key painting and the enormous *Ciència i Caritat* (Science and Charity) is proof to doubters that Picasso fully mastered the academic techniques of portraiture. In rooms 5–7 hang paintings from his first Paris sojourn, while room 8 is dedicated to the first significant new stage in his development, the Blue Period. His nocturnal blue-tinted views of *Terrats de Barcelona* (Rooftops of Barcelona) and *El Foll* (The Madman) are cold and cheerless, yet somehow alive.

A few cubist paintings pop up in rooms 10 and 11. From 1954 to 1962 Picasso was obsessed by the idea of researching and 'rediscovering' the greats, in particular Velázquez. In 1957, he made a series of renditions of the latter's masterpiece, *Las Meninas*, now displayed in rooms 12-15. It is as though Picasso has looked at the original Velázquez painting through a prism reflecting all the styles he had worked through until then. The last rooms contain engravings and some 40 ceramic pieces completed throughout the latter years of his unceasingly creative life. Things like a plate with a fish on it are typical, if not overly practical at the average dining table!

MUSEU BARBIER-MUELLER D'ART PRE-COLOMBÍ Map p82

☎ 93 310 45 16; www.barbier-mueller.ch; Carrer de Montcada 14; adult/child under 16yr/senior & student €3/free/1.50, 1st Sun of month free; ◷ 11am-7pm Tue-Fri, 10am-7pm Sat, 10am-3pm Sun & holidays; Ⓜ Jaume I

Inside the medieval Palau Nadal you plunge into a world of centuries-old South American art and crafts. The artefacts on show are part of the treasure-trove of pre-Columbian art collected by Swiss businessman Josef Mueller (who died in 1977) and his son-in-law Jean-Paul Barbier, who directs the Musée Barbier-Mueller in the heart of old Geneva in Switzerland. Together, the museums form one of the most prestigious collections of such art in the world.

In blacked-out rooms, the eerily illuminated artefacts flare up in the gloom. South American gold jewellery introduces the collection, followed by rooms containing ceramics, jewellery, statues, textiles and other objects. Every year or two, the composition of the exhibition is altered, with pieces moved around between Barcelona and Geneva and items displayed on loan from other collections.

DISSENY HUB Map p82

☎ 93 256 23 00: www.dhub-bcn.cat; Carrer de Montcada 12; admission adult/child under 16yr/senior & student €5/free/3, free 3-8pm Sun; ◷ 11am-7pm Tue-Sat, 11am-8pm Sun, 11am-3pm holidays; Ⓜ Jaume I

The 13th-century Palau dels Marquesos de Lió (which underwent repeated alterations into the 18th century) is now temporary home to part of the city's Disseny (Design) Hub collection of applied arts, which will eventually come together in the centre being built at Plaça de les Glòries Catalanes (due to open in 2011). This building is used for temporary exhibitions, while the permanent collections are housed in the Palau Reial de Pedralbes (p124). Often the exhibition on the ground floor is free, while the more extensive 1st-floor exhibition is what you pay for (admission includes entry to both locations). The building's courtyard, with its cafe-restaurant, makes a delightful stop.

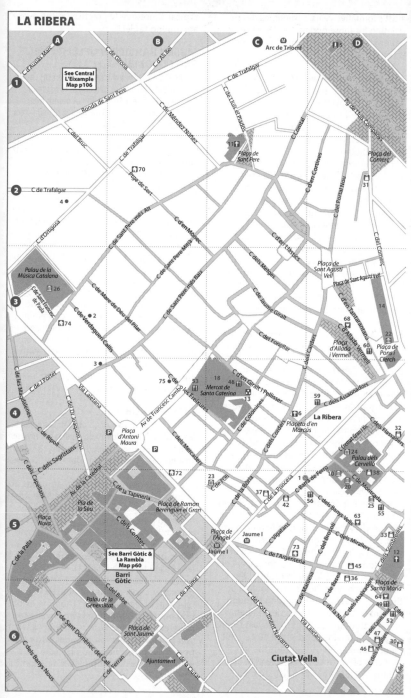

LA RIBERA

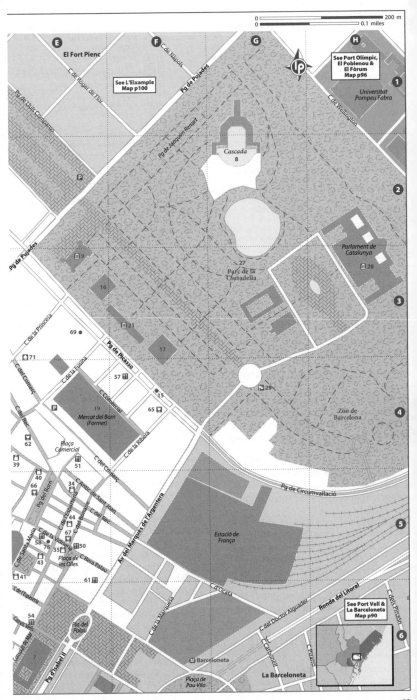

See L'Eixample Map p100

See Port Olímpic, El Poblenou & El Fòrum Map p96

See Port Vell & La Barceloneta Map p90

E El Fort Pienc

F C de Nàpols

G

H

Universitat Pompeu Fabra

C de Wellington

Pg de Pujades

Pg de Joaquim Renart

Cascada
8

Parlament de Catalunya

28

27
Parc de la Ciutadella

Pg de Lluís Companys

Pg de Roger de Flor

P

Pg de Pujades

9

16

21

69

71

C de la Princesa

C del Comerç

C de la Fusina

Pg de Picasso

57

15

65

C Comercial

19
Mercat del Born (Former)

P

C de la Ribera

17

Zoo de Barcelona

29

Pg de Circumval·lació

62

Plaça Comercial

C del Comerç

39

40

66

51

34
Antic de Sant Joan

C del Rec

44

67

C del Bonaire

Pg del Born

C d'En Giralt el Pellisser

Av del Marquès de l'Argentera

Estació de França

58

76

50

35

67

C de la Vidrieria

C de Santa Maria

43

Plaça de les Olles

C Rera Palau

41

61

C de l'Esparteria

C d'Ocata

C de la Marquesa

C del Doctor Aiguader

Ronda del Litoral

C de Pinzón

54

Canvis Vells

7

Pla del Palau

Pg d'Isabel II

M Barceloneta

C Carbonell

C Pizarro

La Barceloneta

Plaça de Pau Vila

83

PALAU DE LA MÚSICA CATALANA

Map p82

☎ 902 475485; www.palaumusica.org; Carrer de Sant Francesc de Paula 2; adult/child/student & EU senior €12/free/10; ⏲ 50min tours every hour 10am-6pm Easter week & Aug, 10am-3.30pm Sep-Jul; Ⓜ Urquinaona

This concert hall is a high point of Barcelona's Modernista architecture. It's not exactly a symphony, but more a series of crescendos in tile, brick, sculpted stone and stained glass.

Built by Domènech i Montaner between 1905 and 1908 for the Orfeó Català musical society, with the help of some of the best Catalan artisans of the time, it was conceived as a temple for the Catalan Renaixença (Renaissance). The palace was built in the cloister of the former Convent de Sant Francesc, and since 1990 it has undergone several major changes.

The *palau*, like a peacock, shows off much of its splendour on the outside. Take in the principal facade with its mosaics, floral capitals and the sculpture cluster representing Catalan popular music. Wander inside the foyer and restaurant areas to admire the spangled, tiled pillars. Best of all, however, is the richly colourful auditorium upstairs, with its ceiling of blue-and-gold stained glass and shimmering skylight that looks like a giant, crystalline, downward-thrusting nipple. Above a bust of Beethoven on the stage towers a wind-blown sculpture of Wagner's Valkyries (Wagner was top of the Barcelona charts at the time it was created). This can only be savoured on a guided tour or by attending a performance – either is highly recommended.

The original Modernista creation, now a World Heritage Site, did not meet with universal approval in its day. The doyen of Catalan literature, Josep Pla, did not hesitate to condemn it as 'horrible', but few share his sentiments today. Montaner himself was also in a huff. He failed to attend the opening ceremony in response to unsettled bills. In 2009, the Palau was at the centre of a fraud scandal, as its president, who subsequently resigned, admitted to having syphoned off millions of euros of its funds.

Tour tickets can be bought as much as a week in advance by phone or online. Space is limited to a maximum of 55 people.

MERCAT DE SANTA CATERINA
Map p82

☎ 93 319 17 40; www.mercatsantacaterina. net, in Catalan; Avinguda de Francesc Cambó 16; ⊙ 7.30am-2pm Mon, 7.30am-3.30pm Tue, Wed & Sat, 7.30am-8.30pm Thu & Fri; Ⓜ Jaume I

Come shopping for your tomatoes at this extraordinary-looking produce market, built by Enric Miralles and Benedetta Tagliabue to replace its 19th-century predecessor. Finished in 2005, it is distinguished by its kaleidoscopically weird wavy roof, held up above the bustling produce stands, restaurants, cafes and bars by twisting slender branches of what look like grey steel trees.

The multicoloured ceramic roof (with a ceiling made of warm, light timber) recalls the Modernista tradition of *trencadís* decoration (a type of mosaic, such as that in Park Güell). Indeed, its curvy design, like a series of Mediterranean rollers, seems to plunge back into an era when Barcelona's architects were limited only by their (vivid) imagination. The market roof bares an uncanny resemblance to that of the Escoles de Gaudí at La Sagrada Família.

The market's 1848 predecessor had been built over the remains of the demolished 15th-century Gothic Monestir de Santa Caterina, a powerful Dominican monastery. A small section of the church foundations is glassed over in one corner as an archaeological reminder (with explanatory panels), the Espai Santa Caterina (admission free; ⊙ 8.30am-2pm Mon-Wed & Sat, 8.30am-8pm Thu & Fri).

PARC DE LA CIUTADELLA Map p82
Passeig de Picasso; ⊙ 8am-6pm Nov-Feb, 8am-8pm Oct & Mar, 8am-9pm Apr-Sep; Ⓜ Arc de Triomf

Come for a stroll, a picnic, a visit to the zoo or to inspect Catalonia's regional parliament, but don't miss a visit to this, the most central green lung in the city. Parc de la Ciutadella is perfect for winding down.

After the War of the Spanish Succession (p25), Felipe V razed a swathe of La Ribera to build a huge fortress (La Ciutadella), designed to keep watch over Barcelona. It became a loathed symbol of everything Catalans hated about Madrid and the Bourbon kings, and was later used as a political prison. Only in 1869 did the central government allow its demolition, after which the site was turned into a park and used for the Universal Exhibition of 1888.

The monumental cascada (waterfall) near the Passeig de Pujades park entrance, created between 1875 and 1881 by Josep Fontserè with the help of an enthusiastic young Gaudí, is a dramatic combination of statuary, rugged rocks, greenery and thundering water. All of it perfectly artificial! Nearby, hire a rowing boat to paddle about the small lake.

To the southeast, in what might be seen as an exercise in black humour, the fort's former arsenal now houses the Parlament de Catalunya (☎ 93 304 66 45; www.parlament.cat; admission free; ⊙ 10am-7pm Sat, 10am-2pm Sun & holidays). A symbol of Catalan identity, the regional parliament also opens to the public on 11 and 12 September. You may follow a circuit alone or join an hourly guided tour (usually in Catalan). Head up the sweeping Escala d'Honor (Stairway of Honour) and through several solemn halls to the Saló de Sessions, the semicircular auditorium where parliament sits. At the centre of the garden in front of the Parlament is a statue of a seemingly heartbroken woman, *Desconsol* (Distress; 1907), by Josep Llimona.

The Passeig de Picasso side of the park is lined by several buildings constructed for, or just before, the Universal Exhibition. The medieval-looking caprice at the top

top picks

FOR KIDS

- Beaches (p94)
- L'Aquàrium (p89)
- Museu de la Xocolata (p86)
- La Sagrada Família (p102)
- Museu Marítim (p73)
- Tibidabo & Parc d'Atraccions (p133)
- Park Güell (p115)
- Transbordador Aeri (p92)

end is the most engaging. Known as the Castell dels Tres Dragons (Castle of the Three Dragons), it long housed the Museu de Zoologia (p95), which is now closed. Montaner put the 'castle's' trimmings on a pioneering steel frame. The coats of arms are all invented and the whole building exudes a teasing, playful air. It was used as a cafe-restaurant during the Universal Exhibition of 1888.

To the south is L'Hivernacle, an arboretum or miniature botanical garden. Next come the former Museu de Geologia (p95) and L'Umbracle, another arboretum. On Passeig de Picasso itself is Antoni Tàpies' typically impenetrable Homenatge a Picasso. Water runs down the panes of a glass box full of bits of old furniture and steel girders.

Northwest of the park, Passeig de Lluís Companys is capped by the Modernista Arc de Triomf, designed by Josep Vilaseca as the principal exhibition entrance, with unusual, Islamic-style brickwork. Josep Llimona did the main reliefs. Just what the triumph was eludes us, especially since the exhibition itself was a commercial failure. It is perhaps best thought of as a bricks-and-mortar embodiment of the city's general *fin de siècle* feel-good factor.

ZOO DE BARCELONA Map p82

☎ 902 457545; www.zoobarcelona.com; Passeig de Picasso & Carrer de Wellington; adult/child under 3yr/senior/child 3-12yr €16/free/8.40/9.60; ☼ 10am-7pm Jun-Sep, 10am-6pm mid-Mar–May & Oct, 10am-5pm Nov–mid-Mar; Ⓜ Barceloneta
The zoo can make a fun distraction for kids, although the comparatively limited space makes it a bit of a squeeze for the 7500 critters (everything from geckos to gorillas) of more than 400 species. A new site being built on the coast of El Fòrum northeast of the city centre will eventually ease the crowding.

MUSEU DE LA XOCOLATA Map p82

☎ 93 268 78 78; http://pastisseria.com; Plaça de Pons i Clerch; adult/child under 7yr/senior & student €4.30/free/3.65; ☼ 10am-7pm Mon-Sat, 10am-3pm Sun & holidays; Ⓜ Jaume I
Chocoholics have a hard time containing themselves in this museum dedicated to the fundamental foodstuff. How not to launch yourself at the extraordinary scale models made out of chocolate? A little salivation for sweet tooths is inevitable

as you trawl around the displays (in part of the former Convent de Sant Agustí), which trace the origins of chocolate, its arrival in Europe and the many myths and images associated with it. Among the informative stuff (with panels in various languages) and machinery used in the production of chocolate are choc models of buildings such as La Sagrada Família, along with various characters, local and international. That part of the display changes every year or so. It's all enough to have you making for the nearest sweet shop, but you don't have to – plenty of chocolate is sold right here! Kids and grown-ups can join guided tours or take part in chocolate-making and tasting sessions, especially on weekends.

Under the Gothic arches of what remains of the convent's one-time cloister is a pleasant cafe-bar, the Bar del Convent (☼ 10am-9pm Mon-Thu, 11am-11pm Fri, 1pm-midnight Sat). Kids often play football in the cloister grounds. You enter at Carrer del Comerç 36.

ARXIU FOTOGRÀFIC DE BARCELONA
Map p82

☎ 93 256 34 20; www.bcn.cat/arxiu/fotografic; Plaça de Pons i Clerch; admission free; ☼ 10am-7pm Mon-Sat; Ⓜ Jaume I
On the 2nd floor of the former Convent de Sant Agustí is the modest exhibition space of this city photo archive. Photos on show are generally related to the city, as the photo collection is principally devoted to that theme, from the late 19th century until the late 20th century. One of the 2010 exhibitions was devoted to Frederic Ballell's scenes of La Rambla, taken in 1907–08.

MUSEU DEL REI DE LA MAGIA
Map p82

☎ 93 319 73 93; www.elreydelamagia.com, in Catalan & Spanish; Carrer de l'Oli 6; admission with/without show €8/3; ☼ 6-8pm Thu, with show 6pm Sat & noon Sun; Ⓜ Jaume I
This museum is a timeless curio. Run by the same people who have the nearby magic shop (p158) on Carrer de la Princesa, it is the scene of magic shows, home (upstairs) to collections of material that hark back to the 19th-century origins of the shop (everything from old posters and books for learning tricks to magic wands and trick

cards) and the place for budding magicians of all ages to enrol in courses. Seeing is believing.

ESGLÉSIA DE SANT PERE DE LES PUELLES Map p82

Plaça de Sant Pere; admission free; M Arc de Triomf

Not a great deal remains of the original church or convent that stood here since early medieval times. The church's pre-Romanesque Greek-cross floor plan survives, as do some Corinthian columns beneath the 12th-century dome and a much-damaged Renaissance vault leading into a side chapel. It was around this church that settlement began in La Ribera. In 985, a Muslim raiding force under Al-Mansur attacked Barcelona and largely destroyed the convent, killing or capturing the nuns.

MERCAT DEL BORN Map p82

Plaça Comercial; M Barceloneta

Excavation in 2001 at the former Mercat del Born, a late-19th-century produce market built of iron and glass, unearthed great chunks of one of the districts flattened to make way for the much-hated Ciutadella (see p85). Historians found intact streets and the remains of houses, dating as far back as the 15th century. Excitement was such that plans to locate a new city library in the long-disused market were dropped. Instead, the site will become a museum and cultural centre.

CASA LLOTJA DE MAR Map p82

La Llotja; ☎ 902 448448; www.casallotja.com; Carrer del Consolat de Mar; M Jaume I

The centrepiece of the city's medieval stock exchange (more affectionately known as La Llotja) is the fine Gothic Saló de Contractacions (Transaction Hall), built in the 14th century. Pablo Picasso and Joan Miró attended the art school that from 1849 was housed in the Saló dels Cònsols. These and five other halls were encased in a neoclassical shell in the 18th century. The stock exchange was in action until well into the 20th century and the building remains in the hands of the city's chamber of commerce. Occasionally they open their doors to the public but the rooms are more generally hired out for events.

SINS OF GLUTTONY IN LA RIBERA
Walking Tour
1 Mercat de Santa Caterina

A glutton's guide to La Ribera has to begin in this modern version of a 19th-century market (p85). A close rival to La Boqueria, its stands overflow with fish, cold meats, cheeses, countless varieties of olives, an olive oil and vinegar specialist, Olisoliva (p158), bar-eateries and a good restaurant.

2 Museu de la Xocolata

Barcelona is awash in specialist chocolate stores, whether traditional *granjas* (milk bars) for enjoying thick hot chocolate with a pastry or modern dens of chocolate delinquency. Where better to get introduced to the history behind this seductive food than the Museu de la Xocolata (see opposite)?

3 Hofmann Pastisseria

You've been to the museum, now try eating the stuff. Hofmann Pastisseria (p158) offers gourmet chocolate bars and all sorts of sweet goodies in jars, as well as fresh pastries and custom-ordered cakes.

4 Casa Gispert

Welcome to the house of nuts. Since the mid-19th century, Casa Gispert (p158) has been toasting up all sorts of nuts and other goodies. The walls are lined with jars of dried fruit, honeyed hazelnuts and other tasty morsels.

5 La Botifarreria

The most startling array of sausages and all sorts of other gourmet goodies are on offer at La Botifarreria (p158). Aromatic cheeses, cold meats, ready-to-eat snacks and more form the colourful armoury.

6 Bubó

Further opportunities for rotting teeth are presented at Bubó (p177). You could appease your conscience with a couple of savoury items first, but resistance to the sweet pastry treats thereafter is futile.

7 El Magnífico

Coffee represents a significant element in Catalan and Spanish tradition. This magnificent store (p158) offers a range of fine coffees from around the world. The family has a long

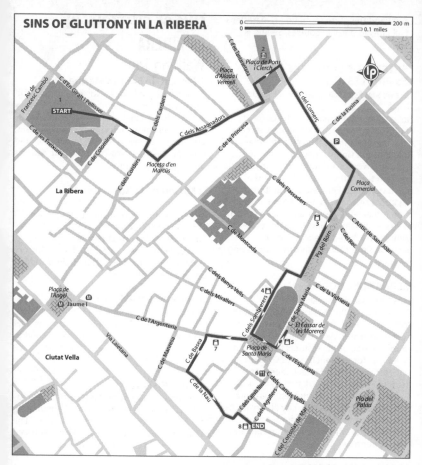

SINS OF GLUTTONY IN LA RIBERA

history in the business, and this is a Barcelona institution.

8 Vila Viniteca
No food experience is complete without wine. To investigate some of the enormous variety of Catalan and Spanish drops, visit Vila Viniteca (p157). There are many foreign wines on hand and it also occasionally hosts tasting events.

PORT VELL & LA BARCELONETA

Drinking & Nightlife p203; Eating p178; Shopping p158; Sleeping p235

Barcelona's old port, once such an eyesore it caused public protests, has been transformed beyond recognition since the 1980s. Abandoned warehouses and general junk are a distant memory, replaced by chic shopping, harbourside munching, movies on the sea, parking for yachts and a huge aquarium.

La Barceloneta is a mid-18th-century fishermen's quarter laid out by military engineer Juan Martín Cermeño to replace housing destroyed to make way for La Ciutadella. The cute houses along narrow streets were later subdivided into four separate 30-sq-metre abodes and subsequently converted into six-storey rabbit warrens. The attentive eye will pick out some of the few remaining original houses.

By the 19th century, La Barceloneta had become an industrial slum, home to the city's gas company, the Nueva Vulcano shipyards, and the La Maquinista ironworks and steam engine plant (which shut down in 1965). One relic left from the industrial era is the Fàbrica del Sol (☎ 93 256 44 30; Passeig de Salvat Papasseit 1), a red brick and yellow-painted building that now houses a city office devoted to environmental sustainability (the solar panel out the back is no coincidence).

What remains of Barcelona's fishing fleet – about 70 vessels and 400 fishermen who land 10 tonnes of fish a day – ties up along the Moll del Rellotge. A complete overhaul of this area is planned for the coming years, as the number of fishermen dwindles.

The area retains a sea-salty authenticity, especially in the numerous seafood eateries scattered about its labyrinthine web of back streets.

Port Vell is at the waterside end of La Rambla. It is not only a haven for yachts: Maremàgnum, a multistorey mall, was built out of what had been nasty old docklands on Moll d'Espanya. It is linked to Moll de la Fusta (Wood Dock) by the Rambla de Mar, a rotating pedestrian bridge. Virtually opposite, the World Trade Center, designed by Henry Cobb, juts out like the prow of a cruise ship into the harbour. To the southwest stretch the ferry docks for boats to the Balearic Islands and Italy, while a second arm of Port Vell, another chic yachties' hang-out, is backed by the tight streets of La Barceloneta.

On La Barceloneta's seaward side, the southernmost beach of Platja de Sant Miquel (popular with a late-arriving, party-exhausted gay set) is capped at its south end by the billowing glass sail of the new hotel W Barcelona (p235), designed by local architect Ricard Bofill.

The strand changes name to Platja de Sant Sebastià and then Platja de la Barceloneta on its way north towards Port Olímpic and is immensely popular in summer. Passeig Marítim de la Barceloneta, a 1.25km promenade from La Barceloneta to Port Olímpic, makes for a pleasant stroll, cycle or rollerblade. Behind it rise some interesting new buildings, including the cylindrical Parc de Recerca Biomèdica de Barcelona (PRBB; Barcelona Biomedical Research Park) and Enric Miralles' Edifici de Gas Natural, a 100m glass tower.

Metro Línia 3 takes you to Port Vell (Drassanes stop), while the yellow Línia 4 is best for La Barceloneta. Several buses also converge on La Barceloneta.

L'AQUÀRIUM Map p90

☎ 93 221 74 74; www.aquariumbcn.com; Moll d'Espanya; adult/child under 4yr/4-12yr/senior over 60yr €17.50/free/12.50/14.50; ☯ 9.30am-11pm Jul & Aug, 9.30am-9.30pm Jun & Sep, 9.30am-9pm Mon-Fri & 9.30am-9.30pm Sat & Sun Oct-May; Ⓜ Drassanes

It is hard to help a slight shudder at the sight of a shark gliding above you, displaying its full munching apparatus. But this, the 80m shark tunnel, is the highlight of one of Europe's largest aquariums. It has the world's best Mediterranean collec-

tion and plenty of gaudy fish from as far off as the Red Sea, the Caribbean and the Great Barrier Reef. All up, some 11,000 fish (including a dozen sharks) of 450 species reside here.

Back in the shark tunnel, which you reach after passing a series of themed fish tanks with everything from bream to sea horses, various species of shark (white tip, sand tiger, bonnethead, black tip, nurse and sandbar) flit around you, along with a host of other critters, from flapping rays to bloated sunfish. An interactive zone,

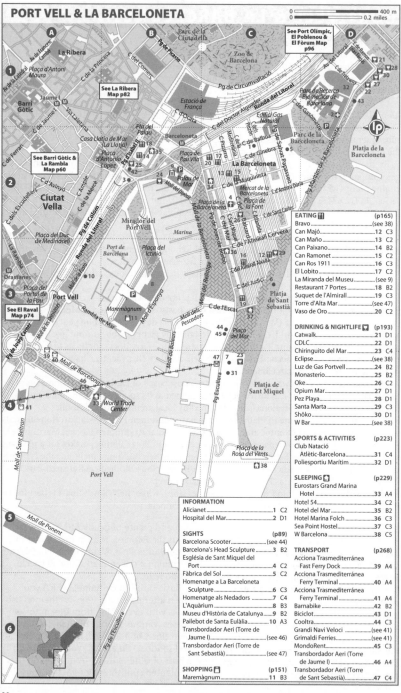

PORT VELL & LA BARCELONETA

See La Ribera Map p82

See Barri Gòtic & La Rambla Map p60

See El Raval Map p74

See Port Olímpic, El Poblenou & El Fòrum Map p96

Planeta Agua, is host to a family of Antarctic penguins and a tank of rays that you watch close up.

Divers with a valid dive certificate may dive (€300; 🕓 9.30am-2pm Wed, Sat & Sun) in the main tank with the sharks.

MUSEU D'HISTÒRIA DE CATALUNYA
Map p90

Museum of Catalonian History; ☎ 93 225 47 00; www.mhcat.net; Plaça de Pau Vila 3; adult/senior & child under 7yr/student permanent exhibition only €4/free/3, permanent & temporary exhibitions €5/free/4, free 1st Sun of month; 🕓 10am-7pm Tue & Thu-Sat, 10am-8pm Wed, 10am-2.30pm Sun & holidays; Ⓜ Barceloneta

The Palau de Mar building facing the harbour once served as warehouses (Els Magatzems Generals de Comerç), but was transformed in the 1990s. Below the seaward arcades is a string of good restaurants. Inside is the Museu d'Història De Catalunya, something of a local patriotic statement, but interesting nonetheless.

The permanent display covers the 2nd and 3rd floors, taking you, as the bumf says, on a 'voyage through history' from the Stone Age through to the early 1980s. It is a busy hodgepodge of dioramas, artefacts, videos, models, documents and interactive bits: all up, an entertaining exploration of 2000 years of Catalan history. See how the Romans lived, listen to Arab poetry from the time of the Muslim occupation of the city, peer into the dwelling of a Dark Ages family in the Pyrenees, try to mount a knight's horse or lift a suit of armour.

When you have had enough of all this, descend into a civil-war air-raid shelter, watch a video in Catalan on post-Franco Catalonia or head upstairs to the rooftop restaurant and cafe.

The temporary exhibitions are frequently as interesting as the permanent display.

PAILEBOT DE SANTA EULÀLIA
Map p90

Moll de la Fusta; adult/child under 7yr/senior & student incl Museu Marítim €2.50/free/1.25; 🕓 noon-7.30pm Tue-Fri, 10am-7pm Sat & Sun & holidays May-Oct, noon-5.30pm Tue-Fri, 10am-5.30pm Sat & Sun & holidays Nov-Apr; Ⓜ Drassanes

Along the palm-lined promenade Moll de la Fusta is moored a 1918 three-mast schooner restored by the Museu Marítim.

top picks

IT'S FREE

Entry to some sights is free on occasion, most commonly on the first Sunday of the month. Quite a few attractions are free from 3pm to 8pm on Sundays. Other are always free. Free days are noted throughout the listings in this chapter. The following are most likely to attract your attention:

- CaixaForum (p139) Always.
- Castell de Montjuïc (p142) Always.
- Catedral (p59) From 8am to 12.45pm and 5.15pm to 8pm Monday to Saturday.
- Centre d'Art Santa Mònica (p57) Always.
- Església de Sant Pau del Camp (p77) Always.
- Església de Santa Maria del Mar (p80) Always.
- Església de Santa Maria del Pi (p66) Always.
- Estadi Olímpic (p144) Always.
- Fundació Joan Brossa (p112) Always.
- Jardí Botànic (p146) Last Sunday of the month.
- Jardins del Laberint d'Horta (p134) Wednesdays and Sundays.
- Museu Barbier-Mueller d'Art Pre-Colombí (p81) First Sunday of the month.
- Museu de Carrosses Fúnebres (p112) Always.
- Museu de la Música (p109) From 3pm to 8pm Sunday.
- Museu d'Història de Barcelona (p63) From 4pm to 8pm first Saturday of the month.
- Museu d'Història de Catalunya (p91) First Sunday of the month.
- Museu d'Història de la Immigració de Catalunya (p149) Always.
- Museu Etnològic (p146) First Sunday of the month.
- Museu Marítim (p73) From 3pm to 8pm Sun
- Museu Nacional d'Art de Catalunya (p138) First Sunday of the month.
- Museu Picasso (p80) First Sunday of the month.
- Palau del Lloctinent (p64) Always.
- Palau Güell (p76) Always (while restoration still incomplete).
- Palau Reial de Pedralbes (p124) First Sunday of the month.
- Park Güell (p115) Always.
- Temple Romà d'August (p68) Always.
- Universitat de Barcelona (p112) Always.

You can see it perfectly well without going aboard, and there's not an awful lot to behold below decks. On occasion it sets sail for demonstration trips up and down the coast.

TRANSBORDADOR AERI
Map p90

**Passeig Escullera; 1-way/return €9/12.50;
⊕ 11am-8pm mid-Jun–mid-Sep, 10.45am-7pm
Mar–mid-Jun & mid-Sep–late Oct, 10.30am-
5.45pm late Oct-Feb; Ⓜ Barceloneta, 🚌 17, 39
or 64**

This cable car strung across the harbour
to Montjuïc provides a bubble-eye view of
the city. The cabins float between Miramar
(Montjuïc) and the Torre de Sant Sebastià
(in La Barceloneta), with a midway stop at
the Torre de Jaume I in front of the World
Trade Center. At the top of the Torre de
Sant Sebastià is a spectacularly located
restaurant, Torre d'Alta Mar (p178).

ESGLÉSIA DE SANT MIQUEL
DEL PORT Map p90

☎ 93 221 65 50; Plaça de la Barceloneta; admission
free; ⊕ 7am-1.30pm Mon-Fri, 8am-1.30pm Sat;
Ⓜ Barceloneta

Finished in 1755, this sober baroque
church was the first building completed
in La Barceloneta. Built low so that the
cannon in the then Ciutadella fort could
fire over it if necessary, it bears images of
St Michael (Miquel) and two other saints
considered protectors of the Catalan
fishing fleet: Sant Elm and Santa Maria de
Cervelló.

Just behind the church is the bustling
marketplace, worth an early morning
browse. Ferdinand Lesseps, the French
engineer who designed the Suez Canal, did
a stint as France's consul-general in Barcelona and lived in the house to the right of
the church.

AROUND THE PORT &
ALONG THE BEACH
Walking Tour
1 Maremàgnum
Reached on foot by the Rambla de Mar foot-
bridge, Maremàgnum (www.maremagnum.es), which
encloses the marina, is a bubbling leisure centre, with chirpy waterside restaurants, bars,
shops and cinemas. In September it hosts a
four-day tastefest of Catalan wines and *cava*
(Catalan sparkling wine; see p19).

2 L'Aquàrium
One of Europe's largest aquariums, L'Aquàrium
(p89) offers a host of sea critters. The most

spectacular is a varied collection of sharks,
seen through a glass tunnel.

3 Museu d'Història de Catalunya
Housed in former warehouses, this museum
(p91) provides a potted history of Catalonia.
It also boasts a top-floor restaurant-bar with
terrace, while downstairs a series of seafood
eateries faces the marina. For a tapas experience, seek the nearby Vaso de Oro (p179).

4 Edifici Gas Natural
Local architect Enric Miralles showed daring
with his somewhat kooky, 100m-high tower,
housing the city offices of a major Spanish gas
company. The Edifici Gas Natural commands
attention with its jutting glass protrusions.

WALK FACTS

Start Maremàgnum
Finish Moll del Rellotge
Distance 4.2km
Duration 1¼ hours
Transport Ⓜ Drassanes

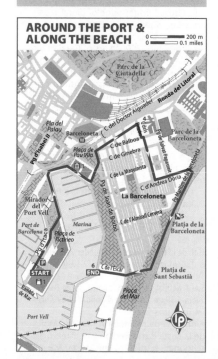

**AROUND THE PORT &
ALONG THE BEACH**

0 ———— 200 m
0 ———— 0.1 miles

5 Platja de la Barceloneta

Barcelona's inner-city beach is packed with people and activity. A series of bars on the sand churn out meals, cocktails and music for the hordes of sun worshippers. Up in the northeast corner, a string of hip bar-restaurants get especially busy on languid summer nights.

6 Moll del Rellotge

A stroll just west from the beach leads to Moll del Rellotge, where you may catch sight of the remaining men and vessels of the city's once-proud fishing fleet. Snooping around here confirms how much modern Port Vell has changed.

PORT OLÍMPIC, EL POBLENOU & EL FÒRUM

Drinking & Nightlife p204; Eating p180; Sleeping p235

On the approach to Port Olímpic from La Barceloneta, the giant copper *Peix* (Fish) sculpture by Frank Gehry glitters brazenly in the sunlight. Port Olímpic was built for the 1992 Olympic sailing events and has now become a classy marina surrounded by bars and restaurants. Behind it rise two lone skyscrapers – the luxury Hotel Arts Barcelona and the Torre Mapfre office block.

From the marina, a string of popular beaches stretches along the coast northeast to the El Fòrum district, which marks the city's northern boundary. Strollers, cyclists and skaters parade on the broad beachside boulevard (dotted with seafood eateries) and admire the ranks of scantily clad flesh on warm summer days. The beaches are dotted with *chiringuitos*, snack bars that stay open until the wee hours for cocktails and dance tunes.

Inland, the southwest end of El Poblenou, a one-time industrial workers' district dubbed Barcelona's Manchester in the 19th century, was converted into the Vila Olímpica, apartments that housed competing athletes and were then sold off after the Olympics. That was just the beginning…

Now, long after the excitement of the games, the rest of El Poblenou is gradually being transformed in an ambitious urban regeneration scheme. At its heart is the hi-tech zone, 22@ bcn, which has been slowly filling with new buildings since 2000. Its symbol is Barcelona's most spectacular modern architectural icon, Jean Nouvel's Torre Agbar, finished in 2005. Tower blocks of hotels, offices and apartments continue to go up. At last count, around 1500 businesses had opened or relocated to 22@bcn since the idea was launched. Research and development centres in a wide range of areas, including media, biotechnology and telecommunications, are setting up shop here.

The El Fòrum and Diagonal Mar projects in the city's northeast corner created something out of nothing: a somewhat soulless high-rise residential area with grand congress buildings, multistar hotels, a giant solar panel, sea-water baths, a new marina, a future zoo and lots of space for summer concerts and fun fairs.

Metro Línia 4 traverses the area, with key stops in Ciutadella Vila Olímpic for the first of the beaches and Maresme Fòrum for the Fòrum area. An alternative that passes the Torre Agbar is the T4 tram, which starts at Ciutadella Vila Olímpic, stops at Fòrum and terminates on the north side of the Riu Besòs in Sant Adrià de Besòs.

BEACHES Map p96

Ⓜ Ciutadella Vila Olímpic, Bogatell, Llacuna or Selva de Mar, 🚊 36 or 41

A series of pleasant beaches stretches northeast from the Port Olímpic marina. They are largely artificial, but this doesn't stop an estimated 7 million bathers from piling in every year!

The southernmost beach, Platja de la Nova Icària, is the busiest. Behind it, across the Avinguda del Litoral highway, is the Plaça dels Campions, site of the rusting three-tiered platform used to honour medallists in the sailing events of the 1992 games. Much of the athletes' housing-turned-apartments are in the blocks immediately behind Carrer de Salvador Espriu.

The next beach is Platja de Bogatell. There's a good skateboard area with half-pipes at

the beach's northern end. Just in from the beach is the Cementiri de l'Est (Eastern Cemetery; ☎ 902 079799; Carrer del Taulat 2; 🕒 8am-6pm), created in 1773. It was positioned outside the then city limits for health reasons. Its central monument commemorates the victims of a yellow-fever epidemic that swept across Barcelona in 1821. The cemetery is full of bombastic family memorials, but an altogether disquieting touch is the sculpture *El Petó de la Mort* (The Kiss of Death), in which a winged skeleton kisses a young, kneeling but lifeless body. There's a good skateboard area with half-pipes at the north end of the beach.

Platja de la Mar Bella (with its brief nudist strip and sailing school) and Platja de la Nova Mar Bella follow, leading into the new residential and commercial waterfront strip, the Front Marítim, part of the Diagonal Mar project in the Fòrum district. It is fronted by the last of these artificial beaches to be created, Platja del Llevant.

TORRE AGBAR Map p96

☎ 93 342 21 29; www.torreagbar.com; Avinguda Diagonal 225; Ⓜ Glòries

Barcelona's very own cucumber-shaped tower, Jean Nouvel's luminous Torre Agbar (which houses the city water company's headquarters), is the most daring addition to Barcelona's skyline since the first towers of La Sagrada Família went up. Completed in 2005, it shimmers at night in shades of midnight blue and lipstick red. Unfortunately, you can only enter the foyer on the ground floor, frequently used to host temporary exhibitions on water-related topics.

Nouvel was also behind the Parc del Centre del Poblenou (Avinguda Diagonal; ☽ 10am-sunset), about halfway between the tower and El Fòrum. It is an odd park, with stylised metal seats and items of statuary. Barcelona is sprinkled with parks whose principal element is cement. The self-proclaimed Gaudíesque cement walls are increasingly covered by sprawling bougainvillea. Inside, some 1000 trees of mostly Mediterranean species are complemented by thousands of smaller bushes and plants. Nouvel's idea is that, with time, the trees will form a natural canopy over the park, watered using local ground water.

EL FÒRUM Map p96

☎ 93 356 10 50; Ⓜ El Maresme Fòrum

Where before there was wasteland, half-abandoned factories and a huge sewage-treatment plant in the city's northeast corner, there are now high-rise apartment blocks, luxury hotels, a marina (Port Fòrum), a shopping mall and a conference centre.

The most striking element is the eerily blue, triangular *2001: A Space Odyssey*–style Edifici Fòrum building by Swiss architects Herzog & de Meuron. The navy blue raised facades look like sheer cliff faces, with angular crags cut into them as if by divine laser. Grand strips of mirror create fragmented reflections of the sky. Now empty, it is being transformed into the Espai Blau (Blue Space), a modern showcase for the Museu de Ciències Naturals (www.bcn.es/museueuciencies), a combination of the old Museu de Zoologia and Museu de Geologia that used to occupy buildings in the Parc de la Ciutadella (p85) and will be installed here in 2011.

Next door, Josep Lluís Mateo's Centre de Convencions Internacional de Barcelona (CCIB) has capacity for 15,000 delegates. The huge space around the two buildings is used for major outdoor events, such as concerts (eg during the Festes de la Mercè) and the Feria de Abril (p17).

A 300m stroll east from the Edifici Fòrum is the Zona de Banys (☽ 11am-8pm in summer), with kayaks and bikes available for rent, the option to learn diving, and other activities. This tranquil seawater swimming area was won from the sea by the creation of massive cement-block dykes. At its northern end, like a great rectangular sunflower, an enormous photovoltaic panel turns its face up to the sun to power the area with solar energy. Along with another set of solar panels in the form of porticoes, it generates enough electricity for 1000 households. Just behind it spreads Port Fòrum, Barcelona's third marina. The area is unified by an undulating esplanade and walkways that are perfect for walking, wheelchair access, bikes and skateboards.

In summer, a weekend amusement park (☽ 11am-2.30pm & 5-9pm Sat & Sun Jun-Sep) sets up with all the usual suspects: rides, shooting galleries, snack stands, inflatable castles and dodgem cars.

The Parc de Diagonal Mar, designed by Enric Miralles, contains pools, fountains, a didactic botanical walk (with more than 30 species of trees and other plants) and modern sculptures.

BURYING THE PAST

Buried beneath the concrete congress centre, bathing zone and marina created in El Fòrum lies the memory of more than 2000 people executed in the fields of Camp de la Bota between 1936 and 1952, most of them under Franco from 1939 onward. To their memory, *Fraternitat* (Brotherhood), a sculpture by Miquel Navarro, stands on Rambla de Prim.

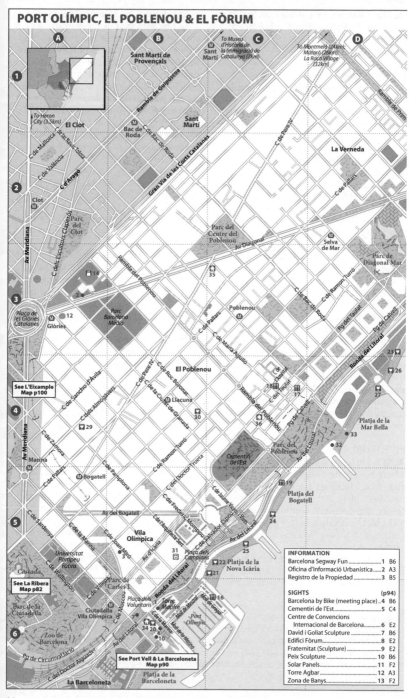

INFORMATION

Barcelona Segway Fun	**1** B6
Oficina d'Informació Urbanística	**2** A3
Registro de la Propiedad	**3** B5

SIGHTS	**(p94)**
Barcelona by Bike (meeting place)	**4** B6
Cementiri de l'Est	**5** C4
Centre de Convencions Internacional de Barcelona	**6** E2
David i Goliat Sculpture	**7** B6
Edifici Fòrum	**8** E2
Fraternitat (Sculpture)	**9** E2
Peix Sculpture	**10** B6
Solar Panels	**11** F2
Torre Agbar	**12** A3
Zona de Banys	**13** F2

THE NEW BARCELONA
Walking Tour
1 Edifici Fòrum

The giant blue triangle that is the Edifici Fòrum (p95) is an impossible-to-miss creation at the heart of the El Fòrum development. Like a UFO, it seems to hover just above the ground.

2 Zona de Banys

This protected bathing area is a popular summer attraction for families. Just behind it looms a giant solar panel, which powers the area. Stretching out further inland from the bathing area, kids playing on swings and other amusements share the space with rollerbladers and strollers.

3 Parc de Diagonal Mar

This park (p95) was created out of nothing as part of the redevelopment of the northeast corner of the city. Surrounded by expensive, high-rise apartment blocks, it is a thoroughly modern park, with an educational botanical walk, modern sculptures, fountains and pools.

4 Beaches

Lining the coast from El Fòrum southwest towards Port Olímpic are the city's beaches (p94). In summer, snack bars–cum–cocktail bars open along these strands for those moments when swimming and sunbathing aren't enough. The water and sand tend to be cleaner than at Platja de la Barceloneta.

5 Cementiri de l'Est

A world away from the hedonism and flesh of Platja de Bogatell, this centuries-old cemetery (p94) makes for a peaceful stroll. Orderly lanes are lined by monumental family mausoleums, and statues of mythical figures, angels and, occasionally, the sorely missed deceased.

WALK FACTS

Start Edifici Fòrum
Finish Port Olímpic
Distance 4.2km
Duration 1¼ hours
Transport 🚇 Maresme Fòrum

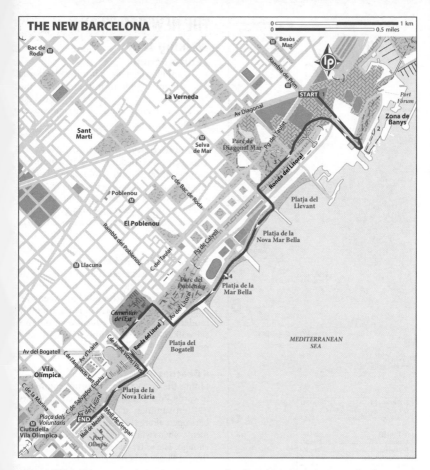

THE NEW BARCELONA

Bac de Roda

Besòs Mar

La Verneda

START 1

Port Fòrum

Zona de Banys

Sant Martí

Av Diagonal

Selva de Mar

Parc de Diagonal Mar

Pg del Taulat

Ronda del Litoral

2

Poblenou

C de Bac de Roda

3

Platja del Llevant

El Poblenou

Rambla del Poblenou

C del Taulat

Pg de Calvell

Platja de la Nova Mar Bella

Llacuna

Parc del Poblenou

4

Platja de la Mar Bella

Av del Litoral

MEDITERRANEAN SEA

Cementiri de l'Est

5

Ronda del Litoral

Platja del Bogatell

C de Jaume Vicens Vives

Av del Bogatell

C de l'Aquilecte Sert

Av d'Icària

Vila Olímpica

C de la Marina

C de Salvador Espriu

Platja de la Nova Icària

Plaça dels Voluntaris

Av del Litoral

Moll de Mestral

Moll de Gregal

END

Ciutadella Vila Olímpica

6

Port Olímpic

6 Port Olímpic

The marina of Port Olímpic is lined on both sides by back-to-back restaurants and bars. In summer it is especially popular with both locals and tourists – it swarms by day as part of Barcelona's busy beachside promenade, and heaves at night as the tacky bars swing into action.

L'EIXAMPLE

Drinking & Nightlife p205; Eating p180; Shopping p159; Sleeping p236

In the 1820s, ranks of trees were planted on either side of the road linking Barcelona (from the Portal de l'Àngel) and the town of Gràcia. Thus was born the Passeig de Gràcia, a strollers' boulevard. A regular horse-drawn coach service linked the city and town. All around were fields and market gardens. In time, gardens were built along the road, along with snack stands and outdoor theatres. It must have been pleasant, given the stifling overcrowding in Barcelona.

The city was bursting at the seams. As the 1850s approached, industrialisation fed a population boom. A progressive government bit the bullet and had the medieval walls knocked down between 1854 and 1856. In 1859, a competition was held to design the city's Eixample (Extension).

Work on L'Eixample began in 1869 to a design by architect Ildefons Cerdà, who specified a grid of wide streets with diamond intersections formed by their chamfered (cut-off) corners. Each block was supposed to have houses on just two sides, open space on the others and parkland in between, but speculators were soon building houses on all four sides of each block. Cerdà's greenery failed to survive the intense demand for L'Eixample real estate. Building continued until well into the 20th century. Wealthy bourgeois families snapped up prime plots along and near Passeig de Gràcia, erecting fanciful buildings in the eclectic style of the Modernistas.

Along L'Eixample's grid streets are the majority of the city's most expensive shops and hotels, a range of eateries and several nightspots. The main sightseeing objective is Modernista architecture, the best of which – apart from La Sagrada Família – are clustered on or near the main shopping avenue, Passeig de Gràcia. The stars include Gaudí's La Pedrera and the Manzana de la Discordia, which comprises three Modernista gems by the three top architects of the period. Never is the old axiom about looking up as you wander more true than here. As you pound the pavement, a seemingly endless parade of eye-catching facades will keep aesthetes pleased. Of course, the equally ancient wisdom about looking down (to avoid stepping into you know what) holds equally true.

L'Eixample is several *barris* in one. La Dreta de l'Eixample (The Right Side of L'Eixample), stretching from Passeig de Gràcia to Passeig de Sant Joan and beyond, contains much sought-after real estate. Beyond, it takes on a dowdy feel, even around La Sagrada Família, a *barri* unto itself. L'Esquerra de l'Eixample (The Left Side of L'Eixample), running southwest from Passeig de Gràcia, changes character several times. As far as Carrer d'Aribau is also prime land. Indeed, the whole area between Carrer d'Aribau, Passeig de Sant Joan, Avinguda Diagonal and the Ronda de Sant Pere has been known since the early 20th century as the Quadrat d'Or (Golden Square). It is jammed

top picks

L'EIXAMPLE

- La Sagrada Família (p102)
- La Pedrera (p104)
- Casa Batlló (p105)
- Fundació Antoni Tàpies (p107)
- Museu del Modernisme Català (p110)

with pricey shops purveying everything from teak furniture to designer clothes, from gourmet nibbles to shoes. The obvious boulevards to start on are Passeig de Gràcia (with a growing line-up of international names and the highest commercial rents in Spain) and the much more appealing parallel, tree-lined Rambla de Catalunya. Flats on Passeig de Gràcia can sell for several million euros.

At night, L'Esquerra de l'Eixample has its own flavour. From Thursday to Saturday, Carrer d'Aribau becomes a busy nightlife axis, with an assortment of bars north of Carrer de Mallorca (and spilling north over Avinguda Diagonal). Closer to the Universitat is the heart of the 'Gaixample', a cluster of gay and gay-friendly bars and clubs in an area bounded by Carrer de Balmes and Carrer de Muntaner. Carrer de Balmes also perks up at night as various music bars, largely frequented by a rowdy, juvenile set, fling open their doors. Just to add a little spice, streetwalkers come out to play along Rambla de Catalunya, while more discreet goings-on take place in the girlie bars and massage parlours nonchalantly sprinkled about the area.

Four Metro lines criss-cross L'Eixample, three stopping at Passeig de Gràcia for the Manzana de la Discordia. Línia 3 stops at Diagonal for La Pedrera, while Línies 2 and 5 stop at Sagrada Família. FGC lines from Plaça de Catalunya take you one stop to Provença, in the heart of L'Eixample.

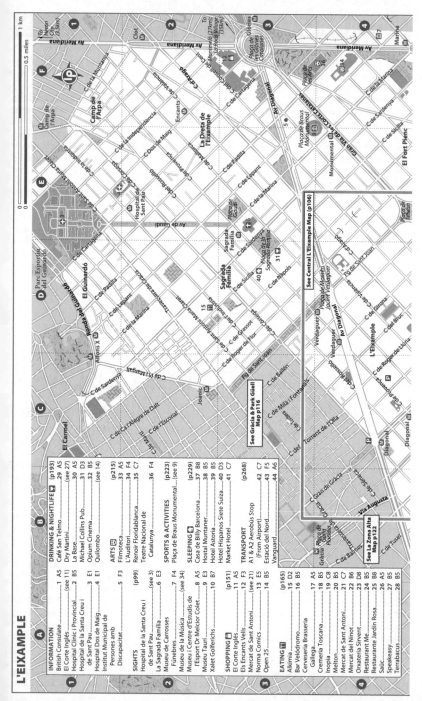

L'EIXAMPLE

INFORMATION
British Consulate	1 A5
El Corte Inglés	(see 11)
Hospital Clínic i Provincial	2 B5
Hospital de la Santa Creu i de Sant Pau	3 E1
Hospital Dos de Maig	4 E1
Institut Municipal de Persones amb Discapacitat	5 F3

SIGHTS (p99)
Hospital de la Santa Creu i de Sant Pau	(see 3)
La Sagrada Família	6 E3
Museu de Carrosses Fúnebres	7 F4
Museu de la Música	(see 34)
Museu i Centre d'Estudis de l'Esport Dr Melcior Colet	8 A5
Museu Taurí	9 E3
Xalet Golferichs	10 B7

SHOPPING (p151)
El Corte Inglés	11 A5
Els Encants Vells	12 F3
Mercat de Sant Antoni	(see 31)
Norma Comics	13 E5
Open 25	14 B5

EATING (p165)
Alkimia	15 D2
Bar Velodromo	16 B5
Cerveseria Brasserie Gallega	17 A5
Cremeria Toscana	18 B5
Inopia	19 C8
Melton	20 B5
Mercat de Sant Antoni	21 C7
Mercat del Ninot	22 B6
Onxateria Sirvent	23 D8
Restaurant Me	24 B5
Restaurante Jardin Rosa	25 B8
Saüc	26 A5
Speakeasy	27 B5
Terrabacus	28 B5

DRINKING & NIGHTLIFE (p193)
Café San Telmo	29 A5
Dry Martini	(see 27)
La Base	30 A5
Michael Collins Pub	31 D3
Opium Cinema	32 B5
Quilombo	(see 14)

ARTS (p215)
Filmoteca	33 A5
L'Auditori	34 F4
Renoir Floridablanca	35 C7
Teatre Nacional de Catalunya	36 F4

SPORTS & ACTIVITIES (p223)
Plaça de Braus Monumental	(see 9)

SLEEPING (p229)
Casa de Billy Barcelona	37 B8
Hostal Muntaner	38 B5
Hotel Astoria	39 B5
Hotel Hispanos Siete Suiza	40 D3
Market Hotel	41 C7

TRANSPORT (p268)
A1 & A2 Aerobús Stop (From Airport)	42 C7
Estació del Nord	43 F5
Vanguard	44 A6

See Gràcia & Park Güell Map p116

See Central L'Eixample Map (p106)

See La Zona Alta Map p122

0 — 0.5 miles
0 — 1 km

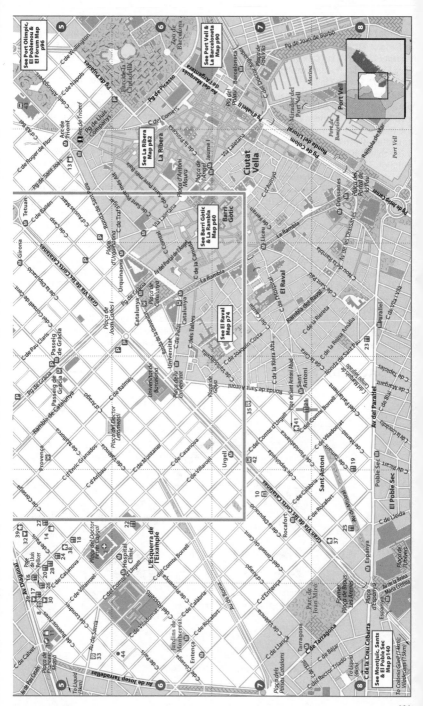

See Port Olímpic, El Poblenou & El Fòrum Map p96

See Port Vell & La Barceloneta Map p90

See La Ribera Map p82

La Ribera

See Barri Gòtic & La Rambla Map p60

Barri Gòtic

Ciutat Vella

El Raval

See El Raval Map p74

Port Vell

L'Eixample

L'Esquerra de l'Eixample

Sant Antoni

El Poble Sec

See Montjuïc, Sants & El Poble Sec Map p140

To Líquid (5km)

To Líquid (4km)

To Colònia Güell (14km); Vilaadecans (15km)

101

LA SAGRADA FAMÍLIA Map p100

☎ 93 207 30 31; www.sagradafamilia.org; Carrer de Mallorca 401; adult/child under 10yr/senior & student €12/free/10, incl Casa-Museu Gaudí in Park Güell €14/free/12; ⏱ 9am-8pm Apr-Sep, 9am-6pm Oct-Mar; Ⓜ Sagrada Família

If you have time for only one sightseeing outing, this should be it. La Sagrada Família inspires awe by its sheer verticality, and in the manner of the medieval cathedrals it emulates, it's still under construction after more than 100 years. When completed, the highest tower will be more than half as high again as those that stand today. Unfinished it may be, but it attracts around 2.8 million visitors a year and is the most visited monument in Spain.

The most important tourist of 2010 was expected to be Pope Benedict XVI, due to arrive in Barcelona on 7 November to consacrate the church in what was promised to be a beautiful ceremony.

The Temple Expiatori de la Sagrada Família (Expiatory Temple of the Holy Family) was Antoni Gaudí's all-consuming obsession. Given the commission by a conservative society that wished to build a temple as atonement for the city's sins of modernity, Gaudí saw its completion as his holy mission. As funds dried up, he contributed his own, and in the last years of his life he was never shy of pleading with anyone he thought a likely donor.

Although a building site, the completed sections and museum may be explored at leisure. Fifty-minute guided tours (€4) are offered. Alternatively, pick up an audio tour (€4), for which you need ID. Enter from Carrer de Sardenya and Carrer de la Marina. Once inside, €2.50 will get you into lifts that rise up inside towers in the Nativity and Passion facades. These two facades, each with four sky-scraping towers, are the *sides* of the church. The main Glory Facade, on which work is underway, closes off the southeast end on Carrer de Mallorca.

Gaudí devised a temple 95m long and 60m wide, able to seat 13,000 people, with a central tower 170m high above the transept (representing Christ) and another 17 of 100m or more. The 12 along the three facades represent the Apostles, while the remaining five represent the Virgin Mary and the four Evangelists. With his characteristic dislike for straight lines (there were none in nature, he said), Gaudí gave his

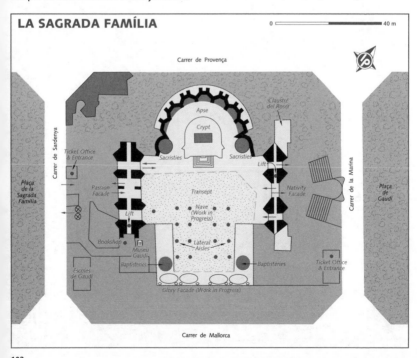

LA SAGRADA FAMÍLIA

towers swelling outlines inspired by the weird peaks of the holy mountain Montserrat outside Barcelona, and encrusted them with a tangle of sculpture that seems an outgrowth of the stone.

At Gaudí's death, only the crypt, the apse walls, one portal and one tower had been finished. Three more towers were added by 1930, completing the northeast (Nativity) facade. In 1936, anarchists burned and smashed everything they could in the church, including workshops, plans and models. Work began again in 1952, but controversy has always clouded progress. Opponents of the continuation of the project claim that the computer models based on what little of Gaudí's plans survived the anarchists' ire have led to the creation of a monster that has little to do with Gaudí's plans and style. It is a debate that appears to have little hope of resolution. Like or hate what is being done, the fascination it awakens is undeniable.

The Nativity Facade is the artistic pinnacle of the building, mostly created under Gaudí's personal supervision. You can climb high up inside some of the four towers by a combination of lifts and narrow spiral staircases – a vertiginous experience. Do not climb the stairs if you have cardiac or respiratory problems. The towers are destined to hold tubular bells capable of playing complex music at great volume. Their upper parts are decorated with mosaics spelling out *'Sanctus, Sanctus, Sanctus, Hosanna in Excelsis, Amen, Alleluia'*. Asked why he lavished so much care on the tops of the spires, which no one would see from close up, Gaudí answered: 'The angels will see them.'

Three sections of the portal represent, from left to right, Hope, Charity and Faith. Among the forest of sculpture on the Charity portal you can see, low down, the manger surrounded by an ox, an ass, the shepherds and kings, and angel musicians. Some 30 different species of plant from around Catalonia are reproduced here, and the faces of the many figures are taken from plaster casts done of local people and the occasional one made from corpses in the local morgue!

Directly above the blue stained-glass window is the Archangel Gabriel's Annunciation to Mary. At the top is a green cypress tree, a refuge in a storm for the white doves of peace dotted over it. The mosaic work

at the pinnacle of the towers is made from Murano glass, from Venice.

To the right of the facade is the curious Claustre del Roser, a Gothic style mini-cloister tacked on to the outside of the church (rather than the classic square enclosure of the great Gothic church monasteries). Once inside, look back to the intricately decorated entrance. On the lower right-hand side, you'll notice the sculpture of a reptilian devil handing a terrorist a bomb. Barcelona was regularly rocked by political violence and bombings were frequent in the decades prior to the civil war. The sculpture is one of several on the 'temptations of men and women'.

The southwest Passion Facade, on the theme of Christ's last days and death, was built between 1954 and 1978 based on surviving drawings by Gaudí, with four towers and a large, sculpture-bedecked portal. The sculptor, Josep Subirachs, worked on its decoration from 1986 to 2006. He did not attempt to imitate Gaudí, rather producing angular, controversial images of his own. The main series of sculptures, on three levels, are in an S-shaped sequence, starting with the Last Supper at the bottom left and ending with Christ's burial at the top right.

The main Glory Facade will, like the northeast and southwest facades, be crowned by four towers (taller than the other eight) – the total of 12 representing the Twelve Apostles. Gaudí wanted it to be the most magnificent facade of the church. Inside will be the narthex, a kind of foyer made up of 16 'lanterns', a series of hyperboloid forms topped by cones.

The semicircular apse wall at the northwest end of the church was the first part finished (in 1894).

Decorative work on the Passion facade continues even today, as construction of the Glory facade moves ahead.

A HIDDEN PORTRAIT

Careful observation of the Passion Facade will reveal a special tribute from sculptor Josep Subirachs to Gaudí. The central sculptural group (below Christ crucified) shows, from right to left, Christ bearing his cross, Veronica displaying the cloth with Christ's bloody image, a pair of soldiers and, watching it all, a man called the Evangelist. Subirachs used a rare photo of Gaudí, taken a couple of years before his death, as the model for the Evangelist's face.

Inside, work on roofing over the church was completed in 2010. The roof is held up by a forest of extraordinary angled pillars. As the pillars soar towards the ceiling, they sprout a web of supporting branches, creating the effect of a forest canopy. The tree image is in no way fortuitous – Gaudí envisaged such an effect. Everything was thought through, including the shape and placement of windows to create the mottled effect one would see with sunlight pouring through the branches of a thick forest. The pillars are of four different types of stone. They vary in colour and load-bearing strength, from the soft Montjuïc stone pillars along the lateral aisles through to granite, dark grey basalt and finally burgundy-tinged Iranian porphyry for the key columns at the intersection of the nave and transept. Tribunes built high above the aisles can host two choirs; the main tribune up to 1300 people and the children's tribune up to 300.

The Museu Gaudí houses material on Gaudí's life and work, including models, photos and other material on La Sagrada Família. You can see a good example of his plumb-line models that showed him the stresses and strains he could get away with in construction. A side hall towards the eastern end of the museum leads to a viewing point above the simple crypt in which the genius is buried. The crypt, where Masses are now held, can also be visited from the Carrer de Mallorca side of the church.

To the right, in front of the Passion Facade, the Escoles de Gaudí is one of his simpler gems. Gaudí built this as a children's school, creating an original, undulating roof of brick

that continues to charm architects to this day. Inside is a recreation of Gaudí's modest office as it was when he died, and explanations of the geometric patterns and plans at the heart of his building techniques.

Guesses on when construction might be complete range from the 2020s to the 2040s. Even before reaching that point, some of the oldest parts of the church, especially the apse, have required restoration work.

LA PEDRERA Map p106

Casa Milà; ☎ 902 400973; www.fundaciocaixa catalunya.es; Carrer de Provença 261-265; adult/child under 13yr/student & EU senior €10/free/6; ⊗ 9am-8pm Mar-Oct, 9am-6.30pm Nov-Feb; Ⓜ Diagonal

This undulating beast is another madcap Gaudí masterpiece, built in 1905–10 as a combined apartment and office block. Formally called Casa Milà, after the businessman who commissioned it, it is better known as La Pedrera (the Quarry) because of its uneven grey stone facade, which ripples around the corner of Carrer de Provença. In spite of appearances, the building is coated in a layer of stone rather than built out of it. The wave effect is emphasised by elaborate wrought-iron balconies. Pere Milà had married the older and far richer Roser Guardiola and knew how to spend her money (he was one of the city's first car owners and Gaudí built parking space into this building, itself a first). With this apartment building he wanted to top anything else done in l'Eixample.

The Fundació Caixa Catalunya has opened the top-floor apartment, attic and roof, together called the Espai Gaudí (Gaudí

TREMORS BELOW GROUND & ABOVE THE LAW

In 2010, a giant tunnel-making machine began to bore a 6km tunnel for the AVE high-speed train that one day will run from France to Madrid via Barcelona. The tunnel will link Estació Sants with the future second railway station in La Sagrera, crossing l'Eixample and passing under streets next to two of Gaudí's masterpieces: La Sagrada Família and La Pedrera.

Since the collapse of several blocks of flats in 2005 in the district of El Carmel because of tunnelling for a Metro line, locals have had little faith in the safety of such projects and neighbourhood groups have protested long and loud against the new tunnel, albeit in vain. Protesting louder than anyone, the administrators of La Sagrada Família tried, and failed, to block the work. In early 2010, work began on the placement of protective panels deep below the road surface in front of the church's Glory Facade to reduce the vibration effects of the passing borer on the foundations.

In 2007, it came to light that La Sagrada Família doesn't have a building permit! In 1885, Gaudí delivered a request to modify the original project but obtained no response. This administrative void has never been filled. And residents on Carrer de Mallorca concerned about the AVE tunnel might have other worries. A 1916 plan to create an open space in front of the Glory Facade would mean knocking down several blocks of flats and moving 150 families elsewhere. It is unclear to what extent the church's administration remains attached to this plan.

Space), to visitors. The roof is the most extraordinary element, with its giant chimney pots looking like multicoloured medieval knights (they say the evil imperial soldiers in the movie series *Star Wars* were inspired by them). Gaudí wanted to put a tall statue of the Virgin up here too: when the Milà family said no, fearing it might make the building a target for anarchists, Gaudí resigned from the project in disgust. Mrs Milà was no fan of Gaudí and it is said that no sooner had the job been completed than she had all his personally designed furniture tossed out!

One floor below the roof, where you can appreciate Gaudí's taste for McDonald's-style parabolic arches, is a modest museum dedicated to his work.

The next floor down is the apartment (El Pis de la Pedrera). It is fascinating to wander around this elegantly furnished home, done up in the style a well-to-do family might have enjoyed in the early 20th century. The sensuous curves and unexpected touches in everything from light fittings to bedsteads, from door handles to balconies, can hardly fail to induce a heartfelt desire to move in at once. All those curves might seem admirable to us today, but not everyone thought so at the time. The story goes that one tenant, a certain Mrs Comes i Abril, had complained that there was no obvious place to put her piano in these wavy rooms. Gaudí's response was simple: 'Madame, I suggest you take up the flute.'

Some of the lower floors of the building, especially the grand 1st floor, often host temporary expositions. On hot August evenings, La Pedrera usually stages a series of brief concerts on the roof.

CASA BATLLÓ Map p106

☎ 93 216 03 06; www.casabatllo.es; Passeig de Gràcia 43; adult/child under 7yr/student, child 7-18yr & senior €17.80/free/14.25; ☽ 9am-8pm; Ⓜ Passeig de Gràcia

One of the strangest residential buildings in Europe, this is Gaudí at his hallucinogenic best. The facade, sprinkled with bits of blue, mauve and green tiles and studded with wave-shaped window frames and balconies, rises to an uneven blue-tiled roof with a solitary tower.

It is one of the three houses on the block between Carrer del Consell de Cent and Carrer d'Aragó that gave it the playful name Manzana de la Discordia, meaning

'Apple (Block) of Discord' (see the boxed text, above). The others are Puig i Cadafalch's Casa Amatller (see below) and Domènech i Montaner's Casa Lleó Morera (p107). They were all renovated between 1898 and 1906 and show how eclectic a 'style' Modernisme was.

Locals know Casa Batlló variously as the *casa dels ossos* (house of bones) or *casa del drac* (house of the dragon). It's easy enough to see why. The balconies look like the bony jaws of some strange beast and the roof represents Sant Jordi (St George) and the dragon. If you stare long enough at the building, it seems almost to be a living being. Before going inside, take a look at the pavement. Each paving piece carries stylised images of an octopus and a starfish, Gaudí designs originally cooked up for Casa Batlló.

When Gaudí was commissioned to refashion this building, he went to town inside and out. The internal light wells shimmer with tiles of deep sea blue. Gaudí eschewed the straight line, and so the staircase wafts you up to the 1st (main) floor, where the salon looks on to Passeig de Gràcia. Everything swirls: the ceiling is twisted into a vortex around its sun-like lamp; the doors, window and skylights are dreamy waves of wood and coloured glass. The same themes continue in the other rooms and covered terrace. The attic is characterised by Gaudí trademark hyperboloid arches. Twisting, tiled chimney pots add a surreal touch to the roof.

CASA AMATLLER Map p106

☎ 93 487 72 17; www.amatller.org; Passeig de Gràcia 41; admission free; ☽ 10am-8pm Mon-Sat, 10am-3pm Sun; Ⓜ Passeig de Gràcia

One of Puig i Cadafalch's most striking bits of Modernista fantasy, Casa Amatller combines Gothic window frames with a

CENTRAL L'EIXAMPLE

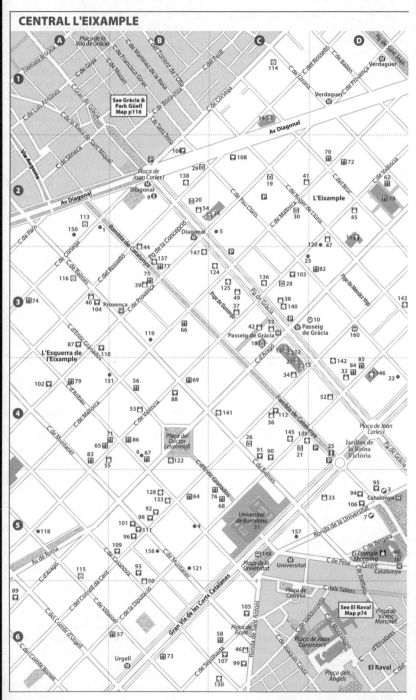

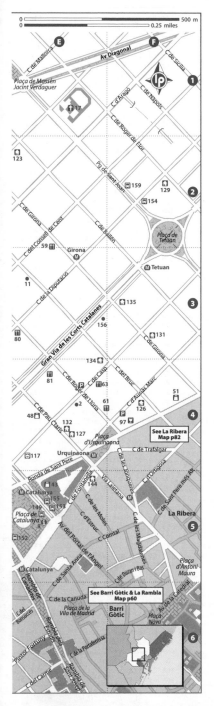

stepped gable borrowed from Dutch urban architecture. But the busts and reliefs of dragons, knights and other characters dripping off the main facade are pure caprice. The pillared foyer and staircase lit by stained glass are like the inside of some romantic castle.

The building was renovated in 1900 for the chocolate baron and philanthropist Antoni Amatller (1851–1910) and it will one day open partly to the public. Renovation due for completion in 2012 will see the 1st (main) floor converted into a museum with period pieces, while the 2nd floor will house the Institut Amatller d'Art Hispanic (Amatller Institute of Hispanic Art).

For now, you can wander into the foyer, admire the staircase and lift, and head through the shop to see the latest temporary exhibition out the back. Depending on the state of renovation, it is also possible to join a 1½-hour guided tour (€10; ⏱ in English noon Fri, in Catalan & Spanish noon Wed) of the 1st floor, with its early-20th-century furniture and decor intact, and Amatller's photo studio. Groups can book guided visits for Monday to Friday.

Amatller was a keen traveller and photographer (his shots of turn-of-the-20th-century Morocco are absorbing and sometimes some are on show). The tour also includes a tasting of Amatller chocolates in the original kitchen.

CASA LLEÓ MORERA Map p106
Passeig de Gràcia 35; Ⓜ Passeig de Gràcia
Domènech i Montaner's 1905 contribution to the Manzana de la Discordia, with Modernista carving outside and a bright, tiled lobby in which floral motifs predominate, is perhaps the least odd-looking of the three main buildings on the block. If only you could get inside – they are private apartments. The 1st floor is giddy with swirling sculptures, rich mosaics and whimsical decor.

FUNDACIÓ ANTONI TÀPIES Map p106
☎ 93 487 03 15; www.fundaciotapies.org; Carrer d'Aragó 255; adult/child under 16yr €7/5.60; ⏱ 10am-8pm Tue-Sun; Ⓜ Passeig de Gràcia
The Fundació Antoni Tàpies is both a pioneering Modernista building (completed in 1885) and the major collection of a leading 20th-century Catalan artist.

The building, designed by Domènech i Montaner for the publishing house Editorial

Montaner i Simón (run by a cousin of the architect), combines a brick-covered iron frame with Islamic-inspired decoration. Tàpies saw fit to crown it with the meanderings of his own mind – to some it looks like a pile of coiled barbed wire, to others… well, it's difficult to say. He calls it *Núvol i Cadira* (Cloud and Chair). Renovation work on it finished in early 2010.

Antoni Tàpies, whose experimental art has often carried political messages (not always easily decipherable) – he opposed Francoism in the 1960s and '70s – launched the Fundació in 1984 to promote contemporary art, donating a large part of his own work. The collection spans the arc of Tàpies' creations (with more than 800 works) and contributions from other contemporary artists. In the main exhibition area (level 1, upstairs) you can see an ever-changing selection of around 20 of Tàpies' works, from early self-portraits of the 1940s to grand items like *Jersei Negre* (Black Jumper; 2008), in which the outline of a man with a hard-on is topped with a pasted on black sweater. Level 2 hosts a small space for temporary exhibitions. Rotating exhibitions take place in the basement levels. At the time of writing, one held about 15 grand Tàpies works and a one-hour documentary on his life, while the other was dedicated to part of Tàpies' eclectic personal collections, anything from centuries-old medical treatises and Japanese calligraphy to lithographs on bullfighting by Francisco Goya.

HOSPITAL DE LA SANTA CREU I DE SANT PAU Map p100
☎ 93 317 76 52; www.rutadelmodernisme.com, www.santpau.es; Carrer de Cartagena 167; adult/senior & student €10/5; ⏰ 10am, 11am, noon & 1pm in English, others in Catalan, French & Spanish; Ⓜ Hospital de Sant Pau

Domènech i Montaner outdid himself as architect and philanthropist with this Modernista masterpiece, long considered one of the city's most important hospitals. He wanted to create a unique environment that would also cheer up patients. The complex, including 16 pavilions – together with the Palau de la Música Catalana (p84), a joint World Heritage Site – is lavishly decorated and each pavilion is unique. Among artists who contributed statuary, ceramics and artwork was the prolific Eusebi Arnau.

The hospital facilities have been transferred to a new complex on the premises, freeing up the century-old structures, which are now being restored to their former glory in a plan to convert the complex into an international centre on the Mediterranean. Whether or not the site will be open to visits was unclear at the time of writing. For the time being, guided tours allow the curious to get inside this unique site.

MUSEU DE LA MÚSICA Map p100
☎ 93 256 36 50; www.museumusica.bcn.cat; Carrer de Lepant 150; adult/senior & student €4/3, free 3-8pm Sun; ⏰ 10am-6pm Mon, Wed-Sat, 10am-8pm Sun; Ⓜ Monumental

Some 500 instruments (less than a third of those held) are on show in this museum housed on the 2nd floor of the administration building in L'Auditori (p217), the city's main classical-music concert hall.

Instruments range from a 17th-century baroque guitar through to lutes (look out for the many-stringed 1641 *archilute* from Venice), violins, Japanese kotos, sitars from India, eight organs (some dating to the 18th century), pianos, a varied collection of drums and other percussion instruments from across Spain and beyond, along with all sorts of phonographs and gramophones. There are some odd pieces indeed, like the *buccèn*, a snake-head-adorned brass instrument.

Much of the documentary and sound material can be enjoyed through audiovisual displays as you proceed. An audio device allows you to listen to how some of the instruments sound, although it is sometimes a trifle hard to hear the recording above the continually changing ambient music.

The museum organises occasional concerts in which well-known musicians perform on rare instruments held in the collection.

FUNDACIÓN FRANCISCO GODIA
Map p106
☎ 93 272 31 80; www.fundacionfgodia.org; Carrer de la Diputació 250; adult/child under 5yr/student €5/free/3.50; ⏰ 10am-8pm Mon & Wed-Sun; Ⓜ Passeig de Gràcia

Francisco Godia (1921–90), head of one of Barcelona's great establishment families, liked fast cars (he came sixth in the 1956 Grand Prix season driving Maseratis) and fine art. An intriguing mix of medieval art, ceramics and modern paintings make up this varied private collection, housed in Casa Garriga Nogués, a stunning, carefully restored Modernista residence originally built for a rich banking family by Enric Sagnier in 1902–05.

The ground floor is given over to a display of Godia's driving trophies (and goggles) and a video on his feats behind the wheel, as well as occasional temporary exhibitions.

The art is up the languidly curvaceous marble stairway on the 1st floor and organised along roughly chronological lines across 17 rooms. The first five are given over mostly to Romanesque and Gothic wooden sculptures. Some of these are especially arresting because of their well-preserved colouring. The early 14th century wood cut of Joseph of Armithea (room 1), with its bright red, pyjama-like outfit, is a case in point. Jaume Huguet is represented in room 5 by *Santa Maria Magdalena*, a bright, Gothic representation of Mary Magdalene dressed in red ermine.

Room 6 is a long and overwhelming rococo room with aqua-green walls and a selection of Godia's extensive ceramics collection, with pieces from all the historic porcelain production centres in Spain (including Manises in Valencia and Talavera de la Reina in Castilla-La Mancha). Admire the fine Modernista stained-glass windows in room 8.

Godia's interests ranged from the Neapolitan baroque painter Luca Giordano to Catalan Modernisme and Valencia's Joaquim Sorolla. Room 17, a gallery around the central staircase, contains several works by Modernista and Noucentista painters, like Ramon Casas, Santiago Rusiñol and Isidre Nonell. There's even a modest Miró.

FUNDACIÓ SUÑOL Map p106

☎ 93 496 10 32; www.fundaciosunol.org; Passeig de Gràcia 98; adult/concession €5/3; ☾ 4-8pm Mon-Sat; Ⓜ Diagonal

Rotating exhibitions of portions of this private collection of mostly 20th-century art (some 1200 works in total) offer anything from Man Ray's photography to sculptures by Alberto Giacometti. Over two floors, you are most likely to run into Spanish artists, anyone from Picasso to Jaume Plensa, along with a sprinkling of others from abroad. It makes a refreshing pause between the crush of crowded Modernista monuments on this boulevard. Indeed, you get an interesting side view of one of them, La Pedrera, from out the back.

MUSEU EGIPCI Map p106

☎ 93 488 01 88; www.museuegipci.com; Carrer de València 284; adult/senior & student €11/8; ☾ 10am-8pm Mon-Sat, 10am-2pm Sun; Ⓜ Passeig de Gràcia

Hotel magnate Jordi Clos has spent much of his life collecting ancient Egyptian artefacts, brought together in this private museum. It's divided into different thematic areas (the Pharaoh, religion, funerary practices, mummification, crafts etc) and boasts a pleasing variety of statuary, funereal implements and containers, jewellery (including a fabulous golden ring from around the 7th century BC), ceramics and even a bed made of wood and leather. In the basement is an exhibition area and library, displaying volumes including original editions of works by Carter, the Egyptologist who led the Tutankhamun excavations. On the rooftop terrace is a pleasant cafe.

MUSEU DEL PERFUM Map p106

☎ 93 216 01 21; www.museudelperfum.com; Passeig de Gràcia 39; adult/student & senior €5/3; ☾ 10.30am-1.30pm & 4.30-8pm Mon-Fri, 11am-2pm Sat; Ⓜ Passeig de Gràcia

Housed in the back of the Regia perfume store, this museum contains everything from ancient Egyptian and Roman (the latter mostly from the 1st to 3rd centuries AD) scent receptacles to classic eau-de-cologne bottles – all in all, some 5000 bottles of infinite shapes, sizes and histories. You can admire anything from ancient bronze Etruscan tweezers to little early-19th-century potpourris made of fine Sèvres porcelain. Also on show are old catalogues and advertising posters.

MUSEU DEL MODERNISME CATALÀ Map p106

☎ 93 272 28 96; www.mmcat.cat; Carrer de Balmes 48; adult/child under 5yr/child 5-16yr/student €10/free/5/7; ☾ 10am-8pm Mon-Sat, 10am-3pm Sun; Ⓜ Passeig de Gràcia

It's hard to believe that Modernisme, Catalonia's answer to art nouveau, was until not so long ago considered a wacky aberration of limited interest. Now everyone seems to be into this architectural and design period (see also p125), so it was only a matter of time before a dedicated museum should open.

MODERNISME UNPACKED

Aficionados of Barcelona's Modernista heritage should consider the *Ruta del Modernisme* pack (www. rutadelmodernisme.com). For €12 you receive a guide to 115 Modernista buildings great and small, a map and discounts of up to 50% on the main Modernista sights in Barcelona, as well as some in other municipalities around Catalonia. The discounts are valid for a year. For €18 you get another guide and map, *Sortim*, which leads you to bars and restaurants located in Modernista buildings around the city. The proceeds of these packs go to the maintenance and refurbishment of Modernista buildings.

The *Ruta del Modernisme* guide (in various languages) is available in bookstores. You can then take it to one of three Centres del Modernisme to obtain the discount cards, or you can buy the lot at those centres. The easiest one to get to and most likely to be open is at the main tourist office at Plaça de Catalunya 17 (p285). The one at Hospital de la Santa Creu i de Sant Pau (p109) is also fairly reliable, while the one at the Pavellons Güell (p124) in Pedralbes is more than likely to be shut out of tour hours.

Housed in a Modernista building, the ground floor seems a like a big Modernista furniture showroom. Several items by Antoni Gaudí, including chairs from Casa Batlló and a mirror from Casa Calvet, are supplemented by a host of items by his lesser-known contemporaries, including some typically whimsical, mock medieval pieces by Josep Puig i Cadafalch.

The basement, showing off Modernista traits like mosaic-coated pillars, bare brick vaults and metal columns, is lined with Modernista art, including paintings by Ramon Casas and Santiago Rusiñol, and statues by Josep Llimona and Eusebi Arnau.

PALAU DEL BARÓ QUADRAS Map p106

Casa Asia; ☎ 93 368 08 36; www.casaasia.es; Avinguda Diagonal 373; ⏱ 10am-8pm Tue-Sat, 10am-2pm Sun; Ⓜ Diagonal

Puig i Cadafalch designed Palau del Baró Quadras (built 1902–06) for the baron in question in an exuberant Gothic-inspired style. The main facade is its most intriguing, with a soaring, glassed-in gallery. Take a closer look at the gargoyles and reliefs, among them a pair of toothy fish and a knight wielding a sword – clearly the same artistic signature as the architect behind Casa Amatller (p105).

Decor inside is eclectic, but dominated by Middle Eastern and Oriental themes. The setting is appropriate for its occupant: Casa Asia is a cultural centre celebrating the relationship between Spain and the Asia-Pacific region. Visiting the varied temporary exhibitions (mostly on the 2nd floor) allows you to get a good look inside this intriguing building. Take in the views from the roof terrace.

CASA DE LES PUNXES Map p106

Casa Terrades; Avinguda Diagonal 420; Ⓜ Diagonal

Puig i Cadafalch's Casa Terrades is better known as the Casa de les Punxes (House of Spikes) because of its pointed turrets. This apartment block, completed in 1905, looks like a fairy-tale castle and has the singular attribute of being the only fully detached building in l'Eixample.

ESGLÉSIA DE LA PURÍSSIMA CONCEPCIÓ I ASSUMPCIÓ DE NOSTRA SENYORA Map p106

Carrer de Roger de Llúria 70; ⏱ 8am-1pm & 5-9pm; Ⓜ Passeig de Gràcia

One hardly expects to run into a medieval church on the grid pattern streets of the late-19th-century city extension, yet that is just what this is. Transferred stone by stone from the old centre in 1871–88, this 14th-century church has a pretty 16th-century cloister with a peaceful garden. Behind is a Romanesque-Gothic bell tower (11th to 16th century), moved from another old town church that didn't survive, Església de Sant Miquel. This is one of a handful of such old churches shifted willy-nilly from their original locations to l'Eixample.

PALAU MONTANER Map p106

☎ 93 317 76 52; www.rutadelmodernisme.com; Carrer de Mallorca 278; adult/child & senior €6/3; ⏱ guided visit in English 10.30am & in Spanish 12.30pm Sat, in Catalan 10.30am, in Spanish 11.30am & in Catalan 12.30pm Sun; Ⓜ Passeig de Gràcia

Interesting on the outside and made all the more enticing by its gardens, this creation by Domènech i Montaner is spectacular on the inside. Completed in 1896, its central feature is a grand staircase beneath a broad, ornamental skylight. The interior is laden with sculptures (some by Eusebi Arnau), mosaics and fine woodwork. Interior and exterior decoration depicts themes related to the printing industry. It is advisable to call ahead if you want to be sure to visit, as the building is sometimes closed to the public on weekends, too.

UNIVERSITAT DE BARCELONA Map p106

☎ 93 402 11 00; www.ub.edu; Gran Via de les Corts Catalanes 585; admission free; ⏲ 9am-9pm Mon-Fri; Ⓜ Universitat

Although a university was first set up on what is now La Rambla in the 16th century, the present, glorious mix of (neo) Romanesque, Gothic, Islamic and Mudéjar architecture is a caprice of the 19th century (built 1863–82). Wander into the main hall, up the grand staircase and around the various leafy cloisters. On the 1st floor, the main hall for big occasions is the Mudéjar-style Paranimfo. Take a stroll in the rear gardens.

FUNDACIÓ JOAN BROSSA Map p106

☎ 93 467 69 52; www.fundaciojoanbrossa.cat; Carrer de Provença 318; admission free; ⏲ 10am-2pm & 3-7pm Mon-Fri; Ⓜ Diagonal

Pop into this basement gallery to get an insight into the mind of one of the city's cultural icons, Joan Brossa, a difficult-to-classify mix of poet, artist, theatre man, Catalan nationalist and all-round visionary. You'll see a panoply of objects of art (like *Porró amb Daus*, a typical Spanish wine decanter with dice), followed by samples of his visual poems (see p40).

MUSEU DE CARROSSES FÚNEBRES

Map p100

☎ 902 076902; Carrer de Sancho d'Àvila 2; admission free; ⏲ 10am-1pm & 4-6pm Mon-Fri, 10am-1pm Sat, Sun & holidays; Ⓜ Marina

If late-18th-century to mid-20th-century hearses (complete with period-dressed dummies) are your thing, then this museum, probably the city's weirdest sight, is where to contemplate the pomp and circumstance of people's last earthly ride. From the reception desk, you are taken into the rather gloomy basement by a security guard. Alongside a metallic Buick hearse and a couple of earlier motorised hearses are lined up 11 horse-drawn carriage-hearses in use in the 19th and early 20th centuries – four of them with horses and accompanying walkers in powdered wigs and tricorn hats. It's a strange little display, easily done in half an hour. The funeral company claims it is the biggest museum of its kind in the world.

MUSEU I CENTRE D'ESTUDIS DE L'ESPORT DR MELCIOR COLET Map p100

☎ 93 419 22 32; Carrer de Buenos Aires 56-58; admission free; ⏲ 9am-2pm & 3-5.30pm Mon-Fri; 🚍 27, 32, 59, 66, 67 or 68

Puig i Cadafalch's Casa Company (1911) looks like an odd Tyrolean country house and is marvellously out of place. A collection of photos, documents and other sports memorabilia stretches over two floors – from a 1930s pair of skis and boots (how did they get down mountains on those things?) to the skull-decorated swimming costume of a champion Catalan water-polo player. A curio on the ground floor is the replica of a stone commemoration in Latin of Lucius Minicius Natal, a Barcelona boy who won a *quadriga* (four-horse chariot) race at the 227th Olympic Games…in AD 129.

MUSEU TAURÍ Map p100

☎ 93 245 58 03; Gran Via de les Corts Catalanes 749; adult/child €6/5; ⏲ 11am-2pm & 4-8pm Mon-Sat, 10am-1pm Sun Apr-Sep; Ⓜ Monumental

Housed in the Plaça de Braus Monumental bullring, this bullfighting museum displays stuffed bulls' heads, old posters, *trajes de luces* (bullfighters' gear) and other memorabilia. You also get to wander around the ring and corrals.

XALET GOLFERICHS Map p100

☎ 93 323 77 90; www.golferichs.org, in Catalan & Spanish; Gran Via de les Corts Catalanes 491; ⏲ 5.30-9.30pm Mon-Sat; Ⓜ Rocafort

This quirky mansion is an oddity of another era on one of the city's busiest boulevards. Its owner, businessman Macari Golferichs, wanted a Modernista villa and he got one. Brick, ceramics and timber are the main building elements of the house, which displays a distinctly Gothic flavour. It came close to demolition in the 1970s, but was saved by the town hall and converted into a cultural centre. Opening times can vary depending on temporary exhibitions and other cultural activities.

ESGLÉSIA DE LES SALESES Map p106

☎ 93 265 39 12; Passeig de Sant Joan; ⏲ 10am-2pm & 5-9pm Mon-Sat; Ⓜ Tetuan

A singular neo-Gothic effort, this church is interesting above all because of who built it. Raised in 1878–85 with an adjacent convent (badly damaged in the civil war and now a school), it was designed by Joan Martorell i Montells (1833–1906), Gaudí's architecture professor. Indeed, the church offers some hints of what was to come with Modernisme, with his use of brick, mosaics and sober stained glass.

MORE MODERNISME IN L'EIXAMPLE
Walking Tour
1 Casa Calvet
Gaudí's most conventional contribution to l'Eixample is Casa Calvet (Carrer de Casp 48), built in 1900. Inspired by baroque, the noble ashlar facade is broken up by protruding wrought-iron balconies. Inside, the main attraction is the staircase, which you can admire if you eat in the swank restaurant (p181).

2 Cases Cabot
Josep Vilaseca (1848–1910) was one of many architects working in Modernista Barcelona whose names have not come down to us as stars. His two contiguous Cases Cabot (Carrer de Roger de Llúria 8-14), built in 1901–04, are quite

different from one another. The doorway of the house at Nos 8–10 has particularly fine decoration.

3 Casa Pia Batlló
Vilaseca's Casa Pia Batlló (Rambla de Catalunya 17), built between 1891 and 1896, is interesting in its use of ironwork, especially along the 1st- and top-floor galleries around the three facades. Stonework is pre-eminent, and pseudo-Gothic touches, such as the witch's hat towers, abound.

4 Casa Mulleras
In among the big three of the Manzana de la Discordia (p105), Casa Mulleras (Passeig de Gràcia 37), built in 1906 by Enric Sagnier (1858–1931), is a relatively demure contribution. The facade

---

WALK FACTS
Start Casa Calvet
Finish Casa Macaya
Distance 3.8km
Duration 1½ hours
Transport Ⓜ Urquinaona

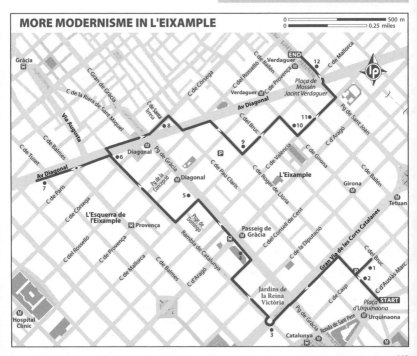

MORE MODERNISME IN L'EIXAMPLE

transmits a restrained classicism, but it's not devoid of light floral decoration and a fine gallery.

5 Casa Enric Batlló

Another apartment building by Vilaseca is Casa Enric Batlló (Passeig de Gràcia 75), completed in 1896 and part of the Comtes de Barcelona hotel (p237). Lit up at night, the brickwork facade is especially graceful.

6 Casa Serra

Puig i Cadafalch let his imagination loose on Casa Serra (Rambla de Catalunya 126), built in 1903–08, a neo-Gothic whimsy that is home to government offices. With its central tower topped by a witch's hat, grandly decorated upper-floor windows and tiled roof, it must have been a strange house to live in!

7 Casa Sayrach

It's worth walking two blocks west of Casa Serra to see Casa Sayrach (Avinguda Diagonal 423-425), built in 1915–18 by Manuel Sayrach (1886–1937). One of the last Modernista buildings, it's home to a chic restaurant and vaguely resembles La Pedrera. While not as nutty as Gaudí's efforts, the stone facade is all curves.

8 Casa Comalat

Built in 1911 by Salvador Valeri (1873–1954), Casa Comalat (Avinguda Diagonal 442) is striking. The Gaudí influence on the main facade, with its wavy roof and bulging balconies, is obvious. Head around the back to Carrer de Còrsega to see a more playful facade, with its windows stacked like cards.

9 Casa Thomas

Completed in 1912, Casa Thomas (Carrer de Mallorca 291) was one of Domènech i Montaner's earlier efforts – the ceramic details are a trademark and the massive ground-level wrought-iron decoration (and protection?) is magnificent. Wander inside to the Cubiña design store (p160) to admire his interior work.

10 Casa Granell

The colourful Casa Granell (Carrer de Girona 122), built between 1901 and 1903 by Jeroni Granell (1867–1931), is a peculiar building, with its serpentine lines (check out the roof) and gently curving decorative facade framing the rectangular windows. If you get the chance, take a peek inside the entrance and stairwell, both richly decorated.

11 Casa Llopis i Bofill

Built in 1902, Casa Llopis i Bofill (Carrer de València 339) is an interesting block of flats designed by Antoni Gallissà (1861–1903). The graffiti-covered facade is particularly striking to the visitor's eye. The use of elaborate parabolic arches on the ground floor is a clear Modernista touch, as are the wrought-iron balconies.

12 Casa Macaya

Constructed in 1901, Puig i Cadafalch's Casa Macaya (Passeig de Sant Joan 108) has a wonderful courtyard and features the typical playful, pseudo-Gothic decoration that characterises many of the architect's projects. It belongs to the La Caixa bank and is occasionally used for temporary exhibitions, when visitors are permitted to enter.

GRÀCIA & PARK GÜELL

Drinking & Nightlife p208; Eating p186; Shopping p162; Sleeping p240

Once a separate village north of l'Eixample, and then in the 19th century an industrial district famous for its Republican and liberal ideas, Gràcia was definitively incorporated into the city of Barcelona (the town had been 'annexed' and then won its 'freedom' several times down the century) in 1897, much to the disgust of the locals.

In those days, it had some catching up to do, as the town had poor roads, schools and clinics, and no street lighting or sewers. In the 1960s and '70s it became fashionable among radical and Bohemian types, and today it retains some of that flavour – plenty of hip local luminaries make sure they are regularly seen around its bars and cafes.

You know you are in Gràcia when you hit the maze of crowded narrow streets and lanes that characterise it. The official district of Gràcia extends beyond, taking in the residential valley of Vallcarca, which nuzzles up alongside Park Güell.

The heart of Gràcia is bounded by Carrer de Còrsega and Avinguda Diagonal in the south, Via Augusta and Avinguda del Príncep d'Astúries to the west, Carrer de Sardenya to the east and Travessera de Dalt to the north.

Plunge into the atmosphere of its narrow streets and small plazas, and the bars and restaurants on and around them. The liveliest are Carrer de Verdi, Plaça del Sol, Plaça de la Vila de Gràcia (formerly de Rius i Taulet) and the tree-lined Plaça de la Virreina. On Plaça de Rovira i Trias, you can sit on a bench next to a statue of Antoni Rovira, Ildefons Cerdà's rival in the competition to design L'Eixample in the late 19th century. Rovira's design has been laid out in the pavement, so you can see what you think.

Metro Línia 3 (Fontana stop) leaves you halfway up Carrer Gran de Gràcia and close to a network of busy squares (see p118).

PARK GÜELL Map p116

☎ 93 413 24 00; Carrer d'Olot 7; admission free; ☾ 10am-9pm Jun-Sep, 10am-8pm Apr, May & Oct, 10am-7pm Mar & Nov, 10am-6pm Dec-Feb; Ⓜ Lesseps or Vallcarca, ▣ 24

North of Gràcia and about 4km from Plaça de Catalunya, Park Güell is where Gaudí turned his hand to landscape gardening. It's a strange, enchanting place where his passion for natural forms really took flight – to the point where the artificial almost seems more natural than the natural.

Park Güell originated in 1900, when Count Eusebi Güell bought a tree-covered hillside (then outside Barcelona) and hired Gaudí to create a miniature city of houses for the wealthy in landscaped grounds. The project was a commercial flop and was abandoned in 1914 – but not before Gaudí had created 3km of roads and walks, steps, a plaza and two gatehouses in his inimitable manner. In 1922 the city bought the estate for use as a public park.

Just inside the main entrance on Carrer d'Olot, immediately recognisable by the two Hansel-and-Gretel gatehouses, is the park's Centre d'Interpretac (closed for restoration at the time of writing) in the Pavelló de Consergeria, which is a typically curvaceous former porter's home that hosts a display

on Gaudí's building methods and the history of the park. There are nice views from the top floor. At the time of writing, it was being refurbished.

The steps up from the entrance, guarded by a mosaic dragon/lizard (a copy of which you can buy in many downtown souvenir shops), lead to the Sala Hipóstila (aka the Doric Temple), a forest of 88 stone columns (some of them leaning like mighty trees bent by the weight of time), intended as a market. To the left curves a gallery whose twisted stonework columns and roof give the effect of a cloister beneath tree roots – a motif repeated in several places in the park. On top of the Sala Hipóstila is a broad open space whose centrepiece is the Banc de Trencadís, a tiled bench curving sinuously around its perimeter and designed by one of Gaudí's closest colleagues, architect Josep Maria Jujol (1879–1949). With Gaudí, however, there is always more than meets the eye. This giant platform was designed as a kind of catchment area for rainwater washing down the hillside. The water is filtered through a layer of stone and sand and drains down through the columns to an underground cistern!

The spired house to the right is the Casa-Museu Gaudí (☎ 93 219 38 11; www.casamuseugaudi. org; adult/child under 10yr/senior & student €5.50/

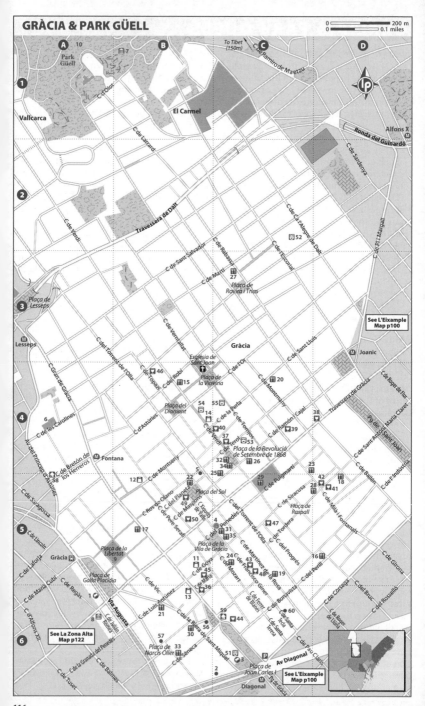

GRÀCIA & PARK GÜELL

0 — 200 m
0 — 0.1 miles

A · **B** · **C** · **D**

To Tibet (150m)

Park Güell

El Carmel

Vallcarca

C de Ramiro de Maetzu

Alfons X

Ronda del Guinardó

C de Olot

C de Jaurès

Travessera de Dalt

C de Verdi

C de l'Alegre de Dalt

52

C de Sant Salvador

C de Rabassa

C de Martí

27

Plaça de Rovira i Trias

C de Viscondel

Plaça de Lesseps

C de Vermellat

C de l'Or

Gràcia

Joanic

Lesseps

C del Torrent de l'Olla

C de Tropai

C del Rabí

46

15

Església de Sant Joan

Plaça de la Virreina

C de Montmany

20

Plaça del Diamant

54 55

14

C de la Perla

38

C de Ramón Cajal

39

C d'Astúries

40

37 53

C de Torrent

Plaça de la Revolució de Setembre de 1868

26

C de Verdi

C de Torrijos

32

34

23

42

18

C de les Carolines

6

C de Bretón de los Herreros

Fontana

12

C de Montseny

5

25

29

C de Puigmartí

28

41

C de Siracusa

Plaça del Sol

Plaça de Raspall

22

C de Ros de Olano

C del Planeta

C de Pere Serafí

45

C de Maspons

4

31

47

C del Torrent de l'Olla

C de Tordera

C de Saragossa

17

50

35

Plaça de la Vila de Gràcia

C de Martínez de la Rosa

16

Av del Príncep d'Astúries

58

Gràcia

8

Plaça de la Llibertat

11

24

43

19

C de Goya

45

48

C de Bonavista

C del Penill

C de Girona

Plaça de Gotla Plácida

C de Vic

9

C de Mozart

13

36

C de Maria Cubí

C de Lincoln

1

Via Augusta

C de Luis Antúnez

21

59

44

60

C de Seneca

C de Balmes

57

33

56

30

51

3

Plaça de Narcis Oller

2

Plaça de Joan Carles I

Av Diagonal

See La Zona Alta Map p122

See L'Eixample Map p100

Diagonal

116

free/4.50; ☻ 10am-8pm Apr-Sep, 10am-6pm Oct-Mar), where Gaudí lived for most of his last 20 years (1906–26). It contains furniture by him (including items that were once at home in La Pedrera, Casa Batlló and Casa Calvet) and other memorabilia. The house was built in 1904 by Francesc Berenguer i Mestres as a prototype for the 60 or so houses that were originally planned here.

Much of the park is still wooded, but it's laced with pathways. The best views are from the cross-topped Turó del Calvari in the southwest corner.

The walk from Metro stop Lesseps is signposted. From the Vallcarca stop, it is marginally shorter and the uphill trek eased by escalators. Bus 24 drops you at an entrance near the top of the park.

The park is extremely popular (it gets an estimated 4 million visitors a year, about 86% of them tourists) and there is talk of limiting access to keep a lid on damage done by the overkill. Its quaint nooks and crannies are irresistible to photographers – who on busy days have trouble keeping out of each other's pictures.

CASA VICENS Map p116
www.casavicens.es; Carrer de les Carolines 22; 🚇 FGC Plaça Molina
The angular, turreted 1888 Casa Vicens was one of Gaudí's first commissions. Tucked away west of Gràcia's main drag, this private house (which cannot be visited and was up for sale at the time of writing)

is awash with ceramic colour and shape. As was frequently the case, Gaudí sought inspiration from the past, in this case the rich heritage of building in the Mudéjar-style brick, typical in those parts of Spain reconquered from the Muslims. Mudéjar architecture was created by those Arabs and Berbers allowed to remain in Spain after the Christian conquests.

MERCAT DE LA LLIBERTAT Map p116
☎ 93 217 09 95; Plaça de la Llibertat; admission free; ☻ 8am-8.30pm Mon-Fri, 8am-3pm Sat; 🚇 FGC Gràcia
Built in the 1870s, the 'Liberty Market' was covered over in 1893 in typically fizzy Modernista style, employing generous whirls of wrought iron. It got a considerable facelift in 2009 and has lost some of its aged charm, but the market remains emblematic of the Gràcia district, full of life and all kinds of fresh produce. The man behind the 1893 remake was Francesc Berenguer i Mestres (1866–1914), Gaudí's long-time assistant.

FUNDACIÓ FOTO COLECTANIA
Map p116
☎ 93 217 16 26; www.colectania.es; Carrer de Julián Romea 6; admission €3; ☻ 11am-2pm & 5-8.30pm Mon-Sat, closed Aug; 🚇 FGC Gràcia
Photography lovers should swing by here to see the latest exhibition; they change over about three times a year. When you reach what seems like offices, head

through to the back on the ground floor, where two floors of exhibition space await. What you see may come from the foundation's own collection of Spanish and Portuguese snappers from the 1950s on, but more likely will be temporary exhibitions of other work.

THE SQUARES OF GRÀCIA
Walking Tour
1 Plaça de Joan Carles I
The obelisk here honours Spain's present king for stifling an attempted coup d'état in February 1981, six years after Franco's death. Under the dictatorship, the avenue that passes through the square was known as Avenida de Francisco Franco. To *barcelonins* it was simply 'La Diagonal'. That name stuck.

2 Casa Fuster
Where Carrer Gran de Gràcia leads you into Gràcia proper, a grand Modernista edifice now turned hotel, Casa Fuster (p240), rises in all its glory.

3 Plaça de Gal.la Placidia
The square recalls the brief sojourn of the Roman empress-to-be Galla Placidia, here as captive and wife of the Visigothic chief Athaulf in the 5th century AD. She had been hauled across from Italy, where she hastily returned upon her captor-husband's death.

4 Plaça de la Llibertat
'Liberty Square' is home to the bustling Modernista produce market of the same name. It was designed by one of Gaudí's colleagues, Francesc Berenguer (see p117), who was busy in this part of town, although he was never awarded a diploma as an architect.

5 Plaça de la Vila de Gràcia
This popular square was, until two years ago, named after the mayor under whom Gràcia was absorbed by Barcelona, Francesc Rius i Taulet. It is fronted by the local town hall (designed by Berenguer). At its heart stands the Torre del Rellotge (Clock Tower), long a symbol of Republican agitation.

6 Plaça del Sol
Possibly the rowdiest of Gràcia's squares, Plaça del Sol ('Sun Square') is lined with bars and eateries and comes to life on long summer nights. The square was the scene of summary executions after an uprising in 1870. During the 1936–39 civil war, an air-raid shelter was installed.

7 Plaça de la Revolució de Setembre de 1868
This busy, elongated square commemorates the toppling of Queen Isabel II, a cause of much celebration in this working-class stronghold. Today, locals gather on benches for a chat or pop into one of the bars or restaurants for refreshment. For agitated stomachs, check out O' Gràcia! (p187).

8 Mercat de l'Abaceria Central
The Mercat de l'Abaceria Central opens out one block away from the revolutionary

---

WALK FACTS

Start Plaça de Joan Carles I
Finish Plaça del Diamant
Distance 2.3km
Duration 1 hour
Transport [M] Diagonal

THE SQUARES OF GRÀCIA

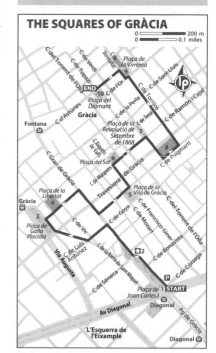

GAUDÍ OFF THE BEATEN TRACK

Gaudí, like any freelancer, was busy all over town. While his main patron was Eusebi Güell and his big projects were bankrolled by the wealthy bourgeoisie, he took on smaller jobs, too. One example is the Casa Vicens (p117) in Gràcia. Another is the Col.legi de les Teresianes (Map p122; ☎ 93 212 33 54; Carrer de Ganduxer 85-105; ℞ FGC Tres Torres), to which he added some personal touches in 1889. Although you can see parts of the wing he designed (to the right through the entrance gate) from the outside, the most unique features are those hardest to see – the distinctive parabolic arches inside. Unfortunately, it is no longer possible to visit the school. Gaudí fanatics might also want to reach Bellesguard (Map p122; Carrer de Bellesguard; ℞ FGC Avinguda Tibidabo, 🚌 60), a private house he built in 1909 on the site of the ancient palace of the Catalan count-king Martí I. You can get a reasonable idea of the house peering in from the roadside. The castlelike appearance is reinforced by the heavy stonework, generous wrought iron and a tall spire. Gaudí also worked in some characteristically playful mosaic and colourful tiles.

square. It is a no-nonsense produce market, where you can dig up cheap clothes, essential kitchen stocks or stop by for coffee at one of the cafes.

9 Plaça de la Virreina

Pleasant terraces adorn this pedestrianised square, notable for its shady trees and presided over by the 17th-century Església de Sant Joan. It was largely destroyed by anarchists during the unrest of the Setmana Tràgica (Tragic Week) of 1909 (see p27). Rebuilt by Berenguer, it was damaged again during the civil war.

10 Plaça del Diamant

Two blocks southwest of Plaça de la Virreina is this once down-at-heel square, which lies at the heart of one of the best known works of 20th-century Catalan literature, Mercè Rodoreda's eponymous novel. It also housed a civil-war air-raid shelter, to which public admission has been mooted for years, with little apparent progress.

Drinking & Nightlife p210; Eating p189; Shopping p163; Sleeping p240

Welcome to posh Barcelona. For some, the Quadrat d'Or in l'Eixample remains prime real estate, but most locals with healthy bank accounts opt for the spacious mansions with private gardens and garages that dot the 'High Zone', a loose name for the heights where Barcelona's topography climbs to the Collserola hills marking the city's inland limits.

The highest point in this wooded range is Tibidabo (512m), with its amusement park and bombastic church. It's great for the fresh air, and on a good day, you can see inland as far as Montserrat. Tibidabo gets its name from the devil, who, trying to tempt Christ, took him to a high place and said, in Latin: *'Haec omnia tibi dabo si cadens adoraberis me'* ('All this I will give you if you fall down and worship me').

Apart from expensive residential living, the other high points in La Zona Alta are the Parc de Collserola, the CosmoCaixa science museum and the monuments of Pedralbes further southwest.

The leafy(ish) suburb of Sarrià is a magnet for much of the serious money in Barcelona. Taken at its broadest, it covers the area arching between Avinguda del Tibidabo (and its cute blue tram) and Via Augusta. At the turn of the 20th century, when this was still largely untouched countryside, wealthy families built whimsical fantasy residences along Avinguda del Tibidabo. More recent are the gated, alarmed mansions further west.

The heart of Sarrià – Plaça de Sarrià and its main street, Carrer Major de Sarrià – is lined with shops, restaurants and bars. Downhill is the equally residential *barri* of Sant Gervasi de Cassoles (just Sant Gervasi to locals), between Gràcia, Avinguda Diagonal and the thundering Ronda del General Mitre freeway.

The better parts of Pedralbes, to the southwest, also attract money for their space and quiet, but there is no shortage of apartment-block clumps interspersed amid the greenery, especially along Avinguda Diagonal. This freeway has its highlights, however, such as the Palau Reial de Pedralbes (p124).

Wedged between Avinguda Diagonal and Carrer de Sants is a more middle-class residential area, Les Corts. Dominated by Camp Nou, the temple of Barcelona's star football team, it is also home to much of the modern Universitat de Barcelona campus (in an area known as the Zona Universitària).

top picks

LA ZONA ALTA

- CosmoCaixa (p120)
- Museu-Monestir de Pedralbes (p121)
- Palau Reial de Pedralbes (p124)
- Camp Nou (p121)
- Jardins del Laberint d'Horta (p134)
- Parc d'Atraccions (p133)

COSMOCAIXA Map p122

Museu de la Ciència; ☎ 93 212 60 50; www.fundacio.lacaixa.es, in Catalan & Spanish; Carrer de Teodor Roviralta 47-51; adult/senior & child under 7yr/student €3/free/2; ☺ 10am-8pm Tue-Sun & holidays; 🚌 60, 🚆 FGC Avinguda Tibidabo
This bright science museum is housed in a Modernista building (completed in 1909). Kids (and kids at heart) are fascinated by displays here and the museum has become one of the city's most popular attractions. The single greatest highlight is the recreation over 1 sq km of a chunk of flooded Amazon rainforest (Bosc Inundat). More than 100 species of Amazon flora and fauna (including anacondas, colourful poisonous frogs and caymans) prosper in this unique, living diorama in which you can even experience a tropical downpour. In another original section, the Mur Geològic, seven great chunks of rock (90 tonnes in all) have been assembled to create a 'geological wall'.

These and other displays on the lower 5th floor (the bulk of the museum is underground) cover many fascinating areas of science, from fossils to physics, and from the alphabet to outer space. To gain access to other special sections, such as the Planetari (planetarium), check for guided visits. Most of these activities are interactive and directed at children, and cost €2/1.50 per adult/child. The planetarium has been adapted so that the vision and hearing impaired may also enjoy it.

Outside, there's a nice stroll through the extensive Plaça de la Ciència, whose modest garden flourishes with Mediterranean flora.

CAMP NOU Map p122

☎ 93 496 36 00; www.fcbarcelona.com; Carrer d'Aristides Maillol; adult/senior & child €17/14; ☉ 10am-8pm Mon-Sat, 10am-2.30pm Sun & holidays early Apr-early Oct, 10am-6.30pm Mon-Sat, 10am-2.30pm Sun & holidays early Oct-early Apr; Ⓜ Palau Reial or Collblanc

Among Barcelona's most-visited museums is the Museu del Futbol Club Barcelona near the club's giant Camp Nou (aka Nou Camp) stadium. Barça is one of Europe's top football clubs, and its museum is a hit with football fans the world over.

Camp Nou, built in 1957 and enlarged for the 1982 World Cup, is one of the world's biggest stadiums, holding 99,000 people. The club has a world-record membership of 173,000.

Football fans who can't get to a game (see p227) may find a visit to the museum, with guided tour of the stadium, worthwhile. The best bits of the museum itself are the photo section, the goal videos and the views out over the stadium. Among the quirkier paraphernalia are old sports board games, the life-sized diorama of old-time dressing rooms, posters and magazines from way back and the *futbolín* (table soccer) collection. You can admire the (in at least one case literally) golden boots of great goalscorers of the past and stacks of trophies. Hi-tech multimedia displays project great moments in Barça history. Sound installations include the club's anthem and match-day sounds from the stadium.

The guided tour of the stadium takes in the team's dressing rooms, heads out through the tunnel, onto the pitch and winds up in the presidential box.

Set aside about 2½ hours for the whole visit.

MUSEU-MONESTIR DE PEDRALBES
Map p122

☎ 93 256 34 34; www.museuhistoria.bcn.cat; Baixada del Monestir 9; adult/child under 7yr/senior & student €7/free/5; ☉ 10am-5pm Tue-Sat, 10am-8pm Sun, 10am-3pm holidays Apr-Sep, 10am-2pm Tue-Sat, 10am-8pm Sun, 10am-3pm holidays Oct-Mar; Ⓡ FGC Reina Elisenda, ⎚ 22, 63, 64 or 75

This peaceful old convent was first opened to the public in 1983 and is now a museum of monastic life (the few remaining nuns have moved into more modern neighbouring buildings). It stands at the top of Avinguda de Pedralbes in a residential area that was countryside until the 20th century, but which remains a divinely quiet corner of Barcelona.

The architectural highlight is the large, elegant, three-storey cloister, a jewel of Catalan Gothic, built in the early 14th century. Following its course to the right, stop at the first chapel, the Capella de Sant Miquel, whose murals were done in 1346 by Ferrer Bassá, one of Catalonia's earliest documented painters. A few steps on is the ornamental grave of Queen Elisenda, who founded the convent. It is curious, as it is divided in two: the side in the cloister shows her dressed as a penitent widow, while the other part, an alabaster masterpiece inside the adjacent church, shows her dressed as queen.

As you head around the ground floor of the cloister, you can peer into the restored refectory, kitchen, stables, stores and a reconstruction of the infirmary – all giving a good idea of convent life. Eating in the refectory must not have been a whole lot of fun, judging by the exhortations to *Silentium* (Silence) and *Audi Tacens* (Listen and Keep Quiet) written around the walls. Harder still must have been spending one's days in the cells on the ground and 1st floors in a state of near-perpetual prayer and devotional reading.

Upstairs is a grand hall that was once the Dormidor (sleeping quarters). It was lined by tiny night cells but they were long ago removed. Today a modest collection of the monastery's art, especially Gothic devotional works, and furniture grace this space. Most is by largely unknown Catalan artists, with some 16th-century Flemish works, and was acquired thanks to the considerable wealth of the convent's mostly high-class nuns.

Next to the convent, the sober church is an excellent example of Catalan Gothic. Just west of the convent, where Carretera d'Esplugues meets Carrer del Bisbe Català, is a peaceful park, the Hort de Pedralbes.

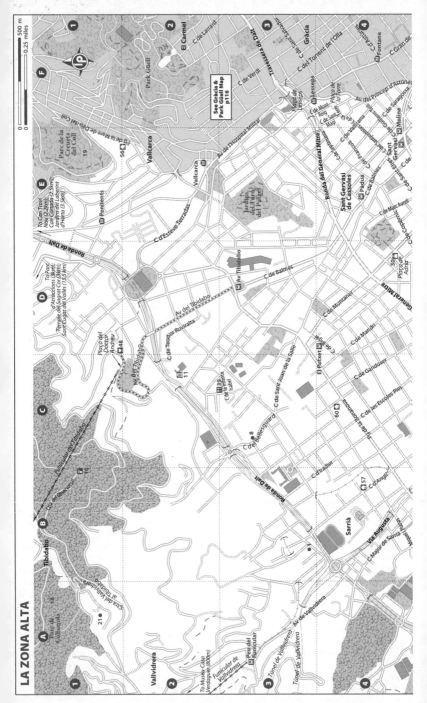

LA ZONA ALTA

See Gràcia & Park Güell Map p116

0 500 m
0 0.25 miles

1
2
3
4

F
El Carmel
Park Güell
Gràcia
C de Larraïd
C de Verdi
Travessera de Dalt
C de Sant de l'Olla
C de Fontana
C Gran de
C de Nil
Plaça de la Torre
Av del Príncep d'Astúries

E
Parc de la Creueta del Coll
Vallcarca
Ctra de la Mare de Déu del Coll
C d'Esteve Terradas
Av de l'Hospital Militar
Plaça de Lesseps
Av V-P
C de Mont-Roig
C de Sant Sve
Magí
C de Verdi
Penitents
To Can Travi Nou (2.2km); Cuina Canela (2.5km); Jardins del Laberint d'Horta (3.5km)
Jardins del Parc del Putxet
Sant Gervasi de Cassoles
Ronda del General Mitre
Pàdua
C de Balmes
Sant Gervasi
C de
C de Mare Aureli
C de Cossart

D
To Parc d'Atraccions (3km); Temple del Sagrat Cor (3km); Sant Cugat del Vallès (13.5km)
Ronda de Dalt
Av del Tibidabo
Av Tibidabo
C de Balmes
C de Teòdor Roviralta
C de Muntaner
Plaça de Adrià
General Mitre

C
Plaça del Doctor Andreu
Av del Tibidabo
Funicular del Tibidabo
Ctra de l'Observatori
11
39
C de la Infanta Isabel
C de Sant Joan de la Salle
El Putxet
C de Martíri
C de Ganduxer
60
C de les Escoles Pies

B
Tibidabo
Ronda de Dalt
C de Bellesguard
8
C de Iradier
57
C d'Anglí
Sarrià
Vía Augusta
C Major de Sarrià

A
Pg de Vallvidrera
Ctra de Vallvidrera al Tibidabo
18
21
Vallvidrera
To Museu-Casa Verdaguer (800m)
Funicular de Vallvidrera
Av de Vallvidrera
Túnel de Vallvidrera

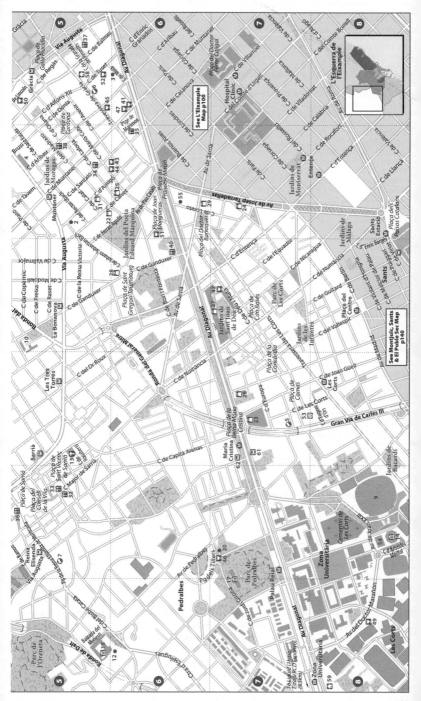

123

PALAU REIAL DE PEDRALBES Map p122

☎ 93 256 34 65; Avinguda Diagonal 686; all collections adult/student & senior €5/3, free 1st Sunday of the month & 3-6pm Sun; ⊙ museums 10am-6pm Tue-Sun, 10am-3pm holidays, park 10am-6pm daily; Ⓜ Palau Reial

Across Avinguda Diagonal from the main campus of the Universitat de Barcelona is the entrance to Parc del Palau Reial. In the park is the Palau Reial de Pedralbes, an early-20th-century building that belonged to the family of Eusebi Güell (Gaudí's patron) until they handed it over to the city in 1926 to serve as a royal residence. Among its guests have been King Alfonso XIII, the president of Catalonia and General Franco.

The palace houses three museums, two of them rolled into one and temporarily housed here.

The Museu de Ceràmica (www.museuceramica.bcn.es) has a good collection of Spanish ceramics from the 10th to 19th centuries, including work by Picasso and Miró. Spain inherited from the Muslims, and then further refined, a strong tradition in ceramics – here you can compare some exquisite work (tiles, porcelain tableware and the like) from some of the greatest centres of pottery production across Spain, including Talavera de la Reina in Castilla-La Mancha, Manises and Paterna

in Valencia, and Teruel in Aragón. There is also some fanciful ceramics from the 20th century – here they have ceased to be a tool with aesthetic value and are purely decorative. The museum also has a collection of ceramics created elsewhere in the world, from 14th century Iranian tiles to Italian Renaissance pieces. Much of this, unfortunately, is not on view at the moment.

The Disseny Hub (Design Hub; www.dhub-bcn.cat) is the fusion of two collections, along with a space for temporary exhibitions in La Ribera (see p81).

The Museu de les Arts Decoratives, across the hall from the Museu de Ceràmica on the 1st floor, brings together an eclectic assortment of furnishings, ornaments and knick-knacks dating as far back as the Romanesque period. The plush and somewhat stuffy elegance of Empire- and Isabelline-style divans can be neatly compared with some of the more tasteless ideas to emerge on the subject of seating in the 1970s.

The Museu Tèxtil i d'Indumentària (www.museu textil.bcn.es), on the 2nd floor, contains some 4000 items that range from 4th-century Coptic textiles to 20th-century local embroidery. The heart of the collection is

(Continued on page 133)

ARCHITECTURE

KIMBERLEY COOLE

Be mesmerised by the trippy detail in the stairs leading up to one of Gaudís Modernista gems, La Pedrera (p104)

Barcelona has lived through at least three great moments of architectural upheaval and creative electricity. The first came as the city, grown rich on its Mediterranean trade and empire-building, transformed into what is now the old city centre into the pageant of Gothic building that has survived in great part to this day (see p33).

The second came, also carried on the wind of boom times, in the late 19th century. The urban expansion programme known as L'Eixample (the Enlargement), designed to free the choking population from the city's bursting medieval confines, coincided with a blossoming of unfettered thinking in architecture. The Modernistas could not have wished for a more propitious period in which to exert their imagination.

Finally, the city is now perhaps riding the last rollers of a great tide of development and architectural creativity that started with the run-up to the 1992 Olympic Games in Barcelona. Plenty is still going on, but with economic crisis biting hard since 2008 and the long-inflated Spanish property market in tatters, it is, for the moment at least, destined to lose intensity.

THE MODERNISTAS

The feverish speculation that took place on the land opened up between Barcelona and Gràcia in the late 19th and early 20th centuries ensured architects had plenty of work. What the developers could not have predicted was the calibre of those architects.

Leading the way was Antoni Gaudí i Cornet (1852–1926). Born in Reus and initially trained in metalwork, he obtained his architecture degree in 1878. Gaudí personifies, and largely transcends, a movement that brought a thunderclap of innovative greatness to an otherwise middle-ranking European city. This startling wave of creativity subsided as quickly – the bulk of the Modernistas' work was done from the 1880s to about 1910.

Modernisme did not appear in isolation in Barcelona. To the British and French the style was art nouveau; to the Italians, Lo Stile Liberty; the Germans called it Jugendstil (Youth Style); and the Austrians, Sezession (Secession). Its vitality and rebelliousness can be summed up in those epithets: modern, new, liberty, youth and secession. A key uniting

TOP MODERNISTA BUILDINGS

La Pedrera (p104)
La Sagrada Família (p102)
Palau de la Música Catalana (p84)
Casa Batlló (p105)
Palau Güell (p115)
Casa Amatller (p105)
Hospital de la Santa Creu i de Santa Pau (p109)
Castell dels Tres Dragons (p86)
Palau del Baró Quadras (Casa Asia) (p111)
Casa Sayrach (p114)

NEIL SETCHFIELD

WAYNE WALTON

The medieval-looking Castell dels Tres Dragons (p86)

Hospital de la Santa Creu i de Sant Pau (p109)

The jewel in Gaudí's crown is undoubtedly the mind-blowing La Sagrada Família (p102)

KRZYSZTOF DYDYNSKI

element was the sensuous curve, implying movement, lightness and vitality. It touched painting, sculpture and the decorative arts, as well as architecture. This leitmotif informed much art nouveau thinking, in part inspired by long-standing tenets of Japanese art.

There is something misleading about the name Modernisme. It suggests 'out with the old, in with the new'. In a sense, nothing could be further from the truth. From Gaudí down, Modernista architects looked to the past for inspiration. Gothic, Islamic and Renaissance design all had something to offer. At its most playful, Modernisme was able to intelligently flout the rule books of these styles and create exciting new cocktails.

As many as 2000 buildings in Barcelona and throughout Catalonia display Modernista traces. Everything from rich bourgeois mansion blocks to churches, from hospitals to factories, went up in this 'style', a word too constraining to adequately describe the flamboyant breadth of eclecticism inherent in it.

The Architects

Gaudí and the two architects who most closely followed him in talent, Lluís Domènech i Montaner (1850–1923) and Josep Puig i Cadafalch (1867–1957), were Catalan nationalists. Puig i Cadafalch, in fact, was a senior politician and president of the Catalan Mancomunitat (a shadow parliament that demanded Catalan autonomy) from 1916 to 1923.

The political associations are significant, as Modernisme became a means of expression for Catalan identity. It barely touched the rest of Spain; where it did, one frequently finds the involvement of Catalan architects.

As Gaudí became more adventurous he appeared as a lone wolf. With age he became almost exclusively motivated by stark religious conviction and devoted much of the latter part of his life to what remains Barcelona's call sign – the unfinished La Sagrada Família (p102). His inspiration in the first instance was Gothic. But he also sought to emulate the harmony he observed in nature. Straight lines were out. The forms of plants and stones were in. Gaudí used complex string models weighted with plumb lines to make his calculations (you can see examples in the upstairs mini-museum in La Pedrera, p104). The architect's work is

DIGGING FOR MODERNISTA GEMS

The **Ruta del Modernisme** (www.rutadelmodern isme.com) is a planned route that guides you to the major Modernista sights and many lesser known ones; see p111 for details. Tourist offices can provide pamphlets and other material on a great range of Modernista buildings. Many are private houses and/or offices and cannot be entered.

Modernista-meets-Dutch at Casa Amatller (p105)

BETHUNE CARMICHAEL

at once a sublime reaching-out to the heavens, and yet an earthy appeal to sinewy movement.

This is as much the case in La Sagrada Família as in other key works, like La Pedrera and Casa Batlló (p105), where all appears a riot of the un-naturally natural, or the naturally unnatural. Not only are straight lines eliminated, but the lines between real and unreal, sober and dream-drunk, 'good sense' and play are all blurred.

For contrast, look from Casa Batlló to Puig i Cadafalch's Casa Amatller (p105) next door, where the straight line is very much in evidence. This architect also looked to the past (observe the playful Gothic-style sculpture) and to foreign influence (the gables are borrowed from the Dutch), and created a house of startling beauty and invention. Domènech i Montaner, too, looked into the Gothic past. He never simply copied, as shown by the Castell dels Tres Dragons – built as a cafe-restaurant for the Universal Exhibition in 1888 (p95) – or the Hospital de la Santa Creu i de Sant Pau (p109). In these buildings, Domènech i Montaner put his own spin on the past, in both decoration and structure.

The Materials & Decoration

Modernista architects relied on the skills of artisans that have now been all but relegated to history. There were no concrete pours (contrary to what is being done at La Sagrada Família today). Stone, unclad brick, exposed iron and steel frames, and copious use of stained glass and ceramics in decoration, were all features of the new style – and indeed it is often in the decor that Modernisme is at its most flamboyant.

The craftsmen required for these tasks were the heirs of the guild masters and had absorbed centuries of know-how about just what could and could not be done with these materials. Forged

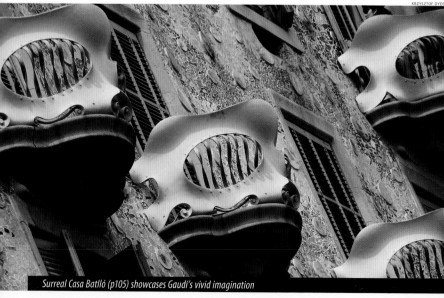

KRZYSZTOF DYDY

Surreal Casa Batlló (p105) showcases Gaudí's vivid imagination

The magnificent Modernista concert hall, designed by Domènech i Montaner, at Palau de la Música Catalana (p84)

iron and steel were newcomers to the scene, but the approach to learning how they could be used was not dissimilar to that adopted for more traditional materials. Gaudí, in particular, relied on these old skills and even ran schools in La Sagrada Família workshops to keep them alive.

Iron came into its own in this period. Nowhere is this more evident than in Barcelona's great covered markets: Mercat de la Boqueria (p57), Mercat de Sant Antoni (p186) and Mercat de la Llibertat (p186), just to name the main ones. Their grand metallic vaults not only provided shade over the produce, but were a proclamation of Barcelona's dynamism and the success of 'ignoble' materials in grand building.

The Rome-trained sculptor Eusebi Arnau (1864–1934) was one of the most popular figures called upon to decorate Barcelona's Modernista piles. The appearance of the Hospital de la Santa Creu i de Sant Pau is one of his legacies and he also had a hand in the Palau de la Música Catalana (p84) and Casa Amatller.

BARCELONA SINCE THE OLYMPIC GAMES

Barcelona's latest architectural revolution began in the 1980s. The appointment then of Oriol Bohigas (1925–), was regarded as an elder statesman for architecture, as head of urban planning by the ruling Socialist party marked a new beginning. The city set about its biggest phase of renewal since the heady days of L'Eixample.

In the run-up to the 1992 Olympics, more than 150 architects beavered away on almost 300 building and design projects. The Port Vell waterfront was transformed. The long road to resurrecting Montjuïc took off with the refurbishment of the Olympic stadium and the creation of landmarks like Santiago Calatrava's (1951–) Torre Calatrava (p144).

Post-1992, landmark buildings still went up in strategic spots, usually with the ulterior motive of trying to pull the surrounding area up by its bootstraps. One of the most emblematic of these projects is the gleaming white Museu d'Art Contemporani de Barcelona (Macba; p76), opened in 1995.

Ricard Bofill's (1939–) team designed the Teatre Nacional de Catalunya (p219) – a mix of neoclassical and modern design.

TOP FIVE CONTEMPORARY BUILDINGS

Torre Agbar (p95)
Mercat de Santa Caterina (p85).
W Barcelona (p235)
Santos Porta Fira (p130)
Edifici Fòrum (p95)

The neoclassical Teatre Nacional de Catalunya (p219)
BILL WASSMAN

Henry Cobb's (1926–) World Trade Center, at the tip of a quay jutting out into the waters of Port Vell, has been overshadowed by Bofill's new W Barcelona hotel (p235), whose spinnaker-like front looks out to sea from the south end of La Barceloneta's beach strip.

One of the biggest recent projects is Diagonal Mar. A whole district has been built (work continues) in the northeast coastal corner of the city where before there was a void. High-rise apartments, waterfront office towers and five-star hotels – among them the eye-catching Hotel Me (p236) by Dominique Perrault, mark this new district. The hovering blue, triangular Edifici Fòrum (p95) by Swiss architects Herzog & de Meuron is the most striking landmark here, along with a gigantic photovoltaic panel that provides some of the area's electricity.

The most visible addition to the skyline came in 2005. The shimmering, cucumber-shaped Torre Agbar (p95) is a product of French architect Jean Nouvel (1945–), emblematic of the city's desire to make the developing hi-tech zone of 22@ (see p47) a reality.

Southwest, on the way to the airport, the new Fira M2 trade fair along Gran Via de les Corts Catalanes (see p47) is now marked by red twisting twin landmark towers (one the Santos Porta Fira Hotel, the other offices) designed by Japanese star architect and confessed Gaudí fan, Toyo Ito (1941–).

The heart of La Ribera got a fresh look with its brand-new Mercat de Santa Caterina (p85). The market is quite a sight, with its wavy ceramic roof and tubular skeleton, designed by one of the most promising names in Catalan architecture until his premature death, Enric Miralles (1955–2000). Miralles' Edifici de Gas Natural, a 100m glass tower near the waterfront in La Barceloneta, is extraordinary for its mirror-like surface and weirdly protruding adjunct buildings, which could be giant glass cliffs bursting from the main tower's flank.

GUY MOBE

Stylish and environmentally friendly, the photovoltaic panel is a landmark in El Fòrum (p95)

The iconic Torre Agbar (p95) looms over Barcelona like a giant cucumber

JOHN HAY

THE CITY TOMORROW

Planned but with an uncertain finishing date is the complete overhaul of the Plaça de les Glòries Catalanes roundabout and surrounding area. The area will be transformed in a series of projects by MBM (Martorell, Bohigas & Mackey). Its Disseny Hub (design museum) is a daring project that looks something like a tip truck. Beneath the roundabout it will create a Cripta del Tresor (Treasure Crypt) as part of the museum space. Zaha Hadid (1950–) will chime in with her redesign of Plaça de les Arts as a cinema and leisure complex in front of the Teatre Nacional de Catalunya.

Work proceeds apace in the Diagonal Mar/Fòrum area. The most significant structure going up is a daring new sliver of a skyscraper headquarters for the national telephone company, Telefónica, designed by Enric Massip-Bosch and dubbed the Torre ZeroZero. It is being erected at the junction of Avinguda Diagonal and Passeig del Taulat.

Further away from the centre, in the long-neglected district of La Sagrera, construction of a major transport interchange for the high-speed AVE train from Madrid, metro and buses will be complemented by a characteristically out-there project from Frank Gehry (1929–), with five twisting steel and glass towers that will feature a large degree of solar energy self-sufficiency.

Meanwhile, Lord Richard Rogers (1933–) is busy transforming the former Les Arenes bull-ring on Plaça d'Espanya into a singular, circular leisure complex, with shops, cinemas, jogging track (!) and more. The facade will be maintained and completion is due by the end of 2011 (six years behind schedule).

Not to be left out, Sir Norman Foster won the design competition for FC Barcelona's planned new-look Camp Nou stadium in 2007. The overhaul will create a kind of glow-in-the-dark sponge-cake affair and is planned for completion in 2012.

Designed by Toyo Ito, this 114m-high tower (p130) marks the new trade fair area on Gran Via de les Corts Catalanes

(Continued from page 124)

the assortment of clothing from the 16th century to the 1930s.

These two collections will form the bedrock of the new Disseny Hub museum being built at Plaça de les Glòries Catalanes and due to open in 2011.

Over by Avinguda de Pedralbes are the stables and porter's lodge designed by Gaudí for the Finca Güell, as the Güell estate here was called. Known also as the Pavellons Güell (☎ 93 317 76 52; www.rutadelmod ernisme.com; guided tour adult/senior & child under 18yr €6/3; ☯ in English 10.15am & 12.15pm, in Catalan 11.15am, in Spanish 1.15pm Fri-Mon), they were built in the mid-1880s, when Gaudí was strongly impressed by Islamic architecture. Outside visiting hours, there is nothing to stop you admiring Gaudí's wrought-iron dragon gate from the exterior.

PARC D'ATRACCIONS off Map p122

☎ 93 211 79 42; www.tibidabo.es; Plaça de Tibid-abo 3-4; adult/child shorter than 0.9m/child shorter than 1.2m & senior €25/free/9; ☯ closed Jan-Feb
The reason most *barcelonins* come up to Ti-bidabo is for some thrills (but hopefully no spills) in this funfair, close to the top funicu-lar station. Among the main attractions are El Pndol, La Muntanya Russa and Hurakan. El Pndol is a giant arm holding four pas-sengers, which drops them at a speed that reaches 100km/h in a period of less than three seconds (a force of four times grav-ity) before swinging outward – not for the squeamish. La Muntanya Russa is a massive new big dipper, which at its high point af-fords wonderful views before plunging you at 80km/h through woods. Hurakan tosses its passengers about with sudden drops and stomach-turning 360-degree turns.

Far tamer options abound, from the Avió (a 1920s prop plane) to a miniature steam train and magic castle.

With your feet more firmly planted on the ground, you can visit the Dididado 4-D cinema (basically 3-D with the appropriate glasses and some sound and movement effects thrown in), which puts on 10-minute films that seem to pop out at you. A curi-ous sideline is the Museu d'Autòmats, around 50 automated puppets going as far back as 1880 and part of the original amusement park. You can still see some of these gizmos at work.

Check the website for opening times.

PARC DE COLLSEROLA Map p122

☎ 93 280 35 52; www.parccollserola.net; Carretera de l'Església 92; ⓡ FGC Peu del Funicular, then funicular to Baixador de Vallvidrera
Barcelonins needing an escape from the city without heading too far into the country-side seek out this extensive, 8000-hectare

TRANSPORT: LA ZONA ALTA

Transport options vary wildly depending on where you want to go. Metro Línia 3 will get you to the Jardins del Laberint d'Horta (Ⓜ Mundet) and Palau Reial de Pedralbes (Ⓜ Palau Reial). From the latter you could walk to the Museu-Monestir de Pedralbes. Otherwise, take an FGC train to the monastery. FGC trains are generally the easiest way of getting close to most of the sights in and around Tibidabo and the Parc del Collserola.

Tibidabo Transport

Take an FGC train to Avinguda Tibidabo from Catalunya station on Plaça de Catalunya (€1.40, 10 minutes). Outside Avinguda de Tibidabo station, hop on the *tramvia blau*, Barcelona's last surviving tram, which runs between fancy Modernista mansions (particularly Casa Roviralta at 31 Avinguda de Tibidabo) to Plaça del Doctor Andreu (one-way/return €2.80/4.30, 15 minutes, every 15 or 30 minutes 10am-8pm daily late June to early September, 10am to 6pm Saturdays, Sundays and holidays early-September to late June) – it has been doing so since 1901. On days and at times when the tram does not operate, a bus serves the route (€1.40).

From Plaça del Doctor Andreu, the Tibidabo funicular railway climbs through the woods to Plaça de Tibidabo at the top of the hill (one-way/return €2.50/4, five minutes). Departures start at 10.45am and continue until shortly after the Parc d'Atraccions closing time.

An alternative is bus T2, the 'Tibibús', from Plaça de Catalunya to Plaça de Tibidabo (€2.60, 30 minutes, every 30 to 50 minutes on Saturdays, Sundays and holidays year-round and hourly from 10.30am Monday to Friday late June to early September). Purchase tickets on the bus, which operates only when Parc d'Atraccions is open. The last bus down leaves Tibidabo 30 minutes after the park closes. You can also buy a combined ticket that includes the bus and entry to the Parc d'Atraccions (€25).

park in the hills. It is a great place to hike and bike and bristles with eateries and snack bars. Pick up a map from the Centre d'Informació (🕐 9.30am-3pm).

Aside from nature, the principal point of interest is the sprawling Museu-Casa Verdaguer (off Map122; ☎ 93 204 78 05; www.museuhistoria. bcn.cat; Vil.la Joana, Carretera de l'Església 104; admission free; 🕐 10am-2pm Sat, Sun & holidays Sep-Jul), 100m from the information centre and a short walk from the train station. Catalonia's revered writer Jacint Verdaguer (see p39) lived in this late-18th-century country house before his death on 10 July 1902. On the ground floor is a typical 19th-century country kitchen, with coal-fired stove and hobs in the middle. Upstairs you can see a raft of Verdaguer memorabilia (from original published works through to photos and documents) as you wander through the rooms. The bed in which he died remains exactly where it was in 1902. Labels are in Catalan only.

Beyond, the park has various other minor highlights, including a smattering of country chapels (some Romanesque), the ragged ruins of the 14th-century Castellciuro castle in the west, various lookout points and, to the north, the 15th-century Can Coll (🕐 9.30am-3pm Sun & holidays, closed Jul & Aug), a grand farmhouse. It's used as an environmental education centre where you can see how richer farmers lived around the 17th to 19th centuries.

Bus 111 runs between Tibidabo and Vallvidrera (passing in front of the Torre de Collserola).

TEMPLE DEL SAGRAT COR off Map p122
☎ 93 417 56 86; Plaça de Tibidabo; admission free; 🕐 8am-7pm
The Church of the Sacred Heart, looming above the top funicular station, is meant to be Barcelona's answer to Paris' Sacré-Cœur. The church, built from 1902 to 1961 in a mix of styles with some Modernista influence, is certainly as visible as its Parisian namesake, and even more vilified by aesthetes. It's actually two churches, one on top of the other. The top one is surmounted by a giant statue of Christ and has a lift (€2; 🕐 10am-7pm) to take you to the roof for the panoramic (and often wind-chilled) views.

TORRE DE COLLSEROLA Map p122
☎ 93 211 79 42; www.torredecollserola.com; Carretera de Vallvidrera al Tibidabo; adult/child & senior/student €5/3/3.50; 🕐 11am-2pm & 3.30-8pm daily Jul & Aug, 11am-2pm & 3.30-8pm Sat, Sun & holidays Sep-Jun; Funicular de Vallvidrera, then 🚌 111
Sir Norman Foster designed the 288m-high Torre de Collserola telecommunications tower, which was built between 1990 and 1992. The external glass lift to the visitors' observation area, 115m up, is as hair-raising as anything at the nearby Parc d'Atraccions. People say you can see for 70km from the top on a clear day. If ever anyone wanted to knock out Barcelona's TV and radio sets, this would be the place to do it: all transmissions are sent from here, and repeater stations across Catalonia are also controlled from this tower. Closing hours shorten in the cooler months.

JARDINS DEL LABERINT D'HORTA
off Map p122
☎ 010; Carrer dels Germans Desvalls; adult/student €2.20/1.40, free Wed & Sun; 🕐 10am-sunset daily; Ⓜ Mundet
Laid out in the twilight years of the 18th century by Antoni Desvalls, Marquès d'Alfarras i de Llupià, this carefully manicured park remained a private family idyll until the 1970s, when it was opened to the

---

A WANDER THROUGH OLD SARRIÀ

Hugging the left flank of thundering Via Augusta, the old centre of Sarrià is a largely pedestrianised haven of peace. Probably founded in the 13th century and only incorporated into Barcelona in 1921, ancient Sarrià is formed around sinuous Carrer Major de Sarrià (Map p122), today a mix of old and new, with a sprinkling of shops and restaurants. At its top end is pretty Plaça de Sarrià (from where Passeig de la Reina Elisenda de Montcada leads west to the medieval Museu-Monestir de Pedralbes), where you'll want to check out Foix de Sarrià (p190), an exclusive pastry shop. As you wander downhill, duck off into Plaça del Consell de la Vila, Plaça de Sant Vicenç de Sarrià and Carrer de Rocaberti, at the end of which is the Monestir de Santa Isabel, with its neo-Gothic cloister. Built in 1886 to house Clarissan nuns, whose order had first set up in El Raval in the 16th century, it was abandoned during the civil war and used as an air-raid shelter.

public. Many a fine party and theatrical performance was held here over the years, but it now serves as a kind of museum-park. The gardens take their name from a maze in their centre, but other paths take you past a pleasant artificial lake *(estany)*, waterfalls, a neoclassical pavilion and a false cemetery. The last is inspired by 19th-century romanticism, characterised by an obsession with a swooning, anaemic (some might say silly) vision of death.

The labyrinth, in the middle of these cool gardens (somehow odd in this environment, with modern apartments and ring roads nearby), can be surprisingly frustrating! Aim to reach the centre from the bottom end, and then exit towards the ponds and neoclassical pavilion. This is a good one for kids.

Scenes of the film adaptation of Patrick Süsskind's novel *Perfume* were shot in the gardens.

To reach the gardens, take the right exit upstairs at Mundet Metro station; on emerging, turn right and then left along the main road (with football fields on your left) and then the first left uphill to the gardens (about five minutes).

PARC DE LA CREUETA DEL COLL
Map p122

☎ 010, 93 413 24 00; www.bcn.cat/parcsijardins, in Catalan & Spanish; Passeig de la Mare de Déu del Coll 77; admission free; ☼ 10am-sunset; Ⓜ Penitents
Not far from Park Güell, this refreshing public park has a pleasant, meandering, splashing pool. The pool, along with swings, showers and snack bar, makes a relaxing family stop on hot summer days and is strictly a local affair. The park area is open all year; only the lake-pool closes outside summer. The park is set inside a deep crater left by long years of stone quarrying. On one side of it, an enormous cement sculpture, *Elogio del Agua* (Eulogy to Water) by Eduardo Chillida, is suspended. You can wander the trails around the high part of this hill-park and enjoy views of the city and Tibidabo. From the Penitents Metro station, it's a 15-minute walk. Enter from Carrer Mare de Déu del Coll.

OBSERVATORI FABRA Map p122

☎ 902 222191; www.observatorifabra.com; Carretera del Observatori; admission €9
Inaugurated in 1904, this Modernista observatory is still a functioning scientific foundation. It can be visited on certain evenings to allow people to observe the stars through its grand old telescope. Visits (generally in Catalan or Spanish) have to be booked. From mid-June to mid-September an option is to join in for the nightly Sopars amb Estrelles (Dinner under the Stars). You dine outside, tour the building, peer into the telescope and get a lecture (in Catalan) on the heavens. The evening starts at 8.30pm and costs €65 per person. The easiest way here is by taxi.

CAMP NOU TO SARRIÀ
Walking Tour
1 Camp Nou
For many, a pilgrimage to the football stadium (p121) of one of Europe's most exciting teams,

WALK FACTS
Start Camp Nou
Finish Carrer Major de Sarrià
Distance 4km
Duration 1½ hours
Transport Ⓜ Palau Reial or Collblanc

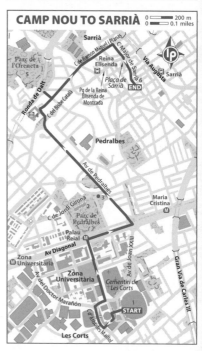

FC Barcelona, is a logical first port of call. A tour of the club's museum includes a peek inside the grounds.

2 Palau Reial de Pedralbes

Set in immaculate grounds, themselves a joy to wander, the elegant Palau Reial de Pedralbes (p124) is fronted by pools and statues. Inside are museums devoted to the decorative arts, textiles and ceramics.

3 Pavellons Güell

At the northern limit of the grounds of Palau Reial de Pedralbes is a Gaudí curiosity. The Pavellons Güell (p124) include a porter's lodge and former stables of the Güell family, the original owners of what later became the Palau Reial.

4 Museu-Monestir de Pedralbes

A stroll up pleasant Avinguda de Pedralbes from the Palau Reial leads to an oasis of another time, the peaceful Museu-Monestir de Pe-dralbes (p121). Still functioning until recently, this Gothic convent provides a tantalising glimpse into the life of nuns down the centuries.

5 Parc de l'Oreneta

Just behind the Museu-Monestir de Pedralbes rise the green slopes of the Parc de l'Oreneta. For a gentle walk and perhaps a picnic lunch, it is a quiet green space that on weekdays attracts few visitors.

6 Carrer Major de Sarrià

Back down at the convent, you could head east for Carrer Major de Sarrià, the attractive pedestrianised high street of what was the medieval village of Sarrià. Wander the pleasant streets and squares in the immediate area and try the city's best *patates braves* (potato chunks bathed in a slightly spicy tomato sauce, sometimes mixed with mayonnaise) at Bar Tomàs (p190).

Drinking & Nightlife p212; Eating p190; Sleeping p241

Montjuïc, overlooking the city centre from the southwest, may only be a hill in dimension, but it's a mountain of activity. Home to some of the city's finest art collections (including the Museu Nacional d'Art de Catalunya, CaixaForum and Fundació Joan Miró), it also hosts several lesser museums, curious sights like the Poble Espanyol, the sinister Castell de Montjuïc and a remake of Mies van der Rohe's 1920s German pavilion. The bulk of the Olympic installations of the 1992 games are also here. Throw in various parks and gardens and you have the makings of an extremely full day (or two). It has its nocturnal side too, with the engaging Font Màgica, several busy theatres and a couple of skeleton-shaking dance clubs.

top picks

MONTJUÏC, SANTS & EL POBLE SEC

- Museu Nacional d'Art de Catalunya (p138)
- CaixaForum (p139)
- Fundació Joan Miró (p143)
- Poble Espanyol (p145)
- Font Màgica (p144)

The name Montjuïc (Jewish Mountain) suggests the presence of a one-time Jewish settlement here, or at least a Jewish cemetery. Some speculate the name also comes from the Latin Mons Jovis (Mt Jupiter), after the Roman god. Before Montjuïc was turned into parks in the 1890s, its woodlands had provided food-growing and breathing space for the people of the cramped Ciutat Vella below.

Montjuïc also has a darker history: its fort was used by the Madrid government to bombard the city after political disturbances in 1842, and as a political prison up until the Franco era. The first main burst of building on Montjuïc came in the 1920s, when it was chosen as the stage for Barcelona's 1929 World Exhibition. The Estadi Olímpic, the Poble Espanyol and some museum buildings date from this time. Montjuïc got a thorough makeover for the 1992 Olympics, and it is home to the Olympic stadium and swimming complex.

For information, head for the Centre Gestor del Parc de Montjuïc in the Font del Gat building (a nice late-Modernista job done in 1919 by Puig i Cadafalch), a short walk off Passeig de Santa Madrona, southeast of the Museu Etnològic. It also has a pleasant bar-restaurant. A couple of other info points operate around the park.

The south side of the hill is bounded by the container port to the southeast and, beyond the southwest cemeteries, the Zona Franca commercial zone.

Sloping down the north face of the hill is the tight warren of working-class El Poble Sec ('Dry Village', so called because its first fountain was only installed in 1854). Though short on sights, it hides various interesting bars and eateries. The only reminders of its more industrial past are the three chimney stacks making up the Parc de les Tres Xemeneies (Three Chimneys Park) on Avinguda del Paral.lel. They belonged to La Canadenca, an enormous power station. The avenue itself was, until the 1960s, the centre of Barcelona nightlife, crammed with theatres and cabarets. A handful of theatres and cinemas survive, and one, the Sala Apolo, managed to convert itself successfully into a club.

El Poble Sec, birthplace of popular singer Joan Manuel Serrat (p41), was long a working-class district, left wing and Republican in orientation. Because it lay downhill from the castle on Montjuïc, development was largely prohibited until the second half of the 19th century. Many of the working-class Catalans have left, replaced by immigrants (now more than a quarter of the local populace), predominantly Caribbean and Latin American.

The swirling traffic roundabout of Plaça d'Espanya marks the boundary between Montjuïc and the *barri* of Sants. From the roundabout unrolls the most majestic approach to the mountain, Avinguda de la Reina Maria Cristina, flanked by buildings of the Fira de Barcelona, the city's main fairgrounds.

Before you rises the monumental facade of the Palau Nacional (which houses the Museu Nacional d'Art de Catalunya). Approaching Montjuïc on foot this way has the advantage of allowing you to follow a series of escalators up to Avinguda de l'Estadi.

Where the grid system of l'Eixample peters out listlessly at Carrer de Tarragona, Sants begins, marked by the city's main railway station. Once a village, the working-class *barri* of Sants was gradually swallowed up by Barcelona in the late 19th century.

Avinguda de Madrid divides Sants from Les Corts, which we have included in the La Zona Alta section (p120).

MUSEU NACIONAL D'ART DE CATALUNYA Map p140

MNAC; ☎ 93 622 03 76; www.mnac.cat; Mirador del Palau Nacional; adult/senior & child under 15yr/student €8.50/free/6, free 1st Sun of month; ☷ 10am-7pm Tue-Sat, 10am-2.30pm Sun & holidays; Ⓜ Espanya

From vantage points across the city, the bombastic neobaroque silhouette of the so-called Palau Nacional (National Palace) can be seen halfway up the slopes of Montjuïc. Built for the 1929 World Exhibition and restored in 2005, it houses a vast collection of mostly Catalan art spanning the early Middle Ages to the early 20th century. The high point is the collection of extraordinary Romanesque frescoes, but there is plenty of other material to keep you busy for hours.

Built under the centralist dictatorship of Miguel Primo de Rivera, there is a whiff of irony in the fact that it has come to be one of the city's prime symbols of the region's separate, Catalan identity.

Head first to the Romanesque art section, considered the most important concentration of early medieval art in the world. It consists of frescoes, woodcarvings and painted altar frontals (low-relief wooden panels that were the forerunners of the elaborate altarpieces that adorned later churches), transferred from country churches across northern Catalonia early in the 20th century. The insides of several churches have been recreated and the frescoes – in some cases fragmentary, in others extraordinarily complete and alive with colour – have been placed as they were when *in situ*.

The two most striking fresco sets follow one after the other. The first, in Àmbit 5, is a magnificent image of Christ in Majesty done around 1123. Based on the text of the Apocalypse, we see Christ enthroned on a rainbow with the world at his feet. He holds a book open with the words *Ego Sum Lux Mundi* (I am the Light of the World) and is surrounded by the four Evangelists. The images were taken from the apse of the Església de Sant Climent de Taüll in northwest Catalonia. In Àmbit

7 are frescoes done around the same time in the nearby Església de Santa Maria de Taüll. This time the central image taken from the apse is of the Virgin Mary and Christ Child. These images were not mere decoration. Try to set yourself in the mind of the average medieval citizen: illiterate, ignorant, fearful and in most cases eking out a subsistence living. These images transmitted the basic personalities and tenets of the faith and were accepted at face value by most.

Opposite the Romanesque collection on the ground floor is the museum's Gothic art section. In these halls you can see Catalan Gothic painting (look out especially for the work of Bernat Martorell in Àmbit 32 and Jaume Huguet in Àmbit 34), and that of other Spanish and Mediterranean regions. Among Martorell's works figure images of the martyrdom of St Vincent and St Llúcia. Huguet's *Consagració de Sant Agustí*, in which St Augustine is depicted as a bishop, is dazzling in its detail.

As the Gothic collection draws to a close, you pass through two separate and equally eclectic private collections, the Cambò bequest and works from the Thyssen-Bornemisza collections. Works by

THE FRESCO STRIPPERS

The Stefanoni brothers, Italian art restorers, brought the secrets of *strappo* (stripping of frescoes from walls), to Catalonia in the early 1900s. At first in the employ of American collectors who wanted to strip out the best of the region's Romanesque art from churches and chapels in the Pyrenees to send to US collectors and museums (such as Boston's Museum of Fine Arts), the Stefanoni were then hired by Barcelona's museum authorities to do the work for them instead. The Stefanoni would cover frescoes with a sheet of fabric, stuck on with a glue made of cartilage. When dry, this allowed the image to be stripped off the wall and rolled up. For three years the Stefanoni roamed the Pyrenean countryside, stripping churches and chapels and sending the rolls back to Barcelona, where they were eventually put back up on walls and inside purpose-built church apses to reflect how they had appeared *in situ*.

the Venetian Renaissance masters Veronese (1528–88), Titian (1490–1557) and Canaletto (1697–1768) feature, along with those of Rubens (1577–1640) and even England's Gainsborough (1727–88).

From here you pass into the great domed central hall. This area is sometimes used for concerts. Up on the next floor, after a series of rooms devoted to mostly minor works by a variety of 17th-century Spanish Old Masters, the collection turns to modern Catalan art. It is an uneven affair, but it is worth looking out for Modernista painters Ramon Casas (Àmbit 71) and Santiago Rusiñol (Àmbit 72). Also on show are items of Modernista furniture and decoration.

If you have any energy left, check out the photography section, which encompasses work from mostly Catalan snappers from the mid-19th century on. Coin collectors will enjoy the Gabinet Numismàtic de Catalunya, with coins from Roman Spain, medieval Catalonia and some engaging notes from the civil war days.

After all this, you can relax in the museum restaurant, which offers great views north towards Plaça d'Espanya. Finally, students can use the Biblioteca del MNAC (⏰ 10am-6pm Mon-Fri, 10am-2.30pm Sat), the city's main art reference library.

The museum's displays account for little more than 20% of its holdings. The rest is kept in storerooms that, since 2010, can be visited on a guided tour (€5). Since the displays themselves already represent an enormous chunk to absorb in a day, a separate day should be set aside for visiting the reserves.

CAIXAFORUM Map p140

☎ 93 476 86 00; www.fundacio.lacaixa.es, in Catalan & Spanish; Avinguda de Francesc Ferrer i Guàrdia 6-8; admission free; ⏰ 10am-8pm Tue-Fri & Sun, 10am-10pm Sat; Ⓜ Espanya

The Caixa building society prides itself on its involvement in (and ownership of) art, in particular all that is contemporary. Its premier art expo space in the city hosts part of the bank's extensive collection from around the globe. The setting is a completely renovated former factory, the Fàbrica Casaramona, an outstanding Modernista brick structure designed by Puig i Cadafalch. From 1940 to 1993 it housed the First Squadron of the police cavalry unit – 120 horses in all.

Now it is home to major exhibition space. On occasion portions of La Caixa's own collection of 800 works of modern and contemporary art go on display, but more often than not major international exhibitions are the key draw (in 2010 anything

MONTJUÏC, SANTS & EL POBLE SEC

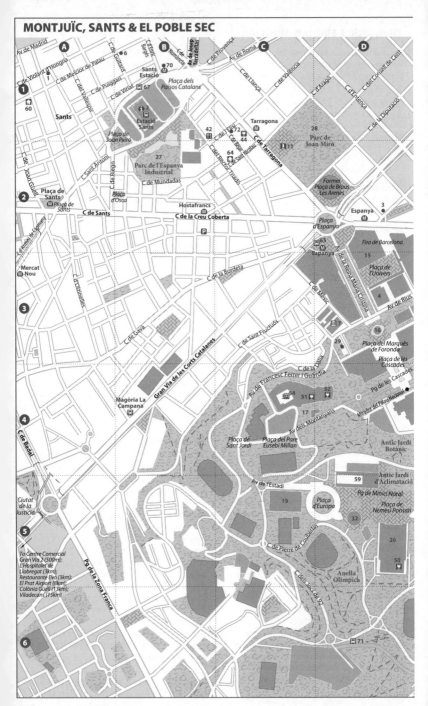

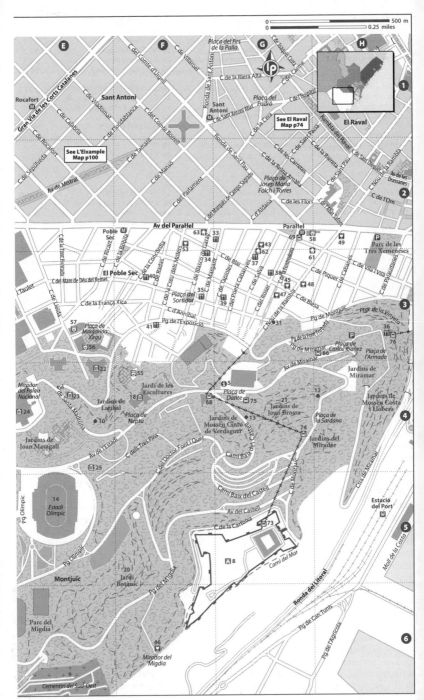

from 2009 press photographers to an extensive exhibition on film-maker Federico Fellini).

In the courtyard where the police horses used to drink is a steel tree designed by the Japanese architect Arata Isozaki. Musical recitals are sometimes held in the museum, especially in the warmer months.

CASTELL DE MONTJUÏC & AROUND
Map p140

☎ 93 329 86 13; ⏱ 9am-9pm Tue-Sun Apr-Sep, 9am-7pm Tue-Sun Oct-Mar; 🚌 193, Telefèric
The forbidding Castell (castle or fort) de Montjuïc dominates the southeastern heights of Montjuïc and enjoys commanding views over the Mediterranean. It dates, in its present form, to the late 17th and 18th centuries. For most of its dark history, it has been used to watch over the city and as a political prison and killing ground. Anarchists were executed here around the end of the 19th century, fascists during the civil war and Republicans after it – most notoriously Lluís Companys in 1940. The castle is surrounded by a network of ditches and walls (from which its strategic position over the city and port become clear).

Until 2009, the castle was home to a somewhat fusty old military museum, closed since the Ministry of Defence handed the fortress over to the city after protracted negotiations. The artillery that once stood in the central courtyard has been removed, but some of the seaward big guns remain in place.

In the coming years, it is planned to establish an international peace centre in the castle, as well as a display on its history. There will also be an interpretation centre dedicated to Montjuïc. While waiting for this to happen, a modest temporary exhibition has been established in one of the castle's bastions, on the right as soon as you enter. Called Barcelona Té Castell (Barcelona Has a Castle), it explains something of the place's history as well as detailing plans for its future. Perhaps when all this is done, the tombstones (some dating to the 11th century) from the one-time Jewish cemetery on Montjuïc will get a more imaginative exhibition space than the drab room once set aside for them in the military museum.

The views from the castle and the surrounding area looking over the sea, port and city below are the best part of making the trip up.

Catalan and Spanish speakers can join free guided tours of the castle on Saturdays and Sundays (11.30am in Catalan, 1pm in Spanish). Group tours (€65 to €80) can also be booked (also in English and French).

Around the seaward foot of the castle is an airy walking track, the Camí del Mar, which offers breezy views of city and sea. Towards the foot of this part of Montjuïc, above the thundering traffic of the main road to Tarragona, the Jardins de Mossèn Costa i Llobera (admission free; 10am-sunset) have a good collection of tropical and desert plants – including a veritable forest of cacti. Near the Estació Parc Montjuïc funicular/Telefèric station are the ornamental Jardins de Mossèn Cinto de Verdaguer (admission free; 10am-sunset). These sloping, verdant gardens are home to various kinds of bulbs and aquatic plants. Many of the former (some 80,000) have to be replanted each year. They include tulips, narcissus, crocus, varieties of dahlia and more. The aquatic plants include lotus and water lilies.

From the Jardins del Mirador, opposite the Mirador Transbordador Aeri (Telefèric) station, you have fine views over the port of Barcelona. A little further downhill, the Jardins de Joan Brossa (admission free; 10am-sunset) are charming, landscaped gardens on the site of a former amusement park near Plaça de la Sardana. These gardens contain many Mediterranean species, from cypresses to pines and a few palms. There are swings and things, thematic walking trails and some good city views.

FUNDACIÓ JOAN MIRÓ Map p140

93 443 94 70; www.bcn.fjmiro.es; Plaça de Neptu; permanent exhibitions adult/senior & child €8.50/6, temporary exhibitions €4/3; 10am-8pm Tue, Wed, Fri & Sat, 10am-9.30pm Thu, 10am-2.30pm Sun & holidays Jul-Sep, 10am-7pm Tue, Wed, Fri & Sat, 10am-9.30pm Thu, 10am-2.30pm Sun & holidays Jun-Sep; 50, 55, 193 or funicular
This shimmering white temple to the art of one of the stars of the 20th-century Spanish firmament rests amid the greenery of its privileged position on the mountain.

Joan Miró, the city's best-known 20th-century artistic progeny, bequeathed this art foundation to his hometown in 1971. Its light-filled buildings, designed by close friend and architect Josep Lluís Sert (who also built Miró's Mallorca studios), are crammed with seminal works, from Miró's earliest timid sketches to paintings from his last years.

The foundation holds the greatest single collection of the artist's work, comprising around 220 of his paintings, 180 sculptures, some textiles and more than 8000 drawings spanning his entire life. Only a small portion is ever on display.

The exhibits give a broad-brush impression of Miró's artistic development. The first couple of rooms (11 and 12) hold various works, including a giant tapestry in his trademark primary colours.

Room 13, a basement space called Espai 13, leads you downstairs to a small room for temporary exhibitions.

Next, oddly enough, comes room 16, the Sala Joan Prats, with works spanning the early years until 1931. Here, you can see how the young Miró moved away, under surrealist influence, from his *relative* realism (for instance his 1917 painting *Ermita de Sant Joan d'Horta*) towards his own unique, recognisable style.

This theme is continued upstairs in room 17, the Sala Pilar Juncosa (named after his wife), which covers the years 1932–55. Before coming up here, you may want to pop down into the basement rooms 14 and 15, together labelled Homenatge a Joan Miró (Homage to Joan Miró), with photos of the artist, a 15-minute video on his life and a series of works from some of his contemporaries, like Henry Moore, Antoni Tàpies, Eduardo Chillida, Yves Tanguy, Fernand Léger and others.

Back upstairs, rooms 18–19 contain masterworks of the years 1956–83, and room 20 a series of paintings done on paper. Room 21 hosts a selection of the private Katsuka collection of Miró works from

WHAT'S HAPPENING ON THE HILL?

To find out what temporary art exhibitions are on at Montjuïc's main art centres (the Museu Nacional d'Art de Catalunya, CaixaForum and the Fundació Joan Miró), take a look at ArtMontjuïc (www.artmontjuic.cat).

1914 to the 1970s. Room 22 rounds off the permanent exhibition with some major paintings and bronzes from the 1960s and 1970s.

The museum library contains Miró's personal book collection.

Outside on the eastern flank of the museum is the Jardí de les Escultures (admission free; ☺ 10am-dusk), a small garden with various pieces of modern sculpture (it is also a wi-fi zone).

ESTADI OLÍMPIC Map p140

Avinguda de l'Estadi; admission free; ☺ 10am-6pm Oct-Mar, 10am-8pm Apr-Sep; ☒ 50, 61 or 193

First opened in 1929, the 65,000-capacity stadium was given a complete overhaul for the 1992 Olympics. You enter from the northern end, in the shadow of the dish in which the Olympic flame burned. At the opening ceremony a long-range archer set it alight by spectacularly depositing a flaming arrow into it. Well, more or less. He actually missed, but the organisers had foreseen this possibility. The dish was alive with gas, so the arrow only had to pass within two metres of it to set the thing on fire. The stadium is used for occasional sporting events and major concerts (the Rolling Stones have played here).

Just east over the road, the Museu Olímpic i de l'Esport (☎ 93 292 53 79; www.fundaciobarcelona olimpica.es; Avinguda de l'Estadi 60; adult/senior & child under 14yr/student €4/free/2.50; ☺ 10am-8pm Tue-Mon Apr-Sep, 10am-6pm Tue-Sat, 10am-2.30pm Sun Oct-Mar) is an all-flashing, all-dancing, information-packed interactive museum dedicated to sport and the Olympic Games. After picking up tickets, you wander down a ramp that snakes below ground level and is lined with

displays on the history of sport, starting with the ancients. From the original Olympics you pass all sorts of objects: anything from a 1930s discus and early-20th-century dumb-bells to a McLaren Formula 1 car and a section devoted to sport and colonialism (ie, games like cricket and polo, which flourished in India under the British Raj). On the basement floor is a special section devoted to Barcelona's 1992 Olympics, with another on the collection of Olympic stamps, art and more of the former head of the International Olympic Committee, Barcelona's Juan Antonio Samaranch.

West of the stadium is the Palau Sant Jordi, a 17,000-capacity indoor sports, concert and exhibition hall opened in 1990 and designed by Isozaki.

The Anella Olímpic (Olympic Ring; ☺ 8am-9pm Apr-Sep, 8am-7pm Oct-Mar) describes the whole group of sports installations created for the games to the west of the *estadi*. Westernmost is the Institut Nacional d'Educació Física de Catalunya (INEFC), a kind of sports university, designed by Ricard Bofill. Past a circular arena, the Plaça d'Europa, with the slender white Torre Calatrava communications tower behind it, is the Piscines Bernat Picornell building, where the swimming events were held (now open to the public; see p225). Separating the pool from the Estadi Olímpic is a pleasant garden, the Antic Jardí d'Aclimatació. You can wander (or skate) around this whole area, graced with little waterfalls and green areas.

FONT MÀGICA Map p140

Avinguda de la Reina Maria Cristina; admission free; ☺ every 30min 7-9pm Fri & Sat Oct-late Jun, 9-11.30pm Thu-Sun late Jun-Sep; Ⓜ Espanya

With a flourish, the 'Magic Fountain' erupts into a feast of musical, backlit liquid life. It is extraordinary how an idea that was cooked up for the 1929 World Exposition has, since the 1992 Olympics, again become a magnet. On hot summer evenings especially, this 15-minute spectacle (repeated several times throughout the evening) mesmerises onlookers. The main fountain of a series that sweeps up the hill from Avinguda de la Reina Maria Cristina to the grand facade of the Palau Nacional, Font Màgica is a unique performance in which the water at times looks like seething fireworks or a mystical cauldron of colour. On the last evening of the Festes de la Mercè in September, a particularly spectacular display includes fireworks.

POBLE ESPANYOL Map p140

☎ 93 508 63 00; www.poble-espanyol.com; Avinguda de Francesc Ferrer i Guàrdia; adult/child 4-12yr/senior & student €8.50/5.50/6.50; ☯ 9am-8pm Mon, 9am-2am Tue-Thu, 9am-4am Fri, 9am-5am Sat, 9am-midnight Sun; Ⓜ Espanya, 🚌 50, 61 or 193
Welcome to Spain! All of it! This 'Spanish Village' is both a cheesy souvenir hunters' haunt and an intriguing scrapbook of Spanish architecture built for the Spanish crafts section of the 1929 World Exhibition. You can wander from Andalucía to the Balearic Islands in the space of a couple of hours' slow meandering, visiting surprisingly good copies of characteristic buildings from all the country's regions.

You enter from beneath a towered medieval gate from Ávila. Inside, to the right, is an information office with free maps. Straight ahead from the gate is the Plaza Mayor (Town Square), surrounded with mainly Castilian and Aragonese buildings. It is sometimes the scene of summer concerts. Elsewhere you'll find an Andalucian barrio, a Basque street, Galician and Catalan quarters and even a Dominican monastery (at the eastern end). The buildings house dozens of restaurants, cafes, bars, craft shops and workshops (such as glassmakers), and some souvenir stores.

Spare some time for the Fundació Fran Daurel (☎ 93 423 41 72; www.fundaciofrandaurel.com; admission free; ☯ 10am-7pm), an eclectic collection of 300 works of art including sculptures, prints, ceramics and tapestries by modern artists ranging from Picasso and Miró to more contemporary figures, including Miquel Barceló. The foundation also has a sculpture garden, boasting 27 pieces, nearby within

the grounds of Poble Espanyol (look for the Montblanc gate). Frequent temporary exhibitions broaden the offerings further.

At night the restaurants, bars and especially the discos become a lively corner of Barcelona's nightlife.

Children's groups can participate in the Joc del Sarró (admission €5; ☯ 10am-6pm). Accompanied by adults, the kids go around the poble seeking the answers to various mysteries outlined in a kit distributed to each group. Languages catered for include English.

PAVELLÓ MIES VAN DER ROHE Map p140

☎ 93 423 40 16; www.miesbcn.com; Avinguda de Francesc Ferrer i Guàrdia; adult/child under 18yr/student €4.50/free/2.30; ☯ 10am-8pm; Ⓜ Espanya
Just to the west of Font Màgica is a strange building. In 1929 Ludwig Mies van der Rohe erected the Pavelló Alemany (German Pavilion) for the World Exhibition. Now known by the name of its architect, it was removed after the show. Decades later, a society was formed to rebuild what was in hindsight considered a key work in the trajectory of one of the world's most important modern architects. Reconstructed in the 1980s, it is a curious structure of interlocking planes – walls of marble or glass, ponds of water, ceilings and just plain nothing, a temple to the new urban environment. A graceful copy of a statue of Alba (Dawn) by Berlin sculptor Georg Kolbe (1877–1947) stands in one of the exterior areas.

MUSEU D'ARQUEOLOGIA DE CATALUNYA Map p140

☎ 93 423 21 49; www.mac.cat; Passeig de Santa Madrona 39-41; adult/child under 16yr & senior/student €3/free/2.10; ☯ 9.30am-7pm Tue-Sat, 10am-2.30pm Sun; 🚌 55 or 193
This archaeology museum, housed in what was the Graphic Arts palace during the 1929 World Exposition, covers Catalonia and related cultures from elsewhere in Spain. Items range from copies of pre-Neanderthal skulls to lovely Carthaginian necklaces and jewel-studded Visigothic crosses. There's good material on the Balearic Islands (rooms X to XIII) and Empúries (Emporion), the Greek and Roman city on the Costa Brava (rooms XIV and XVII). The Roman finds upstairs were mostly dug up in and around Barcelona. The most beautiful piece is a mosaic depicting Les Tres Gràcies (The

Three Graces), unearthed near Plaça de Sant Jaume in the 18th century. Another is of Bellerophon and the Chimera. In the final room, dedicated to the dying centuries of the Roman world, a beautiful golden disk depicting Medusa stands out. The museum is slowly being refurbished and you will almost certainly find some rooms shut.

MUSEU ETNOLÒGIC Map p140

☎ 93 424 64 02; www.museuetnologic.bcn.cat, in Catalan; Passeig de Santa Madrona 16-22; adult/child under 12yr/senior & student €3.50/free/1.75, free 1st Sun of month; ☽ noon-8pm Tue-Sat, 11am-3pm Sun late Jun-late Sep, 10am-7pm Tue & Thu, 10am-2pm Wed & Fri-Sun late Sep-late Jun; ⊜ 55

Barcelona's ethnology museum presents a curious permanent collection that explores how various societies have worked down the centuries, as seen through collections of all sorts of objects. It starts with a general look at ethnology in an introductory section, Orígens (Origins). Thereafter, collections take us first to the Pyrenees region in Catalonia (including traditional instruments and archive images of traditional dances) and Salamanca in central Spain, to look at now largely extinct rural society. Further collections take in Japan, Nuristan (an area straddling Pakistan and Afghanistan), Morocco, Ethiopia, Australia, Papua New Guinea and the Americas (in particular Ecuador's Amazon region). What is on show changes on occasion as only a fraction of the museum's collections can go on show at any one time. Objects from many other countries are wheeled out every now and then, including for temporary exhibitions.

JARDÍ BOTÀNIC Map p140

☎ 93 426 49 35; www.jardibotanic.bcn.es; Carrer del Doctor Font i Quer 2; adult/child under 16yr/student €3.50/free/1.70, free last Sun of month; ☽ 10am-8pm Jun-Aug, 10am-7pm Apr, May & Sep, 10am-6pm Feb, Mar & Oct, 10am-5pm Nov-Jan; ⊜ 50, 61 or 193

Across the road to the south of the *estadi*, this botanical garden was created atop what was an old municipal dump. The theme is Mediterranean flora and the collection of some 40,000 plants includes 1500 species that thrive in areas with a climate similar to that of the Med, including the Eastern Mediterranean, Spain (including the Balearic and Canary Islands), North Africa, Australia, California, Chile and South Africa.

The garden is a work in progress and the plan is to reach 4000 species.

PLAÇA D'ESPANYA & AROUND

Map p140

Plaça d'Espanya; Ⓜ Espanya

The whirling roundabout of Plaça d'Espanya, distinguished by its so-called Venetian towers (because they are vaguely reminiscent of the belltower in Venice's St Mark's Sq), is flanked on its northern side by the facade of the former Plaça de Braus Les Arenes bullring. Built in 1900 and once one of three bullrings in the city, it is being converted into a shopping and leisure centre by Lord Richard Rogers (due for completion in 2011, six years late).

Behind the bullring is the Parc de Joan Miró, created in the 1980s – worth a quick detour for Miró's phallic sculpture *Dona i Ocell* (Woman and Bird) in the western corner. Locals know the park (which apart from Miró is a dispiriting affair) as the Parc de l'Escorxador (Abattoir Park), as that's what once stood here – not surprising given the proximity to the bullring.

A couple of blocks west and just south of Estació Sants is the Parc de l'Espanya Industrial. With its ponds, little waterfalls, green spaces, trees, children's swings, bar, and the odd towers that look for all the world like sci-fi prison-camp searchlight towers, it is a strange park indeed.

CEMENTIRI DEL SUD-OEST Map p140

☎ 93 484 17 00; ☽ 8am-6pm; ⊜ 193

On the hill to the south of the Anella Olímpica stretches this huge cemetery, the Cementiri del Sud-Oest or Cementiri Nou, which extends down the southern side of the hill. Opened in 1883, it's an odd combination of elaborate architect-designed tombs for rich families and small niches for the rest. It includes the graves of numerous Catalan artists and politicians. Among the big names are Joan Miró, Carmen Amaya (the flamenco dance star from La Barceloneta), Jacint Verdaguer (the 19th-century priest and poet to whom the rebirth of Catalan literature is attributed), Francesc Macià and Lluís Companys (nationalist presidents of Catalonia; Companys was executed by Franco's henchmen in the Castell de Montjuïc in 1940), Ildefons Cerdà (who designed l'Eixample) and Joan Gamper (the founder of the FC Barcelona football team, aka Hans Gamper). Many victims of Franco's postwar revenge were buried in unmarked graves here – the last of them in 1974. From the 193 bus stop, it's about an 800m walk southwest. Otherwise, Bus 38 from Plaça de Catalunya stops close to the cemetery entrance.

REFUGI 307 Map p140

☎ 93 256 21 22; www.museuhistoria.bcn.cat; Carrer Nou de la Rambla 169; admission incl tour €3; ☽ tours 11am-2pm Sat & Sun; Ⓜ Paral.lel

Barcelona was the city most heavily bombed from the air during the Spanish Civil War and was dotted with more than 1300 air-raid shelters. Local citizens started digging this one under a fold of Montjuïc in March 1937. In the course of the next two years, the web of tunnels was slowly extended to 200m, with a theoretical capacity for 2000 people. People were not allowed to sleep overnight in the shelter, as when raids were not being carried out work continued on its extension. Vaulted to displace the weight above the shelter to the clay brick walls (clay is porous, which allowed the bricks to absorb the shock waves of falling bombs without cracking), the tunnels were narrow and winding. Coated in lime to seal out humidity and whitewashed to relieve the sense of claustrophobia, they became a second home for many El Poble Sec folks.

When the civil war ended, Franco had some extensions made as he considered the option of entering WWII on Hitler's side. When he dropped that idea, this and other shelters were largely abandoned. In the tough years of famine and rationing during the 1940s and 1950s, families from Granada took up residence here rather than in the shacks springing up all over the area, as poor migrants arrived from southern Spain. Later on, an enterprising fellow grew mushrooms here for sale on the black market.

The half-hour tours (in Catalan or Spanish; book ahead for English or French) explain all this and more.

VIEWS & GARDENS ON MONTJUÏC
Walking Tour
1 Castell de Montjuïc

Long synonymous with oppression, the dark history of Castell de Montjuïc (p142) is today overshadowed by the fine views it commands over the city and sea. The ride up on the Telefèric is the perfect way to get there. And from here on it's all downhill!

2 Jardins del Mirador

A short stroll down the road or the parallel Camí del Mar pedestrian trail leads to

---

WALK FACTS

Start Castell de Montjuïc
Finish Museu Nacional d'Art de Catalunya
Distance 2.5km
Duration 1 hour
Transport Ⓜ Telefèric de Montjuïc (Castell)

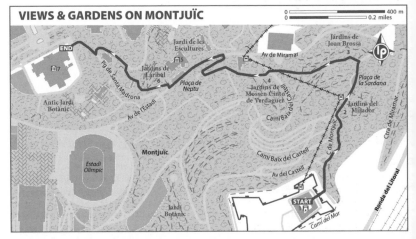

VIEWS & GARDENS ON MONTJUÏC

another fine viewpoint over the city and sea, the Jardins del Mirador. Take a weight off on the park benches or pick up a snack.

3 Jardins de Joan Brossa

Further downhill is the multi-tiered Jardins de Joan Brossa. The entrance is on the left just beyond Plaça de la Sardana, with the sculpture of people engaged in the classic Catalan folk dance. More fine city views can be had from among the many Mediterranean trees and plants.

4 Jardins de Mossèn Cinto de Verdaguer

Exiting the Jardins de Joan Brossa at the other (west) side, you cross Camí Baix del Castell to the painstakingly laid-out Jardins de Mossèn Cinto de Verdaguer. This is a beautiful setting for a slow meander among tulip beds and water lilies.

5 Fundació Joan Miró

Joan Miró left a broad collection of his works to the city in his specially designed hillside foundation (p143). You can discover his earliest, tentative artistic attempts and continue right through to the characteristic broad canvases for which he is known.

6 Jardins de Laribal

Dropping away behind the Fundació Joan Miró, the Jardins de Laribal are a combination of terraced gardens linked by paths and stairways. The pretty sculpted watercourses along some of the stairways were inspired by Granada's Muslim-era palace of El Alhambra. Stop for a snack at the Centre Gestor del Parc de Montjuïc (Map p140; Passeig de Santa Madrona 28; 10am-8pm Apr-Oct, 10am-6pm Nov-Mar).

7 Museu Nacional d'Art de Catalunya

Whichever direction you are coming from, it is worth making the effort to reach this ochre beast of a museum (p138) and see one of Europe's finest collections of Romanesque art, salvaged from countless churches and chapels sprinkled over northern Catalonia. Further collections range from Gothic to Modernisme.

THE OUTSKIRTS

Two key architectural sights lie on the edge of town. Gaudí's crypt in the Colònia Güell provides eye-catching insights into his theories of architecture, while the grand cloisters of the monastery at Sant Cugat del Vallès take us travelling back centuries. Also curious is the immigration museum on the northwest edge of town.

Sant Cugat del Vallès lies about 15km north of central Barcelona, over the Serra de Collserola hills. The Colònia Güell is in Santa Coloma de Cervelló, about 15km west of Barcelona on the west bank of the Riu Llobregat.

COLÒNIA GÜELL off Map p140

☎ 93 630 58 07; www.coloniaguell.net; Carrer de Claudi Güell 6, Santa Coloma de Cervelló; adult/child under 10yr/student & senior €5/free/3.50; ❤ 10am-2pm & 3-7pm Mon-Fri, 10am-3pm Sat, Sun & holidays May-Oct, 10am-3pm daily Nov-Apr; ⑧ FGC lines S4, S7, S8 or S33

Apart from La Sagrada Família, Gaudí's last big project was the creation of a utopian textile workers' complex for his magnate patron Eusebi Güell outside Barcelona at Santa Coloma de Cervelló. Gaudí's main role was to erect the colony's church. Work began in 1908 but the idea fizzled eight years later and Gaudí only finished the crypt, which still serves as a working church.

This structure is a key to understanding what the master had in mind for his *magnum opus*, La Sagrada Família. The mostly brick-clad columns that support the ribbed vaults in the ceiling are inclined at all angles in much the way you might expect trees in a forest to lean. That effect was deliberate, but also grounded in physics. Gaudí worked out the angles so that their load would be transmitted from the ceiling to the earth without the help of extra buttressing. Similar thinking lay behind his plans for La Sagrada Família, whose Gothic-inspired structure would tower above any medieval building, without requiring a single buttress. Gaudí's hand is visible down to the wavy design of the pews. The primary colours in the curvaceous plant-shaped stained-glass windows are another reminder of the era in which the crypt was built.

Near the church spread the cute brick houses designed for the factory workers and still inhabited today. A short stroll away, the 23 factory buildings of a Modernista industrial complex, idle since the 1970s, were brought back to life in the early 2000s, with shops and businesses moving into the renovated complex.

In a five-room display with audiovisual and interactive material, the history and life of the industrial colony and the story of Gaudí's church are told in colourful fashion. Audioguides (€2) are available for visiting the site.

SANT CUGAT DEL VALLÈS off Map p122

☎ 93 675 99 51; www.museu.santcugat.cat, in Catalan; Plaça Octavià, Sant Cugat del Vallès; adult/senior & child under 16yr/student €3/free/1.50; ❤ 10am-1.30pm & 3-8pm Tue-Sat, 10am-2.30pm Sun & holidays Jun-Sep, 10am-1.30pm & 3-7pm Tue-Sat, 10am-2.30pm Sun & holidays Oct-May; ⑧ FGC lines S1, S2, S5 or S55

Marauding Muslims razed the one-time Roman encampment–turned–Visigothic monastery of Sant Cugat del Vallès to the ground in the 8th century. These things happen, so, after the Christians got back in the saddle, work on a new, fortified Benedictine monastic complex was stoically begun. What you see today is a combination of Romanesque and Gothic buildings. The lower floor of the cloister is a fine demonstration of Romanesque design and it's the principal reason for coming. In particular, the decoration of the 72 pairs of columns, with scenes ranging from pious scriptural events to completely medieval fantasy, is captivating. The former monastery holds occasional temporary exhibitions.

From the train station, head left along Avinguda d'Alfonso Sala Conde de Egara and turn right down Carrer de Ruis i Taulet, followed by a left into Carrer de Santiago Rusiñol, which leads to the monastery.

MUSEU D'HISTÒRIA DE LA IMMIGRACIÓ DE CATALUNYA off Map p96

☎ 93 381 26 06; www.mhic.net; Carretera de Mataró 124, Sant Adriàde Besòs; admission free; ❤ 10am-2pm & 5-8pm Tue & Thu, 10am-2pm Wed, Fri & Sat mid-Apr–Sep, 10am-2pm & 4-7pm Tue & Thu, 10am-2pm Wed, Fri & Sat Oct–mid-Apr; Ⓜ Verneda

The star piece of this museum dedicated to the history of immigration in Catalonia is a wagon of the train known as *El Sevillano,* which in the 1950s trundled between Andalucía and Catalonia, jammed with migrants on an all-stops trip that often lasted more than 30 hours! The one-room exhibition in the former country house, Can Serra (now surrounded by light industry, ring roads and warehouses), contains a display of photos, text (in Catalan) and various documents and objects that recall the history of immigration to Catalonia from the 19th century on. There's also an engaging video with images of migrant life decades ago and today.

top picks

- **Caelum** (p154)
- **Papabubble** (p153)
- **Custo Barcelona** (p157)
- **Jamin Puech** (p164)
- **Vila Viniteca** (p157)
- **Antonio Miró** (p160)
- **Cubiña** (p160)
- **Herboristeria del Rei** (p155)
- **Joan Murrià** (p161)
- **Vinçon** (p160)

SHOPPING

If your doctor has prescribed an intense round of retail therapy to deal with the blues, then Barcelona is the place. Across Ciutat Vella (Barri Gòtic, El Raval and La Ribera), L'Eixample and Gràcia is spread a thick mantle of countless boutiques, historic shops, original one-off stores, gourmet corners, wine dens and more designer labels than you can shake your gold card at. You name it, you'll find it here: anything from chocolate to Mango (p161).

Barcelona is a style city and this is evident in its flagship design stores, such as Vinçon and Cubiña, whether you are looking for homewares, gifts or decoration. Even the souvenirs have flair. Fashion, in the broadest possible sense, occupies a sizable wedge of the city's retail space. Local names such as Mango, Custo Barcelona, Antonio Miró and Purificación García jostle side by side with big Spanish names in *haute couture* and *prêt-à-porter* (such as Zara and Adolfo Domínguez). Almost every taste is catered to, with loads of youthful designers, club and street wear, grunge dealers and secondhand operators.

For high fashion, design, jewellery and department stores, the principal shopping axis starts on Plaça de Catalunya, proceeds up Passeig de Gràcia and turns left into Avinguda Diagonal, along which it extends as far as Plaça de la Reina Maria Cristina. The densely packed section between Plaça de Francesc Macià and Plaça de la Reina Maria Cristina is an especially good hunting ground.

The heart of L'Eixample, bisected by chic Passeig de Gràcia, is known as the Quadrat d'Or (Golden Square) and is jammed with all sorts of glittering shops. Passeig de Gràcia has developed into a who's who of international shopping.

The heart of the Barri Gòtic has always been busy with small-scale merchants, but the area has come crackling to life since the mid-1990s. Some of the most curious old stores, such as purveyors of hats and candles, lurk in the narrow lanes around Plaça de Sant Jaume. The once-seedy Carrer d'Avinyó has become a minor young-fashion boulevard. Antique stores line Carrer de la Palla and Carrer dels Banys Nous.

La Ribera is nothing less than a gourmand's delight. Great old stores and some finger-licking newbies deal in speciality foodstuffs, from coffee and chocolate to cheese. Amid such wonderful aromas, a crop of fashion and design stores caters to the multitude of yuppies in the *barri*.

In El Raval you'll discover old-time stores that are irresistible to browsers, and a colourful array of affordable, mostly secondhand clothes boutiques. The central axis here is Carrer de la Riera Baixa, which plays host to everything from '70s threads to military cast-offs. Carrer dels Tallers is also attracting a growing number of clothing and shoe stores (although CDs remain its core business). Art galleries, designer outlets and quality bookstores all huddle together along the streets running east of the Museu d'Art Contemporani de Barcelona towards La Rambla.

Gràcia is also full of quirky little shops. In particular, check out Carrer de Verdi for anything from clothes to bric-a-brac.

In general, shops are open between 9am or 10am and 1.30pm or 2pm and then again from around 4pm or 4.30pm to 8pm or 8.30pm Monday to Friday. Many shops keep the same hours on Saturday, although some don't bother with the evening session.

Large supermarkets, malls and department stores such as El Corte Inglés stay open all day from Monday to Saturday, between about 10am and 10pm. Many fashion boutiques, design stores and the like open from about 10am to 8pm Monday to Saturday.

A few shops open on Sundays and holidays, and the number increases in the run up to key consumer holiday periods.

BARRI GÒTIC & LA RAMBLA

A handful of interesting shops dot La Rambla, but the real fun starts inside the labyrinth. Young fashion on Carrer d'Avinyó, a mixed bag on Avinguda del Portal de l'Àngel, some cute old shops on Carrer de la Dagueria and lots of exploring in tight old lanes awaits.

SALA PARÉS Map p60   Art
☎ 93 318 70 20; www.salapares.com; Carrer del Petritxol 5; Ⓜ Liceu

Picasso had works on sale here a century ago in what is one of the city's most venerable and still-dynamic private galleries. In business since 1877, the gallery has maintained its position as one of the city's leading purveyors of Catalan art, old and contemporary.

LLIBRERIA & INFORMACIÓ CULTURAL DE LA GENERALITAT DE CATALUNYA Map p60 Books
☎ 93 302 64 62; La Rambla dels Estudis 118; Ⓜ Liceu

This is a good first stop for books and pamphlets on all things Catalan, ranging from huge coffee-table tomes on all facets of Catalan art and architecture through to turgid tracts on Catalan law. You can skip the latter, but the former are exquisite. The shop stocks very little in English (and even less in Spanish).

QUERA Map p60 Books
☎ 93 318 07 43; Carrer del Petritxol 2; ⏰ 10am-8pm Tue, 10am-1.30pm & 4.30-8pm Wed-Sat; Ⓜ Liceu

Crammed into a tiny bookshop is a treasure trove of travel material, mostly on Catalonia and the Pyrenees. It specialises in maps and guides, including a host of stuff for walking, and has been in business since 1916.

PAPABUBBLE Map p60 Candied Sweets
☎ 93 268 86 25; www.papabubble.com; Carrer Ample 28; Ⓜ Liceu

It feels like a step into another era in this candy store, where they make up pots of rainbow-coloured boiled lollies, just like some of us remember from corner-store days as kids. Watch the sticky sweets being made before your eyes. For all its apparent timelessness, this is a relatively new venture. Started by Australians in Barcelona, this sweet reminiscence now has shops in Amsterdam, New York, Seoul, Taipei and Tokyo.

CERERIA SUBIRÀ Map p60 Candles
☎ 93 315 26 06; Baixada de la Llibreteria 7; Ⓜ Jaume I

Even if you're not interested in myriad mounds of colourful wax, pop in just so you've been to the oldest shop in Barcelona. Open since 1761 and at this address since the 19th century, it has a voluptuous, baroque feel about it.

VILLEGAS CERÀMICA Map p60 Ceramics
☎ 93 317 53 30; www.villegasceramica.net; Carrer Comtal 31; Ⓜ Urquinaona

For some curious ceramics that have nothing to do with traditional wares, poke your head in here. Arresting items include owl's-head clocks (in which the eyes move back and forth), pottery statues of stretched human figures, Barcelona taxis, ceramic

top picks

SHOPPING STRIPS

- **Avinguda del Portal de l'Àngel** (Map p60) With El Corte Inglés leading the way, this broad pedestrian avenue is lined with everything from shoe shops to patisseries, and feeds into Carrer dels Boters and Carrer de la Portaferrissa, characterised by stores offering light-hearted costume jewellery and young street wear.
- **Avinguda Diagonal** (Map p122) The boulevard is loaded with international fashion names, department stores and design boutiques, suitably interspersed with eateries to allow weary shoppers to take a load off.
- **Carrer d'Avinyó** (Map p60) Once a fairly squalid old-town road (where Picasso and his friends used to frequent houses of ill repute), Carrer d'Avinyó has morphed into a dynamic young fashion street.
- **Carrer de la Riera Baixa** (Map p74) The place to look for a gaggle of stores flogging preloved threads.
- **Carrer del Petritxol** (Map p60) For chocolate shops and art.
- **Carrer del Consell de Cent** (Map p106) The heart of the private art-gallery scene in Barcelona, between Passeig de Gràcia and Carrer de Muntaner.
- **Carrer del Rec** (Map p82) Another threads street, this one-time stream is lined with bright, sometimes quirky boutiques. Check out Carrer del Bonaire and Carrer de l'Esparteria too. You'll find discount outlets and original local designers.
- **Carrer dels Banys Nous** (Map p60) Along with nearby Carrer de la Palla, this is the place to look for antiques.
- **Passeig de Gràcia** (Map p106) This is the premier shopping boulevard, chic with a capital 'C', but mostly given over to big name international brands.
- **Rambla de Catalunya** (Map p106) A prettier boulevard than Passeig de Gràcia, Rambla de Catalunya is laced with all sorts of shops. Stop for a coffee on the central pedestrian strip along the way.

wall-hangings and loads of other original items.

XOCOA Map p60 — Chocolate

☎ 93 301 11 97; www.xocoa-bcn.com; Carrer del Petritxol 11-13; Ⓜ Liceu

Shield your eyes from the ultrabright rose-and-white decor and prepare yourself for a different kind of chocolate. Carefully arranged inside this den of dental devilry are ranks and ranks of original chocolate bars, chocolates stuffed with sweet stuff, gooey pastries and more. It has eight other branches scattered about town.

LA CONDONERIA Map p60 — Condoms

☎ 93 302 77 21; Plaça de Sant Josep Oriol 7; Ⓜ Liceu

Run out of kinky coloured condoms? Need a fresh batch of lubricant? Pick up these vital items and a host of bedside novelties and naughty bits here.

GOTHAM Map p60 — Design

☎ 93 412 46 47; www.gotham-bcn.com; Carrer de Cervantes 7; Ⓜ Jaume I

Look back with fondness at the furniture and lights, which date back to at least the 1960s, and in some cases the '30s. Much of it is restored and given a bright, decorative once-over. Retro design freaks will fall in love with this place.

ESPACIO DE CREADORES

Map p60 — Fashion

☎ 93 318 03 31; Carrer Comtal 22; Ⓜ Catalunya

For a broad selection of cut-price women's fashion and accessories by a long list of Spanish and some international designers, this outlet store claims to slash original prices by up to 70%.

RAG SHOP Map p60 — Fashion

☎ 93 319 78 61; Carrer de la Llibreteria 14; Ⓜ Jaume I

Light dresses, tops and other items, mostly a mix of cotton and modern fibres, like elastane, appeal to those seeking a casual, unfussy look. Skunkfunk, a ballsy Basque Country brand, leads the way here.

SITA MURT Map p60 — Fashion

☎ 93 301 00 06; www.sitamurt.com; Carrer d'Avinyó 18; Ⓜ Liceu

A Catalan fashion company, Sita Murt produces light and sexy women's fashion

for summer, and young, striding out outfits for the girl about town in winter. Much of it is aimed at nights out rather than a day in the office.

URBANA Map p60 — Fashion

☎ 93 269 09 20; Carrer d'Avinyó 46; ☉ 11am-3pm & 4.30-9pm Mon-Sat; Ⓜ Liceu

Colourful, fun city clothes, shoes and accessories await boys and girls in this easygoing store with Basque Country origins. It offers a variety of brands of urban threads, like Supremebeing, Rocketdog and Matilda.

CAELUM Map p60 — Food

☎ 93 302 69 93; Carrer de la Palla 8; ☉ 10.30am-8.30pm Mon-Thu, 10.30am-11.30pm Fri & Sat, 11.30am-9pm Sun; Ⓜ Liceu

Centuries of heavenly gastronomic tradition from across Spain are concentrated in this exquisite medieval space in the heart of the city. Sweets (such as the irresistible marzipan from Toledo) made by nuns in convents across the country make their way to this den of delicacies. You can sip on a tea down in the medieval basement from 3.30pm to closing time, Tuesday to Sunday.

SHOPPING MALLS

Barcelona has no shortage of shopping malls. One of the first to arrive was L'Illa Diagonal (Map p122; ☎ 93 444 00 00; www.lilla.com; Avinguda Diagonal 549; ☉ 10am-9.30pm Mon-Sat; Ⓜ Maria Cristina), designed by star Spanish architect Rafael Moneo. The Centre Comercial Diagonal Mar (Map p96; ☎ 902 530300; www.diagonalmar.com; Avinguda Diagonal 3; ☉ 10am-10pm Mon-Sat; Ⓜ El Maresme Fòrum) by the sea is one of the latest additions.

The city's other emporia include Centre Comercial de les Glòries (Map p96; ☎ 93 486 04 04; www.lesglories.com; Gran Via de les Corts Catalanes; ☉ 10am-10pm Mon-Sat; Ⓜ Glòries), in the former Olivetti factory; Heron City (off Map p100; ☎ 902 401144; www.heroncitybarcelona.com; Passeig de Rio de Janeiro 42; ☉ 10am-10pm Mon-Sat; Ⓜ Fabra i Puig), just off Avinguda Meridiana, about 4km north of Plaça de les Glòries Catalanes; and the Centre Comercial Gran Via 2 (off Map p140; ☎ 902 301444; www.granvia2.com; Gran Via de les Corts Catalanes 75; ☉ 10am-10pm Mon-Sat; Ⓡ FGC Ildefons Cerdà) in L'Hospitalet de Llobregat.

ANTINOUS Map p60 — Gay & Lesbian

☎ 93 301 90 70; www.antinouslibros.com, in Spanish; Carrer de Josep Anselm Clavé 6; Ⓜ Drassanes
Gay and lesbian travellers may want to browse in this spacious and relaxed gay bookshop, which also has a modest cafe out the back. This is the place for porn mags, postcards of muscle-bound fellows and an awful lot of highbrow lit on homosexual issues mixed in with rather lowerbrow lit to groan to.

HERBORISTERIA DEL REI

Map p60 — Herbs & Medicinal Plants
☎ 93 318 05 12; Carrer del Vidre 1; ⏰ 4-8pm Tue-Fri, 10am-8pm Sat; Ⓜ Liceu
Once patronised by Queen Isabel II, this timeless corner store flogs all sorts of weird and wonderful herbs, spices and medicinal plants. It's been doing so since 1823 and the decor has barely changed since the 1860s. However, some of the products have, and you'll find anything from teas to massage oil nowadays. Film director Tom Tykwer shot scenes of *Perfume: The Story of a Murderer* here.

LE BOUDOIR Map p60 — Lingerie & Erotica

☎ 93 302 52 81; www.leboudoir.net; Carrer de la Canuda 21; Ⓜ Catalunya
Need to spice up the bedroom situation? Take a stroll around this sensual shop, where anything from lacy, racy underwear to exuberant sex toys is available. Transparent handcuffs might be fun, or perhaps a bit of slap and tickle with a whip and mask?

EL INGENIO Map p60 — Masks & Costumes

☎ 93 317 71 38; www.el-ingenio.com; Carrer d'en Rauric 6; Ⓜ Liceu
In this whimsical fantasy store you will discover giant Carnaval masks, costumes, theatrical accessories and other fun things. You can pick up some 'devil's batons' to do a little fiery juggling, a monocycle or clown make-up.

OBACH Map p60 — Millinery

☎ 93 318 40 94; Carrer del Call 2; Ⓜ Liceu
Since 1924 this store in the heart of the Call (Jewish quarter) has been purveying all manner of headgear for men. Time seems to have stood still here, and one assumes the bulk of the clientele belongs to a senior generation. Hats off to a remarkably longlived institution.

CASA BEETHOVEN Map p60 — Music

☎ 93 301 48 26; La Rambla de Sant Josep 97; Ⓜ Liceu
This isn't any old sheet-music shop. In business since 1880 and with an air more of a museum than of a store, Casa Beethoven's customers have included Montserrat Caballé, Josep Carreras and Plácido Domingo. It keeps up with the times, however, and you're as likely to find music by Metallica as by Mozart. On Saturdays small concerts are sometimes held.

LA MANUAL ALPARGATERA

Map p60 — Shoes
☎ 93 301 01 72; www.lamanual.net; Carrer d'Avinyó 7; Ⓜ Liceu
The bright white shop front is a local landmark. Everyone from the Pope to Michael Douglas has ordered a pair of *espadrilles* (rope-soled canvas shoes or sandals) from this store, which sholds its own against Nike and co. It also does a line in sun hats and bags.

L'ARCA DE L'ÀVIA

Map p60 — Vintage Clothes & Accessories
☎ 93 302 15 98; Carrer dels Banys Nous 20; Ⓜ Liceu
Grandma's chest is indeed full of extraordinary remembrances from the past, when young ladies used to put together a trousseau of clothes and other items for their wedding. You might find anything from old silk kimonos to wedding dresses from the 1920s. Some items sold here wound up being used in the film *Titanic*.

EL RAVAL

The area boasts a handful of art galleries around the Macba, along with a burgeoning secondhand and vintage clothes scene on Carrer de la Riera Baixa. Carrer dels Tallers is one of the city's main music strips.

IT'S SALE TIME

The winter sales start shortly after Reis (6 January) and, depending on the store, can go on well into February. The summer sales start in July, with stores trying to entice locals to part with one last wad of euros before they flood out of the city on holiday in August. Some shops prolong their sales to the end of August.

LA PORTORRIQUEÑA
Map p74   Coffee

☎ 93 317 34 38; Carrer d'en Xuclà 25; Ⓜ Catalunya
Coffee beans from around the world, freshly ground before your eyes, has been the winning formula in this store since 1902. It also offers all sorts of chocolate goodies. The street is good for little old-fashioned food boutiques.

EL INDIO Map p74   Fabrics
☎ 93 317 54 42; Carrer del Carme 24; Ⓜ Liceu
Take a giant leap back into the late 19th century. You probably won't be in the market for bolts of cloth while in Barcelona, but admire the Modernista shop front before simply wandering in for a look around this time-warp store.

HOLALA! PLAZA Map p74   Fashion
☎ 93 302 05 93; Plaça de Castella 2; Ⓜ Universitat
Backing on to Carrer de Valldonzella, where it boasts an exhibition space (Gallery) for temporary art displays, this Ibiza import is inspired by that island's long established (and somewhat commercialised) hippie tradition. Vintage clothes are the name of the game, along with an eclectic program of exhibitions and activities.

LEFTIES Map p74   Fashion
☎ 93 317 50 70; Carrer de Pelai 2; ◷ 10am-9.30pm Mon-Sat; Ⓜ Universitat

Don't mind being seen in last year's Zara fashions? Lefties (ie leftovers) could be the browsing spot for you, with men's, women's and kids' cast-offs from the previous year at silly prices. You could fill a wardrobe with perfectly good middle-of-the-road threads and your bank manager would be none the wiser.

CASTELLÓ Map p74   Music
☎ 93 318 20 41; Carrer dels Tallers 3 & 7; Ⓜ Catalunya
These two stores are part of a large family business that has been going since 1935 and which is said to account for a fifth of the retail record business in Catalonia.

TERANYINA Map p74   Textiles
☎ 93 317 94 36; Carrer del Notariat 10; Ⓜ Catalunya
Artist Teresa Rosa Aguayo runs this textile workshop in the heart of the artsy bit of El Raval. You can join courses at the loom, admire some of the rugs and other works that Teresa has created and, of course, buy them.

LA RIBERA
The former commercial heart of medieval Barcelona is today still home to a cornucopia of old-style specialist food and drink shops, a veritable feast of aroma and atmosphere. They have been joined, since the late 1990s, by a raft of hip little fashion stores.

THE URGE TO RUMMAGE

Lovers of old books, coins, stamps and general bric-a-brac can indulge their habits uninhibited at several markets. They generally get going from 9am and wind down around 8pm. The coin and stamp collectors' market and the old-book peddlers around the Mercat de Sant Antoni usually pack up by 2pm.

The Barri Gòtic is enlivened by an art and crafts market (Plaça de Sant Josep Oriol; Ⓜ Liceu) on Saturday and Sunday, the antiques-filled Mercat Gòtic (Plaça Nova; Ⓜ Liceu) on Thursday, and a coin and stamp collectors' market (Plaça Reial; Ⓜ Liceu) on Sunday morning.

Just beyond the western edge of El Raval, the punters at the Modernista Mercat de Sant Antoni (Map p100; Ⓜ Sant Antoni) dedicate Sunday morning to old maps, stamps, books and cards.

Once a fortnight, gourmands can poke about the homemade honeys, sweets, cheeses and other edible delights at the Fira Alimentació (Plaça del Pi; Ⓜ Liceu) from Friday to Sunday. Ask at the Oficina d'Informació de Turisme de Barcelona (p284) for the dates.

Some annual markets are also worth looking out for. For 10 days in mid-May (dates change each year), stands set up in the Portal de l'Àngel (Avinguda del Portal de l'Àngel; Ⓜ Catalunya) for the Fira del Llibre Antic (Antique Book Fair). The same spot hosts the Fira de Terrissa (Pottery Fair), which lasts for five days starting around 20 September, coinciding with the Festes de la Mercè (see p18) and the similar Fira de Ceràmica Creativa (Ceramicists Fair), around 23 December to 5 January.

The Fira de Santa Llúcia (Ⓜ Liceu), on and around Avinguda de la Catedral, is held from 28 November to 23 December. You can buy figurines, including many models of that infamous Catalan Christmas character, the *caganer* (crapper; see p19), to make your own Nativity scene.

ANTICH Map p82 — Accessories
☎ 93 310 43 91; www.casaantich.com; Carrer del Consolat de Mar 27-31; Ⓜ Barceloneta
Traditionally this street was lined with purveyors of bags and related travel goods. The Antich clan, in business since 1910, offers a range of travel cases and bags of various known brands. More interesting is its own line of handmade articles, from suitcases to leather tool bags.

OLD CURIOSITY SHOP
Map p82 — Antiques & Bric-A-Brac
☎ 93 310 45 89; Volta dels Tamborets 4; Ⓜ Jaume I
For anything from handmade soaps to French calendar diaries of the 1930s or antique tea sets, this is a fun hole-in-the-wall shop to rummage about it in, hidden in a side lane near the Església de Santa Maria del Mar.

GALERIA MAEGHT Map p82 — Art
☎ 93 310 42 45; www.maeght.com; Carrer de Montcada 25; ☺ 11am-2pm & 3-7pm Tue-Fri, 11am-2pm Sat; Ⓜ Jaume I
This high-end gallery, housed in one of the fine medieval mansions for which this street is known, specialises in 20th-century masters. It is as enticing for the building as the art.

CAFÉ DE LA PRINCESA
Map p82 — Boutique
☎ 93 268 15 18; www.cafeprincesa.com; Carrer dels Flassaders 21; Ⓜ Jaume I
In a dark lane named after the blanket makers that once worked here is this odd combination of cooperative store, art gallery and restaurant (entry to the latter is from Carrer de Sabateret). Its members make many of the oddities on sale, but others are objects imported from such disparate locations as Prague and Denmark. Leather bags, toys and clothes make up just part of the offerings.

EL MAGNÍFICO Map p82 — Coffee
☎ 93 319 60 81; www.cafeselmagnifico.com, in Catalan & Spanish; Carrer de l'Argenteria 64; Ⓜ Jaume I
All sorts of coffee has been roasted here since the early 20th century. The variety of coffee (and tea) available is remarkable – and the aromas hit you as you walk in. Across the road, the same people run the exquisite and much newer tea shop, Sans i Sans (☎ 93 319 60 81; Carrer de l'Argenteria 59).

VILA VINITECA Map p82 — Drink
☎ 902 327777; www.vilaviniteca.es, in Spanish; Carrer dels Agullers 7; ☺ 8.30am-8.30pm Mon-Sat; Ⓜ Jaume I
One of the best wine stores in Barcelona (and Lord knows, there are a few), this place has been searching out the best in local and imported wines since 1932. On a couple of November evenings it organises what has by now become an almost riotous wine-tasting event in Carrer dels Agullers and surrounding lanes, at which cellars from around Spain present their young new wines. At No 9 it has another store devoted to gourmet food products.

COQUETTE Map p82 — Fashion
☎ 93 295 42 85; www.coquettebcn.com; Carrer del Rec 65; Ⓜ Barceloneta
With its spare, cut back and designer look, this fashion is automatically attractive in its own right. Women will love to browse through casual, feminine wear by such designers as Tsunoda, Vanessa Bruno, Chloé Baño and Hoss Intropia. To complement the clothes there are bags, footwear and costume jewellery. The store is a leading light on a street replete with fashion outlets.

CUSTO BARCELONA Map p82 — Fashion
☎ 93 268 78 93; www.custo-barcelona.com; Plaça de les Olles 7; Ⓜ Jaume I
The psychedelic decor and casual atmosphere lend this avant-garde Barcelona

top picks

BEST KEPT SECRETS

- El Rey de la Magia (p158) All the magic tricks you can imagine, in a store with oodles of history.
- Herboristeria del Rei (p155) Ancient herbs and traditional remedies.
- La Portorriqueña (opposite) Timeless coffee merchant in El Raval.
- Sala Parés (p152) A historic private art gallery.
- Caelum (p154) Traditional sweets from Spanish convents.
- El Ingenio (p155) Masks and costumes.
- Siete Besos (p163) A tiny treasure chest of affordable women's fashion amid uptown wealth.
- Papabubble (p153) Boiled sweeties, just like in grandpa's day (well, almost).
- Sergio Aranda (p162) For daring jewellery and pearls for girls.

fashion store a youthful edge. Custo presents daring new women's and men's collections each year on the New York catwalks. The dazzling colours and cut of anything from dinner jackets to hot pants are for the uninhibited. It has five other stores around town.

GAMAYA Map p82 — Fashion
☎ 93 310 67 07; www.gamaya.es; Carrer dels Flassaders 36; Ⓜ Jaume I

A breath of fresh laid-back Ibiza air runs through this new ladies' wear store tucked away on a street that has gone from near abandonment in the 1990s to become a delightful shopping lane today. The lady who runs this shop designs the breezy summer dresses, pants-and-tops combinations and prints herself.

OUTLET DEL BORN Map p82 — Fashion
☎ 93 268 72 49; Carrer de l'Esparteria 12; Ⓜ Barceloneta

Discounted fashions from the previous year from designers like Gonzalo Comella, Hugo Boss, G-Star, Armani Jeans and Viktor & Rolf find their way into this chaotic store, where you can look forward to anything up to half price.

CASA GISPERT Map p82 — Food
☎ 93 319 75 35; www.casagispert.com; Carrer dels Sombrerers 23; Ⓜ Jaume I

Nuts to you at the wood-fronted Casa Gispert, where they've been toasting nuts and selling all manner of dried fruit since 1851. Pots and jars piled high on the shelves contain an unending variety of crunchy titbits: some roasted, some honeyed, all of them moreish.

HOFMANN PASTISSERIA
Map p82 — Food
☎ 93 268 82 21; www.hofmann-bcn.com; Carrer dels Flassaders 44; Ⓜ Jaume I

With old timber cabinets, this bite-sized gourmet patisserie has an air of timelessness, although it is quite new. Choose between jars of delicious chocolates, the day's croissants and more dangerous pastries, or an array of cakes and other sweets.

LA BOTIFARRERIA Map p82 — Food
☎ 93 319 91 23; www.labotifarreria.com; Carrer de Santa Maria 4; Ⓜ Jaume I

As they say, 'sausages with imagination'! Although this delightful deli sells all sorts

of cheeses, hams, fresh hamburger patties, snacks and other goodies, the mainstay is an astounding variety of handcrafted sausages. Not just the pork variety, but stuffed with anything from green pepper and whiskey to apple curry!

OLISOLIVA Map p82 — Food
☎ 93 268 14 72; www.olisoliva.com, in Spanish; Avinguda de Francesc Cambó; Ⓜ Jaume I

Inside the Mercat de Santa Caterina (p85), this simple, glassed-in store is stacked with olive oils and vinegars from all over Spain. Taste some of the products before deciding. Some of the best olive oils come from southern Spain. The range of vinegars is astounding too.

EL REY DE LA MAGIA Map p82 — Magic
☎ 93 319 39 20; www.elreydelamagia.com, in Catalan & Spanish; Carrer de la Princesa 11; ⏰ 11am-2pm & 5-8pm Mon-Fri, 10am-2pm Sat; Ⓜ Jaume I

For more than 100 years, the people behind this box of tricks have been keeping locals both astounded and amused. Should you decide to stay in Barcelona and make a living as a magician, this is the place to buy levitation brooms, glasses of disappearing milk and decks of magic cards.

NU SABATES Map p82 — Shoes & Accessories
☎ 93 268 03 83; www.nusabates.com; Carrer dels Cotoners 14; Ⓜ Jaume I

A couple of modern-day Catalan cobblers have put together some original handmade leather shoes (and a handful of bags and other leather items) in their stylishly renovated locale.

PORT VELL & LA BARCELONETA

Aside from the shopping-mall fun of Maremàgnum, there are precious few outlets for maxing out your cards along the waterfront.

MAREMÀGNUM Map p90 — Shopping Centre
☎ 93 225 81 00; www.maremagnum.es; Moll d'Espanya; ⏰ 10am-10pm; Ⓜ Drassanes

Created out of largely abandoned docks, this chirpy shopping centre, with its bars, restaurants and cinemas, is pleasant enough for a stroll virtually in the middle of the old harbour. You'll find outlets for anything from Calvin Klein underwear to Brazilian flip-flops (Havaianas). Football fans will be drawn to the paraphernalia at FC Barcelona (☎ 93 225 80 45). The big news is that shops here open on Sundays, pretty much unheard of anywhere else in the city.

L'EIXAMPLE

Most of the city's classy shopping spreads across the heart of L'Eixample, in particular along Passeig de Gràcia, Rambla de Catalunya and adjacent streets. All about are dotted a surprising array of specialty stores, selling anything from gloves to glues.

EL BULEVARD DELS ANTIQUARIS

Map p106   Antiques
☎ 93 215 44 99; www.bulevarddelsantiquaris. com; Passeig de Gràcia 55-57; ☽ 10.30am-8.30pm Mon-Sat; Ⓜ Passeig de Gràcia
More than 70 stores (most are open from 11am to 2pm and from 5pm to 8.30pm) are gathered under one roof (on the floor above the more general Bulevard Rosa arcade) to offer the most varied selection of collector's pieces, ranging from old porcelain dolls through to fine crystal, from Asian antique furniture to old French goods, and from African and other ethnic art to jewellery.

ALTAÏR Map p106   Books
☎ 93 342 71 71; www.altair.es; Gran Via de les Corts Catalanes 616; ☽ 10am-8.30pm Mon-Sat; Ⓜ Universitat
Enter the world of travel in this extensive bookshop, which is a mecca for guidebooks, maps, travel literature and all sorts of other books likely to induce a severe case of itchy feet. It has a travellers' notice board and, downstairs, a travel agent.

SHOPPING OUT OF HOURS

Got the munchies at 4am? Forgot to buy the paper from your local kiosk? Need something on a Sunday? Open 25 (Map p100; www.open25.es; Carrer de Còrsega 241) is Barcelona's only 24-hour store, flogging anything from snacks and chocolate bars to magazines and newspapers. Similar, but closed six hours a day, is Opencor (☽ 8am-2am, closed 1 Jan, 1 May, 11 Sep & 25 Dec), with 21 branches around the city at last count. You'll find one at Ronda de Sant Pere 33 (Map p106) and another at Carrer Gran de Gràcia 29 (Map p116).

CASA DEL LLIBRE Map p106   Books
☎ 902 026407; www.casadellibro.com, in Spanish; Passeig de Gràcia 62; ☽ 9.30am-9.30pm Mon-Sat; Ⓜ Passeig de Gràcia
With branches elsewhere in Spain, the 'Home of the Book' is a well-stocked general bookshop with reasonable sections devoted to literature in English, French and other languages. The website is a good place to look for Spanish literature if the shop is a walk too far.

COME IN Map p106   Books
☎ 93 453 12 04; www.libreriainglesa.com; Carrer de Balmes 129bis; Ⓜ Diagonal
English-teachers, those thirsting for the latest thrillers in English and learners of Shakespeare's tongue will all find something to awaken their curiosity in this, one of the city's main English-language bookshops. There are even a few odds and ends in other languages.

LAIE Map p106   Books
☎ 93 318 17 39; www.laie.es, in Catalan & Spanish; Carrer de Pau Claris 85; ☽ 10am-9pm Mon-Fri, 10.30am-9pm Sat; Ⓜ Catalunya or Urquinaona
Laie has novels and books on architecture, art and film in English, French, Spanish and Catalan. Better still, it has a great upstairs cafe where you can examine your latest purchases or browse through the newspapers provided for customers in true Central European style.

CACAO SAMPAKA Map p106   Chocolate
☎ 93 272 08 33; www.cacaosampaka.com; Carrer del Consell de Cent 292; ☽ 9am-9pm Mon-Sat; Ⓜ Passeig de Gràcia; ✗
Chocoholics will be convinced they have died and passed on to a better place. Load up in the shop or head for the bar out the back where you can have a classic *xocolata calenta* (hot chocolate) and munch on exquisite chocolate cakes, tarts, ice cream, sweets and sandwiches.

NORMA COMICS Map p100   Comics
☎ 93 244 84 23; www.normacomics.com, in Spanish; Passeig de Sant Joan 7-9; Ⓜ Arc de Triomf
With a huge range of comics, both Spanish and international, this is Spain's biggest dealer – everything from Tintin to some of the weirdest sci-fi and sex comics can be found here. Also on show are armies of model super heroes and other characters

DANONE'S BARCELONA ROOTS

The yoghurt at the heart of the French foodstuffs multinational Danone was first made and sold in Barcelona in 1919, when Isaac Carasso started a company he called Danone (after Danon, the diminutive of his son Daniel's name). Daniel opened a Paris branch 10 years later, which in 1967 would join a French cheese company to create Gervais-Danone. Six years later, a glass and packaging group, BSN, swallowed up Gervais-Danone and eventually shed its glass business to put food products at the centre of its efforts. By now a thoroughly French multinational, few remember that its popular tub of yoghurt first saw the light of day in post-WWI Barcelona.

produced by fevered imaginations. Kids from nine to 99 can be seen snapping up items to add to their collections.

EL CORTE INGLÉS Map p106   Department Store

☎ 93 306 38 00; www.elcorteingles.es, in Spanish; Plaça de Catalunya 14; ⏰ 10am-10pm Mon-Sat; Ⓜ Catalunya

The 'English Court' is Spain's flagship department store, with everything you'd expect, from computers to cushions, and high fashion to homewares. The top floor is occupied by a so-so restaurant with fabulous city views. El Corte Inglés has other branches, including at Portal de l'Àngel 19-21 (Map p60), Avinguda Diagonal 617 (Map p122) and Avinguda Diagonal 471-473 (Map p100), near Plaça de Francesc Macià.

CUBIÑA Map p106   Design

☎ 93 476 57 21; www.cubinya.es; Carrer de Mallorca 291; Ⓜ Verdaguer

Even if interior design doesn't ring your bell, a visit to this extensive temple to furniture, lamps and just about any home accessory your heart might desire is worth it just to see this Domènech i Montaner building. Admire the enormous and whimsical wrought iron decoration at street level before heading inside to marvel at the ceiling, timber work, brick columns and windows. Oh, and don't forget the furniture.

VINÇON Map p106   Design

☎ 93 215 60 50; www.vincon.com; Passeig de Gràcia 96; ⏰ 10am-8.30pm Mon-Sat; Ⓜ Diagonal

An icon of the Barcelona design scene, Vinçon has the slickest furniture and household goods (particularly lighting), both

local and imported. Not surprising, really, since the building, raised in 1899, belonged to the Modernista artist Ramon Casas. Head upstairs to the furniture area – from the windows and terrace you get close side views of La Pedrera.

XAMPANY Map p106   Drink

☎ 610 845011; Carrer de València 200; ⏰ 4.30-10pm Mon-Fri, 10am-2pm Sat; Ⓜ Passeig de Gràcia

Since 1981, this 'Cathedral of Cava' has been distributing bubbly to the local citizenry. It's a veritable Aladdin's cave of *cava*, with bottles of the stuff crammed high and into every possible chaotic corner of this dimly lit locale.

ADOLFO DOMÍNGUEZ Map p106   Fashion

☎ 93 487 41 70; www.adolfodominguezshop.com; Passeig de Gràcia 32; Ⓜ Passeig de Gràcia

One of the stars of Spanish *prêt-à-porter*, this label produces classic men's and women's garments from quality materials. Encompassing anything from regal party gowns to kids' outfits (that might have you thinking of British aristocracy), the broad range generally oozes a conservative air, with elegant cuts that make no concessions to rebellious urban ideals.

ANTONIO MIRÓ Map p106   Fashion

☎ 93 487 06 70; www.antoniomiro.es, in Spanish; Carrer del Consell de Cent 349; ⏰ 10am-8pm Mon-Sat; Ⓜ Passeig de Gràcia

Antonio Miró is one of Barcelona's *haute couture* kings. The entrance to the airy store, with dark hardwood floor, seems more like a hip hotel reception. Miró concentrates on light, natural fibres to produce smart, unpretentious men's and women's fashion. High-end evening dresses and shimmering, smart suits lead the way. Or you could just settle for an Antonio Miró T-shirt.

ARMAND BASI Map p106   Fashion

☎ 93 215 14 21; www.armandbasi.com; Passeig de Gràcia 49; ⏰ 10am-8pm Mon-Sat; Ⓜ Passeig de Gràcia

Local design star Basi appeals to a thirties and forties crowd with a slick line in casual elegance. Suits that are perfect without ties and made to impress at dinner or in the town's top clubs match with stylish evening dresses. More casual shirts, trousers, tops and frocks broaden the range. Leather jackets and footwear complete the picture.

GI JOE Map p106 · Fashion

☎ 93 329 96 52; Ronda de Sant Antoni 49;
Ⓜ Liceu

Recently moved to this new address, this is
the best central army-surplus warehouse.
Get your khakis here, along with urban
army fashion T-shirts. Throw in a holster, gas
mask or sky-blue UN helmet for a kinkier
effect.

LOEWE Map p106 · Fashion

☎ 93 216 04 00; www.loewe.com; Passeig de
Gràcia 35; ⏱ 10am-8.30pm Mon-Sat; Ⓜ Passeig
de Gràcia

Loewe is one of Spain's leading and oldest
fashion stores, founded in 1846. It specialises in luxury leather (shoes, accessories
and travel bags), and also has lines in
perfume, sunglasses, cuff links, silk scarves
and jewellery. This branch opened in 1943
in the Modernista Casa Lleó Morera.

PURIFICACIÓN GARCÍA

Map p106 · Fashion

☎ 93 487 72 92; www.purificaciongarcia.es, in
Spanish; Passeig de Gràcia 21; ⏱ 10am-8.30pm
Mon-Sat; Ⓜ Passeig de Gràcia

Ms García has an enormous spread of offerings over two floors in this generous corner
store. Not only is the building extraordinary
but so too are her collections, if only because of their breadth. You'll find women's
cardigans and men's ties, as well as light
summer dresses and jeans.

MANGO Map p106 · Fashion & Accessories

☎ 93 215 75 30; www.mango.com; Passeig de
Gràcia 65; ⏱ 10am-9pm Mon-Sat; Ⓜ Passeig de
Gràcia

At home in the basement of a modest
Modernista town house (check out the
white, cast-iron columns inside) and a
dozen other locations around town, Mango
offers locally produced, affordable and

mostly casual fashion for women and men.
Smart but easy evening wear, skirts, jackets,
high heels and leather bags for her contrast
with collarless shirts, jeans, khakis and
T-shirts for him.

ELS ENCANTS VELLS

Map p100 · Flea Market

Fira de Bellcaire; ☎ 93 246 30 30; www.encants
bcn.com, in Catalan; Plaça de les Glòries Catalanes;
⏱ 7am-6pm Mon, Wed, Fri & Sat; Ⓜ Glòries

Also known as the Fira de Bellcaire, the
'Old Charms' flea market is the biggest of
its kind in Barcelona. The markets moved
here in 1928 from Avinguda de Mistral, near
Plaça d'Espanya. It's all here, from antique
furniture through to secondhand clothes.
A lot of it is junk, but occasionally you'll
stumble across a *ganga* (bargain). The most
interesting time to be here is from 7am to
9am on Monday, Wednesday and Friday,
when the public auctions take place. Debate on a future location for the market has
ebbed and flowed for years but at the time
of writing it was still firmly anchored to its
spot on the north flank of the Plaça de les
Glòries Catalanes.

FLORISTERÍA NAVARRO Map p106 · Florist

☎ 93 457 40 99; www.floristeriasnavarro.com;
Carrer de València 320; ⏱ 24hr; Ⓜ Diagonal

You never know when you might need
flowers. What better way to follow up the
first night of a new romance than with a
bunch of roses? No problem, because this
florist never closes!

JOAN MURRIÀ Map p106 · Food

☎ 93 215 57 89; www.murria.cat; Carrer de Roger
de Llúria 85; Ⓜ Passeig de Gràcia

Ramon Casas designed the century-old
Modernista shop front advertisements fea-
tured at this culinary coven. For a century
the gluttonous have trembled here at this

SHOPPING L'EIXAMPLE

HUNTING FOR OLD STUFF

Antique collectors could set aside a Sunday morning for a trip to Mercantic (☎ 93 674 49 50; www.mercantic.com;
Carrer de Rius i Taulet 120, Sant Cugat del Vallès; ⏱ 9.30am-3pm; Ⓡ FGC lines S1, S2, S5 or S55), a collection of
gaily painted timber huts occupied by antique and bric-a-brac dealers selling everything from restored furniture to
dusty old telephones. The first Sunday of the month is delivery day, when the stall-holders take delivery of a new
wave of old stuff. The permanent market, with some 80 stall holders, is open during the week too (9.30am to 8pm
Tuesday to Saturday, 9.30am to 3pm Sunday). There's also an activities and play area for children. A date to watch
is the Antiquaris Barcelona (www.antiquarisbcn.com), an antiques fair usually held between late March and the
first week of April.

DEATH BY CHOCOLATE

Spain has been importing cocoa from its South American colonies since the 16th century and, ever since, the pastry makers of Barcelona have been doing it greatest justice. The city's love affair with chocolate is exemplified in the existence of a museum (p86) dedicated to the stuff. Traditional purveyors of fine chocolates such as Escribà (p185) have long operated alongside *granjas* (milk bars)and other similar outlets for sipping cups of the thick hot stuff (several of which you'll find in the Eating chapter, p166). Since the 1980s, they have been joined by a slew of chocolatiers whose creativity seems to know no bounds. Along with Bubó (p177), Cacao Sampaka (p159) and Xocoa (p154), chocoholics should seek out the following:

Bocamel (Map p82; ☎ 93 268 72 44; www.bocamel.com; Carrer del Comerç 8; Ⓜ Arc de Triomf)

Chocolat Factory (Map p106; ☎ 93 215 02 73; www.chocolatfactory.com; Carrer de Provença 233; Ⓜ Diagonal)

Enric Rovira (Map p122; ☎ 93 419 25 47; www.enricrovira.com; Avinguda de Josep Tarradellas 113; Ⓜ Entença)

Oriol Balaguer (Map p122; ☎ 93 201 18 46; www.oriolbalaguer.com; Plaça de Sant Gregori Taumaturg 2; Ⓡ FGC La Bonanova)

Pastisseria Natcha (Map p122; ☎ 93 430 10 70; www.natcha.cat; Avinguda de Sarrià 45; Ⓜ Hospital Clínic)

Richart (Map p122; ☎ 93 202 02 40; www.richart.com; Carrer de Muntaner 463; Ⓡ FGC La Bonanova)

altar of speciality food goods from around Catalonia and beyond.

NOSOTRAOS Map p106 — Gay & Lesbian
☎ 93 451 51 34; http://nosotras.cat; Carrer de Casanova 56; Ⓜ Urgell
Everything from gay girl calendars to bear T-shirts and books appear in this multi-facted gay and lesbian store in the heart of the 'Gaixample'.

BAGUÉS Map p106 — Jewellery
☎ 93 216 01 74; www.bagues.com; Passeig de Gràcia 41; Ⓜ Passeig de Gràcia
This jewellery store, in business since the 19th century, is in thematic harmony with its location in the Modernista Casa Amatller. Some of the classic pieces of jewellery to come out of the Bagués clan's workshops have an equally playful, Modernista bent.

SERGIO ARANDA Map p106 — Jewellery
☎ 93 451 44 04; www.sergioaranda.com; Carrer de València 201; Ⓜ Diagonal
Trained in the art of jewellery creation in Switzerland, Aranda produces an original line of goods, including jewellery made using ancient coins. He also specializes in pearls, making all sorts of original and even daring necklaces and other items for ladies looking for something combining the extroverted and unique with the classic.

REGIA Map p106 — Perfume
☎ 93 216 01 21; www.regia.es, in Catalan & Spanish; Passeig de Gràcia 39; ☽ 9.30am-8.30pm Mon-Fri, 10.30am-8.30pm Sat; Ⓜ Passeig de Gràcia

Reputed to be one of the best perfume stores in the city and in business since 1928, Regia stocks all the name brands and also has a private perfume museum (p110) out the back. Aside from the range of perfumes, Regia sells all sorts of creams, lotions and colognes. It also has its own line of bath products.

CAMPER Map p106 — Shoes
☎ 93 215 63 90; www.camper.com; Carrer de València 249; Ⓜ Passeig de Gràcia
What started as a modest Mallorcan family business (the island has a long shoemaking tradition) has over the decades become the Clarks of Spain. Camper shoes, from the eminently sensible to the stylishly fashionable, are known for solid reliability and are sold all over the world. It has eight shops in Barcelona.

FARRUTX Map p106 — Shoes
☎ 93 215 06 85; www.farrutx.es; Carrer de Rosselló 218; Ⓜ Diagonal
Another Mallorcan shoemaker, Farrutx specialises in exclusive upmarket footwear for uptown gals. You might fall for high-heeled summer sandals or elegant winter boots. There are matching bags and leather jackets, and even a limited line in men's footwear.

GRÀCIA & PARK GÜELL

A wander along the narrow lanes of Gràcia turns up all sorts of surprises, mostly tiny enterprises producing anything from printed

T-shirts to handmade table lamps. They tend to come and go, so you never quite know what you might turn up. Carrer de Verdi has plenty of interesting threads shops.

HIBERNIAN Map p116 — Books
☎ 93 217 47 96; Carrer de Montseny 17; ⏰ 4-8.30pm Mon, 10.30am-8.30pm Tue-Sat; Ⓜ Fontana
The biggest secondhand English bookshop in Barcelona stocks thousands of titles covering all sorts of subjects, from cookery to children's classics.

ÉRASE UNA VEZ Map p116 — Fashion
☎ 93 217 29 77; Carrer de Goya 7; Ⓜ Fontana
'Once Upon a Time' is the name of this fanciful boutique, which brings out the princess in you (and not a pumpkin in sight). It offers women's clothes, almost exclusively evening wear, to suit most tastes and occasions. Local designers such as Llamazares y de Delgado and Zazo & Brull are behind these sometimes sumptuous creations.

RED MARKET Map p116 — Fashion
☎ 93 218 63 33; Carrer de Verdi 20; Ⓜ Fontana
Several funky fashion boutiques dot this street, best known to locals for the queues outside the art-house cinema. Here you run into bright, uninhibited urban wear and accessories. Red dominates the decor more than the threads, and various brands of various things, from shoes to tops, are on offer.

LA ZONA ALTA

Although many of Barcelona's better-off folks descend from the 'High Zone' to L'Eixample to shop, there are still plenty of trendy little boutiques scattered around La Zona Alta. Passeig de la Bonanova, for example, has quite a liberal spread. It's perhaps a little far off to be of much interest to tourists but can nevertheless make for an interesting shopping experience.

JAMIN PUECH Map p122 — Accessories
☎ 93 414 45 66; www.jamin-puech.com; Carrer de Calvet 44; Ⓡ FGC Muntaner
For beautiful quality bags and accessories designed by a Paris-based French couple who have forged an international reputation since the early 1990s (with shops in Paris, London, New York and Tokyo), it will be hard to resist a stop in this, their only store in Spain. They turn out 100 new models a year, with 'ingredients' ranging from silk to wood, and rattan to leather.

LAVINIA Map p122 — Drink
☎ 93 363 44 45; www.lavinia.es, in Spanish; Avinguda Diagonal 605; ⏰ 10am-9pm Mon-Sat; Ⓜ Maria Cristina
This huge, modern wine store with designer pretensions takes anything but a traditional approach to its products. In classy supermarket style, Lavinia (a shop that originated in Madrid) presents a seemingly endless selection of wine, both from around Spain and the rest of the world. It has a branch at the airport, too.

BEA BEA Map p122 — Fashion
☎ 93 414 29 55; Carrer de Calvet 39; Ⓡ FGC Muntaner
In a bright and spacious locale, women find something to suit most generations and a range of tastes. Younger, carefree styles sit side by side with more classical skirts, jackets and accoutrements for uptown dames. Shoes and bags can also be had,

AN OUTLET OUTING

For the ultimate discount fashion overdose, head out of town for some outlet shopping at La Roca Village (off Map p100; ☎ 93 842 39 39; www.larocavillage.com; La Roca del Vallès; ⏰ 11am-8.30pm Mon-Thu, 11am-9pm Fri, 10am-10pm Sat). Here, a village has been given over to consumer madness. At a long line of Spanish and international fashion boutiques, you'll find clothes, shoes, accessories and designer homewares at (they claim) up to 60% off normal retail prices.

To get here, follow the AP-7 tollway north from Barcelona, take exit 12 (marked Cardedeu) and follow the signs for La Roca. The Sagalés bus company (☎ 902 130014; www.sagales.com) organises shuttles from Plaça de Catalunya (€12 return; 40 minutes; 10am, 4pm and 6pm, Monday to Saturday May to September, Monday, Friday and Saturday October to April). Alternatively, take a slower bus of the same company from Fabra i Puig metro station (€2.90 each way; up to four departures Monday to Friday, does not run in August) or a *rodalies* train to Granollers and pick up the shuttle (Monday to Friday only) or a taxi there.

making this a potential single stop for a full outfit refit.

SIETE BESOS Map p122 Fashion
☎ 93 200 67 34; Carrer d'Amigó 55; ℝ FGC Muntaner

A bijou store surrounded by bigger and shriller competition, the 'Seven Kisses' is an attractive treasure treat for women's fashion. Styles can be cheeky and nonconformist but not at all vintage or jeansy. Pretty, light-hearted dresses vie for your attention with pants and tops, all at pretty reasonable prices, considering the part of town you're in.

LA BOTIGA DEL BARÇA
Map p122 Souvenirs
☎ 93 492 31 11; http://shop.fcbarcelona.com; Carrer de Arístides Maillol; ☾ 10am-9pm Mon-Sat; Ⓜ Collblanc

For some, football is the meaning of life. If you fall into that category, your idea of shopping heaven may well be this store at the football museum next to Camp Nou stadium. Here you will find shirts, key rings, footballs – pretty much anything you can think of, all featuring the famous red and blue colours. It has branches all over town, including at Maremàgnum (p158) and Carrer de Jaume I 18 (Map p60).

EATING

top picks

- **Xiringuito d'Escribà** (p180)
- **Restaurant Me** (p182)
- **Coure** (p189)
- **Ipar-Txoko** (p187)
- **Xemei** (p191)
- **Can Majó** (p179)
- **Cerveseria Brasseria Gallega** (p183)
- **Bodega Sepúlveda** (p184)
- **Can Cortada** (p190)

You could come to Barcelona for the food alone. The options seem limitless, from a rusting grill in a centuries-old farmhouse in the outer suburbs to great pots of fish stew near the waterfront. Barcelona is one of the best places in the country to sniff out what the food writers have predictably dubbed *nueva cocina española*.

For some years now, those lovers of fine dining north of the Pyrenees, the French, have been singing the culinary praises of Barcelona and wider Catalonia. Catalonia has a rich tradition of fine food, and its cuisine, alongside that of the Basque Country to the west, is considered to be Spain's finest. As well as the traditional wide variety of seafood, a whole new culture of inventive gourmet dining has mushroomed in Barcelona since the 1990s, catapulting the city into the foodie limelight. Local chefs, led by the inimitable Ferran Adrià and his contemporaries Sergi Arola and Carles Abellán, have become international cooking icons, raising the status of their kitchens to that of artistic laboratories.

The innards of Ciutat Vella, from El Raval across the Barri Gòtic to La Ribera (especially in the humming El Born area), teem with places offering everything from the classics of Spanish and Catalan cuisine, complete with atmospheric tiled walls and creaking timber-beam roofs, to the latest in molecular inventions. For a shoal of seafood possibilities, explore La Barceloneta.

In L'Eixample, the variety of menus is unlimited. Forget the barnlike tapas joints along Passeig de Gràcia and head southwest to the area bordered by Carrer d'Aribau. Although quieter, you'll find a handful of options in the streets immediately northeast of Passeig de Gràcia, too.

There is no shortage of high-end offerings along and around the west end of Avinguda Diagonal, which cater to the business market and the city's beautiful people. Here, and scattered across La Zona Alta, are some of the most exclusive A-list joints in town.

And what is a great meal without fine wine to accompany it? Aside from being Spain's main producer of bubbly, Catalonia is rich in wine districts, which produce everything from the dark and heavy reds of El Priorat to light whites from the Penedès. Catalonia's vineyards are among the nation's best and most varied.

Food terminology throughout this book is given in Catalan/Spanish (Castilian) or Catalan alone, except in the few cases where the Spanish term is used in both languages. Rather than descend into the murky depths of linguistic polemics, the idea is to reflect what you are most likely to see and hear in the city's restaurants.

HISTORY

The Romans didn't just bring straight roads, a large temple and a functional sewerage system to the little town of Barcino. They also brought with them their culinary habits, which included such fundamentals as olives and grapes. We can perhaps be grateful that another Roman favourite, *garum* (a kind of tart fish paste that could survive long sea voyages), did not survive the demise of the empire.

Catalan cooking is one of several regional Spanish cuisines, all of which have been influenced to some extent by common factors. One particular spin comes from the country's long history of Muslim occupation, reflected in the use of spices such as saffron and cumin and, in desserts, the predominance of honeyed sweets, almonds and fruit. Other major sources of culinary inspiration were imports brought back from South America, where everyday staples such as potatoes, tomatoes and, of course, chocolate came from.

At the heart of Catalan cooking is a diversity of products and traditions. Some dishes are referred to as *mar i muntanya* (surf and turf; a mix of seafood and meats), a term which perhaps best sums up the situation. Barcelona has always been enamoured of edible marine inhabitants (Roman annals suggest big, juicy local oysters were once a common item on ancient menus), while the Catalan hinterland, especially the Pyrenees, has long been the hearth of a much chunkier, heartier cooking tradition. From wintry mountain stews to an array of sausages and a general fondness for charcuterie and venison, the Catalan countryside contributes much to the Spanish dinner table. To these basic ingredients the Catalans add a rich array of

PYJAMA PARTY

If a waiter proposes *'pijama'*, it is not an invitation to head home for bed and jammies. It is rather a suggestion to try one of the country's most lurid desserts. It consists of tinned peach (and maybe pineapple) slices, a clump of flan and two balls of ice cream (say strawberry and vanilla), all covered in whipped cream and chocolate topping! After that you may well want to have a lie down.

sauces, betraying a strong French influence on their culinary habits.

Furthermore, Barcelona has long attracted migrants, at first from the rest of Spain and, since the 1990s, from all over the world. Thus, the city is jammed with Galician seafood restaurants and Basque tapas bars, and since the mid-1990s, foreign cuisines have landed – big time. While cheap and cheerful Chinese establishments have always been here, until the early 1990s, you could count the Japanese, Thai and Indian restaurants on the fingers of one hand. All this has changed. Suddenly *pizzerie,* sushi restaurants, tandoori temptations, Thai, Korean and kebabs are everywhere. The number of non-Spanish restaurants in Barcelona has more than quadrupled since the start of the 21st century.

You name it, Barcelona's got it. It might all seem old hat to veteran foodies arriving from London, Paris, New York or Sydney, but here in Spain the new ethnic eateries are a remarkable addition to what was already an exceptional local scene. And however well-travelled the international palate, surprises are always on hand through local dishes and the ebullient atmosphere of timeless eateries. *¡Buen provecho!*

ETIQUETTE

You may not arrive in Barcelona with jet lag but, due to the rather different Spanish eating habits, your tummy will think it has abandoned all known time zones.

Esmorzar/desayuno (breakfast) is generally a no-nonsense affair eaten at a bar on the way to work. A *cafè amb llet/café con leche* (coffee with milk) with a *pasta* (pastry), such as a cream-filled *canya* (broad, tube-like pastry) or croissant, is the typical breakfast. If you can, try an *ensaïmada*, a Mallorcan import. This whirl-shaped pastry has the consistency of a croissant and is dusted with icing sugar. It can a be a trifle messy to eat, but it's worth it!

If you prefer a savoury start, you could go for the oddly named *bikini,* nothing more than a classic toasted ham and cheese sandwich. A *torrada/tostada* is simply buttered toast.

Dinar/comida (or *almuerzo;* lunchtime), between 2pm and 4pm, is generally the main meal of the day, although modern work and living habits are changing this for some people. Many workers opt for the cheap and cheerful, set-price *menú del día* at lunch, while some restaurants offer more elaborate versions both at lunch and dinner time. (See p171 for more information.) A simpler version is the *plat combinat/plato combinado* (combined dish) – basically a meat-and-three-veg dish that will hardly excite taste buds, but will have little impact on your budget, meaning that you can eat solidly and economically at lunch and then splash out at dinner!

Barcelonins generally don't even start thinking about *sopar/cena* (dinner) much before 9pm. A full meal can comprise an *entrant/entrante* (starter), *plat/plato principal* (main course) and *postre* (dessert). In some places the first two are referred to as the *primer plat/primer plato* (first course) and *segon plat/segundo plato* (second course). You will generally be asked what you would like de primer (for your first course) and then de segon (for your second course). You can skip the starter without causing offence.

Instead of heading for a sit-down meal, some locals prefer to *tapear* or *ir de tapeo* (go on a tapas crawl; also known as *picar* or *pica-pica*). This is the delightful business of standing around in bars and choosing from a range of tasty little titbits. You can stay in one place or move from one to another, and you basically keep munching and drinking until you've had enough.

Generally diners order water and a bottle of wine – separate glasses for each are provided (in Spain the larger glass is generally for the water). In midsummer (mostly at lunchtime), you might also ask for some Casera (lemonade) to mix with your heavy red wine and make *tinto de verano* (summer red).

In many simpler restaurants you will keep the same knife and fork throughout the meal. Once your order is taken and the first course (which could range from a simple *amanida/ensalada rusa* – cold vegetable salad thick with potatoes and mayonnaise – to an elaborate seafood item) is in place, you may find the level of service increases disconcertingly. This especially becomes the case as you reach the end of any given course. Hovering waiters swoop like eagles to swipe your unfinished dish or lift your glass of wine, still tinged with that last sip you wanted to savour. Simply utter '*Encara no he terminat*'/'*Todavía no he terminado*' ('I haven't finished yet') – you'll be flashed a cheerful smile and your waiter will leave you to finish in peace.

Spain is a smokers' paradise and restaurants seem to be a favourite place for this activity. Not only do Spaniards smoke with satisfaction at the conclusion of a filling meal, many smoke between courses, regardless of whether fellow diners have finished or not. A 2006 law provided some relief by requiring all establishments bigger than 100 sq metres to become nonsmoking (with the option of setting up costly, separately ventilated smokers' areas). Smaller places were given the choice of becoming smoking or nonsmoking. No prizes for guessing which most of them went for. Nonsmokers may win in the end, however, as the national government is considering launching a complete ban on smoking in public places – opinion polls suggest (surprisingly to some) that a majority of Spaniards would favour such a ban.

Don't jump out of your seat if people pass your table and address you with a hearty '*bon profit!*'/'*¡buen provecho!*' They're just saying 'enjoy your meal!'

SPECIALITIES

The basics are simple enough: bread and olive oil. And lots of garlic. No Catalan would eat a meal without bread, and olive oil seems to make its way into just about every dish. Catalans find it hard to understand why other people put butter on bread when *pa amb tomàquet/pan con tomate* (bread sliced then rubbed with tomato, olive oil, garlic and salt) is so much tastier! There are many local brands of olive oil, but one of the best is Borges, which has been produced in Tàrrega, in Lleida province, since 1896. Spices, on the other hand, are generally noticeable by their absence. If you're told something is *picante* (spicy, hot) you can generally be sure it is little more than mild.

A typical *carta* (menu) begins with starters such as *amanides/ensaladas* (salads), *sopes/sopas* (soups) and *entremeses* (hors d'oeuvres). The latter can range from a mound of potato salad with olives, asparagus and anchovies to an array of cold meats, slices of cheese and olives. The more upmarket the restaurant, the more imaginative the offerings.

The basic ingredients of later courses can be summarised under the general headings of *pollastre/pollo* (chicken), *carn/carne* (meat), *mariscos* (seafood), *peix/pescado* (fish) and *arròs/arroz* (rice). Meat may be subdivided into *porc/cerdo* (pork), *vedella/ternera* (beef) and *anyell/cordero* (lamb). If you want a *guarnició/guarnición* (side order), you may have to order it separately. This may be the only way to get a decent serve of *verdures/verduras* (vegetables), which for many locals seem to be anathema.

Often much more fun than a full sit-down meal is snacking on bite-sized goodies known as tapas. A *tapa* is a tiny serving; if you particularly like something, you can have a *media ración* or even a full *ración*. Two or three of the latter, depending on what they are, can easily constitute a full meal.

The origin of the *tapa* appears to lie in the old habit of serving drinks with a lid *(tapa)* on the glass, perhaps to keep out pesky bugs. The *tapa* might have been a piece of bread and at some point a couple of morsels on the *tapa* became par for the course – usually salty items bound to work up a greater thirst. In some bars you will still get a few olives or other free snacks with your beer, but since tapas were always more a southern Spanish thing, it is not overly common – in Barcelona, if you want something, you pay for it.

Since the mid-1990s the number of Basque tapas bars has increased exponentially. They generally work like this: you order drinks (try the slightly fizzy white wine, *txacolí*) and ask for a plate. Many of the tapas are *montaditos* (a sort of canapé), which could range from a creamy Roquefort cheese and walnut combination to a chunk of spicy sausage. They all come with toothpicks. These facilitate their consumption, but serve another important purpose too: when you're ready to leave, the toothpicks are counted up and the bill presented.

If you opt for *tapes*/tapas, it is handy to identify some of the common items: *boquerons/boquerones* (white anchovies in vinegar – delicious and tangy); *mandonguilles/albóndigas* (meatballs); *pebrots/pimientos de Padrón* (little green peppers from Galicia, some of which are hot); *patates braves/patatas bravas* (potato chunks bathed in a slightly spicy tomato sauce, sometimes mixed with mayonnaise); *gambes/gambas* (prawns, either done *al all/al ajillo,* with garlic, or *a la plantxa/plancha,* grilled); *chipirons/chipirones* (baby squid); and *calamars/*

calamares a la Romana (deep-fried calamari rings).

The essence of Catalan food lies in its sauces for meat and fish. There are five main types: *sofregit* (fried onion, tomato and garlic); *samfaina* or *chanfaina* (*sofregit* plus red pepper and aubergine or courgette); *picada* (based on ground almonds, usually with garlic, parsley, pine nuts or hazelnuts, and sometimes breadcrumbs); *allioli* (pounded garlic with olive oil, often with egg yolk added to make more of a mayonnaise); and *romesco* (an almond, red pepper, tomato, olive oil, garlic and vinegar sauce, used especially with *calçots*, for which see Catalan Favourites on p170).

The Catalan version of pizza is *coca,* often made in the shape of a long, broad tongue. There are many variations on this theme, savoury and sweet. The former can come with tomato, onion, pepper and sometimes sardines. The sweet version, often almond based, is more common and is a standard item at many a *festa* (festival), such as Dia de Sant Joan in June (see p18). Catalans also like pasta, and *canelons* (similar to Italian cannelloni) is a common dish.

Bolets (wild mushrooms) are a Catalan passion – people disappear into the forests in autumn to pick them. There are many, many types of *bolets;* the large succulent *rovellons* are a favourite. *Trompetas de la muerte* (trumpets of death) are a veritable delicacy and are generally available during summer and autumn. A trip to the Boqueria market in central Barcelona around October will reveal even more varieties.

The main centres of cheese production in Catalonia are La Seu d'Urgell, the Cerdanya district and the Pallars area in the northwest. Although some traditional cheeses are becoming less common, you can still come across things like *formatge de tupí* (goat's cheese soaked in olive oil) in produce markets and specialist cheese shops.

You will also find all sorts of sausages, most using pork as a base. Some generic names include *botifarra, fuet* (a thin, whiplike dried-pork sausage) and *llonganissa*. The names often seem to apply to very different sausages, depending on where you buy them. Some are spicier than others.

Of course, fish and seafood are major components of the region's cuisine. Only 15% of Catalonia's needs are fished in Catalan waters: much of what ends up on Catalan tables comes from the Bay of Biscay, France, the UK and as far off as South Africa (cod in particular in the last case). In 1996 only about 15% of all produce on sale at Barcelona's main wholesale market (Mercabarna) was imported; in 2007, more than half of the fish came from abroad.

Apart from more standard approaches such as serving up steamed, baked or fried fish, the Catalans like to mix it up a little, by way of fish soups and stews. *Suquet,* which combines several types of fish with potatoes, is the best known; while *sarsuela* is richer in its variety of fish ingredients. Other themed stews often go by the name of *caldereta,* where one item (usually lobster) is the star ingredient.

Dessert is a mixed bag. Many of the better restaurants go to great lengths to tempt you into enormous sins of gluttony. At simpler eateries, especially at lunch, dessert might simply be a choice of fruit, *flan* (crème caramel) or *gelat/helado* (ice cream). If you opt for ice cream, don't be surprised to be shown a list of manufactured goodies similar to what you'd grab at the beach.

WHERE TO EAT

Many *tavernes/tabernas, cerveserias/cervezerías* (beer bars) and *cellers/bodegas* (wine cellars) offer some form of solid sustenance. This can range from *entrepans/bocadillos* (filled rolls) or *flautas* (narrow baguettes), tapas and *raciones* to full meals served in *menjadors/comedores* (sit-down restaurants) out the back. For a full meal, you will most frequently end up in a *restaurant/restaurante.* Other establishments you may come across include a *marisquería,* which specialises in seafood; or a *mesón* (literally 'big table'), which might (but not necessarily) indicate a more modest eatery.

VEGETARIANS & VEGANS

Vegetarians, and especially vegans, can have a hard time in Spain, but in Barcelona a growing battery of vegetarian restaurants offers welcome relief. Be careful when ordering salads (such as the *amanida catalana*), which may contain popular 'vegetables' such as ham or tuna.

COOKING COURSES

If you find you like Barcelona's food so much you want to cook some yourself, there are several cooking courses available. For details, see p277.

BEVERAGES

For an introduction to local wines and other alcoholic drinks, see the Drinking & Nightlife chapter (p194).

Coffee, Tea & Hot Chocolate

The coffee in Spain is strong and slightly bitter. A *cafè amb llet/café con leche* (generally drunk at breakfast only) is about half coffee, half hot milk. Ask for *grande* or *doble* if you want a large cup, *en got/vaso* if you want a smaller shot in a glass, or a *sombra* if you want lots of milk. A *cafè sol/café solo* (usually abbreviated to just *un solo*) is a short black or espresso; *un (cafè) tallat/(café) cortado* is a short black with a little milk (more or less the same as a *macchiato* in Italy). Where milk is involved, you'll be asked whether or not you want it *calenta/caliente* (hot). For iced coffee,

CATALAN FAVOURITES

Here are some typical Catalan dishes. For a basic food glossary, see the Language chapter (p287).

Starters

Amanida catalana (Catalan salad) Almost any mix of lettuce, olives, tomatoes, hard-boiled eggs, onions, chicory, celery, green peppers and garlic, with tuna (almost always canned), ham or sausage, and either mayonnaise or an oil and vinegar dressing.

Calçots amb romesco *Calçots* are a type of long spring onion, delicious as a starter with *romesco* sauce. They are only in season in late winter/early spring, when Catalans get together for a *calçotada,* the local version of a BBQ. The *calçots* are the amusing part of the event, as the black ash in which they are grilled inevitably winds up on hands and, when people are feeling naughty, perhaps in their neighbour's face! This is usually followed by an enormous meal with countless meat and sausage courses.

Escalivada Red peppers and aubergines (sometimes onions and tomatoes too), grilled, cooled, peeled, sliced and served with an olive oil, salt and garlic dressing.

Esqueixada Salad of *bacallà/bacalao* (shredded salted cod) with tomatoes, red peppers, onions, white beans, olives, olive oil and vinegar.

Main Courses

Arròs a la cassola/arroz a la catalana Catalan paella, cooked in an earthenware pot, without saffron.

Arròs negre Rice cooked in black cuttlefish ink.

Bacallà a la llauna Salted cod baked in tomato, garlic, parsley, paprika and wine.

Botifarra amb mongetes Pork sausage with fried white beans.

Cargols Snails, almost a religion to some, often stewed with *conill/conejo* (rabbit) and chilli.

Escudella A meat, sausage and vegetable stew, the sauce of which is mixed with noodles or rice and served as a soup. The rest is served as a main course and is known as *carn d'olla*. It's generally available in winter only.

Fideuà Similar to paella, but using vermicelli noodles as the base, it is usually served with tomato and meat and/or sausage or fish. There is also a cuttlefish-ink version. You should receive a little side dish of *allioli* (pounded garlic with olive oil, often with egg yolk added) to mix in as you wish – if you don't, ask for it.

Fricandó A pork and vegetable stew.

Sarsuela/zarzuela Mixed seafood cooked in *sofregit* (fried onion, tomato and garlic sauce) with seasonings.

Suquet de peix A kind of fish and potato hotpot – there are all sorts of variations on this theme, depending on what type of seafood you toss in.

Truita de botifarra Sausage omelette, a Catalan version of the famous Spanish *tortilla*.

Desserts

Crema catalana A cream custard with a crisp, burnt-sugar coating.

Mel i mató Honey and fresh cream cheese – simple but delicious.

Music A serving of dried fruits and nuts, sometimes mixed with ice cream or a sweetish cream cheese and served with a glass of sweet muscatel.

ask for *cafè amb gel/café con hielo* – you'll get a glass of ice and a hot cup of coffee, to be poured over the ice. If you want to skip the caffeine, ask for a *cafè descaféinat/café descaféinado* (decaf) – most people ask for it *de maquina* (from the coffee machine) because *de sobre* (the sachet stuff) is nothing special. If you want your cuppa supercharged, for example with a shot of Baileys (very popular), ask for a *cigaló/carajillo de Baileys* (or whatever your heart desires).

Barcelonins prefer coffee, but you can also get many different styles of *té* (tea) and *infusiones* (herbal teas, such as camomile). Locals tend to drink tea black. If you want milk, ask for it to come *a part/a parte* (separately) to avoid ending up with a cup of tea-flavoured watery milk.

A cup of *xocolata calenta/chocolate caliente* (hot chocolate) is an invitation for sticky fingers – it is generally a thick, dark, sweet tooth's dream and could easily be classed as a food. A local version, topped with thick cream, is known as a *suís*.

Fruit & Soft Drinks

Suc de taronja/zumo de naranja (orange juice) is the main freshly squeezed juice available, often served with sugar. Ask for *natural*, otherwise you may get a puny bottle of runny concentrate. Unfortunately, *natural* also means room temperature in these parts, so if you are proffered a bottle when asking for *natural,* you'll need to explain that you want it *espremut/exprimido* (squeezed).

Refrescos (cool drinks) include the usual brands of soft drinks, local brands such as Kas

and, in summer, *granissat/granizado* (iced fruit crush). A *batut/batido* is a flavoured milk drink.

Orxata/horchata is a Valencian drink of Islamic origin. Made from the juice of *chufa* (tiger nuts), sugar and water, it is sweet and tastes like soy milk with a hint of cinnamon. You'll come across it both fresh and bottled, but this is a drink that should be consumed freshly made. A naughtier version is a *cubanito,* made by adding a fat dollop of chocolate ice cream.

PRACTICALITIES
Opening Hours

Most restaurants and eateries open from 1pm to 4pm and from 8pm to midnight. Bars and cafes that offer tapas generally adhere to similar hours as far as food goes, although you can often purchase snacks from the bar outside these times. A few places open throughout the day, typically from 1pm to 1.30am. Restaurants listed in this chapter are open for lunch and dinner unless stated otherwise. No specific times are given unless they vary considerably from the norm.

If the local opening times have your tummy in a panic, don't worry. Plenty of restaurants in more touristy parts of town open early for foreigners – you pay for this with often mediocre food and the almost exclusive company of other tourists. Many bars and restaurants offering tapas and *raciones* have them on the bar before and after appointed main meal times, which means you can almost always pick up something to eat.

Many restaurants take a day off during the week and most are shut on Christmas Eve and on New Year's Eve (or Christmas Day and New Year's Day). Some close over Easter, and a good deal also shut for most or all of the month of August. Beware that Sunday and Monday evenings can be frustrating, as this is when most places take time off.

Meal times are important events in the daily life of the average *barcelonin*. People take the time to enjoy their food and, where possible, they still have a full sit-down meal at lunchtime. Lunch can easily go on for a couple of hours. Dinner is frequently a lighter affair.

How Much?

Barcelona is not the cheap night out it once was, but lunch can be an economical affair if you opt for the set *menú del día*.

You are rarely likely to spend much more than €100 for a top-quality meal. In the course of

PRICE GUIDE

Some call it *la dolorosa* (the painful one) but sooner or later you will have to ask for *el compte, sisplau* (the bill, please). The price ranges used here indicate the cost per person of a full meal (starter, main and dessert), including a bottle of modest house wine:

€€€	€71 and above
€€	€21 to €70
€	up to €20

this chapter, restaurants are listed in each neighbourhood by price, from top end to budget.

The *menú del día*, a full set meal (usually with several options), water and wine, is a great way to cap prices at lunchtime. They start from around €8 to €10 and can move as high as €25 for more elaborate offerings. Many restaurants listed here offer this cost-saving option.

At high-end restaurants you can occasionally opt for a *menú de degustación*, a tasting menu involving samples of several different dishes. This can be a great way to get a broader view of what the restaurant does and has the advantage of coming at a fixed price.

Booking Tables

At many of the midrange restaurants and simpler taverns with *menjadors/comedores* (dining rooms) you can usually turn up and find a spot without booking ahead. At high-end restaurants, and for dinner especially, it is safer to make a booking. Thursday to Saturday nights are especially busy.

Self-Catering

Shopping in the big produce markets such as Mercat de la Boqueria (Map p60) and complementing your purchases with a quick run around the many *supermercats/supermercados* around town will provide you with all the cheese, sausages, fruit and drink you could need. Supermarkets close to the city centre include Carrefour Express (Map p60; La Rambla dels Estudis 113; 10am-10pm Mon-Sat; Catalunya), near the northern end of La Rambla, and Superservis (Map p60; Carrer d'Avinyó 13; 8.45am-2pm & 5-8.30pm Mon-Thu & Sat, 8.45am-8.30pm Fri; Liceu), in the heart of Barri Gòtic. For freshly baked bread, head for a *forn/panadería* (bakery). For a gourmet touch, the food section of El Corte Inglés (Map p106; 93 306 38 00; Plaça de Catalunya 14; Catalunya) has some tempting local and imported goodies; the Zona Alta branch (Map p122; 93 366 71 00; Avinguda Diagonal 617; Maria Cristina) also has a food section. Specialist food shops abound; see the Shopping chapter (p152) for details. For more on markets, see the boxed text To Market, To Market (p186).

Tipping

Many eating establishments have a cover charge, usually up to a few euros per head. A service charge is often, but by no means always, included in the bill, so any further tipping becomes strictly a personal choice. Catalans (and other Spaniards) are not overwhelming tippers. If you are particularly happy, 5% to 10% on top is generally fine.

BARRI GÒTIC & LA RAMBLA

First things first: skip the strip. La Rambla is fine for people watching, but no great shakes for the palate. Instead venture off into the streets that wind into the Barri Gòtic and your tum will be eternally grateful. Inside the medieval labyrinth, choices abound. If you had

---

MUNCHING IN MUSEUMS

Several museums and other sights house great restaurants and cafes. The most attractive museum snack stop in the Barri Gòtic is the Cafè d'Estiu (Map p60; 10am-10pm Apr-Sep) in the leafy courtyard of the Museu Frederic Marès (p64). A pleasant cafe and snack bar is located in the medieval courtyard of the Disseny Hub (p81) in La Ribera.

At the Museu Marítim (p73), a fine cafe-restaurant (93 317 52 56; 9am-8pm) is housed beneath the vaults of the shipyards. The restaurant sprawls into the gardens outside. Nearby, the Centre d'Art Santa Mònica (p57) on La Rambla has a cafe-restaurant with a pleasant, 1st-floor terrace.

The Museu d'Història de Catalunya (p91) offers a great rooftop terrace cafe and restaurant, La Miranda del Museu (Map p90; 93 225 50 07; cafe 10am-7pm Tue & Thu-Sat, 10am-8pm Wed, 10am-2.30pm Sun & holidays, restaurant Tue-Sun).

On Montjuïc you have a couple of options: the cafe in the Fundació Joan Miró (p142), and Oleum (Map p140; lunch Tue-Sun), a restaurant with good views in the Museu Nacional d'Art de Catalunya (p138).

top picks

TAPAS

- Inopia (p184)
- Tapaç 24 (p183)
- Taktika Berri (p184)
- Bar Celta (p174)
- Cal Pep (p176)
- La Bodegueta Provença (p183)
- Vaso de Oro (p179)

to pinpoint any one area, it would be the half of the *barri* (neighbourhood) between Plaça de Sant Jaume and the waterfront, especially towards Via Laietana. On and around Carrer de la Mercè a huddle of old-time tapas bars survives, down dirty and simple, as if caught in a time warp in postwar Spain. Some are simply dirty; others are wonderful, immutable finds. All are laden with dollops of atmosphere.

PLA Map p60   Fusion €€

☎ 93 412 65 52; www.elpla.com; Carrer de la Bellafila 5; meals €45-50; ⏲ dinner; Ⓜ Liceu; ✖

You could be forgiven for thinking you have waltzed into a dark designer cocktail bar. Actually it's a medieval den (with a huge stone arch) of devious culinary mischief, where the cooks churn out such temptations as *daus de tonyina poc feta a la flama, verduretes i una salsa de cassis i citronella* (lightly flamed tuna cubes with vegetables and a cassis and lemongrass sauce). It has a tasting menu for €29 Sunday to Thursday.

COMETACINC Map p60   Fusion €€

☎ 93 310 15 58; www.cometacinc.com; Carrer del Cometa 5; meals €35; ⏲ dinner daily; Ⓜ Jaume I; ✖

In this grand medieval space, the kitchen constantly produces a changing menu that criss-crosses all boundaries. The elegant candle-lit wooden tables over two floors set an intimate mood for, say, some *tonyina vermella a la brasa amb confitura agre-dolça de albercoc* (charcoal-grilled red tuna with chutney). It also has a fair range of tapas.

AGUT Map p60   Catalan €€

☎ 93 315 17 09; Carrer d'en Gignàs 16; meals €35; ⏲ dinner Tue-Sat, lunch Sun Sep-Jul; Ⓜ Jaume I; ✖

Deep in the Gothic labyrinth lies this classic eatery. A series of cosy dining areas is connected by broad arches while, high up, the walls are tightly lined by artworks. There's art in what the kitchen serves up too, from the oak-grilled meat to a succulent variety of seafood offerings, like the *cassoleta de rap a l'all cremat amb cloïsses* (monkfish with browned garlic and clams).

CAFÈ DE L'ACADÈMIA Map p60   Catalan €€

☎ 93 319 82 53; Carrer de Lledó 1; meals €30-35; ⏲ Mon-Fri; Ⓜ Jaume I; ✖

Expect a mix of traditional dishes with the occasional creative twist. At lunchtime, local Ajuntament (town hall) office workers pounce on the *menú del día* (for €14, or €9.80 at the bar). In the evening it is rather more romantic, as soft lighting emphasises the intimacy of the timber ceiling and wooden decor. Offerings range from *chuletón* (huge T-bone steak) for two to *guatlla farcida de foie d'ànec i botifarra amb salsa de ceps* (quail stuffed with duck foie gras and sausage with a mushroom sauce).

LOS CARACOLES Map p60   Spanish €€

☎ 93 302 31 85; www.los-caracoles.es; Carrer dels Escudellers 14; meals €30-35; ⏲ daily; Ⓜ Drassanes; ✖

Run by the fifth generation of the Bofarull family, 'The Snails' started life as a tavern in 1835 and is one of Barcelona's best-known, if somewhat touristy, restaurants. Several interlocking rooms (consider asking for the small medieval-looking banquet room), with centuries of history seemingly greased into the tables and garlic-clad walls, may well distract you from the rotisserie chickens and snails that are the house specialities. Locals still dine here and the ambience alone makes it worth dropping by, if only for a drink or two at the bar.

CAN PESCALLUNES Map p60   Catalan €€

☎ 93 318 54 83; Carrer de les Magdalenes 23; meals €25-30; ⏲ Mon-Fri; Ⓜ Jaume I

A muted sort of place and decoratively stuck in another era the 'House of the Moon-Fisher' may be, but the family that runs this Catalan eatery are no slouches in the kitchen. Expect generous and well-prepared servings of such items as steak tartare or *bacallà amb samfaina* (cod with samfaina sauce). The first courses are equally good.

BAR CELTA Map p60   Galician €€

☎ 93 315 00 06; Carrer de la Mercè 16; meals €20-25; ⏱ noon-midnight Tue-Sun; Ⓜ Drassanes

This bright, rambunctious bar-cum-restaurant specialises in *pulpo* (octopus) and other sea critters like *navajas* (razor clams). It does a good job: even the most demanding of Galician natives give this spot the thumbs up. Sit at the zinc bar, order a bottle of Ribeiro and the traditional Galician *tazas* (little white cups) and tuck into your *raciones*.

MILK Map p60   Bar-Restaurant €

☎ 93 268 09 22; www.milkbarcelona.com; Carrer d'en Gignàs 21; meals €15-20; ⏱ brunch 11am-4pm Thu-Sun; Ⓜ Jaume I

Known to many as a cool cocktail spot, the Irish-run Milk's key role for Barcelona night owls is providing morning-after brunches. Avoid direct sunlight and tuck into pancakes, salmon eggs Benedict and other hangover dishes in the penumbra. Anyone for a triple whammy hamburger or a Milk's fry-up? Get some hair of the dog with cocktails at €5 to €7.

CAN CONESA Map p60   Snacks €

☎ 93 310 57 95; Carrer de la Llibreteria 1; rolls & toasted sandwiches €3-5; ⏱ Mon-Sat; Ⓜ Jaume I

Locals, especially workers from the Ajuntament and Generalitat (regional government) at lunchtime, have been lining up here for the succulent *entrepans* (filled rolls), toasted sandwiches and other snacks since the 1950s.

CAFÈ DE L'ÒPERA

Map p60   Cafe €

☎ 93 302 41 80; La Rambla 74; ⏱ 9am-3am; Ⓜ Liceu; ✉

Opposite the Gran Teatre del Liceu is La Rambla's most intriguing cafe. Operating since 1929, it is pleasant enough for an early evening libation or coffee and croissants. Head upstairs for an elevated seat above the busy boulevard. Can you be tempted by the *cafè de l'Òpera* (coffee with chocolate mousse)?

CAJ CHAI Map p60   Cafe €

☎ 93 301 95 92; Carrer de Sant Domènec del Call 12; ⏱ 3-10pm Mon, 10.30am-10pm Tue-Sun; Ⓜ Jaume I

Open and bright, this is a tea and herbal-tea connoisseur's paradise. Make your choice, order a pastry and settle in for a nice cuppa and a chat.

SALTERIO Map p60   Cafe €

Carrer de Sant Domènec del Call 4; ⏱ 2pm-1am Mon-Sat; Ⓜ Jaume I

If it got any mellower here, with its gentle Middle Eastern music and low whispering, you'd nod off. The wait for the mint tea is worth it – it's filled with real mint, as good as in Morocco.

EL RAVAL

For contrast alone, El Raval is possibly the most interesting part of the old town. Timeless classics of Barcelona dining are scattered across what was long the old city's poorest *barri*, and since the late 1990s, battalions of hip new eateries and artsy restaurants have also sprung up, especially in the area around the Museu d'Art Contemporani (see p76). Some of the cheapest eats in town, full of character, lurk along El Raval's streets. From Carrer de Sant Pau north towards Carrer de Pelai, the university and Ronda de Sant Antoni is where you'll find most of these haunts.

CASA LEOPOLDO

Map p74   Catalan €€

☎ 93 441 30 14; www.casaleopoldo.com; Carrer de Sant Rafael 24; meals €60; ⏱ lunch & dinner Tue-Sat, lunch Sun Sep-Jul, closed Easter; Ⓜ Liceu; ✉

Long hidden in the slum alleys of El Raval, this was writer Manuel Vázquez Montalbán's favourite restaurant; it figures constantly in the urban wanderings of his detective character, Pepe Carvalho (see p40). Several rambling dining areas in this 1929 classic have magnificent tiled walls and exposed beam ceilings. The mostly seafood menu is extensive and the wine list strong. Surf and turf Catalan classics, like *mandonguilles amb sípia i gambes* (rissoles with cuttlefish and shrimp), are done to perfection.

CAN LLUÍS Map p74   Catalan €€

☎ 93 441 11 87; Carrer de la Cera 49; meals €30-35; ⏱ Mon-Sat Sep-Jul; Ⓜ Sant Antoni

Three generations have kept this spick and span old-time classic in business since 1929. Beneath the olive-green beams in the back dining room you can see the spot where an anarchist's bomb went off in

1946, killing the then owner. Expect fresh fish and seafood. The llenguado (sole) is oven cooked in whisky and raisins.

BODEGA 1800 Map p74 — Catalan €€
☎ 93 317 30 79; http://bodega1800.com; Carrer del Carme 31; meals €25-30; Ⓨ daily; Ⓜ Liceu

Ricardo loves nothing better than to come up with a new canapé or other delicious, bite-sized snack to offer his tippling guests. He has converted an old wine store into a charming wine bar. Linger at the casks inside his little bottle-lined establishment or in the adjacent arcade and be guided through snack and wine suggestions. Wine, no matter which one you want, goes for €2.50 a glass and snacks €3.50 a pop.

L'HAVANA Map p74 — Catalan €€
☎ 93 302 21 06; Carrer del Lleó 1; meals €25-30; Ⓨ lunch & dinner Tue-Sat, lunch Sun; Ⓜ Sant Antoni

Little has changed in this cavernous, family-run place since it opened in the 1940s. The front dining area, with frosted glass windows, Modernista design touches and spaciously spread tables, is a touch more severe than the better-lit rear area. A great starter is the combinat, with three mussels, a smidge of amanida russa (potato salad), esqueixada and more. Meat and fish options follow, and the calamars farcits (stuffed calamari) are filling. Round off with home-made crema catalana.

MAMA I TECA Map p74 — Catalan €€
☎ 93 441 33 35; Carrer de la Lluna 4; meals €25-30; Ⓨ lunch & dinner Sun-Mon & Wed-Fri, dinner Sat; Ⓜ Sant Antoni

A tiny place with a half dozen tables, Mama i Teca is more a lifestyle than a restaurant. The setting is a multicultural and often rowdy street deep in El Raval. Locals drop in and hang about for a drink, and diners are treated to Catalan treats served without rush. How about bacallà al traginer (cod deep fried in olive oil with garlic and red pepper) or a juicy sirloin steak?

ELISABETS Map p74 — Catalan €€
☎ 93 317 58 26; Carrer d'Elisabets 2-4; meals €20-25; Ⓨ Mon-Sat Sep-Jul; Ⓜ Catalunya

This unassuming restaurant is popular for no-nonsense local fare. The walls are lined with old radio sets and the menú del día

(€10.75) varies daily. If you prefer a la carta, try the ragú de jabalí (wild boar stew) and finish with mel i mató. Those with a late hunger on Friday nights can probably get a meal here as late as 1am.

BAR CENTRAL Map p74 — Tapas €
☎ 93 301 10 98; Mercat de la Boqueria; meals €20; Ⓨ lunch Mon-Sat; Ⓜ Liceu

Hiding out towards the back of Barcelona's best-known market is this fabulously chaotic lunchtime bar. Marketeers, local workers and the occasional curious tourist jostle for a stool – get there early or be prepared to wait. Order a few generous raciones, and make one of them the grilled fish of the day.

BAR PINOTXO
Map p74 — Tapas €
☎ 93 317 17 31; Mercat de la Boqueria; meals €20; Ⓨ 6am-5pm Mon-Sat Sep-Jul; Ⓜ Liceu

Of the half-dozen or so tapas bars and informal eateries within the market, this one near the La Rambla entrance is about the most popular. Roll up to the bar and enjoy the people watching as you munch on tapas assembled from the products on sale in the stalls around you.

MESÓN DAVID Map p74 — Spanish €
☎ 93 441 59 34; Carrer de les Carretes 63; meals €15-20, menú del día €8.50; Ⓨ Tue-Sun; Ⓜ Paral.lel

With its smoky timber ceiling, excitable waiting staff and generally chaotic feel, this is a tavern the likes of which they don't make any more – a slice of the old Spain. Plonk yourself down on a bench for gregarious dining, such as house specialities caldo gallego (sausage broth), and the main course of lechazo al horno (a great clump of oven-roasted suckling lamb for €8.90).

RESTAURANTE POLLO RICO
Map p74 — Spanish €
☎ 93 441 31 84; Carrer de Sant Pau 31; meals €15-20; Ⓨ daily; Ⓜ Liceu; ⊗

The 'Tasty Chicken' is true to its name, with fast, cheap, abundant grub. Head upstairs and carve out a space amid the garrulous punters, then rattle off your order to a high-speed waiter. Chicken (quarter chicken and chips costs €4), meat and various other options can be put together to help you fill to bursting. Skip the paella.

ORGANIC Map p74   Vegetarian €

☎ 93 301 09 02; www.antoniaorganickitchen.com, in Spanish; Carrer de la Junta de Comerç 11; meals €14-20; ⏱ 12.45pm-midnight; Ⓜ Liceu; ⊠

As you wander into this sprawling vegetarian spot, to the left is the open kitchen, where you choose from a limited range of options that change from day to day. Servings are generous and imaginative. The salad buffet is copious and desserts are good. The set lunch costs €9.50 plus drinks. The same people have a stand (⏱ 9am-7pm Mon-Sat) in the Mercat de la Boqueria.

BIOCENTER Map p74   Vegetarian €

☎ 93 301 45 83; http://restaurantebiocenter. es; Carrer del Pintor Fortuny 25; meals €10-15; ⏱ lunch & dinner Mon-Sat, lunch Sun; Ⓜ Catalunya; ⊠ 📶

Head past the coffee bar and the dining area, with its warm exposed brickwork and dark wooden tables, to the kitchen at the back to order your *menú del día* (€9.75 plus drink). A huge *plat combinat* (single dish with several portions) costs €7.95. Top up with as much salad as you can handle. This is one of several options on what has become a bit of a vegetarian street.

GRANJA VIADER Map p74   Cafe €

☎ 93 318 34 86; Carrer d'en Xuclà 4; ⏱ 9am-1.45pm & 5-8.45pm Tue-Sat, 5-8.45pm Mon; Ⓜ Liceu

For more than a century, people have flocked down this alley to get to the cups of homemade hot chocolate and whipped cream (ask for a *suís*) ladled out in this classic Catalan-style milk bar–cum-deli. Together with one of the many pastries on display, the offerings here make for the sweet tooth's ideal breakfast. The Viader clan invented Cacaolat, a forerunner of kids' powdered-chocolate beverages.

LA RIBERA

If you'd mentioned El Born (El Borne in Spanish) in the early 1990s, you wouldn't have raised much interest. Now the area is peppered with bars, dance dives, groovy designer stores and restaurants. El Born is where Barcelona is truly cooking – avant-garde chefs and fusion masters have zeroed in on this southern corner of La Ribera to conduct their culinary experiments. If you don't want to play such wild games, there's plenty of the traditional stuff to choose from, too. One or two foreign eateries add variation.

EL PASSADÍS DEL PEP Map p82   Seafood €€€

☎ 93 310 10 21; www.passadis.com; Pla del Palau 2; meals €70-80; ⏱ lunch & dinner Tue-Sat, dinner Mon Sep-Jul; Ⓜ Barceloneta; ⊠

There's no sign, but locals know where to head for a seafood feast. They say the restaurant's raw materials are delivered daily from fishing ports along the Catalan coast. There is no menu – what's on offer depends on what the sea has surrendered on the day. Just head down the long, ill-lit corridor and entrust yourself to their care.

CAL PEP Map p82   Tapas €€

☎ 93 310 79 61; www.calpep.com; Plaça de les Olles 8; meals €45-50; ⏱ lunch Tue-Sat, dinner Mon-Fri Sep-Jul; Ⓜ Barceloneta; ⊠

It's getting a foot in the door here that's the problem. And if you want one of the five tables out the back, you'll need to call ahead. Most people are happy elbowing their way to the bar for some of the tastiest gourmet seafood tapas in town. Pep recommends *cloïsses amb pernil* (clams and ham – seriously!) or the *trifàsic* (combo of calamari, whitebait and prawns).

TANTARANTANA Map p82   Mediterranean €€

☎ 93 268 24 10; Carrer d'en Tantarantana 24; meals €30; ⏱ dinner Mon-Sat; Ⓜ Jaume I

Surrounded as it is by the furiously fashionable, front-line nuclei of *nueva cocina española*, this spot is a refreshing contrast. There is something comforting about the old-style marble-top tables, upon which you can sample simple but well-prepared dishes such as risotto or grilled tuna served with vegetables and ginger. It attracts a 30-something crowd who enjoy the outdoor seating in summer.

WUSHU Map p82   Pan-Asian €€

☎ 93 310 73 13; www.wushu-restaurant.com; Avinguda del Marquès de l'Argentera 1; meals €25-30; ⏱ lunch & dinner Tue-Sat, lunch Sun; Ⓜ Barceloneta; ⊠

This Australian-run wok restaurant serves up an assortment of tasty pan-Asian dishes, including *pad thai*, curries and more. What about kangaroo *yakisoba*? It also offers various BBQ dishes and you can take away. Pull up a pew at the nut-brown tables or sit at the bar. Wash down your meal with Tiger beer or one of a handful of wines.

EATING LA RIBERA

CUINES DE SANTA CATERINA

Map p82   Mediterranean & Asian €€

☎ 93 268 99 18; www.cuinessantacaterina.com; Mercat de Santa Caterina; meals €25-30; ☺ daily; Ⓜ Jaume I; ✗

With a contemporary feel and open kitchens, this multi-faceted eatery inside the Mercat de Santa Caterina offers all sorts of food. Peck at the sushi bar, tuck into classic rice dishes or go vegetarian. They do some things better than others, so skip the hummus and *tarte tatin*. A drawback is the speed with which barely finished plates are whisked away from you, but the range of dishes and bustling atmosphere are fun. Reservations aren't taken, so it's first come first served.

IKIBANA Map p82   Japanese Fusion €€

☎ 93 295 67 32; www.ikibana.es; Passeig de Picasso 32; meals €25-30; ☺ daily; Ⓜ Barceloneta

It feels like you are walking on water as you enter this Japanese-fusion lounge affair. A broad selection of *makis*, tempuras, sushi and more are served at high tables with leather-backed stools. The wide screen TV switches from chilled music clips to live shots of the kitchen your wasabi wandered from. The set lunch is €12.

PLA DE LA GARSA Map p82   Catalan €€

☎ 93 315 24 13; Carrer dels Assaonadors 13; meals €25; ☺ dinner; Ⓜ Jaume I; ✗

This 17th-century house is the ideal location for a romantic candle-lit dinner. Timber beams, anarchically scattered tables and soft ambient music combine to make an enchanting setting over two floors for traditional, hearty Catalan cooking, with dishes such as *timbal de botifarra negra* (a black pudding dish with mushrooms).

BUBÓ Map p82   Patisserie-Restaurant €€

☎ 93 268 72 24; www.bubo.ws; Carrer de les Caputxes 6 & 10; ☺ 4pm-midnight Mon, 10am-midnight Tue-Thu & Sun, 10am-2am Fri & Sat; Ⓜ Barceloneta; ✗

Carles Mampel is a sweet artist, literally. It is difficult to walk by his bar and pastry shop without taking a seat outside to try one of his fantasy-laden creations. They are limitless in style and number. Try saying no to a mousse of *gianduia* (a dark hazelnut cream) with mango cream, caramelised hazelnuts with spices and hazelnut biscuit. To balance things, it offers a series of savoury snacks at €2 to €4 and little sandwiches at €3 to €4.

HABANA VIEJA Map p82   Cuban €€

☎ 93 268 25 04; Carrer dels Banys Vells 2; meals €20-25; ☺ Mon-Sat; Ⓜ Jaume I

Since the early 1990s this Cuban hideaway, the first of its kind in Barcelona and still one of the best, has offered old island faves such as the stringy meat dish *ropa vieja* (literally 'old clothes') and rice concoctions. With its antique light fittings and predilection for timber furnishings, this Ribera house could easily be an Old Havana eatery.

LA LLAVOR DELS ORÍGENS

Map p82   Catalan €

☎ 93 310 75 31; www.lallavordelsorigens. com; Carrer de la Vidrieria 6-8; meals €15-20; ☺ 12.30pm-12.30am; Ⓜ Jaume I; ✗

In this treasure chest of Catalan regional products, the shop shelves groan under the weight of bottles and packets of goodies. It also has a long menu of smallish dishes, such as *sopa de carbassa i castanyes* (pumpkin and chestnut soup) or *mandonguilles amb albergìnies* (rissoles with aubergine), that you can mix and match over wine by the glass. At the L'Eixample branch (Map p106; ☎ 93 453 11 20; Carrer d'Enric Granados 9; ☺ 1pm-1am; Ⓜ Universitat), one of three others around town, you can dine outside.

CASA DELFIN Map p82   Spanish €

☎ 93 319 50 88; Passeig del Born 36; meals €15-20; ☺ noon-1am; Ⓜ Barceloneta

While surrounding restaurants may serve up exquisitely designed Sino-Moroccan-Venezuelan creations, the bustling waiters at the 'Dolphin House' content themselves with serving bountiful Spanish classics. And they are right to do so. Finding a free lunchtime table at the sprawling terrace requires a modest portion of luck. Choose from more than 30 tried-and-true dishes.

EL XAMPANYET Map p82   Tapas €

☎ 93 319 70 03; Carrer de Montcada 22; meals €15-20; ☺ lunch & dinner Tue-Sat, lunch Sun; Ⓜ Jaume I

Nothing has changed for decades in this, one of the city's best-known *cava* bars. Plant yourself at the bar or seek out a table against the decoratively tiled walls for a glass or three of *cava* and an assortment of tapas, such as the tangy *boquerons en vinagre* (white anchovies in vinegar). It's the timeless atmosphere that makes this place.

BAR JOAN Map p82   Catalan €
☎ 93 310 61 50; Mercat de Santa Caterina; menú del día €11; ☺ lunch Mon-Sat; Ⓜ Jaume I
Along with the popular Cuines de Santa Caterina (p177), there are a couple of bar-eateries in the Mercat de Santa Caterina. Bar Joan is known especially to locals for its *arròs negre* (cuttlefish-ink rice) on Tuesdays at lunchtime. It's a simple spot, but always fills up with hungry passers-by, black rice or no black rice.

PORT VELL & LA BARCELONETA

In the Maremàgnum complex (p158) on the Moll d'Espanya you can eat close to the water's edge at a handful of fun, if fairly slapdash, joints. For good food and atmosphere, head around to La Barceloneta, whose lanes fairly bristle with everything from good-natured, noisy tapas bars to upmarket seafood restaurants. Almost everything shuts on Sunday and Monday evenings.

EL LOBITO Map p90   Seafood €€€
☎ 93 319 91 64; Carrer de Ginebra 9; meals €70-80; ☺ lunch & dinner Tue-Sat, lunch Sun; Ⓜ Barceloneta
A coquettish corner spot with pleasingly cluttered decor, dark timber tables and lime-green linen, the 'Little Wolf' is a seafood lover's paradise. Avoid the seriously busy Friday and Saturday nights. The usual procedure is a set menu, with a long procession of sea critters (preceded by a few landlubberly amuse-gueules) coming your way.

TORRE D'ALTA MAR Map p90   Seafood €€€
☎ 93 221 00 07; www.torredealtamar.com; Torre de Sant Sebastià, Passeig de Joan de Borbó 88; meals €70-80; ☺ lunch & dinner Tue-Sat, dinner Sun-Mon; Ⓜ Barceloneta or ⒷⒷ 17, 39, 57 or 64; ☒
Head to the top of the Torre de Sant Sebastià and, instead of taking the Transbordador Aeri, take a ringside seat for the best city dining views and fine seafood, such as a *Gall de Sant Pere amb salsa de garotes* (John Dory with sea-urchin sauce). The setting alone, high up above the city and port, makes this perfect for a romantic couple.

BARCELONA'S GOURMET GAUDÍ

He presents his latest culinary inventions like a child who has just made a fabulous mud pie. Indeed, if Ferran Adrià came up with a mud dish, it wouldn't come as much of a surprise. Born in 1962, this self-taught chef has rocketed to the forefront of international *haute cuisine* with his fearless experimentation. The Gaudí of gourmets, he has been dubbed by his three-star Michelin colleague from the Basque Country, Juan Maria Arzak, 'the most imaginative cook in all history'. The rough-spoken Adrià has been made a doctor *honoris causa* at Barcelona University (UB).

During the 1980s Adrià worked his way up to head chef at a good, if unspectacular, Franco-Catalan restaurant, El Bulli (see p255), in a splendidly wild spot on the Costa Brava. By the early 1990s he was co-owner of the business and had begun to let rip, converting El Bulli into one of the country's most exclusive restaurants, where anything from essence of carrot to solidified edible coffee might have appeared on the menu.

Aided by brother Albert and a staff of more than 50, Adrià has for years run El Bulli for six months of the year – dinner only. Few star chefs can afford the luxury of doing what Adrià decided to do in 2010: close down the restaurant in 2012–14 for a 'creative break'. With plenty of other activities on the boil, he announced he would reopen the restaurant with a new format that had yet to be decided. Losing his three Michelin stars in this way and acclaim for the 'best restaurant in the world' seems to leave him indifferent. 'I don't play the "best restaurants" game,' he said.

He will continue to spend much of his time like a mad scientist in El Bulli Taller, his kitchen workshop on Carrer de la Portaferrissa, virtually across the road from the Mercat de la Boqueria in central Barcelona. He has fast-food eateries in Madrid and Barcelona, a hotel in Seville, runs a restaurant in the Casino de Madrid and has lent his name to bags of potato chips. The gruffly spoken chef gives lectures around the world, has published glossy coffee-table books on his molecular cuisine and has all the hallmarks of a star.

Adrià is not alone. One of his disciples, fellow Catalan Sergi Arola, couldn't resist the call of a place at Hotel Arts Barcelona (p236), where he runs Arola. Another El Bulli alumnus, Carles Abellán, has received acclaim at his Tapaç 24 (p183). Ferran's brother Albert has a hit on his hands with gourmet tapas at Inopia (p184).

SUQUET DE L'ALMIRALL

Map p90   Seafood €€

☎ 93 221 62 33; Passeig de Joan de Borbó 65; meals €45-50; ⟳ lunch & dinner Tue-Sat, lunch Sun; Ⓜ Barceloneta, ⬜ 17, 39, 57 or 64; ✕

A family business run by an alumnus of Ferran Adrià's El Bulli (see boxed text, opposite), the order of the day is top-class seafood with the occasional unexpected twist. The house specialty is *suquet*. A good option is the *pica pica marinera* (a seafood mix, €38) or you could opt for the tasting menu (€44). Grab one of the few outdoor tables.

CAN MAJÓ Map p90   Seafood €€

☎ 93 221 58 18; Carrer del Almirall Aixada 23; meals €30-40; ⟳ lunch & dinner Tue-Sat, lunch Sun; Ⓜ Barceloneta, ⬜ 45, 57, 59, 64 or 157

Virtually on the beach (with tables outside in summer), Can Majó has a long and steady reputation for fine seafood, particularly its rice dishes (€15 to €22) and cornucopian *suquets* (fish stews). The *bollabessa de peix i marisc* (fish and seafood bouillabaisse) is succulent. Or try a big *graellada* (mixed seafood grill). Sit outside and admire the beach goers.

CAN ROS 1911 Map p90   Seafood €€

☎ 93 221 45 79; Carrer del Almirall Aixada 7; meals €30-35; ⟳ Thu-Tue; Ⓜ Barceloneta, ⬜ 45, 57, 59, 64 or 157; ✕

The fifth generation is now at the controls in this immutable seafood favourite. In a restaurant where the decor is a reminder of simpler times, there's a straightforward guiding principle: give the punters juicy fresh fish cooked with a light touch. They also do a rich *arròs a la marinera* (seafood rice), a generous *suquet* and a mixed seafood platter for two.

RESTAURANT 7 PORTES

Map p90   Seafood €€

☎ 93 319 30 33; www.7portes.com; Passeig d'Isabel II 14; meals €30-35; ⟳ 1pm-1am Ⓜ Barceloneta; ✕

Founded in 1836 as a cafe and converted into a restaurant in 1929, this is a classic. In the hands of the Parellada clan, which runs several quality restaurants in and beyond Barcelona, it exudes an old-world atmosphere with its wood panelling, tiles, mirrors and plaques naming some of the famous – such as Orson Welles – who have passed through. Paella is the speciality, or go for the surfeit of seafood in the *gran plat de*

top picks

HOTEL DINING HIGHS

There was a time when about the saddest thing you could do was eat at your hotel. How that has changed in some cases! A number of Barcelona's hotels are home to high-end, elegant restaurants, veritable havens for gourmet highs. You don't need to be a hotel guest to dine in them. Some of the best are the following:

* Actual (Grand Hotel Central, p234)
* Arola (Hotel Arts Barcelona, p236)
* Enoteca (Hotel Arts Barcelona, p236)
* Drolma (Hotel Majèstic, p236)
* Kitchen (Axel Hotel, p238)
* Doscielos (Hotel Me, p236)
* Lasarte & Loidi (Comtes de Barcelona, p237)
* Moo (Hotel Omm, p236)
* Bravo (W Barcelona, p235)

marisc (literally 'big plate of seafood'). We dare you to finish it!

CAN RAMONET Map p90   Seafood €€

☎ 93 319 30 64; Carrer de la Maquinista 17; meals €30; Ⓜ Barceloneta; ✕

Perching at one of the little tables across the lane is the perfect way to pass a warm summer evening, perhaps over some *vieires al cava* (scallops in *cava*). Or step inside and enjoy your tapas around a barrel-cum-table. Rice dishes cost around €20 for two and the catch of the day is around €20 to €25. It claims to have been in business since 1763.

VASO DE ORO Map p90   Tapas €€

☎ 93 319 30 98; Carrer de Balboa 6; meals €20-25; Ⓜ Barceloneta; ✕

This must be one of the world's narrowest bars. At either end, the space balloons a little to allow for a handful of tables. Squeeze in and enjoy the show. Fast-talking, white-jacketed waiters will serve up a few quick quips with your tapas of grilled *gambes* (prawns) or *solomillo* (sirloin) chunks. Want something a little different to drink? Ask for a *flauta cincuenta* – half lager and half dark beer.

CAN MAÑO Map p90   Spanish €

☎ 93 319 30 82; Carrer del Baluard 12; meals €20; ⟳ Mon-Sat; Ⓜ Barceloneta

The owners have been dealing with an onslaught of punters for decades and swear they are going to retire soon (but they never do). You'll need to be prepared to wait before being squeezed in at a packed table for a raucous dinner (or lunch) of *raciones* (listed on a board at the back) over a bottle of *turbio*, a pleasing cloudy white plonk.

CAN PAIXANO Map p90 Tapas €

☎ 93 310 08 39; Carrer de la Reina Cristina 7; meals €15-20; ⏲ 9am-10.30pm; Ⓜ Barceloneta; ☒
Tucked away amid the bright tacky lights of cheap electronics stores in what could almost be a backstreet in southeast Asia, this lofty old champagne bar has long run on a winning formula. The standard poison is bubbly rosé in elegant little glasses, combined with bite-sized *bocadillos* (filled rolls). This place is jammed to the rafters, and elbowing your way to the bar to ask harried staff for menu items can be a titanic struggle.

PORT OLÍMPIC, EL POBLENOU & EL FÒRUM

The Port Olímpic marina is lined on two sides by dozens of restaurants and tapas bars, popular in spring and summer but mostly underwhelming. A more upmarket series of places huddles at the northeast end of Platja de la Barceloneta – it's hard to beat the sand, sea and palm tree backdrop. Otherwise, the search for culinary curios will take you behind the scenes in El Poblenou, where a few nuggets glitter.

ELS PESCADORS Map p96 Seafood €€

☎ 93 225 20 18; www.elspescadors.com; Plaça de Prim 1; meals €50; ⏲ daily, closed Easter week; Ⓜ Poblenou
Set on a cute square lined with low houses and *bella ombre* trees long ago imported from South America, this bustling family restaurant continues to serve some of the city's great seafood-and-rice dishes. There are three dining areas inside: two quite modern, while the main one preserves its old tavern flavour. Better is sitting outside. All the products – fish, meat and vegetables – are trucked in fresh from various parts of Catalonia.

EL CANGREJO LOCO Map p96 Seafood €€

☎ 93 221 05 33; www.elcangrejoloco.com; Moll de Gregal 29-30; meals €45-60, menú del día €23; ⏲ daily; Ⓜ Ciutadella Vila Olímpica; ☒
Of the hive of eating activity along the docks of Port Olímpic, the 'Mad Crab' is the best. It inevitably has a thoroughfare feel, attracting swarms of tourists, but the difference is that the food is generally of a reasonable quality. Fish standards, such as *bacallà* (salted cod) and *rap* (monkfish), are served in various guises and melt in the mouth. The rich *mariscada* (seafood platter) for two includes half a lobster.

XIRINGUITO D'ESCRIBÀ

Map p96 Seafood €€
☎ 93 221 07 29; www.escriba.es; Ronda del Litoral 42, Platja de Bogatell; meals €40-50; ⏲ lunch daily; Ⓜ Llacuna
The clan that brought you Escribà (p185) sweets and pastries also operates one of the most popular waterfront seafood eateries in town. This is one of the few places where one person can order from a selection of paella and *fideuà* (normally reserved for a minimum of two people). Prices are higher than average, but quality matches. You can also choose from a selection of Escribà pastries for dessert – worth the trip alone.

LA PUBILLA DEL TAULAT Map p96 Tapas €€

☎ 93 225 30 85; www.lapubilladeltaulat.com; Carrer de Marià Aguiló 131; meals €20-30; ⏲ Tue-Sun; Ⓜ Poblenou
Get inside the eatery in this late-19th-century building quickly, as you'll find the bar has been stripped of all its tapas delights if you arrive much after 10pm. Tucked away in backstreets still partly lined with low-slung houses of another era, this place is a popular stop. All the classics are present: *patatas bomba* (spicy meat stuffed potatoes), *mejillones al vapor* (steamed mussels), *chocos* (lightly fried cuttlefish slices) and more.

L'EIXAMPLE

This huge grid area can seem daunting, but remember that most of the many varied and enticing restaurants are concentrated in the Quadrat d'Or between Carrer de Pau Claris and Carrer de Muntaner, Avinguda Diagonal and Gran Via de les Corts Catalanes. There is no shortage of perfectly acceptable bar-restaurants (often with street-side tables) that offer reasonable *menús del día* and stock-standard dishes *a la carta*. In among these places are sprinkled real finds, offering both local and international cuisine.

SAÜC Map p100   Catalan €€€

☎ 93 321 01 89; www.saucrestaurant.com; Passatge de Lluís Pellicer 12; meals €70-80, menú del día €27; ☺ Tue-Sat; Ⓜ Hospital Clínic; ⊠

Pop into this basement place down a little Eixample laneway and you enter a soothing sanctuary. Sober designer decor, dominated by ochres, creams and buttercup yellows, allows you to concentrate on what emerges from the kitchen, such as *tàrtar de anguila fumada, poma verda i caviar d'arengada* (smoked eel tartare with green apples and salted sardine caviar). You can request half-size portions at 60% of the price. The tasting menu comprises an appetiser, four courses, then a cheese selection and two desserts (€78).

SPEAKEASY Map p100   International €€

☎ 93 217 50 80; Carrer d'Aribau 162-166; meals €70; ☺ lunch & dinner Mon-Fri, dinner Sat Sep-Jul; Ⓜ Diagonal

This clandestine restaurant lurks behind the Dry Martini (p205). You will be shown a door through the open kitchen area to the 'storeroom', lined with hundreds of bottles of backlit, quality tipples. Dark decorative tones, a few works of art, low lighting, light jazz music and smooth service complete the setting. What's on the menu depends on the markets and the cook's whim. A tempting option is the creamy *burrata di Puglia con yemas de espárragos blancos y jamón Joselito* (a huge hunk of mozzarella from southern Italy with white asparagus hearts and strips of high-quality cured ham).

NOTI Map p106   Mediterranean €€

☎ 93 342 66 73; http://noti-universal.com; Carrer de Roger de Llúria 35; meals €60-70; ☺ lunch & dinner Mon-Fri, dinner Sat; Ⓜ Passeig de Gràcia; ⊠

Once home to the *Noticiero Universal* newspaper, Noti has an ample dining room plastered with mirrors that seem to multiply the steely designer tables. Try a *peix fresc salvatge de la Boqueria, a la planxa, amb carbassó en ratatouille, mantega muntada de llimona* (fresh fish from the Boqueria market with ratatouille of courgette and lemon butter) or perhaps a meat dish – anything from steak tartare to chicken curry. Start

the evening with the cocktail of the day at the bar. It has lunch menus from €14 to €24, and an evening set menu at €36.

CASA CALVET Map p106   Catalan €€

☎ 93 412 40 12; www.casacalvet.es; Carrer de Casp 48; meals €55-70; ☺ Mon-Sat; Ⓜ Urquinaona; ⊠

An early Gaudí masterpiece loaded with his trademark curvy features now houses a swish restaurant (just to the right of the building's main entrance). Dress up and ask for an intimate *taula cabina* (wooden booth). You could opt for *vieires a la planxa amb tagliatelle i tomàquet confitat* (grilled scallops with ribbon pasta and tomato confit). It has various tasting menus for up to €69, and a child's menu for €16.

CASA DARÍO Map p106   Seafood €€

☎ 93 453 31 35; www.casadario.com, in Spanish; Carrer del Consell de Cent 256; meals €50-60; ☺ Mon-Sat Sep-Jul; Ⓜ Passeig de Gràcia; ⊠

Step into the timeless world of silver service and ample helpings of the fruits of the sea. Waiters serve tables with hushed efficiency and present a seafood feast as only the folks from the northwest Atlantic region of Galicia know how. Opt for a set menu (€50) and you will be served endless rounds of seafood wonders, many flown in daily from Galicia. Treat yourself to anything from *cañaíllas* (sea snails) to *nécoras* (small crabs that abound on the Galician coast). It even has a takeaway service.

CINC SENTITS Map p106   International €€

☎ 93 323 94 90; www.cincsentits.com; Carrer d'Aribau 58; meals €50-60; ☺ Tue-Sat Sep-Jul; Ⓜ Passeig de Gràcia

Enter this somewhat overlit realm of the 'Five Senses' to indulge in a tasting menu (from €49 to €69), consisting of a series of small, experimental dishes. What's on offer changes from one day to the next, but think highly elaborate designer portions in a brief menu that balances fish and meat. A key is the use of fresh local product, such as fish landed on the Costa Brava and top-quality suckling pig from Extremadura. Less ambitious, but cheaper, is the set lunch at €30.

CATA 1.81 Map p106   Gourmet Tapas €€

☎ 93 323 68 18; www.cata181.com; Carrer de València 181; meals €50; ☺ dinner Mon-Sat Sep-Jul; Ⓜ Passeig de Gràcia

If you like an Al Capone–style conspiratorial feel, call ahead to book the little room out the back, past the busy, compact kitchen. Surrounded by shelves of fine wines packed to the rafters, you will be treated to a series of dainty gourmet dishes, such as *raviolis amb bacallà* (salt-cod dumplings) or *truita de patates i tòfona negre* (thick potato tortilla with a delicate trace of black truffle). The best option is to choose from one of several tasting-menu options ranging from €28 to €45. Since wines feature so highly here, let rip with the list of fine Spanish tipples.

ALKÍMIA Map p100   Modern Catalan €€

☎ 93 207 61 15; www.alkimia.cat; Carrer de l'Indústria 79; meals €45-50; ⏲ Mon-Fri Sep-Jul; Ⓜ Verdaguer

Jordi Vila, a culinary alchemist, serves up refined Catalan dishes with a twist in this elegant, white-walled locale well off the tourist trail. Dishes such as his *arròs de nyore i safrà amb escamarlans de la costa* (saffron and sweet-chilli rice with crayfish) earned Vila his first Michelin star. He presents a series of set menus from €37 to €79.

RESTAURANT ME Map p100   Pan-Asian €€

☎ 93 419 49 33; www.catarsiscuisine.com; Carrer de París 162; meals €45-50; ⏲ lunch & dinner Thu-Sat, dinner Tue-Wed; Ⓜ Hospital Clínic; ☒

The chef whips up wonders in the kitchen at this surprise fusion establishment. At a time when fusion is often synonymous with nothing in particular, it manages to create superb Asian dishes with the occasional New Orleans or other international intrusion. Some vegetarian options, like the *banh xeo* (Vietnamese pancake filled with bamboo, seitan and mushrooms), accompany such self-indulgent choices as stuffed New Orleans prawns with tartare sauce.

MELTON Map p100   Italian €€

☎ 93 363 27 76; Carrer de Muntaner 189; meals €45; ⏲ Tue-Sat; Ⓜ Hospital Clínic

You know you're onto something when Italians recommend an Italian restaurant. This slick place offers well-prepared pasta and risotto dishes (the latter, for example, with foie gras) and a tempting array of meat and fish mains. For an unusual pasta option, try the *lasagnetta de tòfona negra i múrgules* (little lasagna with black truffle and morel mushrooms).

ALBA GRANADOS

Map p106   Spanish-Mediterranean €€

☎ 93 454 61 16; www.albagranados.com; Carrer d'Enric Granados 34; meals €45; ⏲ lunch & dinner Mon-Sat, lunch Sun; Ⓡ FGC Provença; ☒

In summer ask for one of the romantic tables for two on the 1st-floor balcony. Overlooking the trees, it is a unique spot, with little traffic. Inside, the ground- and 1st-floor dining areas are huge, featuring exposed brick and dark parquet. The menu offers a little of everything but the best dishes revolve around meat, such as *solomillo a la mantequilla de trufa con tarrina de patata y beicon* (sirloin in truffle butter, potato and bacon terrine).

PATAGONIA Map p106   Argentine €€

☎ 93 304 37 35; Gran Via de les Corts Catalanes 660; meals €40-45; ⏲ daily; Ⓜ Passeig de Gràcia; ☒

An elegant Argentinean beef-fest awaits in this stylish restaurant. Start with *empanadas* (tiny meat-crammed pies). You might want to skip the *achuras* (offal) and head for a hearty meat main, such as a juicy beef *medallón con salsa de colmenillas* (a medallion in a morel sauce) or such classics as *bife de chorizo* (sirloin) or Brazilian *picanha* (rump). You can choose from one of five side dishes to accompany your pound of flesh.

YAMADORY Map p106   Japanese €€

☎ 93 453 92 64; Carrer d'Aribau 68; meals €35-40; ⏲ Mon-Sat; Ⓡ FGC Provença

Yamadory, one of the city's first Japanese restaurants, still attracts visiting Japanese business people today. As the door slips closed behind you, the first thing you notice is the hushed atmosphere. Divided into several dining areas with a contemporary Japanese decor, it is notable for its gliding efficiency. Head upstairs to sit on a floor-level tatami. The sushi, sashimi, udon and tempura are all good.

THAI GARDENS Map p106   Thai €€

☎ 93 487 98 98; www.thaigardensgroup.com; Carrer de la Diputació 273; meals €35, menú del día €15; ⏲ daily; Ⓜ Passeig de Gràcia; ☒

One of the first and still one of the best for Thai food in Barcelona. Tables for two set in quiet corners contrast with great round-party sittings amid a veritable forest of tropical greenery. The set menu (€31) allows you to try a broad range of dishes and can be a good idea for larger groups.

DE TAPA MADRE Map p106 Catalan €€
☎ 93 459 31 34; www.detapamadre.com; Carrer de Mallorca 301; meals €35; ⏰ 8am-1am; Ⓜ Verdaguer; ✕

A chatty atmosphere greets you from the bar from the moment you swing open the door. A few tiny tables line the window, but head upstairs for more space in the gallery, which hovers above the array of tapas on the bar below, or go deeper inside past the bench with the ham legs. Choose from a range of tapas or opt for a full meal. The *arròs caldós amb llagostins* (a hearty rice dish with king prawns) is delicious. The kitchen opens all day long, so you can pop by any time hunger strikes.

RELAIS DE VENISE Map p106 French €€
☎ 93 467 21 62; Carrer de Pau Claris 142; meals €35; ⏰ daily Sep-Jul; Ⓜ Passeig de Gràcia; ✕

You can eat anything you want here, so long as it's meat. Indeed, there's just one dish, a succulent beef entrecôte with a secret 'sauce Porte-Maillot' (named after the location of the original restaurant in Paris, which has branches in New York and London), chips and salad (€22), to which you can add a little wine and dessert. It is served in slices and in two waves so that it doesn't go cold.

TERRABACUS Map p100 Tapas & Wine €€
☎ 93 410 86 33; www.terrabacus.com; Carrer de Muntaner 185; meals €30-35, menú del día €18; ⏰ lunch & dinner Tue-Fri, dinner Mon & Sat; Ⓜ Hospital Clínic

Food exists to accompany wine, or so one could be led to believe here. In this 'Land of Bacchus', one of the joys is sampling from the extensive wine list and choosing bites to go down with the nectar. You might try the various cheese platters or select a dish of high-grade Joselito cured ham. More substantial dishes range from risotto to steak tartare.

EMBAT Map p106 Mediterranean €€
☎ 93 458 08 55; www.restaurantembat.es; Carrer de Mallorca 304; meals €30-35; ⏰ lunch Tue & Wed, lunch & dinner Thu-Sat; Ⓜ Girona

Enthusiastic young chefs turn out beautifully presented dishes in this basement eatery, whose brown and cream decor might not enchant all comers. You can

eat three courses for around €20 to €25 at lunch, indulging perhaps in *raviolis de pollo amb bacon i calabassó* (chicken ravioli bathed in a sauce of finely chopped bacon, zucchini and other vegetables) followed by melt-in-the-mouth *lluç amb pa amb tomàquet, carxofes i maionesa de peres* (a thick cut of hake on a tomato-drenched clump of bread dressed with artichoke slices and a pear mayonnaise).

TAPAÇ 24 Map p106 Tapas €€
☎ 93 488 09 77; www.carlesabellan.com; Carrer de la Diputació 269; meals €30-35; ⏰ 9am-midnight Mon-Sat; Ⓜ Passeig de Gràcia

Carles Abellán, master of Comerç 24 in La Ribera, runs this basement tapas haven known for its gourmet versions of old faves. Specials include the *bikini* (toasted ham and cheese sandwich – here the ham is cured and the truffle makes all the difference), a thick black *arròs negre de sípia* (squid-ink black rice), the McFoie-Burguer and, for dessert, *xocolata amb pa, sal i oli* (delicious balls of chocolate in olive oil with a touch of salt and wafer). You can't book.

CERVESERIA BRASSERIA GALLEGA
Map p100 Tapas €€
☎ 93 439 41 28; Carrer de Casanova 238; meals €30; ⏰ Mon-Sat; Ⓜ Hospital Clínic

You could walk right by this modest establishment without giving it a second glance. If you did, you'd notice it was chock full of locals immersed in animated banter and surrounded by plates of abundant Galician classics. The fresh *pulpo a la gallega* (spicy octopus chunks with potatoes) as starter confirms this place is a cut above the competition. Waiters have little time for loitering, but always a quick quip. The setting is simple, the meat dishes succulent and the *fideuà* full of seafood flavour.

LA BODEGUETA PROVENÇA
Map p106 Tapas €€
☎ 93 215 17 25; Carrer de Provença 233; meals €25-30; ⏰ daily; Ⓜ Diagonal

The 'Little Wine Cellar' offers classic tapas presented with a touch of class, from *calamares a la andaluza* (lightly battered calamari rings) to *cecina* (dried cured veal meat). The house speciality is *ous estrellats* (literally 'smashed eggs') – a mix of scrambled egg white, egg yoke, potato and then ingredients ranging from foie gras to black pudding *(morcilla)*. Wash down with a good Ribera del Duero or *caña* (little glass) of beer.

INOPIA Map p100 — Gourmet Tapas €€
☎ 93 424 52 31; www.barinopia.com; Carrer de Tamarit 104; meals €25-30; ⊗ dinner Tue-Sat, lunch Sat; Ⓜ Rocafort

Albert Adrià, brother of Barcelona's star chef Ferran and something of a kitchen celebrity himself, runs this popular corner tapas temple. If you can't grab one of the handful of tables, don't worry, just stand inside or out and select a *pintxo de cuixa de pollastre a l'ast* (chunk of rotisserie chicken thigh) or the lightly fried, tempura-style vegetables. Wash down with house red or Moritz beer.

KOYUKI Map p106 — Japanese €€
☎ 93 237 84 90; Carrer de Còrsega 242; meals €25-30; ⊗ lunch & dinner Tue-Sat, dinner Sun; Ⓜ Diagonal

This unassuming basement Japanese diner is one of those rough-edged diamonds that it pays to revisit. Sit at a long table and order from the cheesy menu complete with pictures courtesy of the Japanese owner – you won't be disappointed. The variety of *sashimi moriawase* is generous and constantly fresh. The *tempura udon* is a particularly hearty noodle option. Splash it all down with Sapporo beer.

TAKTIKA BERRI Map p106 — Basque €€
☎ 93 453 47 59; Carrer de València 169; meals €45-50, tapas €20-30; ⊗ lunch & dinner Mon-Fri, lunch Sat; Ⓜ Hospital Clínic

Get in early as the bar teems with punters from far and wide, anxious to wrap their mouths around some of the best Basque tapas in town. The hot morsels are all snapped up as soon as they arrive from the kitchen, so keep your eyes peeled. The seated dining area out the back is also good. In the evening, it's all over by about 10.30pm.

BODEGA SEPÚLVEDA Map p106 — Catalan €€
☎ 93 323 59 44; www.bodegasepulveda.net; Carrer de Sepúlveda 173bis; meals €25; ⊗ lunch & dinner Mon-Fri, dinner Sat; Ⓜ Universitat; ⊗

This tavern has been showering dishes (which they like to call tapas) on its happy diners since 1952. The main dining area is out the back and downstairs, with a small, low-ceilinged nonsmoking area upstairs. The range of dishes is a little overwhelming and mixes traditional (cold meats, cheeses

and Catalan faves like *cap i pota*, a dish of chunks of fatty beef in gravy) with more surprising options like *carpaccio de calabacín con bacalao y parmesán* (thin zucchini slices draped in cod and parmesan cheese). You can hang out until 1am.

BAR VELÓDROMO Map p100 — Tapas €€
☎ 93 430 60 22; Carrer de Muntaner 213; meals €25; ⊗ daily; Ⓜ Hospital Clínic

The reopening of this once-classic tavern in 2009 brings back a fine-looking establishment in which to take breakfast, stop for an aperitif or sit down for a meal. The low, corner building retains much of its original look, with timber omnipresent. Food largely consists of tapas and smallish renderings of fairly typical Catalan and Spanish dishes. More than anything, this place is about its history and atmosphere.

CERVESERIA CATALANA Map p106 — Tapas €€
☎ 93 216 03 68; Carrer de Mallorca 236; meals €25; ⊗ daily; Ⓜ Passeig de Gràcia; ⊗

The 'Catalan Brewery' is good for breakfast, lunch and dinner. Come in for your morning coffee and croissant, or wait until lunch to enjoy choosing from the abundance of tapas and *montaditos* (canapés). You can sit at the bar, on the pavement terrace or in the restaurant at the back. The variety of hot tapas, salads and other snacks draws a well-dressed crowd of locals and outsiders. It has expanded the premises to deal with demand.

CASA AMALIA Map p106 — Catalan €€
☎ 93 458 94 58; Passatge del Mercat 4-6; meals €20-25; ⊗ lunch & dinner Tue-Sat, lunch Sun Sep-Jul; Ⓜ Girona

This restaurant is popular for its hearty Catalan cooking using fresh produce, mainly sourced from the busy market next door. The orange and white decorated joint has split level dining that makes the most of its space. On Thursdays during winter it offers the Catalan mountain classic, *escudella*. Otherwise, you might try light variations on local cuisine, such as the *bacallà al allioli de poma* (cod in an apple-based aioli sauce). The four-course *menú del día* is exceptional lunchtime value at €12.

CASA ALFONSO Map p106 — Spanish €
☎ 93 301 97 83; www.casaalfonso.com; Carrer de Roger de Llúria 6; meals €20; ⊗ 9am-1am Mon-Sat; Ⓜ Urquinaona

In business since 1934, Casa Alfonso is perfect for a morning coffee or a tapas stop at the long marble bar. Timber panelled and festooned with old photos, posters and swinging hams, it attracts a faithful local clientele at all hours for its *flautas* (thin custom-made baguettes with your choice of filling), hams, cheeses, hot dishes and homemade desserts. Consider rounding off with an *alfonsito* (a miniature Irish coffee).

EL RINCÓN MAYA Map p106 Mexican €

☎ 93 451 39 46; Carrer de València 183; meals €20; ☽ lunch & dinner Tue-Sat, dinner Mon; Ⓜ Passeig de Gràcia

Getting a seat in this Mexican eatery can be a trial. The setting is warm, modest and, thankfully, devoid of the excesses of pseudo-Mexican decor. The pocket-sized serves of nachos, guacamole and fajitas all burst with flavour. You'll also discover lesser-known items like *tacos de pibil* (pork tacos) and *tinga*, little pasta pockets of chicken. There are also more-substantial dishes for €9.50. The owner-chef spent much of his life in the restaurant business in Mexico City.

RESTAURANTE JARDÍN ROSA

Map p100 Chinese €

☎ 93 325 71 95; Avinguda Mistral 54; meals €15-20; ☽ daily; Ⓜ Espanya

As in any other city, there's no shortage of cheap and cheerful Chinese joints, but this is the real McCoy. Go for the first part of the menu where you'll find anything from pig's-blood soup and black chicken in ginger to frogs' legs and strips of eel with leek. The chintzy decor one normally associates with Chinese eateries is considerably more sober here.

AMALTEA Map p106 Vegetarian €

☎ 93 454 86 13; www.amalteaygovinda.com; Carrer de la Diputació 164; meals €10-15; ☽ Mon-Sat; Ⓜ Urgell; ✕

The ceiling fresco of blue sky sets the scene in this popular vegetarian eatery. The weekday set lunch (€10.50) offers a series of dishes that change frequently with the seasons. At night, the set two-course dinner (€15) offers good value. The homemade desserts are tempting. The place is something of an alternative lifestyle centre, with yoga, t'ai chi and belly-dancing classes.

CAFÈ DEL CENTRE Map p106 Cafe €

☎ 93 488 11 01; Carrer de Girona 69; ☽ 8.30am-midnight Mon-Fri; Ⓜ Girona

Step back a century in this cafe, in business since 1873. The timber-top bar extends down the right side as you enter, fronted by a slew of marble-topped tables and dark timber chairs. It exudes an almost melancholy air by day but gets busy at night.

CAFÈ ZURICH Map p106 Cafe €

☎ 93 317 91 53; Carrer de Pelai 39; ☽ 8am-11pm Sun-Fri, 10am-midnight Sat; Ⓜ Catalunya; ✕

It doesn't have the atmosphere of the cafe of the same name that once occupied this prime spot, but not even the hardest of hearts can deny the location is impeccable. Pull up an outdoor pew for the human circus that is Plaça de Catalunya, or huddle over a paper on the mezzanine on a winter's day. In summer it stays open as late as 1am.

COSMO Map p106 Cafe €

☎ 93 453 70 07; www.galeriacosmo.com; Carrer d'Enric Granados 3; ☽ 10am-10pm Mon-Thu, noon-2am Fri & Sat, noon-10pm Sun; Ⓜ Universitat; ☇

This groovy space with psychedelic colouring in the tables and bar stools, high white walls out back for exhibitions and events, a nice selection of teas, pastries and snacks, all set on a pleasant pedestrian strip just behind the university is perfect for a morning session on your laptop or a civilised evening tipple while admiring the art.

CRUSTO Map p106 Cafe €

☎ 93 487 05 51; www.crusto.es; Carrer de València 246; ☽ Mon-Sat; Ⓜ Passeig de Gràcia

A French-inspired bakery and pastry shop, the wonderful perfume of freshly baked bread, baguettes, croissants and countless pastries will be enough to convince you that it's worth pulling up a stool here for a long and tasty breakfast.

ESCRIBÀ Map p106 Chocolate €

☎ 93 454 75 35; www.escriba.es; Gran Via de les Corts Catalanes 546; ☽ 8am-3pm & 5-9pm Mon-Fri, 8am-9pm Sat, Sun & holidays; Ⓜ Urgell; ✕

Antoni Escribà carries forward a family tradition (since 1906) of melting *barcelonins'* hearts with remarkable pastries and criminal chocolate creations. Try the Easter *bunyols de xocolata* (little round pastry balls filled with chocolate cream). Escribà has

TO MARKET, TO MARKET

One of the greatest sound, smell and colour sensations in Europe is Barcelona's most central produce market, the Mercat de la Boqueria (Map p60; www.boqueria.info; La Rambla). It spills over with all the rich and varied colour of plentiful fruit and vegetable stands, seemingly limitless varieties of sea critters, sausages, cheeses, meat (including the finest Jabugo ham) and sweets. It is also sprinkled with half a dozen or so unassuming places to eat, and eat well, with stallholders at lunchtime. According to some chronicles, there has been a market on this spot since 1217. Mind you, nowadays it's no easy task getting past the gawping tourists to indicate the slippery slab of sole you're after, or the tempting piece of Asturian *queso de cabra* (goat's cheese).

La Boqueria is not the only market in Barcelona. The city is bursting with bustling markets, which for the most part are tourist free. Try Mercat de Sant Antoni (Map p100; Carrer del Comte d'Urgell; Ⓜ Sant Antoni); Mercat de Santa Caterina (Map p82; Avinguda de Francesc Cambó; Ⓜ Jaume I); Mercat del Ninot (Map p100; Carrer de Mallorca 157; Ⓜ Hospital Clínic); Mercat de la Llibertat (Map p116; Plaça de la Llibertat; Ⓡ FGC Gràcia); Mercat de l'Abaceria Central (Map p116; Travessera de Gràcia 186; Ⓜ Fontana) and Mercat de la Concepció (Map p106; Carrer de València 332; Ⓜ Girona). Markets generally open from Monday to Saturday from around 8am to 8pm (although some close around 2pm on Saturday). They are all at their animated best in the morning.

another branch in a Modernista setting at La Rambla de Sant Josep 83 (Map p60).

MAURI Map p106 — Pastries €

☎ 93 215 10 20; Rambla de Catalunya 102; ⏱ 8am-9pm Mon-Sat, 8am-3pm Sun; Ⓜ Diagonal; ☒

Since it opened in 1929, this grand old pastry shop has had its regular customers salivating over the endless range of sweets, chocolate croissants and gourmet delicatessen items.

CREMERIA TOSCANA Map p100 — Gelato €

☎ 93 539 38 25; Carrer de Muntaner 161; ⏱ 1-9pm Tue-Sun Oct-Easter, 1pm-midnight Tue-Sun Easter-Sep; Ⓜ Hospital Clínic; ☒

Yes, you can stumble across quite reasonable ice cream in Barcelona, but close your eyes and imagine yourself across the Mediterranean with the real ice-cream wizards. Creamy *stracciatella* and wavy *nocciola*… and myriad other flavours await at the most authentic gelato outlet in town. Buy a cone or a tub! There's another branch with similar hours in El Born (Map p82; ☎ 93 268 07 29; Carrer dels Canvis Vells 2; Ⓜ Barceloneta).

ORXATERIA SIRVENT Map p100 — Ice Cream €

☎ 93 441 76 16; Ronda de Sant Pau 3; ⏱ 11am-2pm & 4-9pm Oct-Apr, 11am-9pm June-Sep; Ⓜ Sant Antoni or Paral.lel

Barcelonins' favourite source of *orxata/horchata* (tiger-nut drink) since 1926, this busy locale serves up the best you'll try without having to catch the train down to this drink's spiritual home, Valencia. You can get it by the glass or take it away. This place also purveys ice cream, *granissat* (iced fruit crush) and *turrón* (nougat).

GRÀCIA & PARK GÜELL

Spread across this busy *barri* are all sorts of enticing options, from simple tapas bars to top-class seafood. Gràcia is loaded with Middle Eastern and, to a lesser extent, Greek restaurants, which are chirpy and good value. Several classic Catalan taverns tick along nicely with a strong local following. There's little of interest, however, around Park Güell.

BOTAFUMEIRO Map p116 — Seafood €€€

☎ 93 218 42 30; www.botafumeiro.es; Carrer Gran de Gràcia 81; meals €70-80; ⏱ 1pm-1am; Ⓜ Fontana; ☒

It is hard not to mention this classic temple of Galician shellfish and other briny delights, long a magnet for VIPs visiting Barcelona. You can bring the price down by sharing a few *medias raciones* to taste a range of marine offerings or a *safata especial del Mar Cantàbric* (seafood platter) between two. Try the *percebes*, the strangely twisted goose barnacles harvested along Galicia's north Atlantic coast, which many Spaniards consider the ultimate seafood delicacy.

RESTAURANT ROIG ROBÍ

Map p116 — Catalan €€€

☎ 93 218 92 22; www.roigrobi.com; Carrer de Sèneca 20; meals €70-80; ⏱ lunch & dinner Mon-Fri, dinner Sat; Ⓜ Diagonal; ☒

This is an altar to refined traditional cooking. The *textures de carxofes amb vieires a la plantxa* (artichokes with grilled scallops) are like a whiff of artichoke wafting over the prized shellfish. It also does several seafood-and-rice dishes and offer half portions for those with less of an appetite.

CON GRACIA Map p116   Asian-Mediterranean €€€
☎ 93 238 02 01; www.congracia.es; Carrer de Martínez de la Rosa 8; meals €70-80; ☽ lunch & dinner Tue-Fri, dinner Sat; Ⓜ Diagonal

This teeny hideaway (seating about 20 in total) is a hive of originality, producing a delicately balanced mix of Mediterranean cuisine with Asian touches. On offer is a regularly changing surprise tasting menu or the set 'traditional' one (€59), which includes such items as *sopa de foie y miso con aceite de trufa blanca* (miso and foie gras soup with white truffle oil) and a nice Chilean sea bass. At lunch, only groups are accepted. Book ahead.

IPAR-TXOKO Map p116   Basque €€
☎ 93 218 19 54; Carrer de Mozart 22; meals €40-50; ☽ Tue-Sat Sep-Jul; Ⓜ Diagonal

Inside this Basque eatery, the atmosphere is warm and traditional. Hefty timber beams hold up the Catalan vaulted ceiling, and the bar (tapas available) has a garish green columned front. Getxo-born Mikel turns out traditional cooking from northern Spain, including a sumptuous *chuletón* (T-bone steak for two – look at the size of that thing!) or a less gargantuan *tortilla de bacalao* (a thick salted-cod omelette). Then there are curiosities, like *kokotxas de merluza*, heart-shaped cuts from the hake's throat. The wine list is daunting but Mikel is on hand to explain everything – in English, too.

BILBAO Map p116   Northern Spanish €€
☎ 93 458 96 24; Carrer del Perill 33; meals €40; ☽ Mon-Sat; Ⓜ Diagonal

It doesn't look much from the outside, but Bilbao is a timeless classic, where reservations for dinner are imperative. The back dining room, with bottle-lined walls, stout timber tables and a yellowing light evocative of a country tavern, will appeal to carnivores especially, although some fish dishes are also on offer. Consider opting for a *chuletón* (T-bone steak), washed down with a good Spanish red.

TIBET Map p116   Catalan €€
☎ 93 284 50 45; Carrer de Ramiro de Maetzu 34; meals €35; ☽ lunch & dinner Wed-Sat & Mon, lunch Sun; Ⓜ Alfons X, 🚌 24 or 39

In a semi-rustic setting not far from Park Güell, this restaurant has as much to do with Tibet as the author of this book does with Eskimos. For 50 years it has been sizzling meat on the grill and dishing up snails, one of the house specialities. There's not an item of seafood in sight.

SURENY Map p116   Catalan €€
☎ 93 213 75 56; Plaça de la Revolució de Setembre de 1868; meals €30-35; ☽ Tue-Sun; Ⓜ Fontana

Appearances can be deceiving: the cooks in this unremarkable-looking corner restaurant dedicate themselves to producing gourmet tapas and *raciones*, ranging from exquisite *vieiras* (scallops) to a serving of *secreto ibérico*, a particular tasty cut of pork meat (near the porcine equivalent of the armpit, perhaps that's the 'secret'). The *menú del día* is decent value at €9.90.

CAL BOTER Map p116   Catalan €€
☎ 93 458 84 62; Carrer de Tordera 62; meals €30-35; ☽ Tue-Sun; Ⓜ Joanic

A classic eatery that draws families and noisy groups of pals for *cargols a la llauna* (snails sautéed in a tin dish), *filet de bou a la crema de foie* (a thick clump of tender beef drowned in an orange and foie gras sauce), and other Catalan specialities, including curious *mar i muntanya* (surf and turf) combinations like *bolets i gambes* (mushrooms and prawns). Finish with a *xarrup de llimona amb mar de cava* (lemon sorbet drowned in *cava*). The *menú del día* (lunch Tuesday to Friday) comes in at a good-humoured €9.80.

O' GRÀCIA! Map p116   Catalan €€
☎ 93 213 30 44; Plaça de la Revolució de Setembre de 1868 15; meals €30-35; ☽ Tue-Sat; Ⓜ Fontana; ✗

This is an especially popular lunch option, with the *menú del día* outstanding value at €10.50. The *arròs negre de sepia* (black rice with cuttlefish) makes a good first course, followed by a limited set of meat and fish options with vegetable sides. Serves are decent, presentation careful and service attentive. There's a more elaborate tasting menu at €24.50.

ENVALIRA Map p116   Catalan €€
☎ 93 218 58 13; Plaça del Sol 13; meals €30; ☽ lunch & dinner Tue-Sat, lunch Sun; Ⓜ Fontana

Surrounded by cool hang-outs, Lebanese eateries and grunge bars, you'd barely notice the modest entrance to this delicious relic. Head for the 1950s time-warp dining room out the back. Serious waiters deliver all sorts of seafood and rice dishes to your table, from *arròs a la milanesa* (savoury rice dish with chicken, pork and a light cheese gratin) to a *bullit de lluç* (slice of white hake boiled with herb-laced rice and a handful of clams).

LAC MAJÙR Map p116 Italian €€
☎ 93 285 15 03; Carrer de Tordera 33; meals €25; Mon-Sat; Ⓜ Verdaguer
You could easily miss this cosy slice of northwest Italy while striding along the quiet and unusually leafy lane outside. Inside, all sorts of home-cooking delights await, including the house specials, gnocchi and *trofie*. The latter are twists of pasta, usually served with pesto sauce, from Liguria. Try the mascarpone and ham variant followed by, say, a *saltimbocca alla romana* (a veal slice cooked with ham, sage and sweet Marsala wine).

LA PANXA DEL BISBE Map p116 Tapas €€
☎ 93 213 70 49; www.lapanxadelbisbe.com; Carrer de Rabassa 37; meals €25; Ⓨ Tue-Sat; Ⓜ Joanic
With low lighting and a hip, young feel, the 'Bishop's Gut' is a great place to indulge in some gourmet tapas, washed down with a fine wine, like the Albariño white from Galicia, for a surprisingly modest outlay.

EL GLOP Map p116 Catalan €€
☎ 93 213 70 58; www.tavernaelglop.com; Carrer de Sant Lluís 24; meals €25; Ⓜ Joanic
Step inside this raucous eatery decked out in country Catalan fashion, with gingham tablecloths and no-nonsense, slap-up meals. The secret is hearty serves of simple dishes, such as *bistec a la brasa* (grilled steak), perhaps preceded by *albergínies farcides* (stuffed aubergines) or *calçots* in winter. Try the *tocinillo*, a caramel dessert, to finish. Open until 1am, it's a useful place to have up your sleeve for a late bite.

A CASA PORTUGUESA
Map p116 Portuguese €
☎ 93 368 35 28; www.acasaportuguesa.com; Carrer de Verdi 58; snacks €20; Ⓨ dinner Tue-Fri, lunch & dinner Sat, Sun & holidays; Ⓜ Fontana
As well as being a convivial halt for a glass or two of fine wine (ask waiters for advice) or a simple *vinho verde* ('green wine', a typical, simple Portuguese white wine), it

is a good spot to fill up on snacks (cheeses, little pies and pastries), all in the name of getting to know the Iberian neighbours better. There is always a buzzing atmosphere and exhibitions are frequently held. Try a couple of *pastéis de Belém* (delightful little cream tarts) and stock up on goodies from Portugal, Brazil and other one-time Portuguese colonies.

LA LLAR DE FOC Map p116 Catalan €
☎ 93 284 10 25; Carrer de Ramón i Cajal 13; meals €20; Ⓜ Fontana
For a hearty sit-down meal at rock-bottom prices, the 'Hearth' is hard to beat. At lunch, it has a €9 *menú del día*. You could start with a mixed salad or *empanadita* (big slice of tuna pie), followed by chicken in a mild curry sauce or *costellas* (ribs). Go for flan for dessert, as the ice creams are on a stick.

HIMALI Map p116 Nepalese & Vegetarian €
☎ 93 285 15 68; Carrer de Milà i Fontanals 60; meals €15-20; Ⓨ Tue-Sun; Ⓜ Joanic
Spacious and simple, with gruff service and paper place mats, this is a great spot for Nepalese chow and vegetarian dishes. A vegetarian set dinner menu costs €14.95; the carnivores' version, €16.95. Carnivores can also opt for mixed grills with rice and naan, or *kukhurako fila* (roast chicken in walnut sauce). Mains come in at €8 to €10.

NOU CANDANCHÚ Map p116 Tapas €
☎ 93 237 73 62; Plaça de la Vila de Gràcia 9; meals €15-20; Ⓨ Wed-Mon; Ⓜ Fontana
The liveliest locale on the square, Nou Candanchú is a long-time favourite for various reasons. Many flock to its sunny terrace just for a few drinks. Accompany the liquid refreshment with one of the giant *entrepans* (filled rolls) for which this place is famous. Otherwise, it offers a limited range of tapas and reasonable grilled-meat dishes.

EL ROURE Map p116 Tapas €
☎ 93 218 73 87; Carrer de la Riera de Sant Miquel 51; meals €15-20; Ⓨ Mon-Sat; Ⓜ Fontana
This old-time locals' bar is what Hemingway meant by a 'clean, well-lighted place'. Sidle up to the bar or pull up a little wooden chair and tuck into a choice of good-value tapas from the bar, washed down by a few cold Estrellas. The *bunyols de bacallà* are delightful battered balls of cod that demand to be gobbled up. The place is full to bursting most of the time.

VRENELI Map p116   Cafe €

☎ 93 217 61 01; Plaça de la Vila de Gràcia 8;
🕑 8am-9pm Tue-Fri, 9am-9pm Sat & Sun;
Ⓜ Fontana

For banana or carrot cake and a cup of coffee on a grey winter's day, this long, narrow bar with soft mood music is a good place to come in out of the cold.

LA NENA Map p116   Cafe & Chocolate €

☎ 93 285 14 76; Carrer de Ramon i Cajal 36;
🕑 9am-2pm & 4-10pm Mon-Sat, 10am-10pm Sun & holidays; Ⓜ Fontana

A French team has created this delightful chaotic space for indulging in cups of rich hot chocolate (known as *suïssos*) served with a plate of heavy homemade whipped cream and *melindros* (spongy sweet biscuits), fine desserts and even a few savoury dishes (including crêpes). The place is strewn with books and the area out back is designed to keep kids busy, making it an ideal family rest stop.

MONTY CAFÉ Map p116   Cafe €

☎ 93 368 28 82; www.montycafe.com; Carrer de la Riera de Sant Miquel 29; 🕑 8am-10pm Mon & Tue, 8am-midnight Wed & Thu, 8am-2am Fri & Sat; Ⓜ Diagonal; 🛜

Italian-run and nicely laid back, this cafe with terracotta floor, art on the walls and classic marble-top tables has a series of varied, secondhand lounges down one side and a bar at the back. Great for coffee, a long list of teas and cocktails, it also offers food, from pasta to *bruschette*. It's a great place to lounge around over your laptop.

LA ZONA ALTA

Some of the grandest kitchens in the city are scattered across La Zona Alta, from Tibidabo across Sant Gervasi (as far down as Avinguda Diagonal, west of Gràcia) to Pedralbes. Plenty of places of all cuisines and qualities abound, often tucked away in quiet, unassuming residential streets far from anything of interest to tourists. Eating in La Zona Alta can be both a culinary and, with a couple of notable exceptions, a genuinely local experience.

VIA VENETO Map p122   Catalan €€€

☎ 93 200 72 44; www.viavenetorestaurant.com; Carrer de Ganduxer 10; meals €90-120; 🕑 lunch & dinner Mon-Fri, dinner Sat, closed 3 weeks in Aug; �",🚇 FGC La Bonanova; ⊠

Dalí used to regularly waltz into this high-society eatery after it opened in 1967. The vaguely art-deco setting (note the oval mirrors), orange-rose tablecloths, leather chairs and fine cutlery may cater to more conservative souls, but the painter was here for the kitchen exploits. Catalan dishes dominate and the mouth waters at the mere mention of, say, *rodaballo al horno con espárragos blancos, alcachofas y navajas del Delta del Ebro* (oven-cooked turbot with white asparagus, artichokes and razor clams). The service is so good you barely notice the waiters' presence.

HOFMANN Map p122   Mediterranean €€€

☎ 93 218 71 65; www.hofmann-bcn.com; Carrer de Granada del Penedès 14-16; meals €80-100; 🕑 Mon-Fri; 🚇 FGC Gràcia; ⊠

What's cooking here are the trainee chefs, helped along by their instructors. Dishes are generally elegant renditions of classic Mediterranean food, followed by such delicious desserts that some people prefer a starter and two sweets, skipping the main course altogether.

LA BALSA Map p122   Mediterranean €€

☎ 93 211 50 48; www.labalsarestaurant.com; Carrer de la Infanta Isabel 4; meals €70; dinner only Mon, lunch & dinner Tue-Sat, lunch only Sun, in Aug dinner only 9pm-midnight; 🚇 FGC Avinguda Tibidabo; ⊠

With its grand ceiling and the scented gardens that surround the main terrace dining area, La Balsa is one of the city's top dining experiences. The menu changes frequently and is a mix of traditional Catalan and off-centre inventiveness. Lounge over a cocktail at the bar before being ushered to your table. The place is famous for its August dinner buffet (around €30).

COURE Map p122   Catalan €€

☎ 93 200 75 32; Passatge de Marimon 20; meals €45-50; 🕑 Tue-Sat; 🚇 FGC Muntaner; ⊠

The minimalist decor gives away that a chef with avant-garde ideas is at work in his laboratory-kitchen. The end results are far from over the top, leaning to nicely elaborated dishes such as the *cochinillo ibérico con manzana al horno* (oven-roasted suckling pig with apple). The set lunch menu (€18) is a great-value sample, popular with office workers all over the area. There's also a tasting menu at €45. A curtain of copper chains hides the dining area from the bar in the entrance (the name is a play on words, meaning both 'copper' and 'to cook').

CAN TRAVI NOU off Map p122 Catalan €€
☎ 93 428 03 01; www.gruptravi.com; Carrer de Jorge Manrique, Parc de la Vall d'Hebron; meals €45-50; ☺ lunch & dinner Mon-Sat, lunch Sun; Ⓜ Montbau; Ⓟ ☒

This expansive 18th-century mansion has several dining areas that stretch out across two floors. The warm colours, grandfather clock and a wholesome, rustic air make for a magical setting for a Catalan splurge. The *risotto de formatge* (cheese risotto) makes a hearty starter, but the generous mains will please you even more. The *arròs caldós amb llamàntol i cloïsses* (rice stew with lobster and clams) is irresistible and it also does some tender grilled steaks.

CAN CORTADA off Map p122 Catalan €€
☎ 93 427 23 15; www.gruptravi.com; Avinguda de l'Estatut de Catalunya; meals €40; Ⓜ Montbau; Ⓟ ☒

More than anything else, it is the setting and the hearty welcome that make this 11th-century estate (complete with the remains of a defensive tower) worth the excursion. Try for a table in the former cellars or on the garden terrace. Lots of Catalan fare, like *pollastre amb escamarlans* (chicken and crayfish), dominates the menu.

INDOCHINE Map p122 Pan-Asian €€
☎ 93 201 99 84; www.indochinebarcelona.com; Carrer d'Aribau 247; meals €35-40; ☺ Tue-Sun; Ⓡ FGC Molina; ☒

This uptown Asian eatery could almost pass for a florist. Once through the French doors and greenery you will be presented with a selection of Thai, Vietnamese and Cambodian dishes. Although somewhat westernised, the food is enticing. You could start with a light green-papaya salad and follow with *pescado al estilo camboyano* (Cambodian-style fish, lightly steamed and done in a vegetable sauce). Those with flexible legs can sit on the floor.

CASA FERNÁNDEZ Map p122 Spanish €€
☎ 93 201 93 80; www.casafernandez.com; Carrer de Santaló 46; meals €30; ☺ 1pm-1am; Ⓡ FGC Muntaner

Immensely popular with bar hoppers suddenly aware they have skipped dinner when it's gone midnight, this bustling, cheerful eatery is a classic. Food is hearty

and service hectic but pretty fast even when the place is brimful with carousers. There's plenty of choice of local and foreign beers and a reasonable wine selection.

BAR TOMÀS Map p122 Tapas €
☎ 93 203 10 77; Carrer Major de Sarrià 49; meals €15-20; ☺ Thu-Tue; Ⓡ FGC Sarrià

Many *barcelonins* have long claimed that Bar Tomàs is by far the best place in the city for *patates braves*, prepared here with a special variation on the traditional spicy tomato and mayonnaise sauce. The place is a rough-edged bar, but that doesn't stop the well-off citizens of Sarrià piling in, particularly for lunch on weekends.

CAFFÈ SAN MARCO Map p122 Cafe €
☎ 93 280 29 73; Carrer de Pedro de la Creu 15; ☺ 9am-9.30pm; Ⓡ FGC Reina Elisenda

For one of the best coffees you're likely to have, it is hard to beat this place. It boasts a charming atmosphere where you can settle in to read the paper or simply watch passers-by.

FOIX DE SARRIÀ Map p122 Pastries €
☎ 93 203 04 73; www.foixdesarria.com, in Spanish; Plaça de Sarrià 12-13; ☺ 8am-8pm; Ⓡ FGC Reina Elisenda

Since 1886 this exclusive pastry shop has been selling the most exquisite cakes and sweets. You can take them away or head out back to sip tea, coffee or hot chocolate while sampling the little cakes and other wizardry.

MONTJUÏC, SANTS & EL POBLE SEC

Montjuïc is largely bereft of notable eating options, for the obvious reason that it is mostly parks and gardens. In gruff old El Poble Sec, however, you'll turn up all sorts of priceless nuggets, from historic taverns offering Catalan classics to a handful of smart, new-wave eateries. The pickings in Sants are slimmer, but there are still some worthy exceptions.

ROSAL 34 Map p140 Gourmet Tapas €€
☎ 93 324 90 46; www.rosal34.com; Carrer del Roser 34; meals €45-65; ☺ Tue-Sat; Ⓜ Poble Sec

Exposed brick and stone walls and a sinuous bar, accompanied by wafting lounge sounds, set the scene for a gourmet experience. You can opt for one of two tasting menus (€48/60) or search the menu for such numbers as *saltejat de xipironets de platja amb trompeta de la mort i ou escalfat* (sautéed small beach cuttlefish with mushrooms and egg).

MIRAMAR Map p140   Mediterranean & Asian €€
☎ 93 443 66 27; www.club-miramar.es; Carretera de Miramar 40; meals €40-50; ⊙ lunch & dinner Tue-Sat, lunch Sun; ⬚ 50 & 193

With several terraces and a cool designer main dining area, this restaurant's key draw is the views it offers over Barcelona's waterfront. Hovering just above the Transbordador Aeri cable-car station, you can linger over a coffee or tuck into an elegant meal with a creative Catalan and Mediterranean slant, or opt for an extensive Asian menu.

XEMEI Map p140   Venetian €€
☎ 93 553 51 40; Passeig de l'Exposició 85; meals €45; ⊙ Wed-Mon; Ⓜ Poble Sec; ⊠

Xemei ('twins' in Venetian, because it is run by a pair of twins from Italy's lagoon city) is a wonderful slice of Venice in Barcelona. To the accompaniment of gentle jazz, you might try an entrée of mixed *cicheti* (Venetian seafood tapas), followed with *bigoi in salsa veneziana* (thick spaghetti in an anchovy and onion sauce). The *suprema de San Pedro* (tender white John Dory) is a fine choice, as is the Tuscan meat intruder *tagliata* (sliced rare beef with rocket and shavings of Parmesan cheese).

HIGH IN THE SKY

For a five-star dining experience beneath a transparent UFO-style dome, 105m above ground, grab a cab to Restaurant Evo (off Map p140; ☎ 93 413 50 30; www.hesperia.com; Gran Via de les Corts Catalanes 144; ⊙ dinner Mon-Fri, lunch & dinner Sat; Ⓜ Hospital Bellvitge; Ⓟ ⊠), located in Hotel Hesperia Tower in L'Hospitalet de Llobregat. This is gourmet dining literally under the stars (of which one comes from Michelin). Lean lines dictate decor, with lacquer-finished tables, low white chairs and the inside of the dome lit up. The high point is the presentation of Mediterranean market cooking (say, the *consomé de faisà amb els seus raviolis de foie i tòfona negra* – a pheasant consommé with foie-gras ravioli and black truffle).

TAPIOLES 53 Map p140   International €€
☎ 93 329 22 38; www.tapioles53.com; Carrer de Tapioles 53; meals €35-45; ⊙ dinner Tue-Sat; Ⓜ Paral.lel; ⊠ 🛜

A stylish place housed in a former umbrella factory, this barely lit gem has a limited yet constantly changing international menu. Ingredients are sourced daily from the city's markets. Asian touches are sometimes present, but you might just as easily find yourself with a Moroccan-style *tajine*. Start at the bar and proceed to one of the stout wooden tables. Book ahead.

ZARAUTZ Map p140   Basque €€
☎ 93 325 28 13; Carrer de l'Elisi 13; meals €30-35; ⊙ 8am-11.30pm Mon-Sat Sep-Jul; Ⓜ Tarragona; ⊠

A short hop away from the train station, you can take in some quality Basque tapas at the bar any time of the day, or retire to the restaurant for a full meal, such as *carpaccio de carn amb formatge Idiazábal* (beef carpaccio with a tangy Basque cheese). The owner is a dessert specialist, so save some room. It's a rough-and-tumble-looking joint, but don't let that put you off.

LA BODEGUETA Map p140   Catalan €€
☎ 93 442 08 46; www.labodeguetabcn.com; Carrer de Blai 47; meals €30; ⊙ lunch Fri-Sun, dinner daily; Ⓜ Paral.lel

For a homey Catalan atmosphere (complete with wine barrels, an old Frigidaire and gingham tablecloths), pop by this cheery spot. Options are limited to classic local favourites, including an array of charcoal-grilled meat dishes, such as a thick *entrecot con Cabrales* (steak with strong northern Spanish cheese). Balance with a *graellada de verdures* (mixed grilled vegetables) and wash down with a generous ceramic jug of house red.

TAVERNA CAN MARGARIT
Map p140   Catalan €€
☎ 93 441 67 23; Carrer de la Concòrdia 21; meals €25-30; ⊙ dinner Mon-Sat; Ⓜ Poble Sec

For decades this former wine store has been dishing out dinner to often raucous groups. Traditional Catalan cooking is the name of the game. Surrounded by aged wine barrels, take your place at old tables and benches and perhaps order the *conejo a la jumillana* (fried rabbit served with garlic, onion, bay leaves, rosemary, mint, thyme and oregano). Dishes are abundant, wine flows freely and time seems to have stood still.

QUIMET I QUIMET Map p140 Tapas €€

☎ 93 442 31 42; Carrer del Poeta Cabanyes 25; meals €25-30; ☺ noon-4pm & 7-10.30pm Mon-Fri, noon-6pm Sat; Ⓜ Paral.lel; ✕

Quimet i Quimet is a family-run business that has been passed down from generation to generation. There's barely space to swing a calamari in this bottle-lined, standing-room-only place, but it is a treat for the palate. Look at all those gourmet tapas waiting for you! Let the folk behind the bar advise you, and order a drop of fine wine to accompany the food.

LA TOMAQUERA Map p140 Catalan €

☎ 93 441 85 18; Carrer de Margarit 5; meals €20; ☺ Tue-Sat; Ⓜ Poble Sec

The waiters shout and rush about this classic, while carafes of wine are sloshed about the long wooden tables. You can't book, so it's first in, first seated (queues are the norm). Try the house speciality of snails or go for hearty meat dishes. The occasional seafood option, such as *cassola de cigales* (crayfish hotpot) might also tempt. And cash is king.

LA BELLA NAPOLI Map p140 Pizza €

☎ 93 442 50 56; www.bellanapoli.net; Carrer de Margarit 14; pizza €7-21; ☺ daily; Ⓜ Paral.lel

There are pizza joints all over Barcelona. And then there's the real thing: the way they make it in Naples. This place even *feels* like Naples. The waiters are mostly from across the Med and have that cheeky southern Italian approach to food, customers and everything else. The pizzas are good, ranging from the simple *margherita* to a heavenly black-truffle number.

DRINKING & NIGHTLIFE

top picks

Heading out into the night in Barcelona will rarely leave you in the cold. The sheer number of bars, pubs and taverns could keep the curious drinker shifting from one spot to the next for weeks, if not months.

Most locals do their partying from Thursday to Saturday. The hefty influx of tourists, students and foreign residents with irregular hours means that you can usually find places busy in the Barri Gòtic, El Born (La Ribera) and El Raval any night, while other areas that attract mostly local punters are quiet until Thursday.

There is also a good spread of clubs and, although city by-laws make it virtually impossible to open major new dance and gig venues, Barcelona is already blessed with a rich line-up of places to hide in until dawn, and a handful where you can stay inside until the middle of the day (on weekends).

The live music scene is vigorous, if a little limited in terms of variety. Barcelona does not have a big local band scene. That said, depending on the night, you can see anything from ear-splitting Spanish pop-rock (popular with the locals but perhaps a little tiresome for the international set) to the latest in house, hip hop and funk. You can catch a live jazz set on just about any night, and flamenco (often cheesy but sometimes top class) is another perennial favourite. A handful of major venues welcome all sorts of acts, Spanish and international, throughout the year.

ETIQUETTE

One rule of drinking etiquette to observe closely in bars: never ask for or suggest having one last drink. Catalans always order the *penúltima* (next but last), even if it really is the last drink of the evening. To mention the *última* (last) is bad luck, since it sounds like one's last drink on earth. Of course, the problem with ordering a *penúltima* is that it frequently ends up being just that…

GETTING THE LOCAL LOW-DOWN

There is no shortage of guides to Barcelona's nightlife, both in print and on the web. Guia del Ocio (www. guiadelociobcn.es, in Spanish; €1), the city's weekly entertainment mag, is available from news-stands. Look for the free mags and booklets distributed around some bars. They include *Micro*, Go Mag (www.go-mag.com), Metropolitan (www.barcelona-metropolitan.com), *Salir* and the rivers of flyers that flow through many bars. For the latest events, register online with Lecool (www.lecool.com). Also take a look at Agentes de la Noche (www.agentesdelanoche.com, in Spanish), Barcelonarocks.com (www.barcelona rocks.com), Clubbingspain.com (www.clubbing spain.com, in Spanish) and LaNetro.com (http://bar celona.lanetro.com). These sources are a good starting point but may not always be up to date. Also bear in mind that, in most cases, many places pay for their listing, so impartiality cannot be guaranteed.

SPECIALITIES

Wine

Spain is a wine-drinking country and *vi/vino* (wine) accompanies all meals (except breakfast!). Spanish wine, whether *blanc/blanco* (white), *negre/tinto* (red) or *rosat/rosado* (rosé), tends to have quite a kick, in part because of the climate but also because of grape varieties and production methods. That said, the long-adhered-to policy of quantity over quality has given way to a subtler approach. It is still possible to find cheap, kick-arse wine that makes your mouth pucker, but the palette of varieties has become infinitely more sophisticated since the 1980s.

At the bottom end of the market (apart from true *garrafón* in the form of almost giveaway Tetra Paks), an entirely drinkable bottle of table wine can easily enough be had for around €5 in supermarkets and from wine merchants (especially the old kind, a slowly dying breed, where they will fill your bottle from giant barrels).

The same money in a restaurant won't get you far. Apart from *vi/vino de la casa* (house wine), which is commonly ordered at lunchtime by the litre or half-litre, you will pay an average of €10 to €15 for a reasonable bottle, and considerably more for something classier. You can also generally order wine by the *copa* (glass) in bars and restaurants, although the choice will be more limited.

Not generally available in bars is the acquired taste of *calimocho*, a mix of Tetra Pak red wine and Coke, beloved of penniless partying students across the country.

As in the other major EU wine-producing countries, there are two broad categories: table wine and quality wine. The former ranges from the basic *vi de taula/vino de mesa* to *vi de la terra/vino de la tierra,* the latter being a wine from an officially delimited wine-producing area. If an area meets certain strict standards, it receives DO *(denominación de origen)* status. Outstanding wine regions get DOC *(denominación de origen calificada)* status. In Catalonia, there are 12 DOs (appellations), including a regional one (DO Catalunya; www.do-catalunya.com) and a general one for *cava*. Some of the DOs cover little more than a few vineyards. Classifications are not always a guarantee of quality, and many drinkers of Spanish wine put more faith in the name and reputation of certain producers or areas than in the denomination labels.

The bulk of DO wines in Catalonia are made from grapes produced in the Penedès area, which pumps out almost two million hectolitres a year. The other DO winemaking zones (spread as far apart as the Empordà area around Figueres in the north and the Terra Alta around Gandesa in the southwest) have a combined output of about half that produced in Penedès. The wines of the El Priorat area, which tend to be dark, heavy reds, have been promoted to DOC status, an honour shared only with those of the Rioja (categorised as such since 1926). Drops from the neighbouring Montsant area are frequently as good (or close) and considerably cheaper.

Most of the grapes grown in Catalonia are native to Spain and include White Macabeo, Garnacha and Xarel.lo (for whites), and Black Garnacha, Monastrell and Ull de Llebre (Hare's Eye) red varieties. Foreign varieties (such as chardonnay, riesling, chenin blanc, cabernet sauvignon, merlot and Pinot noir) are also common.

The bulk of production in and around the Penedès area is white wine. Of these the best-known drop is *cava*, the regional version of champagne. The two big names in bubbly are Freixenet and Codorníu. Connoisseurs tend not to get too excited by these, however, preferring the output of smaller vintners. The main name in Penedès wine is Miguel Torres – one of its stalwart reds is Sangre de Toro. See p257 for tips on wineries to visit.

There is plenty to look out for beyond Penedès. Raïmat, in the Costers del Segre DO area of Lleida province, produces fine reds and a couple of notable whites. Good fortified wines come from around Tarragona (p259) and some nice fresh wines are also produced in the Empordà area in the north.

Sangria is a red wine and fruit punch (usually with lemon, orange and cinnamon), sometimes laced with brandy. It's refreshing going down, but can leave you with a sore head. Indeed, the origins of the drink go back to the days when wine quality was not great and the vinegary taste needed a sweetener. Another version is *sangría de cava*, a punch made with sparkling white. *Tinto de verano* (summer red) is a mix of wine and Casera, which is a brand of *gaseosa*, similar to lemonade. It is both a means of sweetening tart table wine and avoiding lunchtime hangovers. As its name suggests, it is also popular as a refreshing summertime lunch tipple.

A popular and simple accompaniment to seafood, found especially in Galician eateries, is *turbio*, a cloudy white wine that goes down a treat.

Beer

The most common way to order *cervesa/cerveza* (beer) is to ask for a *canya*, which is a small draught beer *(cervesa/cerveza de barril)*. A larger beer, which comes in a straight glass (about 300mL), is sometimes called a *tubo*. A pint is a *gerra/jarra* and is usually relevant only in pseudo-Irish pubs. A small bottle of beer is called a *flascó/botellín*. A 200mL bottle is called a *quinto* (fifth) and 330mL is a *tercio* (third). Either bottle is often referred to as a *mediana*. If you just ask for a *cerveza*, you may get bottled beer, which tends to be marginally more expensive.

BARCELONA'S NEW OLD BEER

Moritz, a crisp lager that was once Barcelona's most popular beer, has made an extraordinary comeback since 2004. Brewed from 1856 by a company founded by Alsatian brewer Louis Moritz, Moritz went broke in 1978 but his descendants (who kept the brand) are back in action. The three late-19th-century buildings at Ronda Sant Antoni 39-43 that housed the subterranean former Moritz brewery (Map p106) are slowly being turned into a leisure and cultural centre (under the direction of French architect Jean Nouvel).

SOMETHING GOOD BURNING

With Catalan impresarios making money hand over fist in sugar plantations in Cuba and other South American colonies from the late 18th century, it is hardly surprising they developed a taste for one of its by-products, *rom/ron* (rum). In 1818 the Pujol liquor company set up a rum distillery in Catalonia, and since then Ron Pujol has been one of the dominant local brands for this sweet firewater. Today it produces all sorts of rum and rum-based drinks, including the classic Ron Pujol (42% alcohol), Pujol & Grau (38%; a lighter, white rum) and Ron 1818, based on the original recipe made in the Antilles. Closer to the Brazilian *cachaça* is Caña Pujol (50%). But the great Catalan drink, especially popular in summer festivals, is *rom cremat* (burned rum). Litres of rum are poured into a shallow ceramic bowl, to which 100g of sugar is added per litre, strips of lemon zest and a stick of cinnamon. The lot is then set alight and constantly *remanat* (stirred and ladled) for about 20 to 30 minutes. About a third of the alcohol is burned off. When the surface appears to be completely alight, with no spaces, your rum is well burned and ready. A small cup of good coffee is poured into the mix to extinguish (this takes some minutes). If you then have to put on a lid to put out remaining flames, you've stuffed it and haven't burned the rum properly!

The main Catalan brewery is Damm, established by Alsatian immigrants in the 19th century. Its lager-style Estrella Damm is the most common beer in Barcelona (other more recent Damm variants include the potent and flavoursome malt Voll Damm, dark Bock Damm, the smooth AK Damm, high-octane Keler, ready-made shandy Damm Lemon and alcohol-free Free Damm). San Miguel, founded in Lleida in the 1940s, is also widely drunk and the company (with several breweries around Spain) is owned by the Mahou beer conglomerate. Damm produces about 15% of all Spain's beer, as does San Miguel. Some bars serve the crisp lager from northwest Spain, Estrella de Galicia. A growing number of bars, and not just the fake Irish pub variety, serve up a variety of UK, Irish and other European beers and ales.

A *clara* is a shandy – a beer with a hefty dash of lemonade (or lemon Fanta).

Other Drinks

There is no shortage of imported and local top-shelf stuff in Barcelona – *coñac* (brandy) is popular. Larios is a common local brand of gin, but those in the know prefer bigger-name brands in their gin and tonics.

On occasion you may be asked if you'd like a *chupito* to round off a meal. This is a little shot of liqueur; the idea is to help digestion. Popular and refreshing Spanish *chupitos* are *licor de manzana verde* (green apple liqueur) and *licor de melocotón* (peach liqueur), both transparent, chilled and with around 20% alcohol.

A popular drink across Spain that swings between sweet liqueur and something a little harder is Ponche Caballero. If you wander into a Galician restaurant, you might come across its version of grappa, a clear firewater made with crushed grapes and called *orujo*.

The Catalan firewater is *ratafia*, a particularly Pyrenean drop, tasting vaguely similar to Kahlúa.

South American cocktails, such as the Brazilian cachaca-based *caipirinha* and the Cuban rum-based mojito, are especially popular – many bars will whip these up for you.

For tap water in restaurants you could ask for *aigua de l'aixeta/agua de grifo*, but you're bound to get a funny look. People rarely opt for Barcelona tap water (and with good reason – it's bloody awful). *Aigua/agua mineral* (bottled water) comes in innumerable brands, either *amb gas/con gas* (fizzy) or *sense gas/sin gas* (still).

WHERE TO DRINK
Bars

There is no shortage of places to get a drink or six in Barcelona. Indeed, there is more drinking, bar hopping and carousing to be done here than most average mortals can bear. The trick is finding the right zone for you on the right night.

Most visitors converge on Ciutat Vella (Old City) and, as a result, you can be sure of plenty of activity seven nights a week. The lower end of the Barri Gòtic, especially on and around Plaça Reial and Carrer dels Escudellers, is usually packed, from the series of tourist-infested pseudo-Irish boozers on Carrer de Ferran, to cool dance locals and relatively quieter bars hidden away in side lanes. In La Ribera the place to be is Passeig del Born and the lanes that branch off it.

In El Raval the scene is more spread out – from the student faves of Carrer de Joaquín Costa to the mixed set on and around Rambla del Raval, Carrer Nou de la Rambla and Carrer de Santa Mònica. Some of the city's classic old bars are scattered about here.

Waterfront action comes in three flavours. It is by far busiest in summer, when a set of hip bars along Platja de la Barceloneta attracts a crowd of chilled-out folk, while the barnyard action of Port Olímpic is home to a strange mix of youngsters from the 'burbs, sailing folk, and marauding stag- and hennight groups from abroad. The third scene is the summer-only beach bar option (see the boxed text, p204).

In L'Eixample, Carrer d'Aribau is charged. The action spreads north across Avinguda Diagonal into La Zona Alta, with bars and several clubs that, as a rule, attract a mostly well-dressed, uptown crowd with the occasional cashed-up tourist thrown into the mix. The bars of Gaixample (gay L'Eixample) are clustered around the Carrer del Consell de Cent end of Carrer d'Aribau.

The squares and some streets of Gràcia are laced with bars, as sleepless local residents are constantly reminded. The scene in the area is remarkably homogenous – basically a young, somewhat rowdy, grungy student set. They are mostly locals but out-of-towners, especially of the Erasmus-student-program variety, mix in as well.

A handful of options sparkle in El Poble Sec, with further venues spread across the city, from La Barceloneta to Montjuïc and La Zona Alta.

You can pay anything from €2 to €4 for a 330mL bottle of Estrella beer (draught costs a little less) – it all depends on where and when you order it. Indeed, drink prices reflect the area you're in. In Gràcia, you're likely to find good cocktails and *combinats* (mixed drinks) for €5.50, and many bars offer happy hours. In the old town the same drinks will nudge closer to €8, while in L'Eixample, La Zona Alta and the waterfront (and of course the clubs) you are looking at €10 to €12 for the same poison.

Most bars are at their liveliest from around 11pm and close between 2am (Sunday to Thursday) and 3am (Friday and Saturday). A handful of places, bless 'em, keep their doors open as late as 5am.

Note that drinking in the streets, on the beach and other public places away from bars is illegal and can attract hefty fines.

Clubs

Barcelona's clubs (*discotecas*) come alive from about 2am until 6am, and are at their best from Thursday to Saturday. Indeed, many open only on these nights.

A surprising variety of spots lurk in the old-town labyrinth, ranging from plush former dance halls to grungy subterranean venues that fill to capacity.

Along the waterfront it's another ball game. At Port Olímpic a sun-scorched crowd of visiting yachties mixes it up with tourists and a few locals at noisy, back-to-back dance bars right on the waterfront. The best spots are over on the La Barceloneta side.

A sprinkling of well-known clubs is spread over the classy parts of town, in L'Eixample and La Zona Alta. As a rule of thumb they attract a beautiful crowd, while the bulk of the city's gay nightlife is concentrated in L'Eixample.

Cover charges range from nothing to €18. If you go early, you'll often pay less. In almost all cases the admission price includes your first drink. Bouncers have last say on dress code and your eligibility to enter. Some places stage live music before converting into clubs.

Live Music Venues

Barely a night goes by without a band filling the night air with the sounds of anything from world music to jazz. A handful of well-established jazz clubs is always busy, while bands, local and international, turn up in clubs around the city. A smattering of little bars around town stage live music.

Jazz fans are also in for a treat in November, when the city's annual jazz festival is staged (see p19).

Start time is rarely before 10pm. Admission charges range from nothing to €30 – the higher prices often include a drink. Note that some of the clubs listed in this chapter sometimes stage concerts. Some bars also intermittently proffer live music.

To see big-name acts, either Spanish or from abroad, you will pay more and probably wind up at venues such as the 17,000-capacity Palau Sant Jordi on Montjuïc, the Teatre Mercat de les Flors or the Fòrum. Truly big acts play the Estadi Olímpic and, on rare occasions, Camp Nou football stadium.

Casino

The city's casino, Casino de Barcelona (Map p96; ☎ 93 225 78 78; www.casino-barcelona.com; Carrer de la Marina 19-21; ⏱ 10am-5am Sun-Thu, 10am-5.30am Fri & Sat; Ⓜ Ciutadella Vila Olímpica) in Port Olímpic, is the place for those who are feeling lucky or fiscally well endowed. As well as the usual one-armed bandits and more-sophisticated games, there are restaurants, bars and a club.

BARRI GÒTIC & LA RAMBLA

La Rambla holds little interest, so leave it to those content to settle for expensive pints and plunge into the narrow streets and back alleys of the lower end of the Barri Gòtic. Check out Carrer dels Escudellers, Carrer Ample (and the parallel Carrer d'en Gignàs and Carrer del Correu Vell) and the area around Plaça Reial.

BARCELONA PIPA CLUB Map p60　　Bar
☎ 93 302 47 32; www.bpipaclub.com; Plaça Reial 3; ◷ 10pm-4am Sun-Thu, 10pm-5am Fri & Sat; Ⓜ Liceu

This pipe smokers' club is like an apartment, with all sorts of interconnecting rooms and knick-knacks – notably the pipes after which the place is named. Buzz at the door and head two floors up. Generally it is for members only until 11pm, but you might sneak in earlier.

BLONDIE Map p60　　Bar
www.blondie-bcn.com; Carrer d'en Roca 14; ◷ 7pm-2am Sun-Thu, 7pm-3am Fri & Sat; Ⓜ Liceu

Long a dark little dive that had slowly sunk into oblivion, this simple, backstreet bar has subtle, multicoloured lighting, Estrella Galicia beer (the country's crispest lager) and something of a conspiratorial air. Italian run, it lures folk in for happy hour from 7pm to 10pm. You could find yourself locked in until 4am.

EL PARAIGUA Map p60　　Bar
☎ 93 302 11 31; www.elparaigua.com; Carrer del Pas de l'Ensenyança 2; ◷ 10am-midnight Sun-Thu, 11am-2.30am Fri & Sat; Ⓜ Liceu

A tiny chocolate box of dark tinted Modernisme, the 'Umbrella' has been serving up drinks since the 1960s. The turn-of-the-20th-century decor was transferred here from a shop knocked down elsewhere in the district and cobbled back together to create this cosy locale. Take a trip in time from Modernisme to medieval by heading downstairs to the brick and stone basement bar area. Part of the walls date to the 11th century.

GLACIAR Map p60　　Bar
☎ 93 302 11 63; Plaça Reial 3; ◷ 4pm-2.30am; Ⓜ Liceu

This classic, with marble bar and wood seating inside and aluminium tables and chairs outside beneath the porch, remains a favourite for warm-up drinks and watching the free street theatre of Plaça Reial.

MANCHESTER Map p60　　Bar
☎ 663 071748; www.manchesterbar.com; Carrer de Milans 5; ◷ 7pm-2.30am Sun-Thu, 7pm-3am Fri & Sat; Ⓜ Liceu

A drinking den that has undergone several transformations down the years now treats you to the sounds of great Manchester bands, from the Chemical Brothers to Oasis, but probably not the Hollies. It has a pleasing rough-and-tumble feel, with tables jammed in every which way. Cocktails cost €4 from 7pm to 10pm.

MARULA CAFÈ Map p60　　Bar
☎ 663 071748; www.marulacafe.com; Carrer dels Escudellers 49; ◷ 11pm-5am Sun-Thu, 11pm-5.30am Fri & Sat; Ⓜ Liceu

A fantastic new funk find in the heart of the Barri Gòtic, Marula will transport you to the 1970s and the best in funk and soul. James Brown fans will think they've died and gone to heaven. It's not, however, a monothematic place and occasionally the DJs slip in other tunes, from breakbeat to house. Samba and other Brazilian dance sounds also penetrate here.

SCHILLING Map p60　　Bar
☎ 93 317 67 87; Carrer de Ferran 23; ◷ 10am-2.30am Mon-Thu, 10am-3am Fri & Sat, noon-2am Sun; Ⓜ Liceu

A gay-friendly favourite with a classy lowlit feel. Perch at the bar, take a little table or slink out the back to the lounges, while

top picks
GAY & LESBIAN CLUBS

various snacks are served up. Whatever you choose, it's a congenial place for a drink and some knowing eye contact.

SINATRA Map p60 — Bar

☎ 93 412 52 79; Carrer de les Heures 4-10; ⏱ 6pm-2.30am Sun-Thu, 6pm-3am Fri & Sat; Ⓜ Liceu

Lurking back a block from boisterous Plaça Reial is this no less raucous location. It's largely patronised by foreigners (Spanish-speaking staff are hard to locate!) who flop into splotchy cowhide-pattern lounges, perch on long stools beneath the mirror ball and sip Desperados beer while listening to '80s tracks.

SÍNCOPA Map p60 — Bar

Carrer d'Avinyó 35; ⏱ 6pm-2.30am; Ⓜ Liceu

Lovers of self-conscious grunge will want to pop in here for the mellow music and conversation. It's a saunter from Plaça de George Orwell (or Plaça del Trippy to those who hang around here taking drugs).

SOUL CLUB Map p60 — Bar

☎ 93 302 70 26; Carrer Nou de Sant Francesc 7; ⏱ 10pm-2.30am Mon-Thu, 10pm-3am Fri & Sat, 8pm-2.30am Sun; Ⓜ Drassanes

Each night the DJs change the musical theme, which ranges from deep funk to Latin grooves. The tiny front bar is for drinking and chatting (get in early for a stool or the sole lounge). Out back is where the dancing is done. On Sundays they start early with a little live jazz.

BLVD Map p60 — Club

☎ 93 301 62 89; www.boulevardcultureclub.com; La Rambla 27; ⏱ midnight-6am Mon-Sat May-Sep, Thu-Sat Oct-Apr; Ⓜ Drassanes

Flanked by striptease bars (in the true spirit of the lower Rambla's old days), this place has undergone countless reincarnations. The culture in this club is what a long line-up of DJs brings to the (turn)table. With three different dance spaces, one of them upstairs, it has a deliciously tacky feel, pumping out anything from 1980s hits to house (especially on Saturdays in the main room). There's no particular dress code.

KARMA Map p60 — Club

☎ 93 302 56 80; www.karmadisco.com, in Spanish; Plaça Reial 10; admission €8; ⏱ midnight-5.30am Tue-Sun; Ⓜ Liceu

Sick of the metallic sounds of the new century? What about some good, main-

stream indie music (during the week)? At weekends it becomes unpredictable, with anything from rock to 1980s disco fever. The odd Madonna track even pops up. A golden oldie in Barcelona, tunnel-shaped Karma is small and becomes quite tightly packed with a good-natured crowd of locals and out-of-towners.

LA MACARENA Map p60 — Club

☎ 637 416647; Carrer Nou de Sant Francesc 5; admission up to €5; ⏱ midnight-5am; Ⓜ Drassanes

You simply won't believe this was once a tile-lined Andalucian flamenco musos' bar. Now it is a dark dance space, of the kind where it is possible to sit at the bar, meet people around you and then stand up for a bit of a shake to the DJ's electro and house offerings, all within a couple of square metres.

HARLEM JAZZ CLUB Map p60 — Live Music

☎ 93 310 07 55; www.harlemjazzclub.es; Carrer de la Comtessa de Sobradiel 8; admission up to €10; ⏱ 8pm-4am Tue-Thu & Sun, 8pm-5am Fri & Sat; Ⓜ Drassanes

This narrow, smoky, old-town dive is one of the best spots in town for jazz. Every now and then it mixes it up with a little rock, Latin or blues. It attracts a mixed crowd who maintain a respectful silence during the acts. Usually there are two sessions with different musos each night. Get in early if you want a seat in front of the stage.

SIDECAR FACTORY CLUB
Map p60 — Live Music

☎ 93 302 15 86; www.sidecarfactoryclub.com; Plaça Reial 7; admission €7-15; ⏱ 10pm-5am Mon-Thu, 10pm-6am Fri & Sat; Ⓜ Liceu

With its entrance on Plaça Reial, you can come here for a meal before midnight or a few drinks at ground level (which closes by 3am at the latest), or descend into the red-tinged, brick-vaulted bowels for live music most nights. Just about anything goes here, from UK indie through to country punk, but rock and pop lead the way. Most shows start at 10pm (Thursday to Saturday). DJs take over at 12.30am to keep you dancing until dawn.

JAMBOREE Map p60 — Live Music & Club

☎ 93 319 17 89; www.masimas.com/jamboree; Plaça Reial 17; admission €5-15; ⏱ 9.30pm-6am; Ⓜ Liceu

Since long before Franco said *adiós* to this world, Jamboree had been bringing joy to the jivers of Barcelona, with headline jazz and blues acts of the calibre of Chet Baker and Ella Fitzgerald. Nowadays, concerts usually start around 11pm, although 9pm sessions are also frequent, and after all the live stuff finishes at about 2am, Jamboree takes on a different hue, as a club. Sounds under the low arches range fairly inevitably from hip hop through funk to R&B.

EL RAVAL

What happened in the El Born area in the mid-1990s is slowly happening here now – new bars and clubs are opening up along the long, slummy alleys. Beside them, some great old harbour-style taverns still thrive – dark, wood panelled and bare except for the odd mirror and vast arrays of bottles behind the bar. Unlike El Born, the lower end of El Raval has a long history of dodginess and the area around Carrer de Sant Pau retains its edgy feel: drug dealers, pickpockets and prostitutes mingling with the streams of nocturnal hedonists.

BAR AURORA Map p74   Bar
☎ 635 902454; Carrer de l'Aurora 7; ☽ 8am-2.30am Mon-Thu, 8am-3am Fri & Sat, 3pm-midnight Sun; Ⓜ Sant Antoni

Once a dark and crowded early opener, the Aurora has morphed under Italian management into a cheery, laid-back multicoloured spot. Set over a couple of floors with variegated lighting, low music and a good vibe, this place is worth wandering just off the Rambla del Raval as you search for beer or a mixed drink.

BAR MARSELLA Map p74   Bar
Carrer de Sant Pau 65; ☽ 10pm-2am Mon-Thu, 10pm-3am Fri & Sat; Ⓜ Liceu

Hemingway used to slump over an *absenta* (absinthe) in this bar, which has been in business since 1820. It still specialises in absinthe, a drink to be treated with some respect. Your glass comes with a lump of sugar, a fork and a little bottle of mineral water. Hold the sugar on the fork, over your glass, and drip the water onto the sugar so that it dissolves into the absinthe, which turns yellow. The result should give you a warm glow.

BAR MUY BUENAS Map p74   Bar
☎ 93 442 50 53; Carrer del Carme 63; ☽ 9am-2am Mon-Thu, 9am-3am Fri & Sat, 7pm-2am Sun; Ⓜ Liceu

This bar started life as a late-19th-century corner store. The Modernista decor and relaxed company make this a great spot for a quiet mojito. You may catch a little live music or even a poetry reading, and can nibble on a limited menu of Middle Eastern titbits.

BAR PASTÍS Map p74   Bar
☎ 93 318 79 80; www.barpastis.com; Carrer de Santa Mònica 4; ☽ 7.30pm-2am Sun-Fri, 7.30pm-3am Sat; Ⓜ Drassanes

A French cabaret theme (with lots of Piaf in the background) dominates this tiny, cluttered classic. It's been going, on and off, since the end of WWII. You'll need to be in here before 9pm to have a hope of sitting, getting near the bar or anything much else. On some nights it features live acts, usually performing French chansons. Tuesday night is Tango night.

BARRAVAL Map p74   Bar
☎ 93 329 82 77; Carrer de l'Hospital 104; ☽ 7pm-2.30am Tue-Thu, 7pm-5am Fri, noon-5am Sat, noon-5pm Sun; Ⓜ Liceu

With its designer looks, greys, black and subtle lighting, this is a hard-to-categorize, all-in-one evening-out location split over two floors. Mediterranean fusion dishes reign in the early evening as people crowd in for dinner. From 11pm, DJs fill the air with mixes of jazz, funk, R&B, soul and Latin sounds. Wednesday nights there is a free snack buffet for tipplers.

BETTY FORD Map p74   Bar
☎ 93 304 13 68; Carrer de Joaquín Costa 56; ☽ 6pm-1.30am Sun & Mon, 2pm-1.30am Tue-Thu, 2pm-2.30am Fri & Sat; Ⓜ Universitat

This enticing corner bar is one of several good stops along the student-jammed run of Carrer de Joaquín Costa. It does some nice cocktails and the place fills with an even mix of locals and foreigners, generally not much over 30 and with an abundance of tats and piercings. Those with a hunger fear not – they cook up some decent burgers here, too.

BOADAS Map p74   Bar
☎ 93 318 88 26; Carrer dels Tallers 1; ☽ noon-2am Mon-Thu, noon-3am Fri & Sat; Ⓜ Catalunya

One of the city's oldest cocktail bars, Boadas is famed for its daiquiris. The bow-tied waiters have been serving up unique drinkable creations since Miguel Boadas opened it in 1933. Joan Miró and Hemingway drank here. Miguel was born in Havana, where he was the first barman at the immortal La Floridita. It specialises in short, intense drinks, such as the house special, the sweetish Boadas, with rum, Dubonnet and curaçao.

BODEGA LA PENÚLTIMA Map p74   Bar
Carrer de la Riera Alta 40; ☽ **7pm-2am Tue-Thu, 7pm-3am Fri & Sat, 7pm-1am Sun;** Ⓜ **Sant Antoni**
There is a baroque semi-darkness about this dark timber and sunset-yellow place, which gives off airs of an old-time wine bar. In Spanish lore, one never drinks *la última* (the last one) as it is bad luck. Rather, it is always the 'second last' *(penúltima)* round. A mixed group crowds into the lumpy lounges around uneven tables at the back or huddles at the bar for endless second-last rounds of wine, beer or cocktails.

CASA ALMIRALL Map p74   Bar
☎ **93 318 99 17; Carrer de Joaquín Costa 33;** ☽ **5.30pm-2.30am Sun-Thu, 7pm-3am Fri & Sat;** Ⓜ **Universitat**
In business since the 1860s, this unchanged corner bar is dark and intriguing, with Modernista decor and a mixed clientele. There are some great original pieces in here, like the marble counter, and the cast-iron statue of the muse of the Universal Exposition, held in Barcelona in 1888.

KENTUCKY Map p74   Bar
☎ **93 318 28 78; Carrer de l'Arc del Teatre 11;** ☽ **10pm-3am Tue-Sat;** Ⓜ **Liceu**
A haunt of visiting US Navy boys, this exercise in smoke-filled Americana kitsch is the perfect way to finish an evening – if you can squeeze in. All sorts of odd bods from the *barri* and beyond gather. An institution in the wee hours, this place often stays open as late as 5am.

LA CONFITERÍA Map p74   Bar
☎ **93 443 04 58; Carrer de Sant Pau 128;** ☽ **11am-2am;** Ⓜ **Paral.lel**
This is a trip into the 19th century. Until the 1980s it was a confectioner's shop, and although the original cabinets are now lined with booze, the look of the place has barely changed in its conversion into a laid-back bar. A quiet enough spot for a house *vermut* (€3; add your own soda) in the early evening, it fills with theatregoers and local partiers later at night.

LONDON BAR Map p74   Bar
☎ **93 318 52 61; Carrer Nou de la Rambla 34-36;** ☽ **7.30pm-4am Tue-Sun;** Ⓜ **Liceu**
Open since 1909, this Modernista bar started as a hang-out for circus hands and was later frequented by the likes of Picasso, Miró and Hemingway (didn't they have any work to do?). As popular as it was in Picasso's time, this place fills to the brim with punters at the long front bar and rickety old tables. On occasion, you can attend concerts at the small stage right up the back.

MARMALADE Map p74   Bar
☎ **93 442 39 66; www.marmaladebarcelona .com; Carrer de la Riera Alta 4-6;** ☽ **7pm-3am;** Ⓜ **Sant Antoni**
From the street you can see the golden hues of the backlit bar way down the end of a long lounge-lined passageway. To the left of the bar by a bare brick wall is a pool table, popular but somehow out of place in this chic, ill-lit chill den (with attached restaurant). Happy hour (cocktails for €4) is from 7pm to 9pm.

NEGRONI Map p74   Bar
Carrer de Joaquín Costa 46; ☽ **7pm-2am Mon-Thu, 7pm-3am Fri & Sat;** Ⓜ **Liceu**
Good things come in small packages and this teeny cocktail bar confirms the rule. The black and beige decor lures in a largely student set to try out the bar's cocktails, among them the flagship Negroni, a Florentine invention with one part Campari, one part gin and one part sweet vermouth.

RESOLÍS Map p74   Bar
☎ **93 441 29 48; Carrer de la Riera Baixa 22;** ☽ **10am-1am Mon-Sat;** Ⓜ **Liceu**
Long a drab dive, the bar is a tasteful image of its former self. The timber panelling, mirror-backed bar and teeny tables all hark back to other times, but without the grime.

MOOG Map p74   Club
☎ **93 301 72 82; www.masimas.com/moog; Carrer de l'Arc del Teatre 3; admission €10;** ☽ **midnight-5am;** Ⓜ **Drassanes**
This fun and minuscule club is a standing favourite with the downtown crowd. In the main dance area, DJs dish out house, techno and electro, while upstairs you can groove to a nice blend of indie and occasional classic-pop throwbacks.

JAZZ SÍ CLUB Map p74 Live Music
☎ 93 329 00 20; tallerdemusics.com; Carrer de Requesens 2; admission €5-8; ⏰ 6-11pm; Ⓜ Sant Antoni

A cramped little bar run by the Taller de Músics (Musicians' Workshop) serves as the stage for a varied program of jazz through to some good flamenco (Friday nights). Thursday night is Cuban night, Sunday is rock and the rest are devoted to jazz and/or blues sessions. It makes for a mellow start to a long night in El Raval. Concerts start around 9pm but the jam sessions can get going as early as 6.30pm.

ROBADORS 23 Map p74 Live Music
Carrer d'en Robador 23; ⏰ music from 8.30pm Wed; Ⓜ Liceu

On what remains a classic dodgy El Raval street, where a hardy band of streetwalkers, junkies and other misfits hangs out in spite of all the work being carried out to gentrify the area, a narrow little bar has made a name for itself with its Wednesday night gigs. Jazz is the name of the game and the free concerts start at 8.30pm. You'll want to get there earlier for a spot.

LA RIBERA

Where the townsfolk once enjoyed a good public execution or rousing medieval joust along Passeig del Born, they now reach a heightened state of animation in a countless array of bars along this elongated square and in the web of streets winding off it and around the Església de Santa Maria del Mar. Much gentrified since the mid-1990s, the area around Passeig del Born has an ebullient, party feel. North of Carrer de la Princesa, things quieten down quite a bit, but there's a scattering of bars about, some barely glanced at by foreign visitors.

GIMLET Map p82 Bar
☎ 93 310 10 27; Carrer del Rec 24; ⏰ 10pm-3am; Ⓜ Jaume I

Transport yourself to a Humphrey Bogart movie. White-jacketed bar staff with all the appropriate aplomb will whip you up a gimlet or any other classic cocktail (around €10) your heart desires. Barcelona cocktail guru Javier Muelas is behind this and several other cocktail bars around the city, so you can be sure of excellent drinks, some with a creative twist.

KICKING ON

The magic word is 'afters'. While the law imposes a closing time of 3am at the latest for bars in Barcelona, those in need of further fun and not in the mood for clubs do not necessarily have to head home for a beer from the fridge. Indeed, those still in need of fun even after the clubs disgorge their punters at 6am can find succour. Ask around for the nearest 'afters' (which may not be near but, hey, taxis are affordable). A handful of these mysterious places, with locked doors and spyholes, are scattered about the city. We can't give away any names – by their very nature (in the legal twilight zone) they don't advertise themselves. But take heart – if you find one, you'll be able to drink away until 8am or later. It's no wonder some people confuse day with night in Barcelona!

LA FIANNA Map p82 Bar
☎ 93 315 18 10; www.lafianna.com; Carrer dels Banys Vells 15; ⏰ 6pm-1.30am Sun-Wed, 6pm-2.30am Thu-Sat; Ⓜ Jaume I

There is something medieval about this bar, with its bare stone walls, forged iron candelabra and cushion-covered lounges. But don't think chill out. This place heaves and, as the night wears on, it's elbow room only. Earlier in the evening you can indulge in a little snack food, too.

LA VINYA DEL SENYOR Map p82 Bar
☎ 93 310 33 79; Plaça de Santa Maria 5; ⏰ noon-1am Tue-Sun; Ⓜ Jaume I

Relax on the *terrassa*, which lies in the shadow of Església de Santa Maria del Mar, or crowd inside at the tiny bar. The wine list is as long as *War and Peace* and there's a table upstairs for those who opt to sample by the bottle rather than the glass.

MIRAMELINDO Map p82 Bar
☎ 93 319 53 76; Passeig del Born 15; ⏰ 8pm-2.30am; Ⓜ Jaume I

A spacious tavern in a Gothic building, this remains a classic on Passeig del Born for mixed drinks, while soft jazz and soul sounds float overhead. Try for a comfy seat at a table towards the back before it fills to bursting. Several similarly barn-sized places line this side of the *passeig*.

MUDANZAS Map p82 Bar
☎ 93 319 11 37; Carrer de la Vidrieria 15; ⏰ 10am-2.30am; Ⓜ Jaume I

This was one of the first bars to get things into gear in El Born and it still attracts a faithful crowd. It's a straightforward place for a beer, a chat and perhaps a sandwich. Oh, and it does a nice line in Italian grappas.

MAGIC Map p82   Club
☎ 93 310 72 67; Passeig de Picasso 40; ⏲ 11pm-6am Wed-Sun; Ⓜ Barceloneta
Although it sometimes hosts live acts in its sweaty, smoky basement, it's basically a straightforward, subterranean dance club offering rock, mainstream dance faves and Spanish pop.

UPIAYWASI Map p82   Club
☎ 93 268 01 54; Carrer d'Allada Vermell 11; ⏲ 5pm-2am Mon-Thu, 5pm-3am Fri & Sat, 4pm-1am Sun; Ⓜ Barceloneta
Slide into this dimly lit cocktail bar, which crosses a chilled ambience with Latin American music. A mix of lounges and intimate table settings, chandeliers and muted decorative tones lends the place a pleasingly conspiratorial feel.

PORT VELL & LA BARCELONETA

The northeastern end of the beach on the Barceloneta waterfront near Port Olímpic is a pleasant corner of evening chic that takes on a balmy, almost Caribbean air in the warmer months. A selection of restaurant-lounges and trendy bar-clubs vies for your attention. Several other attractive options are scattered about away from this core of night-time entertainment.

CDLC Map p90   Bar
☎ 93 224 04 70; www.cdlcbarcelona.com; Passeig Marítim de la Barceloneta 32; ⏲ noon-3am; Ⓜ Ciutadella Vila Olímpica
Seize the night by the scruff at the Carpe Diem Lounge Club, where you can lounge in Asian-inspired surrounds. Ideal for a slow warm-up before heading to the nearby clubs, if you can be bothered lifting yourself back up onto your feet, that is. You can come for the food or wait until about midnight, when they start to roll up the tables and the DJs and dancers take full control.

LUZ DE GAS PORTVELL Map p90   Bar
☎ 93 484 23 26; Moll del Dipòsit; ⏲ noon-3am Mar-Nov; Ⓜ Barceloneta

Sit on the top deck of this boat and let go of the day's cares. Sip wine or beer, nibble tapas and admire the yachts. On shore they play some good dance music at night.

OKE Map p90   Bar
Carrer del Baluard 54; ⏲ 11am-2am; Ⓜ Barceloneta
An eclectic and happy little crowd, with a slight predominance of Dutch, hangs about this hippie-ish little bar near La Barceloneta's market. Lounges, tables and chairs seem to have been extracted willy-nilly from garage sales. Juices, cocktails and snacks are the main fare, along with animated conversation wafting out over the street.

PEZ PLAYA Map p90   Bar
Carrer de Ramon Trias Fargas 2-4; ⏲ 8pm-3am Thu-Fri, 4pm-3am Sat-Sun; Ⓜ Ciutadella Vila Olímpica
A mean mojito is served up in this cheerful, makeshift beachside dance bar. It's a bare-bones structure, mostly open to the balmy night air, and attracts a mixed crowd with broad musical tastes, without the urban-Buddha chilling thing. Just a good fun place to sip and jive.

SANTA MARTA Map p90   Bar
Carrer de Guitert 60; ⏲ 10.30am-7pm Sun, Mon, Wed & Thu, 10.30am-10pm Fri & Sat; Ⓜ Barceloneta, 🚌 45, 57, 59 & 157
Foreigners who have found seaside nirvana in Barcelona hang out in this chilled bar back from the beach. A curious crowd of Rastas, beach bums and switched-on dudes chat over light meals and beer inside or relax outside over a late breakfast. It has some tempting food too: a mix of local and Italian items, with a range of filled rolls (bocatas) for €5, or a dish of mozzarella di bufala (buffalo-milk cheese) for €8.

SHÔKO Map p90   Bar
☎ 93 225 92 00; www.shoko.biz; Passeig Marítim de la Barceloneta 36; ⏲ 8pm-3am Tue-Sun; Ⓜ Ciutadella Vila Olímpica
Too cool for anything really, let alone school, this chilled restaurant and bar is all far-out concepts. Wafting over your mixed Asian-Med food is an opiate blend of Shinto music and Japanese electro. As the food is cleared away, the place turns into a funky-beat kinda place, into which you may or may not enter without dinner, depending on the bouncer's mood.

CATWALK Map p90   Club

☎ 93 224 07 40; www.clubcatwalk.net; Carrer de Ramon Trias Fargas 2-4; admission €15; ☽ midnight-6am Thu-Sun; Ⓜ Ciutadella Vila Olímpica

A well-dressed crowd piles in here for good house music, occasionally mellowed down with more body-hugging electro, R&B, hip hop and funk. Alternatively, you can sink into a fat lounge for a quiet tipple and whisper. Popular local DJ Jekey leads the way most nights.

OPIUM MAR Map p90   Club

☎ 902 267486; www.opiummar.com; Passeig Marítim de la Barceloneta 34; ☽ 8pm-6am; Ⓜ Ciutadella Vila Olímpica

Whites, shimmering silver and dark contrasts mark the decor of this seaside dance place. While much of the action (accompanied by the thumping beat of house and techno) revolves around the central bar, there are plenty of separate spaces to sneak off to as well. It only begins to fill with a 20- and 30-something crowd from about 3am and is best in summer, when you can spill outside overlooking the beach. The beachside outdoor section works as a chilled restaurant-cafe by day (1pm to 8pm). Tuesday nights is Erasmus students night (so what about studying?).

MONASTERIO Map p90   Live Music

☎ 616 287197; www.salamonasterio.com, in Spanish; Passeig d'Isabel II 4; ☽ 9pm-2.30am Sun-Thu, 9.30pm-3am Fri & Sat; Ⓜ Barceloneta

Wander downstairs to the brick vaults of this jamming basement music den. There's a little of everything, from jazz on Sunday night, blues jams on Thursdays, rock and roll on Tuesdays and up-and-coming singer-songwriters on Mondays. It has Murphy's on tap, along with several other imported beers.

PORT OLÍMPIC, EL POBLENOU & EL FÒRUM

Several options present themselves along the coast. The line-up of raucous bars along the marina at Port Olímpic is one. More chilled are the beach bars (see the boxed text, below). In deepest Poblenou you'll find some clubs, among them one of Barcelona's classics, Razzmatazz.

RAZZMATAZZ Map p96   Club & Live Music

☎ 93 272 09 10; www.salarazzmatazz.com; Carrer dels Almogàvers 122 & Carrer de Pamplona 88; admission €15-30; ☽ live music generally Tue-Sat, clubs 1-6am Fri & Sat; Ⓜ Marina or Bogatell

Bands from far and wide occasionally create scenes of near hysteria in this, one of the city's classic live-music and clubbing venues. Bands generally appear Thursday to Saturday evenings (and occasionally Tuesdays and Wednesdays), with different start times. On weekends the live music then gives way to club sounds. Five different clubs in one huge postindustrial space attract people of all dance persuasions

---

CHILLIN' ON THE BEACH

Summer lounging on the beach is not just about towels on the sand. Scattered along Barcelona's strands is a series of hip little beach bars bringing chilled club sounds to the seaside. Sip on your favourite cocktail as you take in the day's last rays. There's no need to head straight home at sundown either, as these places keep humming from about 10am until as late as 2am (Easter to October), depending on the forces of law and order and how good business is. Along the beaches of La Barceloneta (from Platja de Sant Miquel up to Port Olímpic), there are several spots. A good one is Chiringuito del Mar (Map p90).

Better are those northeast of Port Olímpic. There are three on Platja de Nova Icària: Dockers (Map p96; http://dockers bcn.com, in Spanish), El Bierzo (Map p96) and Inercia (Map p96; www.inerciabeach.com). The Pachá club people have one each on Platja de Bogatell and Platja de la Nova Mar Bella: El Chiringuito (Map p96; www.elchiringuitogroup. com). Mochima (Map p96; www.mochimabar.com, in Spanish), popular with a mixed crowd, has a bar on Platja de la Mar Bella and another a little further up on Platja de la Nova Mar Bella. Nueva Ola (Map p96) is the last of these bars, at the northern end of Platja de la Nova Mar Bella.

By far the best beach booty experience takes place outside Barcelona, a train ride to the northeast in Mataró. Lasal (www.lasal.com; ☽ May-Sep), on Platja Sant Simó (northeast of the marina), offers top local DJs, food and a great party atmosphere.

MAKING A SPLASH

Guys and gals board their metal steeds on hot summer nights to bear down on one of the top outdoor club scenes in town (or rather out of town, since it's in neighbouring L'Hospitalet de Llobregat). Liquid (off Map p100; ☎ 670 221209; www.liquidbcn.com; Complex Esportiu Hospitalet Nord, Carrer de Manuel Azaña 21-23; ☼ Jun–Sep) says what it is. A palm-studded islet is surrounded by a bottom-lit azure moat that tempts surprisingly few folks to plunge in while dancing the night away in this megaclub. Local and foreign DJs keep the punters, a mixed crowd from all over town, in the groove in a series of different internal spaces, as well as poolside.

and ages. The main space, the Razz Club, is a haven for the latest international rock and indie acts. The Loft does house and electro, while the Pop Bar offers anything from garage to soul. The Lolita room is the land of techno pop and deep house, and upstairs in the Rex Room guys and girls sweat it out to high-rhythm electro-rock.

SALA MEPHISTO Map p96 — Live Music

☎ 659 163652; www.mephistobcn.com; Carrer de Roc Boronat 33; ☼ 10pm-6am Fri & Sat; Ⓜ Llacuna
Heavy metal, Gothic and hard-rock fans converge on this one-time workshop for concerts by groups from all over Europe. The music determines the crowd, so expect pale people in theatrically dark clothing. Long-haired lads with tats and leather mingle with pale wraiths in flowing black dresses and heavy make-up. It's all in the name of good fun. Heavy metal lovers should especially check the place out from 1am on Saturdays.

L'EIXAMPLE

Much of middle-class L'Eixample is dead at night, but several streets are exceptions. Noisy Carrer de Balmes is lined with a rowdy adolescent set. Much more interesting is the cluster of locales lining Carrer d'Aribau between Avinguda Diagonal and Carrer de Mallorca. They range from quiet cocktail bars to '60s retro joints. Few get going much before midnight and are generally closed or dead Sunday to Wednesday. Lower down, on and around Carrer del Consell de Cent and Carrer de la Diputació, is the heart of Gaixample, with several gay bars and clubs (see the boxed text, p198).

ÁTAME Map p106 — Bar

☎ 93 454 92 73; Carrer del Consell de Cent 257; ☼ 7pm-3am; Ⓜ Universitat
Cool for a coffee in the early evening, Átame (Tie Me Up) heats up later in the night as the gay crowd comes out to play.

There is usually a raunchy show on Friday nights and a happy hour on Thursdays.

BACON BEAR Map p106 — Bar

Carrer de Casanova 64; ☼ 6pm-2.30am; Ⓜ Urgell
Every bear needs a cave to go to, and this is a rather friendly one. It's really just a big bar for burly gay folk. On weekends the music cranks up enough for a bit of bear-hugging twirl.

CAFÉ SAN TELMO Map p100 — Bar

☎ 93 439 73 09; Carrer de Buenos Aires 60; ☼ Mon-Sat; Ⓜ Diagonal
This narrow bar has an appealingly busy feel, with big windows along Carrer de Casanova revealing the crowds and traffic of nearby Avinguda Diagonal. Perch at the bar for a couple of low-key drinks early in your night out (some of the area's key bars and clubs are just over the other side of Avinguda Diagonal).

DACKSY Map p106 — Bar

☎ 93 217 50 72; Carrer del Consell de Cent 247; ☼ 1pm-2am Sun-Thu, 1pm-3am Fri & Sat; Ⓜ Universitat
Eye-candy bartenders know their stuff when it comes to mixing, shaking and/or stirring their way to your heart with a fine selection of cocktails in this chilled lounge in the heart of the Gaixample action. It makes a perfect start to the evening, or a nice way to finish off if clubbing is not on the night's agenda.

DRY MARTINI Map p100 — Bar

☎ 93 217 50 72; www.drymartinibcn.com; Carrer d'Aribau 162-166; ☼ 5pm-3am; Ⓡ FGC Provença
Waiters with a discreetly knowing smile will attend to your cocktail needs here. The house drink, taken at the bar or in one of the plush green leather lounges, is a safe bet. The gin and tonic comes in an enormous mug-sized glass – a couple of these

and you're well on the way! Out the back is a restaurant, Speakeasy (p181).

GARAJE HERMÉTICO Map p106   Bar
Avinguda Diagonal 440; ⏰ 11pm-4am; Ⓜ Diagonal

It's a smoke-filled, pool-playing, rock 'n' roll kinda world in this popular late-night haunt, where those without disco desire but in search of one (or two) more drinkies converge when most of the other bars in Barcelona have closed. It's a no-nonsense place and full of beans after 3am.

LA CHAPELLE Map p106   Bar
☎ 93 453 30 76; Carrer de Muntaner 67; ⏰ 6pm-2am Mon-Thu, 6pm-3am Fri & Sat; Ⓜ Universitat

A typical, long, narrow Eixample bar with white-tiled walls like a 1930s hospital, it houses a plethora of crucifixes and niches that far outdoes what you'd find in any other 'chapel'. This is a relaxed gay meeting place that welcomes all comers. No need for six-pack bellies here.

LA FIRA Map p106   Bar
www.lafiraclub.com, in Spanish; Carrer de Provença 171; admission €8-12; ⏰ 10.30pm-3am Wed-Sat; Ⓡ FGC Provença

A designer bar with a difference. Wander in past distorting mirrors and ancient fairground attractions from Germany. Put in coins and listen to hens squawk. Speaking of squawking, the music swings wildly from whiffs of house through '90s hits to Spanish pop classics. You can spend the earlier part of the night trying some of the bar's shots – it claims to have 500 varieties (but we haven't counted them up).

LES GENS QUE J'AIME
Map p106   Bar
☎ 93 215 68 79; Carrer de València 286; ⏰ 6pm-2.30am Sun-Thu, 6pm-3am Fri & Sat; Ⓜ Passeig de Gràcia

This intimate basement relic of the 1960s follows a deceptively simple formula: chilled jazz music in the background, minimal lighting from an assortment of flea-market lamps and a cosy, cramped scattering of red velvet-backed lounges around tiny dark tables.

MEDITERRÁNEO Map p106   Bar
☎ 678 211253; Carrer de Balmes 129; ⏰ 11pm-3am; Ⓜ Diagonal

This smoky, studenty jam joint is a great hang-out that attracts a mostly casual student set. Order a beer, enjoy the free nuts and chat at one of the tiny tables while waiting for the next act to tune up at the back. Sometimes the young performers are surprisingly good.

MICHAEL COLLINS PUB Map p100   Bar
☎ 93 459 19 64; www.michaelcollinspubs.com; Plaça de la Sagrada Família 4; ⏰ noon-3am; Ⓜ Sagrada Família

Locals and expats alike patronise this place, one of the city's best-loved Irish pubs. To be sure of a little Catalan-Irish *craic*, this barn-sized storming pub is just the ticket. It's ideal for football fans wanting big-screen action over their pints, too.

MILANO Map p106   Bar
☎ 93 481 38 27; www.camparimilano.com; Rond de la Universitat 35; ⏰ noon-2.30am; Ⓜ Catalunya

You don't quite know what to expect as you head downstairs into this cocktail den. Then you are confronted by its vastness and the happily imbibing crowds ensconced at tables or perched at the broad, curving bar to the right.

MUSEUM Map p106   Bar
Carrer de Sepúlveda 178; ⏰ 6.30pm-3am; Ⓜ Universitat

'Kitsch gone mad' is the artistic theme here, where chandeliers meet mock Renaissance sculpture and light pop. Drinks are served behind a stage-lit bar and can be hard to come by from 1.30am on. Twinks and muscle builders mix happily in this gay starter bar perfectly located for a hop over to Metro (see p208) later on.

NEW CHAPS Map p106   Bar
☎ 93 215 53 65; www.newchaps.com; Avinguda Diagonal 365; ⏰ 9pm-3am Sun-Thu, 9pm-3.30am Fri & Sat; Ⓜ Diagonal

Leather lovers get in some close-quarters inspection on the dance floor and more, especially in the dark room, downstairs past the fairly dark loos in the vaulted cellars. It's a classic handlebar-moustache gay-porn kinda place.

PLATA BAR Map p106   Bar
☎ 93 452 46 36; Carrer del Consell de Cent 235; ⏰ 8pm-3am; Ⓜ Universitat

SMOKE SCREEN

Although national smoking laws in place since January 2006 mean that in any bars or clubs bigger than 100 sq metres smoking should be restricted to specific areas or banned altogether, this seems to be honoured rather more in the breach. There is talk of a tougher law in the offing, but it's anyone's guess when the chatter might be translated into deeds. So for now, at least, you will still emerge from a big night out smelling like an ashtray.

A summer seat on the corner terrace of this wide-open bar attracts a lot of lads in the course of an evening hopping the area's gay bars. Inside, metallic horse-saddle stools are lined up at the bar and high tables, the music drifts through modes of dance and trance and waiters whip up drinks from behind a couple of candelabra on the bar.

PREMIER Map p106   Bar

☎ 93 532 16 50; Carrer de Provença 236; ☼ 6pm-2.30am Mon-Thu, 6pm-3am Fri & Sat; ⓡ FGC Provença

A little cross-pollination has happened in this funky little French-run wine bar. The rather short wine list is mostly French – or you can opt for a Moritz beer or a mojito. Hug the bar, sink into a lounge or hide up on the mezzanine. Later in the evening, a DJ adds to the ambience. One warning – it gets smoky in here.

PUNTO BCN Map p106   Bar

☎ 93 453 61 23; www.arenadisco.com; Carrer de Muntaner 63-65; ☼ 6pm-3am; Ⓜ Universitat

It's an oldie but a goody. A big bar over two levels with a crowd ranging from their 20s to their 40s and beyond, this place fills to bursting on Friday and Saturday nights. It's a friendly early stop on a gay night out, and you can shoot a round of pool if you feel so inclined.

QUILOMBO Map p100   Bar

☎ 93 439 54 06; Carrer d'Aribau 149; ☼ 7pm-2.30am daily Jun-Sep, Wed-Sun Oct-May; ⓡ FGC Provença

Some formulas just work, and this place has been working since the 1970s. Set up a few guitars in the back room, which you pack with tables and chairs, add some cheapish pre-prepared mojitos and plastic tubs of nuts, and let the punters do the rest. They pour in, creating plenty of *quilombo* (fuss).

AIRE Map p106   Club

☎ 93 487 83 42; www.arenadisco.com, in Spanish; Carrer de València 236; ☼ 11pm-3am Thu-Sat; Ⓜ Passeig de Gràcia

A popular locale for lesbians, the dance floor is spacious and there is usually a DJ in command of the tunes, which range from hits of the '80s and '90s to techno. As a rule, only male friends of the girls are allowed entry, although in practice the crowd tends to be fairly mixed. Things can heat up on Thursday nights with live music.

ANTILLA BCN Map p106   Club

☎ 93 451 45 64; www.antillasalsa.com, in Spanish; Carrer d'Aragó; ☼ 11pm-6am; Ⓜ Urgell

The *salsateca* in town, this is the place to come for Cuban *son*, merengue, salsa and a whole lot more. If you don't know how to dance to any of this, you may feel a little silly (as a guy) but women will probably get free lessons. The guys can come back at another time and pay for classes (see p277).

ARENA CLASSIC Map p106   Club

☎ 93 487 83 42; www.arenadisco.com, in Spanish; Carrer de la Diputació 233; admission €6-12; ☼ 12.30-6.30am Fri & Sat; Ⓜ Passeig de Gràcia

Around the corner from Arena Madre, this place is a little more sedate than its partner, and tends to get more of a mixed crowd. The dominant sound is commercial house music.

ARENA MADRE Map p106   Club

☎ 93 487 83 42; www.arenadisco.com, in Spanish; Carrer de Balmes 32; admission €6-12; ☼ 12.30-5.30am; Ⓜ Passeig de Gràcia

Popular with a hot young crowd, Arena Madre is one of the top clubs in town for boys seeking boys. Keep an eye out for the striptease shows on Mondays and drag queens on Wednesdays, along with the usual combination of disco and Latin music to get those butts moving. Heteros are welcome but a minority.

CITY HALL Map p106   Club

☎ 93 238 07 22; www.grupo-ottozutz.com, in Spanish; Rambla de Catalunya 2-4; admission €12; ☼ midnight-5am Mon-Thu, midnight-6am Fri & Sat; Ⓜ Catalunya

A corridor leads to the dance floor of this place, located in a former theatre. House and other electric sounds dominate, including a rather forward-sounding session of cutting-edge funk called *Get Funkd!* on Tuesdays. Wednesday night is electro-house, while different guest DJs pop up on Thursdays. Out back from the dance floor is a soothing terrace.

DBOY Map p106   Club
☎ 93 453 05 10; www.dboyclub.com; Ronda de Sant Pere 19-21; ☽ midnight-6am Sat; Ⓜ Urquinaona

With pink laser lights and dense crowds of fit young lads, this is one of the big dance-club locations on a Saturday night. Electronic music dominates the dance nights here and, in spite of the 6am finish, for many this is only the start of the 'evening'. From 5am on, buses line up to ferry punters to the suburb of Viladecans, where the party continues at *Souvenir* (http://09.matinee group.com; Carrer del Noi de Sucre 75) until 3.30pm on Sunday afternoon, which just leaves time for a snooze at the beach afterwards.

DIETRICH GAY TEATRO CAFÉ
Map p106   Club
☎ 93 451 77 07; Carrer del Consell de Cent 255; ☽ 10.30pm-3am; Ⓜ Universitat

It's show time at 1am, with at least one drag-queen gala each night in this cabaret-style locale dedicated to Marlene Dietrich. Soft house is the main musical motif and the place has an interior garden. In between performances, gogo boys heat up the ambience.

LA BASE Map p100   Club
Carrer de Casanova 201; ☽ 10pm-3am Mon-Fri, midnight-5am Sat & Sun; Ⓜ Hospital Clínic

This heavy, heated gay bar and club has something for just about everyone: nude nights, rude nights, leather cruising evenings and dark rooms. There's even music!

METRO Map p106   Club
☎ 93 323 52 27; www.metrodiscobcn.com; Carrer de Sepúlveda 185; ☽ 1am-5am Mon, midnight-5am Sun & Tue-Thu, midnight-6am Fri & Sat; Ⓜ Universitat

Metro attracts a casual gay crowd with its two dance floors, three bars and very dark room. Keep an eye out for shows and parties, which can range from parades of models to bingo nights (on Thursday nights, with sometimes-interesting prizes).

On Wednesday nights there's a live sex show.

OPIUM CINEMA Map p100   Club
☎ 93 414 63 62; www.opiumcinema.com; Carrer de París 193-197; ☽ 9pm-2.30am Tue-Thu, 9pm-3am Fri & Sat; Ⓜ Diagonal

Reds, roses and yellows dominate the colour scheme in this wonderful former cinema. Barcelona's beautiful people, from a broad range of ages, gather to drink around the central rectangular bar, dance a little and eye one another up. Some come earlier for a bite. Wednesday nights are for R&B and Brazilian music.

THE ROXY BLUE Map p106   Club
☎ 93 272 66 97; www.roxyblue.es; Carrer del Consell de Cent 294; ☽ midnight-5am Wed & Thu, midnight-6am Fri & Sat; Ⓜ Passeig de Gràcia

Blue is indeed the predominant colour in this split-level miniclub. Tastes in music swing from New York beats to Brazil night on Sunday. On weekends you are likely to find queues of 20-somethings waiting to pile in. Sit out the music on long leather lounges or investigate the couple of different bars.

BEL-LUNA JAZZ CLUB Map p106   Live Music
☎ 93 302 22 21; www.bel-luna.com, in Spanish; Rambla de Catalunya 5; admission €5-15; ☽ 9pm-2am Sun-Thu, 9pm-3am Fri & Sat; Ⓜ Catalunya

This basement restaurant-cum-bar-cum-club is not the prettiest location but attracts a full jazz program, seven nights a week, with local and visiting acts. You can join in for dinner, but frankly you're better off dining elsewhere. When the last act finishes, the place turns into a kind of preclub club with tunes from the 1980s and '90s.

GRÀCIA & PARK GÜELL

Gràcia is a quirky place. In many ways it's its own world, with rowdy young beer swillers who should probably be studying, trendy music bars and a couple of the city's big clubs.

ALFA Map p116   Bar
☎ 93 415 18 24; Carrer Gran de Gràcia 36; ☽ 11pm-3.30am Thu-Sat; Ⓜ Diagonal

Aficionados of good old-fashioned rock love this unchanging bar-cum-minidisco, a Gràcia classic. Records hang from the ceiling as if to remind you that most of the music comes from the pre-CD era, '60s to

'80s and the occasional later intruder. Take up a stool for a drink and chat or head for the no-frills dance area just beyond. There's another bar right up the back.

BAR CANIGÓ Map p116   Bar
☎ 93 213 30 49; Carrer de Verdi 2; ⏱ 5pm-2am Mon-Thu, 5pm-3am Fri & Sat; Ⓜ Fontana
Especially welcoming in winter, this corner bar overlooking Plaça de la Revolució de Setembre de 1868 is an animated spot to simply sip on an Estrella beer around rickety old marble-top tables, as people have done here for decades. There's also a pool table.

LA BAIGNOIRE Map p116   Bar
☎ 677 408993; Carrer de Verdi 6; ⏱ 7pm-2.30am Sun-Thu, 7pm-3am Fri & Sat; Ⓜ Fontana
This inviting, tiny wine bar is always packed. Grab a stool and high table and order fine wines by the glass (beer and cocktails available too). It's perfect before and after a movie at the nearby Verdi cinema.

LA CIGALE Map p116   Bar
☎ 93 457 58 23; Carrer de Tordera 50; ⏱ 6pm-2.30am Sun-Thu, 6pm-3am Fri & Sat; Ⓜ Joanic
A very civilised place for a cocktail (or two for €8 before 10pm). Prop up the zinc bar, sink into a secondhand lounge chair around a teeny table or head upstairs. Music is chilled, conversation lively and you're likely to see Charlie Chaplin in action on the silent flat-screen TV. You can also snack on wok-fried dishes. The same brothers run La Fourmi (Map p116; ☎ 93 213 30 52; Carrer de Milà i Fontanals 58; Ⓜ Joanic) around the corner, which is just as pleasant and equally good for breakfast.

LE JOURNAL Map p116   Bar
☎ 93 218 04 13; Carrer de Francisco Giner 36; ⏱ 6pm-2.30am Sun-Thu, 6pm-3am Fri & Sat; Ⓜ Fontana
Students love the conspiratorial basement air of this narrow bar, whose walls and ceiling are plastered with newspapers (hence the name). Read the headlines of yesteryear while reclining in an old lounge. For a slightly more intimate feel, head upstairs to the rear gallery. It's a smokers' paradise.

MUSICAL MARIA Map p116   Bar
Carrer de Maria 5; ⏱ 9pm-3am; Ⓜ Diagonal
Even the music hasn't changed since this place got going in the late 1970s. Those longing for rock 'n' roll crowd into this animated bar, listen to old hits and knock back beers. Out back there's a pool table and the bar serves pretty much all the variants of the local Estrella Damm brew.

NOISE I ART Map p116   Bar
☎ 93 217 50 01; Carrer de Topazi 26; ⏱ 6pm-2.30am Tue & Wed, 7pm-3am Thu-Sat, 6pm-1.30am Sun; Ⓜ Fontana
Step back into the 1980s in this retro den. Red, green and other primal colours dominate the decor in a place where you might encounter Boney M on the video music play. Drape yourself on the circular red lounge, have a light meal (served up on old LPs) at red-lit tables alongside floor-to-ceiling glass windows, or perch yourself at the bar. The daiquiris may not be the best you've ever had, but probably the biggest!

RAÏM Map p116   Bar
Carrer del Progrés 34; ⏱ 1pm-2am; Ⓜ Diagonal
The walls in Raïm are alive with black-and-white photos of Cubans and Cuba. Tired old wooden chairs of another epoch huddle around marble tables, while grand old timber-lined mirrors hang from the walls. They just don't make old Spanish taverns like this anymore.

SABOR A CUBA Map p116   Bar
☎ 600 262003; Carrer de Francisco Giner 32; ⏱ 10pm-2.30am Mon-Thu, 10pm-3am Fri & Sat; Ⓜ Diagonal
Ruled since 1992 by the charismatic Havana-born Angelito is this home of *ron y son* (rum and sound). A mixed crowd of Cubans and fans of the Caribbean island come to drink mojitos and shake their stuff in this diminutive, good-humoured hang-out.

SOL SOLER Map p116   Bar
☎ 93 217 44 40; Plaça del Sol 21-22; ⏱ noon-1am; Ⓜ Fontana
A pleasant place with old tile floors, wood panelling and little marble tables perfect for an early beer or glass of red and a chat. Drop by earlier in the day for wi-fi (available to 6.30pm) and, if hunger strikes, order in some bar snacks (the chicken wings are delicious).

TAVERNA LA VIOLETA Map p116   Bar
Carrer de Sant Joaquim 12; ⏱ 9am-11pm Mon-Thu, 9am-2am Fri, 9am-1am Sat; Ⓜ Fontana
They just don't make bars like this anymore. A broad and sociable space with a pool

room next door, this crumpled, cheerful bar was long something of a working-class meeting centre. Drinking goes on much as before at its mostly marble-topped tables, but the bulk of the punters are now of the student variety. The atmosphere is good-natured and rowdy, and you can pick up tapas and *bocadillos* (filled rolls).

MARTIN'S Map p116 · Club
www.martins-disco.com; Passeig de Gràcia 130; admission Sat €12; ☉ 12.30-6am Tue-Sun; Ⓜ Diagonal

Under new management, Martin's is a gay club with a long history in Barcelona. The general dance floor is supplemented by a section for bears, a fetish zone and big, bad dark room for getting it on.

ELÈCTRIC BAR Map p116 · Live Music
www.electricbarcelona.com; Travessera de Gràcia 233; ☉ 7pm-2am Sun-Thu, 7pm-3am Fri & Sat; Ⓜ Joanic

Concerts get under way between 10pm and 11pm in this long and somewhat dingy bar. Generally, we're looking at home-grown bands revelling in the chance to bring jazz, blues, funk, bossa nova and much more to a small stage and apprecia-tive crowd. It can get pretty crowded in here but often the bands are fresh and fun.

HELIOGÀBAL Map p116 · Live Music
www.heliogabal.com; Carrer de Ramón i Cajal 80; ☉ 9pm-2am Sun-Thu, 9pm-3am Fri & Sat; Ⓜ Joanic

This compact bar is a veritable hive of cultural activity where you never quite know what to expect. Aside from art exhibi-tions and poetry readings, you will often be pleasingly surprised by the eclectic live-music program. Jazz groups are often followed by open jam sessions, and ex-perimental music of all colours gets a run. While many performers are local, interna-tional acts also get a look-in.

LA ZONA ALTA

North of Avinguda Diagonal, the *pijos* (cashed-up mamma's boys and papa's girls) are in charge. Whether you sample the bars around Carrer de Marià Cubí (and surround-ing streets) or try the clubs around Carrer d'Aribau or Tibidabo, expect to be confronted by perma-tanned Audi and 4WD-driving folks in designer threads. What do you care? The eye candy more than compensates for the snobbery.

BERLIN Map p122 · Bar
☎ 93 200 65 42; Carrer de Muntaner 240; ☉ 10am-2am Mon-Wed, 10am-2.30am Thu, 10pm-3am Fri & Sat; Ⓜ Diagonal or Hospital Clínic

This elegant corner bar offers views over Avinguda Diagonal. There is a cluster of tables outside on the 1st floor and designer lounges downstairs. Service can be harried but the location is excellent for starting an uptown night. All ages and creeds snuggle in and many kick on to Luz de Gas (p212), virtu-ally next door, afterwards.

HOTEL HANG-OUTS

Hanging out in certain hotel bars has become cool in Barcelona. So much so that locals like to hang out in some of them too! The ground-floor Lobby Lounge & Bar in Hotel Omm (p236) is one of *the* places for beautiful people to preen and be seen. When you're finished lounging around upstairs, you can head into the basement Mon Key Club (☉ 11.30pm-3am Wed-Sat), a smallish but *fashion* dance venue, straight downstairs from the lobby.

In a more enticing setting still is the W Bar (☉ noon-2am) in the new landmark W Barcelona (p235) and the ultra-cool top-floor Eclipse bar higher up in the building, with mesmerising views over the waterfront and out to sea (try the watermelon martinis). The Bankers' Bar in the Mandarin Oriental (p236) is perfect for a chic cocktail session.

Other options include the 6th-floor bar with summer terrace and pool in Hotel Me (p236) and the too-cool-for-school gay stops at Hotel Axel (p238), the Underground (☉ 11pm-2am Mon-Fri, 6pm-2am Sat & Sun) cocktail bar and the summer rooftop Skybar (☉ 11am-midnight Mon, Tue & Thu-Sat, 11am-2am Wed, noon-midnight Sun). Generally, the latter opens only to hotel guests until 10pm or 11pm.

The poolside rooftop cocktail bar, La Dolce Vita (☉ 9am-1pm Jun-Sep) at Hotel Majèstic (p236) is another fine option. Hotel Granados 83 has a small, quiet rooftop bar, the 8 Terrace Bar (Map p106; ☉ 6pm-1am Sun-Thu, 6pm-2am Fri & Sat), by the pool.

On La Rambla, Hotel 1898 (p231) runs the Bar Lobo, a terrace bar out the back. In the depths of El Raval, the Barceló Raval (p233) attracts the beautiful people downstairs in the B-Lounge, a classy tapas and cocktail bar.

BOCAYMA Map p122   Bar
☎ 93 237 94 08; Carrer de l'Avenir 50; ⏲ 11pm-2am Tue & Wed, 11pm-3am Thu-Sat; ☒ FGC Muntaner

Bocayma starts in quiet fashion with patrons gathered around its low tables lined up on one side of the rear bar area. Two backlit bars also keep the drinks coming to this low-lit honey pot of good-looking 20- and 30-somethings. After 1am the music takes off and punters rev up for an outing to nearby clubs. It often opens beyond its official hours.

BUBBLIC BAR Map p122   Bar
☎ 93 414 54 01; www.bubblicbar.com; Carrer de Marià Cubí 183; ⏲ 11pm-2am Tue & Wed, 11pm-3am Thu-Sat; ☒ FGC Muntaner

Many bars around here are tight on space, and the nonsmoking section upstairs in this bar is not much different. In the smoke-filled dungeon, however, several bars run alongside dance areas where you can shake your moving parts to a mixed medley of anything from rock to house and trance.

MARCEL Map p122   Bar
☎ 93 209 89 48; Carrer de Santaló 42; ⏲ 10am-2am Mon-Thu, 10am-3am Fri & Sat; ☒ FGC Muntaner

A classic meeting place, Marcel has a homey but classy old-world feel, with a timber bar, black and white floor tiles and high windows. It offers a few snacks and tapas as well. Space is somewhat limited and customers inevitably spill out onto the footpath.

BÚCARO Map p122   Club
☎ 93 209 65 62; Carrer d'Aribau 195; admission Fri & Sat €10; ⏲ 11pm-3.30am Sun-Wed, 11pm-5am Thu-Sat; Ⓜ Diagonal

Take a 'quiet' drink at the lounges scattered at the front end of the bar, and be regaled with anything from 1980s hits through to Latin pop. Out the back are two more bars and a swirl of people moving between them and the tiny dance floor, with sounds ranging from Spanish pop to house.

ELEPHANT Map p122   Club
☎ 93 334 02 58; www.elephantbcn.com, in Spanish; Passeig dels Til.lers 1; admission Fri & Sat €15; ⏲ 11.30pm-3am Wed, 11.30pm-5am Thu-Sun; Ⓜ Palau Reial; Ⓟ

Getting in here is like being invited to a private fantasy party in Beverly Hills. Mod-els and wannabes mix with immaculately groomed lads who most certainly didn't come by taxi. A big tentlike dance space is the main game here, but smooth customers slink their way around a series of garden bars in summer too.

MIRABLAU Map p122   Club
☎ 93 418 58 79; Plaça del Doctor Andreu; ⏲ 11am-4.30am Sun-Thu, 11am-5am Fri & Sat

Gaze out over the entire city from this privileged balcony restaurant on the way up to Tibidabo. Wander downstairs to join the folk in the tiny dance space. In summer you can step out onto the even smaller terrace for a breather.

OSHUM CLUB Map p122   Club
☎ 93 118 86 01; www.oshumclub.com; Avinguda del Doctor Marañón 17; admission €15; ⏲ 11.30pm-5.30am Thu-Sat; Ⓜ Palau Reial

This concept club has moved in to replace what for years was the Ibiza-inspired Pachá, becoming one of the city's most coveted club nights out. The main, ground floor is enormous, with a stage and several separate VIP sections. Upstairs, the Avantlounge room is a more intimate space, bathed in shimmering light and a strange, bloblike seating arrangement in the middle.

OTTO ZUTZ Map p122   Club
☎ 93 238 07 22; www.grupo-ottozutz.com; Carrer de Lincoln 15; admission €15; ⏲ midnight-5.30am Tue-Sat; ☒ FGC Gràcia

Beautiful people only need apply for entry to this three-floor dance den. Downstairs, shake it all up to house, or head upstairs for funk and soul on the 1st floor. DJs come from the Ibiza rave mould and the top floor is for VIPs (although at some ill-defined point in the evening the barriers all seem to come down). Friday and Saturday it's hip hop, R&B and funk on the ground floor and house on the 1st floor.

SALA BECOOL Map p122   Club
☎ 93 362 04 13; www.salabecool.com; Plaça de Joan Llongueras 5; admission €10-13; ⏲ midnight-6am Thu-Sun; ☒ 27, 32, 59, 66, 67 or 68

Electro is the leitmotif in this middle-sized dance place dominated by a single giant mirror ball at the stage end, where earlier in the night you might catch a concert (from 9pm). The secondary Redrum space runs at a slower pace, with indie music to the fore.

SUTTON THE CLUB Map p122   Club
☎ 93 414 42 17; www.thesuttonclub.com; Carrer de Tuset 13; admission €15; ⏰ midnight-5.30am Thu, midnight-6am Fri & Sat, 6.30-11.30pm Sun; Ⓜ Diagonal

A classic disco with mainstream sounds on the dance floor, some hopping house in a side bar and a fair spread of eye candy, this place inevitably attracts just about everyone pouring in and out of the nearby bars at some stage of the evening. The main dance floor is akin to a writhing bear pit. Jump in! The people are mostly beautiful and the bouncers don't like T-shirts or sports shoes.

BIKINI Map p122   Club & Live Music
☎ 93 322 08 00; www.bikinibcn.com; Carrer de Déu i Mata 105; admission €10-20; ⏰ midnight-6am Wed-Sun; Ⓜ Entença, 🚌 6, 7, 33, 34, 63, 67 or 68

This grand old star of the Barcelona nightlife scene has been keeping the beat since the darkest days of Franco. Every possible kind of music gets a run, depending on the night and the space you choose, from Latin and Brazilian hip jigglers to 1980s disco. It frequently stages quality local and foreign acts, ranging from funk guitar to rock. Performances generally start around 9pm or 10pm (the club doesn't happen until midnight).

LUZ DE GAS Map p122   Club & Live Music
☎ 93 209 77 11; www.luzdegas.com; Carrer de Muntaner 244-246; admission up to €20; ⏰ 11.30pm-6am; Ⓜ Diagonal, then 🚌 6, 7, 15, 27, 32, 33, 34, 58 or 64

Several nights a week this club, set in a grand former theatre, stages concerts ranging through soul, country, salsa, rock, jazz and pop. You can hang back in the relative obscurity of the bars or plunge down into the pit and boogie away before the grand stage. It's like being at a rock concert of old. From about 2am, the place turns into a club that attracts a well-dressed crowd with varying musical tastes, depending on the night. It gets a little sweaty in the dedicated club room Sala B, which opens on Friday and Saturday nights only.

MONTJUÏC, SANTS & EL POBLE SEC

A couple of curious bars in El Poble Sec (literally 'Dry Town'!) make a good prelude to the clubs that hold sway up in the wonderfully weird fantasy world of the Poble Espanyol (p145). A couple of clubs on the lower end of Avinguda del Paral.lel are worth seeking out too.

BARCELONA ROUGE Map p140   Bar
☎ 93 442 49 85; Carrer del Poeta Cabanyes 21; ⏰ 11pm-2am Tue-Thu, 11pm-3am Fri & Sat; Ⓜ Poble Sec; 🛜

Decadence is the word that springs to mind in this bordello-red lounge–cocktail bar, with acid jazz, drum and bass and other soothing sounds drifting along in the background. No, you're not addled with drink and drugs, the corridor leading out back to the bar really is that crooked. The walls are laden with heavy-framed paintings, dim lamps and mirrors, and no two chairs are alike. Stick to simple drinks, as the €10 glamour cocktails are on the watery side. It also offers sandwiches and snacks.

GRAN BODEGA SALTÓ Map p140   Bar
http://bodegasalto.net; Carrer de Blesa 36; ⏰ 7pm-3am Wed-Sat, noon-2am Sun; Ⓜ Paral.lel

You can tell by the ranks of barrels that this was once an old-fashioned wine store. Now, after a little homemade psychedelic redecoration, with odd lamps, figurines and old Chinese beer ads, this is a magnet for an eclectic barfly crowd. Mohicans and tats abound, but the crowd is mixed and friendly.

LA CASETA DEL MIGDIA Map p140   Bar
☎ 93 301 91 77, 617 956572; www.lacaseta.org; Mirador del Migdia; ⏰ 6pm-2.30am Thu-Sat, noon-1am Sun Jun-Sep, noon-7pm Sat & Sun Oct-May; Ⓜ Paral.lel, then funicular

The effort of getting to what is, to all intents and purposes, a simple *chiringuito* (makeshift cafe-bar) is well worth it. Walk below the walls of the Montjuïc castle along the dirt track or follow Passeig del Migdia (watch out for signs for the Mirador del Migdia). Stare out to sea over a beer or coffee by day. As sunset approaches the atmosphere changes, as lounge music (from samba to funk) wafts out over the hammocks. If the cocktails don't inebriate you, the smell of the pines will. It also puts on BBQ food at lunch and crêpes after 4.30pm.

MAUMAU UNDERGROUND Map p140   Bar
☎ 93 441 80 15; www.maumaunderground.com; Carrer de la Fontrodona 35; ⏰ 11pm-2.30am Thu-Sat; Ⓜ Paral.lel

Funk, soul, hip hop – you never know what you might run into in this popular

Poble Sec music and dance haunt, housed in a former factory. Above the backlit bar, a huge screen spews forth weird and wonderful images, which contribute to the relaxed lounge effect. On occasion it might transmit the latest Barça match instead.

TINTA ROJA Map p140   Bar
☎ 93 443 32 43; www.tintaroja.net, in Spanish; Carrer de la Creu dels Molers 17; ⏰ 8.30pm-2am Thu, 8.30pm-3am Fri & Sat; Ⓜ Poble Sec
A succession of nooks and crannies, dotted with what could be a flea market's collection of furnishings and dimly lit in violets, reds and yellows, makes the 'Red Ink' an intimate spot for a drink and the occasional show in the back – with anything from actors to acrobats. Tango aspirants can take class here on Wednesday nights. You never quite know what to expect in this one time *vaqueria*, where they kept cows out the back and sold fresh milk at the front!

DISCOTHEQUE Map p140   Club
☎ 902 023865; www.discotheque.info; Carrer de Tarragona 141; admission €15; ⏰ midnight-6am Fri & Sat, 7pm-1am Sun; Ⓜ Tarragona
Inspired by the megaclubs in Ibiza, this is one of Barcelona's big hitters. House is the main baseline in this sprawling designer club, where the nights can get rather hot and scantily clad. The Sunday Café Olé session is a mix of chill, dance music and suggestive stage dance shows to accompany DJs on the end-of-weekend blast.

PLATAFORMA Map p140   Club
☎ 93 329 00 29; Carrer Nou de la Rambla 145; admission €10; ⏰ midnight-6.30am Thu-Sat; Ⓜ Paral.lel
With two adjoining if smallish dance spaces, 'Platform' has the sense of a slightly clandestine location in an otherwise quiet residential street. Inside this friendly, straightforward dance dive, far from the glitzy Ibiza look, popular tunes from the 1980s and 1990s (along with timeless rock, and drum and bass on Thursdays) attract nostalgics in their 30s and younger partiers.

TERRRAZZA Map p140   Club
☎ 687 969823; www.laterrrazza.com; Avinguda de Francesc Ferrer i Guàrdia; admission €10-20; ⏰ midnight-5am Thu, midnight-6am Fri & Sat; Ⓜ Espanya
One of the city's top summertime dance locations, Terrrazza attracts squadrons of the beautiful people, locals and foreigners alike, for a full-on night of music and cocktails partly under the stars inside the Poble Espanyol complex.

THE ONE Map p140   Club
www.theonebarcelona.com, in Spanish; Avinguda de Francesc Ferrer i Guàrdia; admission €18; ⏰ midnight-6am Fri & Sat; Ⓜ Espanya
A new name for a classic dance place inside the fantasy land of Poble Espanyol has come with a new look. The main dance floor, with the latest in lighting effects and video screens, gets jammed with people from all over town as the night wears on. Friday nights has a house-Ibiza flavour, while Saturday nights tend to be more raucous. A lift and stairs lead up to a more chilled area with several VIP sections. Shuttle buses run from Plaça de Catalunya and Plaça d'Espanya from midnight to 3.30am and back down into town from 5am to 6.30am.

SALA APOLO Map p140   Club & Live Music
☎ 93 441 40 01; www.sala-apolo.com, in Catalan & Spanish; Carrer Nou de la Rambla 113; admission €6-12; ⏰ 12.30-6am Fri & Sat, midnight-5am Sun-Thu; Ⓜ Paral.lel
This is a fine old theatre, where red velvet dominates and you feel as though you're in a movie-set dancehall scene featuring Eliot Ness. 'Nasty Mondays' and 'Crappy Tuesdays' are aimed at a diehard, we-never-stop-dancing crowd. Earlier in the evening, concerts generally take place. Tastes are as eclectic as possible, from local bands to name international acts. Wednesday night is Rumba night (see p43) in Sala 2, the smaller of the two spaces.

SANT JORDI CLUB Map p140   Club & Live Music
Passeig Olimpic 5-7; 🚌 50, 55, 193 or funicular
With capacity for more than 4500 people, this concert hall, annexed to the Palau Sant Jordi, is used for big gigs that do not reach the epic proportions of headlining international acts. For concert information, keep your eyes out for listings sections in newspapers, flyers and magazines like the Guía del Ocio. Admission prices and opening times vary with the concerts.

top picks

Barcelona's reputation as a party city is well established, but the presence of wall-to-wall bars does not preclude other cultural pursuits. Indeed, the city bristles with stages that host anything from comic opera to high drama. Dance companies are thick on the ground and popular local theatre companies, when not touring the rest of Spain, keep folks strapped to their seats. Flamenco also has a place here. International acts, from orchestras to contemporary dance troupes, regularly stop by Barcelona.

Institutions as diverse as CaixaForum (p139), the Fundació Joan Miró (p143), La Casa Elizalde (p282), the Centre de Cultura Contemporània de Barcelona (CCCB; p77), Museu d'Art Contemporani de Barcelona (Macba; p76) and La Pedrera (p104) stage concerts of varying types, from world music to blues, from classical to *klezmer* (Jewish music).

The daily papers are good for cinema listings and the Palau de la Virreina arts information office (Map p60; ☎ 93 301 77 75; La Rambla de Sant Josep 99; ⏰ 10am-8pm; Ⓜ Liceu) has oodles of information on theatre, opera, classical music and more.

The easiest way to get hold of tickets *(entradas)* for most venues throughout the city is through the Caixa de Catalunya's Tel-Entrada (www.telentrada.com) service or ServiCaixa (www.servicaixa.com). With the latter service, you can pick up tickets purchased online at La Caixa bank's ServiCaixa ATMs (note that not all La Caixa's holes in the wall offer this service). Another one to try for concerts is Ticketmaster (www.ticketmaster.es). There's a ticket office *(venta de localidades)* on the ground floor of El Corte Inglés (Map p106; ☎ 902 400222; www.elcorteingles.es, click on venta de entradas, in Spanish; Plaça de Catalunya) and at some of its other branches around town (you can also buy tickets through El Corte Inglés by phone and online), and at the FNAC store on the same square.

You can purchase some half-price tickets in person no more than three hours before the start of the show you wish to see at the Palau de la Virreina (Map p60). The system is known as Tiquet-3.

For exhibitions and other free activities, check out www.forfree.cat.

For cinema bookings, see p220.

CLASSICAL MUSIC & OPERA

Barcelona is blessed with a fine line-up of theatres for grand performances of classical music, opera and more. The two historic music houses are the Gran Teatre del Liceu and the Palau de la Música Catalana. The former is the city's opera house and the latter puts on an infinitely more eclectic programme, from choral to Portuguese *fado*. Both have been given a 21st-century remake, the Liceu because it was burned to the ground and the Palau because it so badly needed it. The modern l'Auditori is home to the city's orchestra.

The *Guía del Ocio* (€1; www.guiadelociobcn.es, in Spanish) has ample listings, but the monthly *Informatiu Musical* leaflet has the best coverage of classical music (as well as other 'highbrow' genres). You can pick it up at tourist offices and the Palau de la Virreina, which also sells tickets for many events.

CONCERT DE CARILLÓ Map p60
www.gencat.net/presidencia/carillo; Palau de la Generalitat, Plaça de Sant Jaume; admission free; ⏰ noon first Sun of month Oct-Jul & 9pm various days in Jul; Ⓜ Jaume I
Some 5000kg of bronze in 49 bells (a carillon) swings into action for monthly 'concerts' in the seat of the Catalan government, allowing spectators a rare chance to get inside. In the pretty Gothic Pati dels Tarongers, an internal terrace lined with orange trees at the heart of the building, the audience is treated to a midday performance of just about anything, from classical through bossa nova, all with bells on. There are no reservations.

FUNDACIÓ MAS I MAS
☎ 93 319 17 89; www.masimas.com; Carrer de Trafalgar 4 (offices); admission €7-20
This foundation promotes chamber and classical music, offering concerts in a couple of locations. Classical concerts, usually involving Catalan performers, are

held regularly in the Sala Oriol Martorell of l'Auditori (p217), starting at around 8.30pm. For intense 30-minute sessions of chamber music, see its program of performances at l'Ateneu (Map p60; ☎ 93 343 21 61; Carrer de la Canuda 6), a hallowed academic institution-cum-club.

GRAN TEATRE DEL LICEU Map p60

☎ 93 485 99 00; www.liceubarcelona.com; La Rambla dels Caputxins 51-59; ☺ box office 2-8.30pm Mon-Fri & 1hr before show Sat & Sun; Ⓜ Liceu

Barcelona's grand old opera house, restored after fire in 1994, is one of the most technologically advanced theatres in the world (see also p67). To take up a seat in the grand auditorium, returned to all its 19th-century glory but with the very latest in acoustic accoutrements, is to be transported to another age. Red plush seating and stage curtains stand in regal contrast to the glistering gold of the five tiers of boxes. Tickets can cost anything from €7 for a cheap seat behind a pillar to €200 plus for a well-positioned night at the opera.

L'AUDITORI Map p100

☎ 93 247 93 00; www.auditori.org; Carrer de Lepant 150; admission €10-60; ☺ box office 3-9pm Mon-Sat; Ⓜ Monumental

Barcelona's modern home for serious music lovers, L'Auditori (designed by Rafael Moneo) puts on plenty of orchestral, chamber, religious and other music. L'Auditori is perhaps ugly on the outside (to the less kind-hearted it looks like a pile of rusting scrap metal) but beautifully tuned on the inside. It is home to the Orquestra Simfònica de Barcelona i Nacional de Catalunya.

PALAU DE LA MÚSICA CATALANA
Map p82

☎ 902 442882; www.palaumusica.org; Carrer de Sant Francesc de Paula 2; ☺ box office 10am-9pm Mon-Sat; Ⓜ Urquinaona

A feast for the eyes, this Modernista pudding is also the city's traditional venue for classical and choral music. Just being here for a performance is an experience. Sip a pre-concert tipple in the foyer, its tiled pillars all a-glitter. Head up the grand stairway to the main auditorium, a whirlpool of Modernista whimsy that is seen at its best before lights are dimmed for the show. The Palau has a wide-ranging programme. You

could pay €10 or less for a cheap seat in a middling concert and up to €150 or more for prestigious international performances.

PALAU ROBERT Map p106

☎ 93 238 40 00; www.gencat.cat/palaurobert; Passeig de Gràcia 107; admission €4; Ⓜ Diagonal

Once a month concerts are held in the peaceful gardens at the back of this fine building or its main hall. Concerts are usually held around 8pm on a Wednesday. You need to pick up a pass the afternoon before (between 5pm and 7pm) or on the morning of the performance (from 10am to noon), as places are limited.

DANCE

Some fine local contemporary dance companies (see p44), along with international visiting companies from time to time, maintain a fairly busy performance programme across town. Look for leaflets at Palau de la Virreina and watch theatre listings. For ballet and other big spectacles, you need to wait for acts to arrive from abroad.

FLAMENCO

Although some major flamenco artists grew up in Barcelona's *gitano* (Roma) neighbourhoods, seeing good performances of this essentially Andalucian dance and music is not always easy. A few *tablaos*, where punters see flamenco while eating dinner, are scattered about. They are touristy but occasionally host good acts, so you need to keep a keen eye out for the names. You can also catch flamenco on Friday nights at the Jazz Sí Club (p202). Flamenco clubs (*peñas*) are scattered about Barcelona's outer suburbs but are a rather hermetic phenomenon. If you are in Barcelona in May, try to catch the Festival de Flamenco de Ciutat Vella (p18) or the festival in the district of Nou Barris in the same month. Earlier in the year, a series of concerts from mid-February to April composing the De Cajón Festival Flamenco (p17) is another opportunity. For other occasional concerts, check out www.barcelonaflamenco.com.

SALA TARANTOS Map p60

☎ 93 319 17 89; www.masimas.net; Plaça Reial 17; admission from €7; ☺ performances 8.30pm, 9.30pm & 10.30pm daily; Ⓜ Liceu

Since 1963, this basement locale has been the stage for some of the best flamenco to pass through or come out of Barcelona.

You have to keep your eye on the place because top-class acts are not a daily diet. For lower-grade stuff, a half-hour *tablao* takes place three times a night.

TABLAO CORDOBÉS Map p60
☎ 93 317 57 11; www.tablaocordobes.com; La Rambla 35; show €37, with dinner €60-68; ⏰ shows 8.15pm, 10pm & 11.30pm; Ⓜ Liceu

This *tablao* is typical of its genre and has been in business since 1970. Artists perform on a tiny hardwood stage with a vaulted backdrop that is supposed to make us think of Granada's El Alhambra. Generally, tourists book for the dinner and show, although you can skip the food and just come along for the performance (about 1¼ hours). Some great names have come through here, so it is not always cheese.

TABLAO DE CARMEN Map p140
☎ 93 325 68 95; www.tablaodecarmen.com; Carrer dels Arcs 9, Poble Espanyol; show only €35, with tapas/dinner €45/69; ⏰ shows 7.30pm & 10pm Tue-Sun; Ⓜ Espanya

Named after the great Barcelona *bailaora* (flamenco dancer) Carmen Amaya, the set-up here is similar to that at the Tablao Cordobés, although it is somewhat larger and the pseudo-Andalucian decor has a colder, more modern look.

PALACIO DEL FLAMENCO Map p106
☎ 93 218 72 37; www.palaciodelflamenco.com; Carrer de Balmes 139; show €32, with dinner €65-75; ⏰ shows 7.45pm & 10.45pm Mon-Sat; Ⓜ Diagonal

A relative newcomer on the Barcelona *tablao* circuit, the Palace of Flamenco is basically the same arrangement as its older confrères, with two sessions an evening. No attempt is made at creating a folkloric atmosphere. Rather, a series of long dinner tables spreads back away from the busy stage.

SARDANA
In Barcelona the best chance you have of seeing people dancing the *sardana* is either at noon on Sunday or 6pm on Saturday in front of La Catedral. They are also performed sometimes in Plaça de Sant Jaume (p65). For more information, contact the **Agrupació Cul-**

tural Folclòrica de Barcelona (☎ 93 315 14 96). You can also see the dance during some of the city's festivals. For more on this traditional dance, see p45.

CONTEMPORARY
TEATRE MERCAT DE LES FLORS
Map p140
☎ 93 426 18 75; www.mercatflors.org; Carrer de Lleida 59; admission €15-20; ⏰ box office 11am-2pm & 4-7pm Mon-Fri & 1hr before show; Ⓜ Espanya

Next door to the Teatre Lliure, and together with it known as the Ciutat de Teatre (Theatre City), this is a key venue for top local and international contemporary dance acts. Dance companies perform all over Barcelona but this spacious modern stage is number one.

THEATRE
Most local theatre is performed in Catalan or Spanish, although foreign companies, especially of a more avant-garde hue, are occasionally welcomed too. Some well-established Barcelona companies (see p44) provide a broad palette of drama, comedy and even musicals. Smaller, experimental theatre groups also have an enthusiastic local following, and dozens of often tiny repertory theatres are scattered across the city. The monthly guide *Teatre BCN* can be picked up at the Palau de la Virreina.

SALA BECKETT Map p116
☎ 93 284 53 12; www.salabeckett.com; Carrer de Ca l'Alegre de Dalt 55bis; ⏰ box office 10am-2pm & 4-8pm Mon-Fri & 1hr before start of show; Ⓜ Joanic

One of the city's principal alternative theatres, the Sala Beckett is a smallish space that does not shy away from challenging theatre, contemporary or otherwise, and usually a heterodox mix of local productions and foreign drama.

TEATRE GOYA Map p74
☎ 93 343 53 23; www.teatregoya.cat; Carrer de Joaquín Costa 68; admission €23-30; ⏰ box office 5.30pm to start of show; Ⓜ Sant Antoni

A classic stage that long had its shutters down, the Goya was reopened to much fanfare in 2009. The programme is generally mid- to highbrow, complementing

THE FURIOUS FURA DELS BAUS

Keep your eyes peeled for any of the eccentric (if not downright crazed) performances of Barcelona's La Fura dels Baus (www.lafura.com) theatre group. It has won worldwide acclaim for its brand of startling, often acrobatic, theatre in which the audience is frequently dragged into the chaos. The company grew out of Barcelona's street-theatre culture in the late 1970s and, although it has grown in technical prowess and received great international acclaim, it has not abandoned the rough-and-ready edge of street performances. In 2010, the group underlined this in its *Degustación de Titus Andrónicus*, in which public and actors shared the same space. Also present were two cooks working away in the kitchen throughout the piece. Whatever La Fura does, surprise is on its side.

partner theatre, the Teatre Romea. Among the first pieces shown (in Catalan), were Oscar Wilde's *An Ideal Husband* and David Mamet's *November*.

TEATRE LLANTIOL Map p74

☎ 93 329 90 09; www.llantiol.com; Carrer de la Riereta 7; admission €6-10; Ⓜ Sant Antoni

At this curious place in El Raval all sorts of odd stuff, from concerts and ballads to magic shows, is staged. On Saturday nights at 12.30am there is a regular cabaret-variety slot, a bit of a throwback to another era. About once a month you can see stand-up comedy in English here too. Check out the Giggling Guiri (www.comedyinspain.com) programme for upcoming acts, mostly from the UK. For other occasional UK stand-up comedy acts, keep an eye on www.glounge bcn.com.

TEATRE LLIURE Map p140

☎ 93 289 27 70; www.teatrelliure.com; Plaça de Margarida Xirgu 1; admission €13-26; Ⓨ box office 5-8pm; Ⓜ Espanya

Housed in the magnificent former Palau de l'Agricultura building on Montjuïc (opposite the Museu d'Arqueologia) and consisting of two modern theatre spaces (Espai Lliure and Sala Fabià Puigserver), the 'Free Theatre' puts on a variety of quality drama (mostly in Catalan), contemporary dance and music.

TEATRE NACIONAL DE CATALUNYA
Map p100

☎ 93 306 57 00; www.tnc.cat; Plaça de les Arts 1; admission €12-32; Plaça de les Arts 1; Ⓨ box office 3-7pm Wed-Fri, 3-8.30pm Sat, 3-5pm Sun & 1hr before show; Ⓜ Glòries or Monumental

Ricard Bofill's ultra-neoclassical theatre, with the bright, airy foyer, hosts a wide range of performances, principally drama (anything from King Lear in Catalan to La

Fura dels Baus) but occasionally dance and other performances.

TEATRE NOU TANTARANTANA Map p74

☎ 93 441 70 22; www.tantarantana.com; Carrer de les Flors 22; Ⓨ box office 1hr before show; Ⓜ Paral.lel

Apart from staging all sorts of contemporary and experimental drama (anything from Harold Pinter to local creations), this cosy theatre (which has room for about 150 spectators) also has a kids' programme, including pantomime and puppets. These shows tend to start at 6pm (noon on Sundays). The adult theatre productions are at 9pm Wednesday to Saturday, and 7pm Sunday.

TEATRE ROMEA Map p74

☎ 93 301 55 04; www.teatreromea.com, in Catalan & Spanish; Carrer de l'Hospital 51; admission €17-28; Ⓨ box office 4.30pm until start of show Wed-Sun; Ⓜ Liceu

Deep in El Raval, this 19th-century theatre was resurrected at the end of the 1990s and is one of the city's key stages for quality drama. It usually fills up for a broad range of interesting plays, often classics with a contemporary flavour, in Catalan and Spanish. In 2010, for instance, offerings ranged from comedy by Venice's great 18th-century playwright, Carlo Goldoni, to a local production musing on the decadence of modern European society.

TEATRE TÍVOLI Map p106

☎ 902 332211; www.grupbalana.com; Carrer de Casp 8-12; admission €20-50; Ⓨ box office 5pm to start of show; Ⓜ Catalunya

A grand old theatre with three storeys of boxes and a generous stage, the Tívoli has a fairly rapid turnover of drama and musicals, with pieces often not staying on for more than a couple of weeks.

THE ARTS THEATRE

TEATRE VICTÒRIA Map p140

☎ 93 329 91 89; www.teatrevictoria.com, in Catalan & Spanish; Avinguda del Paral.lel 67-69; admission €15-45; ⏱ box office 5pm to start of show; Ⓜ Paral.lel

This modern (and, on the street, rather nondescript-looking) theatre is on what used to be considered Barcelona's version of Broadway. It often stages ballet (including the Bolshoi in 2010), contemporary dance and even flamenco.

TEATRENEU Map p116

☎ 93 285 37 12; www.teatreneu.com; Carrer de Terol 26; ⏱ box office 1hr before show; Ⓜ Fontana or Joanic

This lively theatre (with a bustling, rambling downstairs bar facing the street) dares to fool around with all sorts of material, from monologues to social comedy. Aside from the main theatre, two cafe-style spaces serve as more intimate stage settings for small-scale productions. Films are also shown.

CINEMAS

Spain is proud of its dubbing industry, which could sound warning bells. In Barcelona, fortunately, there is no shortage of cinemas showing foreign films with subtitles and original soundtracks. They are marked 'vo' (*versión original*) in movie listings.

The best movie listings are found in the daily *El País* newspaper. A ticket usually costs €6.50 to €8.25, but most cinemas have a weekly *día del espectador* (viewer's day), often Monday or Wednesday, when they charge around €5 to €5.75. In addition to the following mainstream cinemas, classic movies are sometimes shown in such diverse locations as La Pedrera (p104), Sala Apolo (p213), CaixaForum (p139), the CCCB (p77) and civic centres.

Outdoor cinema screens are set up in summer at or near the Castell de Montjuïc (p142) and in the Fòrum (p95). Look out for information in the newspapers from July to mid-September.

CASABLANCA KAPLAN Map p116

☎ 93 218 43 45; Passeig de Gràcia 115; Ⓜ Diagonal

A smallish, popular local cinema (with three screens) that always shows movies in the original language.

CASA AMÈRICA CATALUNYA

Map p106

☎ 93 238 06 61; www.americat.net; Carrer de Còrsega 299; Ⓜ Girona

This cultural centre often has movies from throughout Latin America.

CINEMES GIRONA Map p106

☎ 93 118 45 31; Carrer de Girona 173-175; Ⓜ Girona

Often you'll find this cinema nearly empty, which in one sense is good – you should have no concerns about it selling out!

FILMOTECA Map p100

☎ 93 410 75 90; Avinguda de Sarrià 31-33; admission €2.70; Ⓜ Hospital Clínic

Also known as Cine Aquitania, it specialises in film seasons that concentrate on particular directors, styles and eras of film. The Filmoteca is the film archive of the Generalitat (regional government) and will eventually be transferred to a new location being built in El Raval.

MÉLIÈS CINEMES Map p106

☎ 93 451 00 51; www.cinesmelies.net; Carrer de Villarroel 102; admission €3-5; Ⓜ Urgell

A cosy cinema with two screens, the Méliès specialises in old classics from Hollywood and European cinema.

RENOIR FLORIDABLANCA

Map p100

☎ 93 426 33 37; www.cinesrenoir.com, in Spanish; Carrer de Floridablanca 135; Ⓜ Sant Antoni

With seven screens, this is one of a small chain of art-house cinemas in Spain showing quality flicks. It is handily located just beyond El Raval, so you can be sure that there is no shortage of post-film entertainment options nearby.

RENOIR-LES CORTS

Map p122

☎ 93 490 55 10; www.cinesrenoir.com, in Spanish; Carrer de Eugeni d'Ors 12; Ⓜ Maria Cristina or Les Corts

With six cinemas, this is a somewhat distant alternative from central Barcelona for original versions.

VERDI Map p116

☎ 93 238 79 90; www.cines-verdi.com; Carrer de Verdi 32; Ⓜ Fontana

A popular original-language movie house in the heart of Gràcia, handy to lots of local eateries and bars for pre- and post-film enjoyment.

VERDI PARK Map p116
☎ 93 238 79 90; www.cines-verdi.com; Carrer de Torrijos 49; Ⓜ Fontana

Sister to the Verdi, the Verdi Park is a block away and follows the same art-house philosophy.

YELMO CINES ICÀRIA
Map p96

☎ 93 221 75 85; www.yelmocineplex.es, in Spanish; Carrer de Salvador Espriu 61; Ⓜ Ciutadella Vila Olímpica

This vast cinema complex screens movies in the original language on 15 screens, making for plenty of choice. Aside from the screens, you'll find several cheerful eateries, bars and the like to keep you occupied before and after the movies.

SPORTS & ACTIVITIES

top picks

Barcelona offers those with a hangover every chance to eliminate toxins by flexing other muscles besides the elbow. Options abound, from swimming and sailing to marathon running. For those whose feelings of guilt over the excesses of the previous night don't translate to physical exertions, the city's football and basketball teams provide class-A excitement when they play at home. Or indulge in a massage, day spa or a spot of floating!

For information on where you can practise sports in Barcelona, try the Servei d'Informació Esportiva (Map p140; ☎ 93 402 30 00; Avinguda de l'Estadi 30-40, Montjuïc; ☯ 8am-7pm Mon-Fri), in the same complex as the Piscines Bernat Picornell on Montjuïc.

HEALTH & FITNESS

The folks of Barcelona are as health-conscious as those of any other city and the number of places to indulge in a little 'wellness' of one sort or another is multiplying.

SPAS & MASSAGE

Many of the better hotels have wellness centres, among them Hotel Arts Barcelona (p236), Hotel Omm (p236), Hotel Axel (p238), Hotel Majèstic (p236), W Barcelona (p235) and the Hesperia Tower in L'Hospitalet. You can also get soothing spa treatment outside Barcelona (see p248).

AIRE DE BARCELONA Map p82

☎ 902 555789; www.airedebarcelona.com; Passeig de Picasso 22; thermal baths & aromatherapy €25; ☯ 10am-2am; Ⓜ Arc de Triomf
With low lighting and relaxing perfumes wafting around you, this hammam could be the perfect way to end a day. Hot, warm and cold baths, steam baths and options for various massages, including on a slab of hot marble, make for a delicious hour or so. Book ahead and bring a swimming costume.

AQUA URBAN SPA Map p116

☎ 93 238 41 60; www.aqua-urbanspa.com; Carrer Gran de Gràcia 7; 75min session €51; ☯ 9am-9.30pm Mon-Fri, 9am-8.30pm Sat; Ⓜ Diagonal
With sessions for anything from stress to tired legs (helpful for diehard sightseers!), this spa offers smallish pool and shower areas, along with steam baths, Roman baths and a series of beauty treatment options.

FLOTARIUM Map p116

☎ 93 217 36 37; www.flotarium.com; Plaça de Narcís Oller 3; 1hr session €35; ☯ 10am-10pm; Ⓜ Diagonal

Float in zero gravity and feel the stress ebb away. Each flotarium, like a little space capsule with water, is in a private room, with shower, towels and shampoo, and Epsom salts that allow you to float as if in the Dead Sea.

MAILUNA Map p74

☎ 93 301 20 02; www.mailuna.net, in Spanish; Carrer de Valldonzella 48; 1hr massage €55; ☯ 5-11.30pm Mon, 1-11.30pm Tue-Sat; Ⓜ Universitat
Mailuna is a bit of wellness universe. Not only does it offer all sorts of massages (Ayurvedic, Swedish, Thai and more), it's also a restaurant, aromatherapy setting, wellness goods store and more. Stop for tea and you'll feel better already.

MASAJES A 1000 Map p106

☎ 93 215 85 85; Carrer de Mallorca 233; first 20min €18, every 5min thereafter €4.50; ☯ 8am-11pm; Ⓜ Passeig de Gràcia
Stressed out by sightseeing of the nearby Modernista gems on Passeig de Gràcia? Pop by for a quick, invigorating massage. The chain has four outlets around Barcelona.

RITUELS D'ORIENT Map p122

☎ 93 419 14 72; www.rituelsdorient.com, in Spanish; Carrer de Loreto 50; baths only €28; ☯ women only 1-9pm Tue, 10.30am-8pm Wed, 1-4pm Fri, mixed 1-10pm Thu, 4-10pm Fri, 10.30am-8pm Sat; Ⓜ Hospital Clínic
Luxuriating in hammams, indulging in massages, exfoliation and other treatments is the name of the game in this slice of what could be the Middle East. Dark woods, window grills, soft lighting and candles, cushion-covered sofas to relax on – all combine to evoke something of the mystery we all like to imagine for such a place. If you have time to hang about for four hours, try the 'Ritual

Elixir de las Mil y una Noches' (Thousand and One Nights Ritual), which includes a facial, 40-minute massage, exfoliation and wrapping up your body in a *ghassoul* mud pack.

SILOM SPA Map p106

☎ 93 272 66 62; www.silomspa.com, in Spanish; Carrer de València 304; massages €35-100; ☻ 11am-9.30pm Mon-Sat; Ⓜ Girona

A touch of the Orient is the promise in this city spa, where you can combine a series of Thai, aromatic and other massages with aroma baths. Options for couples abound and you can get a facial while you're at it. The masseurs are all Thai.

GYMS

Barcelona is crawling with places for a workout, but most gyms cater to long-term members.

POLIESPORTIU FRONTÓ COLOM
Map p60

☎ 93 302 32 95; www.frontocolom.com; La Rambla de Santa Mònica 18; admission €13.45; ☻ 7am-10.30pm Mon-Fri, 9am-8pm Sat, 9am-2.30pm Sun & holidays; Ⓜ Drassanes

Smack in the heart of the old city, this gym offers a fitness room with all manner of exercise equipment, including a section with bicycles, step and other cardio machines, and a small swimming pool. There are various multiday passes too.

RUNNING

Joggers have several attractive options in Barcelona. The waterfront esplanade and beaches are all perfect for an early morning run, before the crowds come out. Locals with serious running credentials take to Parc de Collserola, which is laced with trails. More convenient are the gardens and parkland of Montjuïc. Running in the city itself is crazy. It's too crowded and air pollution won't make your lungs happy.

SWIMMING

Barcelona has several good options for those who want to get in some more serious lap swimming than is possible at the city's beaches.

CLUB NATACIÓ ATLÈTIC-BARCELONA
Map p90

☎ 93 221 00 10; www.cnab.org; Plaça de Mar s/n; adult/under 10yr €10.55/6.13; ☻ 6.30am-11pm

SWIMMING AU NATUREL

Skinny-dippers have several options in Barcelona. In addition to the ill-defined nudists' strip at the southwest end of Platja de la Mar Bella (Map p96) and the predominantly gay strip at Platja de Sant Miquel (Map p90), you can also get it all off year-round at the Piscines Bernat Picornell, the Olympic pool on Montjuïc. On Saturday nights, between 9pm and 11pm, the pool (with access to sauna and steam bath) is open only to nudists (adult/6-14yr & senior/under 6yr €5.40/3.80/free). On Sundays between October and May the indoor pool also opens for nudists only from 4.15pm to 6pm.

Mon-Fri, 7am-11pm Sat, 8am-5pm Sun & holidays Oct–mid-May, 8am-8pm Sun & holidays mid-May–Sep; Ⓜ Barceloneta, 🚍 17, 39, 57 or 64

This athletic club has one indoor and two outdoor pools. Of the latter, one is heated for lap swimming in winter. Admission includes use of the gym and private beach access. Membership costs €35.70 a month, plus €71 joining fee.

PISCINES BERNAT PICORNELL Map p140

☎ 93 423 40 41; www.picornell.cat, in Catalan; Avinguda de l'Estadi 30-38; late Sep-late Jun adult/15-24yr/senior & 6-15yr/under 6 yr €9.65/6.50/5.95/free, outdoor pool only late Jun–late Sep adult/15-24yr/senior & 6-15yr/under 6yr €5.30/5.25/3.70/free; ☻ 6.45am-midnight Mon-Fri, 7am-9pm Sat, 7.30am-4pm Sun, outdoor pool, hr vary; 🚍 50, 61 or 193

Included in the standard entry price to Barcelona's official Olympic pool on Montjuïc is use of the gym, saunas and spa bath. Membership costs €53.50 to join and €36.10 a month. Nude bathing is also possible here, see boxed text above.

POLIESPORTIU MARÍTIM Map p90

☎ 93 224 04 40; www.claror.cat, in Catalan; Passeig Marítim de la Barceloneta 33-35; Mon-Fri €15, Sat-Sun & holidays €17.80; ☻ 7am-midnight Mon-Fri, 8am-9pm Sat, 8am-4pm Sun & holidays Sep-Jul, 7am-10.30pm Mon-Fri, 8am-9pm Sat, 8am-3pm Sun Aug; Ⓜ Ciutadella Vila Olímpica

Water babies will squeal with delight in this thalassotherapeutic (sea-water therapy) sports centre. In addition to the small pool for lap swimming, there is a labyrinth of hot, warm and freezing-cold spa pools, along with thundering waterfalls for massage relief.

YOGA

Barcelona is full of yoga centres catering to many different tastes, from the very technical swastthya yoga to the sweat-inducing bikram variety. Happy Yoga (Map p74; www.happyyoga.com) specialises mainly in kundalini and hatha and has various centres around town. A search on 'yoga Barcelona' on the internet will throw up a host of yoga centres and schools.

ACTIVITIES
CYCLING

Although cycle lanes have been laid out along many main arteries, the city centre is not the most relaxing place for a bike ride. Hillier (but much less stressful) is Montjuïc, or you could head up into the Parc de Collserola (p133) with a mountain bike. For information on bicycle hire, see p269.

GOLF

Head out of town if you enjoy belting small round objects around the greenery.

CLUB DE GOLF SANT CUGAT
off Map p122

☎ 93 674 39 08; www.golfsantcugat.com, in Catalan & Spanish; Carrer de la Villa, Sant Cugat del Vallès; Mon–Thu €65, Fri–Sun & holidays €150; ☒ 8am–dusk Mon–Fri, 7am–dusk Sat & Sun; ☒ FGC Sant Cugat

This 18-hole course was designed by Scottish experts in 1917 to meet the needs of a firm of British and American engineers working on electricity projects in Catalonia.

SAILING

On sunny weekends the Mediterranean off Barcelona is alive with the swollen sails of pleasure craft. Feel free to join in.

BASE NAUTICA MUNICIPAL Map p96

☎ 93 221 04 32; www.basenautica.org; Avinguda de Litoral s/n; ☒ Poblenou

Have you come to Barcelona to become a sea dog? If so, head to this place, just back from Platja de la Mar Bella, and enrol in a course in pleasure-boat handling, kayaking (€125 for 10 hours' tuition), windsurfing (€185 for 10 hours' tuition) or catamaran (€216 for 12 hours' tuition).

SPECTATOR SPORTS
BASKETBALL

FC Barcelona's Winterthur FCB basketball team is almost as successful as the city's glamorous football outfit, with 15 premier league victories, 21 Copas del Rey and four European titles since 1946. One of its star players, local boy 2.16m Pau Gasol, has played in the NBA league in the USA since 2001 (now with the Los Angeles Lakers) but he returns home to play in the national Spanish team.

The team plays (generally on Saturday afternoons) in the Palau Blaugrana (Map p122; ☎ 902 189900; www.fcbarcelona.com; Carrer d'Aristides; ☒ Palau Reial or Collblanc), next door to the Camp Nou football stadium in Les Corts. Tickets can be purchased direct at Palau Blaugrana, on the phone or online. Ticket prices oscillate between €12 and €63, depending on the seat and match.

BULLFIGHTING

Hemingway called it death in the afternoon and, like so many things in Barcelona, it is a subject of controversy and political demagogy. In 2004 the city council narrowly voted for a symbolic declaration that Barcelona was antibullfighting. In late 2009, the regional parliament voted to debate a ban on bullfighting in the region and animal-rights groups that oppose la lidia (bullfighting) were delighted. Many of those in favour of a ban accept the common claim that bullfighting is a Spanish cultural imposition on Catalonia, largely loathed by many Catalans. During the Civil War years, vegetarian anarchists banned bullfighting in Republican Barcelona.

Nevertheless, the main political parties seemed unconvinced by calls for the ban and no decision had been taken by mid-2010.

The bullfight season is staged at the Plaça de Braus Monumental (Map p100; ☎ 93 245 58 02; cnr Gran Via de les Corts Catalanes & Carrer de la Marina; ☒ ticket office 11am–2pm & 4-8pm Tue–Sun; ☒ Monumental). The fighting starts between 6pm and 7pm, mostly on Sunday afternoons from around Easter to late September. Tickets are available at the arena, through ServiCaixa or at http://tauroentrada. com. You can also pick up tickets at Toros Taquilla Oficial (Map p106; Carrer de Muntaner 26; ☒ 11am–2pm & 4-8pm Wed–Sat; ☒ Universitat). Prices range from €20 to €120. The higher-priced tickets are for the front row in the shade – any closer and you'd be fighting the bulls yourself.

On an afternoon ticket there are generally six bulls and perhaps three star matadors (those bullfighters who do most of the fighting and then kill the bull at the end). The matador leads a *cuadrilla* (team) of other fighters who make up the rest of the colourful band that appears in the ring. It is a complex business, but in essence the matadors aim to impress the crowd and jury with daring and graceful moves as close to an aggressive, fighting bull as possible. While the death of the bull is generally inevitable (its meat is later sold), this in no way implies the bullfighter always gets off scot-free. It is a genuinely dangerous business, and being gored and tossed by several hundred kilos of bull is no fun.

FOOTBALL

Football in Barcelona has the aura of religion and for much of the city's population, support of FC Barcelona is an article of faith. But the city has another hardy (if less illustrious) side, RCD Espanyol. FC Barcelona is traditionally associated with the Catalans and even Catalan nationalism, while Espanyol is often identified with Spanish immigrants from other parts of the country.

It all started on 29 November 1899, when, four years after English residents had first played the game here, Swiss Hans Gamper founded FC Barcelona (Barça). His choice of club colours, the blue and maroon of his hometown, Winterthur, have stuck. The following year, Espanyol was formed. It distinguished itself from the other sides, ironically, by being formed solely of Catalans and other Spaniards. Most other sides, including FC Barcelona, were primarily made up of foreigners.

By 1910, FC Barcelona was the premier club in a rapidly growing league. The first signs of professionalism emerged – paid transfers of players were recorded and Espanyol's management charged spectators. Barça, who had 560 members (compared to about 173,000 today), claimed victory at that year's national championship.

A match at Camp Nou (Map p122; ☎ 902 189900; Carrer d'Aristides Maillol; ☒ box office 9am-1.30pm & 3.30-6pm Mon-Fri; Ⓜ Palau Reial or Collblanc) can be breathtaking. The stadium is going to get a spectacular sprucing up in coming years (see p131).

After several years in the wilderness, FC Barcelona hit its straps and won the 2004–05 and 2005–06 championships. Another lull followed but then in 2009, the side swept the pools, taking the championship, the Copa del Rey (Spanish equivalent of the UK's FA Cup) and the European Cup! The 2009–10 season, although not quite as glorious, saw FC Barcelona take the championship again, with Madrid biting at its heels.

Barça is one of only three teams never to have been relegated to the second division (the others are Real Madrid and Athletic de Bilbao). Since the league got fully under way in 1928, Barça has emerged champion 19 times, second only to arch-rival Real Madrid (with 31 victories). Between them, the two have virtually monopolised the game – only seven other teams have managed to come out on top (four of them only once or twice) in 70 years of competition.

Tickets are available at Camp Nou, as well as by phone and online. You can also purchase them through the ServiCaixa ticketing service. To purchase tickets by phone or online, nonclub members must do so at least 15 days before the match. Tickets can cost anything from €31 to €225, depending on the seat and match. The ticket windows open on Saturday morning and in the afternoon until the game starts. If the match is on Sunday, it opens Saturday morning only and then on Sunday until the match starts. Usually tickets are *not* available for matches with Real Madrid.

You will almost definitely find scalpers lurking near the ticket windows. They are often club members and can sometimes get you in at a significant reduction. Don't pay until you are safely seated.

Espanyol, based at the brand new Estadi RCD Espanyol (off Map p122; ☎ 93 292 77 00; www.rcdespanyol.com; Avinguda del Baix Llobregat, Cornellà; Ⓜ Cornellà

SPORTS & ACTIVITIES SPECTATOR SPORTS

A WOMAN'S TOUCH

On FC Barcelona's official website (www.fcbarcelona.com) you'll find information not only on the champion football side, but on the club's basketball, handball and even its roller-skate hockey teams. But you'd never know that FC Barcelona has a women's football team. Indeed, you'd be hard pressed finding out that 22 women's teams fight it out each year for the Superliga Femenina premiership. FC Barcelona's women's team is full of fight, but it's a different ball game. On average, fewer than 500 spectators come to watch FC Barcelona women's matches and in the short history of the league (which started in 2001) it has tended to hang around in the bottom half of the table. For more information on women's football in Spain, check out www.futfem.com, in Spanish.

CASTLES IN THE AIR

It's difficult to know how to classify making human castles, but to many a Catalan, the *castellers* (castle builders) are as serious in their sport as any footballer.

The 'building' of *castells* (castles) is particularly popular in central and southern Catalonia. Teams from all over the region compete during summer and you are most likely to see *castellers* in town festivals. The amateur sport began in the 1880s, and although Barcelona's home teams are not among the best, it is always fun to watch. When teams from other towns come to compete, it can be quite exciting.

Without delving too deeply into the complexities, the teams aim to erect human 'castles' of up to 10 storeys. These usually involve levels of three to five people standing on each others' shoulders. A crowd of teammates and supporters forms a supporting scrum around the thickset lads at the base. To successfully complete the castle, a young (light!) child called the *anxaneta* must reach the top and signal with his/her hand. Sometimes the castle then falls in a heap (if it has not already done so) but successful completion also involves bringing the levels back down to earth in orderly fashion. The death of an *anxaneta*, who struck her head in a fall from the top of a *castell* in 2006, provoked calls for these children to wear helmets. In the end, nothing came of the demands, as it was pointed out that there had been just three fatal accidents in the entire history of the activity.

Home and away teams sometimes converge on Plaça de Catalunya, Plaça de Sant Jaume and other city squares for friendly competitions during the city's various festivals. Ask the tourist office (p285) for more details. Beyond Barcelona, competition events can be seen in many towns, including Vilafranca del Penedès (p257) and Tarragona (p259).

Centre), traditionally plays second fiddle to Barça, although it does so with considerable passion.

FORMULA ONE

Every April/May since 1991, the dashing knights in shining motorised armour have come to the Montmeló track, about a 30-minute drive north of Barcelona. A seat for the Grand Prix race at the Circuit de Catalunya (Map p100; ☎ 93 571 97 00; www.circuitcat.com) can cost anything from €110 to €435. If you purchase before mid-March, tickets are slightly cheaper. Purchase tickets by phone, at the track, online or with ServiCaixa, or at advance ticket-sales desks in El Corte Inglés department stores. You can get a regular *rodalies* train to Montmeló (€1.60, 30 minutes) but will need to walk about 3km or find a local taxi (about €12 to €15) to reach the track. On race days the Sagalés bus company (Map p106; ☎ 902 130014; www.sagales.com) runs buses to the track from Passeig de Sant Joan 52 (€8 return), between Carrer de la Diputació and Carrer del Consell de Cent.

SAILING

The annual Trofeo Conde de Godó (www.regatagodo.com, in Spanish) is Barcelona's prestigious yachting competition, held off the city's coast over two-three days at the end of May and drawing crews from around the country.

In December 2010, the Barcelona World Race (www.barcelonaworldrace.com) two-person yachts were due to leave the city in the start of its second round-the-world regatta (first held in 2007). The race takes two to three months to complete.

SLEEPING

top picks

- Hotel Banys Orientals (p234)
- Hotel Axel (p238)
- Alberg Mare de Déu de Montserrat (p241)
- W Barcelona (p235)
- Hotel Omm (p236)
- Hostal Goya (p239)
- Hotel Neri (p231)
- Hotel Constanza (p238)
- Comtes de Barcelona (p237)
- Hostel Mambo Tango (p241)

SLEEPING

There has been little let-up in Barcelona's hotel-building boom since the early 2000s. This is good news for everyone. Some fine, up-to-the-minute hotels in a broad price bracket have opened in historic buildings and key locations, the number of options near the sea has increased and high-end digs have popped up in various strategic spots. Between 1997 and 2007 alone, hotel space in the city doubled.

As competition grows, many of the more established spots are obliged to upgrade – at the upper levels, this means more hotel pools, spas, designer bars and chic dining. The economic downturn that hit Spain even harder than many other countries from 2008, has dampened enthusiasm in the hotel business, putting a brake on price increases. Some places have even cut rates since 2008. Oddly, while many budget places offer free wi-fi, the bulk of top-end hotels charge a hefty extra fee.

ACCOMMODATION STYLES

The city has hundreds of hotels in all categories and a good range of alternatives, including numerous youth hostels.

If dorm living is not your thing but you are still looking for a budget deal, check around the many *pensiones* and *hostales*. These are family-run, small-scale hotels, often housed in sprawling apartments. Some are fleapits, others immaculately maintained gems.

Hotels cover a broad range. At the bottom end there is often little to distinguish them from better *pensiones* and *hostales*, and from there they run up the scale to five-star luxury.

A cosier (and sometimes more cost-effective) alternative to hotels can be short-term apartment rental. A plethora of firms organise short lets across town. Typical prices are around €80 to €100 for two people per night. For four people you might be looking at an average of €160 a night.

Among these services are: Aparteasy (Map p106; ☎ 93 451 67 66; www.aparteasy.com; Plaça del Doctor Letamendi 10); Feelathomebarcelona.com (Map p74; ☎ 651 894141; www.feelathomebarcelona.com; Carrer Nou de la Rambla 15); Barcelona On Line (Map p106; ☎ 902 887017, 93 343 79 93; www.barcelona-on-line.es; Carrer de València 352); Friendly Rentals (Map p82; ☎ 93 268 80 51; www.friendly rentals.com; Passatge de Sert 4); Lodging Barcelona (Map p106; ☎ 93 458 77 58; www.lodgingbarcelona.com; Carrer de Balmes 62); Rent a Flat in Barcelona (Map p106; ☎ 93 342 73 00; www.rentaflatinbarcelona.com; Carrer de Fontanella 18); Oh-Barcelona.com (Map p106; ☎ 93 467 37 82; www.oh -barcelona.com; Spain House, Carrer de Roger de Llúria 50); and MH Apartments (☎ 93 323 87 90; www.mhapartments.com).

If your budget is especially tight, look at the economical options on Barcelona 30.com (☎ 902 585680; www.barcelona30.com).

For a fuller list of officially recognised organisations renting holiday apartments in the city and province Barcelona, have a look at the Associació d'Apartaments Turístics de Barcelona (Apartur; Map p82; ☎ 902 052303; www.apartur.com; Passatge de Sert 4).

If you fancy sleeping on a yacht tied up in Port Vell marina, have a look at the Barcelona Boat Company.

If you're looking to do a short-term house swap, check out the ads on www.loquo.com. Want to sleep on a local's couch? Try your luck at www.couchsurfing.com. For long-term rentals, see Moving to Barcelona (p263).

CHECK-IN & CHECK-OUT TIMES

Always confirm your arrival, especially if it's going to be late in the afternoon or evening. Generally there is no problem if you have paid a deposit or left a credit-card number. While you can check in at any time of the morning, you may not get access to your room until after noon. Most of the time you will be able to leave your luggage at reception and go for a wander until the room is ready.

Check-out time is generally noon, although some places can be a little draconian and set a leaving time of 11am or, in rare cases, even 10am!

RESERVATIONS

Booking ahead is recommended, especially during peak periods such as Easter, Christmas/New Year, trade fairs and throughout much of summer (although August can be quite a slack month owing to the heat). You

PRICE GUIDE

Prices in this chapter are divided into three categories and are high-season maximums. Prices can fluctuate enormously, especially at the higher end. If a place interests you but seems too expensive, check it out anyway – you may find lower rates for your dates. Booking online and far in advance can bring appreciable rate cuts and the more expensive digs frequently have a raft of special offers. Many hotels have varying prices for several kinds of rooms. All these variables are impossible to set out in the listings below. Rooms come with private bathrooms (which at low-end places often means a shower, not a full bathtub) unless otherwise stated. These price categories are for doubles:

€€€	over €250 a night
€€	€70-250 a night
€	under €70 a night

may be asked for a credit-card number and be charged a night's accommodation if you fail to show up. If you prefer to check rooms personally, you could book for the first night or two and then seek an alternative place once in Barcelona.

You can book accommodation at the tourist office at Plaça de Catalunya (p285).

ROOM RATES

Depending on the seasons and hostel, you will pay from €15 to €25 for a dorm bed in a youth hostel. In small *pensiones* or *hostales* you are looking at a minimum of around €35/55 for basic *individual/doble* (single/double) rooms, mostly without a private bathroom. (It is occasionally possible to find cheaper rooms, but they can be unappetising.) For around €100 to €140, there are extensive options for good doubles across a broad range of hotels and areas. The top-end category in this guide starts at €250 for a double, but can easily rise to €500 (and beyond for suites).

Some places, especially at the lower end, offer triples and quads, which can be good value for groups. If you want a double bed (as opposed to two singles), ask for a *llit/cama matrimonial* (Catalan/Spanish). Single travellers are penalised, frequently paying around two-thirds (or more) of the double-room rate (especially in those places that have no single rooms).

Some hotels, particularly at the lower and mid levels, maintain the same prices year round. Others vary the rates for *temporada*

alta (high season), *temporada media* (mid-season) and *temporada baja* (low season). Low season is roughly November to Easter, except during the Christmas/New Year period. Whenever there is a major trade fair (they are frequent), high-season prices generally apply. Conversely, business-oriented hotels often consider weekends, holiday periods and other slow business times to be low season. Booking on the web is often cheaper than turning up at the door.

Virtually all accommodation is subject to IVA, the Spanish version of value-added tax, at 7%. This is often included in the quoted price at cheaper places, but less often at more expensive ones. Ask: *'¿Está incluido el IVA?'* ('Is IVA included?'). In some cases you will be charged IVA only if you ask for a receipt.

BARRI GÒTIC & LA RAMBLA

La Rambla is lined with hotels, *pensiones* and fleapits, and in the labyrinth of the Barri Gòtic are scattered countless others. Carrer de Ferran is lined with popular but mostly cramped, noisy options – a little too close to ranks of pseudo-Irish pubs for comfort. Many of the smaller joints are nothing special, catering to an at times rowdy party crowd. But there are some real gems too.

HOTEL 1898 Map p60   Hotel €€€
☎ 93 552 95 52; www.hotel1898.com; La Rambla 109; d €295-388; Ⓜ Liceu; Ⓟ 🍴 🖥 🛜 🏊
The former Compañía de Tabacos Filipinas (Philippines Tobacco Company) has been resurrected as a luxury hotel. Some of the rooms are smallish but deluxe rooms and suites have their own terraces, and all combine modern comfort and elegance, with hardwood floors and tasteful furniture. Etro toiletries await in the bathrooms. Some of the suites (up to €1600) have access to a private indoor pool, while all guests can use the outdoor one.

HOTEL NERI Map p60   Design Hotel €€
☎ 93 304 06 55; www.hotelneri.com; Carrer de Sant Sever 5; d from €235; Ⓜ Liceu; 🍴 🖥 🛜
Occupying a beautifully adapted, centuries-old building that backs on to the quiet Plaça de Sant Felip Neri, this is a tranquil stop. The sandy stone and timber furnishings lend the building a sense of history.

The rooms have a slick feel, with cutting-edge technology, including plasma-screen TVs and infra-red lights in the stone-clad designer bathrooms. Choose from a menu of sheets and pillows, and sun yourself on the roof deck, where you can also take a shower and order a drink.

HOTEL COLÓN Map p60   Hotel €€
☎ 93 301 14 04; www.hotelcolon.es; Avinguda de la Catedral 7; s/d from €105/195; Ⓜ Jaume I; ⊠ ▯
The privileged position opposite the cathedral lends this hotel special grace. A range of rooms (142 in all), from modest singles to diaphanous doubles and suites, offers elegant accommodation. Decoration varies considerably (from hardwood floors to carpet) and the top-floor superior rooms with terrace are marvellous (and go for about €300).

HOTEL CONTINENTAL Map p60   Hotel €€
☎ 93 301 25 70; www.hotelcontinental.com; La Rambla 138; s/d €87/97; Ⓜ Catalunya; ⊠ ▯
You can imagine being here in 1937, when George Orwell returned from the front line during the Spanish Civil War, and Barcelona was tense with factional strife. Rooms at the Continental are a little spartan, but have romantic touches such as ceiling fans, brass bedsteads and frilly bedclothes. You will pay €20 more for a double with a balcony overlooking La Rambla. Take breakfast in bed… or head down to the buffet any time – it's open 24 hours.

HOTEL JARDÍ Map p60   Hotel €€
☎ 93 301 59 00; www.hoteljardi-barcelona .com; Plaça de Sant Josep Oriol 1; d €65-95; Ⓜ Liceu; ⊠
The 'Garden Hotel' has no garden but several attractive doubles with balcony overlooking one of the prettiest squares

---

ROOMS FOR TRAVELLERS WITH DISABILITIES

Many hotels claim to be equipped for guests with disabilities but reality frequently disappoints. Check out www.accessiblebarcelona.com for help with finding genuinely accessible accommodation. The same people also run www.accessible.travel. For more information on facilities for travellers with disabilities in Barcelona, see p285.

---

in the city. If you can snare one of them, it is well worth climbing up the stairs. If you can't get a room with a view, you are better off looking elsewhere.

HOSTAL CAMPI Map p60   Hostal €
☎ 93 301 35 45; www.hostalcampi.com; Carrer de la Canuda 4; d €67, s/d without bathroom €34/57; Ⓜ Catalunya
This is an excellent budget deal that appeals mostly to younger backpackers. The best rooms at this friendly, central *hostal* are doubtless the doubles with their own loos and showers. They are extremely roomy and bright, with attractive tile floors and are kept spotless. Located just off La Rambla, you are protected from much of the street noise. The building dates to the late 18th century.

ALBERG HOSTEL ITACA Map p60   Hostel €
☎ 93 301 97 51; www.itacahostel.com; Carrer de Ripoll 21; dm €14-20, d €55; Ⓜ Jaume I; ▯ ⊚
A bright, quiet hostel near La Catedral, Itaca has spacious dorms (sleeping six, eight or 12 people), with parquet floors, spring colours and a couple of doubles with private bathroom. It also has a couple of nearby apartments for six people (€120 per night). You can make use of the kitchen and book exchange.

EL RAVAL
You're right in the thick of things when staying in this mildly wild side of the old town. Accommodation options are broad, from fleapits on dodgy lanes through to the latest in designer comfort. Hostels and cheap hotels abound.

CASA CAMPER Map p74   Design Hotel €€€
☎ 93 342 62 80; www.casacamper.com; Carrer d'Elisabets 11; s/d €228/255; Ⓜ Liceu; ⊠ ⊠ ▯
An original designer hotel in the middle of El Raval, Casa Camper belongs to the Mallorcan shoe company of the same name. The massive foyer looks more like a contemporary art museum entrance, but the rooms are the real surprise. Slip into your Camper slippers and contemplate the Vinçon furniture. Across the corridor from your room (which faces hanging gardens) is a separate, private sitting room with balcony, TV and hammock. You can contemplate the city from the rooftop.

WHOTELLS Map p74 — Hostal €€
☎ 93 443 08 34; www.whotells.com; Carrer de Joaquín Costa 28; apt from €230; Ⓜ Universitat; ✂ 🖳
Decked out with Muji furniture and very comfortable, these apartments can sleep from four to six people and give a sense of being at home away from home. Prices fluctuate enormously in response to demand. Cook up a storm in the kitchen with products bought in the nearby La Boqueria market, or flop in front of the LCD TV. They have other apartment buildings in L'Eixample and La Barceloneta.

BARCELÓ RAVAL Map p74 — Design Hotel €€
☎ 93 320 14 90; www.barceloraval.com; Rambla del Raval 17-21; d €150-210; Ⓜ Liceu; ✂ 🖳 🛜 🞵
As part of the city's plans to pull up the El Raval district's bootstraps, this oval shaped designer hotel tower makes a 21st-century splash. The rooftop terrace offers fabulous views and the B-Lounge bar-restaurant is the toast of the town for meals and cocktails. Three classes of room all offer slick appearance (lots of white and contrasting lime greens or ruby-red splashes of colour), Nespresso machine and iPod loaders.

HOTEL SAN AGUSTÍN
Map p74 Hotel €€
☎ 93 318 16 58; www.hotelsa.com; Plaça de Sant Agustí 3; s €123-144, d €171; Ⓜ Liceu; ✂ 🖳 🛜
This former 18th-century monastery opened as a hotel in 1840, making it the city's oldest (it's undergone various refits since then!). The location is perfect – a quick stroll off La Rambla on a curious square. Rooms sparkle, and are mostly spacious and light-filled. Consider an attic double (€134) with sloping ceiling and bird's-eye views.

HOTEL PRINCIPAL Map p74 — Hotel €€
☎ 93 318 89 70; www.hotelprincipal.es; Carrer de la Junta del Comerç 8-12; s/d/tr €105/120/160; Ⓜ Liceu; Ⓟ ✂ 🖳 🛜
This hotel has clean-lined rooms complete with parquet floors, hairdryers and original art depicting Barcelona. All 110 rooms, spread across three adjoining buildings, have double glazing and flat-screen TVs, and you can sink into a deckchair to sunbathe on the roof. For €170, it has a big room with private terrace.

HOTEL ESPAÑA Map p74 — Hotel €€
☎ 93 318 17 58; www.hotelespanya.com; Carrer de Sant Pau 9-11; s €96, d €118-145; Ⓜ Liceu; ✂
Best known for its eccentric Modernista restaurants, in which architect Domènech i Montaner, sculptor Eusebi Arnau and painter Ramon Casas had a hand, this hotel has been given an overhaul and offers clean, straighforward rooms in a building that still manages to ooze a little history. In the 1920s it was a favourite with bullfighters.

HOSTAL CHIC & BASIC Map p74 — Hostal €€
☎ 93 302 51 83; www.chicandbasic.com; Carrer de Tallers 82; s €60, d €93-114; Ⓜ Universitat; ✂ 🖳
The theme colour is predominantly white, with exceptions like the screaming orange fridge in the communal kitchen and chill-and-basic area where you can make yourself a cuppa or sandwich. Rooms are also themed lily white, from the floors to the sheets. Finishing touches include the plasma-screen TVs and the option of plugging your iPod or MP3 player into your room's sound system. The street can get noisy.

HOSTAL GAT RAVAL Map p74 — Hostal €€
☎ 93 481 66 70; www.gataccommodation.com; Carrer de Joaquín Costa 44; d €82, s/d without bathroom €58/74; Ⓜ Universitat; ✂ 🖳 🛜
There's pea-green and lemon-lime decor in this hip 2nd-floor *hostal* located on a bar-lined lane dominated by resident migrants and wandering bands of uni students. The individual rooms are pleasant and secure, but only some have private bathrooms. The staff also run the more upmarket Hostal Gat Xino (Map p74; ☎ 93 324 88 33; www.gataccommodation.com; Carrer de l'Hospital 149-155; s/d/ste with terrace €80/115/140; Ⓜ Liceu; ✂ 🖳 🛜) nearby.

HOTEL PENINSULAR Map p74 — Hotel €€
☎ 93 302 31 38; www.hpeninsular.com; Carrer de Sant Pau 34; s/d €55/78; Ⓜ Liceu; ✂ 🖳 🛜
An oasis on the edge of the slightly dicey Barri Xinès, this former convent (which was connected by tunnel to the Església de Sant Agustí) has a plant-draped atrium extending its height and most of its length. The 60 rooms are simple, with tiled floors and whitewash, but mostly spacious and well-kept. There is wi-fi throughout.

HOTEL ANETO Map p74   Hotel €

☎ 93 301 99 89; www.hotelaneto.com; Carrer del Carme 38; s/d €45/65; Ⓜ Liceu; ⚹

This budget bargain is in a handy spot on one of the more attractive streets of El Raval's upper half. The best of the 15 rooms are the doubles with the shuttered balconies looking on to the street.

BARCELONA MAR HOSTEL

Map p74   Hostel €

☎ 93 324 85 30; www.barcelonamar.com; Carrer de Sant Pau 80; dm €18-22, d €60; Ⓜ Paral.lel; ⚹ 💻 🛜

This is a no-nonsense hostel with double rooms and dorms that sleep six to 16 people. Not only are you within stumbling distance of plenty of bars on Rambla del Raval and beyond, it's open 24 hours and there's free access to internet, lockers, kitchen and luggage storage. Quiet it ain't and you need to watch your pockets in this neighbourhood.

LA RIBERA

Several fine hotels are located on the fringes of the busy Born area and a growing number of the sometimes bombastic buildings on thundering Via Laietana have been or are in the process of being converted into top-end hotels.

GRAND HOTEL CENTRAL

Map p82   Design Hotel €€

☎ 93 295 79 00; www.grandhotelcentral.com; Via Laietana 30; d €224; Ⓜ Jaume I; ⚹ 💻 🅿

With super-soundproofed rooms not smaller than 21 sq metres, this design hotel, complete with rooftop pool, is one of the standout hotel offerings along Via Laietana. Rooms are decorated in style, with high ceilings, muted colours (beiges, browns and creams), dark timber floors and subtle lighting. Some of the bigger rooms are the size of studio apartments.

CHIC & BASIC Map p82   Hotel €€

☎ 93 295 46 52; www.chicandbasic.com; Carrer de la Princesa 50; s €96, d €132-171; Ⓜ Jaume I; ⚹ 💻

In a completely renovated building with high vaults in the facade are 31 spotlessly white rooms. There are high ceilings, enormous beds (room types are classed as M, L and XL!) and lots of detailed touches such as LED lighting, TFT TV screens and the retention of many beautiful old features of the original building, such as the marble staircase. Have a drink in the ground-floor White Bar.

HOTEL BANYS ORIENTALS

Map p82   Boutique Hotel €€

☎ 93 268 84 60; www.hotelbanysorientals.com; Carrer de l'Argenteria 37; s/d €93/107; Ⓜ Jaume I; ⚹ 💻 🛜

Book well ahead to get into this magnetically popular designer haunt. Cool blues and aquamarines combine with dark-hued floors to lend this clean-lined, boutique hotel a quiet charm. All rooms, on the small side, look onto the street or back lanes. There are more spacious suites (€139) in two other nearby buildings.

PENSIÓ 2000 Map p82   Pensión €

☎ 93 310 74 66; www.pensio2000.com; Carrer de Sant Pere més Alt 6; s/d €52/65, without bathroom €35/45; Ⓜ Urquinaona; 💻

This 1st-floor, family-run place is opposite the anything-but-simple Palau de la Música Catalana. Seven reasonably spacious doubles (which can be taken as singles) all have mosaic-tiled floors. Two have ensuite bathroom. Eat brekkie in the little courtyard.

top picks

STYLE HOTELS

- Casa Camper (p232) Original idea with Vinçon furniture and hammocks.
- Barceló Raval (p233) A tower of contemporary style in the heart of El Raval.
- Hotel Banys Orientals (p234) Bite-sized boutique gem in the old town.
- Hotel Sixtytwo (p237) Designer lines, Bang & Olufsen TVs and a peaceful inner garden.
- Hotel Axel (p238) A lifestyle stay that attracts a good-looking gay set with chic rooms and to-be-seen-in bars.
- Hotel Omm (p236) Fantasy-filled hotel with a 'peeling' facade.
- Hotel Me (p236) Daring tower loaded with up-to-date design and a tempting bar-pool combination.
- Chic & Basic (p234) A fine apartment building converted into a white (k)night of style.

PORT VELL & LA BARCELONETA

The handful of seaside options around Port Vell and La Barceloneta ranges from a rowdy youth hostel to a couple of grand five-stars, one of which is destined to become an iconic, waterfront landmark.

W BARCELONA Map p90   Hotel €€€

☎ 93 295 28 00; www.w-barcelona.com; Plaça de la Rosa del Vents 1; r €283-385; Ⓜ Barceloneta; 🚌 17, 39, 57 or 64; Ⓟ ✂ 🖳 ⛲

The spinnaker-shaped tower of glass contains 473 rooms and suites that are the last word in contemporary hotel chic. In an admirable location at the end of a beach, it has rooms in a variety of shapes, orientations and sizes. Self-indulgence is a byword and guests can flit between the gym, infinity pool (with bar) and Bliss@spa. There's avant-garde dining on the 2nd floor in Carles Abellán's Bravo restaurant and hip cocktail sipping in the top-floor Eclipse bar.

EUROSTARS GRAND MARINA HOTEL
Map p90   Hotel €€

☎ 93 295 99 08; www.grandmarinahotel.com; Moll de Barcelona; r €150-255; Ⓜ Drassanes; Ⓟ ✂ 🖳 ⛲

Housed in the World Trade Center, the Grand Marina has a maritime flavour that continues into the rooms, with lots of polished timber touches and hydro-massage bathtubs. Some rooms on either side of the building offer splendid views of the city, port and open sea. The rooftop gym and outdoor pool have equally enticing views.

HOTEL DEL MAR Map p90   Hotel €€

☎ 93 319 33 02; www.gargallohotels.es; Pla del Palau 19; s/d €139/171; Ⓜ Barceloneta; ✂ 🖳

The nicely modernised Sea Hotel is strategically placed between Port Vell and El Born. Some of the rooms in this classified building have balconies with waterfront views. You're in a fairly peaceful spot but no more than 10 minutes' walk from the beaches and seafood of La Barceloneta, and the bars and mayhem of El Born.

HOTEL 54 Map p90   Hotel €€

☎ 93 225 00 54; www.hotel54barceloneta.com; Passeig de Joan de Borbó 54; s/d €130/140; Ⓜ Barceloneta; ✂ 🖳 🛜

This place is all about location. Modern rooms, with dark tile floors, designer bathrooms and LCD TVs are sought after for the marina and sunset views. Other (cheaper) rooms look out over the lanes of La Barceloneta. You can also sit on the roof terrace and enjoy the harbour views.

HOTEL MARINA FOLCH Map p90   Hotel €€

☎ 93 310 37 09; www.hotelmarinafolchbcn.com; Carrer del Mar 16; s/d €40/75; Ⓜ Barceloneta; ✂

A simple dig above a busy seafood restaurant, this hotel has just one teeny single and 10 doubles of varying sizes and quality. The most attractive are those looking out towards the marina. The rooms are basic enough but kept spick and span, and the location is unbeatable, just a couple of minutes from the beach.

SEA POINT HOSTEL Map p90   Hostel €

☎ 93 231 20 45; www.seapointhostel.com; Plaça del Mar 1-4; dm €16-25; Ⓜ Barceloneta; 🚌 17, 39, 57 or 64; ✂ 🖳 🛜

Right on the beach in a rather ugly high-rise (but hey, you don't have to look at the high-rise) is this busy backpackers' hostel. Rooms are cramped and basic but you will not find a room closer to the beach. It organises activities such as bike tours (and rentals). You pay extra for lockers, sheets and towels.

PORT OLÍMPIC, EL POBLENOU & EL FÒRUM

For years the breathtakingly located Hotel Arts Barcelona has been *the* place to stay in Barcelona. It gets some tower-hotel competition in the Fòrum area, mostly aimed at a business crowd and generally considerably cheaper.

HOTEL ARTS BARCELONA

Map p96   Hotel €€€

☎ 93 221 10 00; www.hotelartsbarcelona.com; Carrer de la Marina 19-21; r from €485; M Ciutadella Vila Olímpica; P ⊠ ♿ 🖳 🛜 🖭

In one of the two sky-high towers that dominate Port Olímpic, this is Barcelona's most fashionable hotel, frequented by VIPs from all over the planet. It has more than 450 rooms with unbeatable views, and prices vary greatly according to size, position and time of year. Luxury suites shoot into five-figure sums. Services range from enticing spa facilities on the 42nd and 43rd floors, to fine dining in Arola, run by the Michelin-starred Sergi Arola.

HOTEL ME Map p96   Hotel €€

☎ 902 144440; www.me-barcelona.com; Carrer de Pere IV 272-286; r from €155; M Poblenou; P ♿ 🖳 🛜 🖭

Designed by Dominique Perrault, this daring, slim tower consisting of two filigree slabs of glass caked one vertically on the other, overlooks Jean Nouvel's Parc del Centre del Poblenou and offers designer digs in which whites, creams and reds dominate much of the decor. Rooms come in an array of sizes and comfort levels. You may get views of the city or the sea. The 6th-floor Angels & Kings Club, with its terrace and swimming pool, can get quite lively.

POBLENOU BED & BREAKFAST

Map p96   Hotel €€

☎ 93 221 26 01; www.hostalpoblenou.com; Carrer del Taulat 30; s €60, d €80-90, tr €100; M Llacuna; ♿ 🖳 🛜

Experience life in this colourful working-class neighbourhood, just back from the beach and increasingly home to a diverse population of loft-inhabiting gentrifiers. The 1930s house, with its high ceilings and beautiful tile floors, offers 10 rooms, each a little different and all with a fresh feel, light colours, comfortable beds and, occasionally, a little balcony. You can have breakfast in the rear terrace or parade along the infectiously busy Rambla del Poblenou.

L'EIXAMPLE

It comes as little surprise that this extensive bourgeois bastion should also be home to the greatest range of hotels in most classes. The grid avenues house some of the city's classic hotels and a long list of decent mid-range places.

HOTEL MAJÈSTIC Map p106   Hotel €€€

☎ 93 488 17 17; www.hotelmajestic.es; Passeig de Gràcia 68; d from €399; M Passeig de Gràcia; P ⊠ ♿ 🖳 🛜 🖭

This sprawling, central option has the charm of one of the great European hotels. The rooftop pool is great for views and relaxing, or you can pamper yourself in the spa after a workout in the gym. The standard rooms (no singles) are smallish but comfortable and with marble bathrooms. Various categories of larger rooms allow you to spread out more.

MANDARIN ORIENTAL

Map p106   Design Hotel €€€

☎ 93 151 88 88; www.mandarinoriental.com; Passeig de Gràcia 38; d from €355; M Passeig de Gràcia; P ♿ 🖳 🛜 🖭

At this imposing former bank, 98 rooms combine contemporary designer style with subtle Eastern touches. Straight lines, lots of white and muted colours dominate the look. Many of the standard rooms (no smaller than 32 sq metres) have tempting tubs in the bathroom and all rooms overlook either Passeig de Gràcia or an interior sculpted garden. You can indulge in the spa and gym or linger over a cocktail in the stylish Banker's Bar (complete with safety deposit boxes).

HOTEL OMM Map p106   Design Hotel €€€

☎ 93 445 40 00; www.hotelomm.es; Carrer de Rosselló 265; d from €345; M Diagonal; P ♿ 🖳 🖭

Design meets plain zany here, where the balconies look like strips of skin peeled back from the shiny hotel surface. The idea would no doubt have appealed to Dalí. In the foyer, a sprawling, minimalist and popular bar opens before you. Light, clear tones dominate in the ultramodern rooms, of which there are several categories. After a hard time tramping the city, chill in the Spaciomm spa, which offers everything from a water circuit (including underwater massage) to oxygen treatment for the skin and rocking gravitational beds.

HOTEL MURMURI Map p106   Design Hotel €€€
☎ 93 550 06 00; www.murmuri.com; La Rambla de Catalunya 104; d €170-450; Ⓜ Diagonal; ⊠ ⊠ 🖳 📶

Large rooms with a contemporary feel and efficient service distinguish this hotel, splendidly located at the top end of La Rambla de Catalunya. Many rooms have balconies overlooking the boulevard. With touches like iPod adaptor and smart lobby bar, it is a good spot, as long as you obtain a decent internet room rate – the official start price for standard rooms of €450 is, to put it politely, inflated. When business is slow, these same rooms can go for €170.

HOTEL HISPANOS SIETE SUIZA
Map p100   Hotel €€€
☎ 93 208 20 51; www.hispanos7suiza.com; Carrer de Sicilia 255; r 1/2/4 people €160/280/320; Ⓜ Sagrada Família; Ⓟ ⊠ 🖳 📶

Within spitting distance of the towering madness that is La Sagrada Família is this original lodging option. Wander in past seven vintage Hispano-Suiza cars to one of several apartments, which generally have two double rooms with separate bathrooms (note the super showers!), a lounge, kitchen, washer-drier and terrace. There is also a suite (for up to six people).

COMTES DE BARCELONA
Map p106   Hotel €€
☎ 93 445 00 00; www.condesdebarcelona.com; Passeig de Gràcia 73-75; s/d €177/230; Ⓜ Passeig de Gràcia; Ⓟ ⊠ 🖳 📶 🖳

Also known by its Spanish name, the most attractive half of the Comtes (Condes) de Barcelona occupies the 1890s Modernista Casa Enric Batlló. Across the road stands a more modern extension. Inside both, clean, designer lines dominate, with hardwood floors, architectural touches reminiscent of the Modernista exterior and luxurious rooms. The standard rooms are, at 25 sq metres, the smallest. The pool on the roof is a great place to relax after a hard day's sightseeing. There's also a gym, sauna and a pair of prestige restaurants to choose from onsite.

HOTEL SIXTYTWO Map p106   Design Hotel €€
☎ 93 272 41 80; www.sixtytwohotel.com/en/; Passeig de Gràcia 62; d €140-245; Ⓜ Passeig de Gràcia; Ⓟ ⊠ 🖳 📶

Under new ownership, this 21st-century designer setting (housed in a well-preserved 1930s edifice) boasts rooms with Bang & Olufsen TVs and soft backlighting above expansive beds. Inside the block is a pretty garden to chill in, or you could opt for a massage in your room. All rooms enjoy the same designer features (and Etro bath products) but the more tempting (and dearer ones) have balconies or little private terraces.

ST MORITZ HOTEL Map p106   Hotel €€
☎ 93 481 73 50; www.hcchotels.com; Carrer de la Diputació 262bis; s/d €171/193; Ⓜ Passeig de Gràcia; Ⓟ ⊠ ⊠ 🖳 📶

This upmarket hotel, set in a late-19th-century building, has 91 fully equipped rooms and boasts an elegant restaurant, terrace bar and small gym. Some of the bigger rooms, with marble bathrooms, even have their own exercise bikes. The place was refurbished in 2009, lending it a fresh new feel. You can dine in the modest terrace garden.

SUITES AVENUE Map p106   Hotel €€
☎ 93 487 41 59; www.derbyhotels.es; Passeig de Gràcia 83; apt from €192; Ⓜ Diagonal; Ⓟ ⊠ 🖳 📶 🖳

Fancy apartment-style living is the name of the game in this apart-hotel. Self-contained little apartments with own kitchen and access to a terrace, gym and pool (not to mention the mini-museum of Hindu and Buddhist art) lie behind the daring facade by Japanese architect Toyo Ito.

FIVE ROOMS Map p106   Boutique Hotel €€
☎ 93 342 78 80; www.thefiverooms.com; Carrer de Pau Claris 72; s/d €166/176; Ⓜ Urquinaona; 🖳 ⊠ 📶

Like they say, there are five rooms in this 1st-floor flat virtually on the border between L'Eixample and the old centre of town. Each of them is different and features include broad, firm beds, stretches of exposed brick wall, restored mosaic tiles and minimalist decor (with brilliant white dominating). Breakfast is an abundant continental mix.

HOTEL ASTORIA Map p100   Hotel €€
☎ 93 209 83 11; www.derbyhotels.es; Carrer de Paris 203; s/d from €120/130; Ⓜ Diagonal; Ⓟ ⊠ 🖳 📶 🖳

Nicely situated a short walk from Passeig de Gràcia, this three-star is equally well placed

GAY STAYS

Barcelona has a few excellent gay-friendly options, one in the heart of the old town and fairly simple, another a full design explosion in the heart of the 'Gaixample'. You could start a room search at Gay Apartments Barcelona (www.gayapartmentbarcelona.com).

Hotel Axel (Map p106; ☎ 93 323 93 93; www.axelhotels.com; Carrer d'Aribau 33; r from €142; Ⓜ Universitat; ⊠ ☒ ☐ 🛜 ☒) Favoured by a mixed fashion and gay set, Axel occupies a sleek corner block and offers modern touches in its 105 designer rooms. A subtle, light colour scheme, plasma TVs and (in the double rooms) king-sized beds are just some of the pluses. The hotel was completely overhauled in 2010. Take a break in the rooftop pool, the Finnish sauna or the spa bath. The rooftop Skybar is open for cocktails from May to September.

Hotel California (Map p60; ☎ 93 317 77 66; www.hotelcaliforniabcn.com; Carrer d'En Rauric 14; s/d €80/115; Ⓜ Liceu; ☒ ☐ 🛜) This (gay) friendly and central hotel has 31 straightforward but fastidiously sparkling-clean rooms, with light, neutral colours, satellite plasma TV and good-sized beds. Double glazing helps ensure a good night's sleep and, given the modest prices, the rooms have surprising details such as hairdryers. Meet new friends in the bustling breakfast room and avail yourself of room service 24 hours a day.

Casa de Billy Barcelona (Map p100; ☎ 93 426 30 48; www.casabillybarcelona.com; Gran Via de les Corts Catalanes 420; d €70-120; Ⓜ Rocafort; ☐) Set in a rambling apartment, a stone's throw from the Gaixample bars, this is an intriguing, gay-friendly stop. The rooms are largely decorated in flamboyant art deco style and guests may use the kitchen. There is a two-night-minimum policy.

for long nights out in the restaurants, bars and clubs of adjacent Carrer d'Aribau. Room decor and types vary wildly – you might have black-and-white floor tiles or dark parquet. The hotel has its own mini gym and a display of art by Catalan painter Ricard Opisso.

HOTEL CONSTANZA
Map p106   Boutique Hotel €€
☎ 93 270 19 10; www.hotelconstanza.com; Carrer del Bruc 33; s/d €110/130; Ⓜ Girona or Urquinaona; ☒ ☐
This boutique beauty has stolen the hearts of many a visitor to Barcelona. Even smaller single rooms are made to feel special with broad mirrors and strong colours. Design touches abound, and little details like flowers in the bathroom add charm. Suites and studios are further options. The terrace is a nice spot to relax for a while, looking over the rooftops of the L'Eixample.

MARKET HOTEL Map p100   Boutique Hotel €€
☎ 93 325 12 05; www.markethotel.com.es; Passatge de Sant Antoni Abad 10; s €105, d €115-125, ste €140; Ⓜ Sant Antoni; ☒ ☐
Attractively located in a renovated building along a narrow lane just north of the grand old Sant Antoni market (now shut for renovation), this place has an air of simple chic. Room decor is a pleasing combination of white, dark nut browns, light timber and

reds. Downstairs is a busy restaurant serving up Catalan and Med cuisine.

HOTEL D'UXELLES Map p106   Hotel €€
☎ 93 265 25 60; www.hotelduxelles.com; Gran Via de les Corts Catalanes 688; s/d €90/109; Ⓜ Tetuan; ☒ ☐
A charming simplicity pervades the rooms here. Wrought-iron bedsteads are overshadowed by flowing drapes. Room decor varies (from blues and whites to beige-and-cream combos), with a vaguely Andalucian flavour in the bathrooms. Some rooms have little terraces (€16 extra). Get a back room if you can, as Gran Via is noisy. Hotel d'Uxelles has similar rooms in another building across the road.

HOTEL PRAKTIK
Map p106   Boutique Hotel €€
☎ 93 343 66 90; www.hotelpraktikrambla.com; Rambla de Catalunya 27; s €69, d €99-129; Ⓜ Passeig de Gràcia; ☒ ☐ 🛜
For years a pleasant, somewhat chaotic *hostal* occupied this Modernista gem. It has been transformed into a boutique number. While the high ceilings and the bulk of the original tile floors have been maintained, daring ceramic touches, spot lighting, contemporary art, a chilled reading area and deck-style lounge terrace have transformed this place and its 43 rooms beyond recognition. The handy location on a tree-lined boulevard is an added plus.

HOSTAL GOYA Map p106   Hostal €€

☎ 93 302 25 65; www.hostalgoya.com; Carrer de Pau Claris 74; s €70, d €96-113; Ⓜ Passeig de Gràcia; ✕

The Goya is a modestly priced gem on the chichi side of L'Eixample. Rooms have a light colour scheme that varies from room to room. In the bathrooms, the original mosaic floors have largely been retained, combined with contemporary design features. The more expensive doubles have a balcony.

HOSTAL CENTRAL Map p106   Hostal €€

☎ 93 245 19 81; www.hostalcentralbarcelona. com; Carrer de la Diputació 346; s/d/tr €50/85/106; Ⓜ Tetuan; ✕ ✕ 🛜

In a pretty early-20th-century apartment building you'll find 13 renovated rooms (all nonsmoking and most with own bathroom). They are not excessively big but are pleasant and clean.

HOSTAL OLIVA Map p106   Hostal €€

☎ 93 488 01 62; www.hostaloliva.com; Passeig de Gràcia 32; d €85, s/d without bathroom €38/66; Ⓜ Passeig de Gràcia; ✕ 🛜

A picturesque antique lift wheezes its way up to this 4th-floor hostal, a terrific, reliable cheapie in one of the city's most expensive neighbourhoods. Some of the single rooms are barely big enough to fit a bed but the doubles are big enough, light and airy (some with tiled floors, others with parquet and dark old wardrobes).

HOSTAL GIRONA Map p106   Hostal €€

☎ 93 265 02 59; www.hostalgirona.com; Carrer de Girona 24; s/d €70/85; Ⓜ Girona

This 2nd-floor family-run hostal is a simple but clean and friendly spot of the old world. Some of the rooms have been freshened with bright colour schemes and all have modern bathrooms. Rooms range from rather small, if cute, singles with communal bathroom to airy doubles with balcony (but beware of traffic noise in summer, when you'll have to keep the windows open).

FASHION HOUSE Map p106   B&B €€

☎ 637 904044; www.bcnfashionhouse.com; Carrer de Bruc 13; s/d/tr without bathroom €55/80/110; Ⓜ Urquinaona; ✕ 🖳 🛜

The name is a little silly but this typical, broad 1st-floor L'Eixample flat contains eight rooms of varying size done in tasteful style, with 4.5m-high ceilings, parquet floors and, in some cases, a little gallery onto the street. Bathrooms are located along the broad corridor, one for every two rooms. Breakfast is served in the main dining room or in the garden out back.

HOSTAL CÈNTRIC Map p106   Hostal €€

☎ 93 426 75 73; www.hostalcentric.com; Carrer de Casanova 13; s €45-72, d €63-99; Ⓜ Urgell; ✕ 🖳

The hostal, in a good central location just beyond the old town, has rooms starting from basics with shared bathroom and ranges to renovated rooms with private bathroom facilities and air-con. Midrange ones are similar, but a little older and without air-con. Prices can drop considerably on all room types in slower moments.

SOMNIO HOSTEL Map p106   Hostel €€

☎ 93 272 53 08; www.somniohostels.com; Carrer de la Diputació 251; dm €25, s/d without bathroom €40/72, d €80; Ⓜ Passeig de Gràcia; ✕ 🖳 🛜

A crisp, tranquil hostel with 10 rooms (two of them six-bed dorms and all with a simple white and light-blue paint job), Somnio is nicely located in the thick of things in L'Eixample and a short walk from the old town. Rain showers and thick flex mattresses are nice features in this 2nd-floor dig. You can get a simple breakfast (€5) in the bite-sized lobby, or have a beer.

HOSTAL MUNTANER Map p100   Hostal €

☎ 93 410 94 74; www.hostal-centro.net; Carrer de Muntaner 175; s/d €40/75, s/d without bathroom €25/40; Ⓜ Hospital Clínic; Ⓟ ✕

Within a five-block walk of Passeig de Gràcia and Diagonal, this is a busy residential location surrounded by restaurants and bars (especially along nearby Carrer d'Aribau, a block away). Crisp, simple rooms are comfy and light. Be aware of traffic noise at the front of the house – a room deeper inside will guarantee tranquillity.

HOSTAL ARIBAU Map p106   Hostal €

☎ 93 453 11 06; www.hostalaribau.com; Carrer de Aribau 37; s/d/tr €60/65/80, s/d without bathroom €45/55; Ⓜ Universitat; ✕

Handily located within brisk walking distance of Ciutat Vella and in a busy part of L'Eixample, this is a straightforward family-run hostal with 11 rooms. Some rooms have a balcony (but this also means a fair degree of traffic noise, so is not for light sleepers).

GRÀCIA & PARK GÜELL

Staying up in Gràcia takes you out of the mainstream tourist areas and gives you a more authentic feel for the town. All the touristy bits are never far away by Metro and the restaurant and bar life in Gràcia is great on its own. A few largely nondescript *hostales* are scattered about on and around Carrer Gran de Gràcia. And there's a fine five-star to consider.

HOTEL CASA FUSTER Map p116   Hotel €€€
☎ 93 255 30 00, 902 202345; www.hotelcasa fuster.com; Passeig de Gràcia 132; s/d from €294/321; Ⓜ Diagonal; Ⓟ ✗ 🗙 🖳 🛜 �→

This sumptuous Modernista mansion (built in 1908–11) at the top end of the city's showcase boulevard has been transformed into one of Barcelona's most luxurious hotels. Standard rooms are plush, if smallish. Period features have been restored at considerable cost and complemented with hydro-massage tubs, plasma TVs and king-size beds. The rooftop terrace (with pool) offers great views and relaxation. The Café Vienés, once a meeting place for Barcelona intellectuals in the building's heyday, is the perfect spot for an aperitif before heading out at night.

APARTHOTEL SILVER Map p116   Hotel €€
☎ 93 218 91 00; www.hotelsilver.com; Carrer de Bretón de los Herreros 26; s €79-120, d €85-145; Ⓜ Fontana; 🗙 🖳 🛜

There are no fewer than five types of rooms here, from chintzy, tiny basic rooms to the very spacious 'superior rooms'. Aim for the better rooms. All come with a kitchenette and some have a terrace or balcony. There is a little garden too.

LA ZONA ALTA

Except for a certain business clientele, this mostly residential area is a little too far from the action for most people. Several exceptional places are well worth considering if being in the centre of things is not a priority.

HOTEL REY JUAN CARLOS I
Map p122   Hotel €€€
☎ 93 364 40 40; www.hrjuancarlos.com; Avinguda Diagonal 661-671; d from €299; Ⓜ Zona Universitària; Ⓟ ✗ 🗙 🖳 �→

top picks

HOTEL POOLS

- **Comtes de Barcelona** (p237) Unbeatable rooftop indulgence.
- **Hotel Arts Barcelona** (p236) Look down on the beach and do some short laps.
- **Hotel Majèstic** (p236) Panoramic views from the rooftop dipping pool.
- **Hotel Rey Juan Carlos I** (p240) Keep fit in the indoor and outdoor pools.
- **Eurostars Grand Marina Hotel** (p235) Small but nicely placed for portside views.
- **W Barcelona** (p235) Gaze out to sea or back towards the beach from the infinity pool, cocktail in hand.

Like an ultramodern lighthouse at this southwest gateway to the city, the glass towers of this luxury mega-hotel hold more than 430 spacious rooms, most with spectacular views. The hotel has pools and a gym, along with extensive gardens belonging to the farmhouse that stood here until well into the 20th century. Room prices can sink surprisingly low in slow periods. With the Metro close by, you can be in central Barcelona in about 20 minutes.

HOTEL TURÓ DE VILANA
Map p122   Design Hotel €€
☎ 93 434 03 63; www.turodevilana.com; Carrer de Vilana 7; s/d €187/214; Ⓡ FGC Les Tres Torres or 🚌 64; Ⓟ 🗙 🖳

This bright, designer hotel in residential Sarrià has hardwood floors, a warm colour scheme, marble bathrooms and plenty of natural sunlight in its 20 rooms. There is not a lot to do in the immediate vicinity, but for those who like the idea of being able to dip in and out of central Barcelona at will, this is an attractive option.

HOTEL ANGLÍ Map p122   Hotel €€
☎ 93 206 99 44; www.eurostarshotels.com; Carrer d'Anglí 60; d €180; Ⓡ Sarrià; Ⓟ ✗ 🗙 🖳 �→

Hotel Anglí is a comfortable business hotel. Glass dominates the three-storey design and the semi-transparent tower is lit up in various hues at night. Huge firm beds are set in rooms where floor to ceiling windows and expanses of mirrors add to the sense of light. The buffet breakfast is good and from the rooftop pool you can contemplate the Collserola hills. It seems to have recession blues, as prices can drop as low as €80 for a double.

HOTEL MEDIUM CONFORT
Map p122   Hotel €€

☎ 93 238 68 28; www.mediumhoteles.com; Travessera de Gràcia 72; s/d €90/95; 🚊 FGC Gràcia; 🅿 🔀 🖳 🛜

This strangely named two-star lodging is a comfortable business-oriented hotel in an area handy for some uptown bars and restaurants, and is only a short stroll from Gràcia. It sometimes offers tempting deals on price (€50 for a double is not unheard of), and while rooms do not bubble over with character, they're neat, modern and spacious. You can sit out on the terrace for a coffee.

ALBERG MARE DE DÉU DE MONTSERRAT Map p122   Hostel €

☎ 93 210 51 51; www.xanascat.cat; Passeig de la Mare de Déu del Coll 41-51; dm under 26yr or ISIC cardholders/others €21.55/25.95; 🚆 Vallcarca then 🚌 28 or 92; 🅿 🖳

This 209-bed hostel is 4km north of Barcelona's city centre. The main building is a magnificent former mansion with a Mudéjar-style lobby set in a leafy location above the city. Most rooms sleep six and you can buy towels for €4 if you've lost yours. The common areas are extensive and relaxed. The website provides details of all youth hostels in Barcelona and wider Catalonia, so you can look into your options if this one doesn't appeal.

top picks

ROOMS WITH A VIEW

- Hotel Arts Barcelona (p236) Waterfront rooms with panoramic views up and down the coast.
- W Barcelona (p235) Rooms looking across the beach, around the city and/or right out to sea.
- Hotel Rey Juan Carlos I (p240) Bird's-eye views across the city from the west.
- Eurostars Grand Marina Hotel (p235) Low-level views back up La Rambla, across the port.
- Hotel 54 (p235) Sunset views across the marina.
- Hotel Colón (p232) Front-row seat for La Catedral in the heart of the old city centre.

MONTJUÏC, SANTS & EL POBLE SEC

Several options are strung out along and near the El Poble Sec side of Avinguda del Paral.lel, as well as near the train station in Sants.

URBAN SUITES
Map p140   Hotel & Apartments €€

☎ 93 201 51 64; www.theurbansuites.com; Carrer de Sant Nicolau 1-3; ste from €165; 🅜 Sants Estació; 🅿 🔀 🖳 🛜

Directed largely at the trade fair crowd, this contemporary spot with 16 suites and four apartments makes for a convenient and comfortable home away from home. You get a bedroom, living room and kitchen, DVD player and free wi-fi, and the configuration is good for families. Prices fluctuate enomously.

MELON DISTRICT Map p140   Hostal €

☎ 93 329 96 67; www.melondistrict.com; Avinguda Paral.lel 101; s €45-55, d €50-60; 🅜 Paral.lel; 🅿 🔀 🖳 🛜

Whiter than white seems to be the policy in this student residence, where you can stay the night or book in for a year. Erasmus folks and an international student set are attracted to this hostel-style spot, where the only objects in the rooms that aren't white are the green plastic chairs. There are meeting lounges, kitchen facilities, a cafe and a laundrette on the premises. See also p264.

HOSTAL ABREVADERO Map p140   Hostal €

☎ 93 441 22 05; www.hostalabrevadero.com; Carrer de Vila i Vilà 79; s/d €45/59; 🅜 Paral.lel; 🅿 🔀 🖳

A bright *hostal*, with simple rooms (some quite spacious), this place is worth contemplating if you want to stay just outside the old centre and close to Montjuïc. Light-hued yellows and whites in the decor and spotless bathrooms are standard. There are lockers for left luggage too.

HOSTEL MAMBO TANGO Map p140 Hostel €

☎ 93 442 51 64; www.hostelmambotango .com; Carrer del Poeta Cabanyes 23; dm €26; 🅜 Paral.lel; 🖳 🛜

A fun, international hostel to hang out in, the Mambo Tango has basic dorms (sleeping from six to 10 people) and a welcoming, somewhat chaotic atmosphere. This playful vibe is reflected in the kooky colour scheme in the bathrooms. Advice on what to do and where to go out is always on hand.

ALBERGUINN Map p140 Hostel €

☎ 93 490 59 65; www.alberguinn.com; Carrer de Melcior de Palau 70-74; dm €25; Ⓜ Sants; 🖳 🛜

Handily located near Sants railway station and in a gritty, untouristy part of the city, Alberguinn offers crisp, clean dorm accommodation. You'll find lockers, washing machines, a kitchen and a common room for watching TV.

EXCURSIONS

contents

EXCURSIONS

Barcelona is just the beginning. Once you break through the choking ring of satellite suburbs and dormitory towns surrounding the capital, one of Spain's most diverse regions unfolds before you. Catalonia (Catalunya to the locals), a land with its own language and a proud history setting it apart from the rest of Spain, offers everything from golden beaches to wicked ski runs, medieval monasteries to Roman ruins, top-quality wines to the art of Salvador Dalí. A weekender to Barcelona could easily be converted into a couple of weeks exploring the bustling city's hinterland.

The region, covering 31,932 sq km and with a total population of 7.48 million, is bounded by the mighty Pyrenees range and the French frontier to the north, the Mediterranean Sea to the east and the inland region of Aragón to the west.

Barcelona is the big boy nowadays, but in the times of ancient Rome it was Tarragona that lorded it over this neck of the empire. The sunny port boasts plenty of reminders of its Roman glory days. Northeast of Barcelona, the intensely Catalan town of Girona, where you'll be lucky to hear Spanish (Castilian), flourished during the Middle Ages. Its tightly packed medieval centre remains largely intact. Further north, Figueres is synonymous with the hallucinatory genius of Salvador Dalí.

Catalonia is not, however, all high culture. Myriad beaches, coves and seaside locales dot the rugged spectacle of the Costa Brava. Another fine strand southwest of town is Sitges, which is loaded with bars and is an obligatory stop on the gay partygoer's European circuit. Those who take their hedonism with more restraint can trundle around the Penedès wine country west of Barcelona. The jagged mountain range of Montserrat makes the perfect antidote to a seaside hangover.

ANCIENT CITIES

Tarragona (p259) is a busy port and beachside city with an unfair amount of sunshine. Southwest of Barcelona, it is *the* place in Catalonia for those wanting to know what the Romans ever did for any of us. Apart from the well-preserved vestiges of the city's amphitheatre, circus (where chariot races were held) and forum, Tarragona has an archaeological museum replete with ancient artefacts. Inland and to the northeast of Barcelona lies another Roman settlement, Girona (p246). With its cluttered medieval buildings in the crowded old-town centre, Girona makes an enchanting contrast to the sprawl of the region's capital.

DALÍ MANIA

Zany Salvador Dalí, with his upturned handlebar moustache, outlandish dream paintings and outrageous lifestyle, is surely the most colourful character to emerge from 20th-century Catalonia. For all his globetrotting, he left the greater part of his artistic legacy on home turf. The core rests in his theatre-museum-mausoleum in Figueres (p249), a half-hour north of Girona by train. Enthusiasts can seek out more of his work in several nearby locations, including the magical coastal towns of Cadaqués (p254) and Port Lligat (p251).

WINE, PARTIES & PIETY

Barely 50km west of Barcelona stretch the vineyards of one of Spain's premier wine-making regions, the Penedès (p257). Most of the national production of *cava*, the local version of bubbly, pours out of this region. Alongside known names such as Freixenet and Codorníu, countless smaller wineries are in constant ferment.

Barely 20km south of Vilafranca del Penedès, Sitges (p255) was a modest fishing village a century ago. It is now a party animal's haven, with a notable gay leaning.

On another plane altogether is Catalonia's most revered mountain and monastery, Montserrat (p252), northwest of Barcelona. People come here to venerate the Black Madonna, explore the monastery's art treasures and walk in the weirdly shaped mountains.

RUGGED COAST

Too often dismissed because of its tainted package-holiday image, the bulk of the Costa Brava (Rugged Coast; p253) is a joyous spectacle

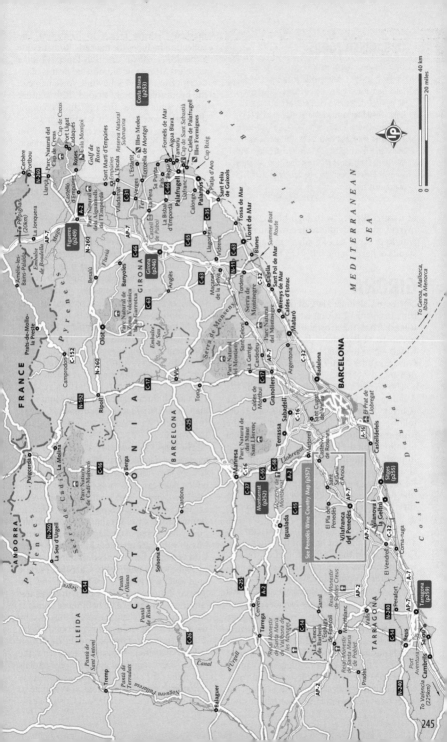

ORGANISED TOURS

The Catalunya Bus Turístic (Map p60; ☎ 93 285 38 32; Plaça de Catalunya) offers a series of day tours from Barcelona to various parts of the region. Routes include a day in Vic, north of Barcelona, visiting the old town and huge weekly market (€35; ☿ Tue); Girona and Figueres (€71, ☿ Tue-Sun); a Penedès wine and *cava* jaunt with three winery tours and lunch (€59; ☿ Wed-Fri & Sun); and Montserrat and Sitges (€69; ☿ Tue-Sun). All tours leave at 8.30am from Plaça de Catalunya from late March to October.

of nature. Blessed with high blustery cliffs, myriad inlets and minuscule coves alternating with long expanses of golden sand and thick stands of hardy pine, it begs to be explored.

GIRONA

Northern Catalonia's largest city, Girona (Gerona in Spanish) is draped in a valley 36km inland from the Costa Brava and 103km northeast of Barcelona. Its medieval centre, which seems to struggle uphill above the Riu Onyar, exudes a quiet, contemplative magnetism.

The Roman town of Gerunda lay on the Via Augusta, the highway from Rome to Cádiz (Carrer de la Força in Girona's old town follows part of its line). Wrested from the Muslims by the Franks in AD 797, Girona became capital of one of Catalonia's most important counties, only falling under the sway of Barcelona in the late 9th century. Its medieval wealth produced a plethora of fine Romanesque and Gothic buildings that survived repeated assaults and sieges to give us pleasure today.

The narrow streets of the old town climb in a web above the east bank of the Riu Onyar. Commanding the northern half of the city with its majestic baroque facade placed high over a breezy square and stairway, the Catedral (☎ 972 42 71 89; www.catedraldegirona.org; Plaça de la Catedral; museum adult/child under 7yr/child 7-16yr/senior & student €5/free/1.20/3, Sun free; ☿ 10am-8pm Apr-Oct, 10am-7pm Nov-Mar) makes an obvious starting point for exploration. Most of the edifice, which has been altered repeatedly, is a great deal older than its exterior suggests. Wander inside to appreciate this. First you find yourself in Europe's widest Gothic nave (23m), but other treasures await. Head through the door

marked 'Claustre Tresor' to the museum. The collection includes the masterly Romanesque *Tapís de la Creació* (Creation Tapestry) and a priceless Mozarabic illuminated Beatus manuscript from AD 975. Beyond, you emerge in the beautiful, wonkily shaped, 12th-century Romanesque cloister; the 112 stone columns display whimsical, albeit weathered, sculpture. During services (especially 10am to 2pm Sundays) you can only visit the museum and cloister.

Next door to the cathedral, in the 12th- to 16th-century Palau Episcopal, the Museu d'Art (☎ 972 20 38 34; www.museuart.com; Pujada de la Catedral 12; adult/child under 16yr/senior & student €2/free/1.50; ☿ 10am-7pm Tue-Sat Mar-Sep, 10am-6pm Tue-Sat Oct-Feb, 10am-2pm Sun & holidays) boasts an extensive collection that ranges from occasionally delirious-looking Romanesque woodcarvings to rather more dour early-20th-century paintings.

Girona's second great church, the Església de Sant Feliu (Plaça de Sant Feliu; ☿ 11am-1pm & 4-6pm), is downhill from the cathedral. The 17th-century main facade, with its landmark single tower, is on Plaça de Sant Feliu, but the entrance is around the side. The nave has 13th-century Romanesque arches but 14th- to 16th-century Gothic upper levels. The northernmost of the chapels, at the far western end of the church, is graced by a masterly Catalan Gothic sculpture, Aloi de Montbrai's alabaster *Crist Jacent* (Recumbent Christ). It looks like it is made of perfectly moulded ice cream.

The Banys Àrabs (Arab Baths; ☎ 972 21 32 62; www.banysarabs.org; Carrer de Ferran Catòlic; adult/senior & student €2/1; ☿ 10am-7pm Mon-Sat Apr-Sep, 10am-2pm Tue-Sat Oct-Mar, 10am-2pm Sun & holidays), although modelled on Muslim and Roman bathhouses, is actually a 12th-century Christian affair in Romanesque style. It's the only public bathhouse discovered in medieval Christian Spain. Possibly in reaction to the Muslim obsession with water and cleanliness, washing came to be regarded as ungodly in Christian Europe (and water was feared as a source of germs and illness). Europe must have been the smelliest continent on earth! The bathhouse contains an *apodyterium* (changing room), followed by the *frigidarium* (cold-water room), the *tepidarium* (hot-water room), and the *caldarium* (a kind of sauna). Across the street from the Banys Àrabs, steps lead up into lovely gardens that follow the city walls in what is called the Passeig Arqueològic (Archaeological Walk) up to the 18th-century Portal de Sant Cristòfol gate,

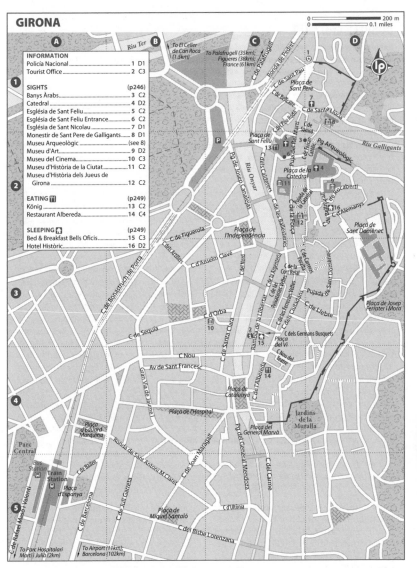

GIRONA

from which you can walk back down to the cathedral.

About 100m north of the Banys Àrabs across the bubbling Riu Galligants stands the 11th- and 12th-century Romanesque Monestir de Sant Pere de Galligants (☎ 972 20 26 32; www. mac.cat/cat/Seus/Girona; Carrer de Santa Llúcia; adult/senior & child €2.30/free; ☉ 10.30am-1.30pm & 4-7pm Tue-Sat Jun-Sep, 10am-2pm & 4-6pm Tue-Sat Oct-May, 10am-2pm

Sun & holidays), a modest monastery with a lovely cloister. Get up close to the pillars that line the cloister. The closer you look, the weirder the medieval imagination seems – all those bizarre animals and mythical monsters! The monastery houses the Museu Arqueològic, with exhibits that range from prehistoric to medieval times, including Roman mosaics and medieval Jewish tombstones. Opposite the monastery is the pretty Lombard-style 12th-

BUBBLES AND MUD

For some, a day at the beach just isn't enough (and a little impractical in winter!). Never fear, for wellness is here. Indeed, it always was. Since Roman days, thermal baths have operated in various parts of Catalonia. Now there are 18 across the region, with several of them less than 40km from Barcelona.

In La Garriga, a pretty town 36km north of the city, are two fine historic installations that have been modernised. Termes La Garriga (☎ 93 871 70 86; www.termes.com; Carrer dels Banys 23; 9.30am-8pm Mon-Sat, 9.30am-2pm Sun) sits atop waters that bubble out at temperatures as high as 60°C. All sorts of treatments are possible, from mud baths to aroma massage. For €33.35 you can spend half a day (three hours) wandering between a couple of pools, a sauna and various showers. Booking is mandatory. The other option is the luxurious five-star Gran Hotel Blancafort (☎ 93 861 92 04/9; www.spablancafort.com; Carrer de la Mina 7; d package incl dinner & baths access from €250), out of the centre. After bathing, go for a stroll around town, especially along the street hugging the railway line, and admire Modernista mansions built by Barcelona's wealthy elite as summer retreats around the turn of the 20th century.

In the seaside town of Caldes d'Estrac, 36km northeast of Barcelona, the Romans loved to slop around in the thermal waters. Emulate them in the Balneari de Caldes d'Estrac (☎ 93 791 26 05; Carrer de la Riera 29; admission €6.40; 9am-1.30pm & 4-8pm Mon-Sat, 8am-3pm Sun), built in the early 19th century. Come on the train for a day and split your time between the baths (you are given about 20 minutes) and other extra treatments, lunch and the beach. Or stay at Hotel Colón (☎ 93 791 04 00; www.hotel-colon.net; Plaça de les Barques; d with/without sea views €122/108, ste €230) and use its spa facilities.

Caldes de Montbui, 28km north of Barcelona, hosts two thermal-bath hotels. You can use the spa facilities even if you don't stay in the hotels. Broquetas Balneario (☎ 93 865 01 00; www.grupbroquetas.com; Plaça de la Font del Lleó 1) is the town's historic spa hotel, located in front of the Roman baths and a public fountain (Font del Lleó) from which water has been spouting forth at a scorching 74°C since the 16th century. Founded in the 18th century and rebuilt several times, it is a predominantly Modernista building. It boasts an original 2nd-century-AD Roman *vaporarium* (steam bath). A session in its spa facilities (9am-1.30pm & 4.30-8.30pm Mon-Fri, 9am-1.30pm & 4.30-9.30pm Sat & Sun), including *vaporarium*, outdoor heated pool and indoor thermal pool with cervical showers, costs €34.65; book ahead. Hotel Termes Victoria (☎ 93 865 01 50; www.termesvictoria.com; Carrer de Barcelona 12) is a luxury spa hotel, with spa facilities (thermal pool session €16; 8am-1pm & 4-9pm Mon-Sat, 8am-2pm Sun) open to the public. The town itself is hardly stunning but is worth a wander. Visit the Museu Thermalia (93 865 41 40; Plaça de la Font del Lleó 20; adult/senior & student €3.15/1.90; 11am-2pm & 5-8pm Tue-Sat, 11am-2pm Sun May-Sep, 10am-2pm & 4-7pm Tue-Sat, 10am-2pm Sun Oct-Apr), which outlines this thermal town's history in a medieval building that was, until the 1970s, a hospital and public baths. The Museu Delger (Carrer del Dr Delger; 11am-1pm 1st & 2nd Sun of month), an 18th-century mansion stuffed with period furniture, is worth a look. For access to Museu Delger, ask at the tourist office (☎ 93 865 41 40; www.caldesdemontbui.org; Plaça de la Font del Lleó 20; 11am-2pm & 5-8pm Tue-Sat, 11am-2pm Sun), in the same building as the Museu Thermalia.

Caldes d'Estrac and La Garriga are easily reached by *rodalies* trains from Barcelona. Caldes de Montbui is more easily reached by car, or Sagalés bus (☎ 902 130014; www.sagales.com) from Passeig de Sant Joan (€2.70, 65 minutes).

century Romanesque Església de Sant Nicolau. It is unusual for its octagonal bell tower.

South along Carrer de la Força, about 100m off the stairway leading up to Plaça de la Catedral, the Museu d'Història de la Ciutat (City History Museum; ☎ 972 22 22 29; www.girona.cat/museuciutat; Carrer de la Força 27; adult/senior & child under 16yr/student €3/free/2; 10am-2pm & 5-7pm Tue-Sat, 10am-2pm Sun & holidays) traces Girona's history from ancient times to the present. Dioramas, explanatory boards, videos and all sorts of objects ranging from neolithic tools to the whining musical instruments used to accompany the *sardana* (traditional Catalan folk dance) help bring the town's story to life. Learn about the 18-month

siege of the town by Napoleon's troops, which cost half Girona's population their lives, and inspect the Capuchin monks' 18th-century cemetery (the monks moved into the then Gothic mansion in 1732), where cadavers were hung in niches.

Carrer de la Força lies at the heart of the Call (the Jewish quarter). Until 1492, when Jews had to convert to Catholicism or leave Spain, Girona was home to Catalonia's second most important Jewish community after Barcelona. For an idea of medieval Jewish life, visit the Museu d'Història dels Jueus de Girona (Jewish History Museum, Centre Bonastruc Ça Porta; ☎ 972 21 67 61; Carrer de la Força 8; adult/child under 16yr/senior & student

TRANSPORT: GIRONA

Distance from Barcelona 103km

Direction Northeast

Travel time Up to 1½ hours

Car Take the AP-7 freeway via Granollers.

Train At least 20 trains per day run from Barcelona Sants station (€6.50 to €8.80).

€2/free/1.50; 10am-8pm Mon-Sat Jul-Aug, 10am-2pm Mon, 10am-6pm Tue-Sat Sep-Jun, 10am-2pm Sun & holidays). Named after Jewish Girona's most illustrious figure, Bonastruc ça Porta, a 13th-century cabbalist philosopher and mystic, the centre offers a limited array of artefacts but has an engaging display of information and images relating to the Jewish presence in the city, dealing with Jewish community life, the synagogues, the Jewish diaspora and persecution in Spain during the Inquisition.

There is not a great deal to see in the modern half of Girona, on the west bank of the Riu Onyar. One outstanding exception is the Museu del Cinema (☎ 972 41 27 77; www.museudelcinema. org; Carrer de Sequia 1; adult/child under 16yr/senior & student €5/free/2.50; 10am-8pm Tue-Sun May-Sep, 10am-6pm Tue-Fri, 10am-8pm Sat, 11am-3pm Sun Oct-Apr), housed in the Casa de les Aigües. Shadow puppets and magic lanterns introduce the Col.lecció Tomàs Mallol, a display that details the precursors to and story of the motion-picture business. Take a close look at some of the images for fairground magic lantern shows in the 18th century, like the devilish character working a bellows in someone's backside!

INFORMATION

Parc Hospitalari Martí i Julià (☎ 972 18 25 00; Carrer del Doctor Castany) Hospital.

Policía Nacional (☎ 091; Carrer de Sant Pau 2)

Tourist office (☎ 972 22 65 75; www.girona.cat/turisme; Rambla de la Llibertat 1; 8am-8pm Mon-Fri, 8am-2pm & 4-8pm Sat, 9am-2pm Sun)

EATING

König (☎ 972 22 57 82; Carrer dels Calderers 16; meals €8-15; daily) For a quick sandwich, *entrepà* (filled roll) or simple hot dish, 'King' boasts a broad outdoor terrace shaded by thick foliage.

Restaurant Albereda (☎ 972 22 60 02; www.restaurantalbereda.com, in Catalan & Spanish; Carrer de l'Albereda 9; meals €40-45; Tue-Sun;) One of the town's top dining venues, Restaurant Albereda serves Catalan cuisine with interesting twists, such as the *fidueada de ceps i calamarcets* (a noodle dish with mushrooms and tiny squids). There are also two tasting menus for €30 and €50.

SLEEPING

Hotel Històric (☎ 972 22 35 83; www.hotelhistoric.com; Carrer de Bellmirall 4a; s/d €109/122;) A bijou hotel in a historic building in the heart of old Girona. The eight pretty, spacious rooms are individually decorated, and there are also apartments available in the same building and in another building nearby (from €60 to €114).

Bed & Breakfast Bells Oficis (☎ 972 22 81 70; www.bellsoficis.com; Carrer dels Germans Busquets 2; r €40-99;) With just five rooms, this family-run option is perfectly placed just off Rambla de la Llibertat. The rooms are all very different. The two best ones have balconies overlooking the Rambla. The biggest (€99) has ample space for four people.

FIGUERES

Just 12km inland from the Golf de Roses, Figueres (Figueras in Spanish) might generously be described as a humdrum town with a single serious attraction: Salvador Dalí. Born here in a two-storey 1898 Modernista house (being restored and destined one day to be a museum on Dalí's early days) at Carrer de Monturiol in 1904, Dalí maintained ties with his home territory in all his long years of peregrination between Barcelona, Madrid, Paris and the USA.

Towards the end of the Spanish Civil War in 1939, Figueres' theatre was largely destroyed by fire and subsequently left to rot. In 1961, the by-now world-renowned eccentric Dalí had the money to buy the site and work on one of his wackier projects, the Teatre-Museu Dalí (☎ 972 67 75 00; www.salvador-dali.org; Plaça de Gala i Salvador Dalí 5; adult/senior & student €11/8; 9am-8pm daily Jul-Sep, 9.30am-6pm Tue-Sun Mar-Jun & Oct, 10.30am-6pm Tue-Sun Nov-Feb), which he completed in 1974. It is at once art gallery, final testament and mausoleum. It was, and remains, the greatest act of self-promotion of a man who had made a supreme art form of such activities. But make no mistake, Dalí was a unique artistic talent, as the contents of his theatre-museum amply demonstrate. It is a multidimensional trip through one of the most fertile (or febrile) imaginations of the 20th century.

The building aims to surprise from the outset. The fuchsia wall along Pujada del Castell is topped by a row of Dalí's trademark egg shapes and what appear to be female gymnasts ready to leap. Bizarre sculptures greet visitors outside the entrance on Plaça de Gala i Salvador Dalí. One can only imagine the parish priest at the adjacent centuries-old Església de Sant Pere looking with disapproval (Franco was still in charge in those days) upon this loopiness as it emerged from the theatre ruins.

Inside, the ground floor (level one) includes a semicircular garden on the site of the original theatre stalls. In its centre is a classic piece of weirdness, *Taxi Plujós* (Rainy Taxi), composed of an early Cadillac – said to have belonged to Al Capone – and a pile of tractor tyres, both

TRANSPORT: FIGUERES

Distance from Barcelona 139km

Direction Northeast

Travel time 1½ to 2¼ hours

Car Take the AP-7 freeway via Granollers and Girona. From central Girona it should not take more than 30 minutes.

Train At least 18 trains daily from Barcelona Sants station via Girona (€9.40 to €12.80).

surmounted by statues, with a fishing boat balanced precariously above the tyres. Put a coin in the slot and water washes all over the inside of the car. The Sala de Peixateries (Fish Shop Room) off here holds a collection of Dalí oils, including his *Autoretrat Tou Amb Tall de Bacon Fregit* (Soft Self-Portrait with Fried Bacon) and *Retrat de Picasso* (Portrait of Picasso). Beneath the former stage of the theatre is the crypt, with Dalí's surprisingly plain tomb.

The stage area (level two), topped by a glass geodesic dome, was conceived as Dalí's Sistine Chapel. If proof were needed of Dalí's acute sense of the absurd, *Gala Mirando el Mar*

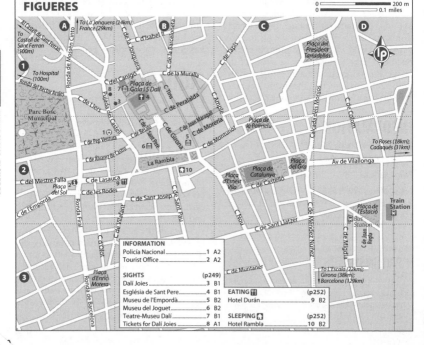

DALLYING WITH DALÍ DELIRIUM

Dalí left his mark in several locations around Catalonia, particularly at his seaside residence in Port Lligat and inland 'castle', Castell de Púbol.

Port Lligat, a 1.25km walk north of Cadaqués, is a tiny fishing settlement on a quiet, enchanting bay. God knows what serious-minded fishermen thought of Dalí's seaside residence, antics and international jet-set pals. Between 1930 and 1982, Dalí spent time (equal to more than half his adult life) here, in what was originally a fisherman's hut. Dalí had not come by choice. His father had forbidden him to return to the family house in Cadaqués after Dalí presented in Paris what was for his father an intolerable painting. Across an image of the Sacred Heart, Dalí had written: *Parfois je crache par plaisir sur le portrait de ma mère* (Sometimes I spit for fun on my mother's picture). His father never forgave him this insult to his deceased wife. By Dalí's standards, the myriad white chimney pots and two egg-shaped towers on the house he 'grew' out of the original cabin are rather understated. It is now a museum, Casa-Museu Salvador Dalí (☎ 972 25 10 15; www.salvador-dali.org; adult/student & senior €10/8; ☼ 9.30am-9pm mid-Jun–mid-Sep, 10.30am-6pm Tue-Sun mid-Sep–early Jan & early Feb–mid-Jun); bookings essential.

The Castell de Púbol (☎ 972 48 86 55; www.salvador-dali.org; Plaça de Gala Dalí; adult/student & senior €7/5; ☼ 10am-8pm daily mid-Jun–mid-Sep, 10am-6pm Tue-Sun mid-Mar–mid-Jun & mid-Sep–Oct, 10am-5pm Tue-Sat Nov-Dec), in the village of La Pera, just south of the C-66 road between Girona and Palafrugell, forms the southernmost point of the Dalí triangle. He bought the Gothic and Renaissance mansion – which includes a 14th-century church – in 1968 for his wife, Gala, who lived here without him (apparently lusting after local young lads to the end of her days) until her death at 88 in 1982. An inconsolable Dalí then moved in himself, but abandoned the place after a fire (which nearly burnt him to a crisp) in 1984 to live out his last years in Figueres. Dalí did the castle up in his own inimitable style, with lions' heads staring from the tops of cupboards, statues of elephants with giraffes' legs in the garden and a stuffed giraffe staring at Gala's tomb in the crypt.

Mediterráneo (Gala Looking at the Mediterranean Sea) would be it. From the other end of the room, the work appears, with the help of coin-operated viewfinders, to be a portrait of Abraham Lincoln. One floor up (level three) is the Sala de Mae West, a living room where the components, viewed from the right spot, make up a portrait of Ms West: a sofa for her luscious, wet lips; twin fireplaces for nostrils; Impressionist paintings of Paris for those come-to-bed eyes.

A separate section displays Dalí Joies (Dalí Jewels; adult/senior & student €6/4), the magnificent Owen Cheatham collection of 37 pieces of jewellery in gold and precious stones designed by Dalí. Dalí did the designs on paper (his first commission was in 1941) and the jewellery was made by specialists in New York. Each piece, ranging from the disconcerting *Ull del Temps* (Eye of Time) through to the *Cor Reial* (Royal Heart), is unique. Admission for Teatre-Museu Dalí includes entry to Dalí Joies. In August, it also opens at night from 10pm to 1am (admission costs €12) for a maximum of 500 people (booking essential); you are treated to a glass of *cava*.

On La Rambla, the town's main boulevard about 100m south of the dazzling display of Dalíesque dizziness, lie what are, by comparison, two rather staid museums. The Museu de l'Empordà (☎ 972 50 23 05; www.museuemporda.org; La Rambla 2; adult/senior & child/student €2/free/1; ☼ 11am-8pm Tue-Sat May-Oct, 11am-7pm Tue-Sat Nov-Apr, 11am-2pm Sun & holidays) is a worthy institution that combines Greek, Roman and medieval archaeological finds with a sizable collection of art, mainly by Catalan artists. Admission is free with a Teatre-Museu Dalí ticket. The Museu del Joguet (☎ 972 50 45 85; www.mjc.cat; Carrer de Sant Pere 1; admission €5; ☼ 10am-7pm Mon-Sat, 11am-6pm Sun Jun-Sep, 10am-6pm Tue-Sat, 11am-2pm Sun & holidays Oct-May) has more than 3500 Catalonia- and Valencia-made toys from the pre-Barbie 19th and early 20th centuries. One wonders to which children the Groucho Marx doll would have appealed.

The sprawling 18th-century Castell de Sant Ferran (☎ 972 50 60 94; www.lesfortalesescatalanes.info, in Spanish, Catalan & French; adult/child under 10yr/senior & student €3/free/2.50; ☼ 10.30am-7pm Easter week, 10.30am-8pm Jul-Aug, 10.30am-3pm Sep-Jun), on a low hill 1km northwest of the centre, was built to withstand the most vicious of sieges but never got the chance show its mettle. Built in 1750, it saw almost no action. Spain's Republican government held its final meeting of the civil war in the dungeons on 1 February 1939. The *castell* is still partly owned by the military, who don't at all mind divisions of tourists manoeuvring around inside.

INFORMATION

Hospital (☎ 972 50 14 00; Ronda del Rector Aroles)

Policía Nacional (☎ 091; Carrer de Pep Ventura 8)

EXCURSIONS FIGUERES

Tourist office (☎ 972 50 31 55; www.figueres.cat, in Spanish; Plaça del Sol; ☷ 8.30am-9pm Mon-Fri, 9am-9pm Sat, 9am-3pm Sun Jul-Aug, 8.30am-8pm Mon-Fri, 9am-8pm Sat Sep, 8.30am-3pm & 4.30-8pm Mon-Fri, 9.30am-1.30pm & 3.30-6.30pm Sat Easter-Jun & Oct, 8.30am-3pm Mon-Fri Nov-Easter) Hours can be a trifle unpredictable.

EATING

Hotel Durán (☎ 972 50 12 50; www.hotelduran.com; Carrer de Lasauca 5; meals €30-40) The Durán clan has been serving up fine traditional food in this hotel-restaurant since 1855. See if you can visit the wine cellar (where it's also possible to dine), in which Salvador Dalí used to hang around quite a bit.

SLEEPING

Hotel Rambla (☎ 972 67 60 20; www.hotelrambla.net; La Rambla 33; s/d €54/67; P ☒ ☐) Right in the heart of the city with comfortable, modern rooms behind a 19th-century facade, this place is one of the best in town. Larger doubles cost a little more (€80).

MONTSERRAT

Shimmering bizarrely in the distance as you drive the C-16 toll road between Terrassa and Manresa is the emblematic mountain range of Catalonia, Montserrat (Serrated Mountain). So dear is it to Catalan hearts that it has long been a popular first name for girls (Montse for short). Lying 50km northwest of Barcelona, the serried ranks of wind- and rain-whipped rock pillars (reaching a height of 1236m) were formed from a conglomeration of limestone, pebbles and sand that once lay beneath the sea. With the historic Benedictine monastery, one of Catalonia's most important shrines, perched at 725m on the mountain range's flank, it makes a great outing.

From the range, on a clear day, you can see as far as the Pyrenees, Barcelona's Tibidabo hill and even, if you're lucky, Mallorca.

The Monestir de Montserrat (☎ 93 877 77 01; www.abadiamontserrat.net; ☷ 9am-6pm) was founded in 1025 to commemorate a vision of the Virgin on the mountain. Wrecked by Napoleon's troops in 1811, then abandoned as a result of anticlerical legislation in the 1830s, it was re-built from 1858. Today a community of about 80 monks lives here. Pilgrims come from far and wide to venerate La Moreneta (Black Madonna), a 12th-century Romanesque wooden sculpture of Mary with the infant Jesus that has been Catalonia's official patron since 1881. A bit like children refusing to believe claims that Santa Claus does not exist, Catalans chose to ignore the discovery in 2002 that their Madonna is not black at all, just deeply tanned by centuries of candle smoke.

The two-part Museu de Montserrat (☎ 93 877 77 77; Plaça de Santa Maria; adult/student €6.50/5.50; ☷ 10am-6pm) has a collection ranging from ancient artefacts,

---

TRANSPORT: MONTSERRAT

Distance from Barcelona 46km

Direction Northwest

Travel time One hour

Bus A daily bus (€53) from Barcelona with Julià Tours (Map p106; ☎ 93 317 64 54; Ronda de la Universitat 5, Barcelona) leaves for the monastery at 9.30am (returning at 3pm). The price includes travel, all entry prices, use of funiculars at Montserrat and a meal at the self-service restaurant. Be at the office a quarter of an hour before departure.

Car Take the C-16. Shortly after Terrassa, follow the exit signs to Montserrat, which will put you on the C-58. Follow it northwest to the C-55. Head 2km south on this road to the municipality of Monistrol de Montserrat, from where a road snakes 7km up the mountain.

Train The R5 line trains operated by FGC (☎ 93 205 15 15) run from Plaça d'Espanya station in Barcelona to Monistrol de Montserrat up to 18 times daily starting at 5.16am. They connect with the cremallera (rack-and-pinion train; ☎ 902 312020; www.cremalleradmontserrat.com; one way/return €5.15/8.20), which takes 17 minutes to make the upward journey. One way/return from Barcelona to Montserrat with the FGC train and cremallera costs €10.10/18.10. Alternatively, you can get off the train at the previous stop, Montserrat Aeri, and take the Aeri de Montserrat telecabin (☎ 93 237 71 56; www.aerimontserrat.com; one way/return €5.40/8.50; ☷ 9.40am-7pm Mar-Oct, 10.10am-5.45pm Mon-Sat, 10.10am-6.45pm Sun & holidays Nov-Feb), which takes five minutes. For various all-in ticket options, check out the above website or www.fgc.net.

including an Egyptian mummy (the collection of Egyptian artefacts counts more than 1000 items, including a mummified crocodile), to occasional works by Caravaggio, Monet, Degas, Picasso and others (including an ample parade of Catalan painters). The Espai Audiovisual (adult/senior & student €2/1.50, free with Museu de Montserrat; ☻ 9am-6pm) is a walk-through multimedia space that illustrates the monks' daily life.

From Plaça de Santa Maria you enter the courtyard of the 16th-century basilica (☻ 7.30am-8pm Jul-Sep, earlier closing rest of year). The facade, with its carvings of Christ and the 12 apostles, dates from 1901, despite its 16th-century plateresque style. For La Moreneta, follow the signs to the Cambril de la Mare de Déu (La Moreneta; ☻ 8-10.30am & 12.15-6.30pm daily), to the right of the basilica's main entrance.

The Escolania (www.escolania.cat; admission free; ☻ performances 1pm & 6.45pm Mon-Thu, 1pm Fri, noon & 6.45pm Sun late Aug-late Jun), reckoned to be Europe's oldest music school, has a boys' choir, the Montserrat Boys' Choir, which sings in the basilica once a day, Sunday to Friday. See the latest performance times (which can change) on the web page. It is a rare (if brief) treat as the choir does not often perform outside Montserrat. The choir has sung hymns since the 13th century. The 40 to 50 escolanets, aged between 10 and 14, go to boarding school at Montserrat and must endure a two-year selection process to join the choir.

To see where the holy image of the Virgin was discovered, take the Funicular de Santa Cova (one way/return €1.80/2.90; ☻ every 20min Apr-Oct, 11am-4.25pm Nov-Mar) down from the main area. You can explore the mountain above

the monastery by a network of paths leading to some of the peaks and to 13 empty and rather dilapidated little chapels. The Funicular de Sant Joan (one way/return €4.50/7.20; ☻ every 20min 10am-5.40pm Apr–mid-Jul, Sep & Oct, 10am-7pm mid-Jul–Aug, 10am-4.30pm Mar & Nov, 11am-4.30pm Dec, closed Jan & Feb) will carry you from the monastery 250m up the mountain in seven minutes. You can also walk.

From the Sant Joan top station, it's a 20-minute stroll (signposted) to the Sant Joan chapel. Enjoy the views as you look west from the trail. More exciting is the hour's walk northwest along a path marked with occasional blobs of yellow paint to Montserrat's highest peak, Sant Jeroni (1236m), from which there's an awesome sheer drop on the northern side.

Check the monastery website for accommodation options. There are several places to eat.

COSTA BRAVA

The rugged Costa Brava stretches from bland Blanes (about 60km northeast of Barcelona) to the French border. At its best, it is magnificent. At its worst, it fully lives up to its reputation as a beach-holiday inferno. Lloret de Mar and parts of the Golf de Roses are the worst offenders, where you can almost hear all that northern European flesh sizzling on the beaches in between lager top-ups. Don't run away! The bulk of the coast is one of nature's grand spectacles, with rugged cliffs plunging into crystalline water, interrupted at improbable points by ribbons of golden sand, tiny hidden coves and shady pine stands. Some towns have managed to retain great charm,

TRANSPORT: COSTA BRAVA

Distance from Barcelona Tossa de Mar 77km; Palafrugell 125km; Empúries 153km; Cadaqués 164km (or 199km via Empúries)

Direction Northeast

Travel time 1½ to three hours

Car Take the AP-7 freeway from Barcelona and peel off at exit 9 for Tossa de Mar, exit 6 for Palafrugell and around, exit 5 for L'Escala and Empúries and exit 4 for Cadaqués (via Roses). You can also follow the coast for parts of the trip. From Barcelona take the C-32 to Blanes and then (often congested) single-lane roads to Tossa de Mar via Lloret de Mar. The single-lane A-2 coast road is slower still. From Tossa it is possible to follow the coast (the initial 21km stretch to Sant Feliu de Guíxols is breathtaking) to Palafrugell and beyond.

Bus The company SARFA (☎ 902 302025; www.sarfa.com) runs buses from Barcelona's Estació del Nord to Tossa de Mar (€10.60, 1½ hours, seven to 18 times daily) and to Palafrugell (€16.15, two hours, seven to 13 times daily). Local buses connect to Calella, Llafranc and Tamariu. Up to four buses a day run from Barcelona to L'Escala and Empúries via Palafrugell (€18.95, 1½ to three hours). For Cadaqués, buses to/from Barcelona (€21.35, 2¼ to 2¾ hours) operate from two to five times daily. Journey times depend on routes and the number of stops made along the way.

and one of the most ancient sites of settlement in Spain, Empúries, is here.

Driving is the easiest way to explore the coast. What follows is a taster. To reach all these spots you need to reckon on at least one overnight stay. In July and August, finding lodgings without a reservation can be problematic.

Leaving the strobe-light silliness of Lloret de Mar behind, the road slices back inland into the coastal hills before setting you down in Tossa de Mar. A small white town backing onto a curved bay that ends in a headland protected by medieval walls and towers, Tossa is an enticing location. Artist Marc Chagall called it his 'blue paradise'. The place has sprawled since Chagall stopped by in the 1930s, but Tossa has retained some of the integrity of a beachside village.

The walls and towers on the headland, Mont Guardí, at the southern end of the main beach, were built in the 12th to 14th centuries. The area they girdle is known as the Vila Vella (Old Town). Wandering around Mont Guardí, you come across ruins of a castle and a lighthouse (with restaurant and bar attached); the sunsets here are superb. Vila Nova (New Town), a tangle of 18th-century lanes, stretches away from the old nucleus and makes for a pleasant stroll. The main beach, Platja Gran, tends to be busy. Further north along the same bay are some quieter, smaller beaches.

The 21km drive from Tossa to Sant Feliu de Guíxols is a treat, the most breathtaking driving stretch of the coast. From here the coastal road continues through the not-unpleasant Spanish resort of Platja d'Aro, on through the more-offensive Palamós and inland to Palafrugell, a local transport hub that funnels you into another prime stretch of the Costa Brava. Again, uncompromising rock walls are interspersed with coves and hideaways. Among the places you can fan out to are Calella de Palafrugell, Llafranc, Tamariu, Aigua Blava and Fornells de Mar. A coastal walking path links the first three.

Jagged cliffs and pine stands give way to a long stretch of beach beyond Sa Punta to L'Estartit, the diving centre of the coast fronted by the marine reserve of the Illes Medes. From here roads redirect you inland to L'Escala, a low-key resort town on the southern tip of the Golf de Roses bay, and the nearby ruins of Empúries (☎ 972 77 02 08; www.mac.cat; adult/senior & child/student €3/free/2.10; ☯ 10am-8pm Jun-Sep, 10am-6pm Oct-May). Founded around 600 BC, it was probably the first, and certainly one of the most important, Greek colonies in Iberia. It came to be called Emporion (literally 'market'). In 218 BC,

Roman legions landed here to cut off Hannibal's supply lines during the Second Punic War. By the early 1st century AD, the Roman and Greek settlements had merged. Emporiae, as the place was then known, was abandoned in the late 3rd century after raids by Germanic tribes.

A small museum separates the Greek town from the larger Roman town on the upper part of the site. While the Museu d'Arqueologia de Catalunya (p145) in Barcelona has a bigger and better Empúries collection, highlights of the larger Roman town include the mosaic floors of a 1st century BC house, the forum and walls. Outside the walls are the remains of an oval amphitheatre.

A string of brown-sand beaches stretches north from the ruins and leads to the cheerful 15th-century hamlet of Sant Martí d'Empúries. On Plaça Major four restaurant-bars compete for your business. You could dine at the homey Can Roura (☎ 972 77 33 80; www.canroura.com; Carrer Major 10; meals €30-35, d €81-115; ☯ Thu-Mon Apr-Jun & Sep, daily Jul & Aug), which serves local dishes and predominantly seafood, and sleep in one of the studio apartments with views over the square.

Next, head for the windswept Parc Natural del Cap de Creus. As well as boasting Spain's most easterly point (Cap de Creus), the area bursts with hiking possibilities, coves and the eternally attractive seaside town of Cadaqués, a strange mix of whitewashed fishing village and minor hedonists' hang-out. The area was the stomping ground of Dalí and a host of other jet-set figures through the 1960s and 1970s. Today it is ideal for strolling, lazing around on nearby beaches and, in the evening, eating and drinking. It can get quite lively on weekends. Nearby is Port Lligat (see Dallying with Dalí Delirium, p251).

INFORMATION

Cadaqués tourist office (☎ 972 25 83 15; www.visitcadaques.org; Carrer del Cotxe 2; ☯ 9am-9pm Mon-Sat, 10am-1pm & 5-8pm Sun Jun–mid-Sep, 9am-1pm & 3-7pm Mon-Thu, 9am-1pm & 3-8pm Fri & Sat, 10am-1pm Sun mid-Sep–May)

Tossa tourist office (☎ 972 34 01 08; www.infotossa.com; Avinguda del Pelegrí 25; ☯ 9am-9pm Mon-Sat, 10am-2pm & 5-8pm Sun & holidays Jun-Sep, 10am-2pm & 4-8pm Mon-Sat Apr, May & Oct, 10am-2pm & 4-7pm Mon-Sat Nov-Mar)

EATING

Casa Anita (☎ 972 25 84 71; www.casa-anita.com; Carrer de Miquel Roset 16, Cadaqués; meals €30; ☯ Tue-Sun Mar-Jan) Everyone from Yul Bryner to Elton John has

COOKING UP A THREE-STAR STORM

Once a simple bar and grill clutching onto a rocky perch high above the bare Mediterranean beach of Cala Montjoi and accessible only by dirt track from Roses, 6km to the west, El Bulli (☎ 972 15 04 57; www.elbulli.com; Cala Montjoi; meals from €200; ☺ Jun–Dec; ☒) is one of the world's most sought-after dining experiences (usually fully booked a year in advance), thanks to star chef Ferran Adrià (see p178). He intends to close it for a creative break from 2012 to 2014, which means he will lose his Michelin stars. While easily Catalonia's internationally best-known dining experience, it has three three-star Michelin stablemates (in all Spain there are only seven; the other three are in the Basque Country).

Can Fabes (☎ 93 867 28 51; www.canfabes.com; Carrer de Sant Joan 6, Sant Celoni; meals €120–300; ☺ lunch & dinner Wed-Sat, lunch Sun, closed Jan) has long attracted a steady stream of 'gastronauts' from Barcelona (53km to the south). Chef Santi Santamaria (the first Catalan chef ever to be awarded three Michelin stars) is a local boy who started up here in 1981. Dishes based on local products (seafood landed at Blanes, for example) are at the core of his cooking, which, while loaded with creative touches, makes no attempt to reach Adrià's kooky levels.

Barely 25km east, on the coast at Sant Pol de Mar, is another foodie's fave. Sant Pau (☎ 93 760 06 62; www. ruscalleda.com; Carrer Nou 10; meals €120–250; ☺ lunch & dinner Tue-Wed & Fri-Sat, dinner Thu, closed most of May & Nov) is a beautifully presented mansion whose garden overlooks the Mediterranean. Observe the cooks at work on local seafood and farm products downstairs before heading upstairs to dine. Carme Ruscalleda is the driving force.

In El Celler de Can Roca (☎ 972 22 21 57; www.cellercanroca.com; Carrer de Can Sunyer 48; meals €120–250; ☺ Tue-Sat), set outside central Girona in a tastefully redone country house, history blends with avant-garde in architecture and cuisine. The enthusiastic team serves up three relatively modestly priced tasting menus (ranging from €90 to €135, plus wine). The style is playful – how about a 'dry gambini' (with a prawn serving the role normally reserved to the olive in a dry martini)?

Twenty-three other restaurants scattered around Catalonia have a Michelin star (and just one has two), in addition to 14 (two with two stars) in Barcelona, so the French clearly find the region fruitful territory for the discerning palate.

---

eaten inside this whitewashed eatery partly carved out of the rock. There is no menu as such, so allow yourself to be advised on oven-cooked fish of the day and other goodies, served at long benches you may well share with perfect strangers.

Sa Jambina (☎ 972 61 46 13; Carrer de Bofill i Codina 21, Calella de Palafrugell; meals €35-45; ☺ lunch & dinner Tue-Sat, lunch Sun mid-Jan–mid-Dec) A few strides back from the beach, Sa Jambina is a family business that takes pride in serving up market-fresh fish and seafood.

Can Sisó (☎ 972 34 07 08; Plaça del Pintor Vilallonga 1, Tossa de Mar; meals €30-35; ☺ lunch & dinner Wed-Sat, lunch Sun; ☒) Set just inside the walls of Tossa's Vila Vella at the foot of the promontory, this place stands out from the bunch. Service is amiable and the accent is on seafood. The *arròs negre* (rice with cuttlefish, drenched in its black ink) is especially worth the wait.

SLEEPING

Hostal Empúries (☎ 972 77 02 07; www.hostalempuries. com; Platja del Portixol, L'Escala; d €130-150; ☒) Looking over the beach by the ruins of Empúries, the elongated hotel is split into the characterful original building, with elegant tiled floors and lots of timber, and a slicker but less appealing designer half. A meal at one of the tall old timber tables overlooking the sea is beaten only by the views from the terraces of the more expensive sea-facing rooms.

Hotel Diana (☎ 972 34 18 86; www.diana-hotel.com; Plaça d'Espanya 6, Tossa de Mar; s/d €90/110, d with sea view €140; ☒) A small-scale, older hotel fronting Platja Gran with 21 simple but light rooms, a Gaudí-built fireplace in the lounge, Modernista decor and stained glass in the central covered courtyard. Prices shoot higher still in August.

Hotel Ubaldo (☎ 972 25 81 25; Carrer de l'Unió 13, Cadaqués; d €55-80; ☒) Set just inside the old town but away from the centre, these quiet and reliable lodgings in two adjacent buildings offer pleasant, simple and mostly airy rooms, some with balcony.

SITGES

Jet-setters, honeymooners and international gay party-goers descend on this once-quiet fishing village from spring to autumn. Just 32km (a half-hour by train) southwest of Barcelona, Sitges boasts a long sandy beach, groovy boutiques for fashionistas, a handful of interesting sights and nightlife that thumps from dusk 'til dawn. In winter, Sitges can be dreary, but it wakes up with a vengeance for Carnaval (see p17) in February, when the gay crowd puts on an outrageous show.

Sitges has been fashionable in one way or another since the 1890s, when it became an avant-garde art-world hang-out. It has been one of Spain's most unconventional, anything-goes resorts since the 1960s.

The main landmark is the parish church, Església de Sant Bartomeu i Santa Tecla, atop a rocky elevation that separates the 2km-long main beach to the southwest from the smaller, quieter Platja de Sant Sebastià to the northeast.

Three museums (☎ 93 894 03 64; per museum adult/child/student €3.50/free/2; ☼ 9.30am-2pm & 4-7pm Tue-Sat, 10am-3pm Sun mid-Jun–Sep, 9.30am-2pm & 3.30-6.30pm Tue-Sat, 10am-3pm Sun Oct–mid-Jun), which offer a combined ticket (adult/child/student €6.50/free/3.50), serve as a timid counterweight to the hedonism. Closed for renovations at time of writing, the Museu Cau Ferrat (Carrer de Fonollar) was built in the 1890s as a house-cum-studio by artist Santiago Rusiñol. The house is full of his own art and that of his contemporaries. The interior, with its exquisitely tiled walls and lofty arches, is enchanting. Next door is the Museu Maricel del Mar (Carrer de Fonollar), with art and handicrafts from the Middle Ages to the 20th century.

The Museu Romàntic (Carrer de Sant Gaudenci 1), housed in late-18th-century Can Llopis mansion, re-creates with its furnishings and dioramas the lifestyle of a 19th-century Catalan landowning family. It also has a collection of several hundred antique dolls – and some of them are mighty ugly! Many of Sitges' grand old residences were built in the 19th century by locals who had made good (often in dubious businesses, such as cotton-raising using slave labour) in South America and were commonly dubbed *Americanos* or *Indianos*.

At night, head down to the 'Calle del Pecado' (Sin St), actually Carrer del Marquès de Montroig, and its extension, Carrer del 1er de Maig, for wall-to-wall bars that will kick your Sitges nocturnal life off with many decibels.

TRANSPORT: SITGES

Distance from Barcelona 32km

Direction Southwest

Travel time 30 minutes

Car The best road from Barcelona is the C-32 toll road. More scenic is the C-31, which hooks up with the C-32 after Castelldefels, but it is often busy and slow.

Train Four *rodalies* trains an hour, from about 6am to 10pm, run from Barcelona's Passeig de Gràcia (€3, 38 to 46 minutes) and Estació Sants to Sitges.

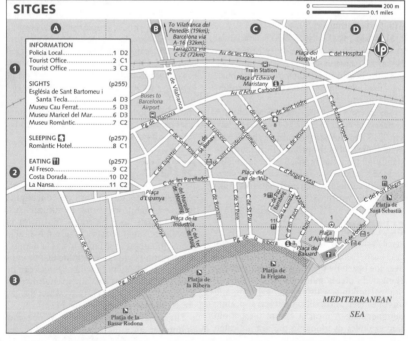

SITGES

| 0 | 200 m |
| 0 | 0.1 miles |

INFORMATION
Policia Local..........................1 D2
Tourist Office.........................2 C1
Tourist Office.........................3 C3

SIGHTS (p255)
Església de Sant Bartomeu i
  Santa Tecla..........................4 D3
Museu Cau Ferrat....................5 D3
Museu Maricel del Mar.............6 D3
Museu Romàntic......................7 C2

SLEEPING (p257)
Romàntic Hotel.......................8 C1

EATING (p257)
Al Fresco................................9 C2
Costa Dorada........................10 D2
La Nansa...............................11 C2

EXCURSIONS SITGES

INFORMATION

Policia Local (☎ 704 101092; Plaça d'Ajuntament)

Tourist office (☎ 93 894 50 04; www.sitgestur.com; Plaça d'Eduard Maristany 2; ☿ 9am-8pm daily mid-Jun–mid-Sep, 9am-2pm & 4-6.30pm Mon-Fri, 10am-2pm & 4-7pm Sat, 10am-2pm Sun mid-Sep–mid-Jun)

Tourist office (☎ 93 811 06 11; Passeig de la Ribera; ☿ 10am-2pm & 4-8pm daily mid-Jun–mid-Sep, 10am-2pm & 4-7pm daily mid-Sep–mid-Jun) A branch office.

EATING

Al Fresco (☎ 93 894 06 00; Carrer de Pau Barrabeig 4; meals €30-40; ☿ dinner Tue-Sat mid-Jan–mid-Dec; ☒) Hidden along a narrow stairway that masquerades as a street, Al Fresco serves a varied array of food in a pleasant setting. You could try anything from an Indian-style chicken curry with green mango to a slab of Angus steak done in red wine and mustard and served with chips. One dish costs €22, or €34 for two (one of which will serve as a starter).

Costa Dorada (☎ 93 894 35 43; Carrer del Port Alegre 27; meals €30; ☿ lunch & dinner Fri-Tue, lunch Wed Jan-Nov) Old-world service in a 1970s atmosphere, perfect for seafood, paella and fideuà (similar to paella but uses vermicelli noodles as the base).

La Nansa (☎ 93 894 19 27; Carrer de la Carreta 24; meals €35; ☿ Thu-Mon, closed Jan) This seafood specialist is cast just back from the town's waterfront and up a little lane in a fine old house. It does a great line in paella and other rice dishes, including a local speciality, cassola d'arròs a la sitgetana (a brothy seafood-and-rice dish). There's a set menu for €24.

SLEEPING

Romàntic Hotel (☎ 93 894 83 75; www.hotelromantic.com; Carrer de Sant Isidre 33; s/d with bathroom from €86/119, s/d without bathroom €72/102) Three adjoining 19th-century villas are sensuously restored in period style, and have a leafy dining courtyard. Prices rise a little for rooms with own terrace and/or facing the garden. If there are no rooms available in this gay-friendly spot, ask about its other boutique hotel, Hotel La Renaixença.

PENEDÈS WINE COUNTRY

Rivers of still white and bubbly, among Spain's best wines, spring forth from the area around

TRANSPORT: PENEDÈS WINE COUNTRY

Distance from Barcelona 48km (to Vilafranca del Penedès)

Direction West

Travel time 30 to 45 minutes

Car Head west along Avinguda Diagonal and follow the signs for the AP-7 freeway, then take either the Sant Sadurní d'Anoia or Vilafranca del Penedès exit.

Train Around two rodalies trains an hour run from Plaça de Catalunya and Estació Sants in Barcelona to Sant Sadurní (€3, 45 minutes from Plaça de Catalunya) and Vilafranca (€3.60, 55 minutes from Plaça de Catalunya).

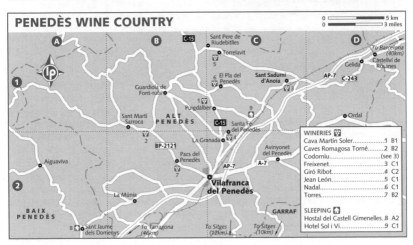

PENEDÈS WINE COUNTRY

WINERIES		
Cava Martín Soler	1	B1
Caves Romagosa Torné	2	B2
Codorníu	(see 3)	
Freixenet	3	C1
Giró Ribot	4	C2
Jean León	5	C1
Nadal	6	C1
Torres	7	B2

SLEEPING		
Hostal del Castell Gimenelles	8	A2
Hotel Sol i Vi	9	C1

the towns of Sant Sadurní d'Anoia and Vilafranca del Penedès. Sant Sadurní d'Anoia, a half-hour train ride west of Barcelona, is the capital of *cava*. Vilafranca del Penedès, 12km further down the track, is the heart of the Penedès DO region (*denominación de origen*; see p194), which produces light, still whites. Some good reds and rosés also gurgle forth here.

A hundred or so wineries around Sant Sadurní produce 140 million bottles of *cava* a year – something like 85% of the national output. *Cava* is made by the same method as French champagne (of course, the French harrumph at such observations) and is gaining ground in international markets. If you happen to be in town during October, you may catch the Mostra de Caves i Gastronomia, a *cava*- and food-tasting festival. For more on *cava*, see www.crcava.es.

The epicentre of the Penedès wine-producing district is the large and somewhat straggly Vilafranca del Penedès. Spreading itself around the pleasant old town centre is a less captivating and sprawling new town.

The mainly Gothic Basilica de Santa Maria stands at the heart of the old town. Construc-

IN SEARCH OF THE PERFECT TIPPLE

To do a tour of the Penedès area, you will need your own transport. For suggestions on wine tourism, browse through www.enoturismealtpenedes.net. Do not, however, expect to wander into any old winery. Many only open their doors to the public at limited times. The more enthusiastic ones will show you how wines and/or *cava* (the Catalan version of champagne) are made and finish off with a glass or two. Tours generally last about 1½ hours and may only be in Catalan and/or Spanish. Groups must book. You can search www.dopenedes.es for wineries. This list should get you started:

Cava Martín Soler (Map p257; ☎ 93 898 82 20; www.cavamartinsoler.com; Puigdàlber; 9am-1pm & 3-7pm Mon-Fri, 10am-1pm, Sat, Sun & holidays) Located 8km north of Vilafranca in a 17th-century farmhouse surrounded by vineyards, this winery only makes *cava*.

Caves Romagosa Torné (Map p257; ☎ 93 899 13 53; www.romagosatorne.com; 10am-1pm & 4-7pm Mon-Sat) This winery at Finca La Serra is on the road to Sant Martí Sarroca. *Cava* is, again, the star. Head on for a look at nearby Sant Martí Sarroca.

Codorníu (Map p257; ☎ 93 891 33 42; www.codorniu.es; Avinguda de Jaume Codorníu, Sant Sadurní d'Anoia; 9am-5pm Mon-Fri, 9am-1pm Sat, Sun & holidays) The Codorníu headquarters is in a Modernista building at the entry to Sant Sadurní d'Anoia when coming by road from Barcelona. One of the biggest names in *cava*, it made its first bottle in 1872.

Freixenet (Map p257; ☎ 93 891 70 00; www.freixenet.es/web/eng; Carrer de Joan Sala 2, Sant Sadurní d'Anoia; adult/child under 9yr/child 9-17yr/senior €6/free/2.20/4.50; 1½hr tours 10am-1pm & 3-4.30pm Mon-Thu, 10am-1pm Fri-Sun) Easily the best-known *cava* company internationally.

Giró Ribot (Map p257; ☎ 93 897 40 50; www.giroribot.es; Finca el Pont, Santa Fe del Penedès; 9am-5pm Mon-Fri, 10am-2pm Sat & Sun) The magnificent farm buildings ooze centuries of tradition. These vintners use mostly local grape varieties to produce a limited range of fine *cava* and wines (including muscat). The times given are for the shop. To visit the cellars, call ahead.

Jean León (Map p257; ☎ 93 899 55 12; www.jeanleon.com; Pago Jean León, Torrelavit; tours per person €6; 9.30am-5pm Mon-Fri, 9.30am-1pm Sat, Sun & holidays) Born in Santander as Ceferino Carrión in 1928, Jean León uses cabernet sauvignon and other grape types imported from prestigious vineyards in France to create a unique name in wines. Visits must be booked.

Nadal (Map p257; ☎ 93 898 80 11; www.nadal.com; El Pla del Penedès; tours per person €6; 10am-2pm & 3-7pm Mon-Fri, 10am-2pm Sat & Sun Mar-Oct, 10am-2pm & 3-7pm Mon-Fri Jan & Feb, 10am-2pm Sat & Sun Nov & Dec) Nadal is just outside the hamlet of El Pla del Penedès. The centrepiece is a fine *masia*, where you can join organised visits.

Torres (Map p257; ☎ 93 817 74 87; www.torres.es; tours per person €6; 9am-5pm Mon-Sat, 9am-1pm Sun & holidays) About 3km northwest of Vilafranca on the BP-2121 near Pacs del Penedès, Torres' El Maset winery is home to the area's premier winemaker. The Torres family tradition dates from the 17th century, but the family company, in its present form, was founded in 1870. Torres produces an array of reds and whites of all qualities, using many grape varieties, including chardonnay, sauvignon blanc, merlot, cabernet sauvignon, Pinot noir and local ones such as Parellada, Garnacha and Tempranillo.

tion began in 1285 and, since then, it has been much restored. It is possible to arrange visits to the top of the bell tower in summer at around sunset. Ask at the tourist office.

The basilica faces the Vinseum (☎ 93 890 05 82; www.vinseum.cat; Plaça de Jaume I 5, Vilafranca; adult/child under 12yr/senior, student and child 12-17yr €5/free/3; ☽ 10am-2pm & 4-7pm Tue-Sat, 10am-2pm Sun & holidays) across Plaça de Jaume I. Housed in a Gothic building, a combination of museums here covers archaeology, art, geology and bird life, along with an excellent section on wine.

INFORMATION

Tourist office (☎ 93 818 12 54; www.turismevilafranca. com; Carrer de la Cort 14, Vilafranca; ☽ 4-7pm Mon, 9am-1pm & 4-7pm Tue-Sat, 10am-1pm Sun) A good source of information on wineries.

EATING

Cal Ton (☎ 93 890 37 41; Carrer Casal 8, Vilafranca; meals €40; ☽ lunch & dinner Wed-Sat, lunch Tue & Sun) Hidden away down a narrow side street, Cal Ton has a crisp, modern decor and inventive Mediterranean chow, which tempts with anything from foie gras with apple to seafood and *cava* pancake.

SLEEPING

Hostal del Castell Gimenelles (☎ 977 67 81 93; www. gimenelles.com; Sant Jaume dels Domenys; r €80-135; ℗) Eight rooms with antique furniture are arranged in a typical, 18th-century Penedès farmhouse and surrounded by vineyards, just west of the town of Sant Jaume dels Domenys. The restaurant offers hearty victuals (set meal €23.50).

Hotel Sol i Vi (☎ 93 899 32 04; www.solivi.com; Subirats; s/d €51/68; ℗ 🛜 🐾) Occupying a renovated *masia* (Catalan country farmhouse) in Subirats, 4km south of Sant Sadurní on the C-243a road to Vilafranca, Hotel Sol i Vi has spacious rooms, a restaurant and country views.

TARRAGONA

A hustling port city, Tarragona was once Catalonia's leading light. Roman and medieval vestiges testify to its two greatest epochs. The Romans established the city as Tarraco in the 2nd century BC, and in 27 BC Augustus elevated it to the capital of his new Tarraconensis province (stretching from Catalonia to

Cantabria in the northwest and to Almería in the southeast). Abandoned when the Muslims arrived in AD 714, it was reborn as a Christian archbishopric in 1089.

The superb Catedral (☎ 977 21 10 80; Pla de la Seu; adult/child 7-16yr/senior & student €3.80/1.20/2.80; ☽ 10am-7pm Mon-Sat Jun–mid-Oct, 10am-6pm mid-Mar–May, 10am-5pm mid-Oct–Nov, 10am-2pm Dec–mid-Mar) was built between 1171 and 1331 on the site of its Visigothic predecessor and a Roman temple (probably dedicated to Caesar Augustus), combining Romanesque and Gothic features, as typified by the main facade on Pla de la Seu. The same combination continues inside in the grand cloister, with Gothic vaulting and Romanesque carved capitals. One of the latter depicts rats conducting what they imagine to be a cat's funeral, until the cat comes back to life! The rooms off the cloister house the Museu Diocesà, with an extensive collection ranging from Roman hairpins to some lovely 12th- to 14th-century polychrome woodcarvings of a breastfeeding Virgin. The interior of the cathedral, which is over 100m long, is Romanesque at the northeast end and Gothic at the southwest (a result of the prolonged construction period). The aisles are lined with 14th- to 19th-century chapels and hung with 16th- and 17th-century tapestries from Brussels. As a mark of reverence for St Thecla, Tarragona's patron saint, her arm is kept as a permanent and rather gruesome souvenir in the Capella de Santa Tecla on the southeast side. All sorts of tall tales abound about St Thecla, who was apparently so impressed by St Paul's preaching on virginity that she called off her impending wedding to follow his advice (and then him). Paul's teaching and

TRANSPORT: TARRAGONA

Distance from Barcelona 96km

Direction Southwest

Travel time 55 minutes to 1¾ hours

Car Take the C-32 toll road along the coast via Castelldefels or the AP-7 (if following Avinguda Diagonal west out of town).

Train More than 40 regional and long-distance trains per day run to/from Barcelona's Estació Sants (some also stop at Passeig de Gràcia). The cheapest fares (for Regional and Catalunya Express trains) cost €5.70 to €6.40 and the journey takes one to 1½ hours. Long-distance trains (such as Talgo, Alaris, Arco and Euromed trains) are faster but more expensive – as much as €19.80 in tourist (standard) class.

her example were not always popular: she escaped several attempts to have her put to death and wound up living as a hermit.

The so-called Museu d'Història de Tarragona (MHT, History Museum; ☎ 977 24 22 20; www.museutgn.com; adult/concession per attraction €3/1.50, all attractions €10/5; 🕑 9am-9pm Tue-Sat, 9am-3pm Sun Easter-Sep, 9am-7pm Tue-Sat, 10am-3pm Sun & holidays Oct-Easter) is actually an ensemble of elements that includes four separate Roman sites (which together with other Roman sites around the province constitute a Unesco World Heritage site).

The Museu Casa Castellarnau (Castellarnau mansion; Carrer dels Cavallers 14) is furnished in 19th-century fashion and sheds light on how the other half lived through the centuries. For the Roman stuff, start with the Fòrum Provincial (Plaça del Rei),

which is dominated by the Torre del Pretori, a multistoreyed building later reused by the city's medieval rulers. A short walk north, Plaça del Fòrum is actually what remains of the Provincial Forum. Stretching west from behind the Torre del Pretori is the Circ Romà (Roman circus), where chariots would thunder along in dangerous, and often deadly, races along a 300m-long track that extended just beyond the present Plaça de la Font. What remains of the vaults of the circus can be entered from Rambla Vella. Nearby, Casa Canals (Carrer d'en Granada) is a fine 19th-century noble family's house abutting the Roman city wall and jammed with period furniture and *objets d'art*. Near the beach is the well-preserved Amfiteatre Romà (Plaça d'Arce Ochotorena; 🕑 9am-9pm Tue-Sat, 9am-3pm Sun Easter-Sep, 9am-5pm

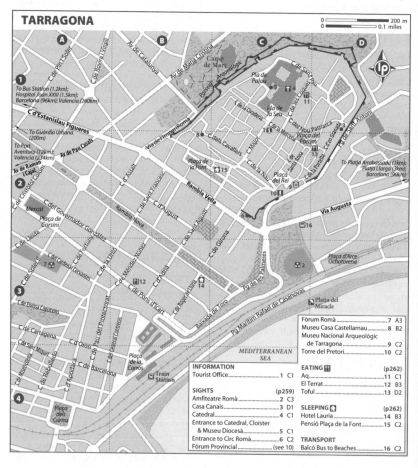

TARRAGONA

0 — 200 m
0 — 0.1 miles

MEDITERRANEAN SEA

Fòrum Romà	7 A3
Museu Casa Castellarnau	8 B2
Museu Nacional Arqueològic de Tarragona	9 C1
Torre del Pretori	10 C2

INFORMATION

Tourist Office	1 C1

SIGHTS (p259)

Amfiteatre Romà	2 C3
Casa Canals	3 D1
Catedral	4 C1
Entrance to Catedral, Cloister & Museu Diocesà	5 C1
Entrance to Circ Romà	6 C2
Fòrum Provincial	(see 10)

EATING (p262)

Aq	11 C1
El Terrat	12 B3
Toful	13 D2

SLEEPING (p262)

Hotel Lauria	14 B3
Pensió Plaça de la Font	15 C2

TRANSPORT

Balcó Bus to Beaches	16 C2

DETOUR: THE MONASTERIES ROUTE

The verdant oasis of La Conca de Barberà lies 30km west of Vilafranca del Penedès. Vineyards and woods succeed one another across rolling green hills (largely hidden from the ribbon of freeway that cuts through them), studded with the occasional medieval village and a trio of grand Cistercian monasteries (a combined ticket to all three is available for €9). With your own vehicle, it is possible to extend a Penedès wineries excursion to some of these magnificent sights. For information on the area around the monasteries, check out the Ruta del Cister (Cistercian Route) website, www.larutadelcister.info.

Following the AP-7 freeway southwest from Vilafranca, take the AP-2 fork about 18km west, then exit 11 north for the medieval Reial Monestir de Santes Creus (Royal Monastery of the Holy Crosses; ☎ 695 186873; Plaça de Jaume el Just; adult/senior & student €4.50/free, guided visit extra €2.20; ☒ 10am-6.30pm Jun-Sep, 10am-5pm Oct-May). Cistercian monks moved in here in 1168 and from then on the monastery developed as a major centre of learning and a launch pad for the repopulation of the surrounding territory. Behind the Romanesque and Gothic facade lies a glorious 14th-century sandstone cloister, chapter house and royal apartments where the comtes-reis (count-kings; rulers of the joint state of Catalonia and Aragón) often stayed when they popped by during Holy Week. The church, begun in the 12th century, is a lofty Gothic structure in the French tradition.

Back on the AP-2, travel another 22km to the medieval town of Montblanc, still surrounded by its defensive walls, and then L'Espluga de Francolí, beyond which you continue 3km to the fortified Reial Monestir de Santa Maria de Poblet (Royal Monastery of St Mary of Poblet; ☎ 977 87 02 54; www.poblet.cat; adult/student €6/3.50; ☒ 10am-12.45pm & 3-6pm Mon-Sat, 10am-12.30pm & 3-5.30pm Sun & holidays mid-Mar–mid-Oct, 10am-12.45pm & 3-5.30pm Mon-Sat, 10am-12.30pm & 3-5.30pm Sun & holidays mid-Oct–mid-Mar), the jewel in the crown of the Conca de Barberà and a Unesco World Heritage site. Founded by Cistercian monks from southern France in 1151, it became Catalonia's most powerful monastery (it is said to be the largest Cistercian monastery in the world) and the burial place of many of its rulers. A community of Cistercian monks moved back in after the Spanish Civil War and did much to restore the monastery to its former glory. High points include the mostly Gothic main cloister and the alabaster sculptural treasures of the Panteón de los Reyes (Kings' Pantheon). The raised alabaster sarcophagi contain such greats as Jaume I (the conqueror of Mallorca and Valencia) and Pere III.

Swinging away north from Montblanc (take the C-14 and then branch west along the LP-2335), country roads guide you up through tough countryside into the low hills of the Serra del Tallat and towards the Reial Monestir de Santa Maria de Vallbona de les Monges (Royal Monastery of St Mary of Vallbona of the Nuns; ☎ 973 33 02 66; adult/child €2.50/2; ☒ 10.30am-1.30pm & 4.30-6.45pm Tue-Sat, noon-1.30pm & 4.30-6.45pm Sun & holidays Mar-Oct, 10.30am-1.30pm & 4.30-6pm Tue-Sat, noon-1.30pm & 4.30-6pm Sun & holidays Nov-Feb). It was founded in the 12th century and is where a dozen nuns still live and pray. You will be taken on a guided tour, probably in Catalan. The monastery has undergone years of restoration, which has finally cleared up most of the remaining scars of Civil War damage. It is possible to stay here overnight on spiritual retreat.

Tue-Sat, 10am-3pm Sun & holidays Oct-Easter), where gladiators hacked away at each other, or wild animals, to the death. In its arena are the remains of 6th- and 12th-century churches built to commemorate the martyrdom of the Christian bishop Fructuosus and two deacons, believed to have been burnt alive here in AD 259. There was certainly no lack of excitement in Roman Tarraco! East of Carrer de Lleida are remains of the Fòrum Romà (Carrer del Cardenal Cervantes), also known as Fòrum de la Colònia and dominated by several imposing columns. The Passeig Arqueològic is a peaceful walk around the perimeter of the old town betwen two lines of city walls; the inner ones are mainly Roman, while the outer ones were put up by the British in the War of the Spanish Succession.

The Museu Nacional Arqueològic de Tarragona (☎ 977 23 62 09; www.mnat.es; Plaça del Rei 5; adult/senior & child under 18yr/student €2.40/free/1.20; ☒ 9.30am-8.30pm Tue-Sat, 10am-2pm Sun & holidays Jun-Sep, 9.30am-6pm Tue-Sat, 10am-2pm Sun & holidays Oct-May) gives further insight into Roman Tarraco, although most explanatory material is in either Catalan or Spanish. Exhibits include part of the Roman city walls, frescoes, sculpture and pottery. A highlight is the large, almost complete Mosaic de Peixos de la Pineda (Fish Mosaic), which depicts local fish and sea creatures that we can only dream about in these times of overfishing. In the section on everyday arts, you can admire ancient fertility aids including an outsized stone penis, symbol of the god Priapus.

The town beach, Platja del Miracle, is clean but crowded. Platja Arrabassada, 1km northeast across the headland, is better, and the aptly named Platja Llarga (Long Beach), beginning 2km further out, stretches for about 3km. Local bus 1 from the Balcó stop on Via

AN AFTERNOON OF WINTER FEASTING

All over Catalonia, but especially in the southwest inland around Tarragona, the locals indulge in a unique feasting frenzy whose culinary centrepiece is a strange, long spring onion, the *calçot* (see also p170), that is grown around here and harvested from late January into March. Country restaurants stage great *calçot* pig-outs on weekends.

A fine place to try this is Ca Vidal (☎ 977 62 52 93; www.cavidal.com; Plaça de l'Església 16; meals €30-35; ☽ lunch & dinner Fri & Sat, lunch Sun-Thu, bookings essential) in the sleepy inland village of Perafort, 10km from Tarragona. After gorging yourself on grilled *calçots* and sloshing back red wine from *porrones* (a kind of carafe with a long spout from which you are supposed to allow the wine to pour through the air into your mouth) in the courtyard, you then head inside this 18th-century stone country house to indulge in seemingly endless serves of grilled meats and sausages.

Augusta goes to Platja Arrabassada and Platja Llarga.

About 11.5km southwest of Tarragona is Port Aventura (☎ 902 202220; www.portaventura.com), a massive and popular Disney-style theme park.

INFORMATION

Guàrdia Urbana (☎ 977 24 03 45; Avinguda Prat de la Riba 37) Local police station.

Hospital Joan XXIII (☎ 977 29 58 00; Carrer del Dr Mallafre Guasch 4)

Tourist office (☎ 977 25 07 95; www.tarragonaturisme. es; Carrer Major 39; ☽ 10am-9pm Mon-Sat, 10am-2pm Sun Jul-Sep, 10am-2pm & 4-7pm Mon-Sat, 10am-2pm Sun & holidays Oct-Jun)

EATING

Toful (☎ 977 21 42 16; Plaça del Fòrum; meals €20-25; ☽ lunch Sun & Tue-Thu, lunch & dinner Fri & Sat) A classic tapas bar in the old town, this place serves up generous servings of old faves like *xipirons* (little battered cuttlefish) and *aletes de pollastre* (oven-cooked chicken wings). During the week you could opt for the lunch menu at €9.80. It becomes a little more elaborate at the weekend (€17). For snacks, you can choose between tapas or the more substantial *raciones* size of most options on the menu.

Aq (☎ 977 21 59 54; www.aq-restaurant.com, in Catalan & Spanish; Carrer de les Coques 7; meals €45-55; ☽ Tue-Sat)

This is a bubbly designer haunt with stark colour contrasts (black, lemon and cream linen), slick lines and intriguing plays on traditional cooking, such as *ventresca de tonyina amb ceba caramelitzada, tomàquet, formatge de cabra i olives* (tuna belly meat with caramelised onion, tomato, goat's cheese and olives).

El Terrat (☎ 977 24 84 85; www.elterratrestaurant. com, in Catalan & Spanish; Carrer de Pons d'Icart 19; meals €45-60; ☽ Tue-Sat) With a pleasingly broad menu (including various rice-based dishes, and others in which foie gras is the standard element), this stylish restaurant, with dark timber floors and a subtle decor of swirling greys, offers a gourmet experience. You might go for a sirloin steak with foie gras and sherry, or the *rèmol amb una parmentier de patata i garotes amb romesco de festucs i olives d'Aragó* (turbot with potato and sea urchins in a pistachio-based sauce with olives from Aragón).

SLEEPING

Hotel Lauria (☎ 977 23 67 12; www.hlauria.es; Rambla Nova 20; s/d €55/75; ☒ ☒) Pleasant enough rooms with parquet floors, good location and a modest pool and sun deck.

Pensió Plaça de la Font (☎ 977 24 61 34; www.hotel pdelafont.com; Plaça de la Font 26; s/d €55/70; ☒) Reasonable *pensión* with its own restaurant on a characterful, busy old town square.

The siren call of Barcelona's pretty seaside location and reputation as a humming metropolis with a broad cultural appeal continues to attract new residents from all over the world.

WHERE TO LIVE

Barcelona is a compact city, making the choice of area to live a comparatively easy matter. Much of the outer suburbs and satellite districts are of limited appeal. With the exception of the privileged minority, most residents live in apartments, which can range from tiny studios (as small as 30 sq metres and on occasion even less) to enormous sprawling affairs (in excess of 200 sq metres). The Spanish property bubble burst in 2008, but Barcelona continues to be one of Spain's most expensive cities. Its compactness and popularity mean that rental property remains at a premium.

Ciutat Vella (the old town) is roughly divided into the three areas of the Barri Gòtic, El Raval and La Ribera. Locals tend to shy away from Ciutat Vella, either because of a lingering reputation for danger or because they feel the area is overrun with tourists. Both are legitimate concerns. Prostitution, petty crime and drugs are still issues at the seaward end of La Rambla and in the streets of El Raval between the waterfront and Carrer del Carme. The most highly prized zone in local eyes is around Carrer de Santa Anna and Carrer del Duc de la Victòria in the Barri Gòtic, while foreigners have tended to be attracted to the buzz of the Born area in La Ribera.

The variety of housing in the old town is enormous. Some apartments are remarkably spacious and may boast attractive features, such as hydraulic mosaic floors, bare stone walls, timber ceiling beams and the like. Other places seem like rabbit hutches. The good and bad frequently have certain disadvantages in common. Narrow streets mean limited natural light in all but top-floor flats. To get to the latter, you might be looking at four or five flights of stairs, as lifts are a rare luxury in these old buildings. Ground- and 1st-floor flats frequently have terraces out the back, perfect for BBQs. The throngs of tourists and nighttime revellers are also a factor to be taken into account, depending on the street you live in.

Seaside options range from the often tiny subdivided flats of La Barceloneta, a still gritty working-class area with much charm that is slowly being gentrified. The Vila Olímpica area is somewhat soulless but offers more modern accommodation. El Poblenou is popular with some expats as it has what they consider a more genuine (read less touristy) feel while offering competitive rent and sale prices and beaches close by. Further northeast, you wind up amid the extravagant high-rise blocks of modern apartments looking out to sea in the Fòrum area – a little too far from the central city action for some tastes.

Popular with younger Catalans and foreigners alike is Gràcia. Many of the long narrow streets of this once separate town are lined with restaurants, bars and shops, lending it a life independent of the rest of the city. Prices can be high.

Between Ciutat Vella and Gràcia sprawls the grid area of L'Eixample. Its heart, the streets around Passeig de Gràcia, is where the more expensive housing tends to be concentrated. Apartments tend to be long, narrow affairs. That means wasted space in long corridors but can be an advantage for those with bedrooms to the rear – far from the noise of traffic and, in certain areas like the streets between Passeig de Gràcia and Carrer de Muntaner, nocturnal weekend revellers. To some, it makes a good compromise, centrally located between most districts of interest, well served by public transport and offering a broad range of options. Prices are moderate to high. The further you are from Passeig de Gràcia, the lower the prices.

The busy, hilly streets of El Poble Sec can be appealing, as prices are not bad by central Barcelona standards. It's a little rough around the edges, which you might like or lump.

La Zona Alta, a rough geographic term for the higher inland areas between Pedralbes and Tibidabo, are firmly favoured by the local bourgeoisie. Real estate is at its most expensive in these areas (including Sant Gervasi and Sarrià).

Families wanting houses and gardens generally have to look further afield and many choose to live beyond the city in and around Sant Cugat. Another popular choice is the seaside town of Sitges (p255). Property anywhere near the centre and waterfront there is as expensive, and often more so, as anything in the poshest parts of Barcelona.

RENTING
Extended Stays

If coming to check Barcelona out for a few weeks, rather than staying in a hotel, the best option is a short-term apartment rental. The Sleeping chapter provides various options for searching out holiday apartment rentals (p230).

You can trawl those websites for longer stays too, although renting your own place or flat-sharing are the two obvious options. Social networks, like Facebook and the travel accommodation website Couchsurfing (www.couch surfing.org) can also be useful tools for seeking out people with whom to share. Check out local websites and publications too (see p267). A particular useful site is www.lloguerjove. com (in English too), where share flats and rentals are advertised.

Many people go through estate agents, liberally sprinkled across the city. Browsing these is a good way to get an initial idea of rents being charged.

Leases & Renter Rights

If renting a room in a share flat (piso compartido), expect to pay about €350 a month or more for a room. Do not accept the first thing you find. And don't be disheartened by your first encounters. You may be confronted with windowless cells in student houses packed to the rafters with people (of course, this can mean the compensation of paying low rent). Older buildings that have long been on the rental market can be in a poor state of repair. Then, occasionally, you can turn up some gems.

Most flat-share arrangements are cash-in-hand affairs with the people already living there. Make sure you understand what is included: electricity, gas, water, phone, internet connections, cable TV and comunidad (building maintenance fees) are all costs and you need to be clear which of these are included in your rent.

If renting a place yourself, you will either go direct to the owner (usually through the websites and publications mentioned on p267) or through an estate agent. The benefit of the former is that you avoid commission and may be able to negotiate a lower rent. The downside is that you will have little or no comeback in case of problems.

Rental leases signed with estate agencies are generally for five years, renewable. It is possible to get shorter contracts. There are generally no rent rises in the life of the contract. As a rule, with at least one month's notice, you may end the contract if you wish to move out. If you have problems in the flat, you can approach the estate agent for help in resolving them. Bear in mind, however, that the general attitude is that tenants have to sort most issues out themselves.

Flats can come either amueblados (furnished) or not (sin muebles). Generally, all flats have the basic kitchen fittings, but on occasion even these are missing and you have to get a plumber to install it all, which basically works out to you doing the owner a little renovation work!

On signing the lease, you pay a month's rent as deposit, at least the first month's rent in advance and the agent's commission (often also one or two month's rent). Check that all the suministros (utilities) are connected before signing. You will have to arrange the name changes on these (again, a friendly estate agent could come in handy here, especially if you have language problems). You will need to provide ID, passport or local resident's number (NIE), and may be asked for some kind of proof of capacity to pay (such as salary slips or an aval bancario, a guarantee from your local bank for up to six months' rent).

Students

Language students learning Spanish and foreign university students, many of them in Barcelona on the one-year Erasmus exchange program, make up the bulk of students in Barcelona. Most opt for flat shares. The Universitat de Barcelona (Map p106; ☎ 93 402 11 00; Gran Via de les Corts Catalanes 585; Ⓜ Universitat), the British Council (Map p122; ☎ 93 241 99 77; Carrer d'Amigó 83; Ⓡ FGC Muntaner) and International House (Map p82; ☎ 93 268 45 11; Carrer de Trafalgar 14; Ⓜ Arc de Triomf) have notice boards with ads for flat shares. Another option is the student residence complexes run by Melon District (☎ 93 217 88 12; www.melondistrict. com; rent from €484 a month in a twin share, to €650 a month in single, depending on length of stay). The better located, Melon District Poble Sec (Map p140; ☎ 93 329 96 67; Avinguda del Paral.lel 101; Ⓜ Paral.lel) can accommodate around 100 people in a combination of single and double rooms with common kitchen areas and single or twin studios.

BUYING AN APARTMENT

Buying property in Barcelona, as anywhere, requires patience and care. The most common way to find an apartment is through estate agents. People also place photocopied notices around town (on walls, street lights, car windscreens, everywhere…). Finally, some vendors content themselves with hanging for sale (*en venda/en venta*) signs on their balconies (although more often than not these are hung by estate agents). Real estate agencies and individuals place classified ads in newspapers like *La Vanguardia*, and on websites such as Loquo (www.loquo.com). Many ads that appear to be private are in fact placed by agents (and anyone can set themselves up as an agent).

The real estate boom from about 1998 to 2008 saw housing prices rise at a phenomenal rate. Since 2008, prices have stabilised and, in some parts of the city, dropped. Sales plummeted but, in early 2010, showed signs of timid recovery. At the time of writing, the average price was around €4600 per sq metre. Though that figure varies considerably from one district to another.

At the height of the boom, estate agents were demanding as much as 10% of the purchase price in commission, which is passed on to the purchaser. However, vendors can negotiate this and a more reasonable figure would hover around 5%. Clearly, if buying direct from a property owner, you can save yourself this cost.

If taking out a mortgage in Barcelona, discuss the options with a local bank before embarking on a serious house search. Since the crisis of 2008, banks have become noticeably more reticent about lending. As a rule, residents need to pay 30% of the house price up front (broken down into 20% of the asking price and the rest to cover costs and taxes, which amount to about 10% of the purchase price). Non-residents generally are asked to pay 50% of the asking price plus the 10% to cover costs.

When you have found a place that interests you, you need to take certain steps to avoid traps. If buying outright and not using a local bank's services, you should consider taking on a conveyancing lawyer. These are best found by word of mouth. Otherwise, try a search on www.elabogado.com/inmobiliario/barcelona.

Firstly, a check needs to be done on the property in the **Registro de la Propiedad** (Map p96; ☎ 93 225 35 51; Carrer de Joan Miró 19-21). For a small fee you can obtain a file on the exact address, in which any outstanding debts, unpaid taxes or problems of ownership should emerge. When buying a property in Barcelona, you take over any debts or outstanding payments. You need to check with the Comunidad de Propietarios (the association of all the owners in the building) that the present owner is up to date with maintenance fees. Finally, you need to know if the building is *afectado*, ie whether it is earmarked for modification, demolition and the like because of future town planning. You can also do this yourself in person at the **Oficina d'Informació Urbanística** (Map p96; Avinguda Diagonal 230; ◷ 9am-1.30pm & 4-5pm Mon-Thu, 9am-1.30pm Fri). Some people buy such properties because they are often cheaper than average, in the hope that the said plans won't be carried out any time soon.

If arranging a local mortgage, the bank will evaluate the property to decide whether the amount being asked is reasonable given its condition and market prices. This is not a full survey of the kind that is common in countries like the UK. Such structural examinations of properties are rarely carried out in Spain.

If you are satisfied you want to buy the property, you may well be invited to make a down payment (commonly 10% of the agreed price) in what is commonly known as a *contrato de arras*. This helps lock in the sale. If you back out later, you lose the money. If the vendor backs out, s/he must pay back this sum and another 10%. The final sale is sealed by signing the *escritura pública* before a notary (usually commissioned by your bank or the estate agent). At this time, you will also pay a whopping 7% VAT on the sale price and expenses (notaries, documentation, registration of the property under your name and so on).

JOBS

With the world economic crisis that began in 2008 and the collapse of the building industry at the same time, unemployment in Spain shot up to just over 20% by April 2010. In the province of Barcelona, the total is not much better, around 17.5% (these figures do not, however, take into account the underground economy – those who work cash-in-hand). In this gloomy context, finding work in Barcelona can be a challenge. Add to this the intensity of competition, with young people from all over Europe attracted by the city's lifestyle, and one can imagine that searching for work in the Catalan capital can be a tough assignment.

Visas & Permanent Residence

Nationals of Switzerland, Norway and Iceland and all EU countries may work in Spain without a visa, but for stays of more than three months they are supposed to register with the Policía Nacional within the first three months. They are then issued with a document bearing the NIE (Número de Identidad de Extranjeros), needed for many everyday activities, such as opening bank accounts. No ID card is issued, merely an unwieldy document. The idea is supposed to make life easier for European citizens, who may identify themselves with their own national ID. But since the NIE is needed for many other transactions in Spain, the net benefit of the measure seems scarce.

All other citizens are supposed to obtain a work permit from a Spanish consulate in their country of residence and, if they plan to stay more than 90 days, a residence visa. If you are offered a contract, your employer will usually steer you through the labyrinth of paperwork. Otherwise, work permits and/or residence visas are hard to come by for non-EU citizens. Quite a few people work, discreetly, without bothering to tangle with the bureaucracy, but this really only works in such areas as bartending, construction, harvesting and the like.

If you manage to get some kind of visa and aim to stay long-term in Spain, you will be aiming for a Permiso de Residencia (resident's permit). If you manage to renew this for a minimum of five years, you are generally granted permanent residence.

Work Options

The easiest source of work for foreigners is teaching English (or another foreign language). Schools are listed under Acadèmies de Idiomes in the Yellow Pages.

Sources of information on possible teaching work – either school or private lessons – include foreign cultural centres (the British Council, Institut Français etc), language schools, foreign-language bookshops and university noticeboards. Cultural institutes you may want to try include the following:

British Council (Map p122; ☎ 93 241 97 00; www.britishcouncil.org/es/spain.htm; Carrer d'Amigó 83; ☒ FGC Muntaner)

Institut Français de Barcelona (Map p122; ☎ 93 567 77 77; www.institutfrances.org; Carrer de Moià 8; Ⓜ Diagonal)

Institute for North American Studies (Map p122; ☎ 93 240 51 10; www.ien.es; Via Augusta 123; ☒ FGC Plaça Molina)

Translating and interpreting could be an option if you are fluent in Spanish (and/or Catalan) and a language in demand. Bar work in Irish pubs and boat scrubbing in the marinas and the like are other possibilities.

For many jobs on a higher level, you will need to have reasonable Spanish and, in some cases, Catalan. The better your ability in these languages, the greater your chances on the local market.

A big impediment can be recognition of foreign diplomas and other qualifications. There is no set rule on which qualifications are recognised but if you are looking for work where they are necessary, you will most likely need to have notarised translations of them prepared.

FAMILY CONSIDERATIONS

Moving with kids can be a complex business. Barcelona offers several international schools, and day-care facilities are available, although competition for places is tough.

MOVING HOUSE

Moving house is a traumatic business at the best of times and can be worse still when heading abroad. Check out various international removal companies in your home city and compare quotes. Pack your belongings well and take the appropriate insurance, as breakage or other damage in transit is always on the cards.

At the destination point, one potential obstacle can be getting bulkier items and furniture upstairs, especially in buildings without a lift (a common situation in the old town, and not uncommon in other parts of town). The most common solution is to hire vehicles with a platform to lift objects to the streetside windows (which generally have to be taken out). This should be taken care of by the removals company you contract.

A web search along the lines of 'removalists Spain' will throw up a plethora of international removals companies. The UK is particularly blessed with such companies.

Places in pre-school day-care centres (*guarderías*) can be hard to come by. *Ludotecas* (play centres for small kids) can be useful for kids of a broader age range, but generally only for a few hours a day, especially for the hours between school finishing times and when busy parents get off work. A good place to start for information is Kids in Barcelona (www.kidsinbarcelona.com), which has a list of English-language and international nurseries, kindergartens and after-school play/activity centres.

A handful of international schools operate in and around Barcelona. The British School of Barcelona (☎ 93 665 15 84; http://britishschoolbarcelona.interaweb.com; Carrer de Ginesta 26, Castelldefels) has delivered quality education since the 1950s, attracting Catalan and international pupils, most of whom go on to attend university in the United Kingdom or Spain. Attracting more of an American student base is the Benjamin Franklin International School (Map p122; ☎ 93 434 23 80; www.bfischool.org; Carrer de Martorell i Peña 9).

USEFUL RESOURCES
Websites
Websites in English on living in Spain abound. There are also some useful ones for the accommodation hunt.

Anuntis (www.anuntis.com, in Spanish) A big general online classified portal where you'll find various small ads websites, such as Segundamano (www.segundamano.es, in Spanish).

Barnavivienda (www.barnavivienda.com, in Spanish) Flat rental.

En Alquiler (www.enalquiler.com, in Spanish) A nationwide property rental site with thousands of flats in Barcelona.

Living in Spain (www.livinginspain.org) A broad site with information on topics ranging from getting married to making wills.

Lloguer Jove (www.lloguerjove.com) Dedicated to flat shares and rental, especially for young people.

Loquo (www.loquo.com) A good place to start looking for apartment rental, share accommodation and a host of other classifieds.

Spain Expat (www.spainexpat.com) This site has a wealth of information on anything from tax to starting your own bar.

Newspapers & Publications
The *Complete Residents' Guide Barcelona*, published by Explorer, is a weighty tome containing all sorts of information for people living in Barcelona. Countless guidebooks in English on living in Spain exist. David Hampshire's regularly updated *Living and Working in Spain* is a good one.

Those in search of properties for sale or rent can trawl classifieds in local papers, especially *La Vanguardia*. The free English-language monthly *Barcelona Metropolitan*, found in bars and some hotels, carries rental classifieds in English, as does another monthly freebie, *Catalunya Classified*. Otherwise, get a hold of *Anuntis*, the weekly classifieds paper. The last few pages of the *Suplement Immobiliària* (Real Estate Supplement) carry ads for shared accommodation under the heading '*lloguer/hostes i vivendes a compartir*'.

AIR

After Madrid, Barcelona is Spain's busiest international transport hub. A host of airlines, including many budget carriers, fly directly to Barcelona from around Europe. One important exception is Ryanair, which uses Girona and Reus airports (buses link Barcelona to both).

Most intercontinental flights require passengers to change flights in Madrid or another major European hub.

Iberia, Air Europa, Spanair and Vueling all have dense networks across the country and, while flights can be costly, you can save considerable time by flying from Barcelona to distant cities like Seville or Málaga.

Websites that list competitive fares include:

www.bookingbuddy.com

www.cheapflights.com

www.cheaptickets.com

www.discount-tickets.com

www.ebookers.com

www.expedia.com

www.flightline.co.uk

www.flynow.com

www.kayak.com

www.lastminute.com

www.openjet.co.uk

www.opodo.com

www.orbitz.com

www.planesimple.co.uk

www.priceline.com

www.skyscanner.net

www.travelocity.co.uk

www.tripadvisor.com

Airlines

The following airlines serve Barcelona.

Air Berlin (AB; ☎ 902 320737, in Germany 01805 737800; www.airberlin.com)

Air Europa (UX; ☎ 902 401501; www.aireuropa.com)

American Airlines (AA; ☎ 902 887300, in the US 1 800 433 73 00; www.aa.com)

British Airways (BA; ☎ 902 111333, in the UK 0844 493 0787; www.britishairways.com)

Cimber Sterling (NB; ☎ in Denmark 70 10 12 18; www.cimber.com)

Continental (CO; ☎ in the US 1 800 231 0856; www.continental.com)

Delta (DL; ☎ 900 800743, in the US 800 221 1212; www.delta.com)

EasyJet (U2; ☎ 902 299992, in the UK 0905 821 0905; www.easyjet.com)

Germanwings (4U; ☎ 8s 025, in Germany 0900 191 91 00; www.germanwings.com)

Iberia (IB; ☎ 902 400500; www.iberia.es)

Jet2 (LS; ☎ 902 881269, in the UK 0871 226 1737; www.jet2.com)

Lufthansa (LX; ☎ 902 220101, in Germany 01805 805805; www.lufthansa.com)

Meridiana (IG; ☎ 807 405018, in Italy 892928; www.meridiana.it)

Norwegian.no (DY; ☎ 815 21 815: www.norwegian.no)

Ryanair (FR; ☎ 807 181881, in the UK 0871 246 0000, in Ireland 0818 303030; www.ryanair.com)

Singapore Airlines (SQ; ☎ 902 380777; www.singaporeair.com)

Spanair (JK; ☎ 902 131415; www.spanair.com)

Swiss (LX; ☎ 901 116712, in Switzerland 0848 700700; www.swiss.com)

Thomson Fly (TOM; ☎ in the UK 0871 231 47 87; www.thomsonfly.com)

Transavia (HV; ☎ 807 075022, in the Netherlands 0900 0737; www.transavia.com)

US Airways (US; ☎ 901 117073, in the US 800 428 4322; www.usairways.com)

Vueling (VY; ☎ 807 200200; www.vueling.com)

Windjet (IV; ☎ 900 996933, in Italy 892020;
w2.volawindjet.it)

Wizz (W6; ☎ 807 450010; http://wizzair.com)

Airports

Barcelona's **El Prat airport** (Map p58; ☎ 902 404704;
www.aena.es) lies 12km southwest of the city at
El Prat de Llobregat. The airport has two main
terminal buildings, the new T1 terminal and
the older T2, itself divided into three terminal
areas (A, B and C).

In T1, the main arrivals area is on the 1st
floor (with separate areas for EU Schengen Area
arrivals, non-EU international arrivals and the
Barcelona-Madrid corridor). Boarding gates for
departures are on the 1st and 3rd floors.

The main **tourist office** (☉ 9am-9pm) is on the
ground floor of Terminal 2B. Others on the
ground floor of Terminal 2A and in Terminal 1
operate the same hours. Lockers (which come
in three sizes) can be found on the 1st floor of
Terminal 1 and at the car park entrance opposite Terminal 2B. You pay €3.80/4.40/4.90
for 24 hours. Lost luggage offices can be found
by the arrivals belts in Terminal 1 and on the
arrivals floor in Terminals 2A and 2B.

Girona-Costa Brava airport (☎ 902 404704; www.aena
.es) is 12km south of Girona and about 90km
north of Barcelona. You'll find a **tourist office**
(☎ 972 18 67 08; ☉ 8am-8pm), ATMs and lost-lug-
gage desks on the ground floor. **Reus airport** (☎ 902
404704; www.aena.es) is 13km west of Tarragona
and 108km southwest of Barcelona. The **tourist
office** (☎ 977 77 22 04; ☉ 8am-10pm) and lost luggage
desks are in the main terminal building.

BICYCLE

Some 156km of (often discontinuous) bike
lanes have been laid out across the city, making it possible to get around on two environmentally friendly wheels. A waterfront path
runs northeast from Port Olímpic towards
Riu Besòs. Scenic itineraries are mapped for
cyclists in the Collserola parkland, and the
ronda verda is a still incomplete 72km cycling
path that extends around the city's outskirts.

You can transport your bicycle on the
Metro on weekdays (except between 7am
and 9.30am or 5pm and 8.30pm). On weekends and holidays, and during July and August, there are no restrictions. You can use
FGC trains to carry your bike at any time
and Renfe's *rodalies* trains from 10am to 3pm
on weekdays and all day on weekends and
holidays.

For information on all aspects of cycling
in Barcelona, take a look at the city's website,
www.bcn.cat/bicicleta (in Catalan/Spanish).

Bicing (www.bicing.com, in Catalan/Spanish) is a
resident-only public bicycle system. Folks pay
an annual fee and ride these red and white
bikes from one stop (scattered all over town,
including near many Metro stations) to another – effectively an alternative system of
public transport.

Hire

Countless companies around town offer bicycles (and anything remotely resembling one,
from tandems to tricycle carts and more).
They include the following:

BarcelonaBiking.com (Map p60; ☎ 656 356300; www
.barcelonabiking.com; Baixada de Sant Miquel 6; per hr/24
hr €5/15; ☉ 10am-8pm) City, road and mountain bikes.

Barnabike (Map p90; ☎ 93 269 02 04; www.barnabike
.com; Carrer del Pas de Sota la Muralla 3; per 2hr/24hr
€6/15; ☉ 10am-9.30pm) Rents out an assortment of
bikes (including kick bikes) and karts, Trikkes (odd three-
wheel contraptions), electric bikes and bikes for kids.

CLIMATE CHANGE & TRAVEL

Every form of transport that relies on carbon-based fuel generates CO_2, the main cause of human-induced climate
change. Modern travel is dependent on aeroplanes and while they might use less fuel per kilometre per person than
most cars, they travel much greater distances. It's not just CO_2 emissions from aircraft that are the problem. The altitude
at which aircraft emit gases (including CO_2) and particles contributes significantly to their total climate change impact.
The Intergovernmental Panel on Climate Change believes aviation is responsible for 4.9% of climate change – double
the effect of its CO_2 emissions alone.

Lonely Planet regards travel as a global benefit. We encourage the use of more climate-friendly travel modes where
possible and, together with other concerned partners across many industries, we support the carbon offset scheme run
by ClimateCare. Websites such as climatecare.org use 'carbon calculators' that allow people to offset the greenhouse
gases they are responsible for with contributions to portfolios of climate-friendly initiatives throughout the developing
world. Lonely Planet offsets the carbon footprint of all staff and author travel.

BEB (Map p106; ☎ 93 451 50 31; www.beb.com.es; Carrer d'Enric Granados 61; rental per day from €20; ☻ 10am-2pm & 4.30-8.30pm) Offers more relaxed cyclists the option of renting motorised bikes. You are provided with bike, battery and charger. Discounts are available for longer periods. Bookings must be made a day in advance.

Biciclot (Map p90; ☎ 93 221 97 78; www.biciclot.net & www.bikinginbarcelona.net; Passeig Marítim de la Barceloneta 33; per hr/day €5.50/€18; ☻ 10am-3pm Mon-Thu, 10am-8pm Fri-Sun & holidays Mar-May, 10am-8pm daily late Jun–late Sep, 10am-8pm Sat-Sun & holidays Oct-Nov,

GETTING INTO TOWN

Barcelona El Prat Airport

The A1 Aerobús (☎ 93 415 60 20) runs from Terminal 1 to Plaça de Catalunya (Map p106; €5, 30 to 40 minutes depending on traffic) via Plaça d'Espanya (Map p140), Gran Via de les Corts Catalanes (corner of Carrer del Comte d'Urgell, Map p100) and Plaça de la Universitat (Map p106) every five to 10 minutes (depending on the time of day) from 6.05am to 1.05am. Departures from Plaça de Catalunya are from 5.30am to 12.30am and stop at the corner of Carrer de Sepúlveda and Carrer del Comte d'Urgell, and Plaça d'Espanya. The A2 Aerobús from Terminal 2 (stops outside terminal areas A, B and C) runs from 6am to 12.30am with a frequency of between eight and 15 minutes and follows the same route as the A1. Buy tickets on the bus or from machines at the airport (if they are working!). Considerably slower local buses (such as the No 46 to/from Plaça d'Espanya and a night bus, the N17, to/from Plaça de Catalunya) also serve Terminals 1 and 2.

Train operator Renfe (www.renfe.es) runs the R2 Nord line every half an hour from the airport (from 6.08am to 11.38pm) via several stops to Estació Sants (the main train station) and Passeig de Gràcia in central Barcelona, after which it heads northwest out of the city. The first service from Passeig de Gràcia leaves at 5.28am and the last at 11.02pm, and about five minutes later from Estació Sants. The trip between the airport and Passeig de Gràcia takes 25 minutes. A one-way ticket costs €3 (unless you have a multiride ticket for Barcelona public transport – see p274).

The airport railway station is about a five-minute walk from Terminal 2. Regular shuttle buses run from the station and Terminal 2 to Terminal 1 – allow for an extra 15 to 20 minutes.

Barcelona HotelBus (www.barcelonahotelbus.com) offers small buses designed for people with luggage a door-to-door service to a series of hotels in central Barcelona and to the Fòrum area. They run about hourly from 8am to 8pm (one way/return €12/20). You can book ahead or just hop on if there is space.

A taxi between either terminal and the city centre – about a half-hour ride depending on traffic – costs €20 to €25. Fares and charges are posted inside the passenger side of the taxi – make sure the meter is used.

Parking is available at each terminal (around €1.65 an hour to a maximum of €18 a day for the first four days, thereafter €14.40). Expensive guarded parking (www.parkingvipbarcelona.com, in Catalan/Spanish; €65 for the first 2 days) is also available.

Mon-Bus (☎ 93 893 75 11) has regular direct buses (which originate in central Barcelona) between Terminal 1 only and Sitges (€2.90; p255). In Sitges you can catch it at Avinguda de Vilanova 14. The trip takes about 35 minutes and runs hourly.

Alsa (☎ 902 422242; www2.alsa.es) runs the Aerobús Ràpid service several times daily from Barcelona airport to various cities including Girona, Figueres, Lleida, Reus, and Tarragona. Fares range from €7.66/14.55 one-way/return to Tarragona up to €26.60/47.90 one way/return to Lleida.

Plana (☎ 977 35 44 45; www.empresaplana.es) has services between the airport and Reus, stopping at Tarragona, Port Aventura and other southwest coastal destinations nearby along the way.

Girona-Costa Brava Airport

Sagalés (☎ 902 130014; www.sagales.com) runs hourly bus services from Girona-Costa Brava airport to Girona's main bus/train station (€2.40, 30 minutes) in connection with flights. The same company runs direct Barcelona Bus (☎ 902 361550) services to/from Estació del Nord bus station (Map p100) in Barcelona (one way/return €12/21, 70 minutes). Regular trains run between Girona and Barcelona (€6.50 to €8.80, up to one hour 40 minutes).

A taxi into Girona from the airport costs €20 to €24. To Barcelona you would pay €130 to €140. Airport parking costs an average €0.95 an hour or €8.90 a day.

For greater flexibility at greater cost, check out Resorthoppa (www.resorthoppa.com). It puts on minibuses to destinations around the region, including Barcelona.

Reus Airport

Hispano Igualadina buses (☎ 902 447726; www.igualadina.com) run between Reus airport and Barcelona (Estació d'Autobusos de Sants; Map p140) to meet flights (€12.50/21 one-way/return, 1½ hours). Local bus 50 serves central Reus (€2.20, 20 minutes) and other buses run to local coastal destinations. Check Ryanair's website (www.ryanair.com) for timetables.

10am-3pm Sat-Sun & holidays Dec-Feb; Ⓜ Ciutadella Vila Olímpica) Handy seaside location.

Bike Rental Barcelona (Map p60; ☎ 666 057655; www.bikerentalbarcelona.com; Carrer d'en Rauric 20; per 2hr/24hr from €6/18 depending on type of bike; ⏲ 10am-8pm).

My Beautiful Parking (Map p60; ☎ 93 304 15 80; www.mybeautifulparking.com; Carrer de Cervantes 5; per 2hr/24hr €6/15; ⏲ 10am-8pm) Parking for bikes and also rents out trekking bikes.

Trixi (Map p60; ☎ 93 310 13 79; www.trixi.info; Plaça dels Traginers 4) Hires out bicycles, kickbikes and 'trixi-kids', tricycles with a kind of front-end trolley for transporting young children.

Un Cotxe Menys (Map p82; ☎ 93 268 21 05; www .bicicletabarcelona.com; Carrer de l'Esparteria 3; per hr/ full day/week €5/15/55; ⏲ 9am-7pm daily Easter-Nov, 11am-2pm Dec-Easter; Ⓜ Jaume I) This business also organises bike tours.

BOAT
Algeria

Algérie Ferries (www.algerieferries.com) has occasional services between Barcelona and Algier. Adult one-way fares start at €120.

Balearic Islands

Passenger and vehicular ferries operated by **Acciona Trasmediterránea** (Map p90; ☎ 902 454645; www.trasmediterranea.es; Ⓜ Drassanes) to/from the Balearic Islands dock around the Moll de Barcelona wharf in Port Vell. Information and tickets are available at the terminal buildings along Moll de Sant Bertran (Map p90) and on Moll de Barcelona (Map p90) or from travel agents. Fares vary enormously according to season, how far in advance you book and whether or not you want a cabin. Fares for a 'Butaca Turista' (seat) from Barcelona to any of the islands are typically around €50 on standard ferries or €80 on high-speed catamaran ferries. Cabins for up to four people are also available on overnight standard ferries.

Another company with links between Barcelona and the Balearic Islands is **Baleària** (☎ 902 160180; www.balearia.com).

Italy

Grandi Navi Veloci (Map p90; ☎ in Italy 010 209 4591; www1. gnv.it; Ⓜ Drassanes) runs high-speed, luxury ferries three (sometimes more) days a week between Genoa and Barcelona. The journey takes 18 hours. Ticket prices depend on season and how far in advance you purchase and vary wildly, starting at about €80 one way for an airline-style seat in summer. They can be bought online or at Acciona Trasmediterránea ticket windows. The same company runs a similar number of ferries between Barcelona and Tangiers, in Morocco (voyage time about 26 hours).

Grimaldi Ferries (Map p90; ☎ 902 531333, in Italy 081 496444; www.grimaldi-lines.com) operates similar services from Barcelona to Civitavecchia (near Rome, 20½ hours, six to seven times a week), Livorno (Tuscany, 19½ hours, three times a week) and Porto Torres (northwest Sardinia, 12 hours, daily). An economy-class airline-style seat costs from €29 in low season to €77 in high season on all routes.

Boats of both lines dock at Moll de Sant Bertran (Map p90) and all vessels take vehicles.

BUS
Barcelona

Transports Metropolitans de Barcelona (TMB; ☎ 010; www.tmb.net) buses run along most city routes every few minutes from between 5am and 6.30am to between around 10pm and 11pm. Many routes pass through Plaça de Catalunya and/or Plaça de la Universitat. After 11pm, a reduced network of yellow *nitbusos* (night buses) runs until 3am or 5am. All *nitbus* routes pass through Plaça de Catalunya and most run every 30 to 45 minutes.

BUS TURÍSTIC

This hop-on hop-off service (audioguides in 10 languages), run by TMB, operates from Plaça de Catalunya (Map p106) and Plaça del Porta de la Pau (Map p60), and covers three circuits (44 stops) linking virtually all the city's main sights. Tickets are available online (www.tmb.net) and on the buses, and cost €22 (€14 for children from four to 12 years) for one day of unlimited rides, or €29 (€18 for children) for two consecutive days. Buses run from 9am to 7.30pm and the frequency varies from every five to 25 minutes. Buses do not operate on Christmas Day or New Year's Day.

The two key routes take about two hours each; the blue route runs past La Pedrera on Passeig de Gràcia and takes in the Sagrada Família, Park Güell and much of the Zona Alta (including Pedralbes and Camp Nou). The red route also runs up Passeig de Grà-cia and takes in Port Vell, Port Olímpic and

Montjuïc. The third (green route), from Port Olímpic to the Fòrum, runs from April to September and takes 40 minutes.

Other private companies run similar services.

Catalonia

Much of the Pyrenees and the entire Costa Brava are served only by buses, as train services are limited to important railheads such as Girona, Figueres, Lleida, Ripoll and Puigcerdà. Various bus companies operate across the region. Most operate from Estació del Nord (Map p100; ☎ 902 260606; www.barcelonanord .com; Carrer d'Ali Bei 80; Ⓜ Arc de Triomf), but Hispano-Igualadina and TEISA do not.

Alsina Graells (☎ 902 422242; www.alsa.es) A subsidiary of Alsa, it runs buses from Barcelona to destinations west and northwest, such as Vielha, La Seu d'Urgell and Lleida.

Barcelona Bus (☎ 902 130014; www.sagales.com, in Catalan & Spanish) Runs buses from Barcelona to Girona (and Girona-Costa Brava airport), Figueres, parts of the Costa Brava and northwest Catalonia.

Hispano-Igualadina (Map p122; ☎ 902 447726; www .igualadina.net; Estació Sants & Plaça de la Reina Maria Cristina) Serves central and southern Catalonia.

SARFA (☎ 902 302025; www.sarfa.com) The main operator on and around the Costa Brava.

TEISA (Map p106; ☎ 93 215 35 66; www.teisa-bus.com; Carrer de Pau Claris 117; Ⓜ Passeig de Gràcia) Covers a large part of the eastern Catalan Pyrenees from Girona and Figueres. From Barcelona, buses head for Camprodon via Ripoll and Olot via Besalú.

Long-Distance

Long-distance buses leave from Estació del Nord. A plethora of companies operates to different parts of Spain, although many come under the umbrella of Alsa (☎ 902 422242; www .alsa.es). For other companies, ask at the bus station. There are frequent services to Madrid, Valencia and Zaragoza (20 or more a day) and several daily departures to distant destinations such as Burgos, Santiago de Compostela and Seville.

Eurolines (www.eurolines.com), in conjunction with local carriers all over Europe, is the main international carrier. Its website provides links to national operators; it runs services across Europe and to Morocco from Estació del Nord, and Estació d'Autobusos de Sants (Map p140; Carrer de Viriat; Ⓜ Sants Estació), next to Estació Sants

Barcelona. Another carrier is Linebús (www.line bus.com, in Spanish).

CAR & MOTORCYCLE
Driving

An effective one-way system makes busy city traffic flow fairly smoothly. Driving in the Ciutat Vella area is largely illegal and frustrating where permitted. Note that, as of 2008, a speed limit of 80km/h is in force in Barcelona and 16 neighbouring municipalities (although there was talk of modifying this in 2010). On ring roads and motorway approaches to the city, either the 80km/h limit or a flexible limit (look out for information screens) is in place. The latter changes depending on traffic flow and perceived pollution levels (the idea is that reducing speed limits cuts down on emissions, as well as saving lives).

The AP-7 *autopista* (motorway) is the main toll road from France (via Girona and Figueres). It skirts inland around the city before proceeding south to Valencia and Alicante. About 40km southwest of Barcelona, the AP-2, also a toll road, branches west off the AP-7 towards Zaragoza. From there it links up with the A-2 dual carriageway for Madrid (no tolls). Several other shorter tollways fan out into the Catalan heartland from Barcelona.

As a rule, alternative toll-free routes are busy (if not clogged). The A-2 (often signposted NII) is the most important. From the French border it follows the AP-7, drops south from Girona to the coast and then southwest into Barcelona, from where it heads west to Lleida and beyond.

Barcelona is 1930km from Berlin, 1555km from London, 1300km from Lisbon, 1200km from Milan, 1145km from Paris, 780km from Geneva and 690km from Madrid.

Coming from the UK, you can put your car on a ferry from Portsmouth to Bilbao with P&O Ferries (☎ in the UK 08716 645645; www.poferries.com) or from Plymouth to Santander with Brittany Ferries (☎ in the UK 08712 440744; www.brittany-ferries.co.uk). From either destination there is still a fair drive to Barcelona. You could also take a ferry to France or the Channel Tunnel car train, Eurotunnel (☎ in the UK 08443 353535; www.eurotunnel.com). The latter runs round the clock, with up to four crossings an hour (35 minutes) between Folkestone and Calais during high season.

Vehicles must be roadworthy, registered and have third-party insurance. Ask your insurer for a European Accident Statement form, which can simplify matters in the event of an accident. A European breakdown assistance policy is a good investment. EU national driver's licences are accepted, as are those from some other non-EU countries (like Switzerland). Otherwise, an international driver's licence is a good idea.

Hire

Avis, Europcar, National/Atesa and Hertz have desks at El Prat airport, Estació Sants and Estació del Nord. Rental outlets in Barcelona include:

Avis (Map p106; ☎ 902 248824, 93 237 56 80; www.avis .com; Carrer de Còrsega 293-295; **M** Diagonal)

Cooltra (Map p90; ☎ 93 221 40 70; www.cooltra.com; Passeig de Joan de Borbó 80-84) You can rent scooters here for around €45 (add insurance). It also organises scooter tours.

Europcar (Map p106; ☎ 93 302 05 43; www.europcar .com; Gran Via de les Corts Catalanes 680; **M** Girona)

Hertz (Map p140; ☎ 93 419 61 56; www.hertz.com; Carrer del Viriat 45; **M** Sants)

MondoRent (Map p90; ☎ 93 295 32 68; www.mondo rent.com; Passeig de Joan de Borbó 80-84) A similar deal on scooter rental to Cooltra.

National/Atesa (Map p106; ☎ 902 100101, 93 323 07 01; www.atesa.es; Carrer de Muntaner 45; **M** Universitat)

Pepecar (Map p60; ☎ 807 414243; www.pepecar.com; Plaça de Catalunya; **M** Catalunya) Specialises in cheap rentals with a mix of cars (the Ford Ka is the cheapest). It has four branches, including one near Sants train station at Carrer de Béjar 68 (Map p140), and another near the airport (free shuttles to/from the airport available). The phone number is expensive to call and customers are encouraged to book on the website.

Vanguard (Map p100; ☎ 93 439 38 80; www.vanguard rent.com; Carrer de Viladomat 297; **M** Entença) For anything from a Fiat Seicento to an Alfa Romeo. It also rents out scooters.

Parking

Parking in the Ciutat Vella is virtually only for residents, with some metered parking available. The narrow streets of Gràcia are little better. The broad boulevards of L'Eixample are divided into blue and green zones, which, for visitors, means the same thing: limited meter parking. Fees vary in central Barcelona from €2.42 to €2.94 per hour. Many car parks charge similar rates. Anything marked in yellow usually means you are permitted to stop for up to 30 minutes for *càrrega* (loading) and *descàrrega* (unloading) only. Most of these zones operate from 8am or 9am to 2pm and 4pm to 8pm Monday to Saturday.

Note that many car parks will not accept camper vans – it can be a real problem parking one of these in central Barcelona.

Parking motorbikes and scooters is easier. On occasion you'll see spaces marked out especially for bikes. Parking on the pavements is illegal, but many do it.

If you get towed, call the Dipòsit Municipal (car pound; ☎ 901 513151; www.bsmsa.cat). Depending on where your car was nabbed, you will be directed to one of several pounds around town. You will pay €150.70 for the tow and €1.96 per hour (maximum of €19.50 per day). The first four hours your car is held are free.

METRO & FGC

The easy-to-use TMB Metro (☎ 010; www.tmb.net) system has seven numbered and colour-coded lines (one, the new Line 9, only partially completed). It runs from 5am to midnight Sunday to Thursday and holidays, from 5am to 2am on Friday and days immediately preceding holidays, and 24 hours on Saturday. Line 2 has access for people with disabilities and a handful of stations on other lines also have lifts. Line 11, a short suburban run, is automated, and in the future the other lines will also run without the need of a driver. See the pull-out map for a map of the Metro system.

Suburban trains run by the Ferrocarrils de la Generalitat de Catalunya (FGC; ☎ 93 205 15 15; www.fgc .net) include a couple of useful city lines. All lines heading north from Plaça de Catalunya stop at Carrer de Provença and Gràcia. One of these lines (L7) goes to Tibidabo and another (L6 to Reina Elisenda) has a stop within spitting distance of the Monestir de Pedralbes. Most trains from Plaça de Catalunya continue beyond Barcelona to Sant Cugat, Sabadell and Terrassa. Other FGC lines head west from Plaça d'Espanya, including one for Manresa that is handy for the trip to Montserrat.

Depending on the line, these trains run from about 5am (with only one or two services before 6am) to 11pm or midnight Sunday to Thursday, and from 5am to about 1am on Friday and Saturday.

TAXI

Taxis charge €2 flag fall plus meter charges of €0.86 per kilometre (€1.10 from 8pm to 7am and all day on weekends). A further €3.10 is added for all trips to/from the airport, and €1 for luggage bigger than 55cm x 35cm x 35cm. The trip from Estació Sants to Plaça de Catalunya, about 3km, costs about €10. You can call a taxi (☎ 93 225 00 00, 93 300 11 00, 93 303 30 33, 93 322 22 22) or flag them down in the streets. The call-out charge is €3.40 (€4.20 at night and on weekends). In many taxis it is possible to pay with credit card and, if you have a local telephone number, you can join the T033 Ràdio taxi service for booking taxis online (www.radiotaxi033.com, in Spanish). You can also book online at www.catalunya taxi.com. General information is available on ☎ 010.

Taxi Amic (☎ 93 420 80 88; www.terra.es/personal /taxiamic, in Spanish) is a special taxi service for people with disabilities or difficult situations (such as transport of big objects). Book at least 24 hours in advance if possible.

Women passengers who feel safer with taxis driven by women can order one on the Línea Rosa (☎ 93 330 07 00).

Trixis

These three-wheeled cycle taxis (Map p56; ☎ 93 310 13 79; www.trixi.info; Plaça dels Traginers 4) operate along the waterfront and around much of the centre (noon to 8pm daily between March and November). They can take two passengers and cost €6/10/18 per 25 minutes/30 minutes/one hour. Children aged three to 12 pay half-price. You can find them near the Monument a Colom and in front of La Catedral.

TRAIN

Train is the most convenient overland option for reaching Barcelona from major Spanish centres like Madrid and Valencia. It can be a long haul from other parts of Europe, where budget flights frequently offer a saving in time and money.

For information on travelling from the UK, contact the Rail Europe Travel Centre (☎ in the UK 0844 848 4064; www.raileurope.co.uk; 1 Lower Regent St, London SW1). For travel within Spain, information is available at train stations or travel agents. A network of rodalies/cercanías serves towns around Barcelona (and the airport). Contact Renfe (☎ 902 320320; www.renfe.es).

Eighteen high-speed Tren de Alta Velocidad Española (AVE) trains between Madrid and Barcelona run daily in each direction, nine of them in under three hours. A typical one-way price is €114 but it comes down if you book a return or book well in advance on the website (which can bring the cost down to about €45). The line will eventually (perhaps by 2012) run right across Barcelona (via a controversial tunnel under construction) and north to the French frontier. France has promised that high speed TGV trains will link Paris with Figueres by 2011.

Another high-speed AVE train, known as Euromed, runs on standard, wide-gauge Spanish tracks, and connects Barcelona with Valencia and Alicante.

Most long-distance (largo recorrido or Grandes Línias) trains have 1st and 2nd classes (known as preferente and turista). After the

---

TICKETS & TARGETES

The Metro, FGC trains, rodalies/cercanías (Renfe-run local trains) and buses come under one zoned-fare regime. Single-ride tickets on all standard transport within Zone 1, except on Renfe trains, cost €1.40.

Targetes are multitrip transport tickets. They are sold at all city-centre Metro stations. The prices given here are for travel in Zone 1. Children under four years of age travel free. Options include the following:

- Targeta T-10 (€7.85) – 10 rides (each valid for 1¼ hours) on the Metro, buses, FGC trains and rodalies. You can change between Metro, FGC, rodalies and buses.
- Targeta T-DIA (€5.90) – unlimited travel on all transport for one day.
- Two-/three-/four-/five-day tickets (€11.20/15.90/20.40/24.10) – unlimited travel on all transport except the Aerobús; buy them at Metro stations and tourist offices.
- T-Mes (€48.85) – 30 days' unlimited use of all public transport.
- Targeta T-50/30 (€32.10) – 50 trips within 30 days, valid on all transport.
- T-Trimestre (€134.10) – 90 days' unlimited use of all public transport.

Fines

The fine for being caught without a ticket on public transport is €50 (a minimum that theoretically can be raised to anything from €150 to €600 if payment is delayed), in addition to the price of the ticket. If you pay on the spot you get 50% off the fine. There's also a minimum €30.50 fine for smoking on the Metro.

AVE, Euromed and several other similarly modern trains, the most common long-distance trains are the slower, all-stops Talgos.

A *trenhotel* is a sleeping-car train with up to three classes: *turista* (for those sitting or in a couchette), *preferente* (sleeping car) and *gran clase* (for those who prefer to sleep in sheer luxury!).

The main train station in Barcelona is Estació Sants (Map p140; Plaça dels Països Catalans; M Sants Estació), located 2.5km west of La Rambla. Direct overnight trains from Paris, Geneva, Milan and Zurich arrive here.

Estació Sants has a tourist office, a telephone and fax office, currency exchange booths open between 8am and 10pm, ATMs and a consigna (left-luggage lockers; small/big locker for 24hr €3/4.50; ⏰ 5.30am-11pm).

TRAM

TMB (☎ 902 193275; www.trambcn.com) runs three tram lines (T1, T2 and T3) into the suburbs of greater Barcelona from Plaça de Francesc Macià and are of limited interest to visitors. The T4 line runs from behind the zoo (near the Ciutadella Vila Olímpica Metro stop) to Sant Adrià via Glòries and the Fòrum. The T5 line runs from Glòries to Badalona (Gorg stop). The T6 runs between Badalona (Gorg) and Sant Adrià. All standard transport passes are valid.

DIRECTORY

BUSINESS HOURS

Generally *barcelonins* work Monday to Friday from 8am or 9am to 1.30pm or 2pm, and then again from between 4pm and 5pm for another three or so hours. In the hot summer months, many work an *horario intensivo* (intensive timetable), from around 7am to 3pm.

Banks tend to open between 8.30am and 2pm Monday to Friday. Some also open from around 4pm to 7pm on Thursday evenings and/or Saturday mornings from around 9am to 1pm. See p283 for post office opening times.

Museum and art gallery opening hours vary considerably, but as a rule of thumb most places are open between 10am and 8pm (some shut for lunch from around 2pm to 4pm). Many museums and galleries close all day Monday and at 2pm Sunday. For shop opening hours, see p152.

CHILDREN

One of the great things about Barcelona is the inclusion of children in many seemingly adult activities. Going out to eat or sipping a beer at a *terrassa* (terrace) on a late summer evening needn't mean leaving children with minders. Locals take their kids out all the time and don't worry too much about keeping them up late. For some ideas and practical tips, take a look at www.kidsinbarcelona.com.

The daytime spectacle of La Rambla (p57) fascinates kids as much as adults. And while the latter might like to sneak a look at the Museu de l'Eròtica, kids will happily lose themselves in the old-fashioned Museu de Cera (wax museum; p69) further down the boulevard. Nearby, head to the top of the Mirador de Colom for the views or to the Golondrinas harbour tour by boat (p282). The shark tunnel and children's activities at L'Aquàrium (p89) are guaranteed success. You might also score points with the nearby 3-D IMAX cinema. Hire a 'trixi-kid' to cycle your young ones around in fun fashion (p274).

The Transbordador Aeri (p92), across the harbour between La Barceloneta and Montjuïc, is another irresistible attraction. To the north of town the Tramvia Blau, the blue tram that runs to the Tibidabo funicular station (see p133), may also raise a smile.

While on Tibidabo, scare the willies out of your youngsters with some of the wild rides at the Parc d'Atraccions amusement park (p133).

Of the city's museums, the ones most likely to capture children's imagination are the Museu Marítim (p73), the Museu de la Xocolata (p86) and the interactive CosmoCaixa (p120).

In summer, you will be rewarded with squeals of delight if you take the kids to one of the city's pools (p225) or the beach (p94). In cooler weather, parks can be a good choice. A roam around Montjuïc, including exploration of its Castell (p142), should appeal. The sheer weirdness of Gaudí's Park Güell (p115) will have older children intrigued, and everyone likes getting lost in the maze of the Jardins del Laberint d'Horta (p134). The Zoo de Barcelona (p86) is a universal child pleaser.

You could take younger kiddies (maximum age 11) along to Happy Parc (Map p106; ☎ 93 317 86 60; www.happyparc.com, in Catalan/Spanish; Carrer de Pau Claris 97; per hr €4; ♡ 5-9pm Mon-Fri, 11am-9pm Sat & Sun) for a play on the slides and other diversions.

For general advice on travelling with children, grab a copy of Lonely Planet's *Travel with Children*.

Babysitting

Most of the mid- and upper-range hotels in Barcelona can organise a babysitting service. A company that many hotels use and that you can also contact directly is 5 Serveis (Map p74; ☎ 93 412 56 76; www.5serveis.com, in Catalan; Carrer de Pelai 50). There are multilingual *canguros* (babysitters). Rates vary, but in the evening expect to pay around €10 an hour plus the cost of a taxi home for the babysitter.

Tender Loving Canguros (☎ 647 605989; www.tlcanguros.com) offers English-speaking babysitters for a minimum of three hours (per hour €8 for one child, €10 for three children), plus a placement fee of €15 and, where necessary, transport costs.

CLIMATE

Barcelona enjoys a Mediterranean climate, with cool winters and hot summers. July and August are the most torrid months, when highs can reach 37°C. The seaside location promotes humidity, but sea breezes can bring relief. A hotel room with a fan or air-conditioning can make all the difference to a good night's sleep.

In the depths of winter, especially in February, it gets cold enough (average lows of 6.7°C) for you to wish you had heating in your room, but by March things begin to thaw out. January tends to be sunny, though not warm.

Rainfall is highest in autumn and winter. During September and into October the city often gets a wash down in cracking thunderstorms.

As Barcelona is downwind from the Pyrenees, cold snaps are always on the cards and the April–May period is particularly changeable. At its best, May can be the most pleasant month of the year – clear and fresh.

CONSULATES

Most countries have an embassy in Madrid. Look them up under Embajada in that city's *Páginas Amarillas* (Yellow Pages). Various countries also maintain consulates in Barcelona:

Australia (Map p116; ☎ 93 490 90 13; Plaça de Gal.la Placídia 1-3; Ⓡ FGC Gràcia)

Canada (Map p106; ☎ 93 412 72 36; Plaça de Catalunya 9; Ⓜ Catalunya)

France (Map p106; ☎ 93 270 30 00; www.consul france-barcelone.org; Ronda de la Universitat 22B; Ⓜ Universitat)

Germany (Map p116; ☎ 93 292 10 00; www.barcelona. diplo.de; Passeig de Gràcia 111; Ⓜ Diagonal)

Ireland (Map p122; ☎ 93 491 50 21; Gran Via de Carles III 94; Ⓜ Maria Cristina)

New Zealand (Map p122; ☎ 93 209 03 99; Travessera de Gràcia 64; Ⓡ FGC Gràcia)

UK (Map p100; ☎ 93 366 62 00; Avinguda Diagonal 477; Ⓜ Hospital Clínic)

US (Map p122; ☎ 93 280 22 27; http://barcelona.us consulate.gov; Passeig de la Reina Elisenda de Montcada 23-25; Ⓡ FGC Reina Elisenda)

COURSES
Language Courses

With its bilingual mix Barcelona may not be the ideal location for embarking on Spanish (Castilian) courses, but there is no short-

age of places to do so. The cost of language courses depends on the school, the length of the course and its intensity. Across Catalonia, more than 220 schools teach Catalan. Pick up a list at the Llibreria & Informació Cultural de la Generalitat de Catalunya (Map p60; ☎ 93 302 64 62; Rambla dels Estudis 118; Ⓜ Liceu).

Non-EU citizens who want to study at a university or language school in Spain should have a study visa. This type of visa is renewable within Spain but only with confirmation of ongoing enrolment and proof that you are able to support yourself.

Some schools worth investigating:

Babylon Idiomas (Map p106; ☎ 93 467 36 36; www .babylon-idiomas.com; Carrer del Bruc 65; Ⓜ Girona) This small school offers a high degree of flexibility – you can study for a week or enlist for a half-year intensive course in Spanish. The big selling point is class size, with a maximum of eight students per class. A week of tuition (30 hours plus five hours of culture) costs €260.

Escola Oficial d'Idiomes de Barcelona (Map p74; ☎ 93 324 93 30; www.eoibd.es; Avinguda de les Drassanes s/n; Ⓜ Drassanes) Part-time courses (around 10 hours a week) in Spanish and Catalan (per semester €185.65) are offered. Because of the demand for Spanish, there is no guarantee of a place.

International House (Map p82; ☎ 93 268 45 11; www .ihes.com/bcn; Carrer de Trafalgar 14; Ⓜ Arc de Triomf) Intensive courses from €410 for two weeks. It can also organise accommodation.

Universitat de Barcelona (Map p106; for Catalan ☎ 93 403 54 77; www.ub.edu/slc; Carrer de Melcior de Palau 140; Ⓜ Sants; for Spanish ☎ 93 403 55 19; www.eh.ub. es; Gran Via de les Corts Catalanes 585; Ⓜ Universitat) Intensive courses (40 hours tuition over periods ranging from two weeks to a month €426) in Catalan and Spanish year-round. Longer Spanish and Catalan courses are also available.

Other Courses

Alicianet (Map p90; ☎ 670 267276; www.alicianet.net; Carrer dels Pinzón 16, La Barceloneta; Ⓜ Barceloneta) Offers various levels of flamenco instruction. One-off classes cost €25 per hour, or you can enrol in courses (up to four hours a week, at €110 a month).

Antilla BCN Escuela de Baile (Map p106; ☎ 93 451 45 64, 610 900558; www.antillasalsa.com; Carrer d'Aragó 141; Ⓜ Urgell) The place to learn salsa and other Caribbean dance, and students can practice moves later on as the dance club opens.

Cook & Taste (Map p60; ☎ 93 302 13 20; www.cookand taste.net; Carrer del Paradís 3; half-day workshop €60;

KEEPING YOUR NOSE CLEAN

Since 2006 tougher city bylaws make drinking in the streets, urinating in the streets and various other vexatious pastimes illegal. You can be fined on the spot and, theoretically, serious misbehaviour can attract penalties of up to €3000. Local police have few qualms about enforcing these laws.

M Liceu) Learn to whip up a paella or stir a gazpacho in this Spanish cookery school.

Dom's Gastronom Cookery School (☎ 93 674 51 60; http://domsgastronom.com; Passeig del Roser 43, Valldoreix; 8 hours of classes over 4 days €100) Cordon bleu–trained chef Dominique Heathcoate holds cookery classes in anything from Catalan, Spanish and French cuisine to tapas and autumn mushroom cooking. Valldoreix is about a 30-minute train ride from Plaça de Catalunya on the line to Sabadell and Terrassa, and Dominique can arrange pick-up from the train station. Groups are catered for.

Escuela de Baile José de la Vega (Map p106; ☎ 93 454 31 14; Carrer d'Aribau 19; per month €55; ☯ Oct-Jun; **M** Universitat) People come from all over town to learn to dance flamenco at this school, which offers classes twice a week.

CUSTOMS

People entering Spain from outside the EU are allowed to bring one bottle of spirits, one bottle of wine, 50mL of perfume and 200 cigarettes into Spain duty free. There are no duty-free allowances for travel between EU countries. For duty-paid items bought in one EU country and taken into another, the allowances are 90L of wine, 10L of spirits, unlimited quantities of perfume and 800 cigarettes.

DANGERS & ANNOYANCES

It cannot be stressed enough that newcomers to Barcelona must be on their guard. Petty theft is a problem in the city centre, on public transport and around main sights. Report thefts to the national police. You are unlikely to recover your goods but you will need to make this formal *denuncia* (police report) for insurance purposes. To avoid endless queues at the *comisaría* (police station), you can make the report by phone (☎ 902 102112) in various languages or on the web at www.policia.es (in Spanish; click on 'Denuncias'). The following day you go to the station of your choice to pick up and sign the report, without queuing. You can also report losses to the Catalan police, the Mossos d'Esquadra (www.gencat

.net/mossos, in Catalan). There's a handy (and busy) police station (Map p74; Carrer Nou de la Rambla 80; **M** Paral.lel) near La Rambla and you can also report petty crime online at www.policia.es/denuncias. You could also try the Guàrdia Urbana (local police; Map p60; La Rambla 43).

DISCOUNT CARDS & TICKETS

The ISIC (International Student Identity Card; www.isic.org) and the European Youth Card (www.euro26.org) are available from most national student organisations and allow discounted access to some sights. Students generally pay a little more than half of adult admission prices, as do children aged under 12 and senior citizens (aged 65 and over) with appropriate ID.

Possession of a Bus Turístic ticket (see p271) entitles you to discounts to some museums.

Articket (www.articketbcn.org) gives you admission to seven important art galleries for €22 and is valid for six months. The galleries are the Museu Picasso (p80), Museu Nacional d'Art de Catalunya (MNAC; p138), the Museu d'Art Contemporani de Barcelona (Macba; p76), the Fundació Antoni Tàpies (p107), the Centre de Cultura Contemporània de Barcelona (CCCB; p77), the Fundació Joan Miró (p143) and La Pedrera (Fundació Caixa Catalunya; p104). You can pick up the ticket through Tel-Entrada (☎ 902 101212; www.telentrada.com) and at the tourist offices at Plaça de Catalunya, Plaça de Sant Jaume and Sants train station.

Something a little different is the Arqueo-Ticket, designed for those with a special interest in archaeology and ancient history. The ticket (€14) gets you entry to the Museu Marítim (p73), Museu d'Història de la Ciutat, Museu d'Arqueologia de Catalunya (p145), Museu Egipci (p110) and Museu Barbier-Mueller d'Art Pre-Colombí (p81). You can get it at participating museums and tourist offices.

If you want to get around Barcelona fast and visit multiple museums in the blink of an eye, the Barcelona Card (www.barcelonacard.com) might come in handy. It costs €26/31.50/36/42 (a little less for children aged four to 12) for two/three/four/five days. You get free transport (and 20% off the Aerobús), and discounted admission prices (up to 30% off) or free entry to many museums and other sights, as well as minor discounts on purchases at a small number of shops, restaurants and bars. The card is available at the tourist offices and online.

The Ruta del Modernisme pack (p111) is well worth looking into for visiting Modernista sights at discounted rates.

Night owls and shopaholics should check out the Go and Connect card (www.goandconnect.com). Valid for one year (€18), the card offers a wide range of discounts (anything from a cut-price haircut to free entry to some clubs).

ELECTRICITY

The electric current in Barcelona is 220V, 50Hz, as in the rest of continental Europe. Several countries outside Europe (such as the USA and Canada) use 110V, 60Hz, which means that some appliances from those countries may perform poorly in Barcelona. It is always safest to use a transformer. Plugs have two round pins, as in the rest of continental Europe.

EMERGENCY

The following are the main emergency numbers:

Ambulance (☎ 061)

Catalan police (Mossos d'Esquadra; ☎ 088)

EU standard emergency number (☎ 112)

Fire brigade (Bombers; ☎ 080, 085)

Guardia Civil (civil guard; ☎ 062)

Guàrdia Urbana (local police; ☎ 092)

Policía Nacional (national police; ☎ 091)

GAY & LESBIAN TRAVELLERS

Barcelona has a busy gay scene, but the region's gay capital is the saucily hedonistic Sitges (p255), a major destination on the international gay party circuit. The gay community takes a leading role in the wild Carnaval celebrations (p17) there in February/March. In Barcelona, the bulk of the nocturnal goings happen in what is known as the 'Gaixample', the part of L'Eixample bounded by Gran Via de les Corts Catalans, Carrer de Balmes, Carrer del Consell de Cent and Carrer de Casanova. As a rule, the city is pretty tolerant and the sight of gay couples arm in arm is generally unlikely to raise eyebrows. That said, attacks on gay men cruising the gardens of Montjuïc at night are reported and care should be exercised.

The free biweekly *Shanguide*, jammed with listings and contact ads, is sometimes available in gay bookshops. Although Madrid-centric, you'll find useful tips on Barcelona too. Magazines with at least some listings and also available in gay bookshops include *Nois* ('boys' in Catalan) and *Gay Barcelona* (www.gaybarcelona.com). The pocket-sized *G* has some Barcelona and Sitges listings. The annual, worldwide *Spartacus* guide (www.spartacus.de) is often on sale at newsstands along La Rambla.

Check out the following websites:

60by80 (www.60by80.com) An excellent gay travellers' website. Click on Barcelona under Cityguides and take it from there.

Coordinadora Gai-Lesbiana (www.cogailes.org) A good site presented by Barcelona's main gay and lesbian organisation, with nationwide links. Here you can zero in on information ranging from bar, sauna and hotel listings through to contacts pages.

Gay Apartments Barcelona (www.gayapartmentbarcelona.com) Aside from the apartments for holiday rent, this site has plenty of info on gay life in Barcelona, from saunas to shops.

GayBarcelona.com (www.gaybarcelona.com) News and views and an extensive listings section covering bars, saunas, shops and more in Barcelona.

GaySitges (www.gaysitges.com) A specific site dedicated to this gay-friendly coastal town (see p255).

Lesbian Spain (www.lesbianspain.com) Some Barcelona-specific information for gay women.

LesboNet.Org (www.lesbonet.org, in Spanish) A lesbian site with contacts, forums and listings.

Shangay.com (www.shangay.com, Spanish only) For news, art reviews, contacts and *Shanguide* listings. You have to register to get full access.

VisitBarcelonaGay.com (www.visitbarcelonagay.com) A busy listings site for visitors to Barcelona, with everything from fetish sections through to saunas and gay accommodation tips.

For gay bookshops, see the Shopping chapter. Organisations include the following:

Casal Lambda (Map p82; ☎ 93 319 55 50; www.lambdaweb.org; Carrer de Verdaguer i Callís 10; Ⓜ Uquinaona) A gay and lesbian social, cultural and information centre in La Ribera.

Coordinadora Gai-Lesbiana Barcelona (Map p140; ☎ 93 298 00 29; www.cogailes.org; Carrer de Violant d'Hongria 156; Ⓜ Plaça del Centre) The city's main coordinating body for gay and lesbian groups. Some lesbian groups are to be found at Ca la Dona (see p285). It also runs an information line, the Línia Rosa (☎ 900 601601).

HOLIDAYS

For *barcelonins* the main holiday periods are summer (July and August), Christmas–New

Year and Easter. August is a peculiar time as Spain largely grinds to a halt. Tourists flock in regardless of the heat, but many locals escape to cooler climes. Finding accommodation can be more difficult around Christmas and Easter. For information on the city's colourful festivals and other events, see p16.

Public Holidays

The following is a list of national public holidays:

New Year's Day (Any Nou/Año Nuevo) 1 January

Epiphany/Three Kings' Day (Epifanía or El Dia dels Reis/Día de los Reyes Magos) 6 January

Good Friday (Divendres Sant/Viernes Santo) March/April

Easter Monday (Dilluns de Pasqua Florida) March/April

Labour Day (Dia del Treball/Fiesta del Trabajo) 1 May

Day after Pentecost Sunday (Dilluns de Pasqua Granda) May/June

Feast of St John the Baptist (Dia de Sant Joan/Día de San Juan Bautista) 24 June

Feast of the Assumption (L'Assumpció/La Asunción) 15 August

Catalonia's National Day (Diada Nacional de Catalunya) 11 September

Festes de la Mercè 24 September

Spanish National Day (Festa de la Hispanitat/Día de la Hispanidad) 12 October

All Saints Day (Dia de Tots Sants/Día de Todos los Santos) 1 November

Constitution Day (Día de la Constitución) 6 December

Feast of the Immaculate Conception (La Immaculada Concepció/La Inmaculada Concepción) 8 December

Christmas (Nadal/Navidad) 25 December

Boxing Day/St Stephen's Day (El Dia de Sant Esteve) 26 December

INTERNET ACCESS

Barcelona is full of internet centres. Some offer student rates and also sell cards for several hours' use at reduced rates. Look also for *locutorios* (public phone centres), which often double as internet centres.

Bornet (Map p82; ☎ 93 268 15 07; Carrer de Barra Ferro 3; per hr/10hr €2.80/20; ☽ 10am-11pm Mon-Fri, 2pm-11pm Sat, Sun & holidays; Ⓜ Jaume I)

Internet MSN (Map p116 ; Carrer del Penedès 1; per min €0.02; ☽ 10am-midnight; Ⓜ Fontana)

WI-FI ACCESS

Many hotels offer their guests wi-fi access (not always for free). A paying wi-fi service operates at the airport and train stations. A growing array of city bars and restaurants are latching on to the service – look for the black-and-white wi-fi signs. The Fresh & Ready fast-food chain is one, and the 16 branches of Starbucks offer 45 minutes of wi-fi with your caramel latte.

MAPS

Tourist offices offer free city and transport maps. Also handy is Michelin's ring-bound *Barcelona*, scaled at 1:12,000.

MEDICAL SERVICES

All foreigners have the same right as Spaniards to emergency medical treatment in public hospitals. EU citizens are entitled to the full range of health-care services in public hospitals, but must present a European Health Insurance Card (enquire at your national health service) and may have to pay up front.

Non-EU citizens have to pay for anything other than emergency treatment. Most travel-insurance policies include medical cover.

For minor health problems you can try any *farmàcia* (pharmacy), where pharmaceuticals tend to be sold more freely without prescription than in places such as the USA, Australia or the UK.

If your country has a consulate in Barcelona, its staff should be able to refer you to doctors who speak your language.

Hospitals include the following:

Hospital Clínic i Provincial (Map p100; ☎ 93 227 54 00; Carrer de Villarroel 170; Ⓜ Hospital Clínic)

Hospital de la Santa Creu i de Sant Pau (Map p100; ☎ 93 291 90 00; Carrer de Sant Antoni Maria Claret 167; Ⓜ Hospital de Sant Pau)

Hospital Dos de Maig (Map p100; ☎ 93 507 27 00; Carrer del Dos de Maig 301; Ⓜ Hospital de Sant Pau)

Some 24-hour pharmacies:

Farmàcia Castells Soler (Map p106; ☎ 93 487 61 45; Passeig de Gràcia 90)

Farmàcia Clapés (Map p60; ☎ 93 301 28 43; La Rambla 98)

Farmàcia Torres (Map p106; ☎ 93 453 92 20; www.farmaciaabierta24h.com, in Spanish; Carrer d'Aribau 62)

MONEY

As in 15 other EU nations (Austria, Belgium, Cyprus, Finland, France, Germany, Greece, Ireland, Italy, Luxembourg, Malta, the Netherlands, Portugal, Slovakia and Slovenia), the euro is Spain's currency. In 2010, the euro zone found itself under considerable pressure as burgeoning public debt in Greece saw the price of government bonds soaring, and the EU and IMF obliged to stump up huge loans to Athens in an effort to calm speculation in the lending markets. All this drove the euro down against other currencies and raised questions over the European monetary union.

Changing Money

Increasingly, the subject of how to take your money abroad, especially within Europe, has only one answer – plastic. Though some people still like to take some cash and travellers cheques. If you wish to be sure to have some ready euros on arrival, fine, but only take in enough to cover needs over the first day or two. Having a little cash at all times is a good idea, just in case cards are stolen and you find yourself in a jam.

Travellers cheques have lost the allure they once had, but as a backup in case cash and or cards are stolen, they are not such a bad idea.

You can change cash or travellers cheques in most major currencies without problems at virtually any bank or *bureau de change* (usually indicated by the word *canvi/cambio*).

Barcelona abounds with banks, many with ATMs, including several around Plaça de Catalunya and more on La Rambla and Plaça de Sant Jaume in the Barri Gòtic.

The foreign-exchange offices that you see along La Rambla and elsewhere are open for longer hours than banks, but they generally offer poorer rates. Also, keep a sharp eye open for commissions at *bureaux de change*.

Interchange (Map p60; ☎ 93 342 73 11; Rambla dels Caputxins 74; ⏰ 9am-11pm; Ⓜ Liceu) represents American Express and will cash Amex travellers cheques, replace lost cheques and provide cash advances on Amex cards.

Credit Cards

Major cards such as Visa, MasterCard, Maestro and Cirrus are accepted throughout Spain. They can be used in many hotels, restaurants and shops. Credit cards can also be used in ATMs displaying the appropriate sign. Check charges with your bank. If your card is lost, stolen or swallowed by an ATM, you can telephone toll free to immediately stop its use:

Amex (☎ 900 994426)

Diners Club (☎ 901 101011)

MasterCard (☎ 900 971231)

Visa (☎ 900 991124)

Travellers Cheques

Travellers cheques are being left behind by plastic. Amex, MasterCard and Visa are widely accepted brands. If you lose your cheques, call a 24-hour freephone number (☎ for Amex 900 994426, for Visa 900 948978 or 900 948973, for Thomas Cook MasterCard 900 948971).

Travelex (www.travelex.com), which issues Amex travellers cheques, also offers prepaid Cash Passports. Load funds onto the card before you travel and use it like any cash card in Visa ATMs worldwide.

NEWSPAPERS & MAGAZINES

A wide selection of national daily newspapers from around Europe (including the UK) is available at newsstands all over central Barcelona and at strategic locations such as train and bus stations. The *International Herald Tribune, Time, Economist, Der Spiegel* and other international magazines are also available.

El País includes a daily supplement devoted to Catalonia, but the region also has a lively home-grown press. *La Vanguardia* and *El Periódico* are the main local Spanish-language dailies. The latter also publishes a Catalan version. The more conservative and Catalan-nationalist-oriented daily is *Avui. El Punt* concentrates on news in and around Barcelona.

The most useful publication for expats is *Barcelona Metropolitan* (www.barcelona -metropolitan.com), with news, views, ads and listings information. *Pilote Urbain* (www.pilote urbain.com) is a French equivalent. *Catalonia Today* is a slim newssheet put out by the owners of *El Punt*.

Conservative Spaniards tend to read the old-fashioned *ABC*, while most of the left-of-centre crowd study *El País*, which identifies with the Partido Socialista Obrero Español (PSOE). *El Mundo* is a robustly right-wing publication in competition with the more respectable *ABC*. One of the best-selling dailies is *Marca*, devoted to sport.

ORGANISED TOURS

Organised tours range from walking tours of the Barri Gòtic or Picasso's Barcelona to organised spins by bicycle.

The Oficina d'Informació de Turisme de Barcelona organises a series of guided walking tours under the name of Barcelona Walking Tours (Map p106; ☎ 93 285 38 34; Plaça de Catalunya 17-S; Ⓜ Catalunya). One explores the Barri Gòtic (adult/child €12.50/5; Ⓨ 10am daily in English, noon Saturday in Spanish and Catalan), another follows in Picasso's footsteps and winds up at the Museu Picasso, to which entry is included in the price (adult/child €19/7; Ⓨ 4pm Tuesday, Thursday and Sunday in English, 4pm Saturday in Spanish and Catalan) and a third takes in the main jewels of Modernisme (adult/child €12.50/5; Ⓨ 4pm Friday and Saturday in English, 4pm Saturday in Spanish, all tours in both English and Spanish at 6pm June to September). It also offers a 'gourmet' tour of traditional purveyors of fine foodstuffs across the old city (adult/child €19/7; Ⓨ 10am Friday and Saturday in English, 10.30am Saturday in Spanish and Catalan). It includes a couple of chances to taste some of the products. All tours last two hours and start at the tourist office.

BICYCLE TOURS

Barcelona is awash with companies offering bicycle tours. Tours typically take two to four hours and generally stick to the old city, the Sagrada Família and the beaches. Operators include the following:

Bike Tours Barcelona (Map p82; ☎ 93 268 21 05; www.biketoursbarcelona.com; Carrer de l'Esparteria 3)

Barcelona By Bike (Map p96; ☎ 93 268 81 07; www.barcelonabybike.com)

CicloTour (Map p74; ☎ 93 317 19 70; Carrer dels Tallers 45; tours €21; Ⓨ 11am daily, 4.30pm mid-Apr–Oct, 7.30pm Thu-Sun Jun-Sep) Three-hour tours starting in Plaça de Catalunya. Just turn up in front of the Hard Rock Café (Map p60) 10 minutes before.

Fat Tire Bike Tours (Map p60; ☎ 93 301 36 12; www.fattirebiketoursbarcelona.com; Carrer dels Escudellers 48)

BarcelonaBiking.com (Map p60; ☎ 656 356300; www.barcelonabiking.com; Baixada de Sant Miquel 6)

Terra Diversions (Map p116; ☎ 93 844 63 88; www.terradiversions.com; Carrer de Santa Tecla 1bis) Mostly mountain-bike tours outside the city.

Barcelona Metro Walks consist of seven routes across the city which combine use of the Metro and other public transport as well as stretches on foot. Tourist information points (p284) sell the €12.50 package, which includes a walks guide, transport pass and map.

Barcelona Guide Bureau (☎ 93 268 24 22; www.barcelona guidebureau.com; Via Laietana 54) places professional guides at the disposal of groups for tailor-made tours of the city. Several languages are catered for. It also offers a series of daily tours, from a six-hour exploration of Barcelona (adult/child €60/40; Ⓨ 9am) to a trip to Montserrat (p252), leaving Barcelona at 3pm and lasting about four hours (adult/child €40/25).

Bus Turístic (Map p60; ☎ 010; www.tmb.net) is a hop-on hop-off service that links virtually all the major tourist sights. See p271 for more information.

For a trip around the harbour, board a Golondrina Excursion Boats (Map p90; ☎ 93 442 31 06; www.lasgolondrinas.com; Moll de les Drassanes; adult/under 4yr/4-10yr/student & senior €13.50/free/5/11; Ⓜ Drassanes) golondrina (swallow) from Moll de les Drassanes in front of Mirador de Colom. The one-hour round trip takes you to Port Olímpic, the Fòrum and back again. The number of departures depends largely on the season and demand. If you just want to discover the area around the port, you can opt for a 35-minute excursion to the breakwater and back (adult/child under four years/child aged four to 10 years €6.50/free/2.60).

Orsom (Map p90; ☎ 93 441 05 37; www.barcelona-orsom .com; Moll de les Drassanes; Ⓨ Apr-Oct; adult/4-10yr/11-18yr & senior €12.50/6.50/9.50; Ⓜ Drassanes) has similar trips to those of Golondrina Excursion Boats, but on a giant catamaran. There are up to three departures per day and the trip lasts about 1½ hours. The third, leaving at 6pm, includes a jazz band and costs a little more (€14.90/6.50/12.90). It also has 45-minute speed-boat tours to and from the Fòrum (adult/four to 10 years/11 to 18 years and senior €10.95/6.50/9.50). Check departure times and availability in advance.

Cultural organisation La Casa Elizalde (Map p106; ☎ 93 488 05 90; www.casaelizalde.com; Carrer de València 302; Ⓜ Passeig de Gràcia) runs several Barcelona walks (which generally occupy a Saturday morning and cost up to €9.25 per person) and one-day or weekend excursions outside the city – tours are in Catalan.

Barcelona Segway Fun (☎ 670 484000; www.barcelona segwayfun.com) offers urban and even country tours on two-wheel people-movers! A one-hour tour costs €30 and leaves from in front of the Torre Mapfre (Map p96) at 12.30pm daily. Segway-mounted guides wait about in front of the Torre Mapfre from 10am daily.

My Favourite Things (☎ 637 265405; www.myft.net; tours from €26-32) offers tours for no more than 10 participants based on numerous themes: anything from design to food. Other activities include flamenco and salsa classes and cycle rides in and out of Barcelona.

See BCN Skytour (Map p90; ☎ 93 224 07 10; www .cathelicopters.com; Heliport, Passeig de l'Escullera; tour per person €80; ☒ 10am-7pm) for a 10-minute thrill at 800m above the city by helicopter that truly gives a bird's-eye view of the city. A 35-minute trip for €240 per person takes in Montserrat (p252). Get to the heliport.

Barcelona Scooter (Map p90; ☎ 93 285 38 32; €45; ☒ 10.30am Sat), run by Cooltra (see p269), offers a three-hour tour around the city by scooter (€50) in conjunction with the city tourism office. Departure is from the Cooltra rental outlet at 3.30pm on Thursdays and 10.30am on Saturdays.

GoCar (Map p82; ☎ 902 301333; www.gocartours.es; Carrer de Freixures 23bis; per hour/day €35/€99; ☒ 9am-9pm Apr-Oct, 10am-7pm Nov-Mar) has GPS-guided 'cars' (actually two-seat, three-wheel mopeds) that allow you to tour around town, park where motorbikes are allowed and listen to commentaries on major sites as you go. The GPS system makes it virtually impossible to get lost.

POST

Correos (☎ 902 197197; www.correos.es, in Spanish) is Spain's national postal service. Barcelona's main post office (Map p60; ☒ 8.30am-9.30pm Mon-Fri, 8.30am-2pm Sat; Ⓜ Jaume I) is just opposite the northeast end of Port Vell at Plaça d'Antoni López. Another handy branch for travellers lies just off Passeig de Gràcia at Carrer d'Aragó 282 (Map p106; ☒ 8.30am-8.30pm Mon-Fri, 9.30am-1pm Sat; Ⓜ Passeig de Gràcia). Many other branches tend to open between 8.30am and 2.30pm Monday to Friday and from 9.30am to 1pm on Saturday.

Segells/sellos (stamps) are sold at most estancos (tobacconists' shops) and at post offices throughout the city.

A postcard or letter weighing up to 20g costs €0.64 from Spain to other European countries and €0.78 to the rest of the world. The same would cost €2.88 and €3.02, respectively, for certificado (registered) mail. Sending such letters urgente, which means your mail may arrive two or three days sooner than usual, costs €3.25 and €3.15, respectively. You can send mail both certificado and urgente if you wish.

Ordinary mail to other western European countries usually takes around three to four days; to North America and Australasia anything from one to two weeks. Delivery times to Spain are similar to those for outbound mail. All Spanish addresses have five-digit postcodes; using postcodes will help your mail arrive a bit quicker.

Lista de correos (poste restante) mail can be addressed to you anywhere in Catalonia that has a post office. It will be delivered to the place's main post office unless another is specified in the address. Take your passport when you pick up mail.

A typical lista de correos address looks like this:
Jenny JONES
Lista de Correos
08080 Barcelona
Spain

RADIO

The Spanish national network, Radio Nacional de España (RNE; www.rtve.es/radio), has several stations: RNE 1 (738AM; 88.3 FM) has general interest and current affairs programmes; RNE 3 (98.6 FM) presents a decent range of pop and rock music; RNE 5 (576AM; 99FM) concentrates on sport and entertainment. Among the most listened-to rock and pop stations are 40 Principales (www.los40.com, in Spanish; 93.9 FM), Onda Cero (www.ondacero.es, in Spanish; 93.5 FM) and Cadena 100 (www.cadena100.es, in Spanish; 100 FM).

Those wanting to get into some Catalan can tune into Catalunya Ràdio (www.catradio.cat; 102.8 FM), Catalunya Informació (92 FM) and a host of small local radio stations.

You can also pick up the BBC World Service (www.bbc.co.uk) on, among others, 6145kHz, 9410kHz and 12,095kHz (short wave). Voice of America (VOA; www.voiceamerica.com) can be found on a number of short-wave frequencies, including 1593kHz, 9685kHz, 11,765kHz and 15,205kHz.

You can tune in to all these stations online too.

TAXES & REFUNDS

Value-added tax, or VAT, is also known as IVA (impuesto sobre el valor añadido, pronounced 'EE-ba'). IVA is 7% on accommodation and restaurant prices and is usually – but not always – included in quoted prices. On most retail goods the IVA is 16%. IVA-free shopping is available in duty-free shops at all airports for people travelling between EU countries.

Non-EU residents are entitled to a refund of the 16% IVA on purchases costing more than €90.15 from any shop, if the goods are taken out of the EU within three months. Ask the shop for a Cashback (or similar) refund form showing the price and IVA paid for each item and identifying the vendor and purchaser. Then present the form at the customs booth for IVA refunds when you depart from Spain (or elsewhere in the EU). You will need your passport and a boarding card that shows you are leaving the EU, and your luggage (so do this before checking in bags). The officer will stamp the invoice and you hand it in at a bank at the departure point to receive a reimbursement.

For more information, check out the Euro Refund website (www.eurorefund.com).

TELEPHONE

The ubiquitous blue payphones are easy to use for international and domestic calls. They accept coins, *tarjetas telefónicas* (phonecards) issued by the national phone company Telefónica and, in some cases, credit cards. *Tarjetas telefónicas* come in €6 and €12 denominations and are sold at post offices and tobacconists.

Public telephones inside bars and cafes, and phones in hotel rooms, are nearly always more expensive than street payphones.

Locutorios (call centres) are another option. You'll mostly find these scattered about the old town, especially in and around El Raval. Check rates before making calls. Increasingly, these double as internet centres.

To call Barcelona from outside Spain, dial the international access code, followed by the code for Spain (☎ 34) and the full number (including Barcelona's area code, ☎ 93, which is an integral part of the number).

The access code for international calls from Spain is ☎ 00. To make an international call, dial the access code, country code, area code and number.

You can dial an operator to make reverse-charge calls to your own country for free – pick up the number before you leave home. You can usually get an English-speaking Spanish international operator on ☎ 1408.

For international directory enquiries, dial ☎ 11825. A call to this number costs €2.

Dial ☎ 1409 to speak to a domestic operator, including for a domestic reverse-charge call *(llamada por cobro revertido)*. For national directory inquiries, dial ☎ 11818.

Mobile-phone numbers start with 6 (from 2011 new ones will begin with 7). Numbers starting with 900 are national toll-free numbers, while those starting with numbers between 901 and 905 come with varying conditions. A common one is 902, which is a national standard-rate number. In a similar category are numbers starting with 803, 806 and 807.

Mobile Phones

Spain uses GSM 900/1800, compatible with the rest of Europe and Australia but not with the North American GSM 1900 or the system used in Japan. If your phone is tri- or quadriband, you will probably be fine. You can buy SIM cards and prepaid call time in Spain for your own national mobile phone (provided what you own is a GSM, dual- or tri-band cellular phone and not code-blocked). You will need your passport to open any kind of mobile-phone account, prepaid or otherwise.

TIME

Spain is one hour ahead of GMT/UTC during winter, and two hours ahead during daylight saving, or summer time (the last Sunday in March to the last Sunday in October). Most other western European countries are on the same time as Spain year-round. The UK, Ireland and Portugal are one hour behind. Spaniards use the 24-hour clock for official business (timetables etc) but generally switch to the 12-hour version in daily conversation.

TOURIST INFORMATION

Several tourist offices operate in Barcelona. A couple of general information numbers worth bearing in mind are ☎ 010 and ☎ 012. The first is for Barcelona and the other is for all Catalonia (run by the Generalitat). You sometimes strike English speakers, although for the most part operators are Catalan/Spanish bilingual. In addition to the following listed tourist offices, information booths operate at Estació del Nord bus station and at Portal de la Pau, at the foot of the Mirador de Colom at the port end of La Rambla. Others set up at various points in the city centre in summer. In addition to what follows, check out www.turismetotal.org for info on Barcelona province.

Oficina d'Informació de Turisme de Barcelona Plaça de Catalunya (Map p106; ☎ 93 285 38 32; www.barcelona turisme.com; Plaça de Catalunya 17-S, underground; ❤ 9am-9pm; M Catalunya); Ajuntament (Map p60; Carrer de la Ciutat 2; ❤ 9am-8pm Mon-Fri, 10am-8pm Sat, 10am-2pm Sun & holidays; M Jaume I); Estació Sants (Map p140; Estació Sants train station; ❤ 8am-8pm late Jun-late Sep, 8am-8pm Mon-Fri, 8am-2pm Sat, Sun & holidays Oct-May; M Sants Estació); El Prat airport (Terminal 1 arrivals, Terminal 2B arrivals hall, Terminal 2A arrivals hall; ❤ 9am-9pm) The Plaça de Catalunya tourist information office concentrates on city information and can help book accommodation. Expect to queue.

Palau de la Virreina Arts Information Office (Map p60; ☎ 93 301 77 75; Rambla de Sant Josep 99; ❤ 10am-8pm; M Liceu) A useful office for events information and tickets.

Palau Robert regional tourist office (Map p106; ☎ 93 238 80 91 or 902 400012 from outside Catalonia; www .gencat.net/probert; Passeig de Gràcia 107; ❤ 10am-7pm Mon-Sat, 10am-2.30pm Sun; M Diagonal) A host of material on Catalonia, audiovisual resources, a bookshop and a branch of Turisme Juvenil de Catalunya (for youth travel).

TRAVELLERS WITH DISABILITIES

Some hotels and public institutions have wheelchair access. All buses in Barcelona are wheelchair accessible and a growing number of Metro stations are theoretically wheelchair accessible (generally by lift, although there have been complaints that they are only any good for parents with prams). Lines 2 and 11 are completely adapted, as are two-thirds of stops on Line 1. In all, about 70% of stops have been adapted (you can check which ones by looking at www.tmb.net and clicking on 'Transport for Everyone'). All stations are due to be fully adapted by 2012. Ticket vending machines in Metro stations are adapted for the disabled and have Braille options for the blind.

You can order special taxis; see p274. Most street crossings in central Barcelona are wheelchair-friendly.

For more information on what the city is doing to improve accessibility, click on 'Barcelona Accessible' at the city council website (www.bcn.cat). Barcelona Turisme (www.vienaeditorial .com/barcelonaaccesible) also publishes the *Acces-*

sible Barcelona Guide in several languages. Other services include the following:

Institut Municipal de Persones amb Discapacitat (Map p100; ☎ 93 413 27 75; Avinguda Diagonal 233) This organisation has information for people with disabilities in Barcelona, aimed mostly at permanent residents.

ONCE (Map p140; ☎ 93 325 92 00; Carrer de Sepúlveda 1; M Plaça d'Espanya) The national organisation for the vision-impaired can help with information, including lists of places such as restaurants where Braille menus are provided.

VISAS

Spain is one of 25 member countries of the Schengen Convention, under which 22 EU countries (all but Bulgaria, Cyprus, Ireland, Romania and the UK) plus Iceland, Norway and Switzerland have abolished checks at common borders.

EU nationals require only their ID cards to visit Spain. Nationals of many other countries, including Australia, Canada, Israel, Japan, New Zealand and the USA, do not require visas for tourist visits to Spain of up to 90 days. Non-EU nationals who are legal residents of one Schengen country do not require a visa to visit another Schengen country.

All non-EU nationals entering Spain for any reason other than tourism (such as study or work) should contact a Spanish consulate, as they may need a specific visa and will have to obtain work and/or residence permits. Citizens of countries not mentioned above should check whether they need a visa with their Spanish consulate.

WOMEN TRAVELLERS

Think twice about going by yourself to isolated stretches of beach or down empty city streets at night. It's inadvisable for women to hitchhike alone – and not a great idea even for two women together.

Topless bathing is OK on beaches in Catalonia and also at swimming pools. While skimpy clothing tends not to attract much attention in Barcelona and the coastal resorts, tastes in inland Catalonia tend to be somewhat conservative.

Ca la Dona (Map p106; ☎ 93 412 71 61; www.caladona .org; Carrer de Casp 38; M Catalunya) The nerve centre of the region's feminist movement, Ca la Dona (Women's Home) includes many diverse women's groups.

Centre Francesca Bonnemaison (Map p82; ☎ 93 268 42 18; www.bonnemaison-ccd.org; Carrer de Sant Pere més

Baix 7; Ⓜ Urquinaona) A women's cultural centre where groups put on expositions, stage theatre productions and carry out other cultural activities.

Institut Català de la Dona (Map p74; ☎ 93 495 16 00; www.gencat.net/icdona; Plaça de Pere Coromines1; Ⓜ Liceu) It can point you in the right direction for information on marriage, divorce, rape/assault counselling and related issues for long-termers. The hotline for victims of assault is ☎ 900 900120.

WORK

Barcelona attracts not only tourists, but flurries of people from all over Europe and beyond hoping to find work and enjoy some of the summer lifestyle on a more long-term basis.

With around 17.5% unemployment (and a national rate just over 20%), the city is perhaps not the easiest place to realise such dreams. That does not make it impossible. Well qualified professionals in areas in demand do find positions. Teaching, bar work and jobs in the marinas are typical options. For more, see p265.

Doing Business

The main business district in Barcelona is along the western end of Avinguda Diagonal. The big banks cluster here with several major business-oriented hotels. Another centre of activity is the World Trade Center in Port Vell. A hi-tech district, known as 22@bcn, is emerging in the former industrial area of Poblenou. The giant congress centre in Fòrum attracts international get-togethers on the northeast coast of the city.

People wishing to make the first moves towards expanding their business into Spain should contact their own country's trade department, such as the Department for Business Innovation and Skills (www.berr.gov.uk) in the UK. The commercial department of the Spanish embassy in your own country should also have information – at least about red tape.

In Barcelona your next port of call should be the Cambra de Comerç de Barcelona (Map p116; ☎ 902 448448; www.cambrabcn.es; Avinguda Diagonal 452; Ⓜ Diagonal). It has a documentation centre and business-oriented bookshop, the Llibreria de la Cambra.

With more than 80 trade fairs a year and a growing number of congresses of all types, Barcelona is an important centre of international business in Europe. The Fira de Barcelona (Map p140; ☎ 902 233200; www.firabcn.es; Plaça d'Espanya; Ⓜ Espanya) organises fairs for everything from fashion to technology, furniture, recycling, jewellery and classic cars. The information office offers business services (such as communications), meeting rooms and other facilities for people working at trade fairs.

The main trade fair (Fira M1; Map p140) is located between the base of Montjuïc and Plaça d'Espanya, with 115,000 sq metres of exhibition space and a conference centre, plus 50,000 sq metres of outdoor space. Fira M2 (Fair No 2), southwest of Montjuïc (en route to the airport) along Gran Via de les Corts Catalanes, totals 200,000 sq metres.

On the waterfront, the World Trade Center (Map p90; ☎ 93 508 80 00; www.wtcbarcelona.com; Ⓜ Drassanes) at Port Vell offers a variety of meeting rooms and conference centres. The Centre de Convencions Internacional de Barcelona (CCIB; Map p96; ☎ 93 230 10 00; www.ccib.es; Rambla de Prim 1-17) in the northeast of the city near the waterfront can host around 15,000 people (see p95) in various halls, auditoriums and meeting rooms.

The Barcelona Convention Bureau (Map p106; ☎ 93 368 97 00; Rambla de Catalunya 123; Ⓜ Diagonal) organises conventions and other events.

LANGUAGE

Catalan (català) and Spanish (more precisely known as castellano, or Castilian) have official-language status in Catalonia. Aranese (aranés), which is a dialect of Gascon, is also an official language in the Val d'Aran.

The recognition of Catalan is the end result of a vigorous regional government campaign that began when the province gained autonomy at the end of the 1970s. Until the Battle of Muret in 1213, Catalan territory extended across southern France, taking in Roussillon and reaching into Provence. Catalan was spoken, or at least understood, throughout these territories and in what is now Catalonia and Andorra. In the couple of hundred years that followed, the Catalans spread their language south into Valencia, west into Aragón and east to the Balearic Islands. The language also reached Sicily and Naples, and the Sardinian town of Alghero is still a partly Catalan-speaking outpost today.

In Barcelona you'll hear as much Spanish as Catalan, and we've provided some Spanish here to get you started (see p290 for some basic Catalan). Your chances of coming across English speakers are also good. Elsewhere in the province, don't be surprised if you get replies in Catalan to your questions in Spanish. However, you'll find that most Catalans will happily speak to you in Spanish, especially once they realise you're a foreigner.

If you want to learn more Spanish than we've included here, pick up a copy of Lonely Planet's comprehensive and user-friendly Spanish phrasebook, or download an iPhone phrasebook through the Apple App store.

SOCIAL
Meeting People
Hello.
¡Hola!
Goodbye.
¡Adiós!
Please.
Por favor.
Thank you.
(Muchas) Gracias.
Yes.
Sí.
No.
No.
Excuse me.
Perdón.
Sorry!
Perdón./Perdóneme.
Do you speak English?
¿Habla inglés?
Does anyone speak English?
¿Hay alguien que hable inglés?
Do you understand?
¿Me entiende?
Yes, I understand.
Sí, entiendo.
No, I don't understand.
No, no entiendo.

Pardon? What?
¿Cómo?

Could you please …?
¿Puede … por favor?
  speak more slowly hablar más despacio
  repeat that   repetir
  write it down   escribirlo

Going Out
What's there to do in the evenings?
¿Qué se puede hacer por las noches?

What's on …?
¿Qué hay…?
  locally   en la zona
  this weekend   este fin de semana
  today   hoy
  tonight   esta noche

Where are the …?
¿Dónde hay … ?
  places to eat   lugares para comer
  nightclubs   discotecas
  pubs   pubs
  gay venues   lugares gay

Is there a local entertainment guide?
¿Hay una guía del ocio de la zona?

PRACTICAL
Question Words

Who?	¿Quién? (sg)
	¿Quiénes? (pl)
What?	¿Qué?
Which?	¿Cuál? (sg)
	¿Cuáles? (pl)
When?	¿Cuándo?
Where?	¿Dónde?
How?	¿Cómo?
How much?	¿Cuánto?
How many?	¿Cuántos?
How much is it?	¿Cuánto cuesta?
Why?	¿Por qué?

Numbers & Amounts

0	cero
1	uno/una (m/f)
2	dos
3	tres
4	cuatro
5	cinco
6	seis
7	siete
8	ocho
9	nueve
10	diez
11	once
12	doce
13	trece
14	catorce
15	quince
16	dieciséis
17	diecisiete
18	dieciocho
19	diecinueve
20	veinte
21	veintiuno
22	veintidós
30	treinta
31	treinta y uno
40	cuarenta
50	cincuenta
60	sesenta
70	setenta
80	ochenta
90	noventa
100	cien
1000	mil
2000	dos mil

Days

Monday	lunes
Tuesday	martes
Wednesday	miércoles
Thursday	jueves
Friday	viernes
Saturday	sábado
Sunday	domingo

Banking

I'd like to change some money.
Quería cambiar dinero.
I'd like to change a travellers cheque.
Quería cobrar un cheque de viaje.

Where's the nearest …?
¿Dónde está … más cercano?

ATM	el cajero automático
foreign exchange office	la oficina de cambio

Do you accept …?
¿Aceptan …?

credit cards	tarjetas de crédito
debit cards	tarjetas de débito
travellers cheques	cheques de viaje

Post

Where's the post office?
¿Dónde está la oficina de correos?

I want to send a …
Quería enviar …

fax	un fax
parcel	un paquete
postcard	una postal

I want to buy (a/an) …
Quería comprar …

envelope	un sobre
stamp/stamps	un sello/sellos

Phones & Mobiles

Where can I find a/an …?
¿Dónde se puede encontrar un …?

I'd like a/an …
Quería un/una …

adaptor plug	adaptador
charger for my phone	cargador para mi teléfono
mobile/cell phone for hire	móvil para alquilar
prepaid mobile/ cell phone	móvil de prepago
SIM card for your network	tarjeta SIM para su red

I want to buy a phonecard.
Quería comprar una tarjeta telefónica.

I want to make a …
Quería hacer …
  call (to …)   una llamada (a …)
  reverse-charge/   una llamada a cobro
  collect call   revertido

Internet
Where's the local internet cafe?
¿Dónde hay un cibercafé cercano?

I'd like to …
Quería …
  get internet   usar el Internet
  access
  check my email   revisar mi correo
                 electrónico

Transport
What time does the … leave?
¿A qué hora sale el …?
  boat   barco
  bus   autobús
  bus (intercity)   autocar
  plane   avión
  train   tren

What time's the … bus?
¿A qué hora hay el … autocar/autobús?
  first   primer
  last   último
  next   próximo

Is this taxi free?
¿Está libre este taxi?
Please put the meter on.
Por favor, ponga el taxímetro.
How much is it to …?
¿Cuánto cuesta ir a …?
Please take me (to this address).
Por favor, lléveme (a esta dirección).

FOOD
  breakfast   desayuno
  lunch   comida
  dinner   cena
  snack   tentempié
  to eat   comer
  to drink   beber

Can you recommend a …?
¿Puede recomendar un …?
  bar   bar
  cafe   café
  coffee bar   cafetería
  restaurant   restaurante

A table for …, please.
Una mesa para …, por favor.
Is service/cover charge included?
¿Está incluido el servicio en la cuenta?
Do you have a menu in English?
¿Tienen una carta en inglés?
I'm a vegetarian.
Soy vegetariano/a. (m/f)
Do you have any vegetarian dishes?
¿Tienen algún plato vegetariano?
I'm allergic to (peanuts).
Soy alérgico/a a (los cacahuetes). (m/f)
What is today's special?
¿Cuál es el plato del día?
What would you recommend?
¿Qué recomienda?
What's the speciality here?
¿Cuál es la especialidad de este restaurante?
I'd like the set lunch, please.
Quería el menú del día, por favor.
The bill, please.
La cuenta, por favor.
I'll have what they're having.
Tomaré lo mismo que ellos.
Good health!/Cheers!
¡Salud!
Thank you, that was delicious.
Muchas gracias, estaba buenísimo.

For more detailed information on food and dining out, see p166.

Food Glossary
Here is a brief glossary of some food terms that could come in handy. Items listed below are in Catalan/Spanish where they start with the same letter. Where the two terms start with different letters, or where only the Catalan or the Spanish term is provided, they are listed separately and marked (C) for Catalan or (S) for Spanish. Entries not marked at all take the same form in both languages.

aceite (S)   oil
aigua/agua   water
alcachofa (S)   artichoke
ametlla/almendra almond
anyell   lamb
arròs/arroz   rice
bacallà/bacalao   salted cod
bogavante (S)   a type of lobster
boquerons/   white anchovies in
  boquerones   vinegar
botifarra   Catalan pork sausage
cafè amb llet/   coffee with milk
  café con leche

A LITTLE BIT OF CATALÀ

These Catalan words and phrases might win you a few smiles and perhaps help you make some new friends.

Hello.	*Hola.*	Wednesday	*dimecres*
Goodbye.	*Adéu.*	Thursday	*dijous*
Yes.	*Sí.*	Friday	*divendres*
No.	*No.*	Saturday	*dissabte*
Please.	*Sisplau./Si us plau.*	Sunday	*diumenge*
Thank you (very much).	*(Moltes) gràcies.*		
You're welcome.	*De res.*	0	*zero*
Excuse me.	*Perdoni.*	1	*un/una* (m/f)
May I?/Do you mind?	*Puc?/Em permet?*	2	*dos/dues* (m/f)
I'm sorry.	*Ho sento./Perdoni.*	3	*tres*
What's your name?	*Com et dius?* (inf)	4	*quatre*
	Com es diu? (pol)	5	*cinc*
My name's ...	*Em dic ...*	6	*sis*
Where are you from?	*D'on ets?*	7	*set*
Do you speak English?	*Parla anglès?*	8	*vuit*
I (don't) understand.	*(No) ho entenc.*	9	*nou*
Could you speak in	*Pot parlar castellà*	10	*deu*
Castilian please?	*sisplau?*	11	*onze*
How do you say ... in	*Com es diu ... en*	12	*dotze*
Catalan?	*català?*	13	*tretze*
I'm looking for ...	*Estic buscant ...*	14	*catorze*
How do I get to ...?	*Com puc arribar a ...?*	15	*quinze*
Turn left.	*Giri a mà esquerra.*	16	*setze*
Turn right.	*Giri a mà dreta.*	17	*disset*
near/far	*a prop/lluny de*	18	*divuit*
		19	*dinou*
Monday	*dilluns*	20	*vint*
Tuesday	*dimarts*	100	*cent*

caldereta	a seafood stew
carxofa (C)	artichoke
cava	Catalan champagne
ceba/cebolla	onion
cervesa/cerveza	beer
chupito (S)/	a shot (small glass of
xupito (C)	spirits)
cordero (S)	lamb
costella/chuleta	cutlet
cranc/cangrejo or	crab
centollo	
formatge (C)	cheese
gambes/gambas	prawns
gelat (C)	ice cream
helado (S)	ice cream
huevos (S)	eggs
llagosta/langosta	lobster
llamàntol (C)	a type of lobster
llenties/lentejas	lentils
menjador (C)	dining room, restaurant
menú del día (S)	fixed-price meal
montaditos (S)	canapés

nueva cocina española	new Spanish cuisine
oli (C)	oil
ous (C)	eggs
paella (S)	rice, seafood and meat dish
patates braves/ patatas bravas	potato chunks in a slightly spicy tomato sauce
pebre/pimienta	pepper
peix/pescado	fish
queso (S)	cheese
rap/rape	monkfish
ratafia (C)	a local, high-octane liquor
ternera (S)	beef
torrada/tostada	open toasted sandwich
trucha (S)	trout
truita (C)	omelette/tortilla, trout
vedella (C)	beef
vi/vino	wine
xai (C)	lamb

EMERGENCIES

Help!
¡Socorro!
It's an emergency!
¡Es una emergencia!
Could you help me, please?
¿Me puede ayudar, por favor?
Where's the police station?
¿Dónde está la comisaría?
Where are the toilets?
¿Dónde están los servicios?

Call …!
¡Llame a …!

an ambulance	una ambulancia
a doctor	un médico
the police	la policía

HEALTH

Where's the nearest …?
¿Dónde está … más cercano/a?

(night) chemist	la farmacia (de guardia)
doctor	el médico
hospital	el hospital

I need a doctor (who speaks English).
Necesito un doctor (que hable inglés).

I have (a/an) …
Tengo …

diarrhoea	diarrea
fever	fiebre
headache	dolor de cabeza
pain	dolor

GLOSSARY

Items listed below are in Catalan/Spanish (Castilian) where they start with the same letter. Where the two terms start with different letters, or where only the Catalan or the Spanish term is provided, they are listed separately and marked (C) for Catalan or (S) for Spanish. If an entry is not marked at all, it is because it takes the same form in both languages.

ajuntament/ayuntamiento – town hall
artesonado (S) – Mudéjar wooden ceiling with inter-laced beams leaving a pattern of spaces for decoration
avinguda (C) – avenue

Barcelonin (C) – inhabitant/native of Barcelona
Barcino – Roman name for Barcelona
barri/barrio – neighbourhood, quarter of Barcelona

caganer (C) – crapper, a character that appears in Catalan nativity scenes
Call (C) – Jewish quarter in medieval Barcelona
capella/capilla – chapel
carrer/calle – street
casa – house
castellers (C) – human-castle builders
cercanías (S) – local trains serving Barcelona's airport, suburbs and some outlying towns
comte/conde – count

església (C) – church

farmàcia/farmacia – pharmacy
festa/fiesta – festival, public holiday or party
FGC (C) – Ferrocarrils de la Generalitat de Catalunya; local trains operating alongside the Metro in Barcelona
fundació/fundació – foundation

garum – a spicy sauce made from fish entrails, found throughout the Roman Empire
gegants – huge figures paraded at festes

Generalitat (C) – Catalan regional government
guiri – foreigner (somewhat pejorative)

hostal – commercial establishment providing one- to three-star accommodation
iglesia (S) – church
IVA – *impost sobre el valor afegit/impuesto sobre el valor añadido*, or value-added tax

masia – Catalan country farmhouse
mercat/mercado – market
Modernisme (C) – the turn-of-the-19th-century artistic style, influenced by Art Nouveau, whose leading practitioner was Antoni Gaudí
Modernista – an exponent of Modernisme
Mudéjar (S) – a Muslim living under Christian rule in medieval Spain; also refers to their decorative style of architecture

palau (C) – palace
passatge (C) – laneway
pensió/pensión – commercial establishment providing one- to three-star accommodation
plaça/plaza – plaza
platja/playa – beach

Renaixença – Rebirth of interest in Catalan literature, culture and language in the second half of the 19th century
rodalies (C) – see *cercanías*

saló (C) – hall
sardana – traditional Catalan folk dance
s/n (S) – *sin número* (without number)

tablao – restaurant where flamenco is performed
teatre – theatre
terrassa/terazza – terrace; often means a café or bar's outdoor tables
turista – second class; economy class

BEHIND THE SCENES

THIS BOOK

This 7th edition of Barcelona was written by Damien Simonis, who also wrote the preceding six editions. It was commissioned in Lonely Planet's London office, and produced by the following:

Commissioning Editors Joe Bindloss, Lucy Monie, Sally Schafer

Coordinating Editor Trent Holden

Coordinating Cartographer Anthony Phelan

Coordinating Layout Designer Carol Jackson

Managing Editors Imogen Bannister, Liz Heynes

Managing Cartographers Shahara Ahmed, Adrian Persoglia, Herman So

Managing Layout Designer Celia Wood

Assisting Editors Andrew Bain, Barbara Delissen, Robyn Loughnane, Simon Williamson

Assisting Cartographers Anita Banh, Hunor Csutoros, Andy Rojas, Amanda Sierp

Cover Research Pepi Bluck

Internal Image Research Aude Vauconsant

Language Content Laura Crawford, Annelies Mertens

Thanks Owen Eszeki, David Connolly, Chris Girdler, Mark Griffiths, Martin Heng, Indra Kilfoyle, Katie O'Connell, Averil Robertson, Wibowo Rusli, Julie Sheridan, Peter Shields, Caroline Sieg

Cover photographs Gaudí's La Pedrera, Rene Mattes/Photolibrary (top); Los Caracoles Restaurant, Krzysztof Dydynski/Lonely Planet Images (bottom)

Acknowledgments Photograph of Damien Simonis (p15) by Peter Sotirakis

All images are copyright of the photographer unless otherwise indicated. Many of the images in this guide are available for licensing from Lonely Planet Images: www.lonelyplanetimages.com.

THANKS
DAMIEN SIMONIS

Keeping up with what's happening in Barcelona is a non-stop affair, and a task made easier and more enjoyable by the company of friends. Thanks to all those who have, over the two years since the last edition, shared tips and discoveries, or simply tagged along for a meal or a drink: María Barbosa Pérez and Enric Muñoz; Ana Blasco; Alexa Botines; Sandra Canudas; Victor Capilla; Josep Cerdà and Maite Zaldivia; Dominique Cerri; Paolo Cesco; Rebecca and Elsa Daraspe; Oscar Elias; Ferran Esteves; Veronica Farré; Fabiana Finetto; Kim Harse (Cosmosoirée); Ralf Himburg and Lilian Müller (and the Thursday gang); Edith López García (and family); Ludmilla Mastromonaco; Teresa Moreno Quintana and Carlos Sanagustin; Niko von Mosch and the Small World crowd; Steven Muller and Veronika Brinkmann; Sonja Müller; Nicole Neuefeind; Brian O'Hare and Marta Cervera; Cristina Pedraza; Susana Pellicer (along with Albert and friends); David Poveda; Helena Ramírez Carreño; Federica Rocco and friends; John Rochlin (and the folks of ASBA); Gemma Sesplugues; Peter (don't call me 'the Greek') Sotirakis; Armin Teichmann; José María Toro (the world's friendliest banker); Joan Trujillo;

THE LONELY PLANET STORY

Fresh from an epic journey across Europe, Asia and Australia in 1972, Tony and Maureen Wheeler sat at their kitchen table stapling together notes. The first Lonely Planet guidebook, Across Asia on the Cheap, was born.

Travellers snapped up the guides. Inspired by their success, the Wheelers began publishing books to Southeast Asia, India and beyond. Demand was prodigious, and the Wheelers expanded the business rapidly to keep up. Over the years, Lonely Planet extended its coverage to every country and into the virtual world via lonelyplanet.com and the Thorn Tree message board.

As Lonely Planet became a globally loved brand, Tony and Maureen received several offers for the company. But it wasn't until 2007 that they found a partner whom they trusted to remain true to the company's principles of travelling widely, treading lightly and giving sustainably. In October of that year, BBC Worldwide acquired a 75% share in the company, pledging to uphold Lonely Planet's commitment to independent travel, trustworthy advice and editorial independence.

Today, Lonely Planet has offices in Melbourne, London and Oakland, with over 500 staff members and 300 authors. Tony and Maureen are still actively involved with Lonely Planet. They're travelling more often than ever, and they're devoting their spare time to charitable projects. And the company is still driven by the philosophy of Across Asia on the Cheap: 'All you've got to do is decide to go and the hardest part is over. So go!'

Michael van Laake and Rocío Vázquez; Nuria Vilches and Simona Volonterio.

This is for Janique, *qui est rentrée chez elle*. For the good times.

OUR READERS

Many thanks to the travellers who used the last edition and wrote to us with helpful hints, useful advice and interesting anecdotes:

Maarten America, Carlos Bertoni, Lars Bruinink, Karina Chircu, Katrien Claus, Valerie Davies, Rebecca Day, Cyrus Elting, Nathan & Rhiannon English, Jackie Fields, Hilary Fine, Saoirse Flood, Robert Geismar, Jared Goodhead, Lisa Gordon, Clare Groome, Alvand Heidary, Don Hotchkiss, Andrew Houston, Anders Jeppsson, Rajnish Kapoor, Athanasios Kavvadias, Deedee Koss, Warner Leedy, Geva Lester, Sebastian Loew, Elizabeth T Massey, Jo Meredith, Jennifer Nash, Norberto Alonso Orcajo, Roly Osborne, Max Perlman, Sarah Phillips, Jaime Rodríguez, Lynn Rubinstein, Kathryn Sargent, Jiri Smitak, Julian Sonksen, Wilma Traldi, Efi Vouchara, Andrea Warburton, Samantha Wayne

SEND US YOUR FEEDBACK

We love to hear from travellers – your comments keep us on our toes and help make our books better. Our well-travelled team reads every word on what you loved or loathed about this book. Although we cannot reply individually to postal submissions, we always guarantee that your feedback goes straight to the appropriate authors, in time for the next edition. Each person who sends us information is thanked in the next edition and the most useful submissions are rewarded with a free book.

To send us your updates – and find out about Lonely Planet events, newsletters and travel news – visit our award-winning website: lonelyplanet.com/contact.

Note: We may edit, reproduce and incorporate your comments in Lonely Planet products such as guidebooks, websites and digital products, so let us know if you don't want your comments reproduced or your name acknowledged. For a copy of our privacy policy visit lonelyplanet.com/privacy.

Notes

Notes

Notes

INDEX

000 map pages
000 photographs

ARTS
CINEMAS

CLASSICAL MUSIC

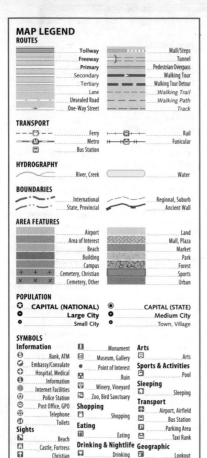

MAP LEGEND

ROUTES
- Tollway
- Freeway
- Primary
- Secondary
- Tertiary
- Lane
- Unsealed Road
- One-Way Street
- Mall/Steps
- Tunnel
- Pedestrian Overpass
- Walking Tour
- Walking Tour Detour
- Walking Trail
- Walking Path
- Track

TRANSPORT
- Ferry
- Metro
- Bus Station
- Rail
- Funicular

HYDROGRAPHY
- River, Creek
- Water

BOUNDARIES
- International
- State, Provincial
- Regional, Suburb
- Ancient Wall

AREA FEATURES
- Airport
- Area of Interest
- Beach
- Building
- Campus
- Cemetery, Christian
- Cemetery, Other
- Land
- Mall, Plaza
- Market
- Park
- Forest
- Sports
- Urban

POPULATION
- CAPITAL (NATIONAL)
- Large City
- Small City
- CAPITAL (STATE)
- Medium City
- Town, Village

SYMBOLS

Information
- Bank, ATM
- Embassy/Consulate
- Hospital, Medical
- Information
- Internet Facilities
- Police Station
- Post Office, GPO
- Telephone
- Toilets

Sights
- Beach
- Castle, Fortress
- Christian
- Islamic

- Monument
- Museum, Gallery
- Point of Interest
- Ruin
- Winery, Vineyard
- Zoo, Bird Sanctuary

Shopping
- Shopping

Eating
- Eating

Drinking & Nightlife
- Drinking
- Cafe

Arts
- Arts

Sports & Activities
- Pool

Sleeping
- Sleeping

Transport
- Airport, Airfield
- Bus Station
- Parking Area
- Taxi Rank

Geographic
- Lookout
- Mountain

Published by Lonely Planet Publications Pty Ltd
ABN 36 005 607 983

Australia (Head Office)
Locked Bag 1, Footscray, Victoria 3011,
☎03 8379 8000, fax 03 8379 8111,
talk2us@lonelyplanet.com.au

USA 150 Linden St, Oakland, CA 94607,
☎510 250 6400, toll free 800 275 8555,
fax 510 893 8572, info@lonelyplanet.com

UK 2nd fl, 186 City Rd, London, EC1V 2NT,
☎020 7106 2100, fax 020 7106 2101,
go@lonelyplanet.co.uk

© Lonely Planet 2010
© Photographers as indicated 2010

Printed by Toppan Security Printing Pte. Ltd.
Printed in Singapore.

Lonely Planet and the Lonely Planet logo
are trademarks of Lonely Planet and are
registered in the US Patent and Trademark
Office and in other countries.

Lonely Planet does not allow its name or
logo to be appropriated by commercial
establishments, such as retailers,
restaurants or hotels. Please let us know of
any misuses: lonelyplanet.com/ip.

Mixed Sources
Product group from well-managed
forests and other controlled sources
www.fsc.org Cert no. SGS-COC-005002
© 1996 Forest Stewardship Council

R.C.L.

FEV. 2011

G